Battling Pornography

Pornography catapulted to the forefront of the American women's movement in the 1980s, singled out by some leading feminists as an agent of female oppression and celebrated by others as an essential ingredient of sexual liberation. In *Battling Pornography*, Carolyn Bronstein locates the origins of anti-pornography sentiment in the turbulent social and cultural history of the late 1960s and 1970s, including women's mixed responses to the sexual revolution and the rise of radical feminism, and explains the gradual emergence of a controversial anti-pornography movement. Based on extensive original archival research, the book chronicles the history of three grassroots organizations and shows that activists first protested images of sexual violence against women in advertisements, Hollywood films, and other mainstream media. They emphasized public education and consumer action and demanded that corporations behave ethically toward women. Over time, feminist leaders made a strategic choice to reorient the movement to pornography to leverage the term's considerable rhetorical and symbolic power. In so doing, they unwittingly attracted right-wing supporters who opposed sexual freedom and ignited a forceful feminist countermovement in defense of sexuality and free speech. *Battling Pornography* presents a fascinating account of the rise and fall of this significant American social movement and documents the contributions of influential activists on both sides of the pornography debate, including some of the best-known American feminists.

Carolyn Bronstein is Associate Professor of Media Studies in the College of Communication at DePaul University. Her research investigates questions of media representation and social responsibility, with an emphasis on gender, and her work has been published in such journals as *Violence Against Women*, *Camera Obscura*, and *Journalism & Mass Communication Quarterly*.

Battling Pornography

The American Feminist Anti-Pornography Movement, 1976–1986

CAROLYN BRONSTEIN
DePaul University

CAMBRIDGE
UNIVERSITY PRESS

CAMBRIDGE UNIVERSITY PRESS
Cambridge, New York, Melbourne, Madrid, Cape Town,
Singapore, São Paulo, Delhi, Tokyo, Mexico City

Cambridge University Press
32 Avenue of the Americas, New York, NY 10013-2473, USA

www.cambridge.org
Information on this title: www.cambridge.org/9781107400399

First published 2011

Printed in the United States of America

A catalog record for this publication is available from the British Library.

Library of Congress Cataloging in Publication data
Bronstein, Carolyn.
Battling pornography : the American feminist anti-pornography
movement, 1976–1986 / Carolyn Bronstein.
p. cm.
Includes bibliographical references and index.
ISBN 978-0-521-87992-7 (hardback) – ISBN 978-1-107-40039-9 (paperback)
1. Pornography – United States – History. 2. Feminism – United States – History.
3. Women – Crimes against – United States – History. I. Title.
HQ471.B727 2011
363.4'7097309047–dc22 2010043981

ISBN 978-0-521-87992-7 Hardback
ISBN 978-1-107-40039-9 Paperback

For my parents

Contents

Figures

Acknowledgments

I would like to thank a number of individuals and institutions that have provided intellectual, financial, and emotional support for this book, and to whom I am deeply grateful. I have been researching and writing about feminist responses to media violence and pornography, and the development of both an anti-pornography movement and a countermovement, for ten years and have received help at every turn from inspiring scholars, dedicated colleagues, encouraging friends, and a patient and loving family. The sociologist Benita Roth has observed, altering a well-known African proverb, that it takes "several villages" to aid one in writing a book, and my own experience confirms the wisdom of her statement. Any flaws that a reader may find in this work rest solely with the author, but everything valuable and insightful in the pages that follow has been made better by the contributions of the people and organizations named here.

My intellectual debts are many and stretch across three institutions: the University of Wisconsin-Madison, Stanford University, and DePaul University.

My professors at the University of Wisconsin-Madison shared their passion for research and modeled the highest standards of academic excellence as I pursued my doctoral studies. I thank the historian James L. Baughman for teaching me how to conduct historical research and how to write a compelling narrative that reveals the significance of past events for contemporary social life. He has championed this book project since its first iteration, offered thoughtful feedback as the project evolved, and never wavered in his enthusiasm for the topic or my approach to it. I am a better scholar for having been his student. I thank the historian Linda Gordon, a mentor whose commitment to women's history and devotion to students inspires me every day, as does her phenomenal and ever-expanding body of work. Linda urged me to write a seminar paper on pornography many years ago, seeing the topic as a perfect fusion of my dual interests in media studies and the history of sexuality. Her intellectual guidance has been critical to my understanding of the role that the pornography debates played within second wave feminism, and she generously read and commented on my work as it evolved from that initial paper.

I also wish to thank the political scientist Donald A. Downs, who offered intellectual and moral support and shared his own experiences writing about the challenging subject of pornography. Robert McChesney, Jo Ellen Fair, and Douglas McLeod read and commented on earlier drafts and provided helpful critiques. Suzanne Pingree published seminal communication research on sexism in 1970s advertising; studying with her enabled me to understand the social context that motivated feminist organizing against violence and gender stereotyping in mass media content. Jim Danky read my work, suggested a host of resources – including the newsletters of many feminist anti-pornography groups at the State Historical Society of Wisconsin – and shared his deep knowledge of women's activism in the 1970s and 1980s.

At Stanford University, my undergraduate mentor, Marion Lewenstein, fostered my interest in media history through her *Literature of the Press* seminar, urged me to consider an academic career, and set the path in motion with a teaching assistantship. Ted Glasser, my Master's advisor, opened up the world of critical thinking through his journalism ethics classes and helped me develop the spirit of inquiry that guided this book from start to finish.

At DePaul University, I thank Dean Jacqueline Taylor of the College of Communication for her leadership, her deep engagement with research, and a steadfast commitment to gender studies evident in her own scholarship. I appreciate many wonderful colleagues who have talked with me about this research and have provided insight and comic relief, including Lexa Murphy, Daniel Makagon, Margaret Storey, Barb Willard, Julie Artis, and Teresa Mastin.

For financial support of the project, I am grateful to the DePaul University Research Council, Dean Jacqueline Taylor, and the College of Communication for providing grants to support the publication of the extraordinary photographs that appear in this book. I also received significant grant funding from the Schlesinger Library at Harvard University that supported two extended visits to read the Women Against Pornography manuscript collection.

I thank the women who organized and populated the major groups under study in this book: Women Against Violence Against Women (WAVAW); Women Against Violence in Pornography and Media (WAVPM); and Women Against Pornography (WAP). I have tremendous respect for activists' efforts to raise consciousness about the psychological and behavioral effects of sexually violent images of women in advertising, entertainment and news media, and pornography. For sharing their perspectives on the media reform campaigns that WAVAW led, and the subsequent anti-pornography efforts of WAVPM and WAP, I am grateful to activists Julia London (WAVAW), Bridget Wynne (WAVPM), and Dolores Alexander (WAP), and the performance artists Suzanne Lacy and Leslie Labowitz-Starus. The women's movement photographer Bettye Lane generously permitted me to reproduce many of her photographs. I thank her for this, and for capturing significant moments in the history of anti-pornography organizing, allowing us to see many of the people and events described in these pages. In the years that have elapsed between the time that I started researching the topic and this book's publication, some leading anti-pornography activists have died, as have some of the women who challenged the movement's basic premises. I note the passing of Ellen Willis, Andrea Dworkin, Frances Patai, Florence Rush, and Dolores Alexander, each of whom played a central role in the life of the movement that this book chronicles.

To conduct my research, I traveled around the United States to numerous libraries and historical archives. Joan Krizack, University Archivist and the head of Special Collections at the Northeastern University Libraries, assisted me with the papers of the Boston chapter of WAVAW. Ann Giagni and Jeri Dietrich, volunteers at the June L. Mazer Lesbian Archives in West Hollywood, California, arranged special off-hours access to the national (Los Angeles) WAVAW files to make sure that I had sufficient time to read the entire collection. Rebekah Kim, Managing Archivist of the GLBT Historical Society in San Francisco, supported my research on WAVPM and somehow made time to scan all of the photographs that I requested. At the Schlesinger Library, archivists Eva Moseley and Susan von Salis offered guidance as I read the WAP manuscript collection. Toward the end of this project, librarian Diana Carey provided assistance with photographs from the WAP records.

At Cambridge University Press, I am grateful to Lewis Bateman for recognizing the project's potential to make a meaningful contribution. Eric Crahan supervised the (lengthy, lengthy) writing and revising process with skill, wit, humor, and a vast knowledge of American history and politics. I thank Eric for his supreme patience as I discovered yet one more manuscript collection that simply had to be included and one more revision that I felt compelled to complete. Eric, I thank you from the bottom of my heart for giving me the time and space that I needed to bring this project to fruition. Jason Przybylski provided superb editorial assistance.

Through my association with Cambridge, I had the great fortune to meet the historian Jane Gerhard, to whom I am indebted for detailed, thoughtful critiques of two different versions of the manuscript. Jane enriched my thinking, pushed me to clarify my arguments, and made recommendations for revisions based on her extensive knowledge of second wave feminist sexual thought that radically improved the quality of the final product. Jane recognized the potential merit of the project after reading the first draft, and her assurance that it would help fill a significant gap in second wave history gave me the confidence to complete the book.

Many other colleagues and friends deserve thanks. Kathy Fitzpatrick has offered constant encouragement and advice on the academic side of life, and an enduring friendship that I count on daily. Linda Steiner shares my passion for the study of media and gender, and her insights, as well as her buoyant spirit, infuse these pages. I thank Ruth Conniff, Shayla Stern, Brooke Liu, Sheila Webb, and Tracy Poe. I thank Carol and Howard Wayne for opening their home to me for two extended stays while I worked at the Schlesinger Library.

This book would not have been possible without the love and support of my wonderful family. I thank my sister, Diane Bronstein Wayne, for lifelong friendship. My three young children have accompanied me on this journey, providing an endless supply of affection, laughter, and fun. Thank you David, Lauren, and Adam. Thank you Janie and Richard Tapper, for taking your grandchildren on vacations and for week-long visits, showering them with love and attention while creating much-needed time for me to finish the manuscript.

My husband, John Tapper, makes everything possible. I thank him for his kind spirit, humor, encouragement, and devotion. I thank him for understanding the many days and nights that I spent away from our family to complete this book, and I love him for being right there waiting for me when I finally emerged.

My parents, Enid and Eugene Bronstein, were my first – and are still my best – teachers. My father, a veteran of World War II and a member of the Greatest Generation, taught me feminist principles as a child. He had no direct experience with the women's movement, only what he read in the newspaper or viewed on television, but he saw women rising and urged my sister and me to develop our talents, pursue meaningful work, and insist on our rights to enjoy both family life and productive, advancing careers. My mother taught me to read at age three and has been helping me accomplish my goals every day since. Her reassuring counsel that I would find a way to finish this book, teach my classes, parent my children, and manage whatever else life sent my way made me believe it was possible. My gratitude to my parents is boundless, as is my love for them. Mom and Dad, thank you for everything. I dedicate this book to you.

Introduction

Battling Pornography

The American Feminist Anti-Pornography Movement, 1976–1986

Beginning with Betty Friedan's 1963 analysis of the role that women's magazines and advertising played in normalizing female subordination within patriarchy and consumer capitalism, media representation provided a significant source of concern for the women's movement. Media constructions offered women limited roles, typically the happy housewife and mother, or the sexual object whose primary function was that of male plaything. Feminist scholars throughout the 1970s paid serious attention to advertising and found that women were rarely depicted in professional working roles or shown without the presence of a male escort in public. Women were primarily featured in ads for cleaning products, clothing, and home appliances, whereas men were shown in advertisements for cars, travel, and banks. Building on this body of image studies, activists and academic researchers including Lucy Komisar, Midge Kovacs, Jean Kilbourne, Gaye Tuchman, and Erving Goffman argued that this visual environment created and maintained conditions of gender inequality.[1]

By the mid-1970s, the "limited roles" critique of sexist media representation expanded to include insights derived from the radical feminist critique of heterosexuality. Feminists looked with new understanding at images that conflated female sexuality and violence, and claimed that they functioned

[1] For a thorough and compelling overview of feminist concern with mass media representation in the early 1970s, see Patricia Bradley, *Mass Media and the Shaping of American Feminism, 1963–1975* (Jackson: University of Mississippi Press, 2005). See also Katharina Lindner, "Images of Women in General Interest and Fashion Magazine Advertisements from 1955 to 2002," *Sex Roles* 51, no. 7/8 (October 2004): 409–421. Some of the influential early studies of advertising representation include: Alice Courtney and Sarah Lockeretz, "A Woman's Place: An Analysis of the Roles Portrayed by Women in Magazine Advertisements," *Journal of Marketing Research* 8 (February 1971): 92–95; Ahmed Belkaoui and Janice M. Belkaoui, "A Comparative Analysis of the Roles Portrayed by Women in Print Advertisements: 1958, 1970, 1972," *Journal of Marketing Research* 13 (May 1976): 168–172; and Lucy Komisar, "The Image of Woman in Advertising," in *Woman in Sexist Society: Studies in Power and Powerlessness*, eds. Vivian Gornick and Barbara K. Moran (New York: Basic Books, 1971), 207–217.

like training manuals for young men growing up in a patriarchal society organized around the domination and oppression of women. Sexually violent media images encouraged the pervasive culture of male violence, contributing to the epidemic of rape and battering newly discovered within the consciousness raising groups popularized by radical feminism. Organizing in grassroots groups around the country, women protested the use of sexually violent images for entertainment and to sell products, arguing that this commercial exploitation fueled an appalling social problem.

These activists connected their insights about real-world media effects to a new body of radical feminist theory that revealed heterosexuality as an institution and ideology that created and maintained male supremacy. The gender stereotypes commonly found in popular media presented women as innately passive, childlike, and vulnerable. Men, by contrast, were aggressive, brutal, and lacked the capacity for restraint, qualities that seemed to encourage rape and other forms of sexual violence. Turning a critical eye to advertising, television, magazines, popular music, and films, feminist activists interpreted mediated violence against women as a powerful tool of patriarchal control. By glorifying sexual violence, mass media taught men to view women as subhuman, as sex objects designed for use and abuse. They also taught women that their primary obligation was to serve men's domestic and sexual needs, excusing violent behavior as a normal aspect of male sexual drive. By connecting sexually oppressive media images to concrete acts of sexual violence, like rape and battering, these feminists laid the groundwork for the rise of an American feminist anti-pornography movement.

This book chronicles the formation and development of an American feminist anti-pornography movement from 1976 to 1986, emphasizing the internal movement dynamics and external structural factors that supported a progression from a campaign against images of sexual violence in mainstream media, especially advertising, to a focus on pornography, including nonviolent, sexually explicit expression. The vast majority of scholarship on the anti-pornography movement concentrates on the latter part of this campaign, specifically the mid-1980s efforts of the legal scholar Catharine MacKinnon and the radical feminist author Andrea Dworkin to introduce anti-pornography ordinances that treated pornography as a form of sex discrimination that violated women's civil rights. This book has a different emphasis. It focuses on the earlier years, tracing the emergence and development of the three most influential feminist media reform groups that led the movement in the 1970s and early 1980s: Women Against Violence Against Women (WAVAW) (Los Angeles, 1976); Women Against Violence in Pornography and Media (WAVPM) (San Francisco, 1976); and Women Against Pornography (WAP) (New York, 1979).[2]

[2] There were a number of other grassroots feminist organizations that helped comprise the anti-pornography movement, and each organization defined the problem of pornography – and the preferred solutions – differently. Some of these other groups included Women Against Sexist Violence in Pornography and Media (WASVP/M) in Pittsburgh, Feminists Against

In restoring the history of these groups, this book locates the origins of the feminist anti-pornography movement in grassroots campaigns against sexually violent and sexist mainstream media content. WAVAW, WAVPM, and WAP took issue with the presentation of women in American advertising and pressured corporations to withdraw campaigns that celebrated sexual violence. WAVAW protested a 1976 advertising campaign for the Rolling Stones' album *Black and Blue*, which portrayed a beaten and bruised woman straddling a photograph of Mick Jagger and the other band members, her eyes closed and mouth hanging open in an expression of intense sexual arousal. WAVPM urged Max Factor to cancel an ad for its *Self-Defense* brand of moisturizing cream that warned women of the need to protect themselves from dirt, grime, and other elements that would "attack" and spoil their beauty. The campaign mocked women's fears of rape and other forms of sexual assault. WAVPM and WAP led a joint protest against the 1981 advertising campaign for the Hanes brand of pantyhose, whose slogan boldly proclaimed that "Gentlemen Prefer Hanes." Feminists criticized the parent corporation for reinforcing what the radical feminist Adrienne Rich termed "compulsory heterosexuality," namely the heterosexist idea that every woman needed to be tied to a man sexually and emotionally. This ad perpetuated the idea that a woman's primary function was to please a man, reduced a woman to her body parts – "'sexy legs' for men to leer at" – and provided daily ideological support for male supremacy and an oppressive patriarchal order.[3]

WAVAW, WAVPM, and WAP tried to disrupt and subsequently improve mainstream media images. They opposed a proliferation of commercial images that glorified violence and reinforced gender stereotypes about women and men that fostered sexist attitudes and behavior. They shared the goal of ending rape, battering, sexual harassment, and other forms of sexual violence. Each organization sought to improve the material conditions of women's lives by calling for reform of a visual environment polluted by sexist and sexually violent messages. Using national consumer action and public education techniques, as well as performance art, feminist conferences, marches, and demonstrations, these organizations led a creative and innovative battle to improve the media, reduce violence against women, and pave the way for true liberation.

At the same time that advertising and other mainstream media captured these groups' attention, the question of pornography – sexually explicit material – always hung in the air. WAVAW, WAVPM, and WAP crafted different approaches to the issue. Members of WAVAW were always careful to describe themselves as anti-media violence, and not as anti-pornography, although the group had initially organized in 1976 to block distribution of

Pornography in Washington, DC, Citizens for Media Responsibility Without Law in Oshkosh, Wisconsin, and People Against Pornography in Chicago. These groups generally had less influence on the movement as a whole, and thus this history focuses on the three main groups.

[3] Alexandra Matusinka, "Hanes' Double Exploitation of Women," *WAP NewsReport* (Spring/Summer 1983), 8.

an X-rated film called *Snuff* that purported to show the on-screen rape, murder, and evisceration of a young woman. As in the case of the Rolling Stones' *Black and Blue*, the organization feared that depictions of violence conflated with sexual enjoyment created dangerous gender stereotypes and lent credibility to the myth that women were sexually aroused by brutal treatment. *Snuff* was an appropriate target for action in WAVAW's view because it featured overt images of physical violence against women, not because it was sexually explicit. Although many organization members resented the increased sexualization of American culture in the 1970s, and the public presentation of women's bodies as sexual objects, they did not consider pornography per se to be a target for action. Organization leaders feared that an all-out war against pornography would lead to sexual repression and censorship, and would distract attention from the intended focus on mainstream media portrayals of violent behavior that showed women as willing victims and men as natural brutes.

In December 1976, San Francisco-area feminists founded WAVPM, identifying pornography from the outset as an important component of their anti-violence agenda. The members of this organization shared WAVAW's commitment to fighting depictions of violence in advertising and other mainstream media, but also believed that pornography was central to women's oppression. WAVPM expanded the movement's definition of media violence and advanced some of the first analyses of the covert, psychological violence against women that sexually explicit images, such as *Playboy* centerfolds, were thought to contain. Within weeks of its founding, WAVPM was leading protest marches through San Francisco's commercial sex districts, arguing that XXX films and adult bookstores created a hostile climate that taught men to view women as sexual playthings. In the words of Andrea Dworkin, one of the anti-pornography movement's most important theorists, pornography "conditions, trains, educates, and inspires men to despise women, to use women, to hurt women."[4] Pornography reinforced the idea that sexual access to women's bodies – whether freely given or taken by force – was every man's right. The radical feminist activist Robin Morgan summed this up in a pithy phrase oft-repeated in the movement: "Pornography is the theory, and rape the practice."[5]

In 1979, the feminist anti-pornography movement seemed to take a decisive turn away from its broad-based set of concerns about media violence with the founding of WAP. Prominent New York radical feminists, including Susan Brownmiller, Gloria Steinem and Robin Morgan launched this organization. These women believed that emphasizing a hot-button issue like pornography, as opposed to media violence, would generate extensive news coverage and

[4] Andrea Dworkin, "Pornography and Grief," in *Take Back the Night: Women on Pornography*, ed. Laura Lederer (New York: William Morrow, 1980), 289.

[5] Robin Morgan, "Theory and Practice: Pornography and Rape," in *Take Back the Night: Women on Pornography*, ed. Laura Lederer (New York: William Morrow, 1980), 139.

community support. The strategic rhetorical shift, coupled with high-profile leaders and generous financial backing from the Mayor's office and business groups who endorsed Times Square gentrification efforts, ensured that WAP would move to the forefront of the feminist anti-pornography movement.

Like their sisters in WAVAW and WAVPM, members of WAP believed that mainstream media images were powerful agents of socialization; they taught men and women about their respective worth in society and communicated insidious gender stereotypes. WAP participated in a range of protests against abusive advertising campaigns, popular films, television programs, and magazines that suggested that women deserved to be exploited and humiliated. But the calculated reorientation to pornography meant that the organization had less time and fewer resources to devote to these broad-based, grassroots media reform efforts, a reality that changed the nature of the movement as a whole. In 1983, WAP leaders endorsed government action and legal strategies to ban violent pornography, concluding that state-supported suppression of this material was the best means of addressing women's second-class status. The organization mobilized on behalf of the MacKinnon-Dworkin anti-pornography ordinances that treated pornography as a violation of women's civil rights. WAP also provided witnesses who gave testimony about the destructive influence of pornography to Attorney General Edwin Meese's 1985 Commission on Pornography. This political body was stacked with religious conservatives and was widely interpreted as a sop to right-wing groups who had helped Ronald Reagan win the presidency, and demanded action on family values issues in return.

Although there was a great deal of heterogeneity among WAVAW, WAVPM, and WAP with respect to their ideas, beliefs, strategies, and tactics, the feminist anti-pornography movement is often described as a monolith, a one-issue movement unified behind a drive for legislative action. The dominant popular view holds that the anti-pornography movement consisted of groups who drummed up widespread national feminist support for the ordinances drafted by MacKinnon and Dworkin, who "somehow became virtually the sole recognized figures for all radical feminism in the 1980s," as Lynn S. Chancer has observed.[6]

In reality, anti-pornography was a complex and multifaceted movement made up of diverse and overlapping feminist groups who articulated their own sets of ideas and goals. These groups never reached consensus on the best way to fight sexualized media violence and they did not simply fall in line behind MacKinnon and Dworkin. Some of the groups, including WAVAW, rejected the focus on pornography altogether, concerned that this approach constituted a threat to individual speech rights and sexual freedom while letting mainstream media, such as advertising and popular films, off the hook. Yet at the same time that these groups exhibited significant differences, it was

[6] Lynn S. Chancer, *Reconcilable Differences: Confronting Beauty, Pornography and the Future of Feminism* (Berkeley: University of California Press, 1998), 20.

clear that they shared theoretical linkages, structural similarities, intellectual origins in the radical feminist critique of heterosexuality, and a sincere desire among members to reform the media landscape in ways that would increase women's rights. WAVAW, WAVPM, and WAP acknowledged one another as "sister organizations" that were part of the same movement, namely "the struggle against commercial and cultural exploitation of violence against women."[7] In opposing sexualized depictions of women that contributed to their oppression, each group played a role in the evolution of a full-fledged feminist anti-pornography movement.

Two distinct purposes guide the account of the feminist anti-pornography movement set forth in this book. First, as a media scholar, I wanted to make sense of the explosive set of social and cultural conditions affecting American women's lives in the mid-1970s that encouraged sexually violent media images to emerge as a key concern. What were the environmental triggers that motivated groups of women at this point in time to train their attention on a subset of media images and identify them as a major cause of female oppression? In a related question, I wondered why a grassroots consumer action and public education campaign against sexual violence in mainstream media, especially advertising, transformed over time into an anti-pornography effort that included nonviolent, sexually explicit expression as a primary target for action. Why did pornography eclipse more mainstream forms of sexualized media violence as the movement progressed, and how did this rhetorical and tactical shift affect each of the groups under study, as well as the direction of the larger movement?

To answer these questions about movement origins and the focus on media images, I examined key social and political developments that affected American women in the years just prior to the formation of WAVAW, WAVPM, and WAP. I found that the groups were populated by individuals who shared common interpretations of a series of conditions during the late 1960s and early 1970s. These included the failed promise of the sexual revolution, the growth of awareness of male violence against women, the development of a radical feminist political critique of heterosexuality, and concern over the commercialization of sex.

As the first few chapters of this book reveal, ideological changes in the Women's Liberation movement in the years prior to the emergence of anti-pornography combined explosively with feminist outrage at the disappointments of the sexual revolution and the discovery of an epidemic of male sexual violence. Although the sexual revolution did enlarge women's right to engage more freely in sexual behavior, it provided little support for women to define their sexuality free of male standards and expectations. Many women felt exploited by a revolution that privileged male desire and enlarged the male right of access. New knowledge about the prevalence of sexual violence, particularly rape, exacerbated women's anger at the oppressive aspects of

7 "On Porn," *WAVAW Newsletter*, no. 8 (1980): 1, 4.

sexuality. Feminists analyzed female vulnerability to sexual pressure and sexual coercion as part of the system of power that men used to maintain and reinforce women's subordination. This mix of conditions supported a feminist consensus opposing depictions of male violence against women as glorifying a symbol and agent of female oppression.

Widespread dissatisfaction with the sexual revolution had many women convinced that the current heterosexual order left women at a significant disadvantage. By the mid-1970s, years of consciousness raising (CR) within the radical feminist wing of the Women's Liberation movement had exposed the callous disregard many men reserved for their female sexual partners, the social pressures that led women to capitulate to unwanted sex, the health risks associated with birth control pills, the devastating effects of venereal disease, and the terror of unwanted pregnancy, which was particularly acute in the pre-*Roe* years when women had no right to safe, legal abortion. Some of this knowledge was channeled into the articulation of political lesbianism, the theory that every committed feminist should oppose patriarchy by withdrawing sexual and social support from men. For a greater number of individuals, however, the disappointments of the sexual revolution hardened into general resentment of men's greater sexual rights and planted seeds of discontent that would support the emergence of anti-pornography sentiment.

Within the CR groups popularized by the Women's Liberation movement, sex provided much fodder for conversation. These intimate discussions not only helped many women realize that the sexual revolution had resulted in fewer favorable outcomes for women than men, but also revealed the pervasive problem of male sexual violence. The discussion of sexual experiences inevitably led women to share painful incidents of coercion, and the prevalence of rape, battering, and incest became known for the first time. Feminists recognized that male violence was part of the fabric of every woman's life through firsthand experience or chronic fear. In the early 1970s, they initiated national campaigns to publicize the problem, provide shelters and counseling for victims, and rewrite sexist laws that exploited women's vulnerabilities. Feminist theorists analyzed violence in revolutionary ways as a patriarchal political tool that benefited all men, because it kept women fearful, timid, and dependent on male protection.[8]

The combination by the mid-1970s of an expansive radical feminist critique of heterosexuality as an institution and an ideology that maintained and reinforced male supremacy, coupled with rage about the sexual oppression of women and the ubiquity of male violence, created a volatile mix of conditions that supported the growth of the anti-pornography analysis. Leading radical

[8] Influential writings incorporating this analysis of violence include: Susan Griffin, "Rape: The All-American Crime," *Ramparts* 10 (1971): 26–35; Andra Medea and Kathleen Thompson, *Against Rape* (New York: Farrar, Straus and Giroux, 1974); Robin Morgan, "Theory and Practice: Pornography and Rape," in *Take Back the Night: Women on Pornography*, ed. L. Lederer (New York: William Morrow, 1980); Susan Brownmiller, *Against Our Will: Men, Women and Rape* (New York: Simon & Schuster, 1975).

feminists began to question where men might *learn* the destructive male values that perpetuated a misogynist culture. Where were men *learning* that it was a male right to abuse, humiliate, and terrorize women? These theorists advanced a social constructionist view of male behavior which held that men learned through media exposure and firsthand observation that it was natural and appropriate for them to dominate women. Mass media images that showed women as domestic servants, or as glorified sexual objects, or worse, as victims of sexual violence, were cultural texts that perpetuated female oppression. These were revolutionary ideas. For women seeking to understand the prevalence of abuse and the male desensitization to violence revealed through radical feminist consciousness raising, the idea that mainstream media and pornography played a role was nothing short of a breakthrough. Susan Brownmiller stated this flatly in her landmark study of rape, *Against Our Will*, when she wrote: "Pornography is the undiluted essence of antifemale propaganda."[9] Pornography reified a hegemonic, aggressive masculinity and taught men to treat women as sex objects, as less than fully human.

The issue of pornography galvanized significant segments of the women's movement in the late 1970s, and appeared to many feminists to be a unifying campaign that might rally all comers. The condemnation of sexually explicit, male-oriented material conformed to the prevailing radical feminist critique of heterosexuality as an institution and an ideology that maintained and reinforced male supremacy, and it resonated with women's anger about greater male sexual license and fear of sexual crime. Pornography was filled with dangerous images of violence against women and was increasingly visible in the public sphere after a series of liberal Supreme Court rulings on obscenity. It was distasteful and horrifying to many women who saw it as a key player in creating and maintaining structural inequalities that deprived women of their civil rights. An anti-pornography campaign would focus on a universal issue that seemed to affect all women because all women were victimized by images that might inspire male brutality. Fighting pornography was a way of launching an all-out war against *male sexual violence*, capturing with one target three areas of tremendous feminist discontent.

My second purpose in writing this book emerged as I studied the early phase of movement history to make sense of the gradual transition to anti-pornography. As I pored over the organizations' manuscript collections to reconstruct their work against media violence, it became clear that the reform accomplished in the first years of the movement, particularly by WAVAW and WAVPM prior to the founding of WAP, had received little critical attention. The successful campaigns that these groups waged against such establishment media conglomerates as Warner Communications were rendered almost invisible in historical scholarship and popular accounts, creating a significant gap in media history and the history of second-wave feminist organizing. By way of comparison, the MacKinnon-Dworkin period of anti-pornography activity

[9] Brownmiller, *Against Our Will*, 394.

has received extensive popular and academic analysis, resulting in a massive body of literature that examines both their theories of pornography's harms and the drive to pass ordinances in Minneapolis, Indianapolis, and several other American cities. This literature originates from every conceivable theoretical perspective, including radical feminist, civil libertarian, third-wave feminist, liberal feminist, socialist feminist, First Amendment, neoconservative, postmodernist, sex radical, religious conservative, and empirical social scientific, among others.[10]

[10] For just a few of the literally thousands of texts, see these examples. For the **liberal/ First Amendment** position: Donald Alexander Downs, *The New Politics of Pornography* (Chicago: University of Chicago Press, 1989); Nadine Strossen, *Defending Pornography: Free Speech, Sex, and the Fight for Women's Rights* (New York: Scribner, 1995); ACLU Arts Censorship Project, *Above the Law: The Justice Department's War Against the First Amendment* (Medford, NY: American Civil Liberties Union, 1991); Ronald Dworkin, "Women and Pornography" in *Prostitution and Pornography: Philosophical Debate about the Sex Industry*, ed. Jessica Spector (Palo Alto, CA: Stanford University Press, 2006), 296–309; **feminist anti-censorship**: Varda Burstyn, ed., *Women Against Censorship* (Toronto: Douglas & McIntyre, 1985); Carole S. Vance, "Negotiating Sex and Gender in the Attorney General's Commission on Pornography," in *The Gender and Sexuality Reader: Culture, History, Political Economy*, eds. Roger N. Lancaster and Micaela di Leonardo (New York: Routledge, 1997), 440–452; Symposium: The Sex Panic: Women, Censorship and 'Pornography,' *New York Law School Law Review* 37, no. 1–4 (1993); Marcia Pally, *Sense and Censorship: The Vanity of Bonfires* (Americans for Constitutional Freedom, 1991); **radical feminist**: Catharine MacKinnon and Andrea Dworkin, *Pornography and Civil Rights: A New Day for Women's Equality* (Minneapolis, MN: Organizing Against Pornography, 1988); Dorchen Leidholdt and Janice Raymond, *The Sexual Liberals and the Attack on Feminism* (New York: Pergamon, 1990); Catherine Itzin, ed., *Pornography: Women, Violence and Civil Liberties* (Oxford: Oxford University Press, 1993); **pro-sex/sex radical/sexual libertarian**: Alison Assiter and Avedon Carol, *Bad Girls & Dirty Pictures: The Challenge to Reclaim Feminism* (Boulder, CO: Pluto Press, 1993); Brenda Cossman, Shannon Bell, Lise Gotell, and Becki Ross, *Bad Attitude/s on Trial: Pornography, Feminism, and the Butler Decision* (Toronto: University of Toronto Press, 1997); Pamela Church Gibson and Roma Gibson, eds. *Dirty Looks: Women, Pornography, Power* (London: British Film Institute, 1993); **liberal feminist**: Martha Nussbaum, *Sex & Social Justice* (New York: Oxford University Press, 1999); Zillah Eisenstein, *The Female Body and the Law* (Berkeley: University of California Press, 1988); Jeanne L. Schroeder, "The Taming of the Shrew: The Liberal Attempt to Mainstream Radical Feminist Theory," *Yale Journal of Law and Feminism* 123, no. 5 (1992): 135–162; **postmodern**: Mary Jo Frug, *Postmodern Legal Feminism* (New York: Routledge, 1992), 145–153; Judith Butler, *Excitable Speech: A Politics of the Performative* (New York: Routledge, 1997); **third wave**: Rene Denfeld, *The New Victorians: A Young Woman's Challenge to the Old Feminist Order* (New York: Warner Books, 1995); Katie Roiphe, *The Morning After: Sex, Fear and Feminism on Campus* (New York: Little, Brown, 1993); **right-wing conservative**: Whitney Strub, *Perversion for Profit: The Politics of Pornography and the Rise of the New Right* (New York: Columbia University Press, 2011); Janice M. Irvine, *Talk About Sex: The Battles Over Sex Education in the United States* (Berkeley: University of California Press, 2002); Louis A. Zurcher Jr. and R. George Kirkpatrick, *Citizens for Decency: Anti-Pornography Crusades as Status Defense* (Austin: University of Texas Press, 1976); **empirical social science**: Edward Donnerstein, Daniel Linz, and Steven Penrod, *The Question of Pornography: Research Findings and Policy Implications* (New York: The Free Press, 1987); Thelma McCormack, "Making Sense of the Research on Pornography," in *Women Against Censorship*, ed. Varda Burstyn (Vancouver: Douglas & McIntyre, 1985).

One result of the dearth of scholarship on the first phase of the movement is that the accomplishments of the earlier groups are often overlooked. Another, more serious result is that the intent of the anti-pornography movement as a whole is frequently mischaracterized. Three examples from recent, widely read books may help illustrate these points. David Allyn, in his history of the sexual revolution *Make Love, Not War*, correctly establishes WAVAW as a predecessor to WAP, but writes that the organization fell apart in 1978. In reality, WAVAW was at the height of its national influence at that point, and would win major concessions from Warner Communications in December 1979 after carrying out a three-year national boycott of its record labels. Allyn also indicates that WAP "borrowed many tactics from the [anti-abortion] right, including the use of a slide show," when in fact the WAP slide show was a modified version of the ones created by WAVAW and WAVPM in 1976–1977.[11] Members of Los Angeles WAVAW had drawn inspiration for this tactic directly from Hollywood films, and the project benefited from the technical expertise of members who worked in the entertainment industry. If Allyn intended to draw a parallel to the widely distributed anti-abortion video, *The Silent Scream*, it should be noted that this video appeared in 1984, almost a decade after WAVAW members began presenting their slide show to community groups.

These are minor factual discrepancies, and I point to them only as a means of illustrating the incomplete historical record that exists with regard to the initial years of feminist anti-pornography organizing. The more serious and common errors date the beginning of anti-pornography to the formation of WAP, write WAVAW and WAVPM out of the picture entirely, and attribute support for anti-sexual ideas and censorship tactics to all movement actors. Journalist Ariel Levy writes in her 2005 book, *Female Chauvinist Pigs*, that a "splinter group of activists" including Steinem and Brownmiller discovered the pornography problem in 1979.[12] Brownmiller, of course, had been railing against pornography since at least 1975, when she pointed out its dangers to a national audience in *Against Our Will*. Steinem had been struggling to define the difference between pornography and erotica in the pages of *Ms.* for at least two years prior to the founding of WAP. Truncating the chronology of anti-pornography in this way erases a significant prior body of feminist activism and obscures the reality that most participants were interested

This is an incomplete list, and I am making rough distinctions here for the sole purpose of making a point about the sheer volume of writing on the MacKinnon-Dworkin and Meese Commission anti-pornography efforts. Some of the works listed here easily fit in two or more categories, and some of the most influential anthologies did not make it onto this list because they include a range of essays exploring anti-pornography efforts from many different ideological positions, for example, Drucilla Cornell, ed. *Feminism & Pornography* (New York: Oxford University Press, 2000).

[11] David Allyn, *Make Love, Not War: The Sexual Revolution: An Unfettered History* (New York: Routledge, 2001), 281, 289.

[12] Ariel Levy, *Female Chauvinist Pigs: Women and the Rise of Raunch Culture* (New York: Free Press, 2005), 60.

in fighting a broad range of sexually violent and sexist mainstream media images. Furthermore, by treating the tail end of the anti-pornography movement, specifically the MacKinnon-Dworkin period, as if it comprised the whole, some postfeminist authors find a basis for excoriating the second wave. Rene Denfeld writes in *The New Victorians*, a scathing critique that takes special aim at anti-pornography, that "to be a feminist today one must support the censorship of sexual material."[13] In fact, the contextualized history of the anti-pornography movement presented here reveals that a majority of movement activists opposed violence, not sex – and that many rejected censorship strategies for fear that gay, lesbian, feminist, and other forms of progressive expression would be squelched along with individual freedoms.

The importance of restoring the full history of the feminist anti-pornography movement thus connects to something far more significant than a sense of second-wave nostalgia, or a desire to celebrate the accomplishments of a band of dedicated activists. When we look at the initial campaigns, such as the nationwide protests against *Snuff* and *Black and Blue*, it is clear that they were based on the radical feminist critique of socially constructed gender differences that falsely divided the sexes into something akin to separate species. These artificial gender roles – woman as passive, willing victim and man as aggressive, lustful brute – were thought to damage men just as badly as women. Early anti-pornography feminists insisted that constant media depictions of these stereotypes warped males' ideas of what real masculinity entailed and encouraged gender-based violence against women, including rape, battering, and sexual harassment. Restoring the full history should help us reconsider the legacy of anti-pornography for American feminism and refute the anti-sexual reputation of the second wave that looms so large in many contemporary accounts. When one takes a long view of anti-pornography organizing, as I do in this book, it becomes clear that the vast majority of activists saw their efforts to eradicate sexually violent media and the artificial gender differences they promoted as a critical step toward authentic sexual liberation for all.

Methodological Considerations

To construct an account of the formation and development of the major groups under study, WAVAW, WAVPM, and WAP, I have drawn from a wide variety of primary and secondary sources. The most significant sources were the internal movement documents created by the organizations themselves. To their credit, each of the groups under study had the foresight to preserve their organizational records and donate them to historical archives. These papers, which include documents ranging from telephone logs, committee memos, and meeting minutes to flyers posted and correspondence sent and received, allowed me to understand the ideas, challenges, conflicts, goals, campaigns, and personalities that animated the groups, and I have drawn extensively from them.

[13] Denfeld, *The New Victorians*, 91.

For the WAVAW organization, I was doubly fortunate, because both the national Los Angeles chapter and the highly active Boston chapter preserved their records. I studied the Los Angeles WAVAW papers (the central organizing chapter) at the June L. Mazer Lesbian Archives in West Hollywood, California. Those papers have since been processed and transferred to the University of California Library, Department of Special Collections. I read the Boston WAVAW chapter papers at the department of Archives and Special Collections of the Northeastern University Libraries. I read the WAVPM manuscript collection at the Gay, Lesbian, Bisexual and Transgender Historical Society in San Francisco. And, finally, I studied the WAP manuscript collection at the Arthur and Elizabeth Schlesinger Library on the History of Women in America, at the Radcliffe Institute at Harvard University. The WAP papers are particularly noteworthy for their breadth, consisting of twenty cartons of organizational records containing news releases, meeting notes, grant proposals, press clippings, correspondence, a slide show, Times Square tour scripts, and many other documents. Because the events under study occurred some thirty years ago, and because extensive archival records for each organization were available, I chose to base my account primarily on the materials generated by movement activists over the course of the natural movement lifecycle. Given the controversy that surrounded the later stages of anti-pornography organizing, and the intense conflict that developed between anti-pornography activists and pro-sex opponents after 1982, I found the archival records to be a reliable and dispassionate guide.[14]

The newsletters produced and distributed by the organizations for their members provided another valuable source of information for the book. The *WAVAW Newsletter*, published by the national chapter in Los Angeles, appeared sporadically from May 1977 until 1980. I found one additional issue of the newsletter that was published in 1982 as part of a brief resurgence of WAVAW activity. The WAVPM newsletter, *WAVPM NewsPage*, was published in Berkeley, California and appeared monthly, with some exceptions, from July 1977 through October 1983. The WAP newsletter, *WAP NewsReport*, was published semiannually in New York and ran from 1979 to 1987. These newsletters constitute a rich resource regarding the anti-media

[14] At the earliest stages of research for this project, I did make contact with several movement activists with the thought of conducting full oral histories to add to this account. However, I found that the bitter conflicts of the 1980s had made women on both sides of the debate wary of any treatment of the movement, fearing the possibility of further vilification of individuals and/or ideological positions. In one instance, a leading anti-pornography movement activist consented to be interviewed only if I would sign a statement that assured her that this book would not include any discussion of the Barnard conference and the conflict surrounding events that took place there. After much consideration, and after the WAVPM papers, and later the Los Angeles WAVAW papers became available, completing my set of archival records for each organization, I decided to focus on the manuscript collections. That said, I did conduct six interviews with movement activists, which I do not characterize as oral histories, but which were focused on gathering biographical data, fact checking, and confirming my general impressions of the unfolding of major events.

violence and anti-pornography organizations' demonstrations, marches, and major actions. Some of the newsletters were available in the manuscript collections and I found more in the Social Action collection at the library of the State Historical Society of Wisconsin (SHSW). I read the newsletters of other feminist anti-pornography organizations, such as Women Against Sexist Violence in Pornography and Media (Pittsburgh) and Feminists Against Pornography (Washington, DC) at the SHSW and the Schlesinger Library to round out my understanding of the national network of anti-pornography organizing.

In addition to exploring the organizations' manuscript collections and newsletters, I conducted six interviews with former WAVAW, WAVPM, and WAP activists, making sure to speak to at least one individual from each group who was highly involved in organization activities. I also used material from four published oral histories with feminists who were associated with anti-media violence or anti-pornography activism, or with pro-sex organizing that challenged anti-pornography.[15] I do not consider the interviews that I conducted to be formal oral histories, nor is this account based primarily on them. Instead, I used the interviews to check facts, to flesh out events or organization dynamics that came to light through the manuscript collections, and particularly in the case of WAVAW, to seek biographical data about founding members. My interview with the first national WAVAW coordinator, Julia London, was especially valuable, because the founding of this group was not as well documented by the feminist press or national media as that of the subsequent two organizations. Suzanne Lacy, the visual artist who worked with WAVPM and the performance artist Leslie Labowitz to create the nation's first *Take Back the Night* march, helped me make sense of the organization's commitment to studying media narratives, such as news and advertising campaigns, and understand how feminists deconstructed images of women that fused sex and violence.

In addition to the archival records, newsletters, and interviews, my primary materials included a wide range of feminist newspapers and magazines that both reported on and shaped the development of the anti-pornography movement, as well as books written by radical feminists about violence against women and pornography.[16] The periodicals were published around the nation and included such titles as *off our backs*, *Big Mama Rag*, *The Lesbian Tide*,

[15] I spoke with Julia London (WAVAW); Bridget Wynne (WAVPM); Dolores Alexander (WAP); Suzanne Lacy (Ariadne, WAVPM); Leslie Labowitz Starus (Ariadne, WAVAW), and another WAP activist who requested anonymity, and used published oral histories for Dolores Alexander (WAP); Dorothy Allison (Barnard conference; pro-sex feminist); Amber Hollibaugh (Barnard conference; pro-sex feminist), and Suzanne Lacy.

[16] Verta Taylor and Nancy Whittier define primary materials as books, periodicals, and narratives written by community members, and organizational papers such as newsletters and correspondence and memos. See Taylor and Whittier, "Collective Identity in Social Movement Communities: Lesbian Feminist Mobilization," in *Frontiers in Social Movement Theory*, eds. A. Morris and C. McClurg Mueller (New Haven, CT: Yale University Press, 1992), 105–106.

Aegis: Magazine on Ending Violence Against Women, *Quest*, and *Plexus*. These periodicals provided a vital link among WAVAW, WAVPM, and WAP and the larger women's movement, and were one of the primary ways that feminists who were unaffiliated with the groups learned about their goals. Tracing feminist newspapers' presentation of the organizations and their explanations of the problem of media violence helped me understand *when* and *how* the central ideas of the anti-pornography movement were presented to the American women's movement.

The articles and books written by feminists who were active in anti-violence organizing should also be regarded as movement building blocks. In many cases, the authors helped found and lead the most influential groups, particularly WAVPM (Diana E. H. Russell, Laura Lederer) and WAP (Susan Brownmiller, Gloria Steinem, Susan Griffin, Robin Morgan, Andrea Dworkin). Some of the most influential books considered here are Brownmiller's *Against Our Will: Men, Women and Rape* (1975); Dworkin's *Pornography: Men Possessing Women* (1979); and *Take Back the Night: Women on Pornography* (1980), a collection of essays edited by Laura Lederer. The writings of legal scholar Catharine MacKinnon, who was not involved on a day-to-day basis with any of the organizations under study, were also influential. Her use of the law to create formal equality for women was visible from the start, stemming first from her landmark book, *Sexual Harassment of Working Women* (1979). In later years, this approach was evident when MacKinnon and Dworkin sought to introduce ordinances that made pornography actionable as a violation of women's civil rights. The books that feminists who opposed anti-pornography politics published were also treated as primary sources. Some of these emerged from direct intramovement conflict, such as the Samois collective's *Coming to Power: Writings and Graphics on Lesbian S/M* (1981), which challenged WAVPM's views regarding appropriate feminist sexuality. The controversial 1982 Barnard Conference on sexuality, which brought the ideological rift between anti-pornography and pro-sex feminists into full view, resulted in a flood of new books that examined the importance of freeing women to explore sexual desire. Among these, two of the most significant were *Pleasure and Danger: Exploring Female Sexuality* (1984), edited by Carole Vance, which contained conference workshop papers; and *Diary of a Conference on Sexuality* (1984), a record of the conference planners' meeting notes that was suppressed by Barnard College administrators in response to WAP pressure.

Broadening out from feminist publications, I also read a range of left-wing, trade, and mainstream journalism that chronicled the growth of anti-media violence and anti-pornography politics as national news. These included such publications as *Rolling Stone*, *Billboard*, *Variety*, *Advertising Age*, *Mother Jones*, the *Nation*, and the *Village Voice*. Two public radio documentaries made in 1978 and 1979 about burgeoning feminist anti-media violence and anti-pornography activism allowed me to listen in on group meetings and hear the voices of the activists discussing their movement in real time, a powerful reminder of the energy, passion, and commitment required to initiate social change. The nation's most influential national newspapers and magazines, such as the *New York Times* and the *Los Angeles Times*, and *Time* and *Newsweek*, also covered the movement, and I drew from their coverage to understand how journalists framed the central movement ideas for the American public.

Finally, I have incorporated secondary data from histories of the women's movement and feminist memoirs, as well as social histories of American life in the 1960s and 1970s; histories of sexuality and sexual thought; social scientific research on sexual behavior; legal analyses of obscenity, pornography, and the First Amendment; social movement studies, including third-wave feminism; and film studies. The memoirs and annotated anthologies written by second-wave feminist activists were informative and useful sources, most notably Brownmiller's *In Our Time: Memoir of a Revolution* (1999), which offers a firsthand account of the formation of and early actions undertaken by WAP.[17]

Terminology

Throughout the book, I use the term *media violence* to refer to a broad set of concerns with the sexist conventions common in advertising and mainstream media. WAVAW challenged a wide range of images that constructed women as sexual objects and as appropriate targets for male violence, taking on the entertainment and advertising industries that produced the mainstream content that organization members viewed as especially insidious. WAVAW was an anti-media violence organization that sought to reform abusive practices by demanding *corporate responsibility*, which members defined as a company's obligation to act ethically when using images of women to sell products. Throughout the book, I refer to the national network of WAVAW chapters as part of a campaign against sexualized media violence. I describe WAVAW as leading an anti-media violence movement, differentiating the organization's orientation from the anti-pornography efforts that followed.

I use the term *anti-pornography* to refer to the shift that took place within the movement once WAVPM and WAP redefined the central problem as the objectification of girls and women through male-oriented, sexually explicit images. Although WAVAW was clearly linked to WAVPM and WAP through its emphasis on violence against women, and through shared concerns with advertising and mainstream media, it is not accurate to describe WAVAW as

[17] A few of the many valuable memoirs and anthologies consulted in the writing of this book include: Ellen Willis, *Beginning to See the Light: Sex, Hope and Rock-and-Roll* (Hanover, CT: Wesleyan University Press, 1992); Andrea Dworkin, *Heartbreak: The Political Memoir of a Feminist Militant* (New York: Perseus Books, 2002); Ruth Rosen, *The World Split Open: How the Modern Women's Movement Changed America* (New York: Viking, 2000); Linda Lovelace with Mike McGrady, *Ordeal* (Secaucus, NJ: Citadel Press, 1980); B. Ruby Rich, *Chick Flicks: Theories and Memories of the Feminist Film Movement* (Durham, NC: Duke University Press, 1998); and Amber L. Hollibaugh, *My Dangerous Desires: A Queer Girl Dreaming Her Way Home* (Durham, NC: Duke University Press, 2000).

anti-pornography. WAVAW did not engage in formal action against sexually explicit images that were free of overt violence, no matter how distasteful and offensive some group members may have found such material. The group restricted its campaign to concrete examples of sexual violence, such as the depiction of the rape and murder of the young actress in *Snuff*, and the bruised but sexually excited model photographed for *Black and Blue*.

WAVPM functioned as a bridge group, with strong ties to both the media education and consumer pressure tactics that characterized WAVAW activism, and the emphasis on pornography and its relationship to violence that defined WAP. WAVPM qualifies as an *anti-pornography* organization, but as one that straddled the divide between the anti-media violence campaign pioneered by WAVAW and the full-fledged anti-pornography movement that emerged under WAP. There were continuities among all three organizations; WAP was active in a number of WAVAW-style media reform efforts, such as protest efforts against sexist advertising campaigns and the development in 1982 of an annual WAP ZAPs advertising award program that singled out the worst offenders. WAP, however, was focused on anti-pornography organizing, as its name clearly stated.

The reader should be aware of some slippage here. For lack of any other commonly accepted term, when I discuss the social factors that influenced the long-term growth, development, and trajectory of an *anti-pornography movement*, I am using that term broadly to encompass the whole of feminist organizing around media from 1976 to 1986. This includes all three organizations, and the overall national trend within American feminism to look critically at the role of media images in creating and maintaining female subordination.

In the later chapters of the book, I use the term *pro-sex* to describe a diverse group of feminist writers, scholars, activists, and artists who objected to the feminist anti-pornography analysis on the grounds that it threatened to deprive women of their rights to sexual exploration and diversity. Their analyses were historically consistent with a rich tradition of nineteenth-century pro-sex thought, which stressed that sexual self-determination was an integral part of human freedom. The contemporary pro-sex feminists feared that anti-pornography discourse denied women the right to pursue their sexual desires, especially when those desires contradicted a narrow cultural feminist standard of acceptable sexual behavior.

These activists dubbed themselves pro-sex in the early 1980s as a way of opposing what they saw as anti-pornography's conservative vision of sexuality and its emphasis on the dangers inherent in the sexual exchange. The implication that anti-pornography feminists were anti-sexual was clear, although that description was unfair to many women active in the anti-pornography movement. The most accurate, albeit clumsy, label for the pro-sex feminists would have been "anti-anti-pornography" because they organized to challenge the main premise and tactics of the anti-pornography movement. Most were not champions of sexist pornography, and many of the most vocal pro-sex critics agreed that pornography frequently contained elements of exploitation and abuse. Today, this strain of thought within American feminism is often referred to as sex-positive or as sexual libertarian. However, because members of the countermovement referred to themselves as pro-sex in the period under study, I have chosen to preserve that terminology.[18] In the final two chapters, I use the term *lesbian sexual radicals* to describe members of a lesbian subculture who contested anti-pornography's objection to sexual practices that relied on dominant and submissive role playing, including lesbian sadomasochism and butch-femme eroticism. Many of the lesbian sexual radicals were affiliated with groups like Samois and the Lesbian Sex Mafia that supported and encouraged non-traditional sexuality.

Plan of the Book

The book is divided into three sections. The first section analyzes the social and cultural conditions that supported the rise of the anti-media violence and anti-pornography movements; the second looks at the formation and development of the three major groups under study and how the movement gradually transitioned from an emphasis on mainstream sexualized media violence to pornography; and finally, the third section examines the rise of a countermovement as feminists outside of anti-pornography challenged the analysis of women's sexual victimization under patriarchy and warned that the campaign threatened women's sexual rights and was vulnerable to right-wing encroachment.

In the first part of the book (Chapters 1–3), I seek to explain the mix of social and cultural conditions that led feminists to focus their attention on the issue of sexualized media violence. I discuss a number of factors that changed American women's consciousness in the mid-1970s, including the disappointments of the sexual revolution, a new awareness of male violence against women, a trenchant critique of the institution of heterosexuality, and the growth of the commercial sex industry. I argue that these conditions contributed to a collective understanding that violent and sexist media presentations were dangerous because they taught men and women that sexual arousal and brutality were natural partners and supported stereotypes of men as sexual

[18] When a number of pro-sex feminists banded together in 1983 to help defeat the MacKinnon-Dworkin anti-pornography ordinances, they adopted the label "anti-censorship" as opposed to pro-sex to describe their political position. As historian and activist Lisa Duggan has explained, they hoped that "censorship" would capture the attention of the American public and would be powerful enough to stand up against "pornography." In describing themselves as anti-censorship, however, the feminists did find themselves caught up with civil libertarians and the free speech discourse, which diluted their attempt to make a specifically feminist defense of sexually explicit expression. Although I discuss these activists and the Feminist Anti-Censorship Taskforce briefly in the book, I refer to them as part of the pro-sex countermovement. See Lisa Duggan, "Introduction," in *Sex Wars: Sexual Dissent and Political Culture*, eds. Lisa Duggan and Nan D. Hunter (New York: Routledge, 1995), 8–9.

aggressors and women as their willing victims. These realizations laid the groundwork for a feminist campaign against the depiction of male sexual violence, which evolved over time into a campaign against the depiction of images of women intended for male sexual consumption.

In Chapter 1, I focus on the sexual revolution and the liberalization of American sexual attitudes that began gradually in the United States in the 1920s and accelerated after the mid-1950s. I emphasize concrete changes in behavior in the 1960s and 1970s, such as increased rates of premarital sex and teen pregnancy, and greater transmission of venereal disease, using this data to show that many women experienced negative outcomes. By the mid-1970s, many women resented the greater social pressure to acquiesce to male demands for sex and to assume the physical risks. For many women, the sexual revolution felt sexist and male-oriented. In this chapter, I argue that the behavioral changes associated with the sexual revolution spawned feelings of disillusionment that would surface in the CR groups popularized by the radical feminist wing of the Women's Liberation movement.

In Chapter 2, I discuss the efforts of the Women's Liberation movement to expose an epidemic of male sexual violence and to formulate a critique of heterosexuality as an institution and an ideology that maintained and reinforced male supremacy. Once women began to discuss sex within the safe spaces of CR groups, they revealed episodes of sexual coercion in startling numbers. Radical feminists like Susan Griffin, Robin Morgan, and Susan Brownmiller analyzed rape as a political tool, a "male protection racket," as Griffin described it, that men used to oppress women and maintain their subordination.[19] The threat of sexual violence kept women in a state of fear, powerless, and dependent on male protection. Angered by the injuries and inequalities that characterized American women's lives, and newly aware of the ways that men controlled women through heterosexuality, radical feminists turned a critical eye to media depictions of male sexual desire. In this chapter, I argue that radical feminists grew wary of images that glorified male-identified sexual behavior, especially images laced with violence, and interpreted them through a powerful new theoretic lens as a patriarchal tool of control.

In Chapter 3, I continue the discussion of the effects of the sexual revolution on American women's lives by exploring the growth of the commercial sex industry and the proliferation of sexually explicit materials in the United States from the mid-1950s onward, paying particular attention to the escalation in the early 1970s. Encouraged by the phenomenal success of magazines like *Playboy*, a burgeoning X-rated film industry, and a decline in national efforts to prosecute obscenity cases, the pornography industry went through a period of unprecedented expansion. In one of the most visible episodes, the X-rated 1972 film *Deep Throat*, hyped by influential news media as the harbinger of a new era for pornography in America, spent ninety-six weeks on *Variety*'s list of the fifty top-grossing films and earned more than $100 million worldwide.

[19] Susan Griffin, "Rape: The All-American Crime," *Ramparts* 10 (1971): 30.

Pornographers marketed male sexual entitlement with unapologetic bravado, and women looked on with horror and alarm as their bodies were packaged and sold for profit in the name of sexual liberation. Worse, former allies on the male Left embraced pornography as a form of rebellious political speech; the editors of countercultural periodicals like *Rat* and *Screw* began publishing their own sexually explicit and patronizing pictorial and editorial content. For women who had embraced the idealism of the Left and the hopefulness of the sexual revolution, the reality of sexual exploitation by men who sought to make a quick buck or prove their *machismo* – or both – was devastating. Armed with new understanding of the depth of the problem of male sexual violence, the failure of the sexual revolution to bring about true equality for women, and a powerful political critique of heterosexuality as an instrument of patriarchal control, the sexualization of American popular culture led many women to think anew about the role of mediated sexual violence in creating and sustaining unequal social conditions for women.

In the second section of the book (Chapters 4–7), I offer an account of the formation and development of each of the three major groups under study, paying particular attention to the kinds of media images that each found objectionable and their preferred strategies for fighting back. I argue that shifts in the groups' preoccupations over time demonstrate that the movement evolved from a focus on overt acts of sexual violence against women in mainstream media to the covert, psychological violence against women that later groups saw in sexually explicit material that did not include violent acts per se. Sexual images that featured behavior associated with male dominance, such as fellatio or penetrative intercourse, were interpreted as violent by later groups, whereas most members of WAVAW would not have regarded this material as within their scope of action, although certainly abhorrent to some. This was a monumental shift. WAVAW consciously avoided the term pornography because it suggested an objection to *all* sexually explicit content rather than violent sexual expression, and excluded mainstream media. WAVPM and WAP included pornography in their names, foreshadowing the move toward a theoretic position that held that pornography itself was a form of violence against women, the *image* of sex and/or sexual violence was every bit as real and as harmful as an *act* of rape, battering, or incest. In this view, pornography injured all women. The first to experience harm were the women photographed or filmed in its production, and the rest were subsequently harmed by its consumption, dehumanized as sexual objects to be used, abused, and discarded.

In Chapter 4, I present the origins and major campaigns of WAVAW, the anti-media violence organization founded by Southern California feminists in 1976. WAVAW formed to prevent distribution of the gory 1975 film, *Snuff*, which claimed to feature the on-camera rape and murder of a young woman. The group gained prominence the following year, when its members protested Atlantic Records' brutal advertising campaign for the Rolling Stones album, *Black and Blue*. The success of this action led WAVAW to focus its attention on sexually violent images in music industry advertising and to initiate a three-year boycott of Warner Communications using the public education and consumer pressure tactics that were the foundation of the organization's activism. From the start, WAVAW rejected the idea of pursuing legal strategies to control expression, preferring to persuade companies to exercise corporate responsibility with respect to the images of women used to sell products.

The Warner campaign illustrated WAVAW's commitment to raising people's consciousness about the real-world effects of the symbolic environment created by the entertainment and news media. Organization leaders argued that it was critical to help members of the public make connections among the images of violence against women so common in advertising, television, and films and women's real-life experiences of abuse and assault. The organization objected to such depictions because they trivialized and condoned male violence, and because images of men as aggressors perpetuated myths about women *and* men, branding women as natural victims and men as their brutish assailants. This book argues that overall feminist support for the anti-pornography movement declined as later groups moved away from the WAVAW consumer action and public education model, and began to characterize male violence as a natural force (biologically driven) rather than a culturally sanctioned behavior that men learned.

In Chapter 5, I introduce WAVPM, the anti-violence and anti-pornography organization founded by a group of Bay Area feminists in December 1976. WAVPM shared WAVAW's commitment to the fight against abusive advertising, and members launched national campaigns against Max Factor cosmetics, Maidenform lingerie, Finnair airlines, and other corporations whose advertising made light of sexual violence. At the same time, WAVPM expressed a commitment to fighting pornography, although the group had difficulty articulating a coherent analysis of its objection to this material. Members carried out a public protest against pornography just six weeks after their initial organizing meeting, leading a picket in front of a strip club owned by San Francisco's well-known porn barons, brothers Jim and Artie Mitchell. WAVPM soon launched a monthly protest march through the city's North Beach neighborhood, the site of many adult businesses. When the June 1978 cover of *Hustler* magazine featured a woman's body being fed head-first into a meat grinder, coming out the other end as bloody hamburger meat, the organization's concerns about violence and pornography met head-on in a single target.

WAVPM occupied an important place in the movement, functioning between 1978 and 1980 as a bridge group in the transition from the anti-media violence campaign led by WAVAW to the anti-pornography movement led by WAP. In Chapter 5, I discuss the first national feminist anti-pornography conference organized by WAVPM in 1978, which brought WAVAW feminists face to face with anti-pornography feminists. Although both groups of activists were committed to eradicating violence against women, the centrality of pornography to the WAVPM agenda took some WAVAW activists by surprise. The question of preferred strategies became controversial for the first time, as a number of WAVPM leaders expressed their desire to move beyond liberal assumptions that any attempt to ban pornography would constitute censorship. Under WAVPM's leadership, pornography began to surpass media violence as the dominant problem – a change that brought criticism from outside the women's movement and began to raise doubts from within.

In Chapter 6, I examine the origins of WAP in New York City in the late 1970s, and the organization's first efforts to present its beliefs about pornography to the public. I discuss an academic conference at the New York University (NYU) School of Law where WAP feminists expressed a desire to explore legal strategies to stem the flow of pornography. In arguing for restrictions, the feminists launched an attack on classic liberalism. They argued that its conception of persons was too abstract and its focus on achieving formal equality before the law failed to factor in the differences that existed between women and men with regard to political, economic, and cultural power. Pornography was a tool that men used to continuously create and reinforce these differences to ensure continued female subordination. Thus, in a society where men were free to produce and distribute pornography, and to use such material to teach young men about domination and young women about submission, there could be no true equality among persons, violating liberalism's central tenet.

Drawing on the feminist social critique of gender discrimination and the rights consciousness inspired by the achievements of the Civil Rights movement, WAP activists insisted that the legal system had the potential to address gender inequality by eliminating the social scourge of pornography. Some members desired state action to accomplish this end. When the civil libertarians, most of whom were male, clung to First Amendment principles and rejected any government interference in the areas of speech and expression, a slow burn ignited among feminists who were tired of lofty arguments that veiled a sexist disregard for women's physical and emotional welfare.

In this chapter, I also discuss an appearance by three WAP founders on the popular daytime talk show, *Donahue*, and the range of viewer response. Some women felt relieved that a feminist group was tackling the problem of sexual objectification and the ways that men used pornography to control women and damage their self-esteem. Conservative Christians who erroneously believed that the feminist group opposed homosexual expression and sex education also voiced support. Women who feared censorship wrote WAP that restrictions on sexual speech would be used to limit feminist and gay and lesbian expression, and to advance anti-feminist goals. Finally, a small number of women argued that they used and enjoyed pornography, and that freedom to explore one's sexuality with all of the tools available under patriarchy was critical to sexual liberation.

The NYU conference and *Donahue* appearances were significant because they demonstrated the existence of multiple, vocal opinion publics on the pornography question, and revealed that conflict would ensue once the movement shifted away from a focus on mainstream media and sexual violence.

Anti-censorship feminists warned that asking the state to protect women from the harms of sex would invite a return to repression; sex radicals argued that their erotic rights would be trampled by an anti-pornography campaign; and liberals maintained that attacks on free speech threatened constitutional freedoms and undermined the rights of adults to read and view whatever material they chose. Whereas the WAVAW program of action against corporations had generated little, if any, controversy, WAP was controversial from the start.

In Chapter 7, I take an in-depth look at WAP's first actions following its establishment in 1979. I argue that WAP's initial year required a difficult balancing act between competing interest groups, and organization leaders made a series of decisions that were unpopular in progressive circles. Some early actions alienated WAP from individuals who questioned the group's overall commitment to feminist principles. This tension was evident when the organization opened its first office at the corner of Ninth Avenue and 42nd Street, in a space provided rent-free by a city agency responsible for a clean-up of Times Square, a crackdown on prostitution, and a gentrification plan that called for a new, corporate-run, tourist-based urban space. WAP's association with the Mayor's office in this initiative gave the group a powerful ally, but left WAP at odds with sex workers and feminists who saw city efforts hurting poor people, especially women who relied on the Times Square sex trade for money. In this chapter, I explore WAP's first four objectives, including the development of a public education program featuring a WAVAW-style slide show; guided tours of Times Square; the 1979 East Coast Feminist Conference on Pornography; and the March on Times Square, which attracted 5,000 participants.

The final section of the book (Chapters 8–9) explores the context of anti-pornography organizing in the early 1980s, just prior to the introduction of the civil rights ordinances authored by Andrea Dworkin and Catharine MacKinnon. These chapters show that the change in emphasis from media violence to pornography shattered the original feminist consensus regarding depictions of sexual violence against women and gave rise to significant concerns about censorship, sexual repression, and right-wing alliances. As WAVAW and WAVPM fell apart due to the loss of charismatic leaders, insufficient funding, and the redefinition of the movement, WAP found itself at the epicenter of an increasingly contentious public debate. The group tried throughout the early 1980s to continue its work and to raise public consciousness about pornography's harms, but fighting intramovement battles – particularly the rise of organized feminist pro-sex resistance – sapped organization time and energy.

In Chapter 8, I discuss a series of demonstrations that WAP organized to communicate concern about the perilous sexual environment that females experienced in a male-dominated society. These events included a series of actions against *Playboy*; a 1980 boycott of *Deep Throat* to call attention to the publication of Linda "Lovelace" Boreman's memoir; and a 1981 protest against a Broadway play based on the Vladimir Nabokov novel, *Lolita*. Through these actions, WAP tried to communicate a feminist objection to pornography, namely that it was a form of visual assault that reduced women to sexual objects and forced them to endure humiliation and abuse. During this period, the organization also began to highlight the problem of sexual exploitation of young girls – a problem that WAP identified as part of a backlash by men who were angry about the gains of the women's movement. Prominent national news media covered these demonstrations and treated WAP leaders as spokespersons for the women's movement. The organization's influence on public discourse surrounding sexuality was unquestionable.

WAP was making an impact on public consciousness, but changing social and political conditions in the United States brought new layers of meaning to a campaign against pornography. Specifically, the rise of the well-organized, well-funded New Right and its anti-feminist, pro-family platform posed a threat to WAP's control of the anti-pornography discourse. The New Right's focus on restoring the authority of the traditional family was part of an effort to beat back changes wrought by feminism and the other liberation movements of the 1960s and 1970s, and to reinvigorate hierarchical sexual structures. Thus, fighting pornography in New Right terms did not mean exposing and eradicating male dominance, as it did in feminist terms, but fighting sexual freedom and nonprocreative sexuality, especially gay and teen sexuality, and strengthening the patriarchal family and men's control over their wives and children. The WAP critique of pornography and sexual exploitation was politically useful to right-wing activists who borrowed feminist rhetoric about harm and degradation to support their own anti pornography efforts. Feminists outside of anti-pornography began to argue that the semblance of a common cause with the Right rendered feminist principles vulnerable.

In Chapter 8, I also begin to discuss emerging critiques of anti-pornography launched by feminists who were wary of the movement's claims to speak for all women. Some feminists argued that WAP collapsed distinctions like class and race to promote a model of universal sisterhood, ignoring the multiple, intersecting aspects of identity that affected each woman's experience of sexuality. They argued that an unremitting emphasis on the harmful aspects of sexuality pitted men and women against each other, reifying socially constructed gender differences as fixed aspects of biology. In this worldview, men were always aggressors and women their helpless victims. These challenges ultimately formed the basis for an organized pro-sex countermovement.

In Chapter 9, I show that the rise of the countermovement initiated the collapse of anti-pornography's control over the American feminist discourse about sexuality. The chapter begins with an analysis of the clash between lesbian sexual radicals and anti-pornography feminists on the West Coast in the late 1970s around questions of sexual diversity. When anti-pornography feminists publicly denounced lesbian sadomasochism for replicating unequal relationships of power, sexual radicals asserted that anti-pornography had created more "internal censorship" for women.[20] Instead of more shame and restriction, they argued, women needed greater encouragement and

[20] Chancer, *Reconcilable Differences*, 206.

opportunity for sexual exploration. These tensions erupted at the 1982 Barnard Conference, where pro-sex feminists challenged WAP and insisted that the feminist conversation about sex had to include questions of pleasure and desire.

The Barnard conference thrust the schism between the two camps into full view and signaled the end of the original feminist consensus that tied WAVAW, WAVPM, and WAP together. In its wake, activists began moving in different directions. Some dropped out of the women's movement entirely. Others switched their allegiance to the pro-sex camp. A number signed on to an anti-pornography movement that was quickly growing more conservative, attracting powerful right-wing constituencies. The political clout of these new conservative supporters created momentum in support of the anti-pornography civil rights ordinances that MacKinnon and Dworkin introduced in 1983. By this time, however, the national base of support for anti-pornography measures was not uniformly feminist – it was comprised of an untidy amalgam of radical feminists and conservative Christians, groups who interpreted the social problem of pornography through very different sets of lenses.

The book concludes with a discussion of WAP and feminist anti-pornography activity in the mid-1980s, when MacKinnon and Dworkin introduced civil rights legislation in Minneapolis and Indianapolis. This chapter shows that the feminist anti-pornography movement ground to a slow halt in the face of insurmountable obstacles. These included a Supreme Court ruling that found the MacKinnon and Dworkin ordinance unconstitutional, a vocal and organized feminist countermovement, a video revolution that brought sexually explicit material directly into Americans' homes, and a concerted effort by right-wing legislators to co-opt feminist rhetoric to support traditional anti-obscenity campaigns. By the time feminist leaders exhausted efforts to achieve legal reform in 1986, the older movement groups, and even WAP to an extent, had fallen into disarray. No national network of grassroots anti-media violence groups remained to carry the movement forward.

1

Seeds of Discontent

The Failed Promise of the Sexual Revolution for Women

In the late 1960s, many young Americans rejected traditional standards of sexual morality that forbade sex outside of marriage, and embraced the "sexual revolution" – the popular movement that equated sexual freedom with personal liberation. They championed a more permissive sexual climate that fostered concrete behavioral changes, such as higher rates of premarital sex, rising divorce rates, shrinking family size, and greater numbers of sexual partners for both women and men. Individuals had more choice regarding their sexual lives, and many openly engaged in sex before marriage, living with someone outside of marriage, or having casual sex with numerous partners, all with relatively little fear of social ostracism. Although these changes may have seemed shocking to mainstream America, they actually built on long-term, gradual trends toward greater sexual freedom that had been at work in American culture since the 1920s. Since that time, Americans' attitudes regarding sexual behavior had moved, somewhat haltingly and with bouts of opposition, in a direction that the historians John D'Emilio and Estelle Freedman refer to as "sexual liberalism."

To the extent that a true sexual revolution occurred in the 1960s and 1970s, it found its fullest expression in a widespread set of attitudinal changes regarding the meaning of sex. Many people came to regard sex as a gratifying touchstone of life – a "self-enriching, joyous phenomenon" – that did not have to be restricted to marriage or serious courtship.[1] Sexual satisfaction was touted as a major ingredient of personal fulfillment and of happy, healthy relationships, especially marriage, and sex was newly legitimized as a pleasurable act independent of reproduction.

The acceleration of sexual liberalism in this period was tied to the cultural radicalism of the late 1960s and 1970s. The Civil Rights movement, domestic protest against the war in Vietnam, politicized youth culture, and feminism created upheavals in the social order that made adherence to traditional sexual

[1] Steven Seidman, *Embattled Eros: Sexual Politics and Ethics in Contemporary America* (New York: Routledge, 1992), 41.

mores seem dated and hypocritical. The countercultural youth who fueled these movements believed that it was absurd to criticize America's involvement in Vietnam and its discriminatory economic and social policies on the one hand while upholding its puritanical sexual regulations on the other. The struggles around sex and the creation of a new sexual morality were thus part and parcel of a larger revolution that involved democratic citizenship, free speech, human rights, equality, and a bid to redefine the kind of individual who had a legitimate public voice. Members of the counterculture challenged social norms, such as marriage, as a means of forcing men and women to conform to artificial gender roles that served the interests of a patriarchal, capitalist state. Men were thrust into the role of breadwinner and head-of-household, and women were forced to assume domestic obligations and child-rearing responsibilities. Looking for ways to overthrow these bourgeois institutions, countercultural youth promoted intimate relationships unregulated by the state as a means of resisting indoctrination.[2]

Many of the counterculture movements were led by student radicals who hoped to transform the social and political order of American society. Their campaigns against the repressive systems maintained by their parents' generation led them to the forefront of the sexual revolution. Some were alienated middle-class college students who had grown up amid the prosperity of post-war America, and who began to connect the war in Vietnam, pervasive racial discrimination, and unequal distribution of wealth throughout American society with what they saw as the immorality of late capitalism. They were expected to follow in their parents' footsteps, shouldering the burden of maintaining the current order, and many shuddered at this vision. Student radicalism and renunciation of conventional morality gave youth "a way to break out of the deadening psychological structures of U.S. middle-class life," as several historians of sexuality have described it.[3] Indeed, the sexual revolution had great appeal as an immediate way to create social change.

Some students found inspiration for sexual radicalism in the writings of the Freudian Left, particularly in the work of Herbert Marcuse and Wilhelm Reich. These social theorists challenged Freud's conservative notion that the inner libidinal self required constant repression for the maintenance of civilized society. Students praised these antiestablishment views and the conviction that the institutions and practices of modern civilization were at odds with human fulfillment. For Marcuse and Reich, no revolutionary transformation could

[2] On the effects of the sexual revolution on American society, see David Allyn, *Make Love, Not War: The Sexual Revolution: An Unfettered History* (Boston: Little Brown, 2000); John D'Emilio and Estelle Freedman, *Intimate Matters: A History of Sexuality in America* (New York: Harper and Row, 1988); Steven Seidman, *Romantic Longings: Love in America, 1830–1980* (New York: Routledge, 1991); and Beth Bailey, *Sex in the Heartland* (Cambridge, MA: Harvard University Press, 1999).

[3] Ann Snitow, Christine Stansell, and Sharon Thompson, "Introduction." in *Powers of Desire: The Politics of Sexuality*, ed. A. Snitow, C. Stansell, and S. Thompson (New York: Monthly Review Press, 1983), 19.

take place in the social and political order without sexual liberation, because sexuality was the wellspring of human freedom, health, and happiness.

Marcuse's *Eros and Civilization* (1955) traced the relationship between political domination and sexual repression. He argued specifically that sexual repression was key to the maintenance of capitalist society. The sexual ethic imposed by the ruling classes was designed to allow members of the proletariat only sufficient sexual release to maintain the physical and mental health required to perform work. Further, human sexuality under capitalism was restricted to genital sexuality, ensuring that the rest of the body was free to be identified as an instrument of labor. Marcuse argued for an uninhibited state of "polymorphous perversity," in which the whole body would become a source of sexual pleasure and no shame would attach to any sexual act.[4] The resexualized body would resist the discipline and order required for the functioning of capitalism and would harness the revolutionary potential of sexuality.

Reich's writings made a direct connection between monogamous marriage and the maintenance of the oppressive social order. In *The Sexual Revolution*, which first appeared in the United States in 1945, he described the patriarchal family as "a factory for authoritarian ideologies and conservative [character] structures."[5] In Reich's view, the main function of the family was the repression of any manifestation of sexuality in children, thus ensuring stunted character development. He reasoned that sexually repressed children would become docile and submissive adults, incapable of rebelling against an unjust and exploitative social system. The only way to prevent these character deficiencies was for human beings to experience total sexual release. For Reich, revolutionary change could not occur without sexual liberation, because to free human beings from social domination meant to free them physically and mentally. Some students influenced by Marcuse and Reich began to eschew traditional ideals of monogamy, marriage, and the family, seeing them as linchpins in the preservation of the dominant social and political order.[6] Instead, they adopted a "Dionysian and polymorphous sexuality" that totally abandoned mainstream standards of respectable behavior.[7]

On campus, radicals popularized the notion of sex as a liberating act that represented everything that was good, right, and natural, and that effectively

[4] Herbert Marcuse, *Eros and Civilization: A Philosophical Inquiry into Freud* (Boston: Beacon Press, 1955), 49.

[5] Wilhelm Reich, *The Sexual Revolution: Toward a Self-Governing Character Structure*, 2nd ed., trans. T. P. Wolfe (New York: Octagon Books, 1971), 72.

[6] For analyses of the influence of Reich on the student movements, see Paul Robinson, *The Freudian Left: Wilhelm Reich, Geza Roheim, Herbert Marcuse*, 2nd ed. (Ithaca, NY and London: Cornell University Press, 1990) and Anthony Giddens, *The Transformation of Intimacy: Sexuality, Love and Eroticism in Modern Societies* (Stanford, CA: Stanford University Press, 1992).

[7] Historian Beth Bailey chronicles these changes at the University of Kansas and nationwide. See Bailey, *Sex in the Heartland*, 9.

challenged the corrupt and artificial American society established by older generations. The counterculture's valorization of authenticity and the self led to a celebration of the body as "the highest expression of an unsullied nature," as the historian Jane Gerhard has described it.[8] The body was a *tabula rasa*, a wellspring of personal fulfillment and self-expression free of the social ills of racism, sexism, capitalism, and the other oppressive systems that structured modern society. Members of the counterculture connected their critique of American life to demands for a more sexually tolerant society. They celebrated sex as a natural act that liberated people from repressive rules. Sexual freedom was thus a revolutionary demand connected to social justice, and when these young people urged "Make love, not war," they did so with the intent of building a more egalitarian society. The struggle for sexual freedom took place nationwide, as students waged battles against authoritarian sexual regulations in concert with antiwar and other political efforts.

This was much more than a vision of individual sexual freedom. Countercultural youth used sex to challenge traditional values, rejecting monogamy and marriage as part of the artificial bourgeois world their parents had created. Most of these youth were deeply disenchanted; polls conducted in 1970–1971 revealed that one-third of America's college-age population felt that marriage was obsolete and raising children was unimportant. "[M]any young Americans no longer saw any reason to heed established conventions about sex, drugs, authority, clothing, living arrangements, food – the fundamental ways of living their lives," the historian Bruce J. Schulman has written of 1970s youth culture.[9]

College students influenced by radical politics were among the nation's most ardent supporters of the sexual revolution, and college campuses in the late 1960s and the 1970s were often sexually free environments. Students targeted university regulations that denied female students the right to live off-campus with their boyfriends, and protested paternalistic rules that prohibited overnight guests in the dormitories. At many schools, students insisted that university health services lift their bans on dispensing birth control pills to unmarried women. They championed "free love," an ethos of no-strings, multiple-partner, fulfillment-oriented sexual conduct, and popularized such expressions as "sex is no different than a handshake" and "chaste makes waste."[10] With the proscriptions on premarital sex lifted and oral contraceptives that separated sex from procreation widely available after 1960, many young people tried to live the revolution.

[8] Jane Gerhard, *Desiring Revolution: Second-Wave Feminism and the Rewriting of American Sexual Thought, 1920 to 1982* (New York: Columbia University Press, 1982), 85.

[9] Bruce J. Schulman, *The Seventies: The Great Shift in American Culture, Society and Politics* (New York: The Free Press, 2001), 16.

[10] For a discussion of the prevalence of these casual sexual attitudes, see Dana Densmore, "Independence from the Sexual Revolution," in *Radical Feminism*, eds. A. Koedt, E. Levine, and A. Rapone (New York: Quadrangle Books, 1973), 107–118.

Young women embraced the freer climate but often became disenchanted once it became obvious that the sexual revolution was happening on male terms. Some came to this realization through cohabitation – "shacking up," as it was commonly called – which meant living with someone of the opposite sex in a committed relationship outside of marriage. Between 1960 and 1970, the number of cohabiting adults increased by a factor of ten, and about 11 percent of the population adopted this type of arrangement by the end of the decade.[11] Cohabitation was especially popular with individuals influenced by the counterculture movements, who believed that they could escape their parents' destiny and "do it right" by living "without the phoniness and hierarchy, the profit and power, the processed food and three-piece suits, the evening news and the suburban ranch house." Instead, these young people would build "alternative families – a separate, authentic, parallel universe."[12] A 1977 study of cohabiting couples found that the majority lived in large cities, often in the Northeastern and Western regions, and were likely to participate in unconventional activities, such as studying an Eastern religion, joining political demonstrations, or using illegal drugs.[13] For many in the counterculture, cohabitation was a way to challenge the institution of marriage – the bedrock of American social life.

At first glance, cohabitation looked like it might revolutionize gender roles. Many women were drawn to the arrangement because it challenged traditional marital roles and promised sexual and social equality, a way to escape the "small, constrained, female lives" that their mothers had endured.[14] In theory, living together without marriage would allow a woman to make a personal and emotional commitment to a man without the ideological baggage and domestic burdens that wives typically assumed. For men, it was an opportunity to forgo the patriarchal role of head-of-household and the pressure of being the primary breadwinner. Cohabitation offered a chance to build an equal partnership, to refuse state intervention into intimate life, and to give each person the opportunity to discover whether the relationship was fulfilling. If not, ending it was (theoretically) as simple as packing one's bags. Although cohabitation seemed to offer advantages to both sexes, it was often no more egalitarian than marriage, and offered women fewer protections.

In 1977, three female sociologists at the University of Nevada set out to compare the division of household labor between cohabiting and married couples. They expected some erosion of gender role specialization in the division of household labor among the former and thought that cohabiting women would spend fewer hours on domestic chores than their married counterparts.

[11] Seidman, *Embattled Eros*, 39. As many as 35% of all college students surveyed in this period indicated that they had lived or were living in a cohabiting arrangement.

[12] Schulman, *The Seventies*, 16.

[13] Richard Clayton and Harwin Voss, "Shacking Up: Cohabitation in the 1970s," *Journal of Marriage and the Family* 39 (May 1977): 280.

[14] Andrea Dworkin, *Right-Wing Women* (New York: Perigee Books, 1983), 90.

Instead, they found almost no difference in the amount and type of work performed by both groups of women. Married or not, women bore most of the responsibility for cooking and cleaning, and in many cases, for raising children. Worse yet, the cohabiting males had fewer domestic obligations than their married male counterparts and did less yard work, snow shoveling, and home repair. Most couples replicated the patterns of division of labor that they had learned from their mothers and fathers, the researchers noted, even though many of the cohabiting women believed themselves to be "in the forefront of the women's liberation movement."[15] Cohabiting women were "the greatest victims of their own ideology," according to the study, because they bore the same brunt of domestic labor as wives, yet enjoyed none of the economic rewards of marriage.[16] By the mid-1970s, some 20 percent of all American men between the ages of twenty and thirty had "shacked up" with a woman for six or more months. Fewer than half of those relationships led to marriage.

By the time the authors Shere Hite and Lillian Rubin published their respective studies of female sexuality and family life in the mid-1970s, many women knew from firsthand experience that the sexual revolution was falling far short of its promise. Although it had succeeded in liberating the discussion of sexual matters and widening the scope of permissible behaviors, the revolution had left sexism largely intact. Hite's 1976 landmark study, *The Hite Report*, shared responses from 3,500 women who had filled out a detailed questionnaire about their sexual lives. Women's anger at the persistence of male chauvinism practically leapt off the pages. One respondent described the sexual revolution as "male-oriented and anti-woman."[17] Another disparaged the sexual revolution as "the biggest farce of the century for females" and described it as "a male production, its principles still concentrated on male values." In her opinion, women had actually lost ground with respect to their sexual rights. "Before at least she had the right to say 'no,'" she lamented. "Now she is a prude or worse if she doesn't put out whenever asked."[18] Many men interpreted the new climate to mean that greater numbers of women were sexually available, and that sex had few strings attached. The women were viewed as passive objects in the sexual exchange – men could use them freely without any sense of obligation or responsibility. For all the rhetoric of revolution, men still held most of the power to determine the conditions of sexual relations.

One of the worst holdovers was the double standard that allowed men to indulge in any number of sexual encounters with no fear of damage to reputation but gave no such freedom to women. A roster of sexual conquests

[15] Rebecca Stafford, Elaine Backman, and Pamela Dibona, "The Division of Labor Among Cohabiting and Married Couples," *Journal of Marriage and the Family* 38 (February 1977): 55.

[16] Stafford, Backman, and Dibona, "The Division of Labor," 53.

[17] Shere Hite, *The Hite Report: A Nationwide Study on Female Sexuality* (New York: Macmillan, 1976), 338.

[18] Hite, 340.

heightened a man's standing among his peers, but any woman who engaged in sexual conduct was subject to a terrible loss of reputation. Many women who tried to explore the possibilities of sexual liberation, acting as sexual equals with men and treating sex as a natural, free, open means of communication, ended up abused and ashamed. A Hite respondent observed that the double standard made it impossible for women to claim the same sexual rights as men. "A man who has many lovers is 'sowing his oats'; a woman who has many lovers is a 'prostitute' or 'nymphomaniac'," she complained.[19]

Some of the women that Rubin interviewed for her 1976 sociological study of family life, *Worlds of Pain*, were equally candid about the disappointments of the sexual revolution. Like Hite's respondents, they were tired of being bombarded by messages from men and media alike that proclaimed a new sexual world in which women had the same opportunities and privileges as men. This, they claimed, was part of a grand scheme to get women to lower their defenses. One respondent explained to Rubin that women were all too aware that sex was full of pitfalls, especially the old double standard. "They know from experience that it [the double standard] is alive and well, that it exists side by side with the new ideology that heralds their sexual liberation," she said. "They know all about who are the 'bad girls' in school, in the neighborhood; who are the 'good girls.' Everybody knows!"[20]

Beyond the psychological harms of the double standard, evidence was mounting that the behavioral component of the sexual revolution had also exacted a serious physical toll. Young women were at greatest risk. Rates of sexual activity among girls aged fifteen to nineteen skyrocketed in the 1970s, and this cohort experienced the negative consequences associated with freer sexual activity. Girls learned that they could not count on men to take precautions with birth control or to fulfill their responsibilities in the case of an unplanned pregnancy. Venereal disease was another widespread problem.

The greatest behavioral changes of the sexual revolution occurred among teenage girls, who experienced a rapid liberalization of attitudes toward premarital sex. These changes began during the late 1960s and accelerated in the early 1970s. One group of researchers compared samples of college men and women in 1965, 1970, and 1975 and determined that whereas men's behaviors and attitudes had remained almost constant, there had been continuing, dramatic increases in both premarital sexual activity and approval for such behavior among college females. Rates of premarital sex among young women increased 9.6 percent between 1965 and 1970 and nearly twice that number – 18.8 percent – between 1970 and 1975. Over the course of the decade, the percentage of college females engaging in premarital sex doubled, rising from less than 30 percent to almost 60 percent.[21] A second group of researchers,

[19] Hite, 338.

[20] Rubin, *Worlds of Pain*, 137.

[21] Karl King, Jack O. Balswick, and Ira Robinson, "The Continuing Sexual Revolution Among College Females," *Journal of Marriage and the Family* 39 (August 1977): 456.

employing national samples rather than college-student samples, found less pronounced change but reported that the percent of women aged fifteen to nineteen engaging in premarital intercourse had increased from 30.1 percent in 1971 to 40.9 percent in 1976.[22] In 1976, more than a third of white seventeen-year-old girls in a national sample reported that they had already experienced sexual intercourse. For black seventeen-year-olds, the figure stood at 68.4 percent.[23]

Heightened levels of sexual activity among teenagers raised concerns on a number of fronts. First, the typical girl experienced her initial premarital sexual encounter with a male partner who was two to three years older.[24] Parents worried that a generation of fifteen- and sixteen-year-old girls had become sexual prey for eighteen- and nineteen-year-old men. Second, the ubiquity of birth control pills in the 1970s placed responsibility for contraception squarely on the shoulders of these young women. Oral contraceptives had become such a fixture of everyday life that it was as if pills were stocked "in the vending machines," one of Hite's respondents complained.[25] Among girls aged fifteen to nineteen who used contraception, reliance on the pill more than doubled between 1971 and 1976, owing largely to the Supreme Court's decision in 1972 that it was unconstitutional for doctors to refuse the pill to unmarried women. By 1976, 58.8 percent of that teen group was using birth control pills. Among black women aged fifteen to nineteen, nearly 75 percent relied on the pill.[26]

Meanwhile, dependence on older methods of contraception, including the condom and withdrawal, which had been the dominant methods in 1971, declined precipitously. These methods had required men to play an active role in contraception and had previously accounted for more than half of contraceptive practice among blacks and 70 percent among whites. By 1976, condom use showed a 27 percent decrease among whites and a 55 percent decrease among blacks. The combined use of condoms and withdrawal declined to the point where they captured less than 20 percent of black and less than 40 percent of white contraceptive efforts.[27]

The pill delivered reliable birth control, but it also came with a host of problems. Users experienced such unpleasant side effects as nausea, weight gain, rashes, and bloating, as well as more serious health risks including heightened

[22] Melvin Zelnik and John F. Kantner, "First Pregnancies to Women Aged 15–19: 1976 and 1971," *Family Planning Perspectives* 10, no. 1 (January/February 1978): 12.

[23] Melvin Zelnik and John F. Kantner, "Sexual and Contraceptive Experience of Young Unmarried Women in the United States, 1976 and 1971," *Family Planning Perspectives* 9, no. 2 (March/April 1977): 56.

[24] Zelnik and Kantner, "Sexual and Contraceptive Experience," 61.

[25] Hite, 356.

[26] Zelnik and Kantner, "Sexual and Contraceptive Experience," 63.

[27] In 1971, condoms were used by 60.6% of combined black and white respondents. By 1976, that number had decreased to 39.3%. See Zelnik and Kantner, "Sexual and Contraceptive Experience," 62–67.

rates of cardiovascular disease and breast cancer.[28] Women became more aware of these dangers in 1969, when the feminist journalist Barbara Seaman published *The Doctor's Case Against the Pill*. By 1972, the link between oral contraceptives and blood clots had been discussed in such popular magazines as *Good Housekeeping* and *Vogue*. Women who relied on birth control pills in lieu of condoms also found themselves unprotected against sexually transmitted diseases. These included syphilis and gonorrhea, which led to infertility if left untreated. In 1973 alone, the U.S. Public Health Service recorded 3 million new cases of venereal disease and estimated that 80 to 90 percent of all infected females failed to seek medical treatment because they showed no clinical signs of the disease.[29]

Although it may have been exhilarating for teenagers to boast that they were "on the pill," the truth was that many took the pills irregularly, or not at all. A 1975 study uncovered a widespread failure among youth to use contraception and indicated that 75 percent of unmarried girls aged fifteen to nineteen never or only sometimes used a method of birth control.[30] The combination of increased sexual activity, decreased rates of use of traditional contraceptive measures (i.e., condoms, withdrawal), and increased expectations that females used the pill soon resulted in less-than-favorable outcomes for young women.

Between 1971 and 1976, the incidence of premarital pregnancy in the United States rose steadily. More than one-third of sexually active teenage girls would experience a premarital pregnancy before turning nineteen, one-quarter by the time they reached seventeen.[31] Between 1971 and 1976, the percentage of first pregnancies conceived out of wedlock among white teenagers rose by about one-third, reflecting both the increased rates of premarital sex during these years and changing mores that relieved men of the obligation to marry a woman if she became pregnant.[32] By 1978, about one million teenage girls – one in ten between the ages of fifteen and nineteen – got pregnant every year.

For unmarried teenagers, abortion was sometimes the only solution to an unplanned pregnancy. In the years prior to the 1973 *Roe v. Wade* decision, which legalized a woman's right to abortion, terminating a pregnancy was a dangerous and costly proposition. Illegal abortions could cost $500, with

28 After 1977, women's use of oral contraceptives decreased sharply. For a discussion of women's growing awareness of dangers associated with the pill, see Linda Gordon, *Woman's Body, Woman's Right: Birth Control in America*, 2nd ed. (New York: Penguin Books, 1990), 422.

29 Shirley K. Bryan, "Venereal Disease and the Teenager," *Journal of Clinical Child Psychology* 3 (1974): 24.

30 Ira L. Reiss, Albert Banwart, and Harry Foreman, "Premarital Contraceptive Usage: A Study and Some Theoretical Explorations," *Journal of Marriage and the Family* (August 1975): 619.

31 Melvin Zelnik, Young J. Kim, and John F. Kantner, "Probabilities of Intercourse and Conception Among U.S. Teenage Women, 1971 and 1976," *Family Planning Perspectives* 11, no. 3 (May/June 1979): 177.

32 Zelnik and Kantner, "First Pregnancies to Women," 13.

the financial burden often falling solely on the woman. Worse, women had no guarantee that the procedure would be performed safely or effectively. By 1976, with seven out of ten teenage pregnancies occurring premaritally, almost 40 percent of pregnant, unmarried white teens sought abortions.[33]

In 1978, the teenage pregnancy epidemic reached such severe proportions that the Senate Human Resources Committee held hearings on the subject. Joseph A. Califano Jr., the Secretary of Health, Education and Welfare, addressed the Committee and described teen pregnancy as one of the most serious and complex social problems facing the nation. Of the one million girls who became pregnant each year, 600,000 saw their pregnancies through to term and generally faced devastating social consequences. Teenage mothers were overwhelmingly likely to drop out of school, earn low wages in dead-end jobs, have large families, and live in poverty. Arthur A. Campbell of the Center for Population Research described this scenario: "The girl who has an illegitimate child at the age of 16 suddenly has 90 percent of her life's script written for her. Her life choices are few, and most of them are bad."[34]

Experts testifying before the Committee identified two leading causes of the epidemic: increased sexual activity and failure to use birth control. Fifty percent of girls were sexually active by age nineteen, although many remained deeply ambivalent about sex. The social pressure to acquiesce in a climate that linked sex with revolution led many to engage in unwanted intercourse. "There just aren't any supports for those who want to be virgins," an expert from the Urban Institute testified. "It really is harder to say no."[35] Author Andrea Dworkin described the tenor of the times in more graphic terms: "[W]omen had no legitimate reason not to want to be fucked ... an aversion to intercourse, or not climaxing from intercourse, or not wanting intercourse at a particular time or with a particular man, or wanting fewer partners than were available, or getting tired, or being cross, were all signs of and proof of sexual repression."[36] The pressure for girls to participate in sexual activity was unremitting.

Although the sexual revolution dramatically affected the lives of young, single Americans, it also touched the lives of married couples in significant ways. Popular literature of the 1970s urged husbands and wives to reinvigorate their physical relationships, to embrace new sexual attitudes and behaviors, and even to indulge in such avant garde inventions as swinging. But this new emphasis on the importance of erotic diversity for personal fulfillment created problems. The sexual adventures that "sexperts" like Hugh Hefner and Helen Gurley Brown romanticized were best conducted by single city dwellers, not by married couples residing in suburban America. For many

33 Zelnik and Kantner, "First Pregnancies to Women," 14–15.

34 Steven V. Roberts, "The Epidemic of Teen-Age Pregnancy," *The New York Times*, June 18, 1978, 1, 15.

35 Roberts, "The Epidemic of Teen-Age Pregnancy," 15.

36 Dworkin, *Right-Wing Women*, 92.

couples, the acceleration of the sexual revolution in the late 1960s and 1970s added a new domestic burden, much of it falling on wives.

Sexual advice for married couples was typically contained in popular sexual self-help literature, such as *Adultery for Adults* (1971), *The Joy of Sex* (1972) – which sold 3.8 million copies in its first two years of publication – *The Erotic Life of the American Wife* (1972), and *The Pleasure Bond* (1974), all of which promised couples the secrets needed to revitalize their relationships. Some manuals were egalitarian in approach, making it clear that the responsibility for an improved sex life rested with both partners.[37] Others, however, placed this obligation directly on women, urging wives to invent new ways to seduce and delight their husbands. For some married women, the overriding message received was that it was prudish and old-fashioned to cling to traditional ideas about respectable sexual behavior. Instead, "modern" women were supposed to engage wholeheartedly in behaviors that they might have been taught to regard as dirty or cheap. The underlying implication was threatening: Wives who failed to keep the sexual component of marriage fresh and exciting might see their husbands walk out the door into the waiting arms of more liberated women.

Millions of Americans were introduced to this way of thinking in the pages of a 1972 how-to book, *The Total Woman.* Written by Marabel Morgan, a born-again Christian housewife from Florida, *The Total Woman* blended the ideology of the sexual revolution with conservative Christian beliefs about a wife's proper and loving role within marriage as a "helper." Morgan argued that every housewife could find happiness by pampering and submitting to her husband. Much of the book was devoted to erotic advice, and she urged women to use costumes and exotic techniques to titillate their husbands, to infuse passion into the marital relationship, and most important, to keep them from straying. She recommended that wives thrill their husbands at the front door every evening wearing something seductive, such as see-through lingerie, a French maid's uniform, or – most famously – Saran Wrap, armed with candles, body oils, and romantic music. The husband's pleasure was paramount, and he deserved the excitement of an affair with a "different woman" every night. "It is only when a woman surrenders her life to her husband, reveres and worships him, and is willing to serve him, that she becomes really beautiful to him," she wrote, joining fundamentalist Christianity to popular-culture eroticism in a quirky blend.[38]

The book was a surprise hit; it was the top-selling book across all genres in 1975 and the ninth nonfiction best-seller of the decade.[39] *The Total Woman*

[37] Steven Seidman discusses the leading manuals that advocated an egalitarian concept of sexual pleasure, including Alex Comfort's 1972 guide, *The Joy of Sex*, and William Masters and Virginia Johnson's 1970 book, *The Pleasure Bond*. Both endorsed the idea that sexual acts ought to be consensual and mutually fulfilling. See Seidman, *Romantic Longings*.

[38] Marabel Morgan, *The Total Woman* (Old Tappan, NJ: Fleming H. Revell, 1973), 96.

[39] Ellen Ross, "'The Love Crisis': Couples Advice Books of the Late 1970s," *Signs: Journal of Women in Culture and Society* 6, no. 1 (1980): 119.

was a consummate product of the sexual revolution: Morgan offered wives greater latitude with regard to their sexual behavior, but did so in a way that privileged male desire and control. *The Total Woman* emphasized a woman's responsibility to cater to her husband's sexual needs, rather than asserting the primacy of her own experience.

Rubin, the family sociologist, discovered that sex loomed large as a domestic burden for many married women. She asked working-class and middle-class wives to share their views on sex in marriage, and reported that many of her respondents felt that the sexual revolution had added pressure, as opposed to pleasure, to their lives. Many wives were accustomed to routine sexual encounters and felt too reticent to discuss sex freely or to be introspective about their own fulfillment. Many felt obliged to create exciting erotic environments for their husbands, à la Morgan, which they regarded as yet another household duty along the lines of cooking, cleaning, and raising children. Resentments began to build.

A majority of the working-class women in Rubin's study found it difficult to adjust to changing sexual norms and to shake off lessons learned earlier in life about respectable sexual conduct. For these women, oral sex was a stumbling block, often regarded as a shameful practice. "He says I'm old-fashioned about sex and maybe I am," complained one woman. "But I was brought up that there's just one way you're supposed to do it. I still believe that way, even though he keeps trying to convince me of his way."[40] Other women in Rubin's study said they felt "cheap" when asked to initiate sex or perform acts different from the "things 'nice girls' do."[41] The middle-class women were more comfortable performing and receiving oral sex, but feared they were frigid if they did not enjoy it. Middle-class women tended to feel guilty about their inhibitions because they believed their hesitation "reflected some inadequacy in their personal sexual adjustment," Rubin concluded.[42]

Both groups of women thought that the sexual revolution had increased the demands on their lives, meaning that they had to say "yes" to sex instead of "no" as they might have done in the past. They felt obligated to try new sexual behaviors and to reach orgasm to please and satisfy their husbands rather than themselves. According to Rubin, life for married women in the 1970s was fraught with emotional dilemmas and conflicts around sex.

The sociologists John Gagnon and William Simon observed in 1970 that the sexual revolution was a notion that had not only entered the realm of public discourse, but had also become a powerful cultural reality. The increased visibility of sex in mainstream society gave people license to participate in "public talk" about it, in turn strengthening the belief that radical change was occurring. As a society, Gagnon and Simon wrote, "we are saddled with and

[40] Lillian B. Rubin, *Worlds of Pain: Life in the Working-Class Family* (New York: Basic Books, 1976), 138.
[41] Rubin, 140.
[42] Rubin, 144.

delighted with an imagery of change – indeed, of revolution – when we talk about sexuality."[43] The proliferation of talk fueled public imagination about the sexual revolution and the extent to which it was transforming American life.

Much of the talk, however, was less than enthusiastic. It was obvious to women that the behavioral and attitudinal changes that were part and parcel of the sexual revolution were not entirely positive. Indeed, by the mid-1970s, many women were disillusioned with what they had come to see as a male revolution, a new sexual contract that put more pressure on women while giving men greater access and fewer obligations. In theory, sexual liberation would have brought about a revolution for women; "free love" as described by Marcuse, Reich, and others had the potential to equalize relationships between the sexes. In practice, however, women often paid a dear price for this so-called liberation, including fewer "legitimate" grounds on which to refuse sexual advances and fewer protections against such unintended consequences as pregnancy and venereal disease. "Opportunities for more sex with more partners did not necessarily translate into sexual liberation for women," Jane Gerhard observed in her study of second-wave feminism and American sexual thought. "Many women rejected accounts of their 'liberation' that viewed them as *Playboy* bunnies."[44] Others tried to salvage what they saw as positive aspects of the sexual revolution, including the separation of sex from reproduction, an emphasis on sexual pleasure and freedom, and a critique of marriage, but for some, optimism was short-lived.

In the next chapter, I discuss ideological changes in the women's liberation movement that put many women at odds with the institution of heterosexuality, including the discovery of an epidemic of male sexual violence, particularly rape, which made any expression of male sexuality seem threatening. Once knowledge of the coercive and violent aspects of male sexuality emerged from the consciousness raising groups organized by the radical feminist wing of the movement, many women looked anew at pornography as a tool of the patriarchy, teaching successive generations that sexual access to women – offered willingly or taken by force – was a male right.

[43] John H. Gagnon and William Simon, "Introduction: Perspectives on the Sexual Scene," in *The Sexual Scene*, eds. J. H. Gagnon and W. Simon (Chicago: Aldine, 1970): 6.

[44] Gerhard, *Desiring Revolution*, 87.

2

Male Violence and the Critique of Heterosexuality

The Influence of Radical Feminism on the Anti-Pornography Movement

Chapter 1 established women's ambivalence toward the freer sexual climate that characterized life in the United States by the late 1960s and early 1970s, and their realization that unfettered sexuality was not the decisive source of liberation that many women had hoped it would be. In this chapter and the one that follows, I explore related cultural conditions – here, the growth of the radical feminist wing of the Women's Liberation movement and in Chapter 3, the rise of the commercial pornography industry – which gave women a framework for interpreting measurable changes in sexual behavior as problematic. Through the lens of radical feminist theory, women saw trends in intimate life such as the increased expectation that contraception was a woman's obligation, as heterosexist means of enlarging men's sexual rights. The pornography industry, in turn, celebrated and marketed male sexual entitlement through depictions of women as eager sexual slaves, and idealized X-rated film heroines like *Deep Throat's* Linda Lovelace as truly liberated women whom American females ought to emulate. This chapter explores theoretic developments in radical feminism that contributed to a powerful critique of heterosexuality as an ideology and institution of male supremacy. Through this critique, many women began to regard (heterosexual) sex as a primary force of oppression. The anti-heterosexual perspective that emerged from radical feminism in this period laid the groundwork for the beginning of an anti-pornography analysis in the mid-1970s.

Theoretic developments emerging from radical feminism supported the growth of the anti-pornography analysis. First, radical feminists uncovered evidence of an epidemic of male sexual violence, which led to new analyses of violence as a tool that men used to maintain women's subordination. Intimate discussions about sex in radical feminist consciousness raising groups inevitably led women to reveal incidents of coercion, and the prevalence of rape, battering, and incest became known for the first time. Feminists realized that male violence was part of the fabric of every woman's life through first-hand experience and chronic fear. In the early 1970s, they initiated national campaigns to publicize the epidemic, provide shelters and counseling for victims, and rewrite sexist laws that exploited women's vulnerabilities. Feminist theorists analyzed violence in revolutionary ways as a political tool that only some men used, but that benefited all because it kept women fearful, timid, and dependent on male protection.[1] This perspective supported feminist organizing against mediated depictions of sexual violence on the grounds that such depictions encouraged men to commit real-life acts of sexual violence against women.

The second major theoretic development that supported the growth of antipornography was an expansive radical feminist critique of heterosexuality as an institution and an ideology that created and maintained male supremacy. After 1968, radical feminists began to argue that heterosexuality was a major source of oppression for women. Within consciousness raising groups, radical feminists spent a great deal of time detailing and analyzing the ways that men controlled women through institutions that were organized around heterosexual norms, especially marriage and the patriarchal family. They came to believe that men's control of women's sexual and reproductive lives, as well as women's self-identity and social status, was the most widespread and deepest form of human oppression.

This political analysis of heterosexuality, which encompassed the new awareness of the power of male violence, led many radical feminists to advocate the destruction of the institution as a means of freeing women. Lesbian feminism, which urged women to direct their emotional and erotic attention to other women as a means of challenging male privilege and ending patriarchal domination, emerged as the preferred strategy. Radical feminists abandoned heterosexuality in droves, leading to the invention of the "political lesbian," a woman so committed to all women's freedom that she made a conscious decision to choose lesbianism as a way of life, depriving men of her sexual, social, and emotional support. Political lesbianism weaved together one's lifestyle and politics; it made lesbianism a valid option for those who had not previously felt erotic desire for other women, but who wanted to reject the male world as a means of putting women first.

The influence of lesbian feminism, and ultimately of the late radical (cultural) feminism that came to dominate the women's movement after 1975, laid the groundwork for opposition to pornography. Cultural feminism celebrated a benevolent, nurturing female way of being; rejected men and aggressive, rapacious "male values"; differentiated between the sexual "styles" enjoyed by women versus men; and emphasized the importance of building a

[1] Influential writings incorporating this analysis of violence include: Susan Griffin, "Rape: The All-American Crime," *Ramparts* 10 (1971): 26–35; Andra Medea and Kathleen Thompson, *Against Rape* (New York: Farrar, Straus and Giroux, 1974); Robin Morgan, "Theory and Practice: Pornography and Rape," in *Take Back the Night: Women on Pornography*, ed. L. Lederer (New York: William Morrow, 1980); Susan Brownmiller, *Against Our Will: Men, Women and Rape* (New York: Simon & Schuster, 1975).

separate women's culture.[2] In a movement climate that grew overtly hostile to and suspicious of any manifestation of heterosexual privilege, male-identified sexual expression like *Deep Throat*, *Playboy*, and *Hustler* loomed large as an attack on women. Pornography championed male sexual desire; was protected by male-controlled courts and smug male liberals who demanded scientific proof of pornography's harms; glorified the violence that men used to ensure women's sexual objectification and subordination; and taught men to despise and abuse women. Pornography violated the female body and the nurturing, life-affirming female values that many feminists prized. It was the perfect expression of male sexuality: violent, genitally focused, and emotionally detached.[3] Ultimately, the radical feminist critique of heterosexuality that led to lesbian feminism and later cultural feminism provided a basis for the formation of anti-pornography sentiment. The radical feminist critique of heterosexual relations evolved into a rejection of men, and later pornography, as a graphic expression of the dangerous "male values" that were central to female oppression. Cultural feminism, which the historian Alice Echols has argued was dominant by the mid-1970s, encouraged women to reject everything associated with men and male values and was a major theoretic influence throughout the 1980s.[4]

The Rise of Radical Feminism

In the late 1960s, the American women's movement was composed of two major branches: the older, liberal women's rights movement and the fledgling, radical Women's Liberation movement. The National Organization for Women (NOW), founded in 1966, was the most prominent organization of the older branch. Members of NOW primarily sought to achieve legislative, economic, and educational reforms to eradicate sex discrimination in existing institutions. Many of the organization's actions were intended to ameliorate the problems of working women. In 1967, NOW urged the federal government to fund child care centers for working mothers and to grant an income tax deduction for child care costs. Led by Betty Friedan, NOW hoped to improve women's status throughout all sectors of American society, and encouraged women to pursue education and employment in male-dominated fields such as medicine, law, business, and government.

The younger wing of the movement was very different in its organization and goals. Whereas NOW tried to advance equal rights for women without

[2] On lesbian feminism and cultural feminism, see Verta Taylor and Leila J. Rupp, "Women's Culture and Lesbian Feminist Activism: A Reconsideration of Cultural Feminism," in *Community Activism and Feminist Politics: Organizing Against Race, Class, and Gender*, ed. N.A. Naples (New York: Routledge, 1998), 57–79.

[3] On cultural feminist views of sexuality, see Rosemarie Tong, *Feminist Thought: A More Comprehensive Introduction*, 3rd edition (Boulder, CO: Westview Press, 2009), 67.

[4] For an excellent discussion of the development of cultural feminist thought, see Jane Gerhard, *Desiring Revolution: Second-Wave Feminism and the Rewriting of American Sexual Thought, 1920 to 1982* (New York: Columbia University Press, 2001), chapter 5.

challenging the basic structures of American society, Women's Liberation aimed for social and political transformation. "We wanted to build a just society, not get a bigger slice of the pie," activist Meredith Tax said of the younger branch's goals.[5] Most of the founding members of the younger branch had been active in the student-led New Left of the 1960s, and they considered themselves more revolution-minded and less tied to the conventional political system than many of the reform-oriented liberal feminists in the older branch.[6] Women's Liberation had no centralized or national membership organization comparable to NOW. Instead, it consisted of hundreds of issue-oriented small groups, such as New York Radical Feminists, D.C. Women's Liberation, Bread and Roses (Boston), and the Chicago Women's Liberation Union. Although groups espoused different theoretical perspectives, including radical feminism, socialist feminism, and Marxist feminism, they were united in the fight against women's oppression. Most groups took direct action to solve problems central to women's lives, such as founding rape crisis centers and battered women's shelters, and providing safe, underground abortions.

Many members of Women's Liberation had roots in the New Left, and organized as a result of their experiences of blatant sexism within that movement. In the 1960s, the New Left consisted of loosely connected groups of predominantly white, college-aged women and men who mobilized in response to the war in Vietnam and a host of other social injustices, such as poverty and racism. Activists challenged such basic American institutions as capitalism, and demanded action for social change. Women who became politicized through New Left groups such as Students for a Democratic Society (SDS) also became aware that they played subordinate roles to male leaders, their ideas routinely ignored.

Within the New Left, sexual inequality did not seem to warrant male concern. Men assumed the leadership roles, and women were expected to type, file, mimeograph, and make coffee. Although women did the lion's share of organizational work, they were rarely given positions of authority. They also faced severe sexual exploitation. Women were pressured to provide sexual services to movement men – with no strings attached, on the basis that free, unrestrained sexuality was an essential ingredient of human liberation. Female activists endured ridicule or ostracism if they objected to rhetoric that confused "the liberation of the self with the liberation of the libido."[7] A gulf developed between New Left men who ignored women's rising demands for leadership roles and treated them as sexual objects and many New Left women, whose

[5] Quoted in Ruth Rosen, *The World Split Open: How the Modern Women's Movement Changed America* (New York: Viking, 2000), 84.

[6] The two branches are described at length in Myra Marx Ferree and Beth Hess, *Controversy and Coalition: The New Feminist Movement* (Boston: Twayne Publishers, 1985). See also Jo Freeman, *The Politics of Women's Liberation: A Case Study of an Emerging Social Movement and Its Relation to the Policy Process* (New York: David McKay Co., 1975).

[7] Maria Farland, "Total System, Total Solution, Total Apocalypse: Sex Oppression, Systems of Property, and 1970s Women's Liberation Fiction," *Yale Journal of Criticism* 18, no. 2 (Fall 2005), 383.

experiences of "compulsory promiscuity" left them feeling abused.[8] Most of the male leadership paid scant attention to women's increasing fury. In 1970, the author Robin Morgan, who would soon become a prominent anti-pornography activist, announced that she was abandoning the male Left in the first women's issue of the underground newspaper, *Rat*. In the powerful essay, "Goodbye to All That," she expressed her disgust that the movement clung to "an image and theory of free sexuality but practice of sex on demand for males," with no regard for its effect on women.[9] The persistence of patronizing and sexist male attitudes, particularly around issues of sexual entitlement, drove many New Left women to create an independent women's movement.

Women's Liberation groups began to spread across the nation in 1968–1969, and members tried to identify the social and cultural origins of female oppression. For many, sexuality was a key factor. A number of these women had experienced bitter disappointments in their heterosexual relationships, discovering that they were not equals with men in the sexual exchange, but were at grave risk for unwanted sexual pressure and such burdens as unplanned pregnancy and venereal disease. Others came into the groups seething from the virulent sexism they experienced within the New Left. These women exchanged stories about sex and politics, and through consciousness raising discovered that their experiences "had been staggeringly the same, ranging from forced sex to sexual humiliation to abandonment to cynical manipulation as both menials and pieces of ass," Andrea Dworkin observed of the early, eye-opening days.[10] They drew on their personal experiences to develop feminist theory about the sexual subordination of women.

Feminists developed numerous theoretical frameworks that helped explain female oppression, but radical feminists drew direct connections to sexuality.[11]

[8] Farland, "Total System, Total Solution, Total Apocalypse," 383. On the use of sex by New Left men to crush female rebellion, see Andrea Dworkin, "Why So-Called Radical Men Love and Need Pornography," in *Take Back the Night*, 148–154.

[9] Robin Morgan, "Goodbye to All That," in *Going Too Far: The Personal Chronicle of a Feminist* (New York: Vintage Books, 1978), 127. On the resentments felt by young women in the New Left, see also Alix Kates Shulman, "Sex and Power: Sexual Bases of Radical Feminism," *Signs* 5, no. 4 (Summer 1980): 590–604.

[10] Andrea Dworkin, *Right-Wing Women* (New York: Perigee Books, 1983), 96.

[11] For a discussion of each of these strains, see Jean Bethke Elshtain, "Ethics in the Women's Movement," *Annals of the American Academy of Political and Social Science* 515 (May 1991): 126–139. Marxist feminists saw class as the primary contradiction. They argued that women's condition could be understood in terms of the kinds of labor assigned to men and women, the means by which this labor was organized, and the social relations that formed as a result of a particular mode of economic production. The subordination of women thus stemmed from capitalism, not from male dominance. Socialist feminists emphasized the interdependent systems of capitalism and patriarchy as the twin sources of women's subordination. They identified capitalism as a gendered mode of economic production, and patriarchy as a system that allowed men to control female labor and reproduction, on which capitalism depended. Philosopher Ann Ferguson has written that the conflict between radical feminists and socialist feminists stems from disagreements about who benefits from male domination. Radical feminists believe that men benefit by exploiting women's labor and by

Radical feminists saw sex as the primary contradiction, and they treated women and men as fundamentally different sex classes with divergent interests and ways of being.[12] They argued that all forms of social domination, including the oppression of women, originated from male supremacy. Men exploited and victimized women, primarily exerting their power through sexuality, through the heterosexual institutions of romantic love, marriage, the family, sexual violence, and through the sexual objectification of women in mass media images, including pornography.[13] If women were to claim equality and free themselves of male domination, they would have to destroy the sex-role system that maintained it.

Over time, radical feminism emerged as the most popular framework within Women's Liberation. Radical feminists, unlike socialist and Marxist feminists, decided to "divorce" the male Left and build an autonomous movement. The founders devoted all of their time and energy to creating radical feminist theory and founding the small groups through which their movement spread. This strategy resulted in significant growth because the activists focused exclusively on radical feminism and did not seek connections with existing leftist groups.[14] Radical feminists also privileged consciousness raising, which allowed women to build theory from their personal experiences, making it accessible and empowering for many. The radical feminist analysis resonated with many women's intuitive belief that it was *men* and

using the existence of economic class divisions and racism as tools to keep women divided. Socialist feminists argue that sexism and racism are tools used by the ruling class to divide men and women in the producing class against each other. Thus, for socialist feminists, a revolution requires working-class men and women to come together to fight domination by the ruling class. For radical feminists, women must come together to fight domination by men. See Ann Ferguson, *Blood at the Root: Motherhood, Sexuality and Male Dominance* (London: Pandora, 1989).

[12] Radical feminists borrowed from black separatism when they argued that men treated women as an inferior class based on their sex. The transfer of ideas was clear; whites treat blacks as an inferior class based on their color, and men treat women as an inferior class based on their sex. Historian Alice Echols has argued that white women who worked in the civil rights movement tended to gravitate toward radical feminism. See Alice Echols, "The New Feminism of Yin and Yang," in *Powers of Desire: The Politics of Sexuality*, eds. Ann Snitow, Christine Stansell, and Sharon Thompson (New York: Monthly Review Press, 1983), 439.

[13] Shulamith Firestone's 1970 book, *The Dialectic of Sex*, was the first major theoretical exploration of radical feminism. In explaining the origins of male dominance, Firestone argues that sex caste, based on women's biological vulnerability to men, predates economic class and thus can be treated as the point of origin of all other social systems of male domination (e.g., capitalism, racism, imperialism). See Firestone, *The Dialectic of Sex: The Case for Feminist Revolution* (New York: Bantam, 1970).

[14] Alice Echols argues that socialist feminists became involved in battles with sectarian leftists who believed that feminism was diverting women's attention from the class struggle. The socialist feminist Barbara Ehrenreich believes that Marxist-Leninist and Maoist groups decimated the nationwide network of socialist feminist women's unions during the years 1975–1977 by infiltrating them and instigating divisive political debates. See Alice Echols, *Daring to Be Bad: Radical Feminism in America, 1967–1975* (Minneapolis: University of Minnesota Press, 1989), 136–137.

their perpetuation of male supremacy through the *male role* that was most directly responsible for the oppression of women.[15]

Violence Awareness

As consciousness raising (CR) spread across the nation, intimate conversations about sexual life inevitably led women to open up to one another about traumatic episodes. The shared experience of submitting to unwanted sex brought out new awareness of the prevalence of rape, molestation, battery, and sexual harassment. Some women had suffered sexual violence at the hands of strangers, whereas others had been abused by family members and friends.[16] The tendency for police, courts, and families to ignore victims' stories or to blame the women themselves was also common. Women who had been attacked often described a "second rape" by the police and courts, who were quick to suggest that the victim's clothing and demeanor had sent an inviting message, and frequently demanded impossible standards of evidence, such as proof of penetration.[17] As women in CR explored these issues, they began to realize that all women lived in fear of sexual violence, circumscribing their daily activities and routines to try to minimize the risk of physical assault.

A fundamental tenet of the Women's Liberation movement was that women had the right to control their own bodies and their own lives. But, the ubiquity of male violence seemed to be eroding the possibility of female autonomy. Beginning in the early 1970s, feminists organized a national campaign against violence, beginning with rape and wife battering, and ultimately encompassing additional forms of violence such as sexual harassment and incest.

The anti-rape movement started in New York City in January 1971. The initial event was a feminist speak-out organized by the New York Radical Feminists, which attracted three hundred people. By 1972, there were rape crisis centers in Berkeley, Detroit, Boston, Ann Arbor, Michigan; Philadelphia, Hartford, Connecticut; and Washington, DC. Four years later, there were at least 400 rape crisis centers operating around the nation, most of which were independent feminist organizations that had no formal ties to public agencies.[18] These centers offered crisis counseling, self-defense classes,

[15] For the growth of the radical feminist sector, see Echols, *Daring to Be Bad*.

[16] Nancy A. Matthews offers excerpts of interviews with early participants in consciousness raising in her 1994 study of the anti-rape movement. In every group, there were women who had been raped, were victims of incest, or were being battered in their homes. See Nancy A. Matthews, *Confrontng Rape: The Feminist Anti-Rape Movement and the State* (New York: Routledge, 1994), chapter 3.

[17] On this experience, see Diana H. Russell, *The Politics of Rape: The Victim's Perspective* (New York: Stein & Day, 1975). Evidence-gathering and DNA-testing methods that are routine today in rape investigations were not available in the 1970s, and corroboration of one's rape by a witness was a common standard of proof that women were asked to meet.

[18] Mary Anne Largen, "Grassroots Centers and National Task Forces: A Herstory of the Anti-Rape Movement," *Aegis: Magazine on Ending Violence Against Women* 32 (Autumn 1981): 46–52.

support groups, and training sessions to teach volunteers how to help women who had been raped.

As female anger about the prevalence of rape mounted, the movement took on an increased public presence. Groups of women confronted individual rapists and staged public rallies demanding legal and institutional reforms, specifically changes in police, court, and hospital procedures.[19] In one well-publicized campaign, the Kitty Genovese Women's Project printed and distributed the names of 2,100 men indicted for sex crimes in Dallas County, Texas.[20] The list was published in March 1977 in a twenty-page newspaper and distributed free of charge to 25,000 Dallas women.[21] Another high-profile development was the first *Take Back the Night* rally in 1977, an annual march that brought thousands of women together to demand their right to safe streets. The anti-rape movement was the first campaign against violence to capture national attention in the early 1970s, but other movements emerged on its heels.

Battering was the second major form of violence that feminist groups mobilized to combat. The battered women's movement resembled the anti-rape movement in the sense that both shared the conviction that violence against women was a key component of male social control. The extent of the problem first came to light in London in 1971, when feminist activist Erin Pizzey founded Chiswick Women's Aid, an advice center for women. Most of the women who sought help had been battered. In 1974, Pizzey published the first major study of wife abuse, *Scream Quietly or the Neighbors Will Hear.*[22]

Although U.S. feminists were deeply concerned about battering, legal remedies for abused women were few and far between. Police officers routinely

[19] Activists tried to change police behavior toward rape victims, particularly brutal questioning about such issues as a woman's clothing, her sexual history, and whether or not she had enjoyed the attack. As for the courts, feminists won major victories overturning state statutes that had required a rape victim to produce a witness (other than herself) to corroborate her story. In hospitals, activists demanded that victims have the right to have an advocate accompany them in the examining area to offer support and information about venereal disease and pregnancy. For a more detailed discussion of these changes, see Matthews, *Confronting Rape*, chapter 4.

[20] This organization was named for Kitty Genovese, a twenty-eight-year-old cocktail waitress who died in Queens, New York, in 1964. She was stabbed fifteen times and raped as she lay dying. Her attack lasted more than thirty minutes and took place on the street in front of the apartment building where she lived. The incident drew national attention when it was reported that thirty-eight of her neighbors had either heard her cries for help or witnessed the attack and failed to intervene or call the police. On the origins of the group, see Nikki Craft, "Kitty Genovese Women's Project: Statement of Purpose," in *Fight Back! Feminist Resistance to Male Violence*, eds. F. Delacoste and F. Newman (Minneapolis, MN: Cleis Press, 1981): 242–246.

[21] The list of names included all the men indicted for sex crimes in Dallas County between the years 1960 and 1976.

[22] For the history of the battered women's movement, see Susan Schechter, *Women and Male Violence: The Visions and Struggles of the Battered Women's Movement* (London: Pluto Press, 1982).

declined to arrest the men in question, preferring to treat this type of violence as a private family matter. Judges ignored battering, discharging the majority of cases. Feminists invented the concept of the battered women's shelter in response to institutional indifference, and the first shelter, Women's Advocates, opened in St. Paul, Minnesota in 1974. Within five years, there were 250 shelters operating in urban areas nationwide. Shelter volunteers documented the number of clients they served to produce the first reliable statistics on battering. During an eleven-month period in 1975, a women's center in Pittsburgh sheltered 191 abused women and 86 children. Some 5,000 women telephoned the center for advice.[23] In Kentucky, researchers used data from a shelter to estimate that 80,000 women in the state had been battered by their husbands during 1979.[24] Beyond proving the sheer enormity of the problem, the statistics showed that domestic violence affected women across socioeconomic and racial lines.

Sexual harassment proved to be another common experience. Many women who had escaped other forms of violence had nonetheless endured hoots, whistles, unwanted touching, and direct propositioning on the streets and in the workplace. Like rape, this kind of harassment represented an abuse of male power. In the mid-1970s, feminists began to protest their vulnerability to unwanted sexual advances. In May 1975, Working Women United, an organization based in Ithaca, New York, held a "Speak-Out on Sexual Harassment" that revealed women's tremendous anger at this common practice.[25] The journalist Letty Cottin Pogrebin published an influential article on the problem in *Ladies' Home Journal* in 1976, and the magazine received "an avalanche of mail" from readers who had suffered the very experiences Pogrebin described.[26] Other women learned about the problem from a 1976 *Redbook* magazine survey that revealed tense relationships between male and female coworkers. Of the 9,000 female respondents, almost 8,000 had received unwanted sexual advances at the office.[27]

Sexual harassment gained additional national exposure at the end of the decade, when Congress mandated a survey of 20,000 federal workers. According to the report, 42 percent of women working for the federal government between May 1978 and May 1980 suffered forms of sexual harassment ranging from subtle, nonverbal behaviors to rape. Thirty percent

[23] Schechter, 56.

[24] Mark A. Schulman, *A Survey of Spousal Violence Against Women in Kentucky*, U.S. Department of Justice, Law Enforcement Assistance Administration, Study No. 792701 (July 1979), 1.

[25] See Deidre Silverman, "Sexual Harassment: Working Women's Dilemma," in *Dear Sisters: Dispatches from the Women's Liberation Movement*, eds. Rosalyn Baxandall and Linda Gordon (New York: Basic Books, 2000), 274–275.

[26] Reader response is described in Peter N. Stearns, *Battleground of Desire: The Struggle for Self-Control in Modern America* (New York: New York University Press, 1999), 247.

[27] Carolyn Safran, "What Men Do to Women on the Job," *Redbook* (October 1976), 217. Eighty-eight percent of the respondents (7,920 out of 9,000) reported sexual harassment.

of all interviewed had experienced severe harassment, including actual or attempted rape, deliberate touching, or the receipt of sexually explicit letters and phone calls.[28]

The problem of child sexual abuse also emerged in the 1970s, creating what the historian Philip Jenkins has described as "an explosion of research and publishing" around a topic that had previously attracted little attention.[29] Florence Rush, a radical feminist and social worker who would become a WAP leader in the 1980s, electrified a New York Radical Feminist Conference on Rape in April 1971. She received a standing ovation for a speech that exposed the extent and severity of the sexual abuse of girls. Working from data collected in a facility for delinquent girls, Rush debunked the idea that this type of sexual abuse occurred at the hands of perverted strangers lurking near playgrounds. Instead, she revealed that "familiar males" – fathers, stepfathers, brothers, uncles, neighbors, and family friends – were the major sexual abusers of children. Between 1978 and 1981, authors inspired by Rush and other pioneers documented a tidal wave of father-daughter incest and sexual molestation. In 1980, Rush published *The Best-Kept Secret: The Sexual Abuse of Children*, a major study that helped cement child sexual abuse as part of the cultural landscape and enlarged feminist discourse about systematic male violence. Rush helped found WAP and was one of the organization's fiercest critics of sexualized portrayals of children in the media. Sociologist Diana E. H. Russell, a founding member of WAVPM, published influential research that indicated that 38 percent of girls were abused before the age of eighteen, and 28 percent before fourteen.[30]

New insight about the prevalence of male violence dovetailed with important theoretic work concerning rape that radical feminists began producing in the early 1970s. Radical feminists analyzed rape from a woman centered perspective and claimed that it was a political tool that men used to oppress and subjugate women. A single rape offered a powerful lesson and reminder for all women about what might befall them without male protection. Indeed, the threat of rape was so frightening for women that most adapted their routines to try to keep safe, staying at home at night, keeping off the streets, and avoiding public transportation, bars, movies, and similar places without a male escort. Rape thus served the interests of all men – whether or not they themselves approved or participated – by constraining women's activities and ensuring that they could not function independently. Furthermore, rape could no longer be dismissed as deviant behavior attributable to a small subgroup of an otherwise benign male population. Instead, all men were viewed as capable

[28] The federal survey was mandated by Congress and conducted by the Merit Systems Protection Board. The results are discussed in Frances Klein, "Violence Against Women," in *The Women's Annual 1981: The Year in Review*, ed. B. Haber (Boston: G. K. Hall) 278–279. For results of the entire survey, see Merit Systems Protection Board (1981).

[29] Philip Jenkins, *Decade of Nightmares: The End of the Sixties and the Making of Eighties America* (Oxford and New York: Oxford University Press, 2006), 118.

[30] Diana E. H. Russell, *Sexual Exploitation* (Beverly Hills, CA: Sage, 1984).

of committing rape, and this threat benefited all men by forcing every woman to seek male protection.

The work of prominent radical feminist theorists such as Susan Griffin and Susan Brownmiller advanced this new understanding of rape. In an influential 1971 article, *Rape: The All-American Crime*, Griffin argued that ordinary men committed rape, not mentally ill or unstable individuals driven to violence by an uncontrollable onset of lust. Rape was a crime of anger, aggression, and violence against women, and it was such a common occurrence that it represented a "normal" interaction between men and women in American culture. She described rape as a kind of "male protection racket" that some men carried out on behalf of all men to maintain their patriarchal power over women.[31] The mere threat of what could happen to any woman who lacked male protection left women weak and dependent, and stripped them as a sex class of any strength or autonomy.

Griffin's essay expressed a number of the powerful ideas about rape and male violence circulating within the Women's Liberation movement. Rape was "a political act of *oppression*" [italics in original] supported by "a consensus in the male class," Pamela Kearon and Barbara Mehrhof wrote in 1971.[32] In 1979, Mehrhof would become a national coordinator of WAP. Andra Medea and Kathleen Thompson maintained that rape was encouraged in sexist societies, and that women were "authorized victims" for men.[33] Robin Morgan expressed similar views. "We won't shuffle past the vulgarity of the sidewalk verbal hassler," she wrote in 1974, "who is not harmless but who is broadcasting the rapist's theory and who is backed up by *the threat of the capacity to carry out the practice* itself" [italics in original].[34] In the early 1970s, feminists described rape as both a symbolic practice and a concrete means of keeping women in a subordinate place, physically and emotionally dependent on men.

These ideas about the patriarchal function of rape were introduced to a national audience in 1975, with the publication of journalist Susan Brownmiller's landmark book, *Against Our Will: Men, Women and Rape*. Brownmiller, a civil rights activist, a founding member of New York Radical Feminists in 1968, and an influential organizer in the anti-rape movement, traced man's use of rape as a weapon of force against women from the earliest civilizations through the present day, and theorized rape as the quintessential act that linked men and women through time and across race, class, and culture. Once primeval men discovered that they *could* rape women, by dint of greater strength and the "anatomical fiat" of the particular structures of male and female genitalia, they passed this knowledge down so that every

[31] Susan Griffin, "Rape: The All-American Crime," *Ramparts* 10 (1971): 30.

[32] Barbara Mehrhof and Pam Kearon, "Rape: An Act of Terror," in *Radical Feminism*, eds. A. Koedt, E. Levine, and A. Rapone (New York: Quadrangle Books, 1973), 233.

[33] Medea and Thompson, 125.

[34] Robin Morgan, "Theory and Practice: Pornography and Rape," in *Take Back the Night: Women on Pornography*, ed. L. Lederer (New York: William Morrow, 1980), 140.

succeeding generation could use both the act of rape and the threat of rape to control women.[35] Rape – or, more generally, male violence or the threat of violence – was thus the linchpin that ensured the maintenance of the social order. Violence was a weapon that men had used throughout history to ensure the continued domination of women. As Brownmiller described this trans-historical mechanism: "It is nothing more or less than a conscious process of intimidation by which *all men* keep *all women* in a state of fear" [italics in original].[36] *Against Our Will* introduced the public to a new way of thinking about rape by explaining that it was not an uncommon occurrence but a mainstay of male supremacy.

Brownmiller's book was especially powerful because it joined theory about rape with statistics that indicated its frequency was on the rise. According to FBI crime statistics, the number of reported rapes increased 62 percent over the five years from 1968 to 1973. Using an "unemotional rock-bottom" working estimate that only one in five rape incidents was actually reported, Brownmiller calculated that more than a quarter of a million rapes took place in the United States in 1973 alone.[37] Working from different data sets just a few years later, the sociologist Allan Griswold Johnson estimated that 20 to 30 percent of the nation's twelve-year-old girls would suffer a violent sexual attack during their lifetimes. The average American woman, he concluded, was just as likely to experience sexual violence as she was to be diagnosed with cancer or go through a divorce.[38]

Brownmiller's best-seller was regarded as a definitive feminist statement, finally bringing national attention to the crisis of sexual violence against women in America.[39] *Against Our Will* commanded the front page of *The*

[35] Brownmiller, *Against Our Will*, 16.

[36] Brownmiller, *Against Our Will*, 15. Many feminists soundly rejected Brownmiller's trans-historical analysis of rape and insisted that rape had been used to achieve different ends with regard to different groups of women and men. A number of black feminists argued that Brownmiller had failed to comprehend the cultural and historical significance of the sexual exploitation of black women during slavery. Author bell hooks contended that the state-sanctioned rape of female slaves "led to a devaluation of black womanhood that permeated the psyches of all Americans and shaped the social status of all black women once slavery ended." See bell hooks, *Ain't I A Woman: Black Women and Feminism* (Boston: South End Press, 1981), 52. In addition, they objected to the way that Brownmiller lumped all men together. White men and women had historically used false rape charges as a powerful weapon against black men. For this analysis, see Deb Friedman, "Rape, Racism and Reality," *FAAR and NCN News* (July/August 1978): 14–19. See also Jacqueline D. Hall, "The Mind that Burns in Each Body: Women, Rape, and Racial Violence," in Snitow, Stansell, and Thompson, 328–349.

[37] Brownmiller, *Against Our Will*, 175.

[38] Allan Griswold Johnson, "On the Prevalence of Rape in the United States," *Signs* 6, no. 1 (Autumn, 1980): 136–146.

[39] Although the book had a tremendous national readership, it is important to note that not all women supported Brownmiller's conclusions about rape. Socialist feminists faulted her for ignoring the centrality of class and race in her analysis. They argued that violence against women had to take into account material realities, including privatization of the family,

New York Times Book Review on October 12, 1975, a major departure for a newspaper that usually relegated women's movement news to the style section. The reviewer, Mary Ellen Gale, staff counsel for the American Civil Liberties Union of Southern California, heaped praise on this "chilling and monumental" book.[40] The review distilled Brownmiller's discussion of rape, describing it as "the hidden foundation for too much of our social order, the cardinal act of defilement by which men assert possession and control over the other half of humanity."[41] After four years of grassroots organizing against rape and battering, feminists enjoyed a new measure of triumph. The most influential newspaper in the country had presented the core ideas of the anti-violence movements and described them in passionate terms as "a demand for justice."[42]

During the early and mid-1970s, a slew of influential feminist writers published work that took a dismal view of men as violent and bestial, capable of feeling nothing but contempt for women. Andrea Dworkin's 1974 book, *Woman Hating*, described a culture that treated rape as a normal male activity. Rape, for Dworkin, was the purest expression of a deep-seated, systemic male hatred of women. Diana E. H. Russell, who would soon found the San Francisco group, Women Against Violence in Pornography and Media, presented rape survivors' harrowing stories in her 1975 book, *The Politics of Rape*. One victim spoke plainly when asked to advise women hoping to escape a similar fate: "To avoid being raped means to not be anywhere where men are.... Don't associate with men," she warned.[43] These books were received by a women's movement that had come to regard male violence, particularly rape, as the single greatest threat to female autonomy.

This focus on – and cultural sensitivity to – male violence marked a revolution in American culture. Two of the most prominent Women's Liberation anthologies published in 1970 had included no articles on rape or battering. Between 1971 and 1975, the issue of violence catapulted to center stage of feminist attention and captured mainstream interest as well.[44] Newspapers began reporting many more rape and domestic violence stories in the mid-1970s than they had in earlier years; the historian Elizabeth Pleck noted that the *New York Times* ran forty-four articles about battering in 1977, whereas prior to that time the newspaper had rarely mentioned the issue. Journalists

exploitation of women's unpaid labor in the home, and limited economic opportunities for women in the public sphere. Many women of color criticized Brownmiller for downplaying the significance of the sexual exploitation of black women during slavery and the racist use of the rape charge by the white community against black men.

[40] Mary Ellen Gale, review of *Against Our Will: Men, Women and Rape*, by Susan Brownmiller, *The New York Times Book Review* (October 12, 1975), sec. 7, p. 1.

[41] Gale, 1975.

[42] Gale, 1975.

[43] Russell, *The Politics of Rape*, 85.

[44] Susan Schechter has made this point with regard to the 1970 anthologies *Sisterhood Is Powerful* and *Voices from Women's Liberation*. See Schechter, 32.

made radical changes to their style of coverage, adopting a more sympathetic approach to the victim, exploring the physical and psychological effects of these events, and treating male violence as a social problem as well as an individual act of crime.[45] Fictionalized accounts of rape that reached Americans through prime-time television programs from 1976 on tended to express greater sympathy for (white) victims and to characterize their trauma as a valid social concern. According to the media scholar Lisa Cuklanz, few of these prime-time storylines from 1976 to 1990 featured minority characters, perhaps as a way of sidestepping the difficult issue of the intertwined nature of racism and rape in American history. However, the episodes did incorporate the reform-minded stance of Women's Liberation that took blame off the victim and placed it squarely on the perpetrator. This was a partial step forward, Cuklanz notes, although television shows rarely explored the role of structural factors that might have encouraged rape, including male socialization, the pervasive objectification of women in the media, and pornography.[46]

Feminists had succeeded in raising rape and battering as political questions, directing blame away from the victim and onto the perpetrators and a patriarchal society at large. Furthermore, they had improved the social and legal services available to women caught in the web of male violence. An obvious next step was to start trying to identify the elements of popular culture that taught men the kind of contempt for women that led to rape and other acts of brutality. As these activists worked to make rape and battering a part of the national consciousness, they also began to question the relationship between the presence of violent sexual images in mainstream media and the incidence of actual male violence against women.

Some of the leading theorists of rape suspected that the mass media might be at least partly to blame. Medea and Thompson made an early connection between mass media images and rape. "As long as we accept the stereotypes that are presented to us in everything from pulp detective stories to Oscar-winning films – that women are naturally passive, childlike, and vulnerable, and that men are naturally aggressive, brutal, and uncontrollable – the rape situation will not change," they wrote.[47] Brownmiller struggled with similar questions. She wondered where "impressionable, adolescent males" might get the "ideology and psychologic encouragement" needed to commit rape.[48]

Brownmiller believed that the answer to this question could be found in two American institutions: prostitution and pornography. She argued that both reinforced the idea that sexual access to women was always a man's right.

[45] Helen Benedict, *Virgin or Vamp: How the Press Covers Sex Crimes* (New York: Oxford University Press, 1992), 37–42; Elizabeth Pleck, *Domestic Tyranny: The Making of Social Policy Against Family Violence from Colonial Times to the Present* (New York and Oxford: Oxford University Press, 1987), 182.

[46] Lisa M. Cuklanz, *Rape on Prime Time: Television, Masculinity and Sexual Violence* (Philadelphia: University of Pennsylvania Press, 2000).

[47] Medea and Thompson, 7.

[48] Brownmiller, *Against Our Will*, 391.

A man who sought out a prostitute or pornographic material purchased access, whereas a rapist took it by force, but both instances reinforced the status quo of male privilege. In Brownmiller's view, pornography was especially similar to rape because each was thrust on unwilling women. Both were "male inventions" designed to humiliate women, to reduce them to "anonymous, panting playthings, adult toys, dehumanized objects to be used, abused, broken and discarded," all for the greater glory of the male ego.[49] In a few short pages, she formalized the connection between mass media images and rape that would motivate the first feminist campaigns to eradicate violence against women in advertising and popular culture. In *Against Our Will*, Susan Brownmiller foreshadowed the rise of the American feminist anti-pornography movement.

The Radical Feminist Critique of Heterosexuality

Within consciousness raising, radical feminists spent a great deal of time analyzing the ways that men controlled women in marriage, in the workplace, in schools, through the law, and through sex. In the early days of the Women's Liberation movement, discussions about sexuality assumed a heterosexual orientation and emphasized women's struggles to improve their relationships with men in and out of bed. Between 1968 and 1970, lesbians remained closeted in women's groups; a woman who came out could not necessarily expect to receive emotional support or understanding from her sisters.[50] Over time, lesbians in the movement became frustrated not only because their sexuality was unwelcome, but also because precious movement time was devoted to solving problems that many lesbians avoided by refusing contact with men. As a result, a number of radical lesbians began to argue that straight women could seek freedom from heterosexual oppression by choosing lesbianism and disentangling themselves from the men in their lives. Political lesbianism, which entailed the redefinition of lesbianism as a political rather than strictly sexual choice, began to dominate radical feminist politics in the early 1970s.

Lesbianism first began to achieve greater visibility in the women's movement as feminists challenged established ideas about heterosexual intercourse. Anne Koedt, a founder of New York Radical Feminists, suggested that men had duped women into believing that penetrative sex was the most pleasurable

[49] Browmiller, *Against Our Will*, 394.

[50] Prior to the development of political lesbianism, many heterosexual feminists clung to a stereotype of the lesbian as hypersexual and male-identified. A number of radical feminists went so far as to condemn lesbians for aping the mannerisms, clothing, and sexual attitudes of heterosexual men. Others believed that lesbians who related to each other through the adoption of butch/femme roles, a gendered form of lesbian eroticism, were mimicking the dominant and submissive structure of heterosexual relationships. To outsiders, butch/femme looked very similar to traditional heterosexual arrangements, with one partner dressing and acting masculine and the other feminine. In this light, lesbianism was more reactionary than radical, and as such was not much use to feminism. See Rosen, 166–167, and Elizabeth Lapovsky Kennedy and Madeline D. Davis, *Boots of Leather, Slippers of Gold: The History of a Lesbian Community* (New York: Penguin Books, 1994), 192.

in an influential 1970 essay. In "The Myth of the Vaginal Orgasm," Koedt used anatomical evidence to challenge the commonly held belief that the seat of the female orgasm was located deep within the vagina. Male authorities including Freud had long insisted that a woman could only experience a mature orgasm through vaginal penetration and penile thrusting. Koedt used medical findings about the absence of nerve endings – and thus sensation – inside the vagina to conclude that female orgasm was actually clitoral. The implications of this discovery were enormous. If women reached orgasm through external clitoral stimulation, they might not require men for sexual satisfaction.

Koedt's widely read essay stimulated new thinking about heterosexuality, especially the idea that men had perpetuated the myth of the vaginal orgasm to ensure their sexual access to women. The discovery of the clitoral orgasm threatened to make men sexually expendable, because it seemed that women could give one another sexual pleasure. "The establishment of clitoral orgasm as fact would threaten the heterosexual *institution*," Koedt wrote. "For it would indicate that sexual pleasure was obtainable from either men *or* women, thus making heterosexuality not an absolute, but an option."[51] [italics in original] The myth of the vaginal orgasm was thus a tool that men used to enforce "compulsory heterosexuality" for women, as the lesbian feminist Adrienne Rich described it in 1980.[52] Even if they did not advocate lesbianism on the basis of Koedt's work, many radical feminists did interpret the essay to mean that women had the potential to create satisfying sexual relationships without men. "Lesbian sexuality," Koedt suggested, "could make an excellent case, based upon anatomical data, for the extinction of the male organ."[53] Women began to consider the deliberate rejection of sexual intercourse with men, and the ideological and practical burdens that accompanied heterosexual relationships.

At the same time that Koedt's article was stimulating new thought, changes in the membership of Women's Liberation brought the issue of lesbianism to the forefront of the movement. Beginning in 1970, lesbians entered Women's Liberation en masse, defecting from both the gay rights movement and the older branch of the women's movement. Many were disillusioned by the indifferent – and often hostile – treatment they had received from gay men, and the fear and suspicion they had aroused among heterosexual feminists in NOW. Lesbians were poised to emerge in the Women's Liberation movement as a powerful force in their own right.

After the Stonewall Riots of 1969, many lesbians joined the gay rights movement and cast their lot with gay men. It soon became apparent, however, that gay male socialization was no better than heterosexual male socialization

[51] Anne Koedt, "The Myth of the Vaginal Orgasm," in *Radical Feminism*, eds. Anne Koedt, Ellen Levine and Anita Rapone (New York: Quadrangle Books, 1973), 206.

[52] Adrienne Rich, "Compulsory Heterosexuality and Lesbian Existence," *Signs* 5, no. 4 (Summer 1980): 631–660.

[53] Koedt, "The Myth of the Vaginal Orgasm," 206.

when it came to relations of power with women. Lesbians encountered the same male chauvinist attitudes that had driven masses of women out of the New Left.[54] Male leaders defined the agenda of gay politics, whereas lesbians were expected to keep quiet about the specific oppressions they faced as *women*, and to function primarily as "the ladies' auxiliary of the gay movement."[55] This type of treatment as "conceptual appendages" led to widespread disillusionment, and many concluded that their oppression as women was as severe as their oppression as lesbians.[56] They hoped that Women's Liberation would provide a supportive environment where lesbian issues would receive attention.[57]

Lesbians working in the women's rights branch of the women's movement fared no better than those in gay liberation. Many became angry and dissatisfied with NOW leaders' homophobia and their failure to acknowledge lesbianism as a feminist issue. Instead, the organization routinely suppressed any discussion of lesbianism for fear that it would discredit the women's movement overall. Betty Friedan, author of *The Feminine Mystique* and the first president of NOW, warned that lesbianism was a "lavender menace" that would compromise the organization's credibility and the legitimacy of the entire question of women's rights.[58] In 1968, Ti-Grace Atkinson, then-president of the New York City chapter of NOW, quit the organization citing its poor treatment of lesbians. At the end of 1969, Rita Mae Brown, a New York-NOW member who had been trying to raise the profile of lesbians within the organization, was summarily dismissed as editor of her chapter's newsletter. Brown resigned her membership in January 1970.[59] That year, journalist Dolores Alexander, the first executive director of NOW, also resigned in protest over NOW's homophobic practices. Alexander continued to lecture on women's rights and at the end of the 1970s, she became one of the founders and national coordinators of WAP.

Displaced from NOW, many of these feminists were drawn into Women's Liberation. Brown gravitated to the newer movement and tried to initiate a conversation about the relationship of lesbianism to feminism. She joined a consciousness raising group affiliated with the New York radical feminist

[54] See Gene Damon, "The Least of These: The Minority Whose Screams Haven't Yet Been Heard," in *Sisterhood Is Powerful*, ed. Robin Morgan (New York: Random House, 1970), 305. See also Shane Phelan, *Identity Politics: Lesbian Feminism and the Limits of Community* (Philadelphia: Temple University Press, 1989), 37–38.

[55] Quoted in Lillian Faderman, *Odd Girls and Twilight Lovers: A History of Lesbian Life in Twentieth-Century America* (New York: Penguin, 1991), 211.

[56] Phelan, 37.

[57] This transition is discussed in both Phelan and Winifred D. Wandersee, *On the Move: American Women in the 1970s* (Boston: Twayne Publishers, 1988).

[58] Judith Hole and Ellen Levine, *Rebirth of Feminism* (New York: Quadrangle Books, 1971), 240.

[59] Sidney Abbott and Barbara Love, *Sappho Was A Right-On Woman: A Liberated View of Lesbianism* (New York: Stein and Day, 1972), 113–115. For Brown's own account of her treatment in NOW, see Rita Mae Brown, *A Plain Brown Rapper* (Oakland,CA: Diana Press, 1976), 88–90.

group Redstockings, but found that its members were reluctant to deal with lesbian issues. The consciousness raising groups had a heterosexual orientation, and discussions centered around "birth control, bad fucks, and abortions," according to one lesbian participant.[60] Brown found little consideration for lesbians in Redstockings. "They could empathize with the prostitute, support the housewife, encourage the single woman and seek child care for the mother, but they wouldn't touch the Lesbian," she observed.[61] As in gay liberation and NOW, lesbians felt devalued and invisible.[62]

Brown began to organize a lesbian feminist movement, recruiting women from radical feminism and gay liberation. Together, they founded a new organization called Radicalesbians, whose members would make lesbianism a central political issue for feminism. In 1970, the Radicalesbians wrote the first major position paper of lesbian feminism, which they titled "The Woman-Identified-Woman."[63] In this manifesto, they argued that lesbianism was the logical means of resistance to patriarchy.

The Radicalesbians and the Introduction of Political Lesbianism

Lesbian feminism made a stunning debut in May 1970 when Brown and forty other Radicalesbians seized the stage at the Second Congress to Unite Women. Wearing light purple t-shirts with the slogan "Lavender Menace" stenciled on the front, the women told the audience what it was like to live in a heterosexist culture that ignored lesbianism as a valid and legitimate form of sexual and political expression. They passed out copies of "The Woman-Identified-Woman" and presented their case for lesbianism as an important political challenge to the heterosexual order.

"The Woman-Identified-Woman" and lesbian feminist politics transformed radical feminism in the early 1970s, redefining lesbianism as a way of life that every woman could – and should – discover if she truly cared about women's freedom. The position paper introduced a new way of thinking about lesbianism that minimized its sexual nature, and framed it as a revolutionary political choice. A lesbian defined herself in relationship to other women, not to men. She rejected male sexual and political domination, male ideology, and the male world that regarded her as inferior. The Radicalesbians argued that a lesbian was a woman who loved women in the broadest sense of the word, prioritizing women's political, emotional, physical, and economic needs over those of any man. She was a woman who devoted herself to other women and to the hope of feminist revolution. "For this we must be available and supportive to one another, give our commitment and our love, give the emotional

[60] Quoted in Echols, *Daring to Be Bad*, 241.
[61] Brown, *A Plain Brown Rapper*, 91.
[62] On lesbians' frustrations with heterosexual radical feminists, see Phelan, 38–39.
[63] For Brown's account of the formation of Radicalesbians by lesbians who were dissatisfied with Women's Liberation and Gay Liberation, see Brown, "Living With Other Women," in *A Plain Brown Rapper*, 74–77.

support necessary to sustain this movement," the Radicalesbians urged. "Our energies must flow toward our sisters, not backward toward our oppressors," they wrote.[64]

The Radicalesbians' manifesto championed lesbianism as the vanguard of feminism and women's best hope to mount a serious, sustained challenge to patriarchy. Members of the Furies, an influential lesbian separatist collective, followed this line of thinking. "Lesbianism is not a matter of sexual preference," they declared, "but rather one of political choice which every woman must make if she is to become woman-identified and thereby end male supremacy."[65] If you were sufficiently angry about male supremacy, and committed to your own liberation as well as the liberation of all women, you could *choose* to be lesbian. Every woman could "'existentially' convert" to lesbianism, severing her relationships with men, escaping her own oppression under patriarchy, and declaring her political solidarity with other women.[66]

The idea that heterosexual women could define themselves as lesbians on the basis of their politics and woman-oriented lifestyle, rather than a genuine sexual attraction to women, gained greatest currency among radical feminists. Lesbianism was a potent force for freedom; by choosing it, a woman asserted her sexual and political independence from men, and her refusal to cooperate in her own oppression or that of other women. In Dworkin's words, "[N]othing is less an expression of love and more an expression of dominance and control than conventional heterosexual relation."[67] If women collectively withdrew from "conventional heterosexual relation," men would have no choice but to cease their sexist behavior, to cede their destructive privileges, and to cooperate in the establishment of a genderless social system.

Lesbianism moved quickly to the forefront of radical feminism, but many activists within Women's Liberation were wary of this development. Socialist feminists questioned the woman-power perspective of political lesbianism, noting that class and race, in addition to sexuality, were key components of oppression. Many women of color – both heterosexual and lesbian – were not prepared to renounce their sexual, emotional and political ties to men of color, and they refused to declare them oppressors on the same level with white men. Some radical feminists criticized political lesbianism because it disparaged all women who engaged in sexual and emotional relationships with men, regardless of their commitment to the movement.

[64] Radicalesbians, "The Woman-Identified-Woman,"in *Radical Feminism*, eds. Anne Koedt, Ellen Levine and Anita Rapone (New York: Quadrangle Books, 1973), 245. On the movement of lesbianism to the forefront of the women's movement, see Chris Weedon, *Feminism, Theory and the Politics of Difference* (New York: John Wiley, 1999), 51–76.

[65] Ginny Berson, "The Furies," in *Lesbianism and the Women's Movement*, eds. Nancy Myron and Charlotte Bunch (Baltimore: Diana Press, 1975), 11.

[66] Lillian Faderman, *Odd Girls and Twilight Lovers: A History of Lesbian Life in Twentieth-Century America* (New York: Penguin, 1991), 202.

[67] Andrea Dworkin, "Marx and Gandhi were Liberals: Feminism and the 'Radical' Left," Pamphlet, Palo Alto, CA: Frog in the Well, 1973, 6. Clipping in the Los Angeles WAVAW Papers, Box 11.

At the onset of these debates, some of the most vigorous opponents to the redefinition of lesbianism as a political choice and a specifically feminist practice were lesbians themselves. Many who identified themselves as such based solely on sexual desire objected because lesbianism was validated as a political act, but not a sexual right. They feared that this approach would ultimately threaten their personal freedom, leading to a prescriptive model of "appropriate" lesbian sexual behavior. "By conflating lesbianism (which I think of as a sexual and erotic experience) with feminism – a political philosophy – the ability to justify lesbianism on grounds other than feminism dropped out of the discourse," the socialist feminist theorist Gayle Rubin wrote of this turn within the movement.[68] Experienced lesbians also knew firsthand that their relationships were not always healthy and egalitarian, and had the potential to replicate the "worst features" of any heterosexual arrangement.[69] Some feared sexual exploitation by the new converts, many of whom were eager to experiment but might choose at any time to return to their male lovers.[70]

The rise of lesbian feminism was highly divisive, and it drove a significant number of activists out of Women's Liberation. However, many heterosexual radical feminists embraced this philosophy, partaking in what the socialist feminist author Wendy Clark has described as a "wholesale appropriation" of lesbianism.[71] Some discovered a strong sexual attraction to women and developed lasting lesbian relationships, but others ultimately returned to heterosexuality as movement pressure receded. Some heterosexual radical feminists tried to continue working in Women's Liberation on their own terms. They resented the chauvinistic premise that lesbianism was a "higher form" of feminism and argued that rejecting men was not the only way to change

[68] Gayle Rubin, Deirdre English, and Amber Hollibaugh, "Talking Sex: A Conversation on Sexuality and Feminism," *Monthly Review* 58 (July/August 1981): 48.

[69] Lynne Segal describes Elizabeth Wilson's response to lesbianism being held up as an ideal practice. Wilson argued that lesbian relationships could be as fraught with inequality as heterosexual relationships. See Lynne Segal, *Straight Sex: Rethinking the Politics of Pleasure* (Berkeley: University of California Press, 1994), 54–55.

[70] In Chapter 9, I discuss the rise of conflict in the late 1970s between lesbian feminists who objected to the desexualization of lesbianism and anti-pornography feminists who insisted that female sexuality should not be oppressive for women. Specifically, the groups clashed over the questions of S/M and butch/femme roles, which the former group defended as lesbian eroticism and the latter group attacked as replicating heterosexual power relations and turning women into sex objects. The latter group redefined acceptable feminist lesbian sex practice in rigid ways that excluded much sexual activity and which critics labeled vanilla sex. The roots of that conflict are found in the debates surrounding political lesbianism, and the idea that there is such an entity as politically correct sex.

[71] Wendy Clark, "The Dyke, The Feminist and the Devil," *Feminist Review* 11 (Summer 1982): 37. Clark wrote that many heterosexual feminists did not take up the lesbian feminist challenge to engage in a thorough critical analysis of heterosexuality, but instead used lesbianism as a form of a shortcut, redefining it as an ideal practice free of the worst excesses of the male order and a critique of male power. This devalued the sexual aspects of lesbianism, which was a negative outcome for women whose relationship to lesbianism was primarily sexual, not political.

society. Heterosexual feminists saw themselves as engaged in the equally valid "heterosexual, heterosocial form of the feminist struggle," which meant confronting men every day, forcing them to change their sexist ways, and teaching them to see and treat women as equals.[72] Some endured fierce personal criticism while remaining connected to the movement. Others dropped out in the face of disapproval and antagonism.

The stunning ideological success of lesbian feminism within Women's Liberation fostered the growth of a separatist movement that advanced the analysis of the centrality of heterosexuality to female oppression. Shortly after the Radicalesbians presented "The Woman-Identified-Woman," a number of lesbian feminists organized groups whose members severed all personal relationships and professional alliances with men. The most radical of these groups also cut off contact with heterosexual women. According to Charlotte Bunch, one of the primary architects of lesbian feminism, separatism allowed lesbians to build community, to strengthen their critique of the ideological and institutional domination of heterosexuality, and to create a political ideology that would force the women's movement to accept lesbians.[73] Some of the influential lesbian separatist groups, such as The Furies, which formed in May 1971 and included Bunch and Brown, published significant writings on the structure of male power in marriage, family, workplace, schools, and organized religion, and argued that each of these institutions was organized around heterosexism. In the workplace, for example, the ideology of heterosexuality made it possible to relegate women to dead-end jobs with low salaries whereas men were rewarded with substantial breadwinner wages. A woman's job was presumed to be of secondary personal and financial importance; her primary responsibility was taking care of her husband and family. Radical lesbian separatists challenged women to look critically at their lives, to acknowledge and refuse the privileges they received from their ties to men (e.g., physical protection on the street, economic support), and to understand how and why the heterosexual norm oppressed all women.

The Gay/Straight Split

The growing influence of lesbian feminism within radical feminism created serious tensions for straight women who wanted both relationships with men *and* a secure place in the movement. Lesbian feminism prescribed a narrow range of acceptable behavior for women in the early 1970s, and separatists insisted that women could only live, work, and be intimate with other women. In effect, lesbian feminism promoted a zero-tolerance policy for heterosexuality. Many lesbian feminists believed that heterosexual women were stabbing them in the back, selfishly clinging to men to maintain social

72 Marie-Jo Dhavernas, "Hating Masculinity Not Men," in *Feminism and Sexuality: A Reader*, eds. Stevi Jackson and Sue Scott (New York: Columbia University Press, 1996), 152.

73 See Charlotte Bunch, "Learning from Lesbian Separatism," in *Passionate Politics: Feminist Theory in Action* (New York: St. Martin's Press, 1987), 182–191.

and economic security even though they recognized lesbianism as the pathway to freedom. Some lesbian feminists refused to maintain ties with straight women. "I have no option but to be separate from them," Rita Mae Brown wrote. "I can't work with people who degrade me, don't deal with behavior that is destructive to me and who don't share their privileges."[74] Lesbian feminists often regarded women who continued to affiliate with men as traitors to the cause. Such persons were "obviously consorting with the enemy and could not be trusted," the sociologist Jo Freeman wrote of the prevailing attitudes toward heterosexual women.[75]

The gay/straight split, as it was called in the movement, drove masses of heterosexual radical women out of Women's Liberation between 1970 and 1972. Many women refused to divorce husbands or leave male lovers, or abandon male comrades-in-arms in movements for social change. As a consequence, some straight women were essentially expelled from their radical feminist groups. Others internalized the idea that a woman who refused to choose lesbianism actively oppressed her sisters, and came to see themselves as unworthy of continued participation. "Given their own personal/ideological need to be in the forefront of social change, and the compelling consistency of the argument that the truly radical feminist was a lesbian, they had to conform or drop out," Jo Freeman observed in 1975.[76] As straight women left the movement, radical feminism coalesced around lesbianism with the result that it became almost "a compulsory new orientation for feminists."[77] According to one historian of the period, the majority of radical feminists identified as lesbian by 1975.[78]

The Shift from Radical Feminism to Cultural Feminism

The struggles around lesbianism threatened to permanently estrange heterosexual radical feminists from lesbian radical feminists, and to make it impossible for heterosexual radical feminists to play active movement roles.[79] By

74 Rita Mae Brown, "Take a Lesbian to Lunch," in *A Plain Brown Rapper*, 95.

75 Jo Freeman, *The Politics of Women's Liberation: A Case Study of an Emerging Social Movement and Its Relation to the Policy Process* (New York: David McKay Co., 1975), 137.

76 Freeman, 134.

77 Clark, 34.

78 Echols, *Daring to be Bad*, 240.

79 These tensions never disappeared, although they did lessen. At a 1979 Women Against Pornography conference, the straight radical feminist Susan Brownmiller was attacked as a "cocksucker" by a lesbian separatist in the audience. The separatist complained that lesbians did all the work in the women's movement, only to be marginalized and hidden from view by feminist organizations like WAP, and betrayed by leaders who went home and slept with men. Brownmiller, in turn, insulted the lesbian separatist by asking her why she was wearing men's clothing (a tie) if she disliked men so much. The implication was that the lesbian wasn't really "woman-identified" and was trying to dress, act, and be like a man. After the incident, Brownmiller defended her comments by explaining that most heterosexual women felt it was close to impossible to work in the women's movement because of the constant slurs against their sexuality. This incident is discussed in Chapter 7.

1973, radical feminist leaders were trying to promote conciliatory strategies to heal the gay/straight split. The pressure to identify as lesbian receded, which provided an opportunity for heterosexual women and lesbians to find common ground. The radical feminist Robin Morgan, who was attacked by the Radicalesbians in 1972 for calling herself a lesbian while she lived with her husband and son, argued that it was time for women to stop treating one another as the enemy.[80] Instead, feminists ought to celebrate women's virtuous, life-loving, nurturing values and oppose men's power-hungry, violent, and destructive ways. "Every woman here knows in her gut the vast differences between her sexuality and that of any patriarchally trained male's," Morgan told a group of West Coast feminists at a 1973 conference. "That the emphasis on genital sexuality, objectification, promiscuity, emotional noninvolvement, and coarse invulnerability, was the *male style*, and that we, as women, placed greater trust in love, sensuality, humor, tenderness, commitment" [italics in original].[81] In a major departure from early radical feminism, Morgan invoked stereotypes of masculine and feminine behavior, describing women's sexuality as more spiritual than corporeal.

Morgan's words signaled the start of a major theoretical shift from radical feminism to cultural feminism. Early radical feminists had argued that differences between men and women were not biological, but social, caused by the corrupt and artificial gender roles that patriarchal society imposed on the sexes.[82] The historian Alice Echols has argued that these radical feminists sought to abolish gender, not to reify the socially constructed differences between women and men. The radical feminist Bonnie Kreps expressed this fundamental tenet: "We believe that the male world as it now exists is based on the corrupt notion of 'maleness vs. femaleness,' that the oppression of women is based on this notion and its attendant institutions."[83] Radical feminists used the critique of heterosexuality to uncover how institutions like the family were carefully structured to create and maintain seemingly natural gender differences between men and women.[84]

Cultural feminism, by contrast, encouraged a fixed view of the differences between women and men, supported biological explanations of gender differences, and regarded "male" and "female" values as categories that corresponded to organic sex-based qualities. Cultural feminism maintained that

[80] Morgan's run-in with Radicalesbians is described in Rosen, 169.

[81] Robin Morgan, "Lesbianism and Feminism: Synonyms or Contradictions?" in *Going Too Far: The Personal Chronicle of a Feminist* (New York: Vintage Books, 1978), 181.

[82] Echols, "The New Feminism of Yin and Yang,", 440.

[83] Quoted in Echols, "The New Feminism of Yin and Yang," 440.

[84] Alice Echols has offered the most complete analyses of these changes within radical feminism, and the disjuncture between early radical feminism and late radical feminism, which she and others have called cultural feminism. See Echols, "The New Feminism of Yin and Yang," and *Daring to Be Bad*. See also Alice Echols, "The Taming of the Id: Feminist Sexual Politics, 1963–83," in *Pleasure and Danger: Exploring Female Sexuality*, ed. Carole S. Vance (Boston: Routledge & Kegan Paul, 1989), 50–72.

there was an innately benevolent, nurturing, and positive female way of life that was opposed by an aggressive, violent, conquering male approach. The male way of life was motivated by rapacious, testosterone-driven urges that made men crave violent encounters like rape and war. Instead of continuing to demand that women reject the men in their lives wholesale, cultural feminists advocated the rejection of male values and aggressive, competitive, and destructive behaviors.

By the time the feminist anti-pornography campaign was in full swing in the late 1970s, the influence of cultural feminism was evident throughout the women's movement. Many anti-pornography activists tended to regard men and women as inherently different types of creatures. Men were rapacious and brutal. "I imagine men filled with desire for violence, the need for violence growing in them every day, as natural as hunger or thirst," the lesbian feminist poet Susan Griffin wrote in the anti-pornography anthology, *Take Back the Night*. "I imagine the average male in a corner of a cage growling with menace."[85] Griffin portrayed men as animals driven by "natural" instincts; violence was an uncontrollable biological drive, no different from hunger or thirst.[86] The departure from the radical feminist view of violence as a political tool that men used selectively to maintain male power and sexual access was striking. Cultural feminists were more likely to agree with Griffin that violence ran through every man's blood, like testosterone.

Many feminists pointed out the shortcomings of cultural feminist arguments that attributed female oppression to male biology. This perspective downplayed the influence of social and cultural factors on personality development, and advanced the dangerous idea that "maleness" could be equated with a natural, irrepressible drive to dominate. A biological argument treated all men as brutes, when some men were women's true allies in struggle and were committed to egalitarian social conditions. Worse, it characterized women as perpetual victims and failed to take women's social, sexual, and political sources of power into account. "The fact that all men, because of their sex, are in the position of oppressor does not mean that all male individuals *are nothing but oppressor* – any more than we are not *nothing but oppressed*," one critic observed [italics in original].[87] Despite the best efforts

[85] Susan Griffin, "Sadism and Catharsis: The Treatment Is the Disease," in *Take Back the Night: Women on Pornography*, ed. Laura Lederer (New York: William Morrow, 1980), 141. *Take Back the Night* was probably the single most influential collection of feminist writings produced by the anti-pornography movement.

[86] The strain of thought that suggests that male and female biology is the problem can be found in Susan Brownmiller's *Against Our Will* as well. Although Brownmiller discussed how tools of male socialization, including the mass media, taught men to hate women, she sometimes lapsed into biological explanation. Explaining the male propensity to rape, Brownmiller argued: "By anatomical fiat – the inescapable construction of their genital organs – the human male was a predator and the human female served as his natural prey." Thus, in Brownmiller's view, male biology – or more precisely, male anatomy – made every man a rapist. See Brownmiller, *Against Our Will*, 16.

[87] Dhavernas, "Hating Masculinity Not Men," 151.

of some feminists to point out that women's subordination was situated in social structures rather than biology, to identify diverse forms of domination, including those based on race and class as well as gender, and to argue that men were capable of changing sexist patterns of behavior, some biologically based explanations did gain currency. Ultimately, these explanations would support anti-pornography analyses that treated every depiction of male sexual desire as violence against women.

Lesbian Feminism and Anti-Pornography

Radical feminist theory exerted a profound influence on the development of the anti-pornography movement. The critique of heterosexuality that led to the development of lesbian feminism and the concept of the political lesbian, coupled with the discovery that women were at grave risk from male sexual violence, particularly rape, affected how the majority of radical feminists – lesbian and straight – viewed sexual relations between men and women. Sex was the linchpin of female oppression, and depictions of male sexual pleasure seemed to many like hateful propaganda that taught men that it was their right to humiliate and abuse women. Organizing first against images of male sexual violence against women in advertising, and later against sexual images designed for the heterosexual male consumer, the trajectory of the anti-pornography movement mirrored theoretic shifts within radical feminism.

When one considers the gay/straight split that ravaged the Women's Liberation movement in the early 1970s, the eventual appeal of anti-pornography as a unifying feminist campaign becomes clear. Radical feminists viewed the institution of heterosexuality as a primary construct that supported the oppression of women, but a serious conflict emerged between groups of feminists who differed as to preferred strategies for dealing with men on a daily basis. As discussed, many radical feminists embraced lesbianism and even separatism, whereas others preferred to confront men and educate them about sexism.

Anti-pornography allowed both groups to attack the heterosexual institution. The women who initiated the early anti-media violence campaigns used the critique of heterosexuality and their knowledge of the male violence problem to deconstruct mass media images, especially advertisements. They saw ads that conflated sexuality and violence as dangerous texts. Women were portrayed as passive victims who were natural targets for male abuse and control, and as sexual objects whose bodies, labor, and emotions existed to serve men. These texts provided daily ideological support for male supremacy. Given the prevailing theoretic climate, it would have been close to impossible to participate in the Women's Liberation movement in the 1970s – especially in radical feminist circles – without learning to look with suspicion and anger at images that were predicated on heterosexual male entitlement.

3

Have You Seen *Deep Throat* Yet?

The Growth of the Commercial Sex Industry in 1970s America

The most famous porn film of all time opened in West Hollywood at the Pussycat Theater on Santa Monica Boulevard in November 1972. The owners of the theater chain submitted advertisements to the *Los Angeles Times*, but the newspaper refused to print the movie title. Determined to spread the word, the management submitted new ad copy that read: "IT is here!" They hoped that savvy patrons would recognize the veiled reference to *Deep Throat* and beat a path to the Pussycat's door.

But *Deep Throat* didn't do major box office right from the start. The West Hollywood Theater which was located in an unincorporated area of Los Angeles known for its significant gay population and as a popular destination for both gay and straight commercial sex, took in a disappointing $24,000 during the first week. The second week's total was down to $18,000. In the third week, ticket sales for *Deep Throat* tumbled to $15,000. The hardcore feature that promised to deliver a blockbuster mainstream audience was failing – badly.

Just as the owners of the Pussycat were lamenting their fortune, something remarkable occurred. *Time* magazine, long a bastion of middle-class values, devoted an entire page to *Deep Throat* and the newly chic pornography business.[1] The editors at the *Los Angeles Times* decided to stop bowdlerizing the Pussycat copy, figuring that if small-town America could tolerate exposure to *Deep Throat* in the pages of its hallowed news weekly, then Californians could surely handle some movie ads. That Friday, the ad for the Pussycat Theater read: "*Deep Throat*. 4th Week. Now." The week's gross skyrocketed to $50,000. In its fifth week, *Deep Throat* earned $90,000. Ultimately, *Deep Throat* would spend ninety-six weeks on *Variety's* list of the fifty top-grossing films and earn more than $100 million in theater and video revenues worldwide.[2]

[1] On the power of *Time* magazine to impart middle-class respectability, see James L. Baughman, *Henry R. Luce and the Rise of the American News Media* (Baltimore: Johns Hopkins University Press, 2001).

[2] On the *Los Angeles Times* reversal, see David Hebditch and Nick Anning, *Porn Gold: Inside the Pornography Business* (London: Faber & Faber, 1988), 193–194. On worldwide grosses,

By printing the name of an X-rated film in a mainstream newspaper in 1972, the editors of the *Los Angeles Times* helped encourage the free flow of pornography through American culture, making its whereabouts and content more accessible to the general public. They contributed to the democratization of pornography, a marked cultural shift that brought sexually explicit materials closer to the mainstream of American life, and brought massage parlors, X-rated films, and glossy skin magazines out into the open, widely available – at least in urban areas – to all who desired them.

Whereas explicit sexuality was almost nonexistent in mainstream popular culture in the 1950s, the mid-1960s and the 1970s brought magazines with pictures of full frontal nudity to corner drug stores and topless dancers to local strip clubs, especially in major metropolitan areas. San Francisco's Carol Doda first danced topless at the famed Condor go-go bar in 1964, and the California Supreme Court would rule in 1968 that topless dancing could have artistic merit and was not in and of itself an obscene act. During this period, adult bookstores, peep shows, go-go bars, XXX movie houses, and sex shops selling everything from vibrators to leather S/M gear sprang up in American cities, and sex districts emerged almost simultaneously in Detroit, Boston, Los Angeles, Baltimore, Chicago, and New York. Adult businesses opened within blocks of such American institutions as the Empire State Building and the White House, installing flashing neon signs and "barkers" who described in graphic detail the sexual entertainment that awaited within. Conservative estimates of national sales from adult bookstores put the figure at close to or exceeding $60 million per year, according to the 1970 report of the President's Commission on Obscenity and Pornography. "In most American metropolises," the urban historian Josh Sides wrote of the emergence of postwar sex districts, "city dwellers could plainly see the sexual revolution writ large on the urban landscape."[3] Sides attributed the proliferation of sex-related businesses in American cities after 1965, and along with them an element of public sexuality, to the libertinism of the sexual revolution, the downturn in prosecutions for obscenity, and the enormous profit potential in commercial sexual entertainment. By the late 1970s, San Francisco alone boasted forty adult movie theaters, dozens of peep shows and strip clubs, and at least fourteen "encounter studios" where patrons engaged in conversations with nude women.[4]

Outside the cities, in America's suburban living rooms, the explosion of sexuality and sexual content mirrored the urban experience. Commercial network television in the 1970s was "wallowing in sex," as the media historian Elana Levine has documented, and the advent of sexually explicit cable television

see Frederick S. Lane III, *Obscene Profits: The Entrepreneurs of Pornography in the Cyber Age* (New York: Routledge, 2000), 29–30.

3 Josh Sides, "Excavating the Postwar Sex District in San Francisco," *Journal of Urban History* 32 (March 2006): 356.

4 On urban sexual liberalism, see Robert O. Self, "Sex in the City: The Politics of Sexual Liberalism in Los Angeles, 1963–79," *Gender & History*, 20, no. 2 (August 2008): 288–311.

programming in the middle of the decade drove the trend forward.[5] Popular 1970s series like *The Love Boat* celebrated a freewheeling hook-up culture that brought passengers from all walks of life to one another's staterooms for a "nightcap" and more, while the jiggling heroines of *Charlie's Angels* became some of the decade's most enduring sex symbols. The iconic 1976 poster of Farrah Fawcett Majors wearing an unlined red bathing suit set national sales records, with demand in February and March of 1977 exceeding three million copies.[6] The 1970s situation comedy, *Three's Company*, used the premise of a trio of roommates in their sexual prime, two female and one male, to offer lighthearted commentary on everything from swinging to homosexuality to divorce. Television shows periodically took up difficult issues related to sexuality, such as rape, abortion, and sexual dysfunction – Levine noted that daytime soap operas ran nineteen different rape storylines between 1978 and 1981 – all of which contributed to the sexualization of American public culture. The historian Jeffrey Weeks concurs that explicit sexuality "pervaded the social consciousness" by the 1970s, and that it was evident on newsstands and prime-time television, in private clubs and adult theaters, on billboards and city streets.[7]

In Chapter 1, I offered concrete changes in sexual attitudes and behavior as evidence of the physical manifestation of the sexual revolution in Americans' lives. This included such shifts as a greater tolerance for nonreproductive sex, increased rates of premarital sex among girls aged fifteen to nineteen, and a decline in men's participation in contraceptive efforts. In Chapter 2, the women's liberation movement and the radical feminist critique of heterosexuality were discussed as political manifestations of the sexual revolution, as women's experiences of sexual exploitation in the New Left and a distinctive set of women's problems discovered through consciousness raising laid the groundwork for a sophisticated analysis of sexuality. Here, I present the expansion of the pornography industry in the 1970s as a marketplace manifestation of the sexual revolution. Throughout the decade, pornographers (and in some cases, activist men in the New Left) marketed male sexual entitlement with supreme confidence and force, and depicted women as willing, panting, mindless objects ripe for male abuse. For women who had embraced the idealism of the sexual revolution and who had viewed men as comrades en route to social transformation, such treatment was a betrayal of the worst order. By the mid-1970s, it was difficult for many to feel anything other than outrage when confronted with the ubiquitous public images of female bodies presented for male sexual consumption.

5 Elana Levine, *Wallowing in Sex: The New Sexual Culture of 1970s American Television* (Durham, NC: Duke University Press, 2007).

6 Fox News, "Behind the Iconic Farah Fawcett Red Bathing Suit Poster," available online at: http://www.foxnews.com/entertainment/2009/06/25/iconic-farrah-fawcett-red-swimsuit-poster/ (accessed February 4, 2010).

7 Jeffrey Weeks, *Sexuality and Its Discontents: Meanings, Myths and Modern Sexualities* (London: Routledge, 1985), 25.

Women's collective disappointment with the sexual revolution evolved from each of these different streams. Many participated in freer sexual behaviors, having more "no strings" sex with greater numbers of partners, only to discover that sexual liberation did not free them from the constraints of gender. Instead, women experienced "an intensification of the experience of being sexually female," a position of vulnerability that was amplified by the relentless commodification of women's bodies promoted by Hefner, Guccione, and the other porn barons.[8] As women saw their bodies and sexuality "turned into the hot stuff of pornography," as Andrea Dworkin has described it, their anger reached a boiling point.[9] In the chapter that follows this one, I focus on watershed events in the formation of the feminist anti-pornography movement. The first of these was the December 1975 release of the X-rated film, *Snuff*, which purported to show the actual on-screen rape, murder, and evisceration of a young woman for male viewers' sexual pleasure.

In the current chapter, I describe a series of legal, governmental, industrial, and social changes that supported the spread of pornography in the 1970s. I review several significant legal decisions that liberalized American obscenity law and freed would-be producers of pornography to create and distribute more sexually explicit cultural product. Next, I discuss the pro-pornography findings of a 1970 federal commission charged with studying the effects of pornography on the American public. The chapter also explores trends toward greater sexual explicitness in the American film industry and the role of the news media in promoting social acceptance of pornography. In the 1970s, on the heels of the critically acclaimed *Deep Throat*, journalists reviewed X-rated movies in major newspapers and magazines, lauded the industry's producers and stars, and portrayed pornography as a favorite indulgence of major celebrities. The widespread availability of sexually explicit, dehumanized images of the female body contributed to women's growing discontent, forcing many to confront the painful truth that pornography reflected ugly, pervasive male attitudes about women's nature and function. Furthermore, the proliferation of violent, sadistic images of women seemed to many like a form of sexual backlash, the male answer to the women's movement and its demands for equality.

Liberalization of American Obscenity Legislation

In the decade following the 1957 Supreme Court case *Roth v. U.S.*, which enlarged the range of materials that qualified for First Amendment protection, the legal protection available to books, magazines, and films containing sexual themes was virtually unlimited. The *Roth* decision cleared the way for such controversial literary depictions of sex as *Lady Chatterley's Lover*,

[8] Andrea Dworkin, *Right-Wing Women* (New York: Perigee Books, 1983), 91.

[9] Dworkin, *Right-Wing Women*, 91.

My Secret Life, and *Tropic of Cancer* to emerge without fear of prosecution. Justice William Brennan had set this course in motion in *Roth*, granting sex both social and constitutional legitimacy as a topic of public discussion. "Sex, a great and mysterious motive force in human life, has indisputably been a subject of absorbing interest to mankind throughout the ages;" he wrote. "[I]t is one of the vital problems of human interest and public concern."[10] The *Roth* decision made it clear, in the words of one legal historian, that "Americans were constitutionally entitled to discuss sex openly and freely."[11] A secondary consequence of *Roth*, which Brennan and his peers may not have foreseen, was the expansion of the pornography industry.

Erotic films, skin magazines, and pulp novels reaped immediate rewards in the aftermath of *Roth*, thanks to a new legal definition of obscenity. To be declared legally obscene, material would have to appeal to the prurient interest in sex; would have no serious literary, artistic, political, or social value; and would be offensive to the average person under contemporary community standards.[12] The Supreme Court revisited this definition in the 1962 case *Manual Enterprises v. Day*, adding a second prong involving "patent offensiveness" to the "prurient interest" clause.[13] *Manual Enterprises* involved a U.S. postmaster's determination that a gay periodical featuring photographs of male nudes was obscene. Justice John Marshall Harlan, writing for the Court, found that pictures of male nudes were not "more objectionable than many portrayals of the female nude that society tolerates."[14] The periodical was not obscene despite its "prurient appeal" to a gay male audience because the photographs lacked "patent offensiveness." This new requirement granted First Amendment protection to expression that could have been censored under *Roth*, adding new hurdles for would-be censors.[15]

Ever greater freedoms for sexually explicit materials came as the Court revisited the *Roth* ruling in the 1964 cases, *Jacobellis v. Ohio* and *Tropic of Cancer*. The *Jacobellis* case involved the conviction of an Ohio movie theater manager for exhibiting *The Lovers*, a critically acclaimed Louis Malle film. *Tropic of Cancer* was a Florida obscenity case, one of fifty active prosecutions aimed at suppressing Henry Miller's semiautobiographical, sexually explicit

[10] *Roth v. United States* and *Alberts v. California*, 354 U.S. 476, 77 S. Ct. 1304, 1 L. Ed. 2d 1498 (1957), 487.

[11] Edward de Grazia, *Girls Lean Back Everywhere: The Law of Obscenity and the Assault on Genius* (New York: Random House, 1992), 322.

[12] On the importance of the Roth case vis-a-vis obscenity doctrine, see Donald A. Downs, *The New Politics of Pornography* (Chicago: The University of Chicago Press, 1989), 13–25.

[13] *Manual Enterprises v. Day*, 370 U.S. 478 (1962). The case is reviewed in Edward de Grazia, *Censorship Landmarks* (New York: Bowker, 1969), 360–375.

[14] *Manual Enterprises v. Day*, 370 U.S. 478 (1962), 490.

[15] For additional discussion of *Manual Enterprises* and its importance regarding a national versus local standard for obscenity (or the "geographic contours of the community"), see Frederick F. Schauer, *The Law of Obscenity* (Washington, DC: The Bureau of National Affairs, 1976), 118–120.

novel.[16] In the *Jacobellis/Tropic of Cancer* opinion, Brennan clarified the constitutional definition of obscenity in ways that provided additional protection to sexually explicit material. First, he addressed the "contemporary community standards" prong of the *Roth* test, insisting that these standards had to be interpreted as national rather than local.[17] *Tropic of Cancer* had been targeted for prosecution in some states but not others, suggesting that a national standard had to be used to ensure that all Americans could enjoy access to adult-themed books and movies, rather than just those living in liberal, urban communities. Second, Brennan instructed the lower courts that a finding of obscenity required that the material in question had to be "utterly without social importance." The courts were required to free any work that contained ideas, no matter how great their prurient appeal might be.[18] If the material contained a shred of social value, Brennan warned, it could not be found obscene. As the political scientist Donald A. Downs has explained, this modification of the *Roth* test guaranteed that "the presence of virtually any idea 'or any other form of social importance' would salvage constitutional protection for a sexual work."[19]

The extent of the new freedoms became apparent in 1966, when the Supreme Court overturned a lower court's ruling that the sexually explicit eighteenth-century novel, *Memoirs of a Woman of Pleasure*, widely known as *Fanny Hill*, was obscene. A graphic fictional account of the daily life of a prostitute, the novel had served "for more than two hundred years," author Walter Kendrick observed, "as a handy synonym for 'obscenity.'"[20] Now, in the wake of *Roth*, *Fanny Hill*'s American publisher insisted that the book had social value; expert witnesses testified in *Memoirs v. Massachusetts* that *Fanny Hill* possessed "literary merit," "historical significance," and "psychological values."[21] Once experts agreed that the novel had social worth, it was not possible to satisfy the criteria for obscenity. In an opinion freeing *Fanny Hill*, Brennan organized the various elements of the definition of obscenity into a strict three-part test: The dominant theme of the material taken as a whole appeals to a prurient interest in sex; the material is patently offensive because it affronts contemporary community standards relating to the description or representation of sexual matters; and the material is utterly without redeeming social value. "[B]ecause all three criteria must be met independently in order to satisfy the test," legal scholar Harry Kalven wrote, "the concession

[16] The Florida case was *Grove Press, Inc. v. Gerstein*, 378 U.S. 577 (1964). *Tropic of Cancer* is written in a surrealistic stream-of-consciousness style. It describes Miller's sexual, emotional, and intellectual experiences during a period of self-imposed exile in Paris in the mid-1930s.

[17] Schauer, *The Law of Obscenity*, 118–120.

[18] See Harry Kalven Jr., *A Worthy Tradition: Freedom of Speech in America*, ed. Jamie Kalven (New York: Harper and Row, 1987), 37–38.

[19] Downs, 15.

[20] On the history of Cleland's novel, originally published in 1748, see Walter Kendrick, *The Secret Museum: Pornography in Modern Culture* (New York: Penguin Books, 1987), 209.

[21] De Grazia, *Girls Lean Back Everywhere*, 437.

to censorship is minimal and very little material is left within the reach of the law."[22] The *Memoirs* decision was a turning point for the pornography industry.

The significance of *Memoirs* for the production and distribution of sexually explicit material did not escape public attention. Indeed, Justice Tom Clark complained that pornographers would be most empowered, for the decision "gives the smut artist free rein to carry on his dirty business."[23] The relaxed legal climate set a juggernaut in motion, as photographers, writers, publishers, motion picture producers and directors, and others discovered that most of the barriers to creating and distributing sexually explicit product had been removed. In the late 1960s and early 1970s, American obscenity regulation "dwindled to a minimum," and pornography flooded the marketplace, largely outside the reach of the law.[24]

One did not have to visit a red-light district to witness the explosion of the pornography industry in the 1970s; the change was evident everywhere. Neighborhood supermarkets and newsstands began selling adult magazines out in the open, shelved next to such staid titles as *Ladies' Home Journal* and *Field & Stream*. Customers snapped up copies of Berth Milton's *Private*, which had become in 1966 – the year of the *Memoirs* decision – the first periodical to legally display sexual penetration. Bob Guccione brought *Penthouse* to the United States from Britain in 1969 and announced that he was going "rabbit hunting," depicting in ads for his magazine the famous *Playboy* bunny caught in the crosshairs of a rifle sight. Guccione and Hugh Hefner pushed each other toward greater sexual explicitness in a battle for circulation, and from 1971 to 1972, industry watchers dubbed their competition the "Pubic Wars."[25] Hefner also filled *Playboy*'s pages with edgy editorial content, giving pornography social capital in certain circles and capturing the attention of upscale, educated male readers. The magazine's circulation soared to 7.2 million in 1972, its all-time high.[26] Larry Flynt, a Cincinnati strip-club owner, began publishing *Hustler* in 1974. Flynt positioned this raunchy, lowbrow men's magazine as the anti-*Playboy*, rejecting Hefner's urbane editorial style in search of a working-class sensibility. These magazines permanently altered American sexual life and confirmed for many radical feminists that women existed to satisfy male sexual desire under the

[22] Kalven, 38.

[23] Quoted in de Grazia, *Girls Lean Back Everywhere*, 442.

[24] Downs, 16.

[25] Lane, 28. *Penthouse* came out with the first full frontal centerfold in August 1971, and Playboy followed suit in January 1972. The circulation of *Playboy* in 1972 exceeded 7 million. In 1973, *Penthouse*'s circulation exceeded 4 million. See also Steven Watts, *Mr. Playboy: Hugh Hefner and the American Dream* (New York: John Wiley, 2008), 298–306; and on the relationship between *Playboy* and Women's Liberation, see Nancy Fraterrigo, *Playboy and the Making of the Good Life in Modern America* (New York: Oxford University Press, 2009), chapter 6.

[26] "Aging Playboy," *Newsweek*, August 4, 1986, 51.

system of patriarchal capitalism. Women's bodies were sexual commodities, little different than other types of objects that one bought, used, enjoyed, and ultimately discarded.

Pornography as a "Social Good": The Johnson Commission

In addition to increased legal protections, pornography received an unexpected government seal of approval in 1970 from a special presidential commission. One year after the 1966 *Memoirs* decision, Lyndon Johnson authorized the formation of an eighteen-member commission to study pornography and its effects on the American public. Congress had held three sets of hearings on the subject of pornography in the fifteen years prior, but none had yielded conclusive results. Johnson intended this commission, chartered with a substantial $2 million dollar research budget, a large support staff, and a two-year study period, to make a definitive ruling as to whether sexually explicit materials were harmful to the public. He assigned four tasks: "to evaluate and recommend definitions of obscenity and pornography"; "to explore the nature and volume of traffic in such materials"; "to study the effect of obscenity and pornography upon the public"; and "to recommend such legislative, administrative, or other advisable and appropriate action ... to regulate effectively the flow of such traffic."[27] William B. Lockhart, dean of the law school at the University of Minnesota and a well-known political liberal, served as chairperson. The other commissioners included scholars, business leaders, clergy, and lawyers. The Commission began its deliberations in January 1968. In September 1970, Richard M. Nixon received the *Report* commissioned by his predecessor.

Much to Nixon's chagrin, the Commission's 700-page analysis recommended that adults should be allowed – even encouraged – to view sexually explicit materials. The *Report* refuted the notion that pornography caused moral degeneracy, declaring that the latest scientific research had found no proof of a link to violent or antisocial behavior. No evidence had been found to support the major claims of conservative antiobscenity groups such as Citizens for Decent Literature (CDL), founded by conservative leader Charles Keating in the 1960s, and the Catholic Church-sponsored National Office for Decent Literature, namely that lewd magazines and films incited such sex crimes as rape and murder, and "deviant" sexual behavior such as homosexuality. Instead, pornography was hailed as an educational tool for learning about human sexuality that could help adults release inhibitions. The Commission recommended that society be more "open and direct in dealing with sexual matters" and that this be accomplished through a "massive sex education effort" that might include pornography.[28] "[G]reater latitude can safely be

[27] *Report of the 1970 Commission on Obscenity and Pornography* (New York: Bantam Books, 1970), 169.

[28] *Report of the 1970 Commission*, 47.

given to adults," the *Report* advised, "in deciding for themselves what they will or will not read or view."[29] The Commission's researchers estimated that 85 percent of all adult American men and 70 percent of all adult American women had already been exposed to pornography, with no social detriment. The *Report* called for zero regulation of pornography, including the repeal of all existing local, state, and federal statutes prohibiting the sale, exhibition, and distribution of obscene material. In its place, the Commission urged the nation to adopt a new openness toward and tolerance for sexuality.

The *Report* was an immediate source of controversy. Two dissenting commissioners, the Rev. Morton J. Hill and the Rev. Winfrey C. Link, published the *Hill-Link Minority Report*, which criticized the supposed liberal bias of the Commission and questioned the validity of its research methodology and findings. Nixon was outraged at the recommendation that adult pornography should be decriminalized and declared the recommendations in the *Report* "morally bankrupt." Placing blame for the debacle squarely on Johnson's administration, Nixon directed the Justice Department to ignore the report. "So long as I am in the White House," he assured America, "there will be no relaxation of the national effort to control and eliminate smut from our national life."[30] Murray Kempton penned a column for the *New York Review of Books* and offered some good-humored observations in Nixon's defense. "[N]o President, in all conscience," Kempton wrote, "ought to have to draw from one of his own commissions the inference that the patrons of grind houses are persons of a sensibility much more refined than his own."[31] The Senate joined the president in a repudiation of the Commission's recommendations, rejecting the *Report* outright by a vote of 96–3. Despite the *Report*'s hostile reception among government elites, a well-funded, scientifically rigorous government commission had announced that pornography was, at worst, harmless.

Under the direction of Chief Justice Warren Burger, a more conservative Supreme Court made a concerted effort in 1973 to place limits on pornography. In *Miller v. California*, the Court overturned Brennan's formulation of a *national* "community standard" for obscenity, arguing that *local* communities ought to have the power to determine their own criteria. Although *Miller* seemed like a powerful new weapon that prosecutors could use against pornographers, the new law failed to curb the booming porn industry. For reasons as varied as insufficient public resources to prosecute obscenity cases, the difficulty of fully explaining the law to juries, and increased public acceptance of sexually explicit materials, enforcement efforts under *Miller* stagnated.[32] In the early 1970s, it seemed like the spread of pornography was unstoppable.

[29] *Report of the 1970 Commission*, 171.

[30] On Nixon's reaction to the *Report*, see Kendrick, 219–220.

[31] Murray Kempton, "A Feelthy Commission," *The New York Review of Books*, November 19, 1970, 24.

[32] On the reasons why *Miller v. California* failed to bring about more obscenity prosecution and stem the rising tide of pornography, see Downs, 18–22. Some of these reasons include relative public tolerance of sexually explicit materials, vagaries of political pressure, low priority

Indeed, the *Final Report* of the 1986 Attorney General's Commission on Pornography later underscored the significance of the previous decade: "The real proliferation of sexually explicit materials in the United States took place in the 1970s."[33]

Trends in the American Adult Film Industry

American adult films between 1950 and 1970 became increasingly explicit as the legal restrictions on obscenity waned. During these years, patrons were exposed to three successive film genres, including exploitation, beaver, and hardcore. Each offered more sexual content than the last, until films like the 1972 *Deep Throat* eradicated the final taboo, displaying penetration and ejaculation on screen.

The exploitation films of the 1950s, known as "Nudie-Cuties" in the industry, used comedic situations to bring male protagonists into contact with naked women. Russ Meyer, a World War II combat cameraman who made his postwar living shooting centerfolds for *Playboy*, was the genre's best-known director, attracting audiences with such pictures as *The Immoral Mr. Teas* (1959). Meyer shot the film – the story of a delivery man who was able to visualize women on the street without clothing – in four days at a cost of $24,000. It was a box-office hit, grossing well over $1 million.[34] The picture's financial success inspired more than 150 imitations; Meyer directed a number of these, including *Eve and the Handyman*, *Europe in the Raw*, and *Wild Gals of the Naked West*.

During the mid-1960s, public demand drove producers and directors to abandon the exploitation genre in favor of more explicit themes and content. The "Nudie-Cutie" gave way to the beaver film, which typically ran about fifteen minutes and featured women removing their clothing, walking around in the nude and assuming sexual postures. The "split beaver" genre offered close-up views of women with their legs spread apart. The "action beaver" featured women masturbating or simulating sexual acts.[35] Formerly shown only in peep show booths in adult bookstores or sold through private mail order, short films such as *Beaver Bondage* and *Ruthless Shaved Beaver* arrived in theaters in 1967. Beaver "loops" – several short films "looped" together to make a feature-length presentation – were the immediate precursors of full-length features like *Deep Throat*.[36] The beaver films carefully avoided

assigned to obscenity cases by prosecutors concerned with other types of crime, insufficient public resources, and the ability of wealthy pornographers to finance and prolong lengthy court battles.

33 Attorney General's Commission on Pornography, *Final Report* (Washington D.C.: U.S. Department of Justice, 1986), vol. 2, 1363.

34 James Cook, "The X-Rated Economy," *Forbes*, September 18, 1978, 92.

35 Linda Williams, *Hard Core: Power, Pleasure and the "Frenzy of the Visible"* (Berkeley: University of California Press, 1989), 96–97.

36 Kenneth Turan and Stephen F. Zito, *Sinema: American Pornographic Films and the People who Make Them* (New York: Praeger Publishers, 1974), 77–78; Williams, chapter 4; Deborah

hardcore behavior, namely penetration and ejaculation, but they were far more risqué than the exploitation films. Action beavers certainly "pushed the outer limits of what constituted legality in public exhibition," but many theater owners were willing to assume this calculated risk. "[F]ines were minimal and the market for the product was growing," the film scholar Linda Williams observed.[37] The public demand for greater explicitness was so great that films showing real, rather than simulated, sexual encounters soon made even the action beaver films obsolete.

By the end of the 1960s, a number of theater owners were feeling public pressure to exhibit hardcore, a genre defined by the presence of the male organ in the act of penetration and climax. In 1969, some twenty-five theaters in the San Francisco area were showing the kind of hardcore short films that had previously been available only at peep show arcades and adult bookstores. Alex de Renzy, a cameraman-turned-filmmaker and theater owner, showed his own hardcore productions at his movie house, the Screening Room. Jim and Artie Mitchell, owners of the O'Farrell Theater, which would become a target of Bay Area anti-pornography efforts, were also among the early hardcore producers and exhibitors. By 1970, theater owners in New York, Dallas, Houston, and even such conservative cities as Indianapolis were advertising and exhibiting both the beaver and hardcore loops that originated in San Francisco, including such gems as *Frisco Beaver Action*, *Frisco Girls*, and *Hot Frisco Shorts*.[38]

In 1969–1970, a new "educational" style of adult film enabled select hardcore pictures to move out of the adult theaters – or grindhouses, as they were called – to play instead in art theaters that could attract an upscale clientele. *Sexual Freedom in Denmark*, directed by John Lamb, and *Censorship in Denmark: A New Approach*, directed by Alex de Renzy, were documentary-style hardcore films that claimed to investigate how the 1968 legalization of pornography in Denmark was affecting Scandinavian sexual behavior. *Censorship in Denmark*, which premiered in a San Francisco art theater in 1969, attracted a well-heeled, middle-class audience that regarded an interview with a porn actress intercut with scenes from her hardcore films as an avant garde cultural experience, not a prurient one. "Many middle-class people who did not realize that there were hardcore films on Eighth Avenue (and would not have gone in any case)," two industry-watchers concluded, "were suddenly perfectly willing to go to a 'nice' theater to see a film that was reviewed in the *New York Times*."[39] Indeed, the fact that establishment publications like the *Times* took favorable notice of *Censorship in Denmark* helped spur the popularity of these films and create additional public demand.

Swedberg, "What Do We See When We See Woman/Woman Sex in Pornographic Movies," *NWSA Journal* 1 (1989): 604.

37 Williams, 97.

38 Turan and Zito, 78–79.

39 Turan and Zito, 82.

Hardcore short films and documentary-style X-rated pictures were typical adult products in the early 1970s, but the push for more frank sexual content soon found industry insiders searching for the next phenomenon. Gerard Damiano, a stag-film producer and ex-hairdresser from Queens, believed that a hardcore feature film with a semblance of a plot and some humor could draw a crossover audience of mainstream moviegoers. Backed by two financiers with ties to organized crime, Damiano began working on *Deep Throat*, a film that would combine explicit sex with a traditional storyline.[40]

Deep Throat starred Linda Lovelace and Harry Reems in the story of a young woman (Lovelace) who failed to reach orgasm during myriad sexual encounters. She consulted a physician (Reems) and learned that her inability to climax was caused by a unique anatomical problem: Lovelace's clitoris was located in her throat, far north of its customary position. Reems advised Lovelace to concentrate her sexual energies on "deep" fellatio, which she would find properly stimulating. She then tried the "throat" technique on him, as well as a series of other men in the film, finally experiencing the "bells and whistles" that had previously eluded her.

Deep Throat broke the mold for adult films, incorporating superior cinematography and high-quality sound with a comprehensive plot that featured clever dialogue, humor, and character development. It set a new standard for adult entertainment, virtually transforming the industry overnight. The old 16-mm "cheapies" with their warped sound, grainy pictures, and routine couplings disappeared and were replaced by costlier, 35-mm films featuring better technical quality, true hardcore action including penetration and ejaculation, and more sophisticated plots. *Deep Throat* brought about a revolution in both the content of X-rated pictures and the composition of the audience that purchased tickets.

The Emergence of "Porno Chic" in American Popular Culture

No movie changed more Americans' minds about the kind of people who went to see "porn flicks" than *Deep Throat*. The tremendous success of this film, produced on a shoestring budget of $25,000 and estimated to have grossed more than $100 million in theater and video revenues worldwide, proved that hardcore features could be popular with a much larger and more varied audience than industry insiders had ever believed possible.[41] The prototypical member of the "raincoat brigade," as patrons of adult theaters were often called, had always been the middle-aged white male, who was highly secretive about his viewing habits. But *Deep Throat* drew a new audience comprised of affluent young men and women, and broader segments of the middle-aged, middle-class population.

[40] Richard Corliss, "That Old Feeling: When Porno Was Chic," *Time.com*. Accessed March 29, 2005. http://www.time.com/time/columnist/prinout/0881610432670o.html.

[41] Cook, 83.

The *Deep Throat* premiere took place on June 12, 1972, at Sam Lake's World Theater on 49th Street in New York City. Public anticipation ran high, thanks in no small part to an advertising campaign that ran in various New York daily newspapers with the tagline: "If you like head, you'll love *Throat*." *Variety* was quick to report the buzz. "Pre-opening word on this latest hard-core feature was hot enough to pack the lunch-time show on opening day," the reviewer crowed. "*Deep Throat*," he concluded, "is a superior piece which stands a head above the current competition."[42] The audience was equally enthusiastic, and the film grossed more than $30,000 in its first week at the World Theater.[43] The producers sought nationwide media exposure after the New York debut, and promoted Lovelace widely as a traditional movie star. She landed on the covers of *Esquire*, *Time*, and *Newsweek*. She appeared on *The Tonight Show* as one of Johnny Carson's guests.

The instant celebrity that *Deep Throat* achieved gave it the status of a hip social event. It became chic to attend adult films, and people went in droves to see the latest hardcore pictures; the middle-class audience discovered a new way to spend five dollars on Saturday night. "The thing that shocked me most about *Deep Throat*," one Hollywood movie executive remarked about the changing demographics, "was that nobody in the audience was a dirty old man with a raincoat. They were all young couples."[44] Another observer at Manhattan's Avon Hudson theater on 45th between Sixth Avenue and Broadway noted that a swank lunch crowd generally filled the place to capacity. "Nattily tailored executives unwrap sandwiches from sleek attaché cases," he commented. "In the late afternoons, tourists wander in."[45] When Damiano's next production, *The Devil in Miss Jones*, opened at New York City's elite 57th Street Playhouse in 1973, well-to-do Manhattanites attended in such record numbers that the weekly box office exceeded $35,000.[46] The commercial success of these features put to rest the idea that only a fringe audience of perverts and sexual deviants frequented porn films. To the contrary, middle-class Americans made up the largest and most rapidly growing segment of the market.

Public acceptance for *Deep Throat* and other adult films of the early 1970s was driven, at least in part, by the serious attention paid them by journalists, celebrities, and intellectuals. Vincent Canby, a film critic for the *New York Times*, called *Deep Throat* "the one porno film in New York chic to see and to be seen at."[47] Author Nora Ephron reviewed *Deep Throat* for *Esquire* magazine

[42] "Deep Throat," *Variety*, June 28, 1972, 26.

[43] Corliss, 3.

[44] Turan and Zito, 158.

[45] Joseph Slade, "Pornographic Theaters off Times Square," in *The Sexual Scene*, rev. ed., eds. J.H. Gagnon and W. Simon (New Brunswick, NJ: Transaction Books, 1973), 271.

[46] Henry Schipper, "Filthy Lucre: A Tour of America's Most Profitable Frontier," *Mother Jones*, April 1980, 60.

[47] Vincent Canby, "What Are We To Think of Deep Throat?" *The New York Times*, January 21, 1973, section 2: 1.

and although she found it "not just anti-female but anti-sexual as well," nonetheless declared that a person who failed to see it "seemed somehow ... derelict."[48] The *Village Voice* published a series of articles profiling the leading porn directors, treating each one as an *auteur* in his own right. Andrew Sarris, a film critic for the *Voice*, went so far as to predict that Lincoln Center would hold an erotic film festival within a few years. That opinion was shared by other mainstream reviewers, one of whom imagined that "... there might be a meeting of pornography, which had quickly established a kind of artistic pedigree, and Hollywood, which was striding toward explicit sexuality."[49] Porn had arrived.

Perhaps the greatest triumph for *Deep Throat* came in the form of a major article describing its successes in the *New York Times*' prestigious Sunday magazine. Journalist Ralph Blumenthal characterized the film as the rage among the jet set: "It has become a premier topic of cocktail-party and dinner-table conversation in Manhattan drawing rooms, Long Island beach cottages and ski-country A-frames."[50] Major celebrities including Johnny Carson, director Mike Nichols, and actors Warren Beatty, Ben Gazzara, and Jack Nicholson had been spotted at local showings. Truman Capote took a group of his friends to see *Deep Throat* after "'Mike Nichols told me I just had to see it'."[51] A group of French United Nations diplomats went, Blumenthal reported merrily, "and insisted on paying with travelers' checks." A large group of the *New York Times* news staff descended on the New Mature World Theater for a noontime screening, followed later that week by a group from the newspaper's *Book Review*. "Members of the in-crowd from Elaine's," Blumenthal wrote of the celebrated bistro that caters to New York's literati, "announced one night that they were going for the second time."[52] This public moment of "porno chic" was unprecedented.

The astonishing success of *Deep Throat* and its successors enabled pornography to enjoy a truly public moment in the 1970s; adult films like *Behind the Green Door* and *Bijou* commingled in theaters with traditional comedies and dramas. *Deep Throat* and *The Devil in Miss Jones* were among the top box-office hits of 1973, earning more than most of Hollywood's mainstream pictures. *The Devil in Miss Jones* actually out-performed *Deep Throat* at the box office; the films ranked as the sixth and eleventh highest-grossing pictures of the year.[53]

The Bloom is off the Rose

The celebration of pornography was short-lived, however. At the same time that people were hailing X-rated films as healthy and lighthearted entertainment that

48 Nora Ephron, "Women." *Esquire* (February 1973): 17.
49 Corliss, 4.
50 Ralph Blumenthal, "Porno Chic," *The New York Times Sunday Magazine*, January 21, 1973, 28.
51 Blumenthal, 28.
52 Blumenthal, 28.
53 Laura Holson, "The Long View," *The New York Times*, September 5, 2004, section 1: 7.

might eradicate sexual repression, opposition voices were beginning to rise. Some belonged to the religious and social conservatives who had opposed the findings of the 1970 presidential commission, including members of such staunch anti-pornography groups as Citizens for Decency Through Law, founded by Charles Keating Jr. in 1957, and Morality in Media, founded by the Rev. Morton A. Hill in 1962. Many of the voices, however, belonged to radical women who felt that pornography told ugly truths about the way that men regarded women, and bolstered the male expectation of unfettered access to female bodies.

By the time of *Deep Throat*'s premiere, the question of pornography had attracted only sporadic attention from the women's movement. When the Johnson Commission returned its favorable 1970 report on pornography and recommended zero legal restriction on sexually explicit materials for adults, some feminists were outraged at what they perceived as a bias in favor of male users. They interpreted the *Report* as a conscious decision to protect male sexual interests and to ignore the real-world harms experienced by women who were coerced into making pornography and women and children who were forced to copy the sexual acts that men learned from X-rated material. Florence Rush, an expert on child sexual abuse who would become a leading member of Women Against Pornography, condemned the Commission for basing its conclusions on a lack of evidence that pornography caused anti-social effects in male users. "[P]ornography does not harm its all-male consumer population. It harms the items consumed," she wrote in response to the *Report*. "Unlike hair dyes and cigarettes, the items consumed in pornography are not inanimate objects but live women and children who are degraded and abused in the process."[54] Rush's indignation mirrored radical feminist attitudes toward the whole of the sexual revolution; women were devalued and treated as sexual commodities, and their safety and bodily integrity regarded as less important than men's right to enjoy unrestricted sexual access.

During the same year that the *Report* was issued, a number of radical feminist responses to pornography suggested the growing importance of the issue. In April 1970, 200 members and supporters of the Chicago Women's Liberation Union (CWLU) picketed the Chicago Playboy mansion, Hugh Hefner's personal residence in the city that served as national corporate headquarters for the Playboy Clubs. They condemned *Playboy* for its chauvinism and for oppressing women by promoting them as "bunnies" and sexual objects, a perspective that had been voiced in 1963 by Gloria Steinem, who published a magazine exposé describing her experiences working undercover in a Playboy Club. Just a few months after the CWLU picket, feminists organized additional demonstrations against the Playboy Clubs in Boston, New York, and San Francisco.

Meanwhile, activist women in the New Left reacted against a tidal wave of sexism emerging from the countercultural press. In one infamous incident, the male editors of the political newspaper, *Rat*, published a "sex-and-porn special" issue at the end of 1969 that so infuriated Jane Alpert, Robin Morgan,

[54] Florence Rush, "Child Pornography," in *Take Back the Night*, 80.

and other radical feminists that they organized a "women's takeover," wresting control of the newspaper away from the men.[55] The first women's issue appeared in February 1970 and featured "Goodbye to All That," Morgan's blistering indictment of the male-dominated New Left and its exploitation of women. "So, *Rat* has been liberated, for this week, at least. Next week? If the men return to reinstate the porny photos, the sexist comic strips, the nude-chickie covers (along with their patronizing rhetoric about being in favor of women's liberation) – if this happens, our alternatives are clear," she wrote. "*Rat* must be taken over permanently by women – or *Rat* must be destroyed."[56] The support for pornography (and opposition to its restriction) among men who located themselves on the political Left became clear during this period, with lasting effect on many feminists. In response, Andrea Dworkin formulated one of her central tenets regarding pornography, namely that the Right's celebration of domesticity and the Left's celebration of sexual liberation represented two sides of the same coin: the practice of male dominance, the ideology of male supremacy, and a belief in the nature of women as whores.[57]

Other feminist writers were also reacting against the sexist content in Left-wing publications that associated pornography with revolt. Jim Buckley, managing editor of the New York *Free Press*, an underground publication, teamed up with Al Goldstein in 1968 to create *Screw*, a sexually explicit tabloid that promised to deliver the unvarnished world of sex to its readers. A number of prominent feminists, including the journalist Leah Fritz, wrote for *Screw*, thinking that the magazine supported the ideals of the Left, including women's right to engage freely in sexual relationships without fear of reprisal. Fritz wrote *Screw*'s "Women's Page" for a year before an onslaught of vicious pictorial and verbal attacks on women in the magazine led her to quit.[58] And several months following the *Rat* takeover, Morgan led a feminist sit-in at the alternative publishing house, Grove Press, triggered by the dismissal of eight employees (including Morgan) for unionizing activities. The protesters charged Grove with publishing pornographic books and magazines that objectified women, and publisher Barney Rosset for earning millions of dollars from their humiliation. They demanded that all profits from the sale of Grove titles that degraded and oppressed women be used to help women who were the victims of such material, including a bail fund to free prostitutes and a medical fund to cover treatment for rape and assault victims.[59]

55 Susan Brownmiller, *In Our Time: Memoir of a Revolution* (New York: The Dial Press, 1999), 76.

56 Robin Morgan, "Goodbye to All That," in *Public Women, Public Words: A Documentary History of American Feminism*, eds. Dawn Keetley and John Pettegrew (New York: Rowman & Littlefield, 2002), 33.

57 See Andrea Dworkin, *Pornography: Men Possessing Women* (New York: Penguin Books, 1981), esp. pp. 203–209.

58 See Leah Fritz, "Pornography as Gynocidal Propaganda," *New York University Review of Law and Social Change* 8 (1978–1979): 219–223.

59 Laura Lederer, "Women Have Seized the Executive Offices of Grove Press Because …" in *Take Back the Night*. 267–271.

Although each of these protests revealed feminist concern with the sexual exploitation of women, the controversial *Deep Throat* brought the question onto the national stage. The film provoked a high-profile clash between women who despised pornography and men who celebrated it as a social good, setting the stage for future conflict. In a 1972 New York City obscenity prosecution directed against nine theater owners who had exhibited *Deep Throat*, prominent male critics, scholars, and medical authorities heaped praise on the film and argued that its message was essentially pro-woman. "It indicates that women have a right to a sex life of their own, and they are not simply an instrumentality of men's sex life ...," argued John Money, a renowned professor of medical psychology at Johns Hopkins University. "[T]here is a theme in the film which implies that women should get sexual satisfaction and sexual gratification."[60] Dr. Edward Hornick, a prominent New York clinical psychiatrist, echoed this point of view. He argued that unlike other adult films, *Deep Throat* did not deal with the sexual exploitation of women by men, but with "a young woman who seeks orgasmic pleasure for herself."[61] Other experts praised Lovelace's character as "a liberated woman" who used men as sex objects just as men used women.[62] The film, according to these male accounts, was a tale of equal opportunity made possible by the sexual revolution. Feminist observers were skeptical, noting that it was terribly convenient that Lovelace's journey of sexual discovery just happened to lead her down the road of conventional male fantasy.

Around the nation, women denounced the film as sexist. At Michigan State University, female students tried unsuccessfully to block a screening on the basis that the movie depicted women as sexual objects. They pointed to a scene in which Lovelace inserts a twelve-inch glass Coca-Cola bottle into her vagina and invites her male partner to drink the soda out with a straw. Many men found this gag hilarious, whereas women viewed it with horror, preoccupied with the physical risk to Lovelace should the bottle break. When they tried to communicate these concerns to male classmates, their words fell on deaf ears. Linda Lovelace, the men insisted, was a "sexually liberated" woman and the film was "a turning point" in pornography because it "brought it out of the back rooms and before a mass audience," increasing everyone's sexual freedom.[63] *Deep Throat*, they were told, was "a valuable contribution to art."[64] Confrontations such as this one persuaded many young women that all the campus talk about sexual equality and a new egalitarian social order was just talk indeed. Women's feelings and concerns were tolerated only so far as they did not interfere with men's sexual pleasure and right of access.

[60] Quoted in Turan and Zito, 145.

[61] Quoted in "Wonder Woman," *Time*, January 15, 1973, available online at http://www.time.com/time/magazine/article/0,9171,906765–1,00.html (accessed November 27, 2007).

[62] Quoted in Canby, 1.

[63] Marianne Rzepka, "'Throat' Not Sexist?" *Her-Self: Women's Community Journal*, 3, no. 2 (1974): 6.

[64] Rzepka, 6.

A number of feminist writers criticized the film for its failure to take a woman's quest for sexual pleasure seriously, relying instead on the absurd and male-oriented premise of Lovelace's peculiar anatomy. Christine Stansell, then a graduate student in history at Yale University, was put off by *Deep Throat*'s rote sexual encounters, which she found about as tempting as "a hot-dog stuffed in a Wonder Bread bun." Stansell had publicly expressed her distaste for sexist pornography two years earlier as an undergraduate at Princeton University, when she and a classmate shredded the *Playboy* pinups hanging on the walls of a male classmate's dorm room and were called before the university disciplinary committee.[65]

Ellen Willis, a founder of the radical feminist group Redstockings and a well-known cultural reporter, complained in *The New York Review of Books* that she found the sex in porn films predictable and mechanistic. The average woman, she argued, would not respond to "all those bodies methodically humping away, their faces sweatless and passionless." *Deep Throat* was no exception. Willis seemed genuinely annoyed that the film, which for her was "about as erotic as a tonsillectomy," made no serious effort to portray an adventurous or lush sexuality that might appeal to women. "[M]ovies like *Throat* don't turn me on, which is, after all, what they are supposed to do," she wrote. "On the contrary, I find them a sexual depressant ... mostly because they deliberately and perversely destroy any semblance of an atmosphere in which my sexual fantasies could flourish."[66] The film illustrated the hollow gains of the sexual revolution: It liberated a woman to search for truly fulfilling sexual relations, but the story's punchline (the clitoris located in the throat) confirmed that men were still in control. Linda Lovelace was "free" to pursue her sexual life, just so long as it conformed to male sexual standards and ensured the continuation of behavior that men enjoyed. Nora Ephron, in the *Esquire* review discussed earlier, came to a similar conclusion, describing *Deep Throat*'s flaws by contrasting it to other adult films that she had seen, some of which were "sweet and innocent and actually erotic."[67] *Deep Throat* was not a good film, in Ephron's estimation, but porn films could be good, and could take women's pleasure seriously.

These reviews and essays revealed more than feminist distaste for shoddy X-rated films. Within every sector of American feminism, there were women who believed that sex had the potential to be an affirming, pleasurable, and expressive experience, and each of these authors expressed their commitment to authentic sexual liberation for women. Far from condemning the existence of pornography per se, Willis offered her own vision of a porn film that would tantalize a female audience. She imagined one that would explore

[65] Christine Stansell, "Films" (review of *Deep Throat*), *off our backs 3* (April 1973): 11. The story about Stansell destroying *Playboy* pinups is recounted in David Allyn, *Make Love, Not War, The Sexual Revolution: An Unfettered History* (New York: Routledge, 2001), 280.

[66] Ellen Willis, "Hard to Swallow," *The New York Review of Books* (January 25, 1973), 23.

[67] Nora Ephron, "Women." *Esquire* (February 1973): 20.

"the psychological and sensual nuances of sex – the power of sexual tension and suspense; the conflict of need and guilt, attraction and fear; the texture of skin; the minutiae of gesture and touch and facial expression that can create an intense erotic ambience."[68] Both writers were disappointed by *Deep Throat*, finding it sexist and objectifying. Willis in particular lamented that the film privileged only the male point of view and male sexual fantasy. She expressed deep frustration that the nation's leading adult film did so little to stimulate women's fantasies and erotic desires.

The mainstream media soon joined feminists and others in repudiating *Deep Throat* and other X-rated films. The glitzy trend that Ralph Blumenthal lauded in 1973 was decidedly over by year's end, influenced in no small part by the onset of a national economic downturn related to the foreign oil crisis, inflation, a precipitous decline in the stock market, and a rise in unemployment, all leading to the worst recession ("stagflation") that the nation had experienced since the Great Depression. In the midst of such gloomy indicators, the wanton celebration of unbridled sexuality no longer suited the tenor of the times. On the order of Mayor John Lindsay, New York City police temporarily closed down *Deep Throat*. The publisher of *The New York Post*, one of New York's most popular daily newspapers, dealt pornography another blow with a new policy in January 1974: no more editorial material about adult films. He barred all X-rated movie reviews, as well as photographs and interviews featuring porn actors. This was a major about-face for *The Post*, whose pages had often featured well-known performers like Lovelace. Industry observers at *Variety* pointed out with some irony that the newspapers that were cracking down on pornography had helped make it popular in the first place with fawning coverage. "The wide world of porno … was considered so chic last year by the fashionably 'in' that most papers couldn't print enough about the phenomenon," one noted. "Reporters rushed to chronicle the trials of *Deep Throat*, reviewers exorcised their own demons in lauding *The Devil in Miss Jones* and columnists devoted deadpan space to making household names of Linda Lovelace, Marilyn Chambers and Georgina Spelvin."[69] Commenting on the change of heart at *The Post* and elsewhere, the reporter from *Variety* observed that "the chic is thoroughly tarnished now."[70]

Moving Toward Anti-Pornography

For many women, the spread of pornography throughout mainstream American culture in the 1970s and the stunning success of *Deep Throat* brought on an epiphany, an "a-ha" moment in American feminism. Here, plainly visible on

[68] Willis, "Hard to Swallow," 23.

[69] Addison Verrill, "Porno Chic Fades; NY Post Muting Its Editorial Play," *Variety* (January 30, 1974): 1. Lovelace, Chambers, and Spelvin were hardcore film stars. Chambers, a former Ivory Soap model, was the lead in *Behind the Green Door*, a 1973 porn film produced and directed by Jim and Artie Mitchell. Spelvin starred in *The Devil in Miss Jones*.

[70] Verrill, 1.

magazine covers at local newsstands and on adult theater marquees, was the boiled-down, painful truth about what men thought of women. Here was male desire writ large – and it indicated a total disregard for women's bodily integrity and their quest for political and social equality. For women who had embraced the idealism of the Left and the hopefulness of the sexual revolution, the sexist reality of pornography was crushing. Ellen Willis expressed her fury that "openly sadistic" images that made women "not only objects but specimens" had become staples of mainstream culture. "It pisses me off that men make fortunes selling these images," she seethed in the *Village Voice*, "and that they pass as respectable, chic, and even liberating."[71]

Some radical feminists began to argue that pornography expressed male hatred and contempt for women, and that the violent genre reflected men's innately aggressive and brutal nature. "The sheer visibility of the porn industry had a consequence which the pornbrokers may not have intended," the radical British anti-pornography feminist Sheila Jeffreys wrote of this period. "Women were able to look at pornography and for the first time had at their disposal a panoramic view of what constituted male sexuality."[72] Violent pornography emerged as the consummate male cultural product, a fierce backlash against women's attempts to claim equality and a powerful reminder of women's vulnerability to physical abuse.

In the following chapter, I focus on two watershed events that precipitated the formation and early growth of Women Against Violence Against Women (WAVAW), the initial grassroots group of the feminist anti-pornography movement. The first event was the December 1975 release of the X-rated film, *Snuff*, which purported to show the actual on-screen murder, dismemberment, and evisceration of a woman in the midst of a forced sexual encounter. The second event occurred in Los Angeles in June 1976, in response to an advertising campaign to promote a new Rolling Stones record album. A billboard appeared over Sunset Boulevard that featured a badly bruised, sexually excited woman bound with ropes. The WAVAW members' reactions to these events show the influence of the social conditions described in previous chapters, including disillusionment with the sexual revolution and the enlargement of male sexual rights; a new awareness of the prevalence of sexual violence; the growth of a lesbian feminist politics that saw heterosexuality as oppressive for women; and frustration with the sexualization of the public sphere and the ubiquitous objectification of women's bodies. This common set of experiences supported the development of the first strands of what would ultimately become the feminist anti-pornography analysis.

[71] Ellen Willis, "Feminism, Moralism and Pornography," *Village Voice*, October 15, 1979, p. 8.

[72] Sheila Jeffreys, *Anticlimax: A Feminist Perspective on the Sexual Revolution* (New York: New York University Press, 1990), 250.

4

"I'm Black and Blue from the Rolling Stones and I Love It!"

Women Against Violence Against Women and the Campaign Against Media Violence

Although women criticized *Deep Throat* widely, the release of the gory 1975 horror film, *Snuff*, precipitated national feminist action. *Snuff* purported to show the actual on-screen rape, murder, and dismemberment of an actress, a claim that motivated women to take a hard look at images of violence against women in mass media. The *Snuff* debacle was followed by a series of national protests against The Rolling Stones and the brutal imagery used to advertise their 1976 album, *Black and Blue*. Grassroots feminist groups dedicated to fighting the proliferation of images linking sex and violence began to form. Rather than focusing on pornography per se, these early groups cast their nets wide and called public attention to the use of violence against women in advertising, fashion, the music industry, and mainstream motion pictures.

This chapter chronicles the formation of Women Against Violence Against Women (WAVAW) on the heels of the *Snuff* and *Black and Blue* controversies in 1975 and 1976. WAVAW was the first national feminist organization to focus exclusively on the problem of sexual violence in the media. "Women Against Violence Against Women," members of the group declared, "is an activist organization working to stop the gratuitous use of images of physical and sexual violence against women in mass media – and the real-world violence against women it promotes – through public education, consciousness-raising, and mass consumer action."[1] The group rejected government restriction as a prudent strategy, and instead demanded that companies exercise "corporate responsibility" with regard to their advertising and the public culture such images created.[2]

[1] Jo Delaplaine, "Stabbing the Beast in the Belly: Women Against Violence Against Women" *off our backs* 7 (November 1977): 9.

[2] Boston WAVAW, "Proposal to Join the Women's Center as an Affiliated Project," n.d., History: Cambridge Women's Center file, Women Against Violence Against Women, Papers, 1977–1984, Northeastern University Archives and Special Collections, Boston, Massachusetts (hereafter cited as Boston WAVAW Papers).

WAVAW set an important precedent for the media violence and anti-pornography campaigns by fighting abusive images of women with consumer action. The organization used such basic protest techniques as letter writing, boycotting, and picketing to force major corporations, including Warner Communications, to adopt new advertising policies and to stop exploiting women. Following in the footsteps of Civil Rights and New Left activist campaigns – WAVAW's national coordinator had organized grape boycotts with the United Farm Workers in the early 1970s – WAVAW harnessed the power of grassroots groups to express outrage and concern, and to demand change. For a small, poorly funded feminist organization, WAVAW achieved impressive results. But as the media violence movement led by WAVAW was overtaken by the anti-pornography movement led by WAVPM and WAP, its consumer action techniques fell out of favor. Instead, members of the later organizations endorsed legal measures to control pornography and broadened their campaigns to include nonviolent sexually explicit expression.

WAVAW was successful not only because of its preferred organizing tactics, but also because the group's arguments made sense to a community of women familiar with dominant radical feminist frameworks regarding sexuality and violence. Members of WAVAW believed that sexual violence was linked to gender polarity; mass media and other social institutions conditioned women to think of themselves as fragile and subordinate, whereas men were taught to be strong and dominant. Gender norms surrounding female and male sexuality mirrored this split. Girls learned that it was appropriate to behave passively in the sexual arena, waiting for men to initiate contact and then exercising proper restraint when confronted with intense male desire. The cultural myth that respectable women had little sex drive was accompanied by another lie – the dangerous and damaging belief that the use of violence would awaken a woman's repressed sexuality. Just as the typical Harlequin romance novel of the period featured a sexual innocent who fell for a cruel, hard man who took her with force, glorified images of sexual violence in the mass media taught men that women secretly liked to be raped. Instead of vilifying men, WAVAW argued that they were victims too, systematically "warped by mass media images of maleness." Media violence taught men that what they saw in magazines, films, and on television accurately reflected what women were really like, and that rough treatment was a normal and necessary part of sexual arousal. Early WAVAW correspondence explained that the media's "crippling, maiming images of what it means to be a woman or a man" devastated both sexes.[3] WAVAW decided to raise public consciousness about the negative social consequences of such images: "It demeans and dehumanizes women as victims and men as victimizers, promoting an atmosphere that denies women their full human rights," the organization stated.[4]

[3] Julia London to Dear Friend [Form letter], 5 July 1977, Women Against Violence Against Women, Papers, 1976–1985, June L. Mazer Lesbian Archives, West Hollywood, California (hereafter cited as Los Angeles WAVAW Papers).

[4] "Slide Program Crucial to WAVAW's Effectiveness," *WAVAW Newsletter*, no. 1 (May 1977): 3.

In the end, most feminists could agree to be "against" violence; the wealth of women's knowledge about rape and battering and a powerful body of feminist theory made violence a key organizing issue. However, what many couldn't agree to be against was sex. By the late 1970s, many American women recognized that the sexual revolution had failed to deliver true liberation for women, but most still held out hope that sex could be experienced as a wellspring of personal pleasure and fulfillment. Ellen Willis and Christine Stansell did not reject *Deep Throat* because it was sexually explicit, but because it promoted a sexist view of female sexual fantasy and desire. As WAVPM and WAP shifted away from a focus on violence in favor of a focus on pornography – which included nonviolent sexually explicit images – feminist community support for the movement began to break down.

Snuff Films and the Formation of WAVAW

I am afraid
when the woman on the screen
was slit
from throat to cunt
when they pulled out her guts
the men in the theater stood yelling
give me a knife
give me a knife
and then went
home
I am afraid
we are at war

– "Declaration of" Catherine
Risingflame Moirai[5]

Rumors started spreading about snuff films in 1975, after the New York City Police Department announced that it had confiscated several films made in South America that contained actual murder footage. For every person who maintained that snuff – an underground genre of pornography featuring the on-camera murder of a woman in the midst of an orgasm – was nothing but a hoax, another claimed to have heard that the films were real. "A kind of whispering campaign kept the question of 'snuff movies' alive for months," a film critic for *Playboy* observed.[6] The persistent buzz inspired a B-movie producer named Allan Shackleton to try to capitalize on the rumors. Shackleton

[5] This is the final stanza of an unpublished poem that expresses the author's fear and anguish at the epidemic of male violence against women. The stanza describes the X-rated film, *Snuff*, and its gruesome depiction of a young woman's rape and evisceration. Moirai lived in the Knoxville, Tennessee area in the mid-1970s. She recalled writing this poem in response to the apparent popularity of snuff films. Catherine Risingflame Moirai, "Declaration of" (n.p., n.d.), Los Angeles WAVAW Papers, Box 2.

[6] Arthur Knight, "Sex in Cinema – 1976," *Playboy*, 23, no. 11 (November 1976): 144.

added a grisly murder scene onto the end of a 1971 horror film and distributed it as an X-rated picture called *Snuff*.

The horror movie that ended up as *Snuff* started out as a low-budget picture called *Slaughter*. Roberta and Michael Findlay, an American husband-and-wife filmmaking team who specialized in "slasher" pictures, made *Slaughter* in Argentina in 1971 on a shoestring budget of $25,000. The plot revolves around a cult of beautiful young women who commit violent crimes to please their sadistic leader, Satan, who is clearly modeled after Charles Manson. At Satan's behest, the young women break into a mansion and savagely murder its wealthy inhabitants. In the film's final scene, the cult members stab a pregnant blonde woman to death in the mansion, recalling the Manson murder of actress Sharon Tate. The Findlays' original version was never released.

Amid the publicity about the underground South American films playing in the United States, Shackleton decided to produce a quickie version of a snuff film for domestic release. Without permission from the Findlays, he tacked a four-minute murder sequence onto the end of *Slaughter*. The original film ended after the cult members stabbed the pregnant woman, but Shackleton added new "behind-the-scenes" footage. As the stabbing scene faded, the audience could see the movie camera pulling back and the film's production crew discussing lighting and technical matters. A young female production assistant approaches the director and confides that she found the stabbing scene sexually arousing. As the audience watches, the director propositions the young woman and leads her to the bed on the set. They are removing each other's clothing when she realizes that the crew is still filming. She protests and tries to get away, but the director holds her down. He picks up the knife used in the previous scene, still lying on the bed, and cries, "Bitch, now you're going to get what you want!" He proceeds to chop off her fingers and toes, and saw off her hands and legs as blood pours from her mouth and limbs. In the final moment, he eviscerates her and brandishes her intestines in the air. The screen goes black and the audience hears a crew member say, "Shit, we ran out of film." Another asks, "Did you get it all?" "Yeah, we got it," the first one replies. "Let's get out of here." No credits roll.[7]

Shackleton released *Snuff* in December 1975 and refused to answer questions about its origins. He rated the film X without submitting it to the Motion Picture Association of America (MPAA). He offered no list of cast members, preferring to use only an anonymous and inflammatory tag line: "Made in South America, where life is cheap." *Variety* observed that Shackleton's plan was to "use the uncertainty of whether the killings are real or simulated to try to gross a bundle."[8] *Snuff* opened in New York in February 1976 and in Los Angeles the following month, generating big ticket sales and a firestorm of controversy in both cities.

[7] Williams, *Hard Core*, 192.

[8] Harlan Jacobson, "If 'Snuff' Killings Are Real, Film Violence Faces New Test," *Variety*, December 10, 1975, 4.

Shortly after *Snuff*'s arrival, New York City feminists organized pickets and demanded that the district attorney investigate the possible murder of the female production assistant. At the National Theater, a Times Square movie house, a group of fifty women tried to discourage ticket sales. The protesters chanted "Don't go in" and carried hand-lettered signs with such messages as "Murder is Not Amusing."[9] They also handed out leaflets to passers-by that explained their fury at the inhumane treatment of women in *Snuff*. "That sexual violence is presented as sexual entertainment, that the murder and dismemberment of a woman's body is commercial film material is an outrage to our sense of justice as women, as human beings," read one.[10]

As tensions rose, reputable individuals disclosed that the *Snuff* murder scene was staged. Under pressure from such prominent New York feminists as Gloria Steinem, Susan Brownmiller, and Susan Sontag, the district attorney for Manhattan conducted an investigation. D.A. Robert Morgenthau announced that the stabbing was simulated after New York City police tracked down and interviewed the actress who was "murdered" on-screen in the final scene. "It is nothing more than conventional trick photography ...," Morgenthau said at a press conference on March 9, 1976. "The actress is alive and well."[11] John Leonard, film critic for the *New York Times*, reached the same conclusion after viewing the film. "Nobody gets vérité killed," he assured readers. "'Marcus Welby, M.D.' could have improved on the special effects."[12] Still, people lined up to buy tickets to see for themselves. Feminists responded with a petition, signed by Susan Sontag, Grace Paley, Dave Dellinger, and other feminist and left-wing intellectuals, that asked Morgenthau to ban *Snuff* on the grounds that its portrayal of a violent murder was an incitement to sexual violence against women. The petition stated that the film constituted a direct threat to women's safety.

The controversy swirling around *Snuff* boosted ticket sales, and the movie performed well at the box office. The picture earned a commanding $66,456 in its first week of release in February 1976 at the National Theatre, with tickets selling for $4 a head.[13] In April 1976, the weekly take for *Snuff* was holding strong at $259,000, making it the ninth biggest seller that week, just behind Warner Bros.' comedy-western, *Blazing Saddles*, which earned $279,950. This was during the same period of time that *One Flew Over the Cuckoo's Nest* was in the first-place slot, earning almost $2 million for the week ending

9 "50 Picket Movie House to Protest Violent Film," *The New York Times*, February 16, 1976, 22.

10 Beverly LaBelle, "*Snuff* – The Ultimate in Woman-Hating," in *Take Back the Night*, 276.

11 "Morgenthau Finds Film Dismembering Was Indeed a Hoax," *The New York Times*, March 10, 1976, 41.

12 John Leonard, "Commentary: Cretin's Delight on Film," *The New York Times*, February 27, 1976, 21.

13 "Snuff." *Variety*, February 25, 1976, 22. Compare *Snuff*'s first-week take to that of another highly successful adult film, *The Opening of Misty Beethoven*. The latter did $55,375 in its first week of release, almost 25 percent less than *Snuff*. For figures on *Misty Beethoven*, see "50 Top-Grossing Films," *Variety*, April 7, 1976, 14.

April 7, followed by *Taxi Driver* in second place, earning slightly less than $1 million.[14] Just three months after its premiere in New York City, *Snuff* had earned more than $600,000.[15] "That 'Snuff' was disclosed here and elsewhere as a hoax some months ago seems not to matter to the media generally nor to the New York public," *Variety* observed of the picture's success.[16]

The Los Angeles feminist community began organizing against *Snuff* in March 1976, after local radio station KFWB aired reports that the controversial film was headed to Southern California. Women affiliated with the Los Angeles and Orange County Feminist Women's Health Centers (FWHC), a national association of women's clinics that offered reproductive services and promoted women's self-knowledge and empowerment, announced a meeting for women interested in forming an action network. That meeting, called on short notice for March 5, 1976, was not well attended. But a second meeting, held one week later at the Woman's Building, a cultural center founded in 1973 in downtown Los Angeles to promote feminist visual arts and social activism, was better publicized. It resulted in an ad hoc coalition including delegates from FWHC, California NOW, Olivia Records, *The Lesbian Tide* (a monthly magazine), Sisterhood bookstores, Radical Feminist Therapy Collective, Feminist Lawyers, Alcoholism Center for Women, Rape Crisis Hotlines, National Abortion Rights Action League, and other community groups. Julia London, a Los Angeles area native and former United Farm Workers organizer, remembered seeing flyers for the meeting and feeling disgusted by the premise of *Snuff*. She was drawn to the group and hoped that her experience and organizing skill could be useful in a fight against the film.[17] The new coalition adopted the name "Women Against Violence Against Women" (WAVAW) from the text of a pamphlet put out by feminists in Washington, DC, who had also organized to stop *Snuff*.[18]

The coalition took immediate action to try to prevent *Snuff* from opening in Southern California theaters. Members organized a telephone campaign to pressure the Los Angeles police department, the district attorney's office, and city councilmen to take legal action. They publicized the telephone numbers

[14] "50 Top-Grossing Films,", 12.

[15] "50 Top-Grossing Films," 12. The $600,000 figure seems insignificant when compared to the grosses for mainstream hit pictures, but *Snuff* played in far fewer theaters and cities. For example, as of April 14, 1976, both *Snuff* and *Taxi Driver* had spent eight weeks on Variety's "50 Top-Grossing Films" chart. *Snuff*, however, played only three cities and forty-five theaters during that period as compared to nineteen cities and ninety-eight theatres for *Taxi Driver*. During the same time period, *Taxi Driver* earned $5,707,234. The *Snuff* grosses are comparable to those of less successful mainstream pictures, such as United Artists' *Breakheart Pass*, which earned $806,252 in the same amount of release time as *Snuff*, or Universal's *Gable and Lombard*, which earned $1,580,598.

[16] "Snuff." *Variety*, February 25, 1976, 22.

[17] Personal conversation with Julia London, December 4, 2008.

[18] Julia London and Lynn Heidelberg, "'Snuff' Shut Down by Protests, Stink Bombs, Bricks," *The Lesbian Tide* (May/June 1976), 4.

of newspapers that were accepting ads for the film, including the *Los Angeles Times* and the *L.A. Free Press*, movie theaters where *Snuff* was scheduled to play, and a telephone number for Ted Mann, chairman of Mann Theatres, a family entertainment chain with multiple theaters planning to exhibit *Snuff*.[19] "Call these numbers. Complain. Don't hesitate to call," read a fact sheet that WAVAW distributed broadly. "If this film is profitable, more will follow. We're not talking about censorship. We're talking about self-defense. Don't hesitate to call. People may think you are calling about pornography. Make sure they know you are talking about murder."[20] On March 12, Allan Shackleton held a press conference announcing that *Snuff* was scheduled to open in twenty-four Southern California theaters. Women from FWHC organized pickets outside of the west Los Angeles hotel where he was staying and sent a letter of complaint to the Argentine Embassy, because *Snuff* had purportedly been filmed in Argentina.[21] Others contacted the local news media, resulting in news coverage favorable to the women's cause. An article published in the Los Angeles *Daily News Tribune* captured the group's rage at the perceived connection between media violence and real-world violence. "We feel the movie is not simply offensive, but it has really crossed the line concerning the amount of violence involved," said a director of the FWHC of Orange County. "Women experience rape, murder and mutilation in their homes and on the street. This type of movie simply titillates the type of person who would commit this sort of crime."[22]

On March 15, just two days before *Snuff* was to open, the new WAVAW group sent a delegation to Mann Theatres' corporate offices to protest the chain's plans to show *Snuff*. They presented the Mann executives with a document titled "Cease and Desist" signed by three dozen women's organizations. "This film capitalizes on the murder and dismemberment of a woman," it stated. "Studies have shown that movies like this encourage and foster similar behavior and acts of atrocities in reality."[23] The theater management refused to pull the film, but a Mann executive invited WAVAW to send two individuals to preview *Snuff* at a special screening scheduled for representatives from the district attorney's office and the police department. On the morning of March 17, two WAVAW members showed up at Mann's Hollywood Fox theater for the screening, but were turned away. The management said that the theater's box office window had been vandalized the night before, and cement poured down its toilets, and Mann no longer had any interest in accommodating WAVAW.[24]

[19] "Chronology," n.d., Box 9, Los Angeles WAVAW Papers.

[20] "Fact Sheet on 'Snuff,'" March 12, 1976, Box 14B, Los Angeles WAVAW Papers.

[21] Kathleen Hodge, Feminist Women's Health Center to Argentine Embassy, March 12, 1976, Box 14B, Los Angeles WAVAW Papers.

[22] Cheryl Pruett, "Film Under Heavy Fire by Women," March 17, 1976, Los Angeles *Daily News Tribune*, p. A-2, clipping in Box 14B, Los Angeles WAVAW Papers.

[23] "Cease and Desist," n.d., Box 14 B, Los Angeles WAVAW Papers.

[24] London and Heidelberg, 5.

On the evening of March 17, *Snuff* opened in twenty Los Angeles and Orange County theaters. In response, 100 women demonstrated outside of Mann's Hollywood Fox theater from 4:00 P.M. to 9:00 P.M., singing anti-*Snuff* chants, displaying protest signs and handing out flyers to would-be moviegoers. Two other groups protested that night; members of the Adult Film Association marched to distance themselves from *Snuff*, and a conservative Christian organization picketed the film for glorifying immoral behavior. The demonstrations received extensive local media coverage, and the publicity helped the fledgling WAVAW organization attract additional members.

Feminist protest continued over the next few days throughout Southern California, with demonstrations taking place in Santa Monica, Santa Barbara, East Los Angeles, and the San Fernando Valley. The fledgling WAVAW group coordinated anti-*Snuff* efforts with Chicana activists from regional Latino groups, the Long Beach and San Bernardino chapters of NOW, and other local feminist organizations, drawing on FWHC resources and staff support. An anonymous group of women broke lobby and box office windows of the Mann Theater chain's Culver City, Criterion (Santa Monica), new Westwood, and Hollywood Fox theaters by hurling bricks through them during the early morning hours of March 18.

The second major WAVAW demonstration took place the following Saturday night. Thirty women picketed three Mann Theatres located in Westwood, the affluent liberal community surrounding the University of California at Los Angeles, and announced a boycott of the theater chain. The demonstrators alerted theatergoers to Mann's support of *Snuff*, and handed out flyers. "This movie encourages violent action in a world which already condones and dismisses many terrorist acts against women such as rape and 'wife-beating,'" the flyer read. "The mutilation of women for the explicit sexual pleasure of men once again connects the strong ties of sex and violence." The flyer urged moviegoers to boycott the Mann chain, foreshadowing WAVAW's inclination to use economic pressure to make media corporations act responsibly toward women. "As long as Mann Theatres feel fine about woman-torture, we feel fine about denying them our economic support," the flyer explained.[25] None of the Westwood moviehouses was showing *Snuff* at the time, but they were among the most profitable theaters in the Mann chain, and the steady foot traffic in the pedestrian-friendly UCLA area meant that the WAVAW protestors could interact with a large number of passers-by. Members of WAVAW estimated that they turned away about a third of Mann's customers that evening.[26]

Within the week, Mann Theaters began to feel the full force of the feminist efforts against *Snuff*. In Orange County, WAVAW members persuaded a municipal judge and local police to view the film, which resulted in a court order that declared the film to be in violation of state obscenity statutes and

[25] *Snuff* flyer, n.d., Box 9, Los Angeles WAVAW Papers.
[26] London and Heidelberg, 5.

the public nuisance provision of the state penal code. Police seized the reels from Mann's Fox Fullerton theater.[27] Two independent Orange County theaters withdrew the film voluntarily in response to the action against Mann, and two theaters belonging to another chain substituted other films for a planned weekend showing. From March 21 to 23, WAVAW organized a three-day educational leafletting campaign at Filmex, an annual Los Angeles film festival that attracted major motion picture industry executives, and collected signatures in support of the Mann boycott.

On March 24, WAVAW achieved its goal to drive *Snuff* out of Southern California. Mann Theatres pulled the film from all of its screens, and the few remaining area theaters owned by other corporations followed suit. By March 24, just one week after opening in L.A. and Orange County, *Snuff* was effectively shut down; none of the twenty exhibiting theaters renewed the film for a second week.[28]

Los Angeles WAVAW's success in ridding the city of *Snuff* became a model for actions in other cities around the country. Women's groups in Detroit turned to WAVAW for help fighting *Snuff* on the heels of the film's closure in Southern California. In Buffalo, San Jose, and Denver, *Snuff* was forced out of town by organized feminist protest. Women in Rochester, New York, formed a WAVAW chapter in the fall of 1977 when *Snuff* arrived at a local movie theater. They began picketing the Holiday Cine, a theater connected to a local Holiday Inn hotel, on October 29, 1977. On October 30, four members of Rochester WAVAW were arrested at the theater and charged with felony criminal mischief for breaking a glass window and destroying the movie poster for *Snuff*.[29] Pickets continued for four days until the film closed on November 1.

Rochester WAVAW stood firm in its attack on *Snuff* as its members prepared to face trial for their actions at the Holiday Cine. "*Snuff* is a graphic expression of a culture that terrorizes women – in films, through rape, battering, and other forms of physical and psychic violence," they explained.[30] At their sentencing hearing, each of the women addressed the judge and tried to make him understand why she had taken action against *Snuff*. "What else can you call it but contempt for women ... when men get off on seeing women submissive, raped, tortured, even murdered?" asked defendant Marg Hall, a part-time mechanic. "When men openly and fearlessly advertise, even brag, that their movie is 'the bloodiest thing that ever happened in front of a camera?' When men can make *Snuff* movies?"[31] On October 4, 1978, the judge ordered

27 "Hearing Scheduled on X-Rated Movie; 'Snuff' Impounded in Fullerton after Protest by Feminists," *Los Angeles Times*, March 22, 1976, p. 7, section 2; clipping in Box 14B, Los Angeles WAVAW Papers.

28 Press Release, "'*Snuff*' Closed in Los Angeles," March 24, 1976, Box 14B, Los Angeles WAVAW Papers.

29 Press Release, "*Snuff* Trial Date Announced," May 10, 1978, Branch Literature file, Boston WAVAW Papers.

30 "*Snuff* Trial Date Announced," Boston WAVAW Papers.

31 "*Snuff* Trial Concludes; 'Restitution' Ordered," *New Women's Times* (November 1978), 5.

the defendants to make restitution of $100 within six months to the owner of the Holiday Cine, finding them guilty of a misdemeanor charge of disorderly conduct.

Although WAVAW was initially an ad hoc coalition of Southern California women who banded together to fight *Snuff*, many founders soon recognized the value of maintaining an organization dedicated to media reform. Lynn Heidelberg, a staff member of the L.A. FWHC and an early WAVAW coalition builder, recommended that the FWHC commit a staff person one day per week to support the fledgling group's initiatives. "I think that the rape movement needs this badly," she wrote of WAVAW's efforts, "and that our being located in L.A. gives us [FWHC] some responsibility to the larger women's movement to work on media violence against women."[32] Heidelberg and Julia London, a twenty-nine-year-old lesbian feminist who had been one of the most active members of the early WAVAW coalition, announced a vision for the new organization. "We intend to maintain a network which can respond to other examples of media violence, to maintain contacts with feminists in other cities who have opposed *Snuff*, to continue to research and analyze the phenomenon of *Snuff* and increased marketing and acceptance of porn-violence, and to raise public consciousness."[33] WAVAW rapidly became a national organization with headquarters in Los Angeles and a network of chapters across the country.

London stepped up to become WAVAW's first national coordinator in 1976, and the organization flourished under her dynamic leadership. Born in Glendale, California, in 1947, London was the only child of a barber and a bookkeeper-turned-beautician who espoused leftist politics. She attended several colleges, including a one-year stint at Reed, and ultimately graduated from the University of California-Irvine in 1973 with a major in American Studies. At UC-Irvine, London completed some initial graduate coursework, studying with the urban anthropologist Edith Folb, an expert on the vernacular of African-American youth living in South Central Los Angeles. London also worked with the African-American documentary filmmaker Carlton Moss, developing a passion for film. Looking back, London credits Folb and Moss for helping her understand that visual images constituted a language that shaped the social environment.[34] This perspective informed her activism against *Snuff* and shaped her desire to build WAVAW into a national force working to end images of violence against women. Most important, London was a seasoned activist, having worked in the early 1970s as an Orange County organizer for the United Farm Workers (UFW), the agricultural labor union led by César Chávez and Dolores Huerta.

[32] Lynn Heidelberg, "Summary: Women Against Violence Against Women," March 26, 1976, Box 9, Los Angeles WAVAW Papers.

[33] London and Heidelberg, 5.

[34] Personal conversation with Julia London, December 4, 2008.

I'm Black and Blue from the Rolling Stones, and I Love It!

From high above the fabled Sunset Strip on a glorious day in June 1976, a bound and bruised woman on a billboard gazed down at the citizens of Los Angeles. She was the centerpiece of a new advertising campaign for the Rolling Stones' album, *Black and Blue*, part of a national promotion by Atlantic Records that featured print ads, radio spots, and in-store displays. At 14 by 48 feet, she dominated the busy skyline, and traffic snarled up and down the boulevard as drivers slowed to get a better look. The woman wore a lacy white bodice, artfully ripped to display her breasts. Her hands were tied with ropes, immobilized above her head, and her bruised legs were spread apart. She straddled an image of the Stones, with her pubic bone positioned just above Mick Jagger's head. Her head was thrown back, eyes closed, and her mouth hung open in an expression of pure sexual arousal, as if the rough treatment had wakened her desire and now she wanted more. The ad copy celebrated the mythic connection between sex and violence, reinforcing the dangerous idea that women get excited when things get a little rough: "I'm Black and Blue from the Rolling Stones and I Love It!"[35]

To anyone familiar with the music of the Rolling Stones, this blatant sexism was not surprising. On tour in 1975, Jagger rode a twenty-foot inflatable stage prop shaped like a penis while singing *Starfucker*, a song about the pleasure he found in having sex with girl groupies. Karen Durbin, editor-in-chief of the *Village Voice* in the mid-1970s, went on the road with the band and described her experiences in their boys' club. "I felt self-consciously female, isolated and engulfed by an all-male world.... [Y]ou spend all of your time with men; it's a peculiar, alien sensation, as if you were visiting a planet where the female population had been decimated by an unnamed plague."[36] Durbin acknowledged that feminism had made few inroads in the rock world, most likely because that world "was still so overwhelmingly dominated by men."[37] Like other feminist critics in this period, Durbin lamented that rockers had opted

[35] I have described this campaign in greater detail in Carolyn Bronstein, "No More Black and Blue: Women Against Violence Against Women and the Warner Communications Boycott, 1976–1979," *Violence Against Women* 14, no. 4 (April 2008): 418–436. With advertising rates for traditional mass media on the rise, the cost-effective billboard made a comeback in the mid-1970s. Outdoor advertising companies promoted billboards as inexpensive, effective means of reaching a wide audience. Industry statistics also indicated that as a man's income rose, the amount of leisure time he spent in his car increased, and thus made it more likely that he would see a billboard. In this light, billboards were an ideal advertising medium for the Rolling Stones. Billboards employing sexual images were especially likely to catch drivers' attention. "The effect of a 14-foot-by-48 foot picture of a bikini-clad suntan-oil model mounted on a six-ton steel structure is, to say the least, distracting,"*Forbes* magazine observed. See "The Low-Priced Spread," *Forbes*, January 15, 1977, 64.

[36] Karen Durbin, "Can the Stones Still Cut It?" *The Village Voice*, June 23, 1975, 1, 8.

[37] Durbin,"Can the Stones Still Cut It?," 8.

FIGURE 4.1. "I'm Black and Blue from The Rolling Stones and I Love It!" The June 1976 Atlantic Records billboard advertising the new Rolling Stones album, *Black and Blue*. The conflation of violence and female sexual arousal led members of WAVAW to call for the removal of the billboard, the cancellation of the advertising campaign, and ultimately a boycott of Warner Communications' music labels. Before it was taken down, an activist spray-painted the graphic symbol of the Women's Liberation movement on the bottom right-hand corner of the billboard. Across the bottom, she wrote: "This is a crime against women!" *Photo courtesy of Northeastern University Libraries, Archives and Special Collections.*

for chauvinism instead of striving to create a more egalitarian alternative culture.[38] She wrote of the Stones: "My politics make me want to believe that they give all their money to the revolution, that they didn't really mean that part about the stupid girl, that in real life they refer to all females over the age of twelve as 'women' and never fail to vote for the Equal Rights Amendment when they're in town."[39] *Black and Blue* made it clear that Durbin's hopes with regard to the band members were far from coming true.

Members of WAVAW were outraged by the *Black and Blue* promotion. The bruised, trussed woman was the centerpiece of Atlantic's new campaign, and an advertisement featuring her image appeared in major music industry magazines and trade publications, including *Rolling Stone*, *High Times*, *Billboard*,

[38] Other feminists who expressed this point of view included Judy Parker of the *Los Angeles Free Press*, Ellen Willis of *Rolling Stone*, Marion Meade of *The New York Times*, and rocker Janis Joplin.

[39] "Stupid Girl" is the title of a well-known Rolling Stones song. Durbin, "Can the Stones Still Cut It?," 8.

Cash Box, and *Record World*. In WAVAW's view, the campaign made light of male violence, especially battering. They feared that associating such violence with a sexy rock-and-roll band like the Rolling Stones gave battering "a veneer of chic sado-masochism."[40] In a news release, WAVAW explained how that billboard made women feel. "We carry in ourselves a deep fear of rape. When we would drive down the Sunset Strip and see the myth about our lust for sexual abuse advertised, our fear and outrage was deepened," the group warned. "We are not *Black and Blue* and we do not love it when we are."[41] It was evident from the WAVAW interpretation of the advertising campaign that many of the group's members had strong ties to the anti-rape and battered women's movements that had grown out of the second wave of American feminism in the early 1970s.[42] Indeed, in a letter written to feminist supporters, London described WAVAW's efforts against *Black and Blue*: "What we are concerned with is more than a billboard. We are concerned with the perpetuation of the myth that women like to be beaten."[43]

London was a student of the feminist performance artist Suzanne Lacy at the Feminist Studio Workshop, and Lacy had exposed her to the sociologist Erving Goffman's early work, *The Presentation of the Self in Everyday Life*. Using this text as a theoretic model, London realized that the performance of sexual excitement in the *Black and Blue* ad would be interpreted by some viewers to mean that women experienced sexual pleasure from violence.[44] Drawing from Goffman, who was then studying the ritual presentation of women's bodies in advertising, London deconstructed the *Black and Blue* image and read it as a powerful endorsement of male violence.

Representatives of the fledgling WAVAW contacted Atlantic Records, a subsidiary of Warner Communications, Inc. (WCI), and the Ryan Outdoor Advertising Agency, owner of the billboard, and voiced their objections to *Black and Blue*. They explained that the ad perpetuated the myths that women are victims who like and expect to be victimized, that victimized women are sexually attractive, and that it is socially acceptable for men to treat women brutally. They demanded the removal of the billboard and the cancellation of the advertising campaign. When neither company complied, WAVAW announced that it would hold a news conference on June 22, 1976 at the site of the billboard, and invited Atlantic Records and Ryan Outdoor to participate. "When

40 "The WAVAW Slide Show," 1977, Boston WAVAW Papers.

41 Press Release, "No More Black and Blue," June 22, 1976, Branch Literature file, Boston WAVAW Papers.

42 These movements are described in greater detail in Chapter 1, which points to women's growing awareness of an epidemic of male violence, especially the prevalence of rape, as a major factor in the rise of the feminist anti-pornography movement. WAVAW's concern with rape was central to many of its analyses. The organization pointed out in its literature, that "the incidence of rape in the U.S. has increased by 134% [since 1970] and it is estimated that nine-tenths of committed rapes go unreported." Press Release, "What is WAVAW?" n.d., Statement of Purpose file, Boston WAVAW Papers.

43 Julia London to Dear Sisters, July 5, 1976, Box 6, Los Angeles WAVAW Papers.

44 Personal conversation with Suzanne Lacy, November 12, 2008.

they treated our objections very casually…," WAVAW members recalled, "we invited them to explain why they felt it was okay to use this kind of technique to sell a product."[45] Just fifteen hours after WAVAW issued this invitation, the billboard was removed. In the interim hours, a feminist activist spray-painted the graphic symbol of the Women's Liberation movement and her own message across the sign: "This is a crime against women."

In response to WAVAW pressure, Atlantic Records scaled back the *Black and Blue* campaign, but did not eliminate it. The company canceled a series of radio spots that began with the sound of a whip cracking and a woman's voice cooing "Ooooh, beat me, beat me, make me '*Black and Blue*'… I love it."[46] However, the trussed and bruised woman continued to appear in print ads in national magazines, and neither Atlantic representatives nor the Rolling Stones themselves seemed to fathom the depth of WAVAW's rage. Bob Greenberg, the West Coast general manager for Atlantic Records, gave a half-hearted statement to *Rolling Stone* magazine, which was one of the many national publications that had carried the *Black and Blue* ad: "It was not the intention of Atlantic, Mick, or the Rolling Stones to offend anyone."[47] Members of the band seemed untroubled by the feminist response. Mick Jagger contended that the billboard offered an accurate portrayal of female sexual desire, and was quoted in *Rolling Stone* as having said, "Well, there are a lot of girls into that, they dig it, they want to be chained up…."[48] According to the rock music critic Richard Harrington, Jagger personally tied up the model (future *Playboy* model Anita Russell) on the set of the photography shoot and shared his vision of the moody "ugly" quality he wanted from the pictures.[49] Keith Richards recalled the controversy in a 1979 interview in *Creem*, a rock music magazine. "I thought it was quite funny," he said. "Goddamn it, a large percentage of American women wouldn't be half as liberated if it wasn't for the Rolling Stones in the first place…. They'd still be believing in dating, rings, and wondering whether it was right to be kissed on the first date or not."[50] The executives at Atlantic Records refused to scrap the campaign. They seemed to share Richards' view that the feminist protesters were little more than irritating "marchers with bees in their bonnets."[51]

[45] "The WAVAW Slide Show," 1977, Boston WAVAW Papers.

[46] "The WAVAW Slide Show," 1977, Boston WAVAW Papers. Rock music critic Richard Harrington asserts that according to Elin Guskind, an advertising copywriter who wrote both the billboard copy and the radio script, the radio commercial was so lurid that WNEW in New York City refused to air it. Personal conversation with Richard Harrington, January 2010.

[47] "Hot Stuff," *Rolling Stone*, July 29, 1976, 25.

[48] Quoted in Ricardo A. Forrest, "Women in Rock: Artsy Image or Insult?" *Neworld: The Multi-Cultural Magazine of the Arts*, 4, no. 5, 1978, 43.

[49] Personal conversation with Richard Harrington, January 2010.

[50] Quoted in Steve Appleford, *The Rolling Stones: It's Only Rock and Roll, Song by Song* (New York: Schirmer Books, 1997), 150. Richards expressed a version of sexual liberation that infuriated many women in the 1970s: We've given you the right to have sex with us, what more could you possibly want?

[51] "Hot Stuff," *Rolling Stone*, July 29, 1976, 25.

These indifferent responses infuriated members of WAVAW. They did not share Richards' interpretation of *Black and Blue* as liberation writ large but saw instead the glorification of violence against women. "We believe that this image validates the physical mistreatment of women," the group wrote in a press release, "and we abhor the depiction of a bound and beaten woman to enhance record sales."[52] Indeed, the record companies were among the worst offenders, tending to present women in submissive positions and employing the "woman as victim" stereotype seen in *Black and Blue*. This type of image raised the specter of rape and battering for WAVAW activists, most of whom had become politicized about violence through the Women's Liberation movement. "We are especially concerned about this issue because of the increasing rate of rape, and because of the horrifying information that has begun to come out about battering," WAVAW members warned. "We cannot allow this kind of behavior to be trivialized, glorified, sensationalized or romanticized in mass media."[53] The proliferation of these images in rock and roll, which tended to capture the attention of young women and men who were still formulating ideas about gender and sexuality, made the situation seem even more serious.

Leaders of the anti-rape and battering movements voiced similar sentiments as they made connections between sexual violence in the media and real-life violence against women. Deb Friedman and Lois Yankowski, members of the Feminist Alliance Against Rape (FAAR), wrote a widely reprinted essay for the women's journal *Quest*, which pointed out how common the depiction of sexual violence had become. "The media do not merely show occasional images of violence and domination, but inundate and overwhelm us with these images," the authors argued. "Women are constantly massacred and brutalized in every conceivable fashion in the media."[54] Friedman and Yankowski urged women to fight back against the proliferation of violent imagery.[55] Foreshadowing one of WAVAW's most significant strategies, the authors predicted that women would have to use pressure tactics, such as boycotts, to gain some measure of control.

52 "No More Black and Blue," Boston WAVAW Papers.

53 "The WAVAW Slide Show," 1977, Boston WAVAW Papers.

54 Deb Friedman and Lois Yankowski, "Snuffing Sexual Violence," *Quest* 3, no. 2 (Fall 1976): 25.

55 The Rolling Stones' billboard was also protested in *Ms.* magazine, in the popular "No Comment" section, which featured offensive advertisements sent in by readers. These ads and photographs were reprinted without editorial comment, and were thus available for deconstruction by the reading audience. Many of the reprinted items suggested that women enjoy sexual abuse or violence, or that beating a woman was a man's prerogative. Many readers sent in advertisements for record albums whose covers featured "brutal chic" imagery. In May 1977, the *Black and Blue* album cover appeared in *Ms.* A reader sent in a photograph of the billboard, which had been spraypainted to read: "This is a crime against women." This "comment" in the "No Comment" section made it perfectly clear that humor about violence against women was anathema to feminists everywhere. See Linda Steiner, "Oppositional Decoding as an Act of Resistance," *Critical Studies in Mass Communication* 5, no. 1 (March 1988): 1–15.

Violence as an Advertising Trend

Record industry insiders who were sympathetic to the WAVAW cause in the wake of *Black and Blue* pointed out that the exploitation of violence against women was a growing trend, particularly in advertising and films. Fashion magazines ran so many images featuring the combination of sex and violence that the term "brutal chic" was coined to describe this approach. The photographer Helmut Newton contributed a photo spread called "The Story of Ohhh..." (a play on the 1954 French novel *The Story of O*, which featured sadomasochistic themes) to *Vogue* magazine in May 1975. It included shots of a woman wincing in pain as a man bit her ear, and another of a man ramming his hand into her breast. In December 1977, *Vogue* published a twelve-page "scenario for modern lovers" shot by fashion photographer and portraitist Richard Avedon. It featured scenes of a young couple traipsing through the fountains and terraces of a water garden, kissing, caressing, and then quarreling. The man is shown seizing the woman's upper arm, twisting it savagely, and hitting her square across the jaw with a closed fist. One sequence showed the woman battered off of her feet in a $140 peach-colored designer jumpsuit. The storyline suggested that the woman did not object to this treatment; on the next page she was shown nudging the man affectionately.[56]

The crossover influence of the fashion industry on record album art was unmistakable. Prominent fashion photographers regularly shot album covers. Francesco Scavullo, best known for photographing models for *Cosmopolitan* magazine covers, shot the disturbing cover image for the 1975 Edgar Winter album, "They Only Come Out at Night." Scavullo was credited with helping the album go gold, with more than $1 million in sales.[57] *Black and Blue* was created in part by the fashion photographer Ara Gallant, who regularly shot models for the cover of *Vogue*.[58] Once fashion photographers adopted themes juxtaposing sex and violence, the record industry followed suit.

To assess the prevalence of imagery that linked brutality with eroticism, WAVAW members started going into music stores and looking at album covers. London and other group members looked through the bins at two Los Angeles record stores and came up with a list of forty-five albums that they deemed offensive to women.[59] They thought they had seen the worst with Atlantic's *Black and Blue*, but soon found numerous images of women tied up and

[56] Laura Lederer, editor of *Take Back the Night: Women on Pornography*, asked Richard Avedon for permission to reprint one of the photographs from this spread so that readers could see the image for themselves. Avedon refused. See Lederer, "Introduction," in *Take Back the Night*, 18–19. On both the Newton and Avedeon spreads, see also "Really Socking it to Women," *Time*, February 7, 1977, 58–59; and Judith Coburn, "S&M," *New Times*, February 4, 1977, p. 43–50.

[57] Susan Rakowski, "What Sells Records in These Zany Times Is Good Graphics," *The Wall Street Journal*, June 15, 1977, 1.

[58] Karen Durbin, "Pretty Poison: The Selling of Sexual Warfare," *The Village Voice*, May 9, 1977, 18+.

[59] Lindsy Van Gelder, "Women's War on LP Cover Violence," *Rolling Stone*, April 21, 1977, 62.

gagged, assaulted, chained, and wearing dog collars and leashes. The cover of the 1973 *Reprise* album by the funk rock group Cold Blood showed a woman lying in the street with her clothes torn open and the contents of her purse strewn about. Her appearance suggested that she had been sexually assaulted and robbed. The cover for the 1972 Ohio Players album, *Pleasure*, featured an emaciated woman with a shaved head. Her hands were criss-crossed above her head and chained. To the WAVAW women, she looked like the victim of a concentration camp or a lynching, but the album's title suggested that she enjoyed this type of treatment.[60] The cover for the 1976 Montrose album, *Jump On It*, displayed a close-up photograph of a woman's pubic area. She was wearing bright red bikini underwear; the color suggested that her vagina was a target. WAVAW members interpreted the album's title as supporting the idea that it was socially acceptable to "jump" a woman and commit sexual assault. This image, like *Black and Blue*, was read as an invitation to rape.

The 1977 album, *Ginseng Woman*, by jazz guitarist Eric Gale, also featured cover art where female sexuality and violence commingled. A naked woman was shown lying face down on the ground with her robe crumpled at her side and her feet bound with an electrical cord. WAVAW members also objected to the 1977 Kiss album, *Love Gun*, as sex and violence were fused in the album title. The cover for the 1976 album *Wild Angel*, by underground rocker Nelson Slater, showed a woman with a chain running through her mouth like a horse's bit. Funk group Bloodstone put out its *Do You Wanna Do a Thing?* album in 1976, with a cover that depicted a gang rape scene. Pure Food and Drug Act, the short-lived band led by Don "Sugarcane" Harris, selected cover art for its 1972 album, *Choice Cuts*, that showed a woman's bare buttocks stamped with the album title. WAVAW insisted that these kinds of images contributed to the sexist ideology of women's subordinate place relative to men, and glorified and trivialized sexual violence. The group recognized an industry-wide problem and noted that many of the abusive albums were released on the Warner label, or that of one of Warner's subsidiary music companies.

Much of what the WAVAW activists saw in the record stores reflected the pervasive sexism of the rock music culture. Although the Rolling Stones were among the most blatant offenders with such songs as *Under My Thumb*, co-written by Jagger and Richards, misogyny was rampant in rock. Pop music was dominated by men whose songs were "a projection of just the kind of chauvinism that women have grown to loathe as a roadblock in their march towards liberation," a writer for *Vogue* observed.[61] She pointed to lyrics like those in Mick Jagger's *Back Street Girl*, which glorified the sexual double standard. "Please, don't be part of my life/Please, keep yourself to yourself/ Please, don't you bother my wife/Don't want you out in my world/Just you be my back street girl." The double standard that dichotomized women as

[60] "The WAVAW Slide Show," 1977, Boston WAVAW Papers.

[61] Julia Marks, "Women in Rock: Don't Sing Me No Songs 'Bout Bad Women!" *Vogue* 157, no. 5 (March 1, 1971): 112.

madonnas and whores, with some women standing in as "good" girls (the wife) and others as "bad" girls (the back street girl used for sex) infuriated women and illustrated the limitations of the sexual revolution. Marion Meade also took rock culture to task for its thinly veiled hatred of women. In an essay for the *New York Times*, she examined Bob Dylan's music and concluded that he "tended to regard nearly every female as a bitch." She described his well-known song, "Just Like a Woman," as a "catalogue of sexist slurs," that defined women's natural traits as "greed, hypocrisy, whining and hysteria."[62] His later songs, Meade wrote, treated women as sexual objects (e.g., "Big Brass Bed"), such that Dylan "has more or less caught up with Jim Morrison's request to 'Light my fire' and with John Lennon's suggestion, 'Why don't we do it in the road?'"[63] By the time the WAVAW activists hit the Los Angeles record stores, the chauvinism inherent in rock music had been coupled with a trendy new emphasis on violence.

Launching the Warner Boycott

In the fall of 1976, WAVAW began planning a campaign to force the record industry to curb its use of images of sexual violence against women. Record companies were certainly not the sole offenders among the entertainment media, but they became a strategic target for WAVAW efforts. Record companies comprised a high-profile and powerful sector of the entertainment industry, and many musical artists exploited images of violence against women in their advertising and promotional materials. A few major corporations dominated the music business, which made it easy to identify a major target for a consumer campaign. London explained WAVAW's decision to focus on the record industry: "It's manageable, not like motion pictures, magazines or books."[64]

Drawing from her experience with the UFW, London suggested that WAVAW initiate a boycott against a major recording industry corporation. The UFW had waged a five-year public boycott of table grapes to support workers' efforts to secure a fair union contract from California's giant agribusiness farms, which gave London direct exposure to the power of mass consumer action. As union representatives pressed community and religious organizations to support the boycott, millions of Americans stopped buying grapes. By the early 1970s, the UFW had organized 50,000 agricultural workers and had forced the grape growers to accept union contracts. London saw firsthand that consumer pressure, direct action, and appeals for social responsibility were powerful techniques that could generate significant public

62 Marion Meade, "Does Rock Degrade Women?" *The New York Times*, March 14, 1971, sec. 2:13, 22.

63 Meade, 1971, 22.

64 Nadine Brozan, "Record Covers Come Under Attack for Portraying Crimes On Women," *The New York Times*, January 1, 1977, 26.

support. She believed that WAVAW could adopt the tactics that had served the farm workers so well, and could use them to force the music industry to curb its portrayal of violence against women.[65] The boycott was intended to pressure the music industry to assume corporate responsibility for the images of women that it produced and promoted and to eradicate the dangerous and gratuitous images of violence against women that were commonplace in music industry advertising and promotions.

Now, WAVAW had to decide which record company would be the target of its campaign. WCI, the parent company of the Warner/Reprise, Elektra/Asylum/Nonesuch, and Atlantic/Atco labels, led the industry in terms of sales and prestige. Their labels carried a wide range of best-selling artists, including America, Bad Company, George Benson, the Doobie Brothers, the Eagles, Fleetwood Mac, Led Zeppelin, Queen, Linda Ronstadt, and Rod Stewart.[66] Just a few months earlier, WCI had announced the best second quarter in the company's history, with the records and music division producing 54 percent of corporate income and 50 percent of sales. Each of the WCI record companies registered increases in sales, posting $15.84 million in profits, up 71 percent from the previous year.[67] Ahmet Ertegun, the chairman of Atlantic Records; Mo Ostin, the chairman of Warner Bros. Records; and Joe Smith, the president of Elektra/Asylum, had come together with Steve Ross, the chairman of WCI, to announce these spectacular earnings. This music world "summit meeting," as *Billboard* described it, was covered by *The New York Times*, the *Wall Street Journal*, the *Los Angeles Times*, and dozens of other national newspapers and entertainment trade papers. When WAVAW convened to select a target for the boycott, WCI was already in the spotlight. Better still, the Rolling Stones recorded on a Warner label, thus making WCI – in WAVAW's eyes – ultimately responsible for *Black and Blue*.

In November 1976, WAVAW, in conjunction with the California state chapter of NOW, sent letters to the chairmen of Warner, Elektra, and Atlantic that demanded a policy statement against the use of violence against women in album advertising.[68] Next, they insisted that the companies cancel any upcoming ads or promotional materials that featured such violence. Finally, WAVAW asked Warner, Elektra, and Atlantic (hereafter, WEA) to recall all albums in retail stores whose covers, like *Jump On It* or *Pleasure*, depicted violence

[65] Personal conversation with Julia London, December 4, 2008.

[66] Stephen Fraiman, "Warner's Year: Music Arm's Sales, Profits," *Billboard*, February 26, 1977, 8.

[67] Stephen Fraiman, "Earnings by Warner at a New High," *Billboard*, July 31, 1976, 1. See also Bob White & John Sippel, "WB & Col Lead '76 Chart Action," *Billboard*, February 26, 1977, 3. The latter article describes Warner/Elektra/Atlantic's overall performance in 1976.

[68] Although WAVAW led the effort against the record companies, the organization's small size and low levels of funding made a partnership with California NOW a smart move. In 1976, California NOW had a statewide membership of 12,000, with fifteen active chapters in Los Angeles alone. On the day of the WAVAW press conference at Tower Records (December 10, 1976), California NOW held simultaneous news conferences at Tower Record stores throughout the state to publicize the issue and state WAVAW/NOW's demands.

against women.[69] WAVAW requested that each company respond by December 6 to indicate compliance. The WAVAW letters were ignored.

On December 10, 1976, leaders of WAVAW and California NOW held a news conference at Tower Records on Sunset Boulevard in Los Angeles to announce a consumer boycott of the three WCI record companies. The feminists assembled at noon with signs, leaflets, and poster-sized photographs displaying WEA's most flagrant record covers. London, the national coordinator for WAVAW, read a statement that connected music industry advertising with violence against women. "WEA's album covers and/or promotion copy have included portrayals of women as willing victims of battering, as implied targets of gang rape, as victims of abduction and targets of abuse, and as being sexually attractive as victims," she said. "This advertising is being used at a time when rape is increasing and when a conservative estimate puts the number of battered women in the United States at one million." [emphasis in original][70] London connected the facts and figures about violence against women to radical feminist theory about the political uses of violence in preserving the patriarchal order. "We refuse to be victims and we refuse to allow the perpetuation and promotion of myths about women being willing victims and men being animals," she said.[71] Following radical feminist theory, she argued that those images deprived women and men alike of their right to "personhood," and instead imposed corrupt and artificial gender differences on both sexes.

The company's behavior was especially disappointing, she added, in view of the music industry's self-regulation regarding the glorification of drug use. In the late 1960s, the record industry had voluntarily adopted a policy to eliminate advertising and other album-related material that sanctioned drugs. WAVAW leaders saw this as a precedent for their campaign against images of violence. "What WAVAW demands," she explained, "is that the industry demonstrate a parallel sensitivity and corporate responsibility when it comes to women."[72] Faced with mounting evidence of Warner's callous disregard, WAVAW called for a consumer boycott of the three Warner record companies until the parent company issued a corporate policy forbidding the use of images of violence against women on album covers and related promotional material.

News coverage of the press conference and the announcement of the boycott was minimal, as was typical for feminist actions at this time, but a few influential trade publications, including *The Hollywood Reporter* and

[69] "WEA Boycott," *WAVAW Newsletter* no. 1 (May 1977): 1.

[70] Press Release, "Statement Presented by Julia London," December 10, 1976, WAVAW Branch Literature file, Boston WAVAW Papers. This document has been reprinted in Rosalyn Baxandall and Linda Gordon, *Dear Sisters: Dispatches from the Women's Liberation Movement* (New York: Basic Books, 2000), 171–172.

[71] Press Release, "Statement Presented by Julia London," December 10, 1976.

[72] Julia London, "Images of Violence Against Women," *Victimology: An International Journal* 3–4 (1977–78): 521.

Billboard, did report the story.[73] *Billboard*, a weekly newspaper covering the music industry, published a major story about the *Black and Blue* controversy and quoted London and members of California NOW extensively. "We are constantly seeing women being abused, raped and gang-rape implied by use of suggestive poses, whips and chains. Very rarely is a woman portrayed as a human being," London told the reporter. Sue Ann Dewing, chair of the Rape and Criminal Justice Task Force of California NOW, also offered a statement. "We want women to become aware and see what an album represents. We are raising the consciousness as to the whole concept of sexual violence as acceptable advertising and society's condonment of this behavior," she told *Billboard*.[74]

From the start, WAVAW was careful to explain to journalists and others that the WEA boycott was a consumer action, not to be confused with a call for government censorship. "We are not advocating censorship but rather encouraging people to realize that as consumers we have the right to make an economic vote in regards to the policies of industry," WAVAW wrote. "We urge people to vote no on the use of degrading and abusive depictions of women."[75] Joining the boycott, the group explained, meant refusing to lend financial support to an industry that told lies about women. WAVAW always presented the boycott in terms of corporate responsibility, sidestepping difficult questions about censorship that plagued later anti-pornography groups. "Just as General Motors has to recall cars with defective parts that create an unsafe environment for motorists, so must any corporation take responsibility for not perpetuating myths that contribute to an environment that is unsafe for women," WAVAW insisted. "Any company that sells a product that is harmful to consumers has a responsibility to take it off the market."[76] By framing their campaign in all-American terms of consumer choice and corporate responsibility, and using parallel examples like the UFW grape boycott, WAVAW generally avoided criticism that the organization's demands infringed on freedom of speech.

Once the boycott was announced, WEA representatives contacted WAVAW. On December 28, 1976, London and Susan Bechaud of WAVAW, Sue Ann Dewing, and Jeane Bendorf, state coordinator of California NOW, met with a dozen Warner executives to discuss the boycott.[77] Bob Merlis,

[73] Jeanne Taylor, "CAL. NOW/WAVAW Confront Warner Conglomerate," *NOW Times*, January 1977, 1, clipping in Press Packet – LA file, Boston WAVAW Papers.

[74] Ed Harrison, "Two Organizations Irate: Women Rebel Over Album Cover 'Art'," *Billboard*, December 11, 1976, 10. By the time of the Tower Records press conference, WAVAW and California NOW had sent letters to Vantage, United Artists, 20th Century, RCA, Phonogram, Motown, London, Columbia, Epic, Chelsea, Capricorn, Buddah, ABC, Amherst, Arista, and MCA Records, warning that the boycott would ultimately be directed against them unless they changed their abusive advertising policies.

[75] "What is WAVAW?," Boston WAVAW Papers.

[76] "The WAVAW Slide Show," 1977, Boston WAVAW Papers.

[77] Ed Harrison, "Problem for Labels: We Will Boycott Nationally: Women," *Billboard*, January 15, 1977, 47.

Warner's national publicity director, attended the meeting, along with the company's director of advertising, director of artist relations, vice president of sales and promotion, art director, and other staff members from the advertising and publicity departments. The Warner team defended the company's refusal to remove existing albums from stores and told the WAVAW representatives that their idea that WEA could police sexual violence in album projects was "unrealistic."[78] The executives maintained that all WEA performers had contractual control over the design of their album covers and promotional materials, and Warner was obligated to go along with whatever creative elements the artist desired. "We're legally bound to go with what the artist wants," Merlis told a reporter from the *New York Times*. "We have no power."[79] According to *Record World*, a trade paper for the music industry, the Warner department heads urged WAVAW to bring their complaints directly to the recording artists.[80] Merlis suggested that the feminists ask sympathetic recording artists, such as Joni Mitchell, to approach Mick Jagger and others directly, to try to "raise their consciousness. He offered the women the telephone number of the manager of any artist on the label. According to the feminist journalist Lindsy Van Gelder, who wrote about the meeting in *Rolling Stone*, London and the other WAVAW representatives viewed this offer as "patronizing and buck-passing."[81]

London and the other WAVAW and NOW members were infuriated. The very suggestion that WEA had "no power" over the albums they produced and sold was insulting. "It seems to us that Warner's rhetoric throughout the meeting," said London, "was a shabby attempt to evade completely the issue of corporate responsibility."[82] Another attendee described the meeting as "farcical" to the *Billboard* reporter.[83] The activists came away from the meeting determined to step up pressure through the consumer boycott.

Following the WEA meeting, London flew to New York City to promote the WAVAW cause among East Coast feminists. Gloria Steinem and Susan Brownmiller invited London to discuss the expansion of the boycott with a group of influential New York feminists and to share the WAVAW slide show with the New York feminist community. London presented the slide show, which consisted of pictures of record album covers, billboards, and magazine advertisements, accompanied by a critical analysis of each image, to a group of women at Brownmiller's Greenwich Village apartment on December 30. The star power of the hosts ensured that the meeting earned a feature

78 Sam Sutherland, "Expanding Boycott," *Record World*, January 8, 1977, clipping in National Office – Press Packet, 1977 file, Boston WAVAW Papers.

79 Brozan, 26.

80 Sutherland, "Expanding Boycott.".

81 Van Gelder, "Women's War on LP Cover Violence," 62.

82 Press Release, "Warner Acknowledges Problem But Refuses to Act," n.d., Press Packet – LA file, Boston WAVAW Papers.

83 Harrison, "Problem for Labels," 47.

story in the *New York Times*.[84] Word-of-mouth and the *Times* article produced a standing-room-only crowd at the Women's Coffeehouse on Seventh Avenue for another slide show and meeting on Sunday, January 2, 1977. Six radio stations broadcast interviews with London, including WNBC AM radio New York City, which featured her on the radio program, "A Woman's Challenge." WAVAW was getting attention across the nation, hailed by many as a modern-day David-and-Goliath effort: a grassroots feminist organization taking a stand against a powerful media corporation.[85] Leveraging this new visibility, WAVAW sent letters to sixteen major record companies, warning that the boycott would ultimately be directed against them as well unless they ceased using images of violence against women.

The Boycott Heats Up

London's trip to New York City sparked a wave of news coverage that caught the attention of some high-level Warner executives. On January 15, 1977, *Billboard* reported that the WAVAW effort was gaining strength and momentum and noted that WAVAW intended to expand the boycott nationally, which it characterized as a serious "problem for labels."[86] Shortly after London's return from New York City, Joe Smith, the chairman of the board of Elektra/Asylum, contacted WAVAW to arrange a meeting. Smith's label concentrated primarily on "writer artist California rock," including such artists as Joni Mitchell, Carly Simon, and Jackson Browne, who were popular with female listeners.[87] Only one Elektra album was included on WAVAW's extensive list of offensive covers, and an insider at Elektra revealed that Smith did not want his company to be "tarred with the same brush" as Warner and Atlantic.[88] The boycott was far more likely to dampen sales of Elektra/Asylum artists than those of rock groups like Led Zeppelin, Queen, and the Rolling Stones, who recorded on other Warner labels. The boycott posed a more realistic threat to Elektra/Asylum than it did to the other Warner music companies.

In February 1977, representatives from WAVAW and California NOW met with Smith. He confirmed what WAVAW had long suspected: Record companies could exert their influence over album covers and advertising images if

[84] The feature story was Nadine Brozan, "Record Covers Come Under Attack for Portraying Crimes On Women," *The New York Times*, January 1, 1977, 26.

[85] Membership data for WAVAW nationwide is scarce, but by February 1978 (one year following London's trip to New York City), WAVAW had 1,000 members and chapters in 25 states. This data is taken from Diane L. Tsoulas, "Women Against Violence Against Women," *Sister Courage* 3, no. 4 (June 1978): 7.

[86] Harrison, "Problem for Labels," 47.

[87] This is Smith's description of the Elektra/Asylum product. See Nat Freedland, "A Day in the Life of Joe Smith," *Billboard*, April 3, 1976, 42–43.

[88] Van Gelder, "Women's War on LP Cover Violence," 62.

they wished to do so. In many instances, the music companies did cede control to recording artists, as Warner's publicity director had argued, but Smith explained that this was a voluntary decision. Record companies could oversee album art, and other forms of advertising and promotion, without losing their artists.[89] Smith refuted what Warner executives had told WAVAW about record companies having "no power" over content.

Following the meeting, Smith issued a public statement promising that Elektra/Asylum (E/A) would no longer use images of physical and sexual violence against women to promote its albums. Smith promised that E/A "would exert its influence in efforts to discourage illustrations showing women as objects of sexual or other violence."[90] "We don't want to put out a product that offends anyone," he told *Variety*. "And it's not only a matter of sales; it's a question of morality and ethics as well."[91] This was a major step toward victory for WAVAW, and London commended Smith for acknowledging corporate responsibility, for his willingness to use his personal influence to heighten industry awareness, and for encouraging self-regulation.[92]

Smith extended one final olive branch. He promised to speak to Mo Ostin, president of Warner Bros. Records, and Ahmet Ertegun, chairman of the board of Atlantic Records, to urge them to meet with WAVAW representatives. On April 1, Smith called London with a compromise offer. Ostin and Ertegun were not willing to meet, but they would agree to add their names to the statement against violence that Smith had issued in February. The companies would implement a policy consistent with that statement, and would publicize it internally at each of the three record companies and externally to each label's roster of recording artists. They would make no assurances about albums where recording artists maintained complete contractual control over design and graphics, and thus it would be possible for violent images to appear from time to time.[93]

WAVAW was sorely disappointed that Ostin and Ertegun were trying to piggy-back on Smith's statement, which had been crafted in light of Elektra's modest contribution to the violence problem, and which did not include a major about-face with regard to existing corporate policy. In a letter to Smith declining the offer, London and Bendorf expressed dismay that Atlantic and Warner showed no real interest in change. "The wording of the statement does not recognize the severity of their offenses – which are far greater than Elektra's – and it would imply that a policy change had not been made on the part of Warner Brothers and Atlantic, and, in fact, would imply that there had been no need for such a change," they wrote [emphasis in original]. "Issuing the joint statement with endorsement by Mo Ostin and Ahmet Ertegun would

[89] "E/A Supports Women's Goals," *Billboard*, March 5, 1977, 74.

[90] "Elektra/Asylum Pledges Respect for Womanhood," *Variety*, February 22, 1977, 1.

[91] "Elektra/Asylum Pledges Respect for Womanhood," 1.

[92] "E/A Supports Women's Goals," 74.

[93] Julia London and Jeane K. Bendorf to Joe Smith, April 15, 1977, Box 15, Los Angeles WAVAW Papers.

obscure the necessity for positive action of significant impact to be taken on their parts...."[94] The WAVAW representatives expressed confidence in Smith's "sincerity and good will" but informed him that the company-wide boycott would continue until all three record companies met WAVAW's terms. "We feel that, given the continuing state of utter lack of direct and serious response from Warner Brothers and Atlantic," they advised Smith, "we are back at ground zero so far as the boycott of W/E/A labels is concerned."[95] Smith responded several days later to London, indicating that he was "extremely disappointed" in WAVAW's decision to continue the boycott. "I honestly believe," he wrote to her, "that you have received an unprecedented commitment from the executives of this corporation that goes far beyond anything you've heard from others. To selectively take action against us while every other company in this industry remains untouched seems to me to be as arbitrary and unfair as you claim Messrs. Ostin and Ertegun are in not meeting with you."[96] At this point, the relationship between Elektra/Asylum and WAVAW began to break down, and WAVAW girded itself for a fight to bring Atlantic and Warner to the bargaining table.

Increasing the Pressure on Warner and Atlantic

In the wake of the inadequate responses from Ostin and Ertegun, WAVAW decided to intensify the boycott directed at Warner and Atlantic. The organization conducted a major letter-writing campaign focused on "the intractable companies" during May 1977.[97] The meetings with Warner executives, East Coast feminists, and Joe Smith had given the WAVAW cause a fairly high profile, and group leaders believed it was time to show Warner and Atlantic the extent of WAVAW's grassroots support. Their goal for May was to generate a minimum of 1,000 letters to Ostin and 1,000 letters to Ertegun to be received by June 1. Members of Los Angeles WAVAW thought they could produce 500 letters in Southern California alone. Ideally, however, letters would arrive from all over the United States, and from men and women of diverse backgrounds. "It is necessary that WEA be confronted with evidence of the scope of public concern around this issue – both the geographic and the social scope," WAVAW members wrote.[98] In fact, WAVAW consciously targeted its May education efforts to civic, religious, and professional groups to assure the widest possible range of letters. Contacts inside the recording industry had informed WAVAW leaders that WEA was afraid that the boycott of their products would spread beyond the feminist community to other groups,

[94] Julia London and Jeane K. Bendorf to Joe Smith, April 15, 1977, Box 15, Los Angeles WAVAW Papers.

[95] London and Bendorf to Smith, Los Angeles WAVAW Papers..

[96] Joe Smith to Julia London, April 22, 1977, Los Angeles WAVAW Papers.

[97] Julia London, Joan Belknap and Beth Grey to Sisters, April 1977, Press Packet – LA file, Boston WAVAW Papers.

[98] London, Belknap and Grey to Sisters, Boston WAVAW Papers.

such as the conservative Christian organizations like Citizens for Decency and Morality in Media.[99] WAVAW hoped that a flood of letters from people associated with groups as varied as the Boy Scouts and the American Medical Association would show WEA that its fears were justified.

The WAVAW chapters poured their efforts into the national May letter-writing campaign. Many concentrated on additional community screenings of the WAVAW slide show. The slide show consisted of thirty images from popular record albums, such as *Black and Blue*, that illustrated the persistent problem of violence against women. The slides contained both blatant and subtle examples of violence, and was crafted to help viewers understand the pervasiveness of this social problem. "The power of our organization and our materials lies in the vivid connection we make between the ads we see everyday in our normal environment and our real life experiences of abuse, assault, victimization, and discrimination that are condoned and reinforced by this almost unnoticed-because-always-there ad environment," [emphasis in original] London wrote in a letter that was sent out to each slide show presenter along with a script prepared in the national office. "The concentration of album graphics in the CR [consciousness-raising] type situation of the slide program creates a powerful emotional experience and energy that can lead to action ... when focused on a definite target."[100] As each slide was shown, the WAVAW speaker offered the critical analysis of the image that appeared in the script and explained how it reflected myths about women enjoying and deserving abuse. At the end of the slide show, the WAVAW representative would turn off the projector, and hand out writing paper and a fact sheet that provided background information and a structured outline to help each viewer write a letter of protest to a WEA company.[101] The audience members wrote letters on the spot, which were then collected and mailed to the record companies.

WAVAW was quite shrewd in soliciting letters from the slide show audiences. First, the letters were often emotional and impassioned, as the writers had just finished watching a slide show that purposely featured the record industry's most offensive artwork. Second, the WAVAW speaker was in a position to give explicit instructions as to what the letters ought to say. For example, the WAVAW representative would ask the letter-writers *not* to identify themselves as WAVAW members or affiliates. "Identify yourself in terms of occupation, life-role, and/or as a member of civic, professional, etc. groups," she advised. "It's OK to mention the boycott and say you're supporting it, but we do not want WEA to imagine that the only people who care about this issue are 'WAVAW people.' It is crucial that they see the extent of support in the broadest possible terms."[102] Letter writers were encouraged

[99] "WEA Boycott," *WAVAW Newsletter* no. 1 (May 1977): 1.
[100] Julia London to Dear Sisters, n.d., Box 14A, Los Angeles WAVAW Papers.
[101] "Women Against Violence Against Women," *Ms.*, January 1978, 86.
[102] "The WEA Boycott: Basic Facts for Letter-Writers," n.d. Branch Literature file, Boston WAVAW Papers.

to mention instances of rape, battering, or other violent episodes that had touched their lives to give the correspondence strong emotional appeal and credibility. The WAVAW speaker also instructed the writers to request a formal response. Every letter, they insisted, ought to demand that the company change all existing violent album covers; send the writer a corporate policy statement regarding the use of violence against women on albums and in associated advertising; and specify a date by which the new album covers would be in stores. Furthermore, they told the writers to warn WCI that they would be spreading news of the company's lack of corporate responsibility to their friends and family members.[103]

Within WAVAW's organizational papers, there are hundreds of examples of the kinds of letters that people wrote after viewing the slide show. One presentation at Los Angeles' Cypress Community College during the May letter-writing campaign resulted in dozens of angry letters to Warner and Atlantic calling for corporate social responsibility. "I am a mother of seven," wrote one woman. "I lived in a battering household thru (sic) 15 years of marriage. I would really like you to reexamine your record jackets and exactly what they are saying about women as victims."[104] Another woman described herself as a mother and a student in a letter to Atlantic's Ertegun, and expressed her horror at the company's album graphics. "We have just witnessed a lecture with slides that is repulsive and horrible to see what is used to sell products. ... Please this is violence and can influence rape and battering. Your responsibility is for better advertising (sic)."[105] A California grandmother expressed her fear that young men might internalize and subsequently act on myths about violence. "I was disgusted and appalled to see some of your record covers," she wrote to Warner's Ostin. "I have a young grandson who will be soon buying records and I will do all I can to be sure that he does not have his values affected by your cheap advertisements. To depict violence against women to sell a product is unthinkable."[106]

Similar letters supporting the boycott poured into the WEA offices from around the country. The feminist folk singer Alix Dobkin wrote from New York to express her support for the national boycott. "I am a regular consumer of recorded music," she wrote to Ostin, "but from now on I will resist Warners products unless I have assurances that you have changed your shameful policies toward women."[107] A woman from Mankato, Minnesota identified herself

[103] "Effective Action Each Individual Can Take," December 25, 1976, Box 5, Los Angeles WAVAW Papers.

[104] Rona Bulone, Anaheim, CA; to Atlantic Records, May 11, 1977, Box 7, Los Angeles WAVAW Papers.

[105] Mildred Allen, Garden Grove, CA; to Ahmet Ertegun, May 11, 1977, Box 7, Los Angeles WAVAW Papers.

[106] Claire Kellman, Crescenta, CA; to Mo Ostin, May 17, 1977, Box 7, Los Angeles WAVAW Papers.

[107] Alix Dobkin, Preston Hollow, NY; to Mo Ostin, August 9, 1977, Box 7, Los Angeles WAVAW Papers.

in a letter sent to both Ostin and Ertegun as a community mental health counselor working with victims of rape, battering, and child abuse. "Sexist and violent record covers must be removed from the market immediately," she demanded. "I can assure you that I am not a lone angry woman, but have a substantial number of women and men behind me."[108] She warned that they would be boycotting all Warner/Atlantic/Elektra records until the offensive covers were eliminated. Nancy Wells, a business manager for a San Pedro, California literary journal, wrote to Ostin in July 1977: "You would not show an animal being violated or beaten – your dog or cat is not photographed being beaten or brutalized," she pointed out. "Our local YWCA has aided 161 women and their children who have been brutalized since May 1977. The men learned it was socially acceptable somewhere in our society, and you are certainly contributing to that image."[109] In Los Angeles, the visual artist and anti-violence activist Suzanne Lacy treated Ertegun to a particularly biting critique, drawing connections between Atlantic's album covers and women's fear of rape:

> Since I doubt that you have ever felt what it is like to be followed home on a dark night (and every woman I know has had this feeling), to be stalked in the street, the least you could do is listen to the voices of the women who have had that experience ... who don't find its depiction on record covers or in the newspapers one bit exciting, titillating or provoking. Your actions in allowing those images to adorn your records are continuing "the rape culture" that exists in the United States.[110]

Through the letter writing campaign, WAVAW did more than advance its agenda with the WEA record companies. The organization informed thousands of people about the Warner boycott, recruited new supporters, and shared the powerful potential of political activism. Many of the slide show attendees who wrote letters to the president of Warner Bros. Records or the chairman of the board of Atlantic Records had never engaged in political action before. WAVAW tried to teach their audiences that every single letter mattered. "While people are writing," the slide show script prompted WAVAW representatives, "ask them to imagine being Mo Ostin or Ahmet Ertegun and receiving 1,000 letters. The presence of 1,000 letters ... all hand written! They cannot be ignored."[111] WAVAW believed that every letter would bring the record companies closer to meeting feminist demands. Indeed, WAVAW records indicate that the May letter-writing campaign was a great success, with more than 1,000 letters pouring into Warner and Atlantic headquarters.

[108] Mary Ellen Stone, Mankato, MN; to Mo Ostin and Ahmet Ertegun, December 6, 1977, Box 7, Los Angeles WAVAW Papers.

[109] Nancy Wells, San Pedro, CA; to Mo Ostin, July 25, 1977, Box 6, Los Angeles WAVAW Papers.

[110] Suzanne Lacy, Venice, CA; to Ahmet Ertegun, September 18, 1977, Box 7, Los Angeles WAVAW Papers.

[111] "The WAVAW Slide Show," 1977, Boston WAVAW Papers.

The companies were so swamped with consumer complaints that they had to resort to sending out form letters that addressed concerns about images of violence against women.

From the start, letter writing was a core component of WAVAW activism. A document distributed by the national chapter explained the twofold purpose of letter writing: "1) to protest in order to create change, and 2) to help you, the letter writer, realize and implement your power as a feminist and a consumer."[112] Early WAVAW organizers, many of whom were seasoned activists, understood that letter writing could give a political neophyte the confidence to move on to bigger projects.[113] Their campaigns aimed to empower women and to show that their actions could bring about change. "You have a right to be angry, upset, or concerned. Use your power," WAVAW urged in reference to abusive record companies. "Tell them you will not buy their product, until the ad campaign is improved, discontinued, etc. Tell your friends and get them to write or call. Our Power lies in numbers!!!" [emphasis in original][114] Each woman opposing WEA was a force to be reckoned with, WAVAW reasoned, because her sentiments were likely to be shared by others. "Sending letters like this, and not buying these companies' records are the most important things you can do," WAVAW advised potential letter writers. "Large corporations take consumer complaints seriously; for every letter they receive, they figure there are another 9 people angry at them."[115] WAVAW's faith in the power of letters was rewarded. Following the May campaign, Ertegun ended a year-long refusal to comment on Atlantic Records' corporate policies.

In July 1977, members of Los Angeles WAVAW and other individuals who had sent letters of complaint to Atlantic Records received a form letter that bore Ertegun's signature. The letter did not address WAVAW demands, and stated only that: "To my knowledge, Atlantic Records has never had an album cover that depicted violence against women." The only exception, Ertegun wrote, was the "alleged portrayal" of violence in the advertisements for *Black and Blue*. And in that instance, Ertegun crowed, "I ordered the campaign terminated and all advertising and billboards were immediately withdrawn." As WAVAW pointed out in its national newsletter, Ertegun had taken down the Sunset Strip billboard and canceled a series of radio spots,

[112] "Letter Writing Tips Or Your Pen Can Make a Difference," n.d., Film Industry file, Boston WAVAW Papers.

[113] London, Belknap and Grey to Sisters, Boston WAVAW Papers. "… [W]riting letters is a very easy (and fast) first step that people can take who have not before been involved with consumer activism; and if we can get them to take a first step, we can often get them to take a second step."

[114] "Letter Writing Tips Or Your Pen Can Make a Difference," n.d., Film Industry file, Boston WAVAW Papers.

[115] Jo Delaplaine, "Stabbing the Beast in the Belly: Women Against Violence Against Women," *off our backs* 7 (November 1977), 9.

but the in-store displays and magazine ads remained. Further, Ertegun failed to mention that he took action only when threatened with imminent public exposure at a WAVAW press conference. "It therefore comes as a surprise to me," he continued in the letter, "that we continue to be singled out for reprimand by groups who seem to be under the impression that we are in some way condoning violence against women."[116] Recipients of the letter were disappointed by Ertegun's response, and baffled by his claim that Atlantic Records had been unjustly singled out and punished for a practice that it "never" followed.

Some women wrote back. "I appreciate your taking the time to send me your form letter in defense of Atlantic Recording Corporation," a woman living in Knoxville, Tennessee replied to Ertegun with thinly veiled contempt. "Can your company be in such desperate financial trouble that you must exploit half of society in order to make money...? ...Why not make a positive statement to the record buying public with an intensive anti-violence campaign rather than the poor job of justification of your present policy."[117] The responses fell on deaf ears; Ertegun was clearly not ready to make concessions to WAVAW.

Increasing the Pressure on Warner Communications

Despite the success of the May letter-writing campaign and an August 1977 story about WAVAW in the *New York Times* that stated that there was "tangible evidence" that the organization was making "inroads" in its campaign, Warner Communications made no formal overture to WAVAW to end the boycott.[118] WAVAW leaders acknowledged that their efforts had limited economic impact on WEA, but they believed that the record companies would tire of the negative publicity. "Its impact on the level of public consciousness and embarrassment for WEA has already more than begun to take effect; and as the campaign spreads throughout the country, that impact will become many times greater," London assured members.[119] In the meantime, members of the national chapter wanted to increase pressure on WEA. London turned to local feminist artists to plan a major media event. She was closely tied to this community through her studies with Suzanne Lacy at the Feminist Studio Workshop.

On August 30, 1977, members of Los Angeles WAVAW partnered with the performance artist Leslie Labowitz and students from the Feminist Studio

116 "Atlantic Issues Misleading Letter," *WAVAW Newsletter* 2 (August 1977): 1–2. See also, Ahmet Ertegun, Chairman, Atlantic Records, to Whom It May Concern, July 1, 1977, Box 10, Los Angeles WAVAW Papers.

117 Bee DeSelm, Knoxville, TN; to Ahmet Ertegun, August 24, 1977, Box 10, Los Angeles WAVAW Papers.

118 Eleanor Charles, "Shelving Violence," *New York Times*, August 7, 1977, section 5, p. 2.

119 London, Belknap and Grey to Sisters, Boston WAVAW Papers.

Workshop to present a street theater performance and media event. Labowitz had just returned from a five-year stint living in Spain and West Germany, where she had studied on a Fulbright grant at the Art Academy in Dusseldorf with her mentor, Joseph Beuys. Beuys was renowned for his conceptualization of art as a social tool, and his belief that art could be used as a form of political action and community building. Labowitz brought this conviction back to Southern California, where she began to collaborate with other artists, particularly Lacy – a student of Judy Chicago and the avant-garde "happenings" artist Alan Kaprow – to develop "a political art that was participatory, egalitarian and reflective of both the personal and collective truth of women's experiences."[120] Kaprow had taught Lacy that art could be politically meaningful by engaging directly with social issues and life events, creating performances that demanded active audience responses.[121] The problem of violence against women was a social issue that lent itself to this kind of collaborative, cathartic confrontation between artist and audience. Labowitz, for one, was shocked by the contrast between her physical freedom and sense of well-being on the streets of Europe during daytime and nighttime hours, and the intense fear that she experienced when traveling around Los Angeles in the evening.[122] When WAVAW approached Labowitz with its desire to create activist art that would critique dominant media representations and change cultural attitudes about violence against women, a mutual commitment to achieving social change was evident.[123]

In response, Labowitz created *Record Companies Drag Their Feet*, a performance that expressed the powerful emotions of anguish and fury that emerged when women were confronted by *Black and Blue* and a music industry that refused to hear their pleas. Three women cast as male record executives dressed up as roosters, wearing brightly painted rooster headpieces and men's business suits. The three "executives" drove up and down Sunset Boulevard in a gold Cadillac convertible, allowing plenty of time for photographers and camera crews to capture their images. Finally, they got out of the car and entered a mock record company office, which the artists had constructed under a billboard advertising the rock group Kiss and their album, *Love Gun*. The office featured a large executive desk covered with stacks of cash and gold records. Behind it, the roosters strutted around with their chests stuck out, imitating arrogant male record executives and parodying the greed of businessmen who knowingly profited from violence against women. Women entered the office and tried to communicate their fears and concerns, but the executives ignored them

120 Suzanne Lacy, "The Name of the Game," *Art Journal* 50, no. 2 (1991): 65.

121 On Lacy's feminist activist performance art, see Vivien Green Fryd, "Suzanne Lacy's Three Weeks in May: Feminist Activist Performance Art as 'Expanded Public Pedagogy,' *NWSA Journal* 19, no. 1 (Spring 2007): 23–36.

122 "Leslie Labowitz Interview," conducted by Ginger-Wolfe Suarez, *InterReview*, Journal 07. Available online at: http://www.interreview.org/issue07.html (accessed January 5, 2010).

123 Personal conversation with Suzanne Lacy, November 12, 2008.

FIGURE 4.2. *Record Companies Drag Their Feet*, created by Leslie Labowitz and the Feminist Studio Workshop in conjunction with WAVAW. Women held up signs in an effort to communicate their concerns to male record executives, but were ignored. The executives standing behind the desk wore brightly colored rooster headpieces to symbolize their cocky attitudes, and the arrogance and greed of businessmen who chose to profit from violence against women. Rape statistics on a giant graph in the background indicated a dramatic annual rise post-1970. Women standing in front of the graph held up examples of offensive album covers, including, at left, the Ohio Players' *Pleasure*, across which they scrawled: "This is a crime against women." This protest took place under a billboard for the rock group Kiss promoting their album, *Love Gun*, a title that clearly linked sexuality with violence. *Photo courtesy of the Millard Sheets Library, Otis College of Art and Design.*

and concentrated on polishing the gold records. Finally, the women resorted to holding up signs:

I Wish the Media Wouldn't Insult, Demean, Dehumanize Me By Their Images;

I Don't Want To Be Treated Like A Piece of Meat;

I Wish I Could Walk Home Alone At Night: Love Is Not Violence.

Other women pointed to a large "counterbillboard" behind the desk meant to oppose the one for *Love Gun*. It featured Federal Crime Index statistics on the frequency of rape from 1970 onward that indicated dramatic annual increases. Other participants held up posters displaying offensive record album covers. At the close of the event, the executives spilled a bucket of red paint over the money on the desk, symbolizing the "blood money" that record companies earned from selling images of violence against women.[124] The performance

[124] Leslie Labowitz and Suzanne Lacy, "Evolution of a Feminist Art," *Heresies* 6 (1978): 84.

FIGURE 4.3. WAVAW leader Julia London (wearing striped shirt, center) and artist Leslie Labowitz (wearing white shirt, right) give a statement to television and newspaper reporters at the conclusion of *Record Companies Drag Their Feet*. A display of offensive album covers released by the Warner, Elektra and Atlantic music companies is visible at the bottom right. *Photo courtesy of Leslie Labowitz-Starus.*

ended when twenty women draped the set with an enormous banner that read: "Don't Support Violence – Boycott!"[125] Labowitz and London subsequently gave a statement to the assembled media representatives, flanked by a display of egregious WEA album covers. The event received extensive television coverage, including spots on every Los Angeles area evening news broadcast and a write-up in *Variety*.[126]

The street theater performance illustrated feminist artists' commitment to create art that was politically meaningful, that engaged directly with social issues and demanded audience responses. By exposing the complicity of the music industry, Labowitz and her partners revealed how men profited from violence against women and explained the destructive effects of violence on women's lives. At the same time, the performance expressed hopefulness in changing the consciousness of music industry executives with regard to their damaging policies and callous attitudes. Feminist activist art sought not only to protest negative images, but also to promote alternative, positive images as an expression of faith in the possibility of a better world, free, in this case,

[125] Leslie Labowitz and Suzanne Lacy, "Feminist Media Strategies for Political Performance," in *The Feminism and Visual Culture Reader*, ed. Amelia Jones (London: Routledge, 2003), 307.

[126] "Media Event Successful," *WAVAW Newsletter* no. 3 (November 1977): 1.

of anti-woman violence.[127] A media event like *Record Companies Drag Their Feet* presented such a feminist perspective, if only briefly, displacing the usual patriarchal viewpoint to reveal hidden aspects of women's lives, such as a constant fear of sexual violence, as well as the demand for better conditions. The WAVAW performance was one of a series of anti-violence performances created in the 1970s by Labowitz, Lacy, and other Los Angeles-based feminist artists, in which the artists attempted to reframe cultural views of violence, especially rape, as a pervasive crime of male power and control.

Over the course of the next several months, WAVAW chapters around the nation pressured the WEA companies to deal with the boycott. By this time, additional chapters had been established in Boston, Philadelphia, New York City, Cleveland, Knoxville, New Haven, Seattle, Portland, and Denver, and each one poured its efforts into deluging the labels with letters and telephone complaints. On May 2, 1978, six members of New York WAVAW created a stir by demonstrating outside the New York Hilton Hotel where the annual Warner Communications' shareholders' meeting took place. The women distributed nearly 1,500 leaflets that described WCI's exploitation of women and the parent company's intransigence in dealing with the issue. On one side of the leaflet, WAVAW reproduced offensive album cover art from Atlantic Records, and on the other they printed Ertegun's form letter response to inquiries about his company's use of images of violence against women.[128] One member of NY-WAVAW, Barbara Trees, distributed almost 500 leaflets inside the hotel to WCI shareholders.

Meanwhile, New York WAVAW's Pamela Brennan attended the WCI meeting. As the owner of one share of WCI stock, Brennan had the right to address the audience.[129] According to her own account of the meeting, she spoke to the 700 shareholders present, reviewing the history of the WAVAW-WEA conflict and denouncing WCI's board of directors for "buck passing" and failing to establish a policy against the use of violence against women. She urged

[127] On this aspect of feminist activist art, see Mary Jo Aagerstoun and Elissa Auther, "Considering Feminist Activist Art," *NWSA Journal* 19, no. 1 (Spring 2007): vii–xiv.

[128] "WAVAW Confronts WCI Shareholders," *WAVAW Newsletter* nos. 5–6 (September 1978): 1.

[129] In 1983, the Securities and Exchange Commission approved new regulations designed to limit activist shareholders' abilities to raise social issues at corporate annual meetings. The bulk of the regulations dealt with shareholders' right to propose resolutions affecting company business, such as resolutions regarding corporate activities in South Africa, the building of nuclear power plants, the sale of infant formula to Third World countries, and the production of napalm. The Commission decided to require that those proposing resolutions hold at least $1,000 worth of a company's stock for a minimum of one year (longer than the lifespan of many activist groups) and to require that a losing resolution obtain at least 5 percent of the vote for it to qualify for resubmission the following year. In addition, the rules would allow a company to omit from the proxy material a proposal if it dealt with substantially the same subject matter as a proposal in the previous year. The regulations were regarded as a major blow by activists who used the public corporate forums, as WAVAW did, to apply pressure to companies to exercise social responsibility. See Robert D. Hershey, Jr. "New Rules on Holders' Proposals," *The New York Times*, August 17, 1983, C1.

the shareholders to demand corporate responsibility, and later reported that her remarks were greeted with enthusiastic applause from the shareholders present.[130] Steven J. Ross, president of Warner Communications, offered the standard response, insisting that most contracts gave the right of creative control over to the artists.[131] The WAVAW cause met with sympathy from the audience, and from at least one board member, Bess Myerson, the former Miss America. Elected to the board of directors of WCI in 1976, Myerson had served as commissioner of consumer affairs of the City of New York from 1969 to 1973, and was well known for her work as a columnist for the *Chicago Tribune-New York Daily News* syndicate and as a contributing editor to *Redbook* magazine. Intrigued by the WAVAW presentation, she contacted members of the organization after the meeting and sat down with Trees and Brennan on May 24, 1978. She agreed to make sure that each member of the WCI board received a copy of a WAVAW packet containing images of the offensive WEA album covers.[132]

The alliance with Myerson cheered the WAVAW chapters, but the financial data from the stockholders' meeting made it clear that the boycott was not crushing Warner's bottom line. For the six months ending June 30, 1978, Warner Communications reported its best second quarter ever, with revenues, net income, and earnings per share at record levels. The company credited continued growth in Warner's two largest divisions, recorded music and filmed entertainment, for the strong figures. Recorded music showed revenue gains of 17 percent for the second quarter of 1977.[133] WAVAW had to hope that the stigma of negative publicity would be enough to persuade Warner to meet the organization's demands.

In July 1978, the Los Angeles WAVAW office began to coordinate a national meeting for all WAVAW chapters. The meeting took place September 15–17 in New York City, and key members from the Los Angeles, Boston, Philadelphia, Rhode Island, New York, Knoxille, Maryland, Connecticut, and North Carolina chapters attended. In total, twenty of the twenty-five WAVAW chapters were represented at the meeting. The top priority was finding a way to inject some new energy into the boycott, followed by discussion of the national organizational structure, which some chapters believed was too loose.[134] Agreeing that the boycott was at a standstill and desiring some

[130] Pam Brennan, Memo, "Meeting with Bess Myerson, WCI Board of Directors and New York-WAVAW (Pam Brennan and Barbara Trees) and How it Came to Be," May 25, 1978, Box 10, Los Angeles WAVAW Papers.

[131] Warner Communications, Inc., "1978 Annual Report," August 4, 1978. Document in Recording Industry File, Boston WAVAW Papers.

[132] Julia London to All WAVAW groups, May 25, 1978, Correspondence: LA file, Boston WAVAW Papers.

[133] "Best-Ever WCI Quarter; Credit Music, Cable, Games and Video," *Variety*, July 23, 1978, 4. See also Warner Communications, Inc., "1978 Annual Report," Boston WAVAW Papers.

[134] Lisa Kellman, National WAVAW Office to WAVAW chapters, July 7, 1978, Correspondence: LA file, Boston WAVAW Papers. See also "National Meeting," *WAVAW Newsletter* no. 5–6 (September 1978): 1.

response from WEA, the chapter representatives decided to increase pressure on the companies by calling for an intensified Christmas season campaign. They would ask holiday shoppers to boycott WEA records when they were out purchasing gifts, a tactic that might finally hold Warner and Atlantic's attention. The WAVAW representatives decided to initiate the effort on November 24, 1978, the day after Thanksgiving and the official start of the holiday buying season.[135] Boston WAVAW designed and printed a special holiday campaign leaflet and poster for all chapters to use. New York WAVAW wrote a news release describing the holiday campaign, and Philadelphia WAVAW mailed it to news outlets, including national newspapers, women's magazines, and feminist journals.[136]

The holiday campaign kicked off in cities across the nation with activities designed to attract the attention of shoppers. New York WAVAW demonstrated in Herald Square, near several major department stores. In Boston, WAVAW and the Take Back the Night Coalition cosponsored a march from the State House to the downtown shopping district. Philadelphia WAVAW picketed Sam Goody's record store, and Los Angeles WAVAW picketed outside of two Westwood Village record stores, Tower Records and the Wherehouse. Thirty members of Los Angeles WAVAW carried signs reading "Stop Violence Against Women" and "Don't Promote Violence with Your Gift."[137] In all cities, shoppers were handed leaflets that stated that domestic violence increased during the holiday season, and that the purchase of records whose covers promoted violence could translate into danger for friends or family members. The leaflets included illustrations of four violent album covers, recording industry sales data, statistics on rape and assault, and the names of the WEA companies. The leaflet challenged every shopper to think twice before buying a WEA album with its provocative headline: "Does your gift do violence to women?"[138]

An End in Sight

As the two-and-a-half year dispute dragged on, WCI began to grow uneasy about the public relations impact of the WAVAW boycott. The boycott was not making a financial dent in Warner's bottom line; earnings in the music division were growing steadily and contributing mightily to company revenues. But the boycott was damaging to WCI's public image, and the WAVAW activists posed a constant, unpredictable threat. WAVAW member Brennan

[135] Press Release, "WAVAW Pushes Boycott of Record Albums for Holidays," October 9, 1978, Correspondence: LA file, Boston WAVAW Papers.

[136] Julia London to WAVAW Chapters, "1978 Holiday Season Campaign," November 5, 1978, Correspondence: LA file, Boston WAVAW Papers.

[137] "30 Women Protest 'Gifts of Violence,'" *Los Angeles Times*, November 25, 1978, section A, p. 27.

[138] News Release, "For Release Saturday, November 25, 1978" Box 7, Los Angeles WAVAW Papers.

alerted 700 Warner stockholders to the conflict at the 1978 annual meeting; all those not present learned of the WAVAW-Warner struggle in the annual report, which contained a full description of the proceedings.[139] WCI executives had to fear that this kind of publicity would help WAVAW spread the boycott to other groups. Conservative Christian organizations such as Morality in Media and Citizens for Decency were well funded, highly organized, savvy about publicity and politics, and had membership bases far exceeding WAVAW's small numbers. Besides this threat, Warner had to deal with periodic high-level media coverage of the boycott, which rarely cast the company in a favorable light. In addition, the WAVAW chapters used the group slide show presentations to generate thousands of letters of complaint addressed to the WEA record companies. Each of those letters had to be answered, draining staff time, energy, and morale. When WAVAW announced the 1978 holiday season push, it became clear to WCI executives that it was time to resolve the situation.

Over the next six months, WCI began to indicate a desire to put the dispute to rest. In a memo to WAVAW members that recounted the chronology of the WEA boycott, Joan Howarth, a twenty-six-year-old lesbian feminist who had graduated from Smith College and was pursuing her law degree at the University of Southern California, noted that the album covers released by Warner Bros. and Atlantic Records "started looking better" in the period following the holiday campaign. The change was dramatic, so much so that WAVAW's surveys of album covers revealed that "at some point they stopped using blatant images of violence against women," albeit without announcing a formal corporate policy. However, the final "breakthrough" with WCI, as Howarth described it, came during the first week of May 1979, just days before the corporation's annual meeting.[140]

In April 1979, the Los Angeles WAVAW chapter presented its slide show to an audience at the University of California at Los Angeles (UCLA) School of Medicine. At the conclusion of the program, the WAVAW representatives asked audience members to write letters. Mary Zupanc, a physician in the audience, wrote to WCI and requested a corporate policy governing the use of images of violence against women. Instead of the usual form letter, Dr. Zupanc received a lengthy response from David Horowitz, one of WCI's highest-ranking executives with primary oversight of the recording division.[141] Horowitz's letter, which arrived just days before the annual meeting, stated that the company

[139] Warner Communications, Inc., "1978 Annual Report," August 4, 1978. Document in Recording Industry file, Boston WAVAW Papers.

[140] Memorandum, Joan Howarth to WAVAW women, August 25, 1979, Box 15, Los Angeles WAVAW Papers.

[141] In October 1976, Warner Communications established an office of the president, which was jointly held by four individuals. Three of the men named to fill this office already held posts with Warner. They included Jay Emmet, Emanuel Gerard, and David Horowitz. The fourth man named was Kenneth Rosen, president of a merchant banking concern. The office of president had previously been held by Steven J. Ross, who remained chairman and CEO of

had already instituted such a policy. "As a matter of Corporate policy, Warner Communications is opposed to the depiction of violence, against women or men, on album covers, in promotional material or otherwise," he wrote. "This policy has been communicated to each of our record companies, which have been enforcing it to the fullest possible extent." The letter assured Zupanc that "[T]oday all album cover art and related promotional materials are carefully reviewed, initially at the Art Department level, and when questions arise, at the upper management level and in discussions with the recording artists involved, to assure that the materials conform to the Company's policy." In a restrained nod to WAVAW, Horowitz continued: "We do give the WAVAW organization credit for raising this issue and directing attention to it with specific reference to album art."[142] Both Horowitz and Zupanc sent copies of the letter to the Los Angeles WAVAW office.

The Horowitz letter stunned WAVAW leaders. When had this policy gone into effect? What guidelines were used in reviewing promotional materials? Julia London and other WAVAW leaders called art directors and marketing specialists at Warner Bros. Records, Atlantic, and Elektra and found "confusion" regarding a policy. One individual told them that he had received a memo; another told them that the standard had always been and continued to be "good taste;" others had no knowledge of a new policy regarding images of violence.[143] Contrary to Horowitz's statements, it was clear that the policy had *not* been communicated effectively to Warner's subsidiary record companies. Members of New York and Boston WAVAW made plans to demonstrate for the second year in a row at the WCI shareholders' meeting in New York City.

Clearly, WCI executives had hoped that a quiet policy shift might be sufficient to end the WAVAW boycott. The letter to Zupanc, with a copy sent to Los Angeles WAVAW, was intended as a low-profile white flag. This approach, had it succeeded, would have spared WCI the unenviable position of publicly announcing a decision to accede to WAVAW's demands. When WAVAW activists turned up to demonstrate at the 1979 annual meeting, armed with proof that WCI employees were not familiar with the new policy, it was clear that the letter would not satisfy them. Following the meeting, WCI officials agreed to make a joint announcement with WAVAW to publicize the new policy.

the company. In announcing the appointments, Ross said that WCI's rapid growth required a group of key leaders to share management responsibility. Horowitz joined Warner in 1973 after serving as vice president and general counsel of Columbia Pictures Industries Inc. See "Four Will Fill Warner Communications Job of Office of the President," *The Wall Street Journal*, October 26, 1976, 22.

142 David H. Horowitz, Office of the President, WCI to Mary Zupanc, M.D., May 4, 1979, Box 9, Los Angeles WAVAW Papers.

143 Memorandum, Joan Howarth to WAVAW women, August 25, 1979, Box 15, Los Angeles WAVAW Papers.

From May 1979 to August 1979, both organizations worked to craft a mutually acceptable statement that would announce the end of the boycott and the introduction of a formal corporate policy banning the use of images of violence against women. WAVAW drafted a statement that held WCI accountable for its contribution to the violence problem, but that commended the organization for its new policy, or as London expressed it, for offering "an important example of an industry leader taking this step."[144] WCI, in turn, drafted a statement that denied any connection with long-term wrongdoing, minimized the extent of the conflict between WCI and WAVAW, and presented the policy as something that had already been in place for a significant period of time. London wrote to Horowitz to remind him that the boycott would not end until a statement was agreed on and until it was jointly released to the media by WCI and WAVAW. "WAVAW is eager to be able to announce an end to this boycott, an announcement that should most appropriately be made when WCI's corporate policy is announced publicly," she wrote.[145]

Slowly, over the course of several months, the organizations found common ground. In addition to hammering out a statement, each imposed terms for the end of the boycott and the immediate aftermath. First, WAVAW insisted that the new corporate policy had to be circulated to all employees of the WEA record companies. Second, WAVAW asked WCI to distribute the news release and policy statement to all national news services, as well as to the entertainment industry trade papers and feminist publications. Finally, Horowitz would be required to arrange a meeting for the art directors of Atlantic, Elektra/Asylum, and Warner Bros. Records and WAVAW representatives to facilitate better mutual understanding of the new policy.[146] In return, WCI exacted a promise that neither WEA record album covers nor advertising images would be shown as examples of abusive images at the joint press conference. Some WAVAW members objected, arguing that WCI expected feminists to sweep years of exploitation under the rug. But London and Howarth argued that WAVAW needed to start treating WCI as an ally, a strategy that might influence other record companies to adopt similar policies. "[T]here is no point in grinding WCI badness into the ground when what they have done now is very commendable and puts WAVAW in a much stronger position to deal with other companies," Howarth wrote.[147] Instead of revisiting Warner's mistakes, she urged WAVAW members to view their partnership as a first step toward additional media reform.

144 Julia London, WAVAW to David Horowitz, Office of the President, WCI, July 25, 1979, Correspondence: LA file, Boston WAVAW Papers.

145 London to Horowitz, Boston WAVAW Papers.

146 The meeting took place on February 12, 1980, at the Beverly Wilshire Hotel in Beverly Hills, California. The WAVAW representatives began the meeting by showing the WAVAW slide show to the art directors and WCI executives present.

147 Joan Howarth, "Press Conference and Release of Statement," n.d., Correspondence: LA file, Boston WAVAW Papers.

After three years of national protests, slide shows, letter writing, staging public performance art, and boycotting, WAVAW achieved victory. On November 8, 1979, WAVAW and WCI made joint statements to the media at dual press conferences in New York and Los Angeles announcing that an agreement had been reached. "The WCI record group opposes the depiction of violence, against women or men, on album covers and in related promotional material," Horowitz read from the carefully crafted statement. "This policy expresses the WCI record group's opposition to the exploitation of violence, sexual or otherwise, in any form.... The WCI record divisions have been implementing this policy internally and today's announcement, made at the request of WAVAW, formalizes that policy."[148] Howarth spoke next, calling off the nearly three-year boycott of the WEA record companies. "By publicizing this policy," she said, "WCI is acknowledging that the commercial use of visual and other images that trivialize women victims is irresponsible in light of the epidemic proportions of real-life violence against women, most particularly rape and domestic battering." She commended WCI for its leadership, downplayed its lack of corporate responsibility in previous years, and predicted further successes in the WAVAW campaign to reform the music industry. "We do look forward to increased receptivity from other companies as a result of the step taken by the WCI record group, one of the most important leaders in the industry," she advised.[149] The end of the boycott was covered by the Los Angeles news media and entertainment trades, including an extended story in the *Los Angeles Times* that discussed the women's plan to step up pressure on the recording industry.[150]

In a memorandum to all the WAVAW chapters that outlined the terms of the agreement, London could barely contain her joy. A grassroots community of women had compelled a major media conglomerate to assume corporate responsibility for the images of violence against women that it used to sell products. "All in all, WAVAW has achieved an <u>important</u> precedent, a first, something to build on and use. We're on our way!!" she wrote. "Three cheers (or more!) to us all who have focused on this and to all our friends inside and outside the movement who have boycotted, talked to store owners, written letters, picketed and organized, and who have supported WAVAW during these last 3 years!" London signed her letter, "In EXALTED sisterhood" [all emphasis in original].[151]

148 News Release, November 8, 1979, Box 15, Los Angeles WAVAW Papers; See also Ed Harrison, "Women and Warners: Forgive and Forget," *Billboard*, November 17, 1979, 3; and Dorothy Townsend, "Firm to Ban Violence on Album Covers," *Los Angeles Times*, November 9, 1979, section 2, p. 1.

149 Howarth, "Press Conference and Release of Statement," Boston WAVAW Papers.

150 Dorothy Townsend, "Firm to Ban Violence on Album Covers," *Los Angeles Times*, November 9, 1979, section 2, p. 1.

151 Memorandum, Julia London to All WAVAW Chapters, "WCI/WAVAW Joint Press Statement on WCI Advertising Policy," October 29, 1979, Correspondence: LA file, Boston WAVAW Papers.

WAVAW Post-Warner: New Challenges

The Warner boycott and the campaign to achieve a corporate policy against violence represented the apex of national WAVAW activity. The Los Angeles office made efforts post-Warner to pressure other record companies to issue similar policies, but most WAVAW chapters turned to local projects once the boycott ended. Without the centralized campaign, it was more difficult for members nationwide to feel connected. The organizational structure had always been loose, with chapters reporting their activities periodically to the national office, and creating local actions as well as participating in the national campaign, but the boycott had served as a unifying force for three years. Once it was over, WAVAW struggled to remain a cohesive organization with concrete goals.

In the national office in Los Angeles, members tried to inaugurate WAVAW "Phase II" by pressuring other record companies to exercise corporate responsibility. In January 1980, on the heels of the WCI victory, the organization sent a letter and information packet about the boycott and the new WCI policy to eighteen major record companies with requests for meetings. WAVAW hoped to use the WCI example to push them to adopt similar anti-violence policies to keep up with the industry leader, or simply out of fear of a boycott. Some momentum was visible in New York, where NY-WAVAW founding member Dorchen Leidholdt, who would later become a WAP leader, had meetings with high-level officers at CBS Records. Most executives offered the same canards as WEA, including claims of artistic control contractually owed to musicians. Without an active boycott in place, the organization found itself at a standstill in its effort to reform music industry advertising. In a 1980 issue of the *WAVAW Newsletter*, the national staff acknowledged that some members were "growing bored with the long fight," and that a new national campaign "would also help all of us feel more connected to a national organization and movement."[152]

During this transitional period, London stepped down as WAVAW's national coordinator, creating even more uncertainty about the organization's future. In the months prior to the end of the WEA boycott, London had warned members that her energy was flagging. "I have finally come to face the fact that I am exhausted, burned-out temporarily," she wrote to members in May 1979. "I have for the last 2 ½ years been doing the work of two people and have also held a part-time subsistence pay job. In the last few months, my efficiency has fallen off, projects have not been well-coordinated, and many which should have been finished by now are still incomplete."[153] Shortly after the culmination of the WCI campaign, London left her position, and the first of a series of new national coordinators recruited from the feminist community stepped up to fill her place. Although London remained involved with the

[152] "WAVAW – Phase II," *WAVAW Newsletter* no. 8 (1980): 1+.

[153] Julia London to Dear Sisters, May 8, 1979, Box 14A, Los Angeles WAVAW Papers.

organization in future years, and even served on its national steering committee, the loss of her dynamic leadership was never overcome. Without her day-to-day vision and guidance, WAVAW was unable to coordinate and sustain a new national media reform campaign.

In the post-Warner period, most chapters dedicated themselves to local projects, particularly protesting violence in mainstream movie advertising. Seattle WAVAW and Los Angeles WAVAW demonstrated against billboards for Paramount Pictures' 1979 film, *Bloodline*, which pictured a dead woman with a thin trail of blood running across her neck.[154] The Los Angeles chapter held a demonstration to oppose director Brian dePalma's 1980 film, *Dressed to Kill*, which they criticized for glamorizing a link between sex and violence. Philadelphia WAVAW picketed several films, including *Bloodline*, *Last Tango in Paris*, and the adult film *The Devil in Miss Jones*. New York WAVAW, Boston WAVAW, and WAP protested United Artists' 1980 film, *Windows*, which featured a lesbian who hired a man to rape a woman she secretly loved, in hopes that the woman would turn to her for support in the aftermath.[155] The film outraged feminists because it presented rape as a crime instigated by one woman against another, a storyline that seemed to absolve the rapist of responsibility for his sexual violence. Chapters around the nation also picketed theaters that showed the 1981 Twentieth Century Fox film, *Tattoo*, which involved a mentally disturbed tattoo artist who kidnapped a female model and tattooed her entire body to perfectly match his own in a bizarre, obsessive declaration of love. The movie was marketed with the tagline, "Every Great Love Leaves Its Mark," prompting Los Angeles WAVAW to argue that the film equated love with acts of violence that left bruises and scars on women's bodies, promoting a dangerous conception of "love" that was "detrimental to the relationships between women and men."[156]

The lack of a cohesive national campaign in the years following Warner was a problem for WAVAW, but the changing nature of the feminist anti-media violence movement had even greater impact. By 1979, WAVAW had two powerful "sister organizations," Women Against Violence in Pornography and Media and Women Against Pornography.[157] As WAVPM and WAP moved into the national spotlight, original set of concerns defined by WAVAW began to morph into something quite different. Specifically, the direction of the movement shifted away from an emphasis on images of overt violence against women in advertising, motion pictures, and everyday popular culture, and away from a focus on harmful effects on men as well as women. In the newer groups, activists talked more about pornography and its role in the objectification and

[154] On Boston WAVAW protest against Windows, see Flyer, "Boycott 'Windows'!!" March 1980, Windows/Cruising file, Boston WAVAW Papers.

[155] "Windows," *WAVAW Newsletter* no. 8 (1980): 6.

[156] Flyer, "Boycott Tattoo," n.d., Box 9, Los Angeles WAVAW Papers.

[157] "Nat'l Meeting," *WAVAW Newsletter* no. 8 (1980): 1.

social subordination of women. These groups were also open to the idea of using legal strategies for control, whereas WAVAW was committed to public education and consumer pressure tactics.

From the start, WAVAW had been careful to avoid defining itself as an "anti-pornography" group. In branch literature prepared by the national office, WAVAW leaders specifically instructed chapter representatives not to talk about pornography. "Talk about violence against women and sex-violence," they urged. Many WAVAW members believed that the term "pornography" would suggest that the organization opposed even nonviolent depictions of sex and endorsed anti-obscenity legislation or censorship. The use of the term might also shroud WAVAW's core objection to the perpetuation of artificial gender roles – woman as victim and man as victimizer – because it was often interpreted as including material related to homosexuality, abortion, and sex education, which had "nothing to do with the destructive and dangerous relationships we are talking about," WAVAW warned.[158] Howarth, one of the most influential members of Los Angeles WAVAW, wrote in the national newsletter that "'pornography' is not a useful word for naming what it is that we are fighting." She pointed out that the term was "both over-inclusive (pulling in erotica and merely sexually explicit materials) and grossly under-inclusive (since it appears to take the heat off of abusive mainstream commercial materials, such as record album advertising)."[159] The group's organizing principles gave members clear direction: "Subsume pornography under violence against women, not the other way around."[160]

Looking at WAVAW's work in retrospect, the organization led an anti-media violence campaign, which was ultimately a very different animal than the feminist anti-pornography campaign that would follow in its footsteps. In the first national newsletter, members described their goals: "Women Against Violence Against Women is an activist organization working to stop the gratuitous use of images of physical and sexual violence against women in mass media – and the real-world violence against women it promotes – through public education, consciousness-raising, and mass consumer action."[161] Their understanding of the violence problem adhered to the radical feminist perspective that portrayals of women as victims and men as brutes perpetuated false gender roles that hurt and demeaned both sexes. They expected media corporations to exercise responsibility when it came to depictions of women and men, rather than resorting to fashionable trends like "brutality chic" that portrayed women as enjoying, deserving, and expecting abusive treatment.

158 LA WAVAW, "Possible Supportive Actions for Persons in Public Relations/Advertising/Marketing," n.d., Branch Literature file, Boston WAVAW Papers.

159 "On Porn: Response by Joan Howarth," *WAVAW Newsletter* no. 8 (1980): 6.

160 LA WAVAW, "Words and Phrases and Ideas for Emphasis," n.d., Organizing Principles file, Boston WAVAW Papers.

161 "Who We Are," *WAVAW Newsletter* no. 1 (May 1977): 4.

WAVAW's consumer action tactics were based on methods that activists had used with great success in Civil Rights and New Left organizing. From its founding, WAVAW rejected government action and argued that women working together could exert sufficient public pressure to achieve social change. Most group members believed that any effort to suppress violent material through legal means would be too dangerous and too divisive for feminists to pursue.

As early as December 1976, when London addressed a group of New York feminists in Susan Brownmiller's apartment, the changes in the movement that would split WAVAW from WAVPM and WAP were visible. Brownmiller was moving in new directions. Praising WAVAW's campaign against abusive record covers in the *New York Times*, she employed the terms "pornography" and "censorship," both of which WAVAW avoided. "Our job is to make it clear that pornography is violence against women, and that is beyond the pale of censorship," Brownmiller said. "I really believe that the feminist movement attack on pornography is important, and this group is launching it."[162] Pornography and censorship were key terms in Brownmiller's lexicon, and as the following chapters will show, they would help define the WAVPM and WAP agendas.

[162] Brozan, 26.

5

Something Inside Me Just Went "Click"

Women Against Violence in Pornography and Media and the Transition to an Anti-Pornography Movement

In August 1977, Max Factor & Co. launched a major advertising campaign to promote its new line of skin cleansers and moisturizers. The multimedia campaign for the new "Self-Defense" products, which included television and radio spots, as well as newspaper advertisements and billboards, was introduced that summer to thirty major U.S. markets. The cosmetics company budgeted $1 million for the initial promotion, or "first flight" of the Self-Defense ads. The "second flight" would include a substantial push during the Christmas holidays. Conceived by the Los Angeles advertising agency of Wells, Rich and Greene, the Max Factor campaign used themes of public safety and environmental pollution to alert women to the danger posed to the skin by smog, dirt, and grime. The agency designed a stark billboard advertisement with blue and white graphics and large block print that resembled an official police bulletin. Its message read like one too. "Warning! A Pretty Face Isn't Safe In This City. Fight Back With Self-Defense."[1]

To a female audience keenly aware of male violence, self-defense was sound advice.[2] At first glance, the Max Factor advertisements concurred. It was important for women to be vigilant on the streets and in their homes, on guard against the threats posed by rapists, muggers, and sexual harassers. Women's groups offered self-defense classes where women could learn karate, judo, and other techniques that could be used to fend off attackers. At second glance, however, it was clear that the Max Factor ads were satirizing the concept of self-defense, mocking women's fears of sexual assault for the purpose of selling cosmetics. "Your face is under constant attack from pollution, smog, the dirt and grime in the air, heat and wind – all drying your skin, making it look

[1] "Environment Hits Skin, Factor Line Fights Back," *Advertising Age*, August 15, 1977, 72.

[2] On the centrality of self-defense to feminist efforts against male violence, see Frédérique Delacoste and Felice Newman, eds., *Fight Back! Feminist Resistance to Male Violence* (Minneapolis, MN: Cleis Press, 1981). See especially "Karate and the Feminist Resistance Movement," 184–196; "Some Facts on Self-Defense," 197–200; and "Do It Yourself Self-Defense," 201–208.

older," the ads warned. "But now, you can fight back. With Self-Defense."[3] The campaign shocked and enraged women for whom violence and sexual exploitation were matters of grave personal and political significance.

Adding insult to injury, many of these women were already predisposed to distrust the beauty industry. Radical feminists urged women to see gendered products such as cosmetics, girdles, and high heels as tools of sexual objectification that lay the groundwork for what Naomi Wolf would later term the "beauty myth." Lotions and creams like "Self-Defense" were advertised in ways that supported the ideology that a woman's major responsibility was to make herself supple and lovely to attract and keep male sexual attention (e.g., to "fight back" against any threat to one's beauty). As Wolf has argued, once the women's movement took hold and challenged the notion that women belonged at home, fulfilling the glorified domestic role, advertisers feared a downturn in consumption. To compensate, they increased the pressure on women to meet narrow standards for appearance that dictated a very thin body and a fashion-model standard of feminine beauty that would be unattainable for most. The Max Factor campaign was an early sign of the transition from *feminine mystique* to *beauty myth*, or the use of rhetorical strategies in advertisements that threatened women as to what might befall them should they abandon the responsibility to pursue idealized beauty standards.

The Self-Defense advertising campaign met with particular hostility in New York City. In an unfortunate turn of events, the "Self-Defense" billboards and subway posters debuted in the midst of a tense summer during which New York police sought the "Son of Sam" serial killer for the murders of six young women. City residents lived in terror as "Son of Sam" eluded authorities at every turn. His brutal slayings and frightening missives promising more violence dominated New York newspaper headlines and the local television news.[4] Advertisements reminding women that "a pretty face isn't safe in this city" took on an alarming double meaning. Most of the campaign copy was similarly regrettable. "Self Defense," crowed the print ads, "protects against the beauty spoilers." The advertising copywriters meant environmental agents like the sun and wind, but some readers interpreted "beauty spoilers" to mean muggers, rapists, and slashers.[5] Many women were disgusted. "I live in Queens near the scene of one of the murders," said a New Yorker. "I noticed the ad the day before 'Son of Sam' was captured. I was immediately struck by – wow! – this is a low way of merchandizing (sic) this product."[6] Another woman described her feelings of exploitation and "inexpressible anger" at the realization that the campaign mocked women's fears of assault and their

[3] Liberation News Service, "A Pretty Face Isn't Safe...," *The Longest Revolution* 2: 1 (October 1977), 7.

[4] Leah Rozen, "Son of Sam – Boon for Dailies," *Advertising Age*, August 15, 1977, 1.

[5] "Max Factor Assaults Women with Ad Campaign," *Women Against Violence in Pornography & Media Newspage* 1, no. 5 (October 1977): 1. (Microforms Collection of the State Historical Society of Wisconsin, Madison, Wis.), hereafter cited as *WAVPM Newspage*.

[6] "Max Factor Assaults Women with Ad Campaign," *WAVPM Newspage*.

efforts to practice "true self-defense," and blatantly manipulated this theme to sell drugstore cold cream.[7]

Within the feminist community, a relatively new anti-violence group stepped up to lead the campaign against Max Factor's "Self Defense." Women Against Violence in Pornography and Media (WAVPM) was an organization based in northern California whose members shared many of the same concerns as WAVAW. Both groups objected to abusive images of women in popular culture, especially advertising, and they connected these images with a culture that demeaned and dehumanized women, and taught men that women were willing victims. Their members shared an analysis of media violence as an ideological tool that reinforced male supremacy and artificial gender roles, and functioned as "a celebration of male power over women and the sexist wish that women's sexuality and values be totally subservient to men's," as WAVPM expressed it.[8] There were tactical similarities too. WAVPM adopted many of the public education, consciousness raising and consumer action techniques favored by WAVAW, including letter writing and picketing. The campaign against Max Factor's "Self Defense" put WAVPM on the map as a nationally recognized sister organization to WAVAW.

WAVAW was leading the movement against sexualized media violence in southern California, just as WAVPM was starting to mobilize northern California women, but the groups diverged in important ways. WAVPM's name, Women Against Violence in Pornography and Media, highlighted the primary distinction: the introduction of "pornography" as a central concern. As discussed in the previous chapter, WAVAW leaders did not use that term. They thought that mainstream commercial media, such as advertising, had a greater impact on people's daily consciousness. They also feared that being against "pornography" would suggest a blanket condemnation of a wide range of sexual expression, including gay, lesbian, and nonviolent sexual images, and would dilute the group's intended focus on acts of violence. Finally, WAVAW members believed that positioning themselves against pornography would raise the specter of new anti-obscenity legislation and censorship, none of which WAVAW endorsed. "Our proclaimed identity is a violence-prevention group committed to long-term strategy and education," members of the Boston WAVAW chapter responded when asked how pornography fit into their organization's agenda.[9] The national WAVAW office in Los Angeles was careful to avoid any mention of pornography in its public statements, although most members regarded the newly formed WAVPM as a sister organization.

[7] Letter, Roberta Spivek to Gene Taylor, Wells, Rich and Greene Advertising Agency, October 27, 1977, Box 2, Folder: Correspondence: Protest Letters, non-WAVPM sponsored, Women Against Violence in Pornography and the Media Records, #96–21, The Gay, Lesbian, Bisexual, Transgender Historical Society, San Francisco, Calif. Cited hereafter as, WAVPM Records, GLBT Historical Society.

[8] Laura Lederer and Diana Russell, "Questions We Get Asked Most Often," *WAVPM NewsPage*, 1, no. 6 (November 1977): 3.

[9] Chapter Literature, "Boston WAVAW History," n.d., Branch Literature file, WAVAW Papers.

A second major difference between WAVAW and WAVPM concerned the groups' beliefs as to whether media violence and/or pornography *caused* actual violence against women. WAVAW did not argue causality; the organization maintained that images of violence *trivialized and condoned* violent behavior against women, and suggested to men that women deserved and enjoyed brutal treatment. In other words, viewing the *Black and Blue* billboard that featured a beaten and bruised woman might lead a man to feel less sympathy for a woman who was raped or to minimize the seriousness of a crime like battering, but it would not necessarily lead him to commit a violent act. Members of WAVPM agreed with WAVAW that the sexual objectification of women, the presentation of women as appropriate targets for violence, and the perpetuation of the myth that women actually enjoyed and expected such treatment were key elements in the maintenance of male social control, but their beliefs also diverged in important ways.

Leaders of the new WAVPM organization argued that the representation of women as sexual objects in violent contexts not only condoned, but actually incited violence against women. Kathy Barry, the radical feminist sociologist, author of *Female Sexual Slavery*, and a founder of WAVPM, insisted that the "causal connections" between pornography and sexual violence were "perfectly evident" to women. "We do not need to follow individual men out of specific pornographic theaters and witness them raping the first woman they see to realize as women what impact pornography has on our lives," she said at WAVPM's 1978 national conference. "We need only appeal to our own common sense."[10] Laura Lederer and Diana E.H. Russell, two of WAVPM's

10 Kathleen Barry, "Beyond Pornography: From Defensive Politics to Creating a Vision," in *Take Back the Night*, 311. Barry's comment about "common sense" also revealed a major divide in the organization over whether or not women needed scientific proof of the causal connection between pornography and violence. Barry argued that demands for evidence placed a "burden of proof" on women and privileged social scientific research conducted with sexist bias and "masculinist values." Many WAVPM members resented the fact that if a male scientist said violence caused rape, people would listen, whereas women's ideas were routinely ignored. Nonetheless, WAVPM's *NewsPage* reported scientific developments that seemed to support the causal connection, although the organization primarily built its arguments on feminist theory. As early as December 1978, members of WAVPM were aware of psychologist Edward Donnerstein's experiments to see whether or not exposure to pornography could provoke aggressive behavior, as measured by male students' willingness to administer electric shocks to women. Donnerstein, a dues-paying member of WAVPM, reported positive findings. There is a massive body of research in the social sciences that deals with the behavioral and attitudinal effects that result from viewing violent content, sexually explicit nonviolent content, and sexually explicit violent content. Long-term studies generally suggest that viewing violence has far greater effect on antisocial behavior and attitudes than nonviolent sexually explicit content. For a comparative analysis of the research as it relates to rape, see Mike Allen et al., "Exposure to Pornography and Acceptance of Rape Myths," *Journal of Communication*, 45 (Winter 1995): 5–26. For a comparative analysis of 1970–1988 research findings on the various types of content, see Daniel Linz, "Exposure to Sexually Explicit Materials and Attitudes Toward Rape: A Comparison of Study Results," *Journal of Sex Research*, 26 (February 1989): 50–84.

founders and most influential leaders, agreed that pornography was an "essential ingredient" of rape. They described the objectification of women's bodies in pornography – viewing women as "things" rather than as human beings – as a key part of the chain of events leading to violence. "Men are reared to view females in this way [as things], pornography thrives off this and feeds it, and rape is one of the consequences," they wrote.[11] As Robin Morgan deftly described it: "Pornography is the theory, and rape the practice."[12] Throughout *NewsPage*, the group's monthly newsletter, WAVPM advanced the idea that a causal connection existed between media violence and actual violence. "We believe there is a relationship between what we see and hear in the media, and how we think and consequently act," was one oft-repeated organizational principle.[13] If pornography caused violence, then perhaps its proliferation in the 1970s could help feminists explain the epidemic of real-world violence against women that had become a central movement concern.

The introduction of causal arguments reflected WAVPM's efforts to make sense of what seemed like a massive increase in the number of cases of rape, battering, sexual harassment, and incest in American society. As discussed earlier, most radical feminists participated in CR groups whose intimate structure allowed women to open up to one another about instances of abuse. Some violent crimes that had lacked names, let alone visibility, such as battering and sexual harassment, were revealed as frequent occurrences. WAVPM's leaders included well-known violence experts such as Russell (rape) and Barry (prostitution), who were sure that what seemed like a rise in violence was caused in part by the objectification of women in pornography and popular culture. "Real life violence against women and little girls in this country is drastically increasing," WAVPM wrote in a national organizing document. "At the same time, the advertising and entertainment industries continue to produce abusive images of women and children at an alarming rate."[14] It seemed clear to members of WAVPM that these trends were connected.

National crime statistics do not bear out an increase in the incidence of violent crime against women during the 1970s, but certainly women's *awareness* of rape and other crimes and willingness to report them to police reached new levels. According to data from the Justice Department's National Crime Victimization Survey, which asks thousands of respondents aged twelve and older about crimes that they have experienced, national rape rates remained stable between 1973 and 1980; on average, three women out of every thousand

[11] Laura Lederer and Diana Russell, "Questions We Get Asked Most Often," *WAVPM NewsPage*, 1, no. 6 (November 1977): 3.

[12] Robin Morgan, "Theory and Practice: Pornography and Rape," in *Take Back the Night*, ed. Laura Lederer (New York: William Morrow, 1980), 139.

[13] This statement was frequently used to describe the organization's beliefs. It appears in numerous issues of *NewsPage*. See "Who Are We?" *WAVPM NewsPage*, 2, no. 2 (March 1978): 3.

[14] "The Destructive Effects of Media Violence," *Write Back, Fight Back! WAVPM Media Protest Packet*: 12, WAVAW Papers.

were raped each year.[15] During the same time period, however, the number of rape cases reported to police rose significantly due to increases in third-party reporting and victim reporting of nonstranger rapes.[16] The most significant changes regarding sexual violence in the 1970s did not have to do with the actual number of incidents, but with changes in public awareness, greater sensitivity to the trauma endured by rape survivors, and victims' increased willingness to report sexual crimes to the authorities. In turn, newspapers reported many more rape stories in the mid-1970s than they had in earlier years and began framing rape as a significant social problem and protecting the identity of women who came forward to tell their stories.[17]

Through feminist efforts, it became possible for women to open up to one another – and to police and court authorities – about rape and battering instead of keeping such experiences bottled up inside. However, awareness was a double-edged sword. Although it was empowering for women to reduce the silence around sexual violence and to learn that legal and social supports were available, it was also frightening to discover that so many women had been victims. "Visibility created new consciousness, but also new fear – and new forms of old sexual terrors: sexual harassment was suddenly *everywhere*; rape was an *epidemic*; pornography was a violent polemic against women," was one feminist's description of the climate in the late 1970s.[18] Within WAVPM, pornography was regarded as a causal agent of what seemed like a tidal wave of violence against women.

The third major difference between WAVAW and WAVPM concerned censorship and whether the respective organizations agreed that seeking government action was a prudent strategy for fighting media violence. In a February 1977 statement of principles, WAVAW flatly rejected legal measures, arguing that the organization would bring consumer pressure to bear on corporations but would not appeal to police or judicial agencies to take action against offensive media content. WAVAW explained that its reasoning did not stem from an abstract commitment to freedom of speech, but from members' beliefs that small grassroots groups were already at a considerable disadvantage relative to powerful corporations when it came to efforts to make their

[15] Bureau of Justice Statistics. *Criminal Victimization, 1973–95*. NCJ-163069 (April 1997). That said, rape is still one of the most underreported crimes. Several decades after the establishment of rape crisis hotlines, increased sensitivity for rape survivors by police and prosecutors, adoption of policies by news organizations to shield victims' identities, and limitations on how much a victim's sexual history can be placed in evidence during trial, the U.S. Department of Justice estimates that 61 percent of rapes and sexual assaults go unreported.

[16] Eric P. Baumer, Richard B. Felson and Steven F. Messner, "Changes in Police Notification for Rape, 1973–2000," *Criminology* 41, no. 3 (August 2003): 841–872.

[17] Helen Benedict, *Virgin or Vamp: How the Press Covers Sex Crimes* (New York: Oxford University Press, 1992), 37–42.

[18] Ann Snitow, "Retrenchment Versus Transformation: The Politics of the Antipornography Movement," in *Women Against Censorship*, ed. Varda Burstyn (Vancouver, BC: Douglas & McIntyre, 1985), 112.

voices heard, and that the state had no particular interest in advancing feminist expression. Members of the organization believed that it was antithetical to women's best interests to give the state more power to regulate expression. Historically, such power had been used to "protect" women from needed information, particularly about contraception and abortion. "[W] e oppose censorship from simple self-interest: we want to protect our own freedom to speak publicly, however limited it may be in practical terms," the organization claimed in its statement of principles.[19] WAVAW was unyielding in its opposition to legal measures, and its members made this position clear to the fledgling WAVPM. "Censorship does not work," a spokesperson for the national WAVAW office told an interviewer from WAVPM's *NewsPage*. "It seems unrealistic to expect patriarchal government to enforce laws created to protect women."[20] Instead, WAVAW chose to emphasize public education and consciousness-raising tactics, as well as consumer action campaigns that might force corporations to stop portraying violence against women to sell products.

WAVPM, at least initially, took a different position. Although the organization formally rejected censorship strategies in 1981, many of the founding members strongly supported legal measures to eradicate violent pornography. Prominent WAVPM leaders endorsed government restriction and condemned the idea that abstract speech rights ought to outweigh women's rights to bodily safety. "I personally believe that portraying women being bound, raped, beaten, tortured, and killed for so-called sexual stimulation and pleasure should be banned ...," the sociologist and anti-rape activist Diana E. H. Russell wrote. "People seem to have forgotten that many individual liberties are curtailed by all societies for the perceived welfare of the whole society."[21] A September 1977 *NewsPage* roundtable on pornography and the First Amendment confirmed the existence of pro-censorship sentiment. One of WAVPM's founders stated explicitly that WAVAW's tactics of consumer action and demands for corporate responsibility were not effective, and that feminists would have to use "every vehicle in our legal system" to achieve change.[22] These ideas appeared throughout the newsletter in the organization's first five years, as WAVPM struggled to persuade women that the law could be useful in a fight to eradicate pornography, rather than simply accepting its existence as inevitable in a sexist society. "[W]e DO think that laws can be written which would protect women, and which would help to upgrade our

[19] Women Against Violence Against Women, "Statement of Principles," February 1977, Box 6, Los Angeles WAVAW Papers.

[20] Susan Bechaud, spokesperson for national WAVAW, quoted in "Pornography and the First Amendment: Is it an Issue?" *WAVPM NewsPage*, 1, no. 4 (September 1977): 2.

[21] Diana E. H. Russell, "Pornography and the Women's Liberation Movement," in *Take Back the Night*, 304.

[22] Pat Loomes, Berkeley Women's Center, quoted in "Pornography and the First Amendment: Is it an Issue?" *WAVPM NewsPage*, 1, no. 4 (September 1977): 2.

status in this culture," WAVPM advised readers in the February 1978 issue of *NewsPage*.[23] At the organization's 1978 national conference on pornography, several speakers endorsed the creation of new laws to ban violent pornography as discriminatory material that fostered gender inequality, a proposition that was controversial in the growing national movement.

In this chapter, I argue that WAVPM functioned as a swing group during a transition period (1978–1980) that culminated in the decline of the anti-media violence effort initiated by WAVAW and the rise of the anti-pornography movement led by WAP. WAVPM had a foot in each camp, with tactical and philosophical ties to both WAVAW and WAP. The organization adopted aspects of WAVAW's focus on abusive images in popular culture and continued its national letter-writing and public education campaigns. But in shifting the terms of the debate to pornography and endorsing legal action, WAVPM also set the stage for the rise of WAP. When WAP organized in New York in 1979, it sealed the movement's transformation from anti-media violence to anti-pornography, sidelining WAVAW on the national scene as pornography emerged as the key movement concern. Here, I analyze WAVPM's activities in the pre-WAP years, during which the organization operated as the leading voice of the nascent anti-pornography movement.

WAVPM Fights Back against Max Factor

When the Max Factor "Self Defense" ad campaign appeared in the Bay Area, women alerted WAVPM. Laura Lederer, a twenty-five-year-old Detroit native and magna cum laude graduate of the University of Michigan, was WAVPM's national coordinator, and she fielded many of the calls. "We were contacted by several women in the community who had seen a large billboard in San Francisco and it was the advertising campaign for Max Factor's new product," she told a reporter for National Public Radio. "The woman who called me on the phone said 'I thought they were telling me to take karate, at first, and then I realized, my god, no, they are actually selling me a moisturizing cream for my face.'"[24] Lederer began organizing a WAVPM response.

WAVPM kicked off a letter-writing campaign to Max Factor and the advertising agency that had created the campaign. The organization urged citizens to inform the cosmetics company that its advertising was contributing to the problem of violence against women. It was important to point out the causal relationship between media images that trivialized violence and subsequent acts of violence against women. "Urban crime rates in general, and assault, rape and murder of women, in particular, are on the rise," WAVPM told its membership through the organization's newsletter. "There is a correlation between the kind of media-violence used by Max Factor in these ads and these

[23] "Action: Legal Research," *WAVPM NewsPage*, 2, no. 1 (February 1978): 2.

[24] Barbara Boyer Walter, narrator, *Women Against Violent Pornography*, Washington, DC, 1978, National Public Radio [sound recording].

anti-social, anti-woman acts."[25] In addition to letter writing, a WAVPM action committee suggested picketing stores that sold the product line, launching a general boycott of Max Factor, and staging a press conference under a "Self-Defense" billboard, all of which resembled WAVAW tactics.

Max Factor initially ignored WAVPM's letters and complaints. Lederer described the first response from the cosmetics company: "You're just a crazy minority – we've gotten 10 letters and you're the only 10 out of 10 million people in the country who have interpreted the billboard that way."[26] The organization stepped up the pressure, deluging Max Factor with letters and telephone calls. One woman sent a letter to the president of Max Factor and the president of Wells, Rich and Greene to announce her boycott of Max Factor products. "Max Factor's advertising campaign capitalizes on women's very real fear of assault and violence, and misrepresents and makes a mockery of the words 'self-defense' and women's recent attempts to learn and practice true self-defense ..." she wrote. "I do not intend to purchase another Max Factor product until this advertising campaign is stopped."[27] Other WAVPM members contacted rape crisis centers and battered women's shelters and asked counselors to write to Max Factor about the effects of violence on women's lives. They gave interviews to local radio programs and picketed drugstores that had window displays of "Self-Defense" products. "We pushed harder," Lederer recalled, "... and as the letters began to come in and we kept in contact with Max Factor through our lawyer, they began to turn around." Victory was in sight. "[S]oon we heard from them that the billboards could be misinterpreted and they are going to redesign the ad campaign and all the billboards are down now.... And they attributed that to our community pressure."[28] Max Factor canceled the "Self-Defense" campaign.[29] The fiasco may have also played a role in the June 1978 resignation of Samuel Kalish, president of Max Factor, which industry observers attributed to the failure of highly touted products, like "Self-Defense," that fell flat with consumers.[30]

[25] "Max Factor Assaults Women with Ad Campaign," *WAVPM Newspage*: 2.

[26] Boyer Walter, *Women Against Violent Pornography*, 1978.

[27] Letter, Roberta Spivek to Gene Taylor, Wells, Rich and Greene Advertising Agency, October 27, 1977, Box 2, Folder: Correspondence: Protest Letters, non-WAVPM sponsored, WAVPM Records, GLBT Historical Society.

[28] Boyer Walter, *Women Against Violent Pornography*, 1978.

[29] According to *WAVPM Newspage*, Warren Leslie, a vice-president of Max Factor & Co., wrote to WAVPM member Sue Schectman to let her know that all the billboards were down, and that Max Factor was in the process of redesigning the ad campaign. He told Schectman that the response from the women's community was the reason the campaign was canceled. See "Past Actions," *WAVPM Newspage* 2, no. 1 (February 1978): 2; and "Final Update: Max Factor Billboard," *WAVPM Newspage*, 2, no. 2 (March 1978): 3.

[30] Kalish, who had a reputation in the cosmetics business for marketing flair, was brought in to shore up the faltering Max Factor operation in 1973. His heavy investments in new marketing programs and product development seemed to be paying off when the Los Angeles-based company earned $23 million in fiscal 1977, a sharp increase over the previous year, but many of the expensively promoted new products, like Self-Defense, turned out to be "consumer duds." Company warehouses became flooded with products that did not catch on, and the

Origins and Structure

WAVPM originated at the December 1976 Bay Area Conference on Violence Against Women, which was sponsored by San Francisco State University and San Francisco Women's Centers. Two of the conference workshops, one on pornography and one on women and media, merged on the last day of the conference in recognition of common issues. For many of the attendees, including Lederer, the conference was electrifying.

Lederer became involved in feminist activism around media violence almost by chance. She graduated from the University of Michigan in 1975 with a bachelor's degree in comparative religions, an interest stimulated by her upbringing by a Jewish father and a Lutheran mother. During her college years, she saw herself as someone more inclined toward academia than activism. Much of this changed in 1976, when she visited a friend in California who was attending the Bay Area violence conference.

Lederer accompanied her friend to the meeting and walked into the workshop on pornography. The four walls of the room were covered with images of women and children. The first wall featured advertisements and photographs from the mainstream media, such as *Time* magazine. The second wall was plastered with pictures collected from adult magazines like *Playboy*. The third wall displayed hardcore pornography, especially images featuring S/M and bestiality, some of which had appeared in *Hustler* and *Penthouse*. The last wall was covered with child pornography. Lederer noticed a striking continuity among the poses, themes, and messages featured on all of the walls, across all of the genres.[31] "I attended the conference on violence against women and I saw there was a workshop on pornography," she recalled. "And I don't know what clicked inside me, but I thought 'I'll go to that' and I entered the room and there was around the room a display of pornography – softcore, hardcore, all mixed together, and something inside me just went 'click' – it was like an instant consciousness raiser."[32] When participants from the merged conference workshops proposed that they keep meeting and form a new organization dedicated to monitoring and protesting abusive images of women, Lederer signed on.

Eighteen women gathered on January 22, 1977 to found the new organization, initially named the Women's Anti-Degradation Alliance. They set several goals for themselves, including supporting WAVAW in its boycott against the WEA record companies, planning and carrying out a march against violence against women, and serving as a "solid united women's force" for the Bay Area, dedicated to the struggle against violence against women.[33] They

company sustained losses in 1978. See "Behind Kalish's exit from Max Factor," *Business Week*, June 19, 1978, 38.

[31] Joanne Cavanaugh Simpson, "Vile Crimes," *Johns Hopkins Magazine* (November 2000). Available online at http://www.jhu.edu/~jhumag/1100web/crimes.html

[32] Boyer Walter, *Women Against Violent Pornography*, 1978.

[33] Agenda, Women's Anti-Degradation Alliance, January 22, 1977 and January 29, 1977, Box 1, Folder: General Meeting, 1977–1983, WAVPM Records, GLBT Historical Society.

purchased a copy of the WAVAW slide show with the intent of creating a similar public education program, and initiated a picket and boycott of a San Francisco music store, Castro Records, that was advertising a sale on Warner-label albums.

Over the course of the next few weeks, members hotly debated the name of the organization, because few believed that Women's Anti-Degradation Alliance accurately captured the desired focus on violence. On January 29, the group voted to change the name to Women Against Media Violence, which lasted just two weeks before concerns arose that the issue of pornography ought to be specified. The members called a special meeting for February 12, 1977 to try to define key concepts for the organization, including pornography and erotica, and to determine a definitive name. After two more iterations, they settled on Women Against Violence in Pornography and Media, pleased with the emphasis on violence and its specific contexts. Founding member Cathy DiVito reminded the membership that the organization had evolved from the violence conference, where the primary concern was violence committed against women in different institutional settings, such as the prison system and the nuclear family.[34] By highlighting the role of media in promulgating violence, the new name was in keeping with the group's origins.

WAVPM got off the ground with few material resources but a wealth of intellectual leadership. Russell, a Harvard-educated sociologist and a professor at Mills College, was the author of *The Politics of Rape*, a widely read and influential study that positioned rape as a manifestation of sexism. Barry was a feminist sociologist whose 1979 book, *Sexual Slavery*, would be regarded as a seminal account of the connections among prostitution, pornography, and violence, and the use of coercion to force women into prostitution and sex trafficking. Susan Griffin was a Bay Area poet and Emmy Award-winning playwright known for her writings on feminism and ecology. Lederer, who would later edit *Take Back the Night*, the most influential collection of feminist anti-pornography writing, found herself in the company of prominent and experienced feminists. She signed on as national coordinator for a take-home salary of $100 a week, and became the editor of WAVPM's newsletter, *NewsPage*.[35]

The fledgling group set about building its membership in the Bay Area, claiming 500 members by December 1978 and almost triple that number by July 1980.[36] Like their leaders, the founding members of WAVPM were mostly white women who identified as radical feminists. Members described the group as equally divided between heterosexual women and lesbians, and

[34] General Meeting Minutes, February 26, 1977, Box 1, Folder: General Meeting, 1977–1983, WAVPM Records, GLBT Historical Society.

[35] Lederer's salary is described in Susan Brownmiller, *In Our Time: Memoir of a Revolution* (New York: Dial Press, 1999), 300. Brownmiller also writes that the salary often went unpaid as the organization struggled with start-up costs.

[36] See both "Membership Report," *WAVPM NewsPage*, 2, no. 11 (December 1978): 3; and Diana E.H. Russell and Laura Lederer, "Questions We Get Asked Most Often," *WAVPM Newspage*, 5, no. 7 (July 1980): 1.

about half of them had previous political experience in anti-war, union, or women's movement organizing.

Many people were drawn to WAVPM after becoming disenchanted and angry about sexism and the sexual exploitation of women, often experienced firsthand. Some found their way to the organization as a result of negative experiences with pornography. Kate Roberts, who joined in April 1978, was having a relationship with a man whose roommate kept pornography in the house, and she felt threatened by the idea that men fantasized about "retouched, plastic looking women" who did not resemble any of the real women Roberts knew.[37] She wanted to work against these kinds of media images of women that promoted feelings of insecurity and low self-esteem, and that likely led to male violence. Eliza Roaringsprings joined WAVPM in 1979 after experiencing sexism on the job as a park district groundskeeper; male coworkers had pinned nude centerfolds on the locker room walls.[38] Susan Stock recalled that she had "the formative experience of comparing myself to the models in my uncle's *Playboy* magazines," and that joining WAVPM in 1978 was a way of fighting back with others who had been humiliated by pornography.[39] Lily Mar, a thirty-two-year-old, first-generation Asian American, joined WAVPM in 1980 in response to her teenage experiences of molestation and rape. She told the membership that she believed that the men who had abused her had been influenced by pornography. "For a long time I didn't speak about these experiences," she wrote in *NewsPage*. "Joining WAVPM was my way to break this silence and to take direct action against sexist violence."[40]

The organization maintained a structure composed of a board of directors and a steering committee of active members. The twelve seats on the board of directors were divided among WAVPM activists and community leaders, and the board initially maintained policy-making and fiscal power over the organization. In later years, the board of directors assumed an advisory role. Active members volunteered for a series of working committees devoted to particular tasks, such as fundraising, the slide show, and membership. Each committee completed its own tasks and made its own decisions, delegating one member to sit on the WAVPM steering committee along with WAVPM staff members. Matters that concerned the entire membership were brought up at general meetings, held monthly. Women who volunteered sixteen hours or more per month were considered active and eligible to vote. The steering committee met every two weeks and the board of directors, which included Russell, Griffin, and Lederer, met four times per year.

The organization had several sources of funding. WAVPM raised money through its $10 annual membership dues, slide show presentation fees of

37 "An Interview with WAVPM Active Members," *WAVPM NewsPage*, 3, no. 3 (April 1979): 2–3.

38 "An Interview with WAVPM Active Members," *WAVPM NewsPage*, 2–3.

39 "An Interview with WAVPM Active Members," *WAVPM NewsPage*, 2–3.

40 "Why Are We Involved in WAVPM?" *WAVPM NewsPage*, 5, no. 2 (November 1981): 1.

$200 per screening, literature packet sales, donations, and grants.[41] Financial statements from May 1978 showed that the organization had a bank balance of $4,000.[42] By October 1978, WAVPM had received more than $14,000 in grants, including $7,500 from the *Ms.* Foundation and $5,000 from two Bay Area feminists. In 1980, the organization hired an outside firm to conduct ongoing door-to-door canvassing in the Bay Area, which resulted in five commission-based workers stumping nightly for WAVPM. These individuals informed people about WAVPM's programs and goals and solicited memberships and donations. Canvassing provided the organization's major source of income through 1983.

WAVPM Demonstrates against Pornography

WAVPM carried out its first public protest against pornography just six weeks after its initial organizing meeting. The members planned an event for March 8, 1977, in honor of International Women's Day, deciding to picket a well-known adult movie theater and strip club. Thirteen WAVPM members protested in front of the Mitchell Brothers Theater on O'Farrell Street, which was owned by San Francisco's leading porn entrepreneurs, brothers Jim and Artie Mitchell. The demonstration focused on the Ultra Room, one of several themed areas where patrons paid $10 to stand in private booths and watch an all-female cast perform live sex acts with sadomasochistic (S/M) overtones. WAVPM member Cathy DiVito described the Ultra Room to a reporter covering the protest for the *San Francisco Examiner*: "It's an S and M den with paddles, whips and swings," she said. "They don't hurt one another but the insinuation is, 'I love it.'"[43] In an attempt to counter that message, the WAVPM protesters carried signs that read "Women Don't Love Torture" and "Who Says Pain Is Erotic?" Pat Loomes, a founding WAVPM member and the executive director of the San Leandro Girls' Club, told the *Examiner* that the group selected the Ultra Room because the violent themes in its live shows contributed to an atmosphere of S/M chic that made the brutal treatment of women seem glamorous. This was similar to the argument that WAVAW had made about the Rolling Stones' *Black and Blue*. In opposing S/M, WAVPM stood behind its founding principles, which stated that the organization would work to put an end to all portrayals of women being "bound, raped, tortured, killed or degraded for sexual stimulation or pleasure."[44]

[41] The $10 dues went into effect on October 1, 1978. Students, unemployed people, unpaid workers and welfare recipients could apply for a discounted rate of $5 per year. "WAVPM NewsPage: New Rates!" *WAVPM NewsPage*, 2, no. 9 (October 1978): 3.

[42] "Financial Statements for WAVPM," *WAVPM NewsPage*, 2, no. 4 (May 1978): 2.

[43] Carol Pogash, "Ultra-bias, Claim Porn Pickets: Live Show Singled out for Protest," *San Francisco Examiner*, March 9, 1977, 22.

[44] "Statement of Purpose," August 5, 1978, Box 1, Folder: Statement of Purpose, 1978, WAVPM Records, GLBT Historical Society.

FIGURE 5.1. WAVPM member Kathy Barry protests the Ultra Room at the Mitchell Brothers Theater, San Francisco, 1977. Barry would publish *Female Sexual Slavery* in 1979, a book that helped launch the international movement against sex trafficking. *Courtesy of the Gay, Lesbian, Bisexual, Transgender Historical Society.*

The major San Francisco newspapers and the alternative press covered the demonstration, alerting Bay Area sex radicals – some of whom did claim to find pain erotic – to WAVPM's position on S/M. Some members of WAVPM rejected not only the commercial exploitation of S/M prevalent in pornography, but also the whole notion of consensual S/M on the grounds that it involved unequal power exchanges and physical and psychic assault, which were thought to be incompatible with feminist principles and the commitment to egalitarian relationships. The Ultra Room protest caught the attention of the writer Pat Califia and the feminist academic Gayle Rubin, who criticized WAVPM's views of sexuality as conservative and puritanical, and in turn founded Samois, a lesbian-feminist S/M rights group based in San Francisco from 1978 to 1983.[45] Samois members believed that lesbian S/M was a feminist act. The participants were by definition marginalized women lacking social capital and who were attempting to explore the concept of power through play. WAVPM's insistence that top/bottom relationships reproduced and supported the hierarchical nature of male sexuality where women were always subordinate to men ultimately led to angry confrontations between members of the two groups. The battles between Samois and WAVPM over the question of fantasy violence and the perpetuation of patriarchal roles continued over the next several years and represented the first volleys exchanged in the feminist sex wars of the 1980s, which pitted anti-pornography activists against pro-sex challengers.

Elated by the media attention paid to their first public action, members of WAVPM planned the group's second anti-pornography demonstration. They announced a rally and a "May Day Stroll" through the city's North Beach district of massage parlors, go-go bars, adult bookstores, and XXX cinemas to be held on May 1, 1977. The rally began at noon, downtown at the Embarcadero Plaza, with speeches by Russell, Griffin, Barry, and the president of the San Francisco chapter of NOW. Following the speeches, the 200 women who had assembled for the event marched up Broadway chanting "People look around/And what do you see/The bodies being sold are you and me!" and "Pornography is a lie about women!"[46] They plastered stickers that read "This is a crime against women" on the windows of sex-oriented businesses along the march route, using the same words that a feminist activist had spray-painted across the *Black and Blue* billboard in Los Angeles. As they marched, they handed out questionnaires about pornography to women who gathered to watch. More than 100 women mailed back completed questionnaires, with the majority of respondents indicating that they supported the demonstration.

Based on the success of the May Day rally and the questionnaire data, WAVPM initiated a series of monthly marches on Broadway in the city's North Beach district. The "Stroll Down Broadway" program took place every third Friday of the month beginning in June 1977 and lasted through the early fall.[47] WAVPM selected a particular theater or sex-related business to picket at the end of each march, and the assembled women handed out flyers condemning violent pornography to would-be patrons and passers-by. As they picketed, they called out anti-pornography chants, such as: "Porn teaches torture/Porn teaches rape/Women are the victims/Of organized

[45] Pat Califia is now Patrick Califia. He is a female-to-male (FTM) transgendered individual. Because Califia's identity as a lesbian was central to the events described in this chapter, and because (s)he was known as Pat Califia at that time, I am using his former name and gender identity in keeping with the historical record.

[46] "A March to Protest Violent Porn," *San Francisco Examiner*, May 2, 1977, 19. See also, Boyer Walter, *Women Against Violent Pornography*, 1978.

[47] "Picket Against Pornography," *WAVPM NewsPage*, 1, no. 2 (July 1977): 1.

hate."[48] The June stroll ended with a picket of the Kearney Cinema, on the grounds that the XXX theater showed propaganda films that taught men that women desired brutal treatment. Women, they argued, felt the consequences of pornography's glorification of sexual violence every day. "We see it in women who are hassled and attacked on the streets," the organization stated in a news release announcing the march. "We see it in wives and girlfriends who get beaten when we 'get out of line.'"[49] The marches gave Bay Area feminists an opportunity to confront San Francisco's "neon jungle" of adult theaters, bookstores, and live sex shows amid the supportive and protective company of other outraged women.[50]

Diana Russell noticed the strength that women exuded during the marches, empowered by one another's presence. She suggested that groups of women might go further than the doorstep of the adult businesses, banding together to venture inside. In this way, women could see for themselves the daily operations of adult theaters and bookstores and get a better grasp of the actual conditions in the sex industry. Just as the WAVAW women had visited record stores and looked at albums to learn about violence in music industry advertising, WAVPM women could investigate the world of massage parlors, XXX theaters, and adult bookstores. Few were familiar with the operations of the pornography industry. They also lacked critical data, such as the percentage of material that featured acts of violence. "We resent what we are *forced* to see [of pornography]," Russell told WAVPM members and supporters at the organization's 1978 national conference. "Yet few of us follow through and say: 'My Goddess! This stuff is hateful. I need to check out what is going on *inside* some of these places!'"[51] Russell's idea was well received.

In the fall of 1977, Lederer organized a group of WAVPM members to visit some of the establishments that the organization had picketed during the summer months. Many of the women came face to face with hardcore pornography for the first time. Lederer described her experiences to a reporter from National Public Radio. "I saw peep shows – the 25-cent jobbers – they went for about a minute, maybe a minute and half," she said. "The floors were totally slimy, wet, stinking. The first ten minutes I was in the bookstore I would not look at any of the men because I was so afraid they would do something to me." As she became more accustomed to the surroundings, her fear gave way to fury. "I started to get a lot more righteous anger in me and I looked the guys right in the face and invariably they would look away."[52] Another WAVPM member described the experience of visiting an adult theater. "There were about 60 men. Most of the seats were taken, so there were a

[48] "Past Actions," *WAVPM NewsPage*, 2, no. 1 (February 1978): 2.

[49] News Release, June 17, 1977, Box 4, Folder: Broadway Protest, 1977, WAVPM Records, GLBT Historical Society.

[50] Boyer Walter, *Women Against Violent Pornography*, 1978.

[51] Russell, "Pornography and the Women's Liberation Movement," in *Take Back the Night*, 302.

[52] Boyer Walter, *Women Against Violent Pornography*, 1978.

lot of people standing along the wall," she said. "They really noticed us, they felt our presence.... It took them about 30 seconds to adjust to the fact that I was standing there taking notes, looking around and counting the number of people in the theater...."[53] These initial feminist explorations were the basis of the guided educational tours of the pornography districts that WAP and WAVPM would offer in New York City beginning in 1979 and San Francisco in 1980, respectively.

WAVPM Protests Abusive Advertising Campaigns

Within the second wave of the American women's movement, a great deal of attention was paid to advertising. The origins of this critique can be traced to Betty Friedan's blistering 1963 indictment of the advertising industry in *The Feminine Mystique*, which exposed the sexist portrayals of women in ads and the psychological manipulation of women to ensure their continued cooperation as avid consumers of packaged food, drug, beauty, and fashion products. Using Friedan's work as a point of departure, numerous critics pointed in the 1970s to the industry's limited depictions of women, who were typically shown in domestic roles or as sex objects whose body parts were used to draw attention to mundane consumer goods. Activist-scholars such as NOW vice president Lucy Komisar and Jean Kilbourne argued that a visual environment devoted to images of women cleaning their homes or tending to a family's needs taught women that their primary responsibilities were to others rather than to themselves, and that a "woman's place" was in the home. Beauty and fashion ads, in turn, imposed unrealistic standards for female appearance, and undermined women's physical and psychological well-being.[54] Komisar testified in 1970 before a special Congressional subcommittee on the subject of discrimination against women and pointed to both lack of hiring and promotion opportunities for women working in the media industries, and to objectionable portrayals of women in news, entertainment and advertising. Two months later, NOW and a coalition of women's rights groups called for a boycott of four products whose advertising they found demeaning: Silva Thins cigarettes, Ivory Liquid detergent, Pristeen feminine hygiene deodorant, and Cosmopolitan magazine.[55] NOW's call for a boycott soon faded, and the

[53] Boyer Walter, *Women Against Violent Pornography*, 1978.

[54] On feminist critiques of advertising, see L. Robinson, "Women, Media, and the Dialectics of Resistance," in *Class, Race, Sex: Dynamics of Control*, ed. A. Swerdow and H. Lessinger (Boston: G.K. Hall, 1983), 308–324; Lucy Komisar, "The Image of Woman in Advertising," in *Woman in Sexist Society*, eds. V. Gornick & B. K. Moran (New York: New American Library, 1972).

[55] For a discussion of the advertising industry's response to the emergence of the women's movement, and to this NOW boycott, see Stephen Craig, "Madison Avenue Versus The Feminine Mystique: How the Advertising Industry Responded to the Onset of the Modern Women's Movement," paper presented at the Popular Culture Association annual meeting, San Antonio, Texas, March 27, 1997. Available online at: http://www.rtvf.unt.edu/people/craig/madave.htm.

organization did not mount a successful national consumer protest. But the rationale for a boycott – the fact that women purchased 85 percent of consumer goods sold – was not lost on WAVAW and WAVPM's founders, all of whom were familiar with NOW actions and tactics. And in a related move that would also be echoed in anti-pornography activism, NOW devised at its 1970 national convention the "Barefoot and Pregnant" awards for sexist advertising. Members distributed thousands of stickers reading "This Ad Insults Women," and urged citizens to slap them on offensive ads wherever they encountered them.

Within academia, critiques of advertising and the depiction of women in the media were also gaining ground. Sociologist Erving Goffman published *Gender Advertisements* in 1976, in which he undertook a systematic study of the presentation of women's bodies in photographs used in magazine advertising. This study proceeded from Goffman's assumption that advertisements were windows into culture that revealed social beliefs about gender and offered rich data about stereotypical masculine and feminine traits. Identifying six primary symbolic behaviors that structured how men and women were depicted in advertising, Goffman pointed to the contorted postures, withdrawn gazes, child-like touches, and recumbent poses reserved for women, and made a powerful argument that advertising reflected and enforced the social dominance of men and the subordination of women. Communication scholar Suzanne Pingree, along with colleagues at the University of Wisconsin-Madison and Stanford University, published an influential study that same year that proposed a "scale for sexism" that could be used to quantitatively measure both the occurrence of sex role stereotyping in advertising and the degree to which sexism was present in any given advertising image. The authors concluded that more than half of the advertisements in a sample drawn from *Time, Newsweek, Playboy*, and *Ms.* magazines portrayed women in subordinate roles. Worse, the ads reflected the two most sexist types of depiction, showing women as either decorative objects or in domestic or "womanly" occupations.[56] Two years later, Judith Williamson published her semiotic analysis, *Decoding Advertisements* (1978), which argued that viewers used their existing referent systems, including their system of beliefs about women's place in society, to activate the latent meanings in ads.

In the field of cinema studies, scholars were also paying attention to the depiction of women and offered new critiques that contained important insights for activists. Film critic Molly Haskell's 1974 study, *From Reverence to Rape*, chronicled the portrayal of women in films from the 1920s to the 1970s and argued that they conformed to a limited pool of stereotypical stock characters, all of whom derived their value as women from their respective

On the NOW boycott, see also Patricia Bradley, *Mass Media and the Shaping of American Feminism, 1963–1975* (Jackson: University of Mississippi Press, 2005).

[56] Suzanne Pingree et al., "Equality in Advertising: A Scale for Sexism," *Journal of Communication*, 26, no. 4 (1976): 193–200.

value to men. Characters like the "Good Girl" and the "Dutiful Wife" perpetuated a system of social organization that assigned power and privilege by sex. Film scholar Laura Mulvey articulated the concept of the controlling "male gaze" in her seminal 1975 essay, "Visual Pleasure and Narrative Cinema," a theoretic concept built on Freudian and Lacanian perspectives. Mulvey argued that the specific act of watching Hollywood films placed the spectator in a heterosexual masculine subject position, with the woman viewed on screen through the male lens as an object for domination and/or erotic desire. The gaze was inherently non-gender-neutral; a woman in the literal act of watching a film brought patriarchal codes to her interpretation, privileging male needs and desires and expecting the storyline, on the basis of socialization, to turn out in ways that conformed to the dominant social order. This male "way of seeing" was understood to reduce women to passive objects subject to control by both the male characters in the film and the male-oriented expectations of viewers. Film and other popular media forms thus inscribed a masculinist discourse that not only reflected existing social arrangements, but also reinforced them.

Members of WAVPM used these burgeoning critiques of the objectification of women to reach an understanding that media played a significant role in subordinating women and creating pervasive gender discrimination. They realized that images on television, in films and advertising, and in pornography presented women as passive victims and sexual objects, and encouraged men to regard women as such. Across all media platforms, women were reduced to their body parts and stripped of social worth. "The most familiar examples of mass media porn are in advertising – the focus on women's asses, the acrobatic spread of the model's legs, the mountainous regions of cleavage, all of which have no relation to the product," journalist and WAVPM board member Valerie Miner complained about modern selling techniques.[57] Another WAVPM member complained that advertisements directed to women were sexist and designed to breed self-hate. "We are told that our bodies are repulsive in their natural state – we are bombarded with feminine 'hygiene' products, diet pills, depilatories, hair coloring, 'control top' pantyhose, and most recently, pantiliners that we are advised to wear 'the other twenty-five days of the month,'" she wrote in *NewsPage*.[58] Members of WAVAW and WAVPM understood, as Goffman observed in 1976, that advertisements did a great deal of ideological work, persuading viewers of their own inferiority. Advertising also reassured women that purchasing a steady stream of beauty

57 Valerie Miner, "Fantasies and Nightmares: The Red-Blooded Media," *Jump Cut: A Review of Contemporary Media*, no. 26 (December 1981). Available online at http://www.ejumpcut.org/archive/onlineessays/JC26folder/Miner

58 Nancy McCready, "Advertising and the Victimization of Women," *WAVPM NewsPage*, 5, no. 6 (June 1981): 2. McCready based her article on studies conducted by George Gerbner at the Annenberg School of Communication at the University of Pennsylvania, and work by other communication researchers and sociologists, including Matilda Butler and William Paisley, Gaye Tuchman, and Lucy Komisar.

and fashion products would help them overcome flaws and move toward an aspirational state of ideal womanhood.[59]

Following the WAVAW example, WAVPM urged its membership to protest negative ads with letter-writing campaigns, boycotts, pickets, and other pressure tactics designed to make corporations act responsibly. The organization purchased a copy of the WAVAW slide show in January 1977 and used it to develop a similar program. WAVPM called its slide show "Abusive Images of Women in Mass Media and Pornography." The WAVAW slide show concentrated on images from advertising, whereas the WAVPM slide show mixed traditional ads with examples of pornography culled from magazines like *Hustler* and posters for X-rated films like *The Opening of Misty Beethoven*. By the end of the organization's first full year of operation, WAVPM members had presented the slide show to more than 200 community groups, including screenings at the main branch of the San Francisco public library, the San Bruno Jail for Women, and the San Francisco State University Women's Studies program.[60] The use of this program as a tool for public education was a major point of continuity from WAVAW to WAVPM.

WAVPM also extended WAVAW's efforts to deluge corporations with protest letters in response to the publication of abusive ads. In 1978, WAVPM formed the *Write Back! Fight Back!* national letter-writing network that alerted hundreds of people and dozens of women's groups across the nation, such as battered women's shelters and rape crisis centers, to the emergence of a negative advertising campaign.[61] Members of the network typically received a mailing describing the advertising campaign, a sample protest letter, and the names and addresses of the corporate executives to whom similar complaints should be sent.

The first letter-writing campaign organized through *Write Back! Fight Back!* was launched in January 1978 to protest an advertisement for Finnair, the national airline of Finland. Created by DeGarmo Advertising, a New York agency, the print campaign ran in national consumer magazines and offered a glimpse of fictional "famous" Finns, such as Henni Salmi, creator of the smorgasbord. The ad that caught WAVPM's attention described Vilho Vatanen, inventor of the sauna. The ad copy read: "How Vilho Vatanen, the Finn, created the world's first sauna when he locked his wife in the smokehouse, set it on fire, beat her soundly with birch leaves, and discovered she loved it."[62] Many women readers thought that the ad trivialized the crime of battering and communicated the dangerous message that women enjoy physical abuse.

Lederer sent a letter to the president of Finnair that explained WAVPM's concern. "[W]e find joking references to wife-beating completely offensive

59 Erving Goffman, *Gender Advertisements* (Cambridge, MA: Harvard University Press, 1976).

60 "End of the Year Report, 1978" Box 2, Folder: End of the Year Report, 1978, WAVPM Records, GLBT Historical Society.

61 *Write Back, Fight Back! WAVPM Media Protest Packet*, WAVAW Papers, 2.

62 "Whimsical Finnair Ads Feature 'Famous' Finns," *Advertising Age*, January 30, 1978, 35.

and dangerous in a society where a woman is raped every 60 seconds, and a woman is beaten every 30 seconds by a man with whom she lives," she wrote.[63] Lederer strongly urged Finnair to "rethink" its ad campaign and warned that WAVPM was adding the sauna ad to its slide show presentation and would be asking viewers to refrain from traveling on the airline. Leif Lundstrom, president of Finnair, responded immediately. "Actually, the ad was meant to convey anything but violence or wife-beating," he explained. "[T]he sauna is a place for peace and family togetherness...."[64] Pat Greenwald, research director at DeGarmo Advertising, insisted that the ad was supposed to be "light-hearted and humorous" and its intent "was in no way to communicate violence."[65] In New York City, members of New York WAVAW supported the protest by demonstrating outside the Finnair ticket office on Fifth Avenue. Finnair promised that the "Vilho Vatanen" ad would not be repeated. The consumer pressure campaigns initiated by WAVAW and WAVPM worked.

In 1980, WAVPM organized another successful effort through the *Write Back! Fight Back!* network. Heublein Spirits Group, a beverage manufacturer, introduced an advertising campaign for its Club Cocktail bottled beverage. The ad, which appeared in national magazines and on billboards, showed a woman smiling beneath a slogan that read: "Hit me with a Club." Member Robin Goldner drafted WAVPM's letter of complaint. "We object to the implication that people ask or want to be hit.... Your light play on words trivializes the quite serious issue of woman-battery and abuse, and thus worsens the plight of the victims."[66] Rather than encouraging the purchase of Club Cocktail, Goldner warned, the advertisements would result in a WAVPM boycott of Heublein products for the duration of the campaign. More than 1,000 individuals alerted through the *Write Back! Fight Back!* network sent similar letters to the beverage company, and many sent copies of the ad to *Ms.* magazine to be included in the *No Comment* section.[67]

Within two months of receiving the initial WAVPM letter, Heublein Spirits canceled the "Hit me with a Club" campaign. In a letter to Pat Carbine, the publisher of *Ms.* magazine, the beverage company's CEO acknowledged that the flood of protest letters had raised the company's consciousness about

[63] Laura Lederer to Leif Lundstrom, February 22, 1978, in *Write Back, Fight Back! WAVPM Media Protest Packet*, WAVAW Papers.

[64] Leif Lundstrom to Laura Lederer, February 28, 1978, in *Write Back, Fight Back! WAVPM Media Protest Packet*, WAVAW Papers.

[65] Betty Liddick, "Women Victims – Statistics to Sales Gimmicks," *Los Angeles Times*, February 16, 1978, clipping in the Los Angeles WAVAW Papers.

[66] Robin Goldner to J. E. Corr, June 6, 1980, in *Write Back, Fight Back! WAVPM Media Protest Packet*, WAVAW Papers.

[67] Many women both inside and outside of the anti-pornography movement sent offensive advertisements to *Ms.* for inclusion in the monthly *No Comment* section. The magazine reproduced the ads without editorial comment, based on the understanding that readers could easily recognize the demeaning messages therein. On *No Comment*, see Linda Steiner, "Oppositional Decoding as an Act of Resistance," *Critical Studies in Mass Communication* 5, no. 1 (March 1988): 1–15.

violence against women. The first few letters stunned management because it had not occurred to anyone that the campaign "could have been interpreted, even in the remotest sense, as encouraging or condoning physical abuse." Most of the executives maintained that few women were likely to read the advertisement that way. But as the pile of protest letters grew, it became obvious that the ad had touched a nerve. "[W]e were moved by the logic and depth of feeling [in the letters]," the CEO wrote to Carbine. "Their arguments were persuasive and difficult to refute and ultimately convinced us that the advertising should be changed."[68] WAVPM chalked up another victory against abusive advertising. The ties between WAVAW and WAVPM were evident in the groups' shared concern about the prevalence of violent and sexist images in advertising.

National Newspapers and Restriction of XXX Advertisements

In a move that combined members' interests in fighting abusive advertising and pornography, WAVPM turned its attention to advertisements *for* pornography. Members of the organization were angry about the explicit ads for XXX films that the leading Bay Area daily newspapers, the jointly operated *San Francisco Chronicle* and the *San Francisco Examiner*, printed. When legitimate newspapers accepted ads for pornographic films that presented women as things to be used sexually, they put "a stamp of objectivity" on portrayals of violence that condoned and normalized male desire for the brutalized female body.[69] The July 29, 1977 issue of the *Chronicle*, for example, included five display ads for adult movies. The ads showed women in sexualized poses, some featuring bondage, whips, and leather gear. WAVPM began circulating petitions around the Bay Area, gathering signatures to demonstrate public opposition. Members hoped that the newspapers would agree to prohibit, or at least limit, these ads.[70]

WAVPM members developed the idea to pressure the *Chronicle* and the *Examiner* after the *New York Times* enacted a strict anti-porn advertising policy. On June 21, 1977, publisher Arthur Ochs Sulzberger announced that the *Times* would strictly limit the size and format of advertisements for films whose primary purpose was to portray sex acts.[71] Sulzberger characterized adult films ads as "a blight on the newspaper's pages" that were not in keeping with the quality and content of the newspaper as a whole.[72] A *Times* editorial further justified the move to regulate X-rated ads, arguing that advertising that glamorized pornography "offends the community in which we publish" as well as the standards of taste that the editors sought to uphold throughout

68 J. E. Corr to Pat Carbine, August 8, 1980, letter reprinted in *Ms.* Magazine (October 1980): 11.

69 Leslie Labowitz and Suzanne Lacy, quoted in Fryd, "Suzanne Lacy's *Three Weeks in May*," 33.

70 Judith Landy, "Porn Turns Mean," *San Francisco Bay Guardian*, January 18, 1979, 12.

71 "Chaste Ads for Porno Films," *The New York Times*, June 21, 1977, A32.

72 Anna Quindlen, "The Times Will Curb Ads for Pornographic Films," *The New York Times*, June 21, 1977, B6.

the newspaper.[73] This move brought the *Times* to the forefront of similar efforts that were beginning nationwide. Among New York City dailies, the *Daily News* and the *New York Post* reserved the right to edit advertisements for XXX films, but neither newspaper had dictated a specific policy governing the space and kind of copy allowed at the time of Sulzberger's announcement. The other major daily newspapers that limited the space available to adult film ads at that time were the *Detroit News*, the *Cleveland Plain Dealer*, and the *Miami Herald*.

The *Times*' new guidelines sharply curtailed the size and permissible content for adult film advertisements. The newspaper would publish only "service information," which amounted to the name of the film (so long as the name itself was not too explicit), and the theater's name, location, and show times. Ads were limited in size to single-column type displays, up to 1 inch deep for a single title and no more than 1 and 3/8 inches deep for two or more titles. The *Times* would not accept illustrations, and each theater was limited to one advertisement per day.[74] These restrictions were among the most stringent in the nation among daily newspapers. Of course, moral uplift had its price. The new policy was expected to cost the newspaper more than $750,000 per year in lost revenue.[75]

Although the *Times* staunchly defended its policy, questions arose as to how the newspaper would apply the new advertising regulations. Which films, members of the public wondered, were "pornographic?" Did any film with sexual content count as pornography, or did artistic erotic expression fall under a different category? How might one distinguish between the two? This difficult question would also come to plague the anti-pornography movement, as its critics argued that a diverse community of people could never reach consensus as to what constituted pornography. Sulzberger made an effort to address the issue, responding that individual decisions would be based on the information submitted in the advertisements, and on editors' good judgment. He insisted that the newspaper would be able to distinguish pornographic films from those for which explicit sex was part of a larger story, noting that the editors had always made such distinctions in selecting appropriate subjects for cultural news coverage and criticism.[76] The newspapers' editors also sought to assure members of the public that it was possible to separate pornographic films from those created with a loftier purpose in mind. "How do we distinguish between such films and those with a wider purpose?" they mused on the *Times*' editorial page. "Overwhelmingly, these films distinguish themselves, in their advertising, and the clientele they seek."[77]

[73] "Chaste Ads for Porno Films,"A32.

[74] "New York Times to Curb Pornographic Film Ads," *The Wall Street Journal*, June 21, 1977, 20.

[75] Quindlen, "The Times Will Curb Ads," B6.

[76] Quindlen, "The Times Will Curb Ads," B6.

[77] "Chaste Ads for Porno Films," A32.

The editors were presented with just such a case less than a month after Sulzberger announced the new advertising policy. In July 1977, the newspaper published display ads for *In the Realm of the Senses*, a Japanese film that featured scenes of explicit sex and male castration. Originally banned by U.S. Customs, the film played to near-sellout audiences in New York City. Bernard Stein, the *New York Times*' advertising acceptability representative, explained that the editors believed *In the Realm of the Senses* had a purpose beyond sexual stimulation. "'It was felt that the scenes depicted transcended the usual Western pornographic films," he told an advertising industry trade publication. "The film has artistic quality."[78]

Some readers were less sanguine about the *Times*' ability to make these judgment calls.[79] One sounded a strong note of caution. "It comes as a shock to see that the *New York Times* has gotten into the censorship business again," he wrote. "First it's cigarettes that you're cutting out and now it's sex; tomorrow it will be liquor."[80] Irving Kristol, the well-known American neo-conservative, also took the newspaper to task. For years, the editors of the *Times* had insisted that censorship of pornography would constitute a violation of the First Amendment. One of their oft-printed arguments had been that no one person or group in a democratic society was sufficiently wise and prudent to be a censor of others. Under the new policy, Kristol complained, the *Times* had appointed itself as censor, deciding which films were worthy of publicity.[81]

Meanwhile, the *Times*' decision was hailed by members of the Broadway theater community that struggled to coexist around 42nd Street with the adult entertainment industry. "The less attention we call to the fact that there is a pornography system operating rather freely here can't help but be beneficial to the community," said Richard Barr, president of the League of New York Theaters, in response to the *Times*' policy. Jack Valenti, president of the Motion Picture Association of America, hailed the step as "the most reasonable measure that's been adopted so far" and one that other newspapers should consider.[82]

[78] Leah Rozen, "Where Did Porn Ads Go?" *Advertising Age*, August 8, 1977, 59.

[79] Some readers did praise the policy. One reader commended the newspaper for a move "that will be applauded soundly by your readers everywhere." He added, "Maybe, in a small way, you have pioneered a return to the moral and ethical standards which have been dimmed by time, and signaled the demise of the age of permissiveness fostered by the motion picture industry over the last decade." See Vincent J. Dolan Jr. to the Editor, *The New York Times*, June 28, 1977, A30.

[80] Francis M. Ellis to the Editor, *The New York Times*, June 28, 1977, A30.

[81] Irving Kristol, "Summer Notes and Footnotes," *The Wall Street Journal*, July 18, 1977, 12. Kristol ultimately became one the nation's leading advocates of the censorship of pornography. He has argued that its proliferation undermines the basis for American democracy.

[82] Judith Cummings, "Theater Leaders Applaud Curb on Ads in The Times," *The New York Times*, June 22, 1977, B18. Concerns about censorship did exist, however. Don Baker, chairman of the advertising committee of the National Association of Theater Owners, which represented 14,000 mainstream movie theaters, worried that newspapers might formulate such restrictive policies that regular movies might be prevented from advertising.

Newspapers around the nation did follow the *Times*' lead in establishing anti-pornography advertising policies. Otis Chandler, publisher of the *Los Angeles Times*, banned all ads for adult theaters in August 1977, forfeiting $1 million in annual revenue. "The truth is, we have been dealing with an indefensible product, one with absolutely no redeeming values, and this phenomenon shows no sign of leaving the contemporary social scene," Chandler explained.[83] The about-face was somewhat remarkable, considering that these changes came just five years after the *Los Angeles Times* and other newspapers had relaxed their standards and accepted ads for *Deep Throat* and other X-rated films.[84] Going a step beyond the *New York Times*, the *Los Angeles Times* even refused to print service information for adult theaters.[85] Chandler credited pressure from community groups and complaints raised at the annual shareholders' meeting for motivating his decision.

Members of WAVPM surveyed the national scene. The *New York Times* had seen fit to restrict such material. Closer to home, the *Los Angeles Times* had banned XXX ads in response to community pressure. They believed that it might be possible to force the San Francisco newspapers to follow suit. "*The Chronicle* and *The Examiner* run pious editorials condemning pornography, but they continue to make over a half a million dollars per year on pornography ads alone," WAVPM advised in *NewsPage*. "We feel this is a perfect place to make our point: by attacking a large corporation which upholds (and profits from) brutalization and degradation of women."[86] WAVPM sent letters to executives at both the *San Francisco Chronicle* and the *San Francisco Examiner*, and pointed out that the ads constituted a danger to every woman.[87] In September 1977, they included petitions along with a regular mailing of *NewsPage* and asked members to gather signatures in support of a ban.

On February 15, 1978, Susan B. Anthony Day, WAVPM held a rally outside the *Chronicle* offices at 5th Street and Mission, demanding a policy against ads for adult theaters. A crowd of 150 women handed out flyers from 11 A.M. to 4:30 P.M. and carried signs with slogans that included: "*Chronicle* Delivers Porn to Your Door" and "No More Profits Off Women's Bodies." Kathy Barry was working on the manuscript for *Female Sexual Slavery* and could not attend the rally, but she sent a letter of support to her WAVPM sisters,

83 "Los Angeles Times Bans All Advertising for Porno Movies," *The Wall Street Journal*, August 24, 1977, 22.

84 For example, Copley Newspapers' *San Diego Union* and *The Evening Tribune* had accepted no ads from theaters running X-rated films until 1973, when it agreed to print ads no larger than two inches that would give only the theater's name and show times and note the fact that an X-rated picture was playing. Neither the film's name nor any other promotional material was printed. In 1975, the newspapers dropped these restrictions and began accepting full display ads. See Philip H. Dougherty, "A Reprise of 1975's Big Events," *The New York Times*, January 5, 1976, 45.

85 "All the Ads Fit to Print," *Time*, September 12, 1977, 80.

86 "Rally at the Chronicle/Examiner," *WAVPM NewsPage*, 2, no. 1 (February 1978): 1.

87 WAVPM to John Murphy, publisher, *San Francisco Examiner*, *WAVPM NewsPage*, 1, no. 3 (August 1977): 3.

FIGURE 5.2. WAVPM members and supporters protest at the San Francisco *Chronicle-Examiner*, 1978. They demanded that the newspaper cease publishing advertisements for adult films and theaters, following in the footsteps of other national newspapers that had enacted bans. *Courtesy of the Gay, Lesbian, Bisexual, Transgender Historical Society.*

telling them that she would be there in spirit. "I am canceling my subscription to it [the *Chronicle*] until we win an agreement of a change in practices from them," she added.[88] In subsequent months, WAVPM supporters deluged the newspapers with letters demanding corporate responsibility. Many warned the newspaper that pornographic films contributed to the violence problem. "Crimes against women, especially rape, are increased with the advertising of these kinds of movies," one letter writer stated, adding that she intended to cancel her newspaper subscription if such ads continued.[89]

[88] Kathy Barry to WAVPM, *WAVPM NewsPage*, 2, no. 1 (February 1978): 4.

[89] Letter, Mary Frances Bachman to Richard Thieriot, Editor, *San Francisco Chronicle*, May 4, 1978, Box 2, Folder: Correspondence: Internal, WAVPM Papers, GLBT Historical Society.

WAVPM exerted a great deal of pressure on the San Francisco newspapers, but the group was not able to secure an advertising policy. The newspapers earned significant revenues from adult theater ads in the mid-1970s, and would have faced severe financial consequences had they restricted them. Furthermore, the San Francisco newspapers catered to an urban readership with diverse sexual preferences, and a ban against sexually explicit advertising would have been likely to elicit strong protest from the city's vocal gay community.

WAVPM Action against *Hustler*

In addition to protesting XXX ads and marching through the North Beach and Tenderloin districts, both of which had a history of commercial sexual activity including straight and gay nightclubs, topless dancing, and prostitution, members of WAVPM were becoming increasingly angry about the proliferation of newsstand pornography. The number of adult magazines sold in San Francisco had risen from zero in 1953 to forty in 1978. Around the nation, women detested the presence of *Hustler*, *Penthouse*, *Oui*, *Swank*, and other "men's magazines" at their local supermarkets, convenience stores, and newsstands. In a *New York Times* opinion piece, the radical feminist Robin Morgan expressed her disgust. "So we've tried averting our eyes – but where to, these days?" she asked. "In the act of buying a paper at my corner newsstand, I am surrounded with material contemptuous of my womanhood. My rhetoric may pronounce such material 'sexist propaganda': my nausea rises in simple humiliation. It hurts."[90] Ellen Willis, a cultural critic for the *Village Voice* and cofounder of the radical feminist group Redstockings, found the situation equally intolerable. "One day it's a glossy magazine cover of a woman sitting with legs spread, her flimsy black slip up around her waist.... Another time, another magazine: A woman with platinum hair ... naked except for a garter belt, stockings and high heels, bends over, ass to the camera ...," she wrote of the prevalence of such images. "The magazines are obtrusively, unavoidably at eye level, the better to ensure that sales will continue to burgeon."[91] Although Morgan and Willis would ultimately join different camps – with Morgan a staunch anti-pornography activist and Willis emerging as a leading pro-sex feminist – they were in agreement at this time regarding the ubiquitous display of sexualized images of the female body. Writing for the *Village Voice* in 1979, Willis noted that pornographic images, many of them openly sadistic, had become such a staple of popular culture that they functioned as a form of "psychological harassment" of women.[92]

[90] Robin Morgan, "Check It Out: Porn, No. But Free Speech, Yes." *The New York Times*, March 24, 1978, A27. Morgan was one of the anti-pornography movement's most influential theorists and leaders. She coined the phrase "Pornography is the theory, and rape the practice," which became the movement battle cry. See her seminal 1974 essay, "Theory and Practice: Pornography and Rape," reprinted in *Take Back the Night*, 134–140.

[91] Ellen Willis, "Sexual Counterrevolution I," *Rolling Stone*, March 24, 1977, 29.

[92] Ellen Willis, "Feminism, Moralism and Pornography," *The Village Voice*, October 15, 1979, 8.

Among the adult magazines, *Hustler* was perhaps the worst offender. Under the direction of publisher Larry Flynt, *Hustler* offered its readers close-up views of female genitalia, known in the industry as "pink-shots," kinky sex scenes, and misogynistic cartoons that found humor in rape, incest, child molestation, and battering. In a well-known study, the filmmaker Laura Kipnis compared *Hustler* to *Penthouse* and *Playboy*, and noted that the magazine "outstripped the other two in its unprecedented explicitness and raunch."[93] Regular features like *Chester the Molester*, a cartoon that detailed the adventures of a middle-aged pedophile who enjoyed raping girls, elicited feminist rage.

Women's concerns aside, *Hustler* was one of the most popular men's magazines. In October 1977, *Hustler* ranked eighth in newsstand sales for all magazines in the United States, just behind *Playboy* and ahead of *Penthouse*.[94] The publication boasted a readership of 10 million, with a monthly paid circulation of 2.5 million. Each newsstand copy sold for $2.25, far more than the average price of national consumer magazines at that time.[95]

The wrath against *Hustler* exploded in June 1978. That month, the magazine published its infamous "all meat" issue. The cover showed a woman, naked and upside down, being fed into a meat grinder, head first. Half of her body had already been processed; it was displayed as chopped hamburger meat sitting on a plate beneath the grinder. Her legs stuck out of the top of the grinder, waving in the air, next to be fed through. When this issue of *Hustler* hit newsstands, it gave new urgency to WAVPM's fight against the "woman-hate" present in pornography.

WAVPM organized a series of demonstrations in front of liquor stores that were selling the "all meat" issue of *Hustler*. On June 3, 1978, seventy-five WAVPM members and supporters picketed Jug's Liquors in San Francisco. "*Hustler* Lies About Women!" they chanted to the beat of a live drum.[96] They carried hand-lettered posters with slogans such as: "*Hustler* Breeds Contempt For Women" and "No More Magazine Mutilation Of Our Bodies."[97] They also gave out leaflets and asked passers-by to sign petitions demanding that

[93] Laura Kipnis, *Bound and Gagged: Pornography and the Politics of Fantasy in America* (New York: Grove Press, 1996), 129. See especially chapter 4, "Disgust and Desire: Hustler Magazine."

[94] Advertisement for Larry Flynt Publications Inc., *Advertising Age*, October 10, 1977, 85. The cost to advertise in *Hustler* was much lower than that of general-interest magazines, and the magazine was primarily supported by newsstand sales. A one-page color advertisement in *Hustler* in 1977 cost $4,000. See "*Hustler* Changes May Help Ads," *Advertising Age*, November 28, 1977, 72.

[95] The demographics for *Hustler* readers in 1978 were as follows: 85% male, 40% had attended college, 23% were professionals, 59% had household incomes of $15,000 or more per year, which was above the national mean at that time. The median reader age was 30. See Jeffrey Klein, "Born Again Porn," *Mother Jones* (February/March 1978), 18.

[96] Boyer Walter, *Women Against Violent Pornography*, 1978.

[97] Photo of Jug's Liquors protest, Folder: Unsorted: Marches and 1978 Conference, WAVPM Papers, GLBT Historical Society. See also Photo, "Women Move Against Hustler," *WAVPM NewsPage*, 2, no. 6 (July 1978): 1.

FIGURE 5.3. Feminist groups around the nation protest the gory cover image of *Hustler* magazine's June 1978 issue. The cover showed a naked, upside-down woman being fed head-first into a meat grinder. *The Schlesinger Library, Radcliffe Institute, Harvard University.*

stores remove the magazine from their shelves. Over the course of the next week, members of WAVPM visited liquor and convenience stores around the East Bay to try to persuade them to stop selling *Hustler*. The WAVPM representatives explained to the store managers that pornography actively contributed to real-life violence against women. On June 10, WAVPM picketed Jay Vee Liquors in Berkeley and Eddie's Liquors in Oakland for refusing to remove *Hustler*.[98] These protests resulted in the temporary removal of the magazine from a number of Bay Area stores and earned the organization coverage by

[98] Lynn Campbell, "Women Move Against Hustler," *WAVPM NewsPage*, 2, no. 6 (July 1978), 1.

FIGURE 5.4. WAVPM members and supporters picketed in front of stores that sold *Hustler* magazine's June 1978 meatgrinder issue. This picket took place on June 3, 1978 outside of Jug's Liquors in San Francisco. Feminists urged the owners of liquor and convenience stores to remove the magazine from their shelves. *Courtesy of the Gay, Lesbian, Bisexual, Transgender Historical Society.*

three Bay Area news programs and three radio networks, including National Public Radio.[99]

There was some irony in the fact that it was the meat issue that pushed WAVPM over the edge with regard to *Hustler*. In November 1977, *Hustler* publisher Larry Flynt had undergone a highly publicized conversion to evangelical Christianity under the guidance of Ruth Carter Stapleton, a charismatic preacher and the sister of President Jimmy Carter.[100] Flynt vowed publicly to transform *Hustler* from a magazine featuring raunchy sex into one focused on "healthy sex" and religion, although many observers viewed his promise as a cynical means of currying public favor to help beat pending obscenity charges. Speaking before a Pentecostal congregation in Houston, Flynt announced that he owed every woman in America an apology. He described plans to

[99] WAVPM General Meeting Minutes, June 10, 1979, Box 1, Folder: General Meeting, 1977–1983, WAVPM Records, GLBT Historical Society.

[100] Klein, "Born Again Porn," 18. Flynt's conversion took place just a few months before he was shot and paralyzed outside a Lawrenceville, Georgia courthouse where he was on trial on an obscenity charge. In the year following his shooting, Flynt renounced his newfound religion. On Flynt's shooting, see Wayne King, "Larry Flynt, Owner of Hustler, Is Shot Near Georgia Court," *The New York Times* (March 7, 1978), 1.

reincarnate "Chester the Molester" as "Chester the Protector," a hero who would protect young girls from seduction. Similarly, he swore that he would retool *Hustler*'s popular "Asshole of the Month" column, which (unreformed) would feature many anti-pornography feminists in the 1980s, including Andrea Dworkin, Diana Russell, Gloria Steinem, Catharine MacKinnon, and WAP's Dorchen Leidholdt, as well as their supporters, including Dworkin's attorney, Gerry Spence. According to Paul Krassner, the civil libertarian and former Yippie leader hired by Flynt to serve as *Hustler*'s publisher during this period, the meat grinder cover was intended to poke fun at the boss's conversion. The illustration appeared next to a promise from the new-and-improved Flynt: "We will no longer hang women up like pieces of meat." Krassner acknowledged that the intended humor was not widely appreciated.[101]

Feminist Perspectives on Pornography: WAVPM's National Conference

As WAVPM's work around pornography expanded, it became clear that the organization needed to develop a comprehensive feminist analysis that would explain pornography's particular harms to women. From the time of its founding, WAVPM had launched direct actions against abusive advertising, like Max Factor's "Self-Defense" campaign, and had organized numerous protests against pornography, such as the marches down Broadway and the *Hustler* pickets. However, members of WAVPM had not yet worked together to develop a comprehensive theory of violent pornography and its effects. "We did not spend our time discussing how do we define pornography," Diana Russell recalled. "We became activists very quickly."[102] A reader of *NewsPage* in the early years might have had a hard time understanding exactly *why* WAVPM opposed pornography. Members often expressed the idea that pornography taught men to hate women and made it easier for men to abuse women in real life, but the organization's formal analysis lacked greater depth. Members of WAVPM, like most women inside the burgeoning anti-pornography movement, were wrestling with basic questions, such as how to define pornography, what differences existed between pornography and erotica, how pornography harmed women and men, and how to identify the best means for controlling its spread.

In the summer of 1978, WAVPM began planning the first national feminist conference on pornography to address some of these unresolved definitional and strategic questions. The organization hired a second full-time coordinator to work on the conference arrangements and to solicit the participation of leading feminists. Lynn Campbell was a twenty-two-year-old lesbian feminist who had begun her life as an activist organizing farmworkers, much like WAVAW's Julia London. Campbell dropped out of Stanford University in 1974 to work for the UFW for a salary of $5 per week plus room and board, honing her

101 "Is This the Real Message of Pornography?" *Harper's* (November 1984): 35.

102 Russell quoted in Brownmiller, *In Our Time*, 299.

organizing skills through leadership roles in the grape boycotts. She was the Bay Area coordinator for the UFW in 1975 and served as one the directors of the Los Angeles County boycott in the summer of 1976.[103] Campbell, remembered by WAVPM colleagues as a "phenomenal" organizer, quickly became a major figure in the burgeoning anti-pornography movement.[104] She worked with Lederer during 1978–1979 on the WAVPM anti-pornography conference and *Take Back the Night* march, and subsequently moved to New York City at Susan Brownmiller's invitation in 1979 to begin organizing Women Against Pornography.

Lederer and Campbell worked for months to pull together the Feminist Perspectives event, which would attract some of the nation's best-known radical feminists and announce to the women's movement that a serious effort was underway to combat pornography. The conference combined informational and strategy workshops, speeches, panel discussions, and the nation's first *Take Back the Night* march. The organizers hoped that participants would generate new theory, increase their understanding of pornography's harms to women, and create action strategies for limiting this dangerous material. Although there was a strong WAVAW presence at the conference, including two WAVAW-led workshops on media violence, pornography claimed center stage.

Feminist Perspectives on Pornography took place at Galileo High School in downtown San Francisco during the weekend of November 17–19, 1978. Some 350 women from 30 states attended.[105] The organizers tried to be inclusive, offering scholarships for conference travel and fees to Black, Chicana, Asian, and Native American women, as well as to older and disabled individuals.[106] Every woman was allowed to determine her own conference registration fee on a sliding scale from $5 to $25; WAVPM asked women to send in whatever amount they could afford. The organization arranged overnight accommodations for most of the out-of-town attendees with local residents and provided reasonably priced food at all conference events. The conference proceedings were translated into sign language, Spanish, Chinese, and Japanese.

Lederer and Campbell lined up an all-star cast. Kathy Barry gave the opening address. Adrienne Rich and Susan Griffin read poetry. Florence Rush, a social worker and expert on child sexual abuse, gave a speech on the subject of child pornography. Susan Brownmiller joined Susan Griffin and two Bay Area feminist attorneys for a panel discussion on pornography and the First Amendment. Andrea Dworkin delivered a powerful, apocalyptic speech, "Pornography and Grief," in which she warned the audience that sex and

[103] Jane Creighton, "Lynn Campbell, 1955–1984," *off our backs* (June 1984), 25.

[104] Personal conversation with Bridget Wynne, an active member of WAVPM in the late 1970s, and a co-coordinator of the organization after Laura Lederer stepped down from this role; November 19, 2008.

[105] Walter Hinkle, "Women Meet, Talk, March on Porn" *San Francisco Chronicle*, November 18, 1978, 27; Laura Lederer, "Introduction," *Take Back the Night*, 15.

[106] "Special Issue: Conference Report," *WAVPM NewsPage*, 2, no. 12 (February 1979): 1.

murder were "fused in the male consciousness."[107] The lesbian feminist poet Audre Lorde, the sole woman of color in this group, discussed the erotic as a source of power, strength, and affirmation, and as something quite different from pornography. Like other anti-pornography feminists who avoided any mention of sexual behavior in descriptions of women's sexuality, Lorde described the erotic as "a resource within each of us that lies in a deeply female and spiritual plane, firmly rooted in the power of our unexpressed or unrecognized feeling."[108] Diana Russell spoke last. She urged the audience to jettison the "liberal-radical line" on pornography that rejected any legal means of restriction on First Amendment grounds. This reasoning was used, Russell pointed out, "to freeze us into saying and doing nothing" to stop pornography.[109] These feminist leaders headlined a conference against *pornography*, making it quite obvious that the anti-media violence movement was in the midst of a decisive shift.

Many WAVAW members attended the conference, eager to understand how WAVPM's work against pornography fit with WAVAW's emphasis on public education and consumer pressure tactics to combat abusive advertising. Julia London and Joan Howarth traveled from Los Angeles. Many women attended from regional WAVAW chapters, including Boston, Rochester, Denver, and Knoxville. Members of WAVAW led three workshops (of twenty-three total) on the strategies that the organization had developed to fight media violence. Mechanic Marg Hall and visual artist Martha Gever, two members of the Rochester chapter who had been charged with destruction of private property at a theater showing *Snuff*, led a workshop on "Sabotage of Pornography." London chaired a session titled "Mobilizing/Communicating/Pressuring," which reviewed the successful WAVAW techniques of letter writing, picketing, and boycotting. In another workshop, London discussed the ongoing Warner effort and future targets for anti-media violence campaigns. Howarth sent a follow-up memo to WAVAW's national coordinating committee that tried to connect the two organizations in positive ways. "Although we haven't focused on porn per se," she wrote, "our workshops were well received."[110] Nonetheless, the disjuncture between the WAVAW and WAVPM agendas was evident.

On Saturday afternoon, a panel of speakers tackled the issue of legal restrictions on pornography and related First Amendment questions. Moderated by the journalist Valerie Miner, the panelists included Brownmiller, Griffin, and San Francisco attorneys Jill Lippitt and Camille LeGrand. Lippitt was a

[107] Andrea Dworkin, "Pornography and Grief," in *Take Back the Night*, 288.

[108] Audre Lorde, "Uses of the Erotic: The Erotic as Power," in *Take Back the Night*, 295. This speech was also reprinted in *WAVPM NewsPage*.

[109] These speeches are included in the anthology *Take Back the Night*, which Lederer edited after the Feminist Perspectives conference. See Diana E. H. Russell, "Pornography and the Women's Liberation Movement," in *Take Back the Night*, 302, 304.

[110] Memorandum, Joan Howarth to National Coordinating Committee, December 13, 1978, Correspondence LA file, WAVAW Papers.

FIGURE 5.5. Workshop participants at WAVPM's Feminist Perspectives on Pornography, the first national feminist conference on pornography (1978). Author and anti-pornography activist Susan Brownmiller sits at the front of the room, clapping. Her chair is directly in front of the podium. *Courtesy of the Gay, Lesbian, Bisexual, Transgender Historical Society. Photo by Jessica Collett.*

member of the WAVPM Board of Directors and was associated with La Casa de las Madres, a shelter for battered women and children. LeGrand specialized in civil law with a focus on violence-related issues, particularly rape and rape legislation. WAVPM had invited her to join the organization in May 1978, but LeGrand had declined on First Amendment grounds, noting in a letter to the group that WAVPM's goal of eliminating pornography through legal means was "dangerous and misplaced."[111] When it came to the advisability of using the law to control pornography, the panelists split down the middle: Brownmiller and Lippitt for, and Griffin and LeGrand against.

Brownmiller's panel comments revealed her anger toward men on the Left who were content to ignore or, worse, support pornography. Offering arguments that would define her early leadership of Women Against Pornography, Brownmiller complained that any feminist effort to discuss pornography's harm to women was invariably greeted by pat liberal responses about the greater importance of protecting First Amendment rights. Male liberals, who ostensibly were willing to empower government to increase personal freedom and equality for all individuals, were first in line to block the efforts of women who demanded limits on pornography. Although feminists pointed out that pornography humiliated, degraded, and dehumanized women, created a

[111] Camille LeGrand to WAVPM, Letter, May 8, 1978, Box 2, Folder: Correspondence: Attorneys, WAVPM Records, GLBT Historical Society.

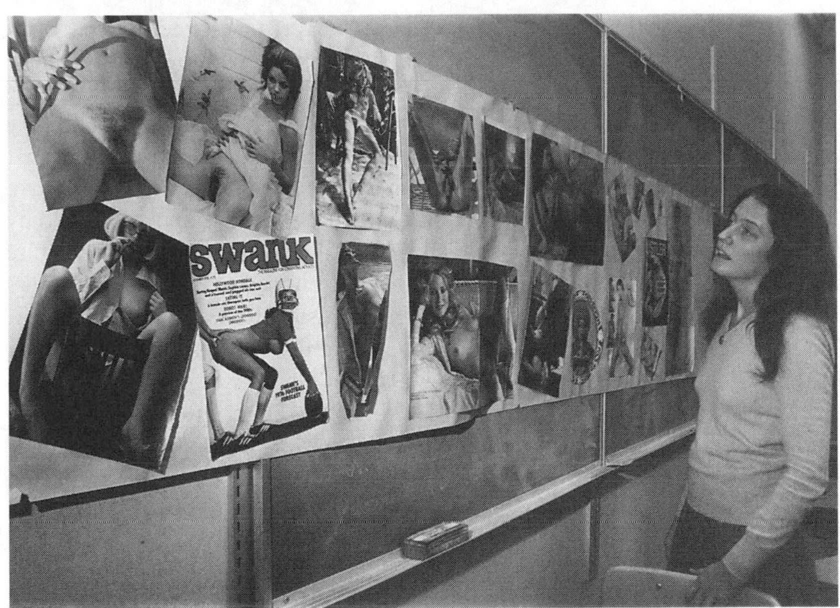

FIGURE 5.6. A Feminist Perspectives on Pornography conference attendee studies a display of sexually explicit images culled from such magazines as *Hustler, Swank, Playboy*, and *Penthouse*. Conference organizers hoped that direct confrontation would raise women's consciousness and stimulate their desire to join the anti-pornography movement. This display also allowed women to confront pornography in a safe space, supported by other women who were trying to grapple with this complex and emotionally charged issue. *Courtesy of the Gay, Lesbian, Bisexual, Transgender Historical Society.*

culture that encouraged men to commit acts of sexual violence, and deprived women of their First Amendment rights by silencing women's voices, liberals refused to consider any action that might promote equality *for women.* "I think the inviolability of the First Amendment has replaced God, motherhood and patriotism as a sacrosanct refuge for those who prefer to rely on sacred cows rather than the working out of complex societal problems in the public arena," Brownmiller told the crowd.[112]

It angered her that many former male allies rejected what seemed to a community of feminists as eminently reasonable demands for equal rights. This was particularly galling knowing that many of the same men were passionate supporters of the Civil Rights movement and had supported government action, such as the measures approved in the landmark 1954 *Brown v. Board*

[112] Helene Rosenbluth, narrator, *Fair Sex, Fair Game: Women Say No to the Sexual Safari*, Los Angeles, 1979, Pacifica Tape Library [sound recording]. This tape features live coverage of the WAVPM conference. The panel discussions and question-and-answer sessions that followed were captured in their entirety. It is a remarkable source of information on WAVPM and on the climate of the early anti-pornography movement.

of Education decision and the 1964 Civil Rights Act, to correct instances of racial discrimination. For many feminists, the violent pornography sold in neighborhood stores was as much a root cause and pedagogical tool of male violence against women as segregated public schools were agents of inequality and racism. In the *Brown v. Board of Education* decision, the Supreme Court noted that the existence of separate schools was a source of psychological harm and social disadvantage for children of color because segregation sanctioned by law was widely interpreted to mean that black children were inferior to white children. The justices noted that the impact of the harm was increased by its protection through the law, which gave segregationist policies social legitimacy. Pornography was also protected by the law, which, through a feminist lens, gave equivalent social legitimacy to the idea that women were inferior to men and normalized male sexual abuse and domination. Pornography humiliated and degraded women, and functioned like segregation to teach women their lesser place in the social order. Pornography was a root cause of discrimination and a legally sanctioned means of encouraging male violence. In Brownmiller's view, pornography was propaganda for gender discrimination and a patriarchal tool of oppression, and it required corrective government action.

Lippitt went even further than Brownmiller in her support of legal measures to control pornography. She urged the audience to set aside fears, convinced that a new generation of feminist attorneys steeped in the discourse of women's rights could write innovative laws designed to eliminate violent pornography while protecting artistic expression. The women's movement had encouraged growing numbers of college-educated women to enter the legal profession, and by the 1970s, federal anti-discrimination and affirmative action policies required law schools to both eliminate sex-based restrictions on admissions and to recruit female law professors. By the mid-1980s, when anti-pornography's campaign to pass legislation was at its zenith, women comprised a third of new entrants to law schools.[113] Feminist lawyers were making a national impact. From changes in sexual assault trial proceedings, to the development of sexual harassment law, to new definitions of domestic violence, these women were creating ways to use the law to bring about greater social equality and advance women's rights. In 1980, a reporter for the *New York Times* observed that feminist legal scholars were "proposing a basic rethinking of everything from the doctrine of negligence to the criminal laws about rape."[114] In such a climate, where law, legal process, and procedure were subject to feminist reinterpretation, the idea of restricting pornography to address pervasive gender discrimination seemed prudent to many. Lippitt supported the creation of legislation that would outlaw "the mass distribution

[113] For a discussion of the movement of women into legal careers and legal education, and the effect on anti-pornography organizing, see Clara Altman, "'All of These Rights': Equality, Free Speech, and the Feminist Anti-Pornography Movement, 1976–1986," Paper presented at the annual meeting of the Law and Society Association, Grand Hyatt, Denver, Colorado, May 25, 2009.

[114] Tamar Lewin, "Feminist Scholars Spurring a Rethinking of Law," *New York Times*, September 30, 1988, B9.

of for-profit films and periodicals which visually and explicitly depict women and children in a violent, degrading and brutal manner."[115]

Yet a number of problems with this approach were evident at the outset. Women at the conference could not agree on what constituted pornography, and it proved equally difficult to reach consensus when labeling material as degrading or oppressive. Indeed, members of WAVPM were already in conflict with lesbian sex radicals who argued that the organization's analysis of S/M as violent threatened their sexuality and erroneously condemned a consensual sexual practice. Finally, the liberal tradition of casting the widest possible net when dealing with the protection of freedom of expression was not easily dismissed. Despite these stumbling blocks, Lippitt's comments received thunderous applause.

Camille LeGrand, well known in feminist circles as an advocate for victims of rape and battering, feared that the kind of legislation Lippitt proposed could be turned against women. A new law might be used to censor feminist, gay, and lesbian materials whereas heterosexist pornography would go untouched. She told the audience that although a new anti-pornography law might not result in a government campaign against feminist works like *Our Bodies, Ourselves*, it was still important to remember that law enforcement was selective and political. Indeed, there were numerous historical examples of feminist efforts to pass laws to reduce female sexual exploitation, only to see those laws subsequently shaped and enforced by government authorities in distinctly anti-feminist ways.[116] For example, the Comstock Act of 1873 made it illegal to send obscene materials through the U.S. mail, and was used to prevent the dissemination of contraceptive devices, as well as information about birth control and abortion.[117] This history suggested that a so-called feminist anti-pornography law might not be applied in feminist ways. One might predict that local officials would challenge sexually explicit lesbian novels while leaving *Hustler* untouched.[118] "There is no law in this country requiring every case to be prosecuted," LeGrand told the audience.[119]

[115] Rosenbluth, *Fair Sex, Fair Game*, 1979.

[116] These included nineteenth-century social purity campaigns to strengthen laws against prostitution and to raise the age of sexual consent for girls. Both ultimately cast women as victims requiring male protection and control, and stripped them of sexual and political rights. See Ellen Carol DuBois and Linda Gordon, "Seeking Ecstasy on the Battlefield: Danger and Pleasure in Nineteenth-Century Feminist Sexual Thought," in *Pleasure and Danger: Exploring Female Sexuality*, ed. Carole S. Vance (New York: Routledge, 1984).

[117] See Linda Gordon, *Woman's Body, Woman's Right: Birth Control in America*, rev. ed. (New York: Penguin Books, 1990).

[118] This was the case with the 1992 *Butler* decision by the Supreme Court of Canada, which enacted anti-obscenity legislation based on the MacKinnon-Dworkin ordinances. The legislation has been used primarily to harass gay and lesbian publishing houses and feminist bookstores, and to enjoin the distribution of books and magazines directed at sexual minority populations, such as lesbian sadomasochists. The first prosecution was directed at *Bad Attitude*, a lesbian sex magazine. See Brenda Cossman, Shannon Bell, Lise Gotell, and Becki L. Ross, eds. *Bad Attitudes on Trial: Pornography, Feminism, and the 'Butler' Decision* (Toronto: University of Toronto Press, 1997).

[119] Kathy Riley, "First Conference on Pornography," *Big Mama Rag*, 7, no. 2 (February 1979), 3.

In a subsequent forum, LeGrand warned moderator Valerie Miner that women did not hold the upper hand when it came to the legal system. "All enforcement against pornography is political," she said. "As long as women hold such little power in this country, that's dangerous."[120] In hopes of turning WAVPM away from this path, she encouraged the organization to reorient its work toward the production of positive media images of women, rather than trying to stamp out a category of expression that the membership generally opposed.[121] Lederer sent LeGrand a blistering response on behalf of WAVPM, in which she described as "appalling" the very suggestion that the organization cease its campaign against pornography. With regard to concerns over the First Amendment, Lederer wrote that she rejected the "slippery slope" argument that any effort to restrict one type of speech would ultimately infringe on overall speech rights. "While I understand your concern about the erosion of first amendment rights," she wrote, "I think we have to remember that women's rights have not only been eroded – they've been totally negated."[122] For Lederer and other early proponents of legal action against pornography, the assumption that women and men benefited equally from freedom of speech was flawed and did not accurately reflect the reality of women's lives. Women had *theoretic* speech rights, but in practice they were silenced by the threat of rape, incest, sexual harassment, battering, and the incessant fear derived from life in a society where women were subject to violent male control. From a rights-based perspective, women were challenging a concept of free speech that neither incorporated a feminist critique nor took into account the material conditions of women's lives. Women, it seemed, had little to lose by questioning a principle that afforded them so little real protection.

Panelist Jill Lippitt did not seem as concerned with the potential for abuse of the law. She argued that women should try to empower themselves through any means possible, and if that meant challenging the First Amendment, then so be it. Women who were afraid that anti-pornography laws would erode speech rights were "naïve" in her view, because powerful forces would always try to suppress feminist voices, with or without the First Amendment. "I say if I can get pornography houses off the street and stop the violent and brutal portrayal of women in the mass media, I will do so without fear of eroding an already eroded First Amendment," she added. She also tried to allay concerns that laws against pornography would be used improperly against literature and art. "I think that this kind of legislation would protect all books and writings and would protect individual artistic expression," she insisted. "[B]ut what it would do is it would outlaw the porno houses and ban the pornographic magazines that featured those kinds of brutal photographic depictions

120 Camille LeGrand quoted in Valerie Miner, "Fantasies and Nightmares: The Red-Blooded Media," *Jump Cut: A Review of Contemporary Media*, 26 (December 1981). Available online at http://www.ejumpcut.org/archive/onlineessays/JC26folder/Miner

121 Camille LeGrand to WAVPM, Letter, May 8, 1978, Box 2, Folder: Correspondence: Attorn eys, WAVPM Records, GLBT Historical Society.

122 Laura Lederer to Camille LeGrand, Letter, August 24, 1978, Box 2, Folder: Correspondence: Attorneys, WAVPM Records, GLBT Historical Society.

of women and children."[123] Sitting in the audience, Denver WAVAW's Kathy Riley perceived a seismic split in the audience between women who supported consumer action strategies, such as boycotts and letter-writing campaigns, and women who believed – like Lippitt – that new laws could and should be devised to halt the spread of violent, woman-hating pornography.

The conference raised a number of difficult questions for Riley and many other WAVAW activists who felt uncomfortable with the dramatic changes taking place in the movement. The conference attendees were united in their recognition of women's oppression, and they believed that images of women in the media that conflated sexuality and violence were a social tool that men used to maintain their dominance over women. Yet the new focus on pornography and the enthusiasm for legal action in some WAVPM quarters were troubling. "Clearly, feminists need to do some thinking about pornography," Riley wrote after attending the conference. "Yet, consider all the problems inherent in even talking about porn: just getting through the misconceptions – the old association of an anti-pornography stance with sexual puritanism or censorship." Beyond the definitional issues, Riley expressed concern that some movement leaders were too ready to use the legal system. "With nearly every feminist issue one can name, changes in the law have been part of our strategy; it's only with porn that many of us question, not what kind of law, but whether we should have any at all."[124]

As the Saturday afternoon panel on pornography and the First Amendment wrapped up, conference-goers prepared for the evening's first national *Take Back the Night* march. This event expressed women's desire to reclaim the streets from rapists, sexual harassers, and pornographers, so that women might venture out free of the constant fear of sexual assault.[125] Andrea Dworkin addressed a packed auditorium of women as hundreds more waited outside Galileo High School, ready to march. "The most terrible thing about pornography is that it tells male truth," an impassioned Dworkin told the crowd. "Pornography functions to perpetuate male supremacy and crimes of violence against women because it conditions, trains, educates, and inspires men to despise women, to use women, to hurt women."[126] Dworkin expressed the central tenet of cultural feminism: an essentialist view of the fixed differences

[123] Rosenbluth, *Fair Sex, Fair Game*, 1979.

[124] Kathy Riley, "First Conference on Pornography," *Big Mama Rag*, 7, no. 2 (February 1979), 3.

[125] Walter Hinkle, "Women Meet, Talk, March on Porn" *San Francisco Chronicle*, November 18, 1978, 27. The slogan "Take Back the Night" was first used in the United States as the theme for this national protest march through San Francisco's Broadway pornography district. Laura Lederer has described it as follows: "Take Back the Night was a profound symbolic statement of our commitment to stopping the tide of violence against women in all arenas, and our demand that the perpetrators of such violence – from rapists to batterers to pornographers – be held responsible for their actions and made to change." Take Back the Night marches became a regular feature of feminist organizing, especially anti-violence organizing, and are still held today. Laura Lederer, "Introduction," in *Take Back the Night* 19.

[126] Andrea Dworkin, "Speech Exhorts March," *off our backs* (January 1979): 4. The full text of Dworkin's speech is reprinted in the Lederer anthology. See Andrea Dworkin, "Pornography and Grief," in *Take Back the Night*, 286–291.

between women and men. She praised women and female values as peaceful, cooperative, and nurturing, whereas men and male values were vilified as aggressive, sadistic, and murderous. Pornography celebrated the "common values" of men. According to Dworkin, women would have to destroy pornography to claim their freedom.

Following this powerful exhortation to march, 3,000 women claimed the streets of San Francisco, marching up Broadway, Kearney Street, and Columbus Avenue in the North Beach district lined with adult bookstores, XXX theaters, and live sex shows. Chanting "No More Profits Off Women's Bodies," they lit up the night with candles, flashlights, and torches. They blocked traffic and jammed Broadway for three city blocks. "Many March participants were deeply affected by the feelings of strength, power, and unity they experienced," Lynn Campbell wrote in *NewsPage*. "For an hour, Broadway belonged not to the barkers, the pimps, the pornographers, or to the theater owners, not to potential rapists, not to whistles, hassles or catcalls. It belonged instead to the songs, voices, rage, vision, strength, and presence of the 5000 women who took back the night."[127] A participant expressed similar feelings in a letter to WAVPM. She described the Saturday night demonstration as one of the most dynamic and moving events she had been part of in ten years of feminist organizing. "The anger, rage, energy and power of 2000–3000 women is incredible, fantastic," she raved.[128] Writing about WAVPM, the urban historian Josh Sides has noted the "emotional weight" associated with activists' ability to claim, even briefly, these notorious sex districts as part of their larger campaign to demand change.[129]

WAVPM turned to the Los Angeles anti-violence artists Suzanne Lacy and Leslie Labowitz to conceptualize a performance art piece to accompany the march. Labowitz had created WAVAW's *Record Companies Drag Their Feet* street theater event in conjunction with London and other artists from the Feminist Studio Workshop. Lacy's 1977 multimedia project, *Three Weeks in May*, was a public intervention designed to call attention to the prevalence of rape in American culture and to critique mainstream news media coverage of sexual violence, and included interviews with rape hotline staffers, an art installation showing the location of rapes occurring in Los Angeles over a three-week period, self-defense demonstrations, speak-outs, and speeches. Lacy and

[127] "We Took Back the Night," *WAVPM NewsPage* 2, no. 12 (February 1979): 3. Campbell and other WAVPM members put the number of marchers at 5,000, but news accounts of the march in both the *San Francisco Chronicle* and *San Francisco Examiner* estimated that 3,000 people participated. An account of the march in the leading feminist newspaper, *off our backs*, confirmed the number of participants as 3,000 (which alleviates concerns that mainstream newspapers might have underreported the numbers because of the radical nature of the march). See "Conference: Speech Exhorts March," *off our backs*, January 4, 1979, 4.

[128] Ellen Being to WAVPM, Letter, November 22, 1978, Box 6, Folder: Take Back the Night, WAVPM Records, GLBT Historical Society.

[129] Josh Sides, "Excavating the Postwar Sex District in San Francisco," *Journal of Urban History*, 32 (2006): 370.

FIGURE 5.7. The first national *Take Back the Night* march, November 18, 1978, San Francisco. The marchers gathered outside of Galileo High School to join the WAVPM conference attendees, some 3,000 strong. *Courtesy of Suzanne Lacy and Leslie Labowitz-Starus, Take Back the Night, San Francisco, 1978. Photo by Rob Blalack.*

Labowitz believed that an ongoing strategy to transform the media was critical to the anti-violence movement, and they regarded their art as a feminist cultural project that could analyze and disrupt mainstream media perspectives.[130] They were committed to demonstrating how images in advertising, television, film, mainstream news, and pornography presented women as sexual objects and willing victims to perpetuate patriarchal control.[131] They were particularly interested in critiquing mainstream news, which they saw as condoning and reproducing acts of male violence through patterns of coverage, and hoped through their art to disrupt and transform the media so that it might carry an activist message of civic protest fused with feminist consciousness.

Lacy and Labowitz recruited artists from San Diego, San Francisco, and Los Angeles, all of whom were part of their newly formed social art network, Ariadne, to help design a float to convey the theme of women's oppression under patriarchy.[132] Measuring six feet wide by ten feet long, the brightly lit

[130] Suzanne Lacy, *Leaving Art: Writings on Performance, Politics, and Publics, 1974–2007* (Durham, NC: Duke University Press, 2010).

[131] Leslie Labowitz, "Developing a Feminist Media Strategy," *Heresies* 3, no. 1 (1980): 28–31.

[132] Lacy and Labowitz cofounded Ariadne: A Social Art Network in 1977 as a project of the Los Angeles Women's Building that focused on issues of violence against women. The organization sought to bring together women artists, politicians, activists, and media workers committed to creating political art and action around the issue of violence against women and making direct social change.

float featured two sides that brought to life Mulvey's theory of the voyeuristic and fetishistic male gaze and the way that male spectators objectified women as madonnas or whores. The front showed a virginal, doll-like figure with porcelain-white skin that was made out of a woman's fashion-store mannequin. She was bedecked with flowers and surrounded with electric candles, resembling Latin American Santa Semana celebrations in which the image of the Madonna is carried through the streets. The back of the float featured a three-headed lamb carcass, covered in red feathers and pearls, with images of pornography pouring out of her open, exposed gut. The two sides were meant to express the dichotomy of the representation of women in media and society, both revered and degraded.[133] Pictures ripped from magazines like *Hustler* and *Penthouse* and offensive record album covers, including the Ohio Players' *Pleasure*, were plastered all around the base of the back side, and marchers tore the images from the float as it went by, as a symbol of their desire to be free from pornography. As the float moved down Broadway, Lacy directed the marchers to ululate loudly, attempting to create an audiovisual experience that would be "more powerful and yet related to that incredible neon barrage and the sounds of the [Broadway] strip."[134] The feminist folk musician Holly Near followed on a flatbed truck, singing her original composition, "Fight Back!" that urged women to channel their fear into rage and unite to make the world a safe place for all women. Near had originally performed "Fight Back!" as part of Lacy's activist art project *In Mourning and in Rage*, created to memorialize the rape-murder victims of the Los Angeles Hillside Strangler in 1977. Rape, murder, and pornography were seen as points on the continuum of male violence against women, so Lacy and Labowitz asked Near to reprise her performance for *Take Back the Night*. Together, these artists created a public event that allowed women to join in the "emotive and cathartic expression of private experience," namely their physical and emotional oppression in a culture of male violence.[135]

Conclusion: Conflicts Over Strategies and Tactics

In her concluding remarks at the WAVPM conference, Diana Russell urged the audience to spread the word about the newly forming movement against pornography. She implored her listeners to recognize that the sexual revolution had confused women, enabling men to pressure them into accepting pornography as part of normal and healthy sexuality. This "male liberal and radical line" had been used to silence women, persuading them that "being against any aspect of the so-called sexual revolution meant being a

[133] *Oral history interview with Suzanne Lacy*, 1990 Mar. 16 & 24 and Sept. 27, Archives of American Art, Smithsonian Institution.

[134] *Oral history interview with Suzanne Lacy*, 1990.

[135] Suzanne Lacy, *Leaving Art: Writings on Performance, Politics, and Publics, 1974–2007* (Durham, NC: Duke University Press, 2010).

FIGURE 5.8. Artists Suzanne Lacy and Leslie Labowitz designed a two-sided float to accompany the *Take Back the Night* march. The front side, shown here, was a Madonna figure bedecked with flowers and surrounded by electric candles. The back side featured a three-headed lamb with images of pornography pouring out of her open, exposed gut. The two sides represented the madonna/whore dichotomy of the representation of women in media and society, both revered and degraded. *Courtesy of Suzanne Lacy and Leslie Labowitz-Starus, Take Back the Night, San Francisco, 1978. Photo by Rob Blalack.*

reactionary, unliberated prude." Men had pressured women to accept the idea that being sexually liberated meant tolerating "male sex trips," including pornography.[136] Now, women were fighting back. With eyes wide open, they saw that the sexual revolution had primarily delivered greater sexual access for

[136] Russell, "Pornography and the Women's Liberation Movement," in *Take Back the Night*, 302.

men, and that pornography was a key tool that men used to control women both in and out of bed.

Although she had great hopes for the new movement, Russell worried aloud that questions about First Amendment issues threatened to derail feminist progress. She asked the audience to set aside concerns about free speech long enough to develop and articulate a feminist analysis of pornography. "[M]ost feminists ... have been so hung up on the censorship issue that they have refused to allow themselves to recognize pornography as a problem for women, refused to analyze what is going on in pornography and why, refused to even allow themselves to *feel* outraged by it," Russell chided.[137] She entreated her listeners to avoid the "short-circuiting" process that typically happened when women ran up against First Amendment arguments that froze them in their tracks and kept them from taking any action against pornography.[138] Although she mentioned that civil disobedience might end up being the best strategy for fighting pornography, she also welcomed legal approaches. "I personally agree with Susan Brownmiller that portraying women being bound, raped, beaten, tortured, and killed for so-called sexual stimulation and pleasure should be banned," Russell told the crowd. "[I] believe these portrayals encourage and condone these crimes against women in the real world."[139] For members of WAVPM, it was no surprise to hear Russell endorse the legal eradication of pornography, as these ideas had appeared in *NewsPage* since 1977.

For many WAVAW members, however, the conference signaled a worrisome sea change. For those in the audience who saw themselves as part of an anti-media violence movement focused on public education, consciousness raising, and consumer action to achieve corporate responsibility, the growing emphasis on pornography coupled with feminist support for legal restriction of sexually explicit material was alarming. Certainly, it raised serious questions about the viability of a unified movement. Seven members of Denver WAVAW attended the conference, most wondering how their tradition of consumer activism might fit with WAVPM's anti-pornography focus. Kathy Riley of Denver WAVAW shared her thoughts in a postconference report in the local women's newspaper, *Big Mama Rag*. "I went for a couple of reasons: mostly to meet other women working in the area of violence against women, but also to work out my confusion and politics on the issue of pornography itself," she wrote. That confusion, she added, meant "how to define the whole of pornography, how to look at it in relation to other feminist issues, and then, only then, how to fight it."[140] In her assessment of the conference, Riley noted that participants couldn't agree on any definition of pornography, and thus tended to skip the first two steps and proceed directly to the third: how to fight it. Deb Friedman of the Feminist Alliance Against Rape made a similar observation,

137 Diana Russell, "In Conclusion," *WAVPM NewsPage* Special Issue: Conference Report (February 1979): 7.

138 Russell, "Pornography and the Women's Liberation Movement," in *Take Back the Night*, 303.

139 Russell, "In Conclusion," *WAVPM NewsPage*, 8.

140 Kathy Riley, "First Conference on Pornography," *Big Mama Rag* 7, no. 2 (February 1979), 3.

noting that the conference was inspiring at times, but also a "disappointment" in that the attendees were not able to decide what constituted pornography and explain how it harmed women. "If we are to get rid of pornography, we need a more coherent analysis than currently exists," she wrote in *Aegis*. "With few exceptions, this was not being called for at the conference."[141] As Riley pointed out, the sessions did not produce a concrete definition of pornography and its social effects, but emphasized ideas for controlling its spread. The level of interest in forging ahead with legal action took some members of WAVAW by surprise, and sent many activists like Riley home feeling uneasy about changes in the movement's direction.

Just two years after leading the national campaign against Max Factor – an effort that succeeded using the tactics and strategies borrowed from sister organization WAVAW – WAVPM was moving in a different direction. Although WAVPM shared broad concerns about violence against women with WAVAW, the organization's attention had shifted to pornography and to legal means for controlling its content and distribution. This marked a major departure from the WAVAW agenda and that organization's commitment to public education and consumer action. "Since when is passing new laws the only legitimate goal of political organizing?" WAVAW's Joan Howarth wondered as talk of legal action against pornography spread. "The task of educating, consciousness-raising and analysis of the visual reflections of sexual politics throughout our culture is difficult, profound political work."[142] Both within and outside the movement, many observers echoed Howarth's concerns, urging caution.

Ellen Willis, a radical feminist writer who became a major voice of the pro-sex movement in the early 1980s, was one of the first women to criticize the anti-pornography movement for seeking legal restrictions. "Though I share the impulse behind them, I think these appeals for an official crackdown are mistaken and dangerous," she warned in *Rolling Stone*. "Feminists who support censorship are offering the state a weapon that will inevitably be used against us."[143] She urged movement activists to stay the course set by WAVAW to try to raise people's consciousness as the first step in reversing the trend of increased social acceptance of sexually violent media images. But many members of WAVPM were undeterred, and the organization's leaders continued to promote the benefits of legal solutions.

By the end of the WAVPM national conference, it was clear that WAVAW and WAVPM had reached an impasse. Social movements are never static; indeed, they consist of a complex and fluid interplay of differently organized groups, subcultures, and individuals who share a common recognition of a social problem, such as pornography, yet may differ widely regarding desirable solutions. The anti-media violence movement represented by WAVAW

141 Deb Friedman, "Conference Reports," *Aegis: Magazine on Ending Violence Against Women* (September/October 1979), 48.

142 Joan Howarth, "Response by Joan Howarth," *WAVAW Newsletter* no. 8 (1980): 6.

143 Willis, "Sexual Counterrevolution I," 29.

had its share of subgroups and individuals with varied and often conflicting viewpoints, but most members clung to a central logic that endorsed public education, consciousness raising, consumer pressure tactics, and the demand for corporate responsibility. The WAVPM conference revealed the existence of another community of activists who defined the social problem and its preferred solution differently, and in ways that were not complementary to WAVAW. As WAVPM moved aggressively in the direction of anti-pornography, the ties linking WAVPM and WAVAW in a broader media violence movement began to unravel.

6

Growing Pains

The Emergence of Women Against Pornography and New Directions for the Feminist Anti-Pornography Movement

In July 1977, about a year and a half before the national Feminist Perspectives on Pornography conference, WAVPM reported exciting news from New York City. A contingent of well-known feminists had decided to form an anti-pornography action group.[1] Organized by Susan Brownmiller, the membership roster read like a who's who of the New York radical feminist community. Gloria Steinem was the most famous feminist in the nation, and the editor of *Ms.* Robin Morgan had edited the important radical feminist anthology, *Sisterhood Is Powerful*, and had published a collection of her own essays. Shere Hite was known for her groundbreaking study of American women's sexual lives. Leah Fritz had been part of the 1968 Miss America protest in Atlantic City, and her collection of essays, *Thinking Like a Woman*, had been published in 1975. Grace Paley was a leading antiwar activist and award-winning short-story writer. Adrienne Rich was a nationally recognized lesbian-feminist poet. Lois Gould was a well-known journalist. Barbara Mehrhof was an anti-rape activist and had been a member of some of the leading radical feminist groups, including Redstockings and THE FEMINISTS.

Many of these women had been present at Brownmiller's Greenwich Village apartment in December 1976 when Julia London traveled to New York to present the WAVAW slide show and discuss the Warner Communications boycott. Impressed by the media violence work being accomplished around the country, they decided to launch a new East Coast-based group called the Women's Anti-Defamation League. The League members were more interested in pornography than advertising per se, and many believed that WAVAW's campaign against abusive record advertising was missing the major target. The new group had a different agenda, to "tackle the mainstreaming of violent hard-core porn," which, the women complained, was increasingly visible on New York streets.[2]

[1] "News from the East Coast," *WAVPM NewsPage*, 1, no. 2 (July 1977), 2.

[2] Susan Brownmiller, *In Our Time: Memoir of a Revolution* (New York: The Dial Press, 1999): 298.

The journalist Molly Ivins reported favorably on the group for the *New York Times*. Although her story was lumped between a preview of the designer Adolfo's fall fashions and a feature story about the baked goods available at Zaro's Bread Basket in Grand Central Station, as was typical for stories about "women's issues" at that time, Ivins managed to explain the women's objections. The League members were organizing against the degradation and dehumanization of women in pornography. More than just insulting, the violent portrayal of women in pornography – brutalized, chained, screaming in pain – robbed women of their humanity. It presented women as sexual objects to be used and abused rather than as people who deserved to be respected and treated as equals. Pornography was a means of humiliating women and keeping them down, teaching them to see themselves as nothing more than sexual playthings and to accept male violence as a normal part of sexuality. "The human body is not obscene, sexuality is not obscene," Gloria Steinem told Ivins. "But this is not sex, it is violence."[3]

Already struggling with the distinction between "erotica" and "pornography," which would always be a sticking point within the movement, Steinem meant to convey that feminists differed from religious conservatives who opposed all explicit depictions of sex, especially nonmarital and homosexual images. Although no one that Ivins interviewed could speak for all of the League members, many would likely have supported Steinem's definition of erotica: images of people "making love," including "a sensuality and touch and warmth, an acceptance of bodies and nerve endings," as Steinem wrote in *Ms.* in 1978.[4] Steinem, Dworkin, and other anti-pornography feminists cited the etymological roots of the words to lend substance to their different meanings: the word *pornography* was derived from the ancient Greek terms *porne* and *graphos*, which taken together meant "the graphic depiction of whores." *Porne* referred to the lowest class of whore, kept in brothels in ancient Greece and available to all male citizens. *Graphos* meant literal depiction, as in writing, etching, or drawing. *Eros*, by contrast, was drawn from a Greek word meaning love, specifically passionate love that contained an appreciation of beauty.

Members of WAVPM also tried to flesh out these definitions and characterized erotica as related to a woman's "wholeness and integrity," as "personal," "natural," "fulfilling," "circular," and as something that "taps into the emotional, creative part of self." Pornography, on the other hand, was "for titillation of men – not with women's interests in mind." It was sexuality as "defined by penis, men," and was said to produce "violence," a "power imbalance," "no reciprocity," and "gratification at someone else's expense."[5]

[3] Molly Ivins, "Feminist Leaders Join Anti-Smut Campaign Despite Reservations," *The New York Times*, July 2, 1977, 18.

[4] Gloria Steinem, "Erotica and Pornography: A Clear and Present Difference," *Ms.* (November 1978): 53–54, 75. Reprinted in *Take Back the Night*, 35–39.

[5] Sue Scope, "Erotica Versus Pornography: An Exploration," *WAVPM NewsPage*, 3, no. 6 (July 1979): 1. See also, "The Uses of the Erotic," *WAVPM NewsPage*, 5, no. 3 (March 1981): 2.

Anti-pornography feminists supported erotica and wished to promote the production and dissemination of this type of positive sexual imagery, but the distinction collapsed over time as it became clear that one woman's erotica was another's pornography.

Ivins also reported in the *Times* that the League was investigating ways to reduce the public visibility of pornography. She noted that the women seemed inclined to seek a city ordinance limiting its display. Steinem heartily agreed. "If someone wants to see it, he should have to go into a store or theater and ask; it now assaults everyone who walks on the streets," she complained.[6] Brownmiller supported this strategy, which she believed fell short of censorship. "We are not going to smash any presses or try to stop anyone from printing," she advised, but she welcomed legislation to keep pornography from appearing in plain sight.[7] Some of the members of the League were eager to explore legal remedies that might deliver more tangible results than the public education and consumer pressure tactics that WAVAW used nationwide.

Over the course of the next few months, other well-known feminists joined the League and began working to craft a feminist statement on pornography. Barbara Deming, an author and advocate of nonviolent social change, came aboard. Andrea Dworkin, author of the 1974 book *Woman Hating*, and one of the anti-pornography movement's foremost rhetoricians, joined too. So did Karla Jay, a member of the radical feminist group Redstockings and an activist in Gay Liberation, and Letty Cottin Pogrebin, an editor of *Ms*.[8] The women met during the spring and summer of 1977 to draft copy for a statement about feminist opposition to pornography. They intended to purchase advertising space in the *New York Times*, where they would publish the statement along with the signatures of hundreds of supporting feminists. The statement would explain the League's objections to pornography from a specifically feminist point of view.

But as Brownmiller has recalled in a memoir, the drafting and editing process became cumbersome with so many famous – and opinionated – writers and activists working on the same material. Dworkin, Rich, and Steinem composed a statement that linked rape and wife beating to violent pornography. Brownmiller, Gould, and Mehrhof wrote something about the dangers of linking images of violence with images of sexual pleasure. Deming thought that the group ought to mention the First Amendment. Adrienne Rich wanted to include a statement about every woman's right to control her own body and determine her sexual preference. Factions developed within the League about how to define pornography and which points ought to appear uppermost in the text. With so many cooks in the kitchen, it became impossible to produce a statement that everyone could support. After months of work,

[6] Ivins, "Feminist Leaders Join Anti-Smut Campaign," 18.

[7] Ivins, "Feminist Leaders Join Anti-Smut Campaign," 18.

[8] The League is also described in Barbara Mehrhof and Lucille Iverson, "Pornography and Violence: When Does Free Speech Go Too Far?" *Majority Report*, August 20–September 2, 1977, 6.

the group "petered out from exhaustion," Brownmiller recalled.[9] It did not help matters when League member Lois Gould published a "Hers" column in the *New York Times* that endorsed the idea that feminists might join hands with the religious Right in a combined anti-pornography effort. This idea was publicly denounced by a number of fellow League members, which only added to the group's turmoil. Although its founders made bright predictions for the future, the Women's Anti-Defamation League never really got off the ground. It would take until 1979 for Brownmiller and others to successfully organize Women Against Pornography (WAP) – the reincarnated Women's Anti-Defamation League.

This chapter chronicles the formation of WAP and describes some of the early events that revealed the organization's interest in exploring legislative remedies. Although WAP did not formally endorse the use of legal measures until 1983, when it supported the anti-pornography ordinances introduced by Andrea Dworkin and Catharine MacKinnon, I argue that some influential WAP leaders alienated liberals and potential feminist supporters by expressing early support for government restriction. Worse, the initial enthusiasm for legal strategies to suppress pornography hampered WAP's ability to communicate a multilayered and specifically feminist objection to violence against women to the national audience, because the issue of free speech quickly came to dominate discussion. Some members of WAP tried to extend earlier analyses of violence by articulating a definition of pornography as material that harmed every woman, physically injuring some in its production and ideologically debasing all in its consumption. Other WAP members, however, muddied the waters with talk of city ordinances and anti-obscenity legislation. Once the word "censorship" had been uttered, WAP would find itself contending with all sorts of unexpected opposition.

In the period just prior to and immediately following WAP's formation, two major events contributed to the perception that the organization supported censorship. The first was a 1978 debate between civil libertarians and leaders of the League that was soon to be reincarnated as WAP. Just two weeks after WAVPM's national pornography conference, representatives of these two groups clashed at an all-day colloquium at the New York University School of Law. Most of the civil libertarians reacted with hostility to the feminists' concerns, worried that restrictions on pornography constituted a threat to First Amendment rights and would encourage government encroachment into the areas of speech and expression. Some of the anti-pornography women were equally unbending with regard to the civil libertarian point of view, feeling that male liberals were quick to stand up against every sort of injustice except those where *women's* rights were violated. The climate in the room, at first cordial, degenerated over the course of the afternoon; the NYU law professor and civil liberties expert Paul Chevigny stood up and walked out in protest while Andrea Dworkin was speaking.

[9] Brownmiller, *In Our Time*, 299.

The second event occurred in July 1979, when WAP founders Susan Brownmiller, Dolores Alexander, and Lynn Campbell were guests on the popular afternoon television program, the *Phil Donahue Show*. While appearing on the talk show, the WAP panelists raised the issue of using legal restriction to control public display of pornography. Although many women in the viewing audience responded favorably to WAP's agenda, others expressed their alarm at the organization's willingness to give additional power to the state to "protect" women. Many pointed out that if WAP engineered a solution whereby the courts could decide what material was – and was not – suitable for public display, gay, lesbian, and feminist expression would surely be censored. The courts were a product of the same patriarchal and heterosexist culture that allowed pornography to flourish; it was naïve to assume that jurists, particularly conservative ones, would apply feminist principles when evaluating books, films, magazines, and the like. *Our Bodies, Ourselves*; *Scream Quietly or the Neighbors Will Hear*, and *Sisterhood Is Powerful* might be the first to go. When WAP, following WAVPM's lead, shifted the public discussion from consciousness raising and consumer pressure to legislative action, feminist anti-pornography organizing became controversial.

NYU Conference: "Obscenity: Degradation of Women versus Right of Free Speech"

On Saturday, December 2, 1978, just two weeks after WAVPM's national Feminist Perspectives on Pornography conference in San Francisco, 300 people turned out for an all-day colloquium on pornography at the New York University School of Law. The meeting was sponsored by the *Review of Law and Social Change*, a law school publication created in 1969 during the height of student radicalism. The colloquium brought feminists and civil libertarians together to discuss whether the state might restrict pornography to mitigate its harms to women and create the possibility for gender-based social equality, or whether women were obliged in the name of free speech to tolerate what they described as a legally and socially sanctioned hate campaign.

The question of free speech rights energized women who were concerned about the tidal wave of popular media images conflating sexuality and violence. They believed in the wake of the Civil Rights movement that the state had a significant role to play in not only guaranteeing social equality, but in taking concrete steps to produce it. WAVPM activists, particularly the feminist attorneys among them, were familiar with federal interventions designed to combat discrimination and substantive social imbalances, such as the Supreme Court's 1954 *Brown v. Board of Education* decision that found racially segregated public schools to be unconstitutional, and the 1964 Civil Rights Act that prohibited discrimination on the basis of race and sex in public employment and accommodations. These efforts to eliminate racial inequality suggested that lawmakers could take formal steps to reduce or eliminate gender inequality as well. Once feminist activists connected the issue of women's social subordination to the presentation of women as inferior beings in pornography, they drew on the equality principles advanced in the Civil Rights movement to demand justice for women.

Feminists, however, faced a major barrier: The agent of discrimination they intended to fight was based in images and speech, both of which enjoyed expansive protection under the First Amendment. Whereas *Brown* and the Civil Rights Act addressed substantive *acts* of discrimination, such as the creation of separate schools for black and white children, feminists were arguing that *expression* – the words and pictures that constituted pornography – were responsible for their oppression.[10] Historically, feminists had objected to obscenity laws that sought to restrict sexual speech, viewing them as a barrier to women's rights; it was nearly impossible to demand access to birth control, abortion, sex education, and overall sexual self-determination in a legal environment where such subjects could not be discussed openly without fear of legal consequence. Faced with the urgent problem of violent pornography, however, many radical thinkers were reconsidering their traditional opposition to censorship. When *Snuff* first appeared in New York City, more than eighty well-known feminists and liberal intellectuals including Susan Sontag, Grace Paley, Eric Bentley, and David Dellinger, signed a petition asking the Manhattan district attorney to ban the film on the grounds that it would incite viewers to commit sexual violence against women.

The 1978 NYU colloquium, "Obscenity: Degradation of Women versus Right of Free Speech," foregrounded this startling new view of modern First Amendment doctrine as a barrier to women's equality. The topic was suggested by Norman Redlich, dean of the law school, after a student in his constitutional law class presented the feminist case for restrictions on speech rights. Redlich had been teaching the subject of obscenity for close to twenty years, and had observed that law students reacted to the topic in predictable ways. "Namely, they tend to think that all laws regulating obscenity are a silly waste of time, and that the first amendment should be interpreted very broadly," Redlich wrote.[11] When he became aware that a sharply different viewpoint was taking shape in the women's movement, Redlich asked Teresa Hommel, a member of WAVPM, former legislative coordinator of NOW-NY, and a third-year law student at NYU, to share these ideas. Hommel presented a feminist analysis of pornography, arguing that it dehumanized women by objectifying them as body parts and presenting them as natural outlets for male sexual aggression. Pornography encouraged rape and other acts of violence, threatening women's safety and establishing a climate of terror that silenced women and perpetuated their oppression. Pornography thus helped

[10] Clara Altman has made this point in her essay, "'All Of These Rights,' Equality, Free Speech, and the Feminist Anti-Pornography Movement, 1976–1986," Paper presented at the annual meeting of the Law and Society Association, Grand Hyatt, Denver, Colorado, May 25, 2009.

[11] Norman Redlich, "Introduction," *New York University Review of Law and Social Change*, 8 (1978–1979), 205.

create and maintain women's subordinate status and made it impossible for women to claim social equality with men. Redlich was moved by Hommel's passion. "It was one of the most stirring and interesting classes that I have ever taught," he recalled.[12]

The colloquium that grew out of Redlich's class was designed to expose the legal community to recent developments in feminist thought about pornography, and to help feminists devise a means of fighting this material that would not violate the First Amendment. The intent was to allow the two groups to learn from each other, to draw from their respective expertise and protect sexual speech while still addressing pornography's harms to women. "We hoped to get the civil libertarians 'unstuck' from addressing only the obsolete moralistic objections to pornography," the colloquium coordinator wrote, and added that the groups would discuss "what legal remedies may be available to women subjected to the dehumanization and the physical threats posed by violent pornography."[13] It was an ambitious program, and the *Review* invited some of New York's leading feminists and civil liberties experts to participate.

The feminist panelists included Susan Brownmiller and Andrea Dworkin, as well as Florence Rush, a social worker and expert on the sexual abuse of children, journalist Leah Fritz, and Phyllis Chesler, a feminist psychologist and author of *Women and Madness* (1972), which argued that women were subject to a punitive double standard in the diagnosis and treatment of mental illness. Each of these women would play a role in the founding of WAP in 1979.[14] Teresa Hommel presented the WAVPM slide show to the colloquium audience on Saturday morning. WAVPM coordinators Laura Lederer and Lynn Campbell flew in from San Francisco and set up a display featuring sexually explicit photographs of women from such magazines as *Playboy*, *Penthouse*, and *Hustler*. Another group of images showed S/M and bestiality, including a woman having sexual intercourse with a pig.

On the civil libertarian side, the panelists included four law professors from NYU, as well as a number of attorneys who specialized in First Amendment cases. Some, like professor Paul Chevigny and attorney Alan Levine, had worked for years for the New York Civil Liberties Union. Two of the women on the lawyers' panel, Brenda Feigen Fasteau and Marjorie Smith, identified themselves as feminists and civil libertarians. Fasteau was a former national vice-president for legislation of NOW and a former director of the American Civil Liberties Union's (ACLU) Women's Rights Project. Smith was the Deputy Commissioner of the New York City Department of Consumer Affairs and

[12] Redlich, "Introduction," 205.

[13] Lisa Lerman, "Preface," *New York University Review of Law and Social Change*, 8 (1978–1979), 181.

[14] Dworkin was not involved with the group day to day, but participated in the group's early actions such as the March on Times Square and the East Coast pornography conference. In this way, her ideas and presence were very much a part of the initial public image of anti-pornography feminism.

a former staff attorney for both the Women's Rights Project of the ACLU and the Prisoners' Rights Project of the Legal Aid Society of New York City. Herald Price Fahringer, attorney for both Larry Flynt, publisher of *Hustler*, and Al Goldstein, publisher of *Screw*, also sat on the civil libertarian panel, much to the disgust of the anti-pornography feminists.

Teresa Hommel opened the morning session with the WAVPM slide show. She described pornography's recurring themes: the association of sexuality and violence; the stereotypical images of men as sexual brutes and women as their passive, willing victims; the presentation of rape and battering as normal aspects of sexuality; and the portrayal of women as subhuman. Hommel showed images from adult fetish magazines like *Roped and Raped* and *Cherry Blossoms*, which featured pictures of Asian women bound and tortured. She presented the advice column from the June 1978 issue of *Genesis* magazine where a "reader" complained about his wife's sexual performance: "'She only blows me in bed for five or six minutes.... What can I do to get her to suck me off longer and wherever I want?'" The magazine replied: "'If this is what you want, then demand it! Women in general like to be dominated, so tell her to get on her knees and ram it down her throat. She'll, no doubt, know that you mean business!'"[15] Hommel offered a series of statistics about women and sexual violence, including a figure from New York Women Against Rape that indicated that one out of every three American women would experience sexual assault. The reporter from *off our backs* wrote that the slide show and rape statistics made "a stunning impact on the audience."[16] The *New York Times* reporter observed that the slides of women in chains being mutilated and battered "drew gasps" from all assembled.[17]

Over the course of the morning session, it seemed to observers that the civil libertarians were sympathetic to the feminists' concerns. However, when the panel discussion turned to the use of legal strategies to control the dissemination of pornography, any possibility for cooperation faded away. Looking back, it was probably unrealistic to hope that such a colloquium could have built bridges between civil libertarians and anti-pornography feminists. These groups defended interests that pornography set in conflict, and they approached the question of censorship with different priorities. The civil libertarians were opposed to any government-enforced limits on free expression, and they took an absolutist position on the First Amendment. They were committed to protecting the fundamental rights guaranteed to the individual by law, and thus viewed any effort to restrict pornography as unwarranted interference with freedom of speech. They argued vehemently that every human being was entitled to equality before the law, and that no one had the right to strip an individual of his or her right to express a viewpoint, even if that viewpoint

[15] Teresa Hommel, "Images of Women in Pornography and Media," *New York University Review of Law and Social Change*, 8 (1978–1979), 207.

[16] brooke, "Life, Liberty, & the Pursuit of Porn," *off our backs*, 9 (January 1979): 5.

[17] Judy Klemesrud, "Women, Pornography, Free Speech: A Fierce Debate at N.Y.U." *The New York Times*, December 4, 1978, D10.

offended other people or groups. "I take the position, and I will defend the position, that there is *nothing* to be said, nothing *rational* to be said, for any government censorship of any writings that relate to sex," Paul Chevigny told the feminists. "It would be an inexcusable interference with the freedom of everyone in this room and everyone in this country."[18] Chevigny voiced support for a central tenet of traditional liberal political philosophy – respect for a society in which government authority is defined and limited by individual consent, and the content of the "good life" is to be defined by each person based on his or her own choices and preferences. His position also revealed a commitment to the modern First Amendment doctrine of speech, which holds that the state must remain neutral toward expression that has intellectual or social value, essentially remaining indifferent to the moral superiority or popularity of one person's viewpoint over another and respecting the equal worth of persons as choicemakers.

The feminist panelists, on the other hand, articulated a communitarian social position and argued that the private preferences protected by classic liberalism provided an inadequate basis for protecting the interests of women as a group. They explained that the liberal principles that protected the rights of individual men to produce and consume pornography effectively silenced women as a class, making it impossible for them to exercise the free speech rights due them under the First Amendment. In pornography, women were presented as inferior to men, as subhuman sex objects who enjoyed humiliation, violence, and pain, and who were appropriate targets for sadistic male torture. Men learned who and what women were from pornography, and accepted this definition of women as a lesser class of human beings, created to serve male needs and desires. Men circulated pornography to foster a climate of terror that would keep women silent and subordinate. Leah Fritz described pornography to the colloquium as "gynocidal propaganda," part of a systematic campaign of brutality directed against women. Andrea Dworkin told the audience that the images of bound and bruised women in pornography were equivalent to "death threats to a female population in rebellion."[19] Pornography was a brutal reminder of what men would do to women who tried to rise up and free themselves from male control.

According to the feminist panelists, it was impossible for women living in such a culture to claim equal rights before the law, knowing that men would not only threaten women who challenged male power, but would back up their threats with the use of terrible sexual violence. Catharine MacKinnon has been the primary architect of this theory, describing the chilling effect on speech that a social imbalance of power creates for women:

> [W]hen you are powerless, you don't just speak differently. A lot, you don't speak. Your speech is not just differently articulated, it is silenced. Eliminated, gone. You aren't

[18] Paul Chevigny, "Opening Statement," in "Panel Discussion: Effects of Violent Pornography," *New York University Review of Law and Social Change*, 8 (1978–1979), 233.

[19] Quoted in brooke, "Life, Liberty & the Pursuit of Porn," 5.

just deprived of a language with which to articulate your distinctiveness, although you are; you are deprived of a life out of which articulation might come. Not being heard is not just a function of lack of recognition, not just that no one knows how to listen to you, although it is that; it is also the silence of the deep kind, the silence of being prevented from having anything to say.[20]

In MacKinnon's view, pornography was not a form of protected speech, but an act of sex discrimination that robbed women of their right to speak and to be heard. Chevigny's defense of classic liberalism was thus an "ideological charade" because its abstract ideal of equality for all persons who would speak masked concrete realities of male power and pervasive gender inequality.[21] Sometimes, the women argued, the interests of the group had to be taken into account and given priority over those of the individual to achieve a common good.

Although MacKinnon was not a participant at NYU, the influence of her groundbreaking work on male sexual dominance of women was evident. Specifically, MacKinnon was at that time advancing an inequality argument about sexual harassment as sex discrimination, namely that sexual harassment was a practice that expressed and reinforced the social inequality of women to men.[22] The WAP panelists at NYU borrowed language and theory from MacKinnon to present pornography as a form of sex discrimination. They argued that pornography silenced women by creating and reinforcing a hostile social environment that made women reluctant to speak at all, choosing silence even in the face of violent abuses like rape and battering. Freedom of speech was meaningless for women living in world where men systematically denied their autonomy and subjectivity. Pornography was a key male weapon in this regard.

The feminist panelists urged the civil libertarians to think differently about freedom of speech. They asked them to understand that creating social conditions that would allow women the full exercise of their civil rights would have to include limits on pornography. Leah Fritz told the lawyers that if they refused to help women secure their First Amendment rights – their rights to talk openly about birth control, rape, the female body, and sexuality – they were essentially guilty of malpractice, and "worth nothing" in their profession. "I will go to them [the lawyers] as I would go to a doctor and I will say it hurts here.... What are you going to do to help me? ... And I do not expect the doctor to say, 'Well, it is against the first amendment for me to help you.' I expect the doctor to offer a suggestion," Fritz said. "I expect him to ... save my life."[23] Dworkin asked the lawyers to think about pornography from

[20] Catharine A. MacKinnon, *Feminism Unmodified: Discourses on Life and Law* (Cambridge, MA: Harvard University Press, 1987), 39.

[21] Donald A. Downs, *The New Politics of Pornography* (Chicago: University of Chicago Press, 1989), xv. On feminist challenges to the liberal tradition, see Martha Nussbaum, *Sex and Social Justice* (New York: Oxford University Press, 1999), chapter 1.

[22] Catharine A. MacKinnon, *Sexual Harassment of Working Women: A Case of Sex Discrimination* (New Haven, CT: Yale University Press, 1979).

[23] Opening statement of Leah Fritz in "Panel Discussion: Effects of Violent Pornography," *New York University Review of Law and Social Change*, 8 (1978–1979), 238.

women's point of view and to weigh women's lived experiences more heavily than abstract rights. "I will tell you what the threat to my freedom of expression is. And if you are serious about freedom for everyone in this country, then you will listen.... I tell you that pornography silences me, that pornography makes me sick every day of my life...."[24] Fritz and Dworkin consciously spoke their pain to the male panelists, expressing the burgeoning feminist critique that the law did not take into account the realities of women's place in the social order. In so doing, they followed such influential thinkers as Aristotle, Jean-Jacques Rousseau, and Adam Smith, all of whom advanced within the liberal tradition the idea that the capacity to feel distress over the harm of others was a cornerstone of ethical public life. Fritz and Dworkin also brought forward a common feminist critique of liberalism as practiced, namely that its unwavering attachment to reason unfairly diminished the consideration that citizens ought to give to emotion in moral and political life.[25]

Brownmiller offered the same argument she had presented two weeks earlier at the WAVPM conference, namely that pornography ought to fall outside the scope of the First Amendment, because the framers had intended only to protect the right of political dissent. "I do not think that those who framed the Bill of Rights ever intended dirty words and dirty pictures to be covered under the same protection that is given to the right of someone to express an unpopular political view," she told the WAVPM audience.[26] Brownmiller shared this idea with colloquium attendees, insisting that the First Amendment had been "stretched out of shape" to protect all kinds of acts that the framers never intended to cover.[27] The feminists asked the lawyers to think beyond traditional conceptions of freedom of speech to consider how pornography stripped women of basic rights, a claim that raised serious concerns among the civil libertarians.

The responses from the lawyers' panel ranged from sympathetic to scolding, but none of its members were willing to consider a solution to the pornography problem that might encroach on the First Amendment. Several of the civil libertarians acknowledged that pornography harmed women but insisted nonetheless that its creators were expressing their personal viewpoints regarding sexual matters – an enterprise which deserved full protection under the law. "I do think women are an oppressed class. I do think pornography is bad for women," Chevigny said. "Nevertheless ... I do not think that the law has any right to control writings with respect to emotions about sex."[28] David Richards, an NYU law professor and gay rights advocate, agreed with his

[24] Opening statement of Andrea Dworkin in "Panel Discussion: Effects of Violent Pornography," *New York University Review of Law and Social Change*, 8 (1978–1979), 239.

[25] These critiques are discussed in Martha S. Nussbaum, *Sex and Social Justice* (New York: Oxford University Press, 1999), chapter 2.

[26] See Helen Rosenbluth, narrator, *Fair Sex, Fair Game: Women Say No to the Sexual Safari*, Los Angeles, 1979, Pacifica Tape Library [sound recording].

[27] Susan Brownmiller, "Pornography and the First Amendment," *New York University Review of Law and Social Change*, 8 (1978–1979), 256.

[28] Paul Chevigny, "Opening Statement," 233.

colleague, arguing that "mere offense at content" was not enough to permit its prohibition. He chastised the effort as misguided, warning that if the feminists focused on an issue as trivial as pornography, they would damage the entire women's movement. "You should be concentrating on the real issues – family structure, occupational structure, sex roles and the like," he urged.[29] Fahringer, the lawyer for Flynt and Goldstein, was downright insulting and derided the women as "insurgents" who were "an embarrassment to the feminist cause." Like Richards, he told the feminists that the women's movement ought to deal with issues directly affecting women's economic and social equality rather than living in fear of the "witchcraft of pornography."[30] He rejected the concept of legal restriction and described himself as "unalterably committed" to the principle that people should be allowed to read and view whatever they pleased, without interference:

> [T]hose who believe that this country's new breed of publishers and filmmakers should have their mouths washed out with soap for using four-letter words or publishing pictures of nude women in obstetric poses must remember that no one is compelled to either see or read what is repulsive to him or her. Those who are appalled by these materials can ignore them. And the few who gain some satisfaction from them should be allowed that small comfort.[31]

Fahringer elevated male "comfort" over women's bodily integrity and social equality, reinforcing feminist fears harking back to the height of New Left organizing that male liberals had no real commitment to improving the material conditions of women's lives, but only of ensuring their continued access to women's bodies. It appeared that none of the civil libertarians would support concrete legal steps to help women control pornography. Even though several admitted that pornography probably did cause harm to women, they did not see the harm as sufficiently great to offset the dangers inherent in censorship and to justify the erosion of the speech rights of pornographers and their eager customers.

As the day wore on, the spirit of cooperation and exchange of ideas that had marked the start of the colloquium began to wear thin. Several of the attorneys pressed the women for "hard facts" that would prove that pornography was dangerous. If reliable evidence could be produced to show that pornography consumption increased the incidence of violent sexual crime or other harm to women, there would be a very strong liberal case for prohibiting it. The demand for facts, however, seemed to cast doubt on the veracity of the

[29] Richards quoted in Judy Klemesrud, "Women, Pornography, Free Speech: A Fierce Debate at N.Y.U." *The New York Times*, December 4, 1978, D10.

[30] Herald Price Fahringer, "'If the Trumpet Sounds An Uncertain Note...'" *New York University Review of Law and Social Change*, 8 (1978–1979), 253. Fahringer has represented more than 100 owners of adult-entertainment businesses in Times Square. On his efforts to save X-rated shops from government-mandated shutdowns, see: Dan Barry, "Federal Court Upholds Law to Curb X-Rated Businesses," *The New York Times*, June 4, 1998, A27.

[31] Fahringer, "'If the Trumpet Sounds An Uncertain Note ...,'" 252.

entire feminist account. Dworkin exploded when the lawyers questioned the reality of a pervasive silencing of women: "Fact: Women are denied freedom of speech by rape, by battering, by medical butchery, by violence on every level, by sexual harassment on the job, by being unable to make the decent living that gives one the freedom to speak one's mind."[32] Brownmiller, in a ringing retort to Fahringer, insisted that women could not simply "avoid" pornography, as he had suggested, because the material was displayed at every New York City newsstand, plastered over all four sides of the ubiquitous booths. The situation had become intolerable, with women's rights trailing behind those of pornographers.

At the end of the day, the feminists likely felt that the civil libertarians had turned a deaf ear to their pleas for help. While several of the lawyers acknowledged that pornography was bad for women, they also dismissed it as "mere offense," not "a real issue," and as harmless "comfort" and entertainment for men. Some displayed a total lack of empathy for the feminist position, failing to understand just how vulnerable many women felt when confronted with pornography. "In this day and age when we have reached the edge of the moon," Fahringer intoned, "I find it hard to believe that our people cannot tolerate magazines like *Hustler*, *Penthouse*, and *Screw*."[33] It seemed that Fahringer had not heard a single word that the feminist panelists had spoken that day, nor had their pained accounts of life in a pornographic public sphere moved him.

Fahringer's words, and those of his fellow panelists, confirmed some feminists' worst suspicions about male liberals. They were willing to march for the civil rights of blacks, to fight for union wages for Chicano agricultural workers, to oppose the draft and the Vietnam War, to campaign for better conditions for prisoners, and to defend the rights of pornographers, Nazis, man-boy lovers, and every other group under the sun. But not women. Even though women felt personally attacked and exploited by pornography, and even though they linked pornography to an epidemic of rape and other forms of sexual violence, they could not get the men to budge. When the women asked for help with pornography, which they saw as the single greatest obstacle to their freedom and the full exercise of their civil rights, the lawyers denied them.

Amid all the fighting and insult trading, two panelists from the civil libertarian side did make a serious effort to address the anti-pornography feminists' concerns. Brenda Feigen Fasteau offered two legal tactics that women might use, clearly foreshadowing the MacKinnon-Dworkin ordinances that WAP would support in the early 1980s. First, she suggested the creation of a tort that would allow women to bring a civil action against a pornographer if they could show that the pornography in question had damaged an individual woman or class of women. Second, she thought that WAP might investigate the

32 Opening Statement of Andrea Dworkin, 239.

33 Fahringer, "If the Trumpet Sounds An Uncertain Note ...," 253.

incitement-to-violence statutes, as pornographic pictures of violence against women might incite men to commit violent crimes. This was the approach that feminists had used to try to get the film *Snuff* banned the year prior. Her comments were received with enthusiasm by the anti-pornography feminists, but met with disapproval from the male civil libertarians who saw any legal action against pornography as eroding individual rights.

Marjorie Smith, the Department of Consumer Affairs official and ACLU staff member, was also sympathetic to arguments from both sets of panelists. As a civil libertarian, she agreed that the attorneys must hold their ground in defense of free speech even though the feminists had presented a compelling case against pornography. "It is fundamental that the suppression of first amendment rights does not become acceptable because the cause is holy," she said.[34] A civil libertarian could not support any effort to curtail an individual's right and opportunity to communicate as broad a spectrum of ideas as desired, even if he or she agreed that pornography was a critical social problem and accepted that pornography undermined women's civil rights. On the other hand, as a feminist, she recognized significant movement support for the idea that pornography contributed to the incidence of real world violence against women, and understood that many women wanted to take concrete steps to combat its harmful effects.

Smith provided an answer that she believed could satisfy the needs of both groups. She said that feminists and civil libertarians alike could support the kind of anti-media violence campaign pioneered by WAVAW. The organization's public education and consumer boycott techniques were consistent with First Amendment principles, as the group did not seek government control of free expression. In the case of the Warner campaign, WAVAW was pressuring a corporation to stop publishing images of physical and sexual violence against women, which Smith found consistent with a 1977 ACLU statement upholding the First Amendment right to picket or boycott "to influence the decisions of those responsible for deciding what material a medium of communication will present."[35] The critical distinction, Smith maintained, was that WAVAW was exerting private pressure, not advocating government regulation. With a private pressure campaign, the Warner record companies were ultimately free to decide whether to curtail objectionable advertising campaigns like *Black and Blue*; no amount of public protest could *force* the companies to change their course, whereas a law could prohibit this type of communication. In Smith's opinion, WAVAW had devised an effective means of challenging media images of violence against women without encroaching on freedom of speech. "[T]he decision to become involved in the group's efforts can be made by a civil libertarian feminist without abandoning civil liberties principles," she concluded.[36]

[34] Marjorie Smith, "Private Action Against Pornography: An Exercise of First Amendment Rights," *New York University Review of Law and Social Change*, 8 (1978–1979), 247.

[35] Smith, "Private Action Against Pornography," 248.

[36] Smith, "Private Action Against Pornography," 250.

Although Smith made a strong argument in favor of WAVAW-style organizing, most of the anti-pornography panelists had already stated a commitment to legal change. These women were well aware of WAVAW's approach but had made a strategic decision to take the campaign against media violence in another direction. The WAVAW protest methods were creative and effective, but they were also time-consuming to mobilize, often slow to bring results, and could be focused on just a few offending corporations at one time. When the NYU panel convened, WAVAW had been campaigning against Warner Communications for two and a half years and had not yet achieved victory. And once concessions were won, it would be up to the feminists themselves to police the organization for compliance because no law would require the corporation to reign in its abusive advertising campaigns.

The anti-pornography feminists wanted to create more dramatic, large-scale change that would happen at a faster pace. They did not care to tackle the pornography problem one company at a time, but desired a legal solution that might bring about sweeping changes to improve the quality of women's lives. There was an electric excitement attached to the idea of harnessing state power to free women from pornography, and the anti-pornography feminists felt it. During these heady years, even as the "thunder on the Right" was growing louder, anti-pornography feminists, encouraged by the legal and social gains achieved by the Civil Rights and women's movements, believed that the law could be shaped to serve women's interests.

Many feminist anti-pornography leaders had experience with and knowledge of government affairs and the law, which created a sense of empowerment and agency within the movement. Brownmiller, then forty-three years old, was especially well versed in the legislative process. She had majored in government at Cornell University in the early 1950s and later wrote and edited a weekly four-page review of the New York State Legislature called the *Albany Report* (1961–1962) that counted among its subscribers practically every major state official. She and other anti-pornography participants, like Hommel who was finishing law school at a time when feminist lawyers were using the law creatively and proactively to battle problems like sexual harassment, felt inspired by the possibility of creating change. Furthermore, as the political scientist Sylvia Bashevkin has observed, the very strength and prominence of the U.S. women's movement during these years may have provided "a false sense of security." Buoyed by their substantial gains, feminist leaders believed in "the inevitability of progress" even while a concerted challenge to their agenda was gathering strength among members of the New Right.[37]

The feminists' enthusiasm for legal solutions was not shared by the civil libertarians. At the end of the conference day, the two groups had reached an impasse. The organizers had hoped that the colloquium would foster a productive exchange, but for the most part, that did not come to pass. If anything, the

[37] Sylvia Bashevkin, "Facing a Renewed Right: American Feminism and the Reagan/Bush Challenge," *Canadian Journal of Political Science* 27, no. 4 (December 1994), 690.

sessions exacerbated the divide. The *Review* coordinator described "a general failure of communication" in her postconference report. She noted that the feminist speakers sought advice from the civil liberties lawyers as to what legal action might be taken to reduce pornography's harms to women, but the lawyers interpreted the objections to pornography as a blanket call for censorship. As a result, the attorneys focused on defending the First Amendment against this "perceived assault." For the coordinator, the inability to set aside differences long enough to listen to one another was deeply disappointing. "The lawyers defended free speech," she wrote, "seeming not to understand that the feminists had come for help."[38]

Internal Shifts for WAVPM and the Rise of WAP

In the weeks following the WAVPM conference and the NYU colloquium, Brownmiller began talking to Laura Lederer and Lynn Campbell about the possibility of moving to New York and relocating the headquarters of the campaign against pornography. WAVPM's national conference, held just two weeks before the NYU event, had received only modest regional media coverage. Brownmiller complained that Bay Area newspapers "had blanked out the nation's first feminist antipornography conference and march."[39]

This assessment was accurate, but the lack of coverage did not reflect a lack of interest in the feminist conference so much as competition from major breaking news stories. As the WAVPM women were meeting at Galileo High School on November 18, journalists learned that California congressman Leo Ryan had been murdered in Jonestown, Guyana. The following day brought reports of the mass murder-suicide of more than 900 members of the San Francisco-based Peoples Temple, orchestrated by their charismatic leader, Jim Jones. The Jonestown Massacre, as it came to be called, was major international news, dominating newspapers and television programs everywhere, especially the Bay Area, given the local angle. One week later, when WAVPM might have hoped for a delayed feature story describing the anti-pornography conference, San Francisco was rocked by the assassinations of Mayor George Moscone and the city's first openly gay supervisor, Harvey Milk. The headline of the *San Francisco Examiner* on the day following the murders read: *A City in Agony*, and the newspaper's pages were filled with stories about the fallen political figures printed alongside news of the dead in Guyana, and the shipment of bodies home to the Bay Area. The WAVPM conference was lost amid the coverage of these two astounding sets of events.

Brownmiller believed that the anti-pornography campaign would have to take root in New York City if it were to succeed on a national level. "The weekend's disappointing outreach had convinced me that New York, the home of both Times Square *and* the national media, was the only place to

[38] Lerman, "Preface," 182, 184.
[39] Brownmiller, *In Our Time*, 302.

launch a national feminist antipornography campaign," she recalled in her memoir.[40] What she didn't say – but what was equally significant – was that New York City was home to the nation's most famous feminists. Brownmiller, Dworkin, Steinem, and the rest of the founding members of the Women's Anti-Defamation League were media stars whose actions commanded attention. "Though these women are all New Yorkers," Molly Ivins had observed in the *New York Times*, "their views tend to have a national impact."[41]

Brownmiller wanted to try again to form an East Coast anti-pornography group, but she needed help. The prominent women she had recruited for the now-defunct League were busy with their careers – writing, teaching, speaking – and did not have the time to do the intensive day-to-day work needed to get a new enterprise off the ground. If Lederer and Campbell would come east and bring their organizing skill and personal drive, Brownmiller could deliver a stellar group of feminists whose actions would earn media attention. She could provide the *visibility* and the *star power* that the campaign needed. The prospect of seeing the feminist anti-pornography movement skyrocket to the national stage captivated the WAVPM women.

Lederer and Campbell agreed to meet with Brownmiller and the former League members in March 1979 to discuss an anti-pornography effort based in New York. Brownmiller sent out letters on personal stationery inviting the League women to a March 27 gathering at her home on Jane Street in the West Village. She reminded her colleagues that they had tried valiantly the year before to "hammer out a feminist position against pornography" before falling apart as a group.[42] During that time, WAVPM had taken up the initiative and organized the Feminist Perspectives conference and *Take Back the Night* march. Brownmiller noted that Lederer and Campbell, whom she dubbed "the San Francisco Angels," would discuss the ideas for the "proposed assault on New York," which included setting up an East Coast network, a New York office, and planning a conference and demonstration. She ended on a cautionary note. "What we couldn't do last year – because none of us was prepared to do the work – can happen this year if we accept our responsibility."[43]

Over the course of the next month, Lederer and Campbell faced major decisions about relocating and spearheading the New York effort. Ultimately, Lederer decided not to accept Brownmiller's offer. She was committed to editing an anthology of feminist anti-pornography essays and speeches originating from WAVPM's national conference because the organization had secured a book contract with a New York publishing house. Lederer spent most of the summer and fall of 1979 focusing on the book project, which

40 Brownmiller, *In Our Time*, 302.

41 Ivins, "Feminist Leaders Join Anti-Smut Campaign," 18.

42 Susan Brownmiller to a former League member, March 4, 1979, Box 1, Folder 1, WAP Records.

43 Susan Brownmiller to a former League member, March 4, 1979, Box 1, Folder 1, WAP Records.

would become *Take Back the Night: Women on Pornography*, the single most influential and widely read collection of feminist anti-pornography writings.

Furthermore, Lederer was tired of the abominable pay, all-consuming work schedule, and lack of appreciation endemic to grassroots organizing. After the Feminist Perspectives conference, she found herself increasingly in conflict with the active members of WAVPM, who wanted a greater collective voice in decision making and the allocation of funds, and who wanted a group to edit *Take Back the Night*, rather than Lederer alone. The organization held a structure meeting in January 1979 that turned into a painful confrontation between Lederer, who had the board of directors on her side, and the active members who were clamoring for more control. One WAVPM member described the meeting as full of "accusation and bitterness" in a letter written to WAVAW's London and Howarth, confiding that many of the active members either wanted to see Lederer forced out or would themselves quit the group.[44] Lederer responded to the structure meeting with an eight-page, single-spaced, typed letter outlining the enormous personal sacrifices she had made for WAVPM, working for just $4,800 a year, without medical insurance, under constant stress, while dealing with "the attacks, the power struggles, the lack of encouragement, [and] the unspoken thanks" that characterized her relationship with the membership. She rejected collective decision making, arguing that too many members lacked "political astuteness" and sufficient knowledge of WAVPM's operations. "I do not want ... to be told what to do ... by someone who may know process and collectivity and personal feelings well but knows nothing about the issue of pornography or the political battle that must be fought," Lederer wrote.[45] It was the beginning of a breakdown of communication and trust between Lederer and the WAVPM membership that would lead to her resignation as national coordinator in January 1980.

Lynn Campbell reached a different decision about the proposed move to New York. Just twenty-four years old, she was eager for a challenge that promised a whirlwind introduction to some of the most dynamic members of the women's movement and the chance to make a national impact. Brownmiller and her colleagues were delighted to learn that they had successfully recruited her. When Campbell moved to New York in the spring of 1979, Brownmiller and others met her at the airport with flowers.[46] Brownmiller, the poet Adrienne

[44] Member of WAVPM to Julia London and Joan Howarth, January 14, 1979, Box 14B, LA WAVAW Papers. Because the author of the letter intended her account of the WAVPM structure meeting to be kept confidential by London and Howarth, I am not revealing her name. She was a Los Angeles WAVAW member who had moved from Southern California to Northern California to attend graduate school. Once in Northern California, she joined WAVPM.

[45] Laura Lederer to WAVPM Women, n.d., Box 2, Folder: Correspondence: Internal, WAVPM Records, GLBT Historical Society.

[46] Just weeks after her arrival in New York City, Campbell was diagnosed with cancer. She worked with WAP though 1979, before her health required that she find a less stressful and time-consuming job. She died in 1984, at the age of twenty-eight. See Jane Creighton, "Lynn Campbell, 1955–1984," *off our backs*, June 1984, 25.

Rich, and the novelist Frances Whyatt contributed $1,000 each to a bank account to pay Campbell's salary and help cover living expenses. Another supporter found her an affordable apartment on East 66th Street.[47] The New York effort was underway.

The group that Campbell moved to New York to organize soon became known as Women Against Pornography, though by all rights it should have been called WAVPM East Coast. Indeed, Lederer and Campbell believed that they were being recruited to build a strong East Coast chapter of WAVPM, one that would work in cooperation with the national office in San Francisco. From April through June, WAVPM's *NewsPage* referred to the activity in New York as an extension of the existing organization's work. Campbell was identified as "WAVPM's East Coast Coordinator." The New York group's planned pornography conference and march on Times Square were described in *NewsPage* as WAVPM-sponsored events designed to expand WAVPM's reach to a national audience.[48] Through June 1979, Campbell sent out all press releases for the New York group on WAVPM letterhead, and referred to the East Coast effort as "WAVPM-New York." She responded to inquiries about membership by sending out WAVPM registration materials, and instructions to send them, along with $10, to WAVPM in San Francisco.[49]

By early summer, it was clear that WAVPM had lost the battle to keep the East Coast group under its aegis. Once the New York group began billing itself as Women Against Pornography, it rarely mentioned that it was a project of the national WAVPM. By July 1979, the group referred to itself as Women Against Pornography exclusively. This turn of events was caused in part by WAVPM's difficulty in securing tax-exempt status for the New York group, but was also greatly influenced by the character of the New York feminist community. The New Yorkers were accustomed to being at the forefront of the women's movement, and the notion that WAP would be a second-string East Coast affiliate of WAVPM did not sit well. Looking back, it seems almost naïve to imagine that the most prominent feminists in the nation would have been satisfied with that arrangement. With Lederer focused on *Take Back the Night* and Campbell having moved east, young, unknown feminists were assuming the leadership of WAVPM. The WAP women were playing in an entirely different league. They would create a new organization with no formal ties to WAVPM, no leadership but their own, and an agenda to make pornography the number one women's rights issue in the nation.

[47] Brownmiller, *In Our Time*, 303.

[48] "Feminists Organize Against Pornography in New York," *WAVPM NewsPage* 3, no. 4 (May 1979), 2.

[49] Lynn Campbell to Vassar Women, April 10, 1979, Box 7, WAP Records. Campbell's apartment address appeared on early press releases (April–May 1979) for "Women Against Violence in Pornography and Media – New York Conference and March." These press releases were sent out by Campbell from her home before WAP secured office space. Also, the $3,000 donated by Brownmiller, Rich, and Wyatt appears in WAP financial records as seed money for the organization. Thus, it was likely used to pay Campbell's salary, as well as to cover early WAP expenses.

Early Actions

Fans of the *Phil Donahue Show* were in for more than the usual talk show treacle when they tuned in on July 18, 1979. Phil's guests were Susan Brownmiller, Lynn Campbell and Dolores Alexander, three founders of the brand-new feminist organization, Women Against Pornography. Alexander and Brownmiller had worked together previously as members of New York Radical Feminists. The WAP founders were appearing on *Donahue* to raise women's consciousness about pornography. Pornography, they insisted, represented hatred of women. It humiliated, demeaned, and objectified women and their bodies, and taught men that violence was a staple of sex. The proliferation of pornography contributed to a culture that regarded rape and other acts of violence against women as normal male behavior, and encouraged that behavior. Further, publications like *Playboy* and *Hustler* manipulated women and preyed on their fears, making them feel inadequate when their own bodies fell short of the airbrushed images that dominated the magazines' pages. Pornography dehumanized women by depicting them as passive sex objects, nothing more than the sum of their body parts, whose only value lay in their provision of sexual services to men.[50]

During the course of the show, audience members asked the panelists to discuss their views regarding possible solutions to the pornography problem. Alexander, then forty-eight years old, was a news reporter, first with New York *Newsday* and later with *Time*. She had worked with Betty Friedan to organize the first chapter of NOW in New York City in 1966 and had become the national organization's first executive director three years later.[51] On *Donahue*, she endorsed the kind of consumer pressure tactics used by WAVAW. Brownmiller, however, insisted that legal action was necessary to control the spread of pornography. She argued that degrading and humiliating images of the female

[50] Here I am summarizing some of the major arguments advanced by anti-pornography feminists. See for example, Helen Longino, "Pornography, Oppression and Freedom: A Closer Look," in *Take Back the Night*, 40–54; Robin Morgan, "Theory and Practice: Pornography and Rape," in *Take Back the Night*, 134–140; Dworkin, *Pornography: Men Possessing Women*; and Brownmiller, *Against Our Will.*

[51] Dolores Alexander was raised in a working-class Italian community in Newark, New Jersey. She attended City College in the late 1950s and subsequently became a journalist. Working as a reporter for New York *Newsday*, she came across a press release announcing the formation of the National Organization for Women (NOW) in 1966. Alexander became NOW's first Executive Director from 1969 to 1970 and was a co-owner of Mother Courage, a lesbian feminist restaurant in New York City's Greenwich Village with partner Jill Ward during the 1970s. According to the oral history of Alexander's life available in the Sophia Smith Voices of Feminism Oral History Project collection at Smith College, she was present at many significant events of the women's movement, including the lesbian purge of NOW, the National Women's Conference in Houston in 1977, and the UN Fourth World Conference on Women in Beijing in 1995. See Dolores Alexander, oral history conducted by Kelly Anderson, Southold, New York, March 20, 2004 and October 22, 2005, Sophia Smith Voices of Feminism Oral History Project. Available online at http://www.smith.edu/library/libs/ssc/vof/vof-narrators.html

body did not deserve protection under the First Amendment, and that such material ought to be legally defined as obscene and banned from display.

Indeed, Brownmiller summarized for the *Donahue* audience the arguments that she put forward in an opinion piece for *Newsday*, the daily newspaper serving Long Island, New York. In "Let's Put Pornography Back in the Closet," which appeared during the same month that the *Donahue* episode aired, Brownmiller maintained that the brazen display of pornography on city streets assaulted women's sensibilities under the guise of free speech. Quoting Chief Justice Warren Burger's 1973 majority opinion in *Miller v. California* to the effect that protecting obscenity was "'a misuse of the great guarantees of free speech and free press,'" Brownmiller argued that the First Amendment was never intended to protect such material, and that the courts ought to be able to place restrictions on its public display. "We are not saying 'smash the presses' or 'ban the bad ones,' but simply 'Get the stuff out of our sight.' Let the legislatures decide – using realistic and humane contemporary community standards – what can be displayed and what cannot," she advised. "The courts, after all, will be the final arbiters."[52] Many people around the nation shuddered at the thought of the U.S. courts empowered to make such decisions, aware that conservative jurists' definitions of pornography were not likely to square with Brownmiller's. She reiterated these ideas for the television audience, adding that liberals who staunchly defended pornography as free speech were going to have to start rethinking that position from the perspective of women's rights.

Although Brownmiller's impassioned comments about banning pornography from public display generated a great deal of audience reaction, they did not comprise the most controversial segment of the show. That occurred when Donahue asked Brownmiller about *Hustler* publisher Larry Flynt, who had been shot and paralyzed four months earlier outside a Georgia courthouse while standing trial on obscenity charges.[53] "Well, Phil," Brownmiller responded, "that may have been the best thing that ever happened to Flynt."[54] Donahue shot back angrily that Brownmiller was no better than Iran's Ayatollah Khomeini, who meted out death sentences to political enemies. A number of women subsequently wrote to WAP to advise Brownmiller that she had displayed bad form when she reveled in Flynt's misfortune. Brownmiller regretted that comment. "... I still feel ashamed that my hard-boiled wisecrack let my colleagues down," she wrote in her memoir.[55] Although the quip about Flynt earned her some criticism, a significant number of the women in the viewing audience were very receptive to Brownmiller's ideas.

Judging from the letters that WAP received after the *Donahue* episode aired, the response from viewers around the nation was quite positive. Dozens of

[52] Susan Brownmiller, "Let's Put Pornography Back in the Closet," *Newsday*, July 17, 1979, p. 41.

[53] Wayne King, "Larry Flynt, Owner of Hustler, Is Shot Near Georgia Court," *The New York Times*, March 6, 1978, p. 1.

[54] Brownmiller, *In Our Time*, 307.

[55] Brownmiller, *In Our Time*, 307.

people wrote to WAP, with many letters coming from women inquiring about membership in the new organization and expressing support for the cause. A number of these writers agreed "100 percent" with the anti-pornography activists and promised to send donations and rally friends and family members for the upcoming WAP March on Times Square. These writers typically identified themselves as mothers and expressed concerns about the values of the society in which they were raising their children, especially their daughters. The letters came from women around the nation, most living in suburban and rural areas.

Many letters of support also arrived from religious conservatives who thought that they shared a common cause with WAP. These writers denounced premarital sex and teen pregnancy in the United States and expressed their hope that a campaign against pornography might help restore decency and what the burgeoning New Right would soon call "family values." One married viewer wrote to WAP that she prayed that an "anti-sex education" curriculum would be established in American schools to keep young people pure. "Please God that morality will some day soon be restored to our precious nation," she added.[56] A small subgroup of viewers believed (incorrectly) that WAP objected to television commercials advertising feminine hygiene products, and these writers congratulated the feminists for condemning this degrading and indecent public talk about women's bodies.

Letters from viewers who supported WAP showered the organization with praise for addressing the pornography problem and its harms to women. "I was beginning to wonder if I was the only one who feels humiliated, embarrassed and degraded by the exploitation of nude bodies in magazines and elsewhere," a twenty-year-old married college student with a two-year-old daughter wrote. "The exploitation of nude women in the popular men's magazines makes me feel so inferior and disgusted I could scream!"[57] A woman who described herself as a feminist living in California understood what WAP meant about pornography being connected to male power and control. "Everything you spoke about on the show really hit home with me. In my first marriage my husband's way of keeping me 'in line' and always feeling inferior, worthless, lacking confidence, was to read the *Playboy* magazine," she wrote.[58] A church-going mother in Louisiana confessed that she had ripped the centerfolds off the walls at her husband's office. "Maybe it wasn't my place to tear them down, but when I'm home every day taking care of two little babies

[56] Married woman to WAP, August 8, 1979, WAP Records, Box 3, Folder 113.

[57] Twenty-year-old college student to WAP, September 13, 1979, WAP Records, Box 6, Folder 287. According to the terms of use of the manuscript collection of Women Against Pornography, I cannot reprint the names of private individuals who wrote or called the organization, nor may I identify them by use of their proper initials. I will try to identify the writers demographically, as in this example, in those cases where the information is available. The letters are available at the Schlesinger Library at the Radcliffe Institute, Harvard University, Cambridge, Massachusetts.

[58] A Feminist in California to WAP, September 12, 1979, WAP records, Box 3, Folder 117.

it hurts me terribly to think my husband is at work ogling over these women."[59] A female factory worker from Michigan wrote that her male coworkers had taped a violent pornographic picture to her locker along with a threat that this would be her fate unless she gave notice.[60] Another viewer expressed grateful feelings of solidarity with WAP because she too felt outrage over the exploitation of women. "Like you, I am fed up with passing a newsstand and seeing an average of four nude women staring at me."[61] Others thanked WAP for giving voice to years of women's pent-up frustrations and anger: "You don't know how good it made me feel to see you on national TV speaking the very things I've been feeling for years."[62] The WAP women struck a chord.

A number of letter writers connected their hatred for pornography to concerns for their children, and the lessons that pornography was sure to teach them about the roles of men and women in society. A mother of three living in Cucamonga, California, told WAP that their cause was "terrific" and that she had already addressed the issue of pornography in her home. "I for one have always hated those magazines," she declared. "My husband used to buy them but now he doesn't after I talked to him.... We have two sons and one daughter and there is just no way we will have them grow up and think that this is what a woman is to be used for."[63] Pornography brought out strong feelings in individuals across the country, and as these letters illustrate, WAP had tapped into an issue that was emotional and raw. Their campaign against pornography appealed broadly to women, not necessarily women who self-identified as feminist or were otherwise politically active, but everyday women who felt belittled, insulted, and degraded by porn. A married woman with two daughters wrote to WAP from her home in Staten Island, New York: "I have never marched for anything before but I'm getting my walking shoes out of storage for that big day in October. I was always angry at the way women were treated in this society – like sex objects – but felt powerless to do anything about it...."[64] She added that her husband also planned to march because he did not want their daughters to grow up in a world that regarded them as nothing more than sexual playthings. These women staunchly supported the idea of a national campaign to eradicate pornography.

The letters from women who were wary of WAP's agenda were just as passionate. Some claimed that they found pornography sexually gratifying and that they used explicit sexual material to expand their sexual knowledge and practice. Foreshadowing a major argument of the pro-sex feminist movement that would emerge to challenge anti-pornography in the early 1980s, these women claimed that women needed more access to sexually explicit material, not less. Censorship of pornography, they warned, was just another

59 Mother in Metairie, Louisiana to WAP, n.d., WAP Records, Box 1, Folder 10.
60 A Michigan woman to WAP, July 1979, WAP Records, Box 3, Folder 117.
61 A woman to WAP, July 30, 1979, WAP Records, Box 3, Folder 105.
62 A woman to WAP, July 31, 1979, WAP Records, Box 3, Folder 106.
63 Mother in Cucamonga, California to WAP, n.d., WAP Records, Box 1, Folder 10.
64 Staten Island wife and mother to WAP, July 1979, WAP Records, Box 3, Folder 117.

means of "protecting" women from sexuality and would teach women to fear sex as dangerous and corrupting rather than to claim it as positive and life-affirming. Part of the task of women's liberation was to reclaim women's sexuality, they argued, and to give women space and freedom from male control so that women might discover their authentic sexual desires. Pornography was a tool that women could use to further that self-discovery. One letter writer living in Rockford, Illinois, described herself as a committed feminist and member of NOW who actively sought out pornography and who opposed WAP: "I couldn't disagree with you more. No one, absolutely no one is being forced to buy any publications ... against their will. I CHOOSE, as do enough others in this 'free' country to make it [pornography] a million dollar business. You would like to see my choice (and anyone who does not agree with your opinion's choice) taken away."[65] She asserted that her enjoyment of pornography was real, and that her affinity for this material was as strong as any WAP member's loathing of it.

Anti-pornography feminists, following MacKinnon and other theorists, chalked such arguments up to "false consciousness," a social and psychological aspect of oppression and domination that encouraged victims to internalize the norms of the more powerful group in society – in this case, men. Through pornography, women learned to eroticize images of their own subordination. If a woman experienced sexual desire when viewing such material, anti-pornography feminists argued that she had been conditioned under patriarchy to respond affirmatively to the needs of men and to believe that she herself desired this type of relationship. "Women who are compromised, cajoled, pressured, tricked, blackmailed, or outright forced into sex (or pornography) often respond to the unspeakable humiliation, coupled with the sense of having lost some irreplaceable integrity, by claiming that sexuality as their own," MacKinnon wrote, in an explanation of this psychological coping mechanism. Women who claimed to love and choose pornography had not yet developed a true feminist consciousness that would reveal porn as the graphic depiction of their own oppression. Pornography was a powerful ideological tool that kept women in their place, socially and sexually subservient to men.

Other women writing to WAP concentrated on questions of dangerous alliances with religious conservatives over the question of pornography, and the potential abuse of censorship powers by right-wing community groups and courts. Their letters urged WAP to cease the pursuit of legal measures to control pornography because such a campaign might easily be turned against women to undo the gains of the women's movement. One *Donahue* viewer living in Maumee, Ohio, criticized the WAP representatives for what she saw as pandering to potential allies on the Right. "I thought that you failed to distinguish strongly and adequately between pornography and sexuality; therefore on the show, you seemed to agree with those reactionary 'back-to-the-Bible' members of the audience." She warned WAP that any partnership

[65] Rockford, Illinois woman to WAP, August 22, 1979, WAP Records, Box 4, Folder 133.

with religious conservatives would ultimately bring about anti-feminist ends. "This is an opportunistic approach and a dangerous one," she wrote. "Here, you ally yourselves with those who condemn and wish to deny sexual and reproductive freedom – abortion and birth control rights, sex education, lesbian rights, and general acceptance of sexual freedom for women."[66] Indeed, the "strange bedfellows" situation that brought anti-pornography feminists and religious conservatives into the same camp in the mid-1980s in support of the MacKinnon-Dworkin anti-pornography ordinances would backfire, much as the letter writer feared. In those instances, right-wing groups and legislators appropriated feminist anti-pornography rhetoric and rewrote the model ordinances to try to accomplish conservative social goals.[67]

Perhaps the most ominous letter came from a woman living in Ogden, Utah. She characterized herself as a feminist and as someone who agreed with WAP that pornography harmed women, but who was also deeply concerned about the pro-censorship position that Brownmiller advocated. "I am a teacher, a patron of the public library, and a supporter of Planned Parenthood in the state," she wrote. "In all three roles, I face opposition from a group called 'Citizens for True Freedom,' which has established itself as the arbiter of the community's morals." She described a chilling situation. The Citizens for True Freedom were waging a successful campaign to get books banned from libraries and school reading lists. So far, they had managed to remove *To Kill a Mockingbird*, *A Raisin in the Sun*, *Our Bodies Ourselves*, and *Ms.* magazine. The head librarian of a local public library had just been fired because she refused to remove a book at the request of the library board. This brush with censorship made the Utah woman cringe when she heard Brownmiller endorse legislation to remove pornographic material from plain sight. "Surely you are aware of the dangers of censorship," she entreated. "You may see *Hustler* and *Playboy* as offensive. I may agree with you. Yet, with the same sense of justification, the Citizens for True Freedom here in Utah seek the removal of all books dealing with sexuality, contraception, abortion, etc. from the public view. I am very afraid that in many ways, I see no difference between the two."[68] Pornography, the teacher acknowledged, was a grave problem. However, it deserved a more thoughtful approach than a call for censorship. "Frankly, your group frightens me," she wrote. "To ask again that time-worn question, where will it end?"[69] Her inquiry was prescient, as the choice to pursue legal remedies would ultimately bring some anti-pornography feminists into alliances with religious conservatives who opposed sexual freedom for women.

[66] Maumee, Ohio wife and mother to WAP, August 14, 1979, WAP Records, Box 3, Folder 117.

[67] On the creation of these alliances, see Downs, *The New Politics of Pornography*.

[68] Ogden, Utah teacher to Susan Brownmiller, September 23, 1979, WAP Records, Box 6, Folder 287.

[69] Ogden, Utah teacher to Susan Brownmiller, September 23, 1979, WAP Records, Box 6, Folder 287.

Reading the letters from *Donahue* viewers today, one can see that their responses foreshadowed the issues that would ignite the pornography wars among feminists in the early 1980s. Some viewers were wildly enthusiastic about WAP's plans, feeling that pornography objectified women, deprived them of equality with men, and robbed women of their speech rights. Others despaired that the organization was making a disastrous choice, inviting the state to regulate sexual speech and opening the door for increasingly active and powerful right-wingers to "protect" women from dangerous, immoral writings about sex and a host of other contested cultural issues. The polarized reactions to the WAP agenda were a defining feature of the new anti-pornography movement that was emerging, distinct from the anti-media violence campaign initiated by WAVAW. WAVAW's goals and tactics had never been controversial among feminists. Founders of WAP, on the other hand, were advocating strategies that raised questions and concerns within feminist and liberal circles that would only intensify over time.

Conclusion: Organizing Under Fire

The debate at NYU and the appearance on *Donahue* were some of the first actions that alerted the public to the emergence of an organized feminist anti-pornography movement. In both instances, prominent feminists expressed support for the legal suppression of pornography. This caught the attention of dissenting feminists and civil libertarians, and the WAP founders learned firsthand just how contentious the struggle over pornography would become. WAP, in other words, organized under fire.

Brownmiller was the leading voice for censorship at the time of WAP's founding, reiterating opinions that she had shared three years earlier in *Against Our Will*. In her book, she expressed ire toward liberals who opposed concrete efforts to stem the tide of pornography, viewing this as a sexist position taken up by men who were indifferent to the plight of women. According to Brownmiller, liberals had mobilized to stop Hitler's malicious attacks on Jews, and to dismantle racist stereotypes of blacks, but they refused to oppose pornography even though it told equally terrible lies about women. "[T]hese very same liberals," Brownmiller wrote, "now fervidly maintain that the hatred and contempt for women that find expression in … 'adult' or 'erotic' books and movies are a valid extension of freedom of speech that must be preserved as a Constitutional right."[70] She reserved her harshest criticism for the ACLU, which she saw as defending pornographers' freedoms at women's expense. "I wonder if the ACLU's position might change if, come tomorrow morning, the bookstores and movie theaters lining Forty-second Street … were devoted not to the humiliation of women by rape and torture, as they currently are, but to … the sadistic pleasures of gassing Jews or lynching Blacks?" she

[70] Brownmiller, *Against Our Will*, 394–395.

asked.[71] Brownmiller argued that pornography was as serious a threat to women as "storm troopers, concentration camps, and extermination" had been for European Jews during World War II, yet liberals were more interested in protecting their own sexual interests and abstract speech rights than in saving women's lives.[72]

In the wake of the early events surrounding the formation of WAP, a climate of distrust and hostility developed between anti-pornography feminists and those who opposed their campaign. Many liberals and dissenting feminists concluded that Brownmiller's support for a ban on the public display of pornography was WAP's official position, and the new organization was greeted with suspicion. Aryeh Neier, then the national executive director of the ACLU, characterized anti-pornography feminists as "the new censors" and observed in *The Nation* that their attack on free speech was misguided and desperate, the tactic of activists who were otherwise "bereft of a strategy for combating oppression."[73] A staff writer at the *Village Voice*, New York's best-known alternative weekly, expressed contempt for Brownmiller's views shortly after the *Donahue* program aired. "Brownmiller, despite her splendid motives and eloquent arguments, is an enemy of the First Amendment," he wrote. "If the government can decide that *one* class of speech is to be denied protection, it can decide that *any* is. And Brownmiller's cavalier reassurance to namby-pambies like me who fear legislative lunacy is hardly comforting."[74] Like Marjorie Smith from the NYU panel, this writer urged feminists to stick with the WAVAW approach, bringing economic and intellectual pressure to bear on those who created and distributed images of violence against women.

[71] Brownmiller, *Against Our Will*, 395.

[72] Brownmiller, *Against Our Will*, 395.

[73] Aryeh Neier, "Expurgating the First Amendment," *The Nation*, June 21, 1980, 1.

[74] Geoffrey Stokes, "Beaver, Buggery, Brownmiller and Black Girls: The First Amendment Bullies," *The Village Voice*, August 20, 1979, 15.

7

Porn Tours

Tensions and Triumphs for WAP

In the summer of 1979, as WAP made its debut on the New York scene, organization leaders identified fundraising and membership initiatives as immediate priorities. Dolores Alexander proposed that WAP ask some well-connected feminist friends to sponsor parties at their summer homes in the Hamptons and on Fire Island. "We need an elitist [sic] group of feminists to put their names to our cause so we can raise money, hold parties, etc.," she wrote in a memo detailing recommendations for action.[1] These gatherings would allow WAP leaders to introduce the organization to the feminist community and solicit support. Alexander, whom Brownmiller described as "a whiz at raising money through the lesbian social network," had many contacts through her work with NOW and Mother Courage, the feminist restaurant in Greenwich Village that she co-owned with partner Jill Ward during the 1970s. She began contacting friends and asking them to host parties.[2]

The WAP women expected friendly cocktail hours, confident that a feminist organization committed to fighting pornography would be well received. To their surprise, they found that the conversations at the gatherings were heated, as guests vehemently opposed to limitations on sexual speech challenged WAP's goals. The word was out throughout New York City's feminist and progressive communities that prominent WAP leaders were calling for legal measures to suppress pornography. Up and down the East Coast, people were buzzing about WAP's appearance on *Donahue* and Brownmiller's *Newsday* essay. At the summer parties, women who viewed the organization's agenda with concern confronted WAP leaders.

1 Memorandum, "Recommendations for Immediate Action," Dolores Alexander to WAP, n.d., WAP Records, Box 1, Folder 3.

2 Brownmiller, *In Our Time*, 307. Mother Courage is described in an oral history transcript narrated by Dolores Alexander. See Dolores Alexander, oral history conducted by Kelly Anderson, Southold, New York, March 20, 2004 and October 22, 2005, Sophia Smith Voices of Feminism Oral History Project. Available online at http://www.smith.edu/library/libs/ssc/vof/vof-narrators.html

One East Hampton fundraiser held at the end of July proved especially contentious. In a letter to the host penned several days after the party, Alexander complained that a number of women who were relatively uninformed about WAP had loudly declared themselves in opposition. One guest told Alexander that she had heard a rumor that WAP was taking right-wing money. Another insisted that people were saying that the organization was too actively embroiled in political and legislative affairs to qualify for tax-exempt status. Alexander denied both claims.[3] A feminist attorney, whom Alexander had repeatedly invited to view the WAP slide show, marched up and announced: "I want you to know that I'm actively working against you."[4] Alexander recalled that, to her surprise, many attendees flatly rejected the premise that pornography was degrading to women, and in fact, they insisted that they used and enjoyed pornography. "[W]hen I gathered lesbian groups together for little parties and to ask for money," she recalled in a recent oral history interview, "... [we] began to understand that these images were titillating to women."[5]

The East Hampton debacle suggested that the support that feminists had shown for the campaign against media violence would not necessarily transfer to a campaign against pornography. Following the party, Alexander received a letter from the feminist attorney explaining her objection: "Both you and Susan [Brownmiller] have specifically stated that you were seeking some sort of legislative proscription against either the use of, or the placement of pornographic materials," she wrote. "I fully respect your right to organize and protest, but vehemently object to seeking support for the cause through the use of legislative and judicial processes."[6] Like many women who attended the East Hampton fundraiser, the attorney feared that state suppression of sexual expression would be deployed in anti-feminist ways. How could Brownmiller recommend that feminists trust the courts to decide what materials women might safely view? The courts were agents of a patriarchal, misogynist, and racist state, and if given the opportunity, would be sure to "protect" women from harmful information about birth control, abortion, and female sexuality. The attorney warned Alexander that legal action could bring dire consequences. "If you were to succeed in legislating sales of pornographic materials, your very successes would someday be used to deny women the rights which you have worked so hard to ensure."[7]

[3] For the record, WAP did have tax-exempt status. The claim about taking right-wing money would depend on how one defined "right-wing," but WAP did take donations and subsidies from organizations bent on cleaning up Times Square. These donations are discussed later in this chapter.

[4] Letter, Dolores Alexander to East Hampton party host, August 3, 1979, WAP Records, Box 6, Folder 270.

[5] Dolores Alexander, oral history.

[6] Letter, Feminist Attorney to Dolores Alexander, August 9, 1979, WAP Records, Box 6, Folder 270.

[7] Letter, Feminist Lawyer to Dolores Alexander.

Alexander received a similar warning from a close friend, a well-known lesbian playwright who rejected an invitation to become involved in WAP. Upon reading the organization's literature and Brownmiller's *Newsday* essay, the playwright reported that she felt "a little sick to my stomach." She was stunned by Brownmiller's assertion that restrictions on the public display of pornography would constitute a desirable free speech abridgment that would strengthen "societal values."[8] Throughout the playwright's career, her plays and novels had been condemned as pornographic for exploring controversial themes like homosexuality; her stage productions had been dismantled and her books removed from store shelves. These experiences led her to believe that social conservatives had more control over the definition of societal values than feminists. If feminists were to call for censorship, and open up that "can of worms," they would invite the return of a more repressive social agenda. "One little worm is going to scamper right to south Miami and crawl up Anita's leg, another is heading west to scout out John Birch," she cautioned.[9] The playwright referred to leaders of the rapidly ascending New Right and growing numbers of conservative Christian activists who had become politicized by progressive social changes including expanded reproductive freedom and gay rights. She summed up the crux of early feminist opposition to WAP, namely the fear that any law that allowed for the suppression of so-called pornography would be controlled by right-wingers whose definition did not square with that of feminists. "I know firsthand about the temperament of censorship," she warned Alexander, "and I know absolutely that once unleashed, it cannot be controlled."[10]

The persistence of feminist opposition to WAP frustrated the anti-pornography activists. They too were concerned about freedom of speech, but they saw pornographers hiding behind the First Amendment and using their speech rights to perpetuate the sexual abuse of women. Influential anti-pornography theorists like Andrea Dworkin argued that instead of lionizing the First Amendment, women ought to recognize that it was meaningless in a society where women had so little power as a class. Pornographers with vast financial and publishing empires had far greater ability to make their speech heard, and they used their enormous reach to impose a corrupt vision of female sexuality on society. Women, by contrast, had nothing more than "token access" to the media.[11] Furthermore, the invention of the video camera in the late 1970s had democratized pornography, enabling average men to make pornography at home starring their wives and children as unwilling subjects. Given circumstances that weighed so heavily against the possibility

[8] Susan Brownmiller, "Let's Put Pornography Back in the Closet," *Newsday*, July 17, 1979, 41.

[9] Anita refers to conservative activist Anita Bryant, who was well known for her 1977 campaign opposing anti-discrimination legislation for gays and lesbians. Letter, Lesbian Playwright to Dolores Alexander, July 23, 1979, WAP Records, Box 6, Folder 270.

[10] Letter, Lesbian Playwright to Dolores Alexander.

[11] Andrea Dworkin, "For Men, Freedom of Speech; For Women, Silence Please," in *Take Back the Night*, 258.

of women's freedom, protecting theoretic speech rights at all costs seemed absurd. Dworkin believed that women had no choice but to reform male laws to make them more responsive to female victimization "because something is better than nothing," she argued in an essay written after the NYU colloquium on pornography and free speech.[12] Liberal feminists who piously cited the First Amendment as a justification for abandoning any effort to control the spread of violent, woman-hating pornography were playing right into the pornographers' hands.

After the East Hampton debacle, WAP leaders worried that fighting the free speech battle would sap the organization's energy, hamper effective action against pornography, and stymie efforts to build a national campaign. These women were fiercely committed to doing something *concrete* about the pornography problem, and they did not believe that WAVAW-style economic pressure applied to a few corporations at a time would deliver results. They wanted to try to use the law to achieve real change that would improve women's lives. "I understand people's fears about the First Amendment," Alexander wrote in the post-mortem to the East Hampton party host. "But obscenity is not protected by the First Amendment.... We have no quarrel with art or literature or reasonable facsimiles thereof. We are opposed to an industry – a multimillion dollar industry that degrades and humiliates women."[13] Overall, the responses to the July fundraiser suggested that WAP's agenda would divide feminists. "I think you must be sorry that you got into this party with us," Alexander wrote her friend. "I know I am. Neither of us could have foreseen the problems that cropped up."[14]

The Ascendance of WAP

In this chapter, I argue that the rise of Women Against Pornography altered the nature of the feminist movement against media violence. With the attention-getting subject matter of their campaign and a high-profile membership, WAP captured media attention and became the dominant organization in a national movement reorganized around pornography. On the one hand, the formation of WAP gave the movement against media violence much needed visibility, yet on the other, the shift to pornography pushed WAVAW and WAVPM to the margins. As the older organizations ceded territory to WAP, journalists narrowed the range of issues presented to the public as part of the anti-violence agenda, and the consumer action model that WAVAW had pioneered fell to the wayside.

The WAP leaders' exclusive focus on pornography was calculated. The reorientation to pornography was engineered by media-savvy individuals who

[12] Dworkin, "For Men, Freedom of Speech," 257.

[13] Letter, Dolores Alexander to East Hampton party host, August 3, 1979, WAP Records, Box 6, Folder 270.

[14] Letter, Dolores Alexander to East Hampton party host.

understood that porn would grab more headlines than violence. "... [W]e are getting so much press, it's making my head spin," Alexander wrote to a friend in August 1979. "[P]ornography is of such interest to men and the male press that it will make it an important issue for us. If we were against say, violence, – by that I mean wife beating, sexual harassment, etc. – we would have a hard time being heard."[15] Brownmiller recalled in her memoir that when she left WAP at the end of 1979, she had accomplished her goal of bringing the problem of pornography into the national spotlight.

In the short run, at least, the WAP strategy enhanced the organization's position. Confining its agenda to anti-pornography initiatives did result in the national media attention that Brownmiller and the other founders desired. However, it was a decision that hastened the demise of the older groups, WAVAW and WAVPM, who were struggling by 1980 to figure out how they might continue to occupy a meaningful place in the movement. With public attention now focused on pornography, the fight against abusive advertising campaigns seemed like a backburner issue. The goals of WAVAW and WAVPM, who continued to characterize their work in broader terms as fighting sexualized media violence against women, were perceived as less urgent.

Other factors contributed to WAP's ascendance, and not least among them were the organization's well-known feminist members and connections to high-profile supporters. WAP's founders were among the most influential actors in the women's movement, including Brownmiller, Gloria Steinem, Adrienne Rich, and Robin Morgan. Each possessed a national reputation in her professional field, whether journalism, activism, academe, or art, and reporters treated them as official sources who could speak authoritatively about the feminist campaign against media violence. Other women who were not active members of WAP, including feminist leaders like Andrea Dworkin and celebrities such as television actress Valerie Harper of the *Mary Tyler Moore Show* and *Rhoda*, were recruited to headline organization events as a means of attracting the news media. Their opinions were often presented as reflecting those held by the WAP membership, with lasting consequences. The true diversity of thought in the organization on various questions – including censorship – was rarely presented to the public. The news media's attention to a relatively small group of women and their opinions influenced the overall trajectory of the movement in ways that did not necessarily reflect members' desires.

A wide body of literature in mass communication discusses newsgathering routines with an eye to how the economic and political interests of news organizations, as well as journalists' professional codes, lead reporters to solicit information from official sources. Decentralized movements such as the New Left and women's liberation were always ambivalent about identifying leaders, so journalists typically appointed charismatic individuals – such as Steinem – who were not necessarily accountable to movement organizations.

[15] Letter, Dolores Alexander to friend, August 3, 1979, WAP Records, Box 6, Folder 270.

Sociologist Todd Gitlin has argued that in the case of the New Left, journalists decided who the leaders and noteworthy personalities for the anti-war movement were, and thereby played an active role in determining what that movement ultimately became.[16] Within anti-pornography, however, which was a far more centralized movement, WAP consciously proffered its best-known feminists and supporters to maximize media attention. Journalists used the views of this select group to frame the movement against media violence for the public, a strategy that failed to adequately represent the range of opinions and strategies present in WAVAW, WAVPM, and even WAP. The concern with abusive advertising, as well as the consumer pressure and public education tactics favored by WAVAW and the majority of WAVPM members, dropped out of the public conversation. Over time, the roots of the feminist anti-pornography movement in a broader campaign against media violence against women faded from public view.

The final factor that aided WAP's rise to the forefront of the movement was the publication of several of the major texts of late radical feminism (cultural feminism), which documented the sexual exploitation of women. Andrea Dworkin's influential book, *Pornography: Men Possessing Women*, and Kathy Barry's *Female Sexual Slavery* were published in 1979, the year of WAP's founding. *Take Back the Night*, the definitive feminist anti-pornography anthology, arrived in 1980. Susan Griffin's important work, *Pornography and Silence: Culture's Revenge Against Nature*, appeared in 1981. Drawing from the theories of women's difference advanced by white feminists such as Dorothy Dinnerstein, Nancy Chodorow, and Carol Gilligan in the late 1970s, these texts emphasized what the historian Jane Gerhard has described as a "psychological essentialism" that characterized men and male values not only as different from women and women's values, but also as the source of women's oppression.[17]

The anti-pornography authors used the theories of women's difference to argue that whereas women desired intimacy, sensuality, and closeness, men's sexuality was violent and rapacious. They saw a continuum between the expected, "normal" violence of the heterosexual male and the patriarchal family (e.g., battering, rape, incest) and the larger-scale expression of male violence, including militarism, capitalism, and environmental destruction. Pornography had a place on that continuum, as a graphic depiction and teaching tool of the violent male impulse toward women. In *Female Sexual Slavery*, for example, Barry argued that men's abuse of women as sexual objects in prostitution and pornography was so pervasive that such representations of women had become accepted as normal. These conditions constituted what she termed the "ideology of cultural sadism," or the mainstreaming of male sexual violence and domination as part of the everyday structure of society.[18]

[16] Todd Gitlin, *The Whole World is Watching: Mass Media in the Making and Unmaking of the New Left* (Berkeley: University of California Press, 1980).

[17] Gerhard, *Desiring Revolution*, 172.

[18] Barry, *Female Sexual Slavery*, 154.

Griffin argued that men in a patriarchal society identified themselves with culture and women with nature and the body. Culture feared nature, and thus men sought to punish and destroy women's bodies and suppress the female in themselves. Pornography was in itself "a sadistic act" that objectified and degraded women, and its images reassured men that they had the ability to torture, murder, and silence women at will.[19] In *Take Back the Night*, Griffin described male nature as "essentially rapacious and brutal." She characterized the average man as an animal "in the corner of a cage growling with menace" who fed his appetite for violence with pornography.[20]

Dworkin also interpreted pornography as male violence. In her view, the major components of male identity were physical and psychic violence. One purpose of pornography was to channel all of this violence toward women and away from other men. In a book review written for the *New York Times*, Ellen Willis described Dworkin's worldview: "Men are predators, women their chief prey. To men, sex means rape; the penis is an instrument of power and terror."[21] In April and May 1981, WAP threw book parties to promote Dworkin and Griffin's work. The analyses set out in this group of high-profile books best corresponded to WAP's focus on pornography, and further pushed the anti-media violence movement toward WAP leadership.

WAP Opens its First Office

On June 16, 1979, WAP unlocked the doors of its first office, located at the corner of Ninth Avenue and 42nd Street, on the edge of Times Square, and declared itself "open for business."[22] This location put the WAP women in close proximity to ninety-six sex-related establishments operating in and around Times Square, including X-rated movie theaters, peep shows, adult bookstores, sex emporiums, live shows, and massage parlors. The WAP office space, which a reporter from the *New York Times* described as a "soul food restaurant and gathering place for transvestites and prostitutes" that had recently been closed down by the city, was provided rent-free to the organization at the request of Carl Weisbrod, the head of Mayor Edward L. Koch's Midtown Enforcement Project.[23]

[19] Griffin, *Pornography and Silence*, 111.

[20] Susan Griffin, "Sadism and Catharsis: The Treatment is the Disease," in *Take Back the Night*, 141.

[21] Ellen Willis, "Nature's Revenge," *The New York Times*, July 12, 1981, available online at http://www.nytimes.com/1981/07/12/books/nature-s-revenge.html

[22] Press Release, "Our Times Square Office – We Swept, Scrubbed, Painted and Moved In," June 22, 1979, WAP Records, Box 8.

[23] Georgia Dullea, "In Feminists' Antipornography Drive, 42nd Street Is the Target," *The New York Times*, July 6, 1979, A12. New York City, in the area of 42nd St. known as Times Square, has the equivalent of Boston's Combat Zone, an area in which legal sex entertainment industries and their illicit counterparts such as prostitution are concentrated in a relatively small area. The stretch of 42nd St. between 6th and 8th Avenues represents the heart

Midtown Enforcement was one of two major players in Koch's attempt to drive sex-related businesses out of the Times Square area to improve the environment for economic development. In cities around the nation, government agencies working in cooperation with law enforcement were fighting the expansion of sex districts on the grounds that they caused urban blight and contributed to the social and moral decline of commercial and residential neighborhoods. In each case, urban public officials cast the spread of sex-related businesses as a threat to neighborhood quality-of-life, giving more weight to urban development and real estate values than sexual freedom. They were supported in these efforts by business and property owners and chambers of commerce, whose interests lay in making the streets "safe and clean for people of all ages and interests," particularly tourists.[24] In Los Angeles, Boston, Detroit, San Francisco, and elsewhere, powerful real estate interests argued that adult businesses invited economic decline, low property values, and criminal behavior including prostitution and the drug trade. They demanded that the spread of commercial sex establishments be curbed to prevent further capital flight – an early battle cry for gentrification. New York City developers working with a $500,000 grant from the Ford Foundation had already come up with a plan to take over a full block of West 42nd Street in Times Square, condemn it as a city urban renewal project, and erect an elaborate, tourist-oriented structure that would contain theaters, exhibitions, and multimedia displays, at a projected cost of $175 million.

Founded in 1976, Midtown Enforcement used zoning regulations, the State Public Health law, and ultimately New York City's 1977 Nuisance Abatement Law to assert control over the Times Square sex district. In short, these tools enabled Midtown Enforcement to close down businesses that were promoting criminal activities, specifically prostitution. The Nuisance law gave Weisbrod's office the power to use civil court actions to shut down businesses where two or more on-site arrests resulted in convictions for prostitution. As such, Midtown Enforcement tracked all arrests taking place on the premises of Times Square establishments and provided the Manhattan district attorney's office with a weekly hot sheet listing the ones that the Mayor's office wanted to see through to conviction, not plea bargained down

of this area and has generally featured X-rated movie theaters, peep shows, adult bookstores, sex emporiums, live shows, and massage parlors. At the start of Edward L. Koch's mayoral administration in New York City in 1978, there were ninety-six sex-related businesses operating in the Times Square area. By March 1982, there were sixty-three. Figures from: Letter, Carl B. Weisbrod, Director, Mayor's Office of Midtown Enforcement to the Editor, *The New York Post*, April 15, 1982, 38. On the history of Times Square's transformation from a sex-oriented urban center to a family-friendly, corporate-sponsored entertainment district, see Daniel Makagon, *Where the Ball Drops: Days and Nights in Times Square* (Minneapolis, MN: University of Minneapolis Press, 2004).

24 Robert O. Self, "Sex in the City: The Politics of Sexual Liberalism in Los Angeles, 1963–79," *Gender & History* 20, no. 2 (August 2008): 297. Here, Self discusses the Hollywood Chamber of Commerce and its drive to "clean up" Hollywood through the late 1960s and into the 1970s.

to lesser charges or dismissed. Once two convictions for prostitution-related activity were on the books, Midtown Enforcement would close down the business under the provisions of the Nuisance Abatement law, on the grounds that it was a "public nuisance" that fostered illegal sexual activity. The cooperation among Midtown Enforcement, the New York police department, and the district attorney's office resulted in a 65 percent increase in arrests for prostitution from 1978 to 1981.

When Midtown Enforcement closed down a "public nuisance," its commercial space became available for use by another tenant. The 42nd Street Redevelopment Corporation, a nonprofit local development agency controlled by the Mayor's office and charged with redeveloping and revitalizing the Times Square area, used various incentive programs to persuade legitimate businesses to set up shop, with the goal of driving out the sex trade.[25] After Midtown Enforcement locked the doors to the soul food restaurant, the Redevelopment Corporation leased the space rent-free to WAP. WAP remained in that office for more than two years, battling a takeover attempt by *Penthouse* publisher Bob Guccione, who tried to buy the building to kick WAP out and open a sex-related business called The Meat Rack. WAP ultimately relocated to 47th Street, when major renovations on buildings adjacent to the original storefront made the office structurally unsafe.[26]

Many neighborhood merchants and area residents welcomed WAP with open arms. "Martin's Paint Store offered a discount on the buckets of whitewash needed to cover the grimy walls," the *New York Times* reported. "Tony's bar provided the hot water and sink space. Others offered folding chairs, castoff furniture and moving day greetings."[27] Brownmiller remembered that St. Malachy's, an actors' chapel located at West 47th Street, donated four desks.[28] "Everybody kept saying, 'It's about time you showed up!'" Lynn Campbell told a *New York Times* reporter.[29]

WAP benefited from the supplies received from neighbors and the free office space arranged by Midtown Enforcement, but members also raised a significant amount of the organization's seed money. Brownmiller donated $10,000 to get WAP off the ground.[30] Adrienne Rich and Frances Whyatt helped pay Campbell's salary. Gloria Steinem gave $100 and pledged to send more once she was paid for her next round of lectures.[31]

[25] Dullea, "In Feminists' Antipornography Drive," A12.

[26] In the fall of 1981, WAP relocated its office to 358 West 47th Street, near Ninth Ave. WAP organized community members to protest Guccione's plan, and eventually the city denied him a business license.

[27] Dullea, "In Feminists' Antipornography Drive," A12.

[28] Brownmiller, *In Our Time*, 304.

[29] Brownmiller, *In Our Time*, 304.

[30] Dolores Alexander, oral history.

[31] In August 1979, Steinem gave an additional $100 and promised: "More will be forthcoming with my next lecture money." Letter, Gloria Steinem to Dolores Alexander, August 28, 1979, WAP Records, Box 6.

FIGURE 7.1. WAP opens its first office at the corner of Ninth Avenue and 42nd Street, and begins the "clean-up" operation – a double entendre that reflected members' efforts to both transform the dingy storefront space and to eradicate the pornography problem that was seen as a blight on Times Square and a danger to women. Notice that the woman at work in the WAP office wears a t-shirt that reads: "Never Another Battered Woman." Dozens of women wore identical t-shirts to the WAP march on Times Square, underscoring the close ties among the anti-rape and anti-battering movements, and the anti-media violence and anti-pornography campaigns. *Photo: Bettye Lane.*

In the months following its founding, WAP also received a number of major corporate donations. In July 1979, the Joe and Emily Lowe Foundation, which primarily supported the arts, gave WAP a $5,000 grant. Off-Track Betting contributed $2,500.[32] In September 1979, Con Edison, a New York utility, donated $1,000. The New York League of Theater Owners and Producers gave WAP a grant of $8,000 in September 1979, and then hosted a benefit performance at the Circle in the Square Theatre on October 14, 1979. The evening featured stars from various Broadway shows, including Jessica James and Gregory Hines, and yielded an additional $1,166 for WAP.[33] After just ten months of organizing, WAP had raised more than $50,000.[34] This was

[32] Financial Statement: Women Against Pornography, February to December 1979, WAP Records, Box 9, Folder 569. See also Press Release, "Our Times Square Office – We Swept, Scrubbed, Painted and Moved In," June 22, 1979, WAP Records, Box 8.

[33] Grant Proposal, "1980–81 Proposal to Support the Local and National Organizing Programs of Women Against Pornography," n.d., WAP Records, Box 9, Folder 569.

[34] Financial Statement: Women Against Pornography, February to December 1979, WAP Records, Box 9, Folder 569.

an impressive amount of start-up capital (roughly equivalent to $150,000 in 2011 dollars) whereas WAVPM and WAVAW always operated on shoestring budgets and were frequently in debt.[35]

WAP made a strategic decision to align itself with powerful city and corporate partners, and in fact, having these supporters may have been the organization's best hope to make inroads into the city's pornography problem. The Mayor's office and the business community were powerful allies for a fledgling feminist group, and gifts of an office free of high-priced Manhattan rent and substantial grant funding must have been exhilarating first steps. There was a precedent for such cooperation, too. WAVPM's Lederer had worked closely with San Francisco Supervisor Dianne Feinstein to try to introduce zoning restrictions similar to those approved by the Detroit City Council in 1972 that prohibited the establishment of sex businesses within 1,000 feet of one another and required owners to obtain the approval of 51 percent of the residents within a 500-foot radius of the proposed site. The Detroit "Anti-Skid Row Ordinance" proved very successful in containing the growth of that city's sex district and reducing the number of sex-related businesses operating in the city within five years.[36] Lederer was very familiar with the Detroit measure because her father was the city's commissioner of buildings and safety and had been an avid ordinance supporter. According to urban historian Josh Sides, Lederer conducted interviews with Detroit city officials and shared her research with Feinstein, ultimately playing an influential role in the development of Feinstein's proposal for a similar zoning ordinance for San Francisco.[37]

Back on the Times Square scene, the Redevelopment Corporation and the New York League of Theater Owners and Producers were problematic donors from a feminist standpoint. Both supported a "clean-up" of Times Square, which generally included sweep arrests of prostitutes and other sex workers, many of whom were poor women of color, vulnerable individuals whom middle-class feminists surely did not wish to harm. Midtown Enforcement encouraged these sweeps and worked hand-in-hand with the police department

35 brooke, "Life, Liberty, and the Pursuit of Porn," *off our backs* 9 (January 1979): 5. For the inflation calculation, see the Consumer Price Index inflation calculator available online at http://www.bls.gov/data/inflation_calculator.htm

36 Sides, "Postwar Sex District," 369. See also Robert O. Self, "Sex in the City: The Politics of Sexual Liberalism in Los Angeles, 1963–79," *Gender & History* 20, no. 2 (August 2008): 303.

37 Sides, "Postwar Sex District," 370–371. Feinstein, who became Mayor of San Francisco in 1978 following the assassination of Mayor George Moscone and Supervisor Harvey Milk, came up against strong opposition when she put the ordinance forward. Most opposed were sex-business owners who insisted that San Francisco was an "open" city in terms of sexual conduct, and the ordinance was puritanical. The San Francisco chapter of the ACLU was also opposed because its members saw the ordinance as an attack on free speech and privacy rights. Residents of areas who feared that sex businesses would open shop locally if the North Beach and Tenderloin areas were better controlled were also opposed. Ultimately, Feinstein was only able to pass a watered-down version of the Detroit ordinance that blocked adult businesses from opening within 1,000 feet of one another. See Sides, 373–374.

and district attorney's office to ensure that the highest possible number of arrests ended in convictions. The League regarded pornography and prostitution as a "cancer" on the Broadway-Times Square neighborhood, not because women were engaged in dangerous and exploitative sex work, but because the environment threatened theater profits and limited the potential for midtown business development. "Not only is the pornography blight highly destructive to our morale, we know it has had a deleterious effect on theatre-goers who have to pick their way through seedy streets past so called 'Adult' bookstores and attendant enterprises ...," the League wrote in a news release supporting WAP efforts.[38] Their objections centered on patrons' comfort as they walked through the Times Square area; they did not express concern that women worked as prostitutes because structural inequalities made it difficult to find secure jobs that paid decent wages, nor did they worry that clean-up efforts left these women vulnerable to sexual coercion and police abuse. The Mayor's office, the League, and WAP shared a common goal, namely the eradication of commercialized sex in Times Square, but they did not share the same interpretation of the underlying social causes and costs of pornography and prostitution.

In addition to accepting financial support, WAP leaders adopted Midtown Enforcement's "clean-up" language to describe their own efforts in the Times Square area. In a news release describing the new office space, WAP announced that the first order of business was "a cleanup operation ... which has symbolic as well as practical value."[39] During its October 1979 March on Times Square, WAP led a chant whose lyrics included: "Clean 'em up – close 'em down, Make New York a safer town." The chorus rang out: "Shut, Shut it down! Shut it down down down!" a rallying cry that seemed to put WAP activists at odds with women who depended on employment in commercial sex establishments, and suggested a lack of sensitivity to the politics of class and race.[40] At the East Hampton fundraiser, Dolores Alexander had denied charges that WAP was accepting right-wing money. But setting up an office in a space that Midtown Enforcement had cleared out by arresting and convicting prostitutes, and taking donations from the Theater League that supported increased police action against sex workers and a clear-cut gentrification agenda, seemed to some observers to come perilously close. In their enthusiasm for launching the organization and tackling the pornography problem, WAP leaders may have been shortsighted in accepting the free rent and funding.[41]

[38] Press Release, New York League of Theatre Owners and Producers, "In League With: Women Against Pornography," n.d., WAP Records, Box 1, Folder 1.

[39] Press Release, "Women Open Times Square Office to Kick Off Anti-Pornography Campaign," n.d., WAP Records, Box 8.

[40] March Chants and Leaflets, WAP Records, Box 1, Folder 15. The chant is also mentioned in Barbara Basler, "5,000 Join Feminist Group's Rally in Times Square Against Pornography," *The New York Times*, October 21, 1979, 41.

[41] Brownmiller, it should be noted, did not seem to have any qualms about accepting money from organizations whose goals diverged from those of WAP. At the East Coast Feminist

Some of these early actions alienated New York progressive groups that might otherwise have regarded the anti-pornography activists with favor. Shortly after opening its office, WAP received a series of letters from individuals and local feminist, gay, and lesbian groups denouncing the organization for cooperating with law enforcement and the business community. Some pledged to work against the arrest and abuse of prostitutes caught in police sweeps. "Efforts to 'clean up' Times Square are nothing new ... and always amount to white middle class crusades against street people," the Gay Activists Alliance chided, pointing out the obvious connection to urban capitalist interests.[42] Six New York City lesbians sent an open letter to feminist groups and alternative newspapers during the fall of 1979 to voice their objection to WAP's clean-up effort. They argued that Times Square was the city's leading symbol of "immorality," and that any plan to clean up the area amounted to an attack on sexual minorities and on poor women who had no viable economic option other than selling their bodies. According to these six women, it was a violation of feminist principles for WAP to support the city's gentrification campaign, considering that feminists traditionally stood with, not against, prostitutes. They described a previous effort in Times Square that had occurred at the time of the 1976 Democratic national convention, when the city passed an anti-loitering law that allowed police to conduct sweep arrests of prostitutes. "The *last time* an attempt was made to 'clean up' Times Square ... feminists showed solidarity with prostitutes by loitering in the Midtown area and circulating petitions against this unconstitutional law," they wrote. "*This time* feminists appear to be calling for the clean-up" [italics in original].[43] They insisted that support for these campaigns deflected attention from the role of white middle-class men in perpetuating prostitution, and exacerbated racism and classism by pitting white, middle-class women against women of color and poor women.

WAP also received a number of letters from sex workers who criticized the organization's early activities. These women asked WAP to reconsider its cooperation with state agencies and local businesses who were trying to gentrify Times Square because working girls would feel the brunt of this effort. "[Y]our movement is hurting women – women on the street – women who do not have nice jobs or husband 'johns,'" insisted an adult film actress. "These are the women who face police violence every night, yet you work hand

Conference on Pornography, discussed later in the chapter, several audience members questioned WAP's willingness to take funds from all sources. Brownmiller responded: "I don't believe that there's any such thing as dirty money." This question would be hotly debated at the conference. See brooke, "Feminist Conference: Porn Again," *off our backs* (November 1979): 24–27.

42 Letter, Chairperson, Gay Activists Alliance to WAP, October 25, 1979, WAP Records, Box 6, Folder 295.

43 Marjory Ackerman, Quinn Bevan, Cathy Cockrell, Eileen Kane, Doris Lunden, and Marty Pottenger, "Use of Times Square," *Plexus* (February 1980): 3.

and hand [sic] with their tormentors to 'clean up' Times Square."[44] Another sex worker insisted that giving the police more power to regulate the area amounted to a direct attack on citizens who were already struggling. Street work was the lowest paid work for prostitutes and posed the highest risk for arrest. "You talk about harassment of women," she wrote. "I guess poor Black women don't count."[45] WAP members familiar with the pressures that prostitutes faced likely knew that the percentage of women of color arrested for street soliciting was much greater than that of white women, and that women of color picked up for prostitution constituted 85 percent of those who served jail time for the offense.[46]

Without question, members of WAP did care about the welfare of women working in prostitution and pornography. Radical feminists were critically concerned about coercion and subjugation in the sex industry, and the physical and sexual abuse that the women forced into such work were made to endure. Regarding the conflict over Times Square, prostitutes and anti-pornography feminists tended to approach the question of sex work from different vantage points. Many of the prostitutes who opposed WAP treated their work as a rational economic choice, a sex-for-money transaction not dissimilar to middle-class arrangements wherein wives provided emotional and sexual services to husbands in exchange for financial support. Some prostitutes earned five times as much money per day as the average woman working in the service sector, making sex work more attractive to some than a respectable low-wage, dead-end job. Liberal feminist discussions of prostitution supported the idea that selling one's sexual services was not fundamentally different from other jobs defined by physical labor (e.g., furniture movers), and what prostitutes needed most was the same guarantee of fair, safe working conditions that unionized workers enjoyed. Furthermore, many prostitutes and liberal feminists believed that the *stigma* attached to sex work was its worst feature, and that decriminalization of prostitution and normalization of sexual commerce were needed to combat this problem.[47]

Radical feminists rejected those views, regarding prostitutes and women working in the sex industry with sympathy and anger as victims of male sexual exploitation. Dancing in strip clubs, walking the street as prostitutes, or working as live actor models in pornography reduced women to sexual commodities and confirmed men's unconditional rights to sexual access. These occupations, as Carole Pateman has argued, were the consummate expression

44 Letter, A sex worker to WAP, July 24, 1981, WAP Records, Box 6, Folder 265.

45 Letter, An angry woman to WAP, October 20, 1983, WAP Records, Box 3, Folder 93.

46 These statistics appear in Linda LeMoncheck, *Loose Women, Lecherous Men: A Feminist Philosophy of Sex* (New York: Oxford University Press, 1997), 142–143.

47 For this perspective, see Laurie Schrage, "Prostitution and the Case for Decriminalization," in *Prostitution and Pornography: Philosophical Debate about the Sex Industry*, ed. Jessica Spector (Stanford, CA: Stanford University Press, 2006), 240–246; Christine Overall, "What's Wrong with Prostitution? Evaluating Sex Work," *Signs* 17, no. 4 (Summer, 1992): 705–724.

of women's subordinate social and political status.[48] A woman might agree to this kind of employment because of her need for money, but the social and physical harm she would endure was so great that the very notion of her exercise of free will was suspect. MacKinnon has described the argument that women willingly enter into prostitution as the "myth of consent." She maintains that the possibility for meaningful consent is absent because the small sum of money paid to the woman can in no way compensate for the threat posed and the dehumanization endured; there is no legitimate price that could be paid.[49] Prostitutes who claimed to freely choose their work were said to suffer from false consciousness, having internalized their own oppression and the self-hatred born of life in a patriarchal society.

To white, middle-class, radical feminists – which described most of WAP's membership – prostitutes were women beaten down by a male-controlled society that taught them that they were inferior, subordinate, and deserving of abuse; their descent into sex work was a manifestation of the gender inequality that characterized women's lives in a patriarchal society.[50] A woman who consented to prostitution, topless dancing, modeling for pornography, or any other kind of sex work was so degraded by gender oppression that her view of herself as exerting agency or power in the exchange was distorted. Prostitution was sexual slavery, and slavery had to be prohibited – even if self-imposed – because it was inconsistent with the liberal conception of free and equal personhood.[51] If cooperating with city agencies – embracing law and order while seemingly condemning individual moral choice – would help WAP move a step closer to eradicating prostitution and pornography, and the women enslaved in those "professions," then the end of saving women from male exploitation and abuse justified the means.

As the letters from various critics – including sex workers – illustrate, some of WAP's early organizing actions and decisions raised concern in progressive and feminist circles. Observers questioned WAP's choice to reject the established campaign against media violence in favor of a fight against pornography; to set up shop in Times Square, which implied a law-and-order battle against vice and immoral sexual activity; to take funds from organizations with vested interests in gentrification; and to cooperate with city agencies that promoted the arrest of prostitutes. WAP acted in good faith to try to alleviate the potential harms done to women by prostitution and pornography, but external correspondence revealed that the organization's early decisions alarmed some feminists from the start.

48 See Carole Pateman, *The Sexual Contract* (Stanford, CA: Stanford University Press, 1988), esp. pp. 192–194.

49 Catharine MacKinnon, "Prostitution and Civil Rights," *Michigan Journal of Gender and Law* 1 (1993): 13–31.

50 See LeMoncheck's excellent discussion of pornography, prostitution, and live actor modeling in *Loose Women, Lecherous Men*, pp. 110–154.

51 See Drucilla Cornell, *At the Heart of Freedom: Feminism, Sex, and Equality* (Princeton, NJ: Princeton University Press, 1998), pp. 45–58.

Four Objectives: Slide Shows, Porn Tours, East Coast Conference, and the March on Times Square

By the time of the office launch in June, WAP had two full-time paid organizers: Lynn Campbell and Dolores Alexander, who had been hired in May 1979.[52] In July 1979, Barbara Mehrhof, a founding member of the radical feminist group Redstockings and a leading member of THE FEMINISTS, came on board as a third full-time paid organizer.[53] Susan Brownmiller put aside her then-current project, the manuscript for *Femininity*, and began working full time for WAP as a fourth organizer, although she drew no salary. These leaders launched a nationwide publicity campaign and initiated four major projects for WAP: slide show presentations, tours of the Times Square pornography district, an East Coast Feminist Conference on Pornography and a March on Times Square.[54]

Slide Shows

The slide show was an important point of continuity from WAVAW to WAVPM to WAP. Each group used the slide show to raise public consciousness and to let audiences see for themselves the kind of offensive and abusive media images that the organizations denounced. When Julia London visited New York City in December 1976, she brought the WAVAW slide show with her and presented it to a group of feminists assembled at Brownmiller's home. WAVPM constructed its slide show using WAVAW's program as a starting point, and WAP built on both of its predecessors' work. A number of images were common to all three groups' slide shows, including the Rolling Stones' *Black and Blue* advertisement and the *Hustler* meat grinder cover. WAP included fewer images from mainstream advertising than WAVAW, adding examples of softcore and hardcore pornography in their place.

The first version of the WAP slide show (1979–1980) included forty-two slides and illustrated what the organization described as the prevailing themes

[52] Grant Proposal, "1980–81 Proposal to Support the Local and National Organizing Programs of Women Against Pornography," n.d., WAP Records, Box 9, Folder 569. The salaries for these full-time organizers were quite modest – $100/week ($4,800/year).

[53] Mehrhof was also co-author with Pam Kearon of the influential article "Rape: An Act of Terror." This article is discussed in Chapter 1. She was a part-time Staff Coordinator at WAP through September 1981. Letter, Barbara Mehrhof to Steering Committee, November 23, 1981, WAP Records, Box 5, Folder 263.

[54] As far as the nationwide publicity campaign went, it should be noted that *The New York Times* paid WAP a great deal of attention, running three major feature stories on the group in the four months from July to October 1979. As previously mentioned, the activities of well-known feminists like Brownmiller and Steinem frequently got attention. However, it seems very likely that the newspaper's own interests played a role in the generous coverage. *The New York Times* owns major real estate holdings in the Times Square area (hence the name), particularly its massive building on West 43rd Street. Gentrification of that area would only serve to increase the value of the newspaper company's real estate.

of pornography. These included women in bondage; women as sexual objects; child molestation; and brutal physical violence, such as rape, murder, and mutilation. Like WAVAW and WAVPM, the organization charged a fee ($200) to present the slide show to a community group, complete with a WAP narrator who offered an analysis of each slide and placed it in the context of the fight against pornography. In 1979 alone, WAP presented the show to 225 groups (4,500 people) at its Times Square storefront and to college audiences, women's groups, and civic, religious, and professional organizations up and down the East Coast.[55] WAP concentrated its efforts on the slide show in the summer months, in hopes of persuading viewers to join the March on Times Square planned for October.

New York Times reporter Georgia Dullea viewed the WAP slide show in July 1979 and reported favorably on its impact as a consciousness raiser. She found herself among a dozen women staring "frozen-faced" as images of women being bound, beaten, and abused flashed across the screen. Dolores Alexander narrated the show and explained pornography's prevailing themes to the audience. She pointed out that women were consistently portrayed as objects rather than as sentient human beings, and she linked objectification to rape. "It is easier to abuse an object than a human being," Dullea quoted Alexander as saying.[56] WAP disseminated an important message, namely that the proliferation of media images of violence against women condoned real-life violence against women. Such images taught men that rape, battery, and other forms of abuse were normal behaviors, and portrayed women as men's willing and deserving victims. This idea was shared among WAVAW, WAVPM, and WAP.

It was relatively easy for WAP to explain its objection to slides that dealt with clear-cut violence, such as a man holding a knife to a woman's throat or binding her arms and legs with an electrical cord. However, the group's emphasis on pornography meant that narrators also had to describe the specific elements that might make a nonviolent sexually explicit image offensive. This boiled down to explaining the difference between "pornography" and "erotica." Feminists around the nation were grappling with this question but finding no easy answer. For Steinem, writing in *Ms.* in 1978, erotica was rooted in "'eros' or passionate love, and thus in the idea of positive choice, free will, the yearning for a particular person." Pornography, on the other hand, "begins with a root 'porno,' meaning 'prostitution' or 'female captives,' thus letting us know that the subject is not mutual love ... but domination and violence."[57] These distinctions may have seemed clear on paper, but it proved difficult to achieve consensus on many images.

[55] Grant Proposal, "1980–81 Proposal to Support the Local and National Organizing Programs of Women Against Pornography," n.d., WAP Records, Box 9, Folder 569.

[56] Dullea, "In Feminists' Antipornography Drive," A12.

[57] Gloria Steinem, "Erotica and Pornography: A Clear and Present Difference," *Ms.* (November 1978): 54.

During the course of the slide show, WAP narrators used the concept of *power* to explain the difference between pornography and erotica. If an image of a sexual exchange involved an abuse of power, then it was pornographic. "Erotica is about sex; pornography is about power," the slide show script read. "It [pornography] uses sex as a vehicle for power and the subjugation of women. It turns every act of sex into rape and ultimately, murder."[58] Through the lens of the group's passionate analysis, it was difficult to look at any heterosexual image without seeing a celebration of male control over women's bodies and women's lives. Images of women serving male needs, sexual or otherwise, seemed to glorify the subordinate and dominant roles characteristic of heterosexual arrangements. It was hard to find an image – particularly a *heterosexual* image – that someone in the group did not interpret as an abuse of power.

The difficulty of achieving consensus on images that did not feature overt violence became clear as WAP exposed people outside of the anti-pornography movement to their ideas. Gay rights activist John D'Emilio, then a doctoral candidate in history at Columbia University, joined WAP for a slide show and Times Square tour in the spring of 1980. He took issue with the show's inclusion of an advertisement for Alexander's, a New York department store. The ad featured two "tween" girls modeling shirts, standing side by side with their chins dropped slightly, smiling coyly up at the camera. Following the WAP slide show script, the narrator explained that the girls were posed just as they would be in hardcore pornography, presented as "sexually compliant, innocent and vulnerable little objects for adult men." These twelve- or thirteen-year-old girls, the script read, are "trying to look seductive, trying to make themselves into sex objects."[59] Photographs of pretty, pouting, pubescent girls in magazine and newspaper ads suggested that children were appropriate sexual targets for adult males who were only too willing to exploit their vulnerability. Furthermore, WAP argued that the image revealed the influence of pornography on mainstream media, as the trend in pornography for the past five years had been to depict females as young and defenseless. Frances Patai, an active WAP member, told a December 1979 tour group that portrayals of young girls as sexual prey were part of a backlash against the women's movement, meant to reassure men who were "unable to cope with mature adult women" that they retained social power.[60]

In an article written for *Christopher Street*, D'Emilio recounted his exchange with WAP about the Alexander's ad, which he did not find pornographic according to the organization's definition. At the beginning of the

[58] Women Against Pornography Slide Show Script, n.d., WAP Records, Folder 160, Box 4. Although the script is undated, it is an earlier script because it is printed on letterhead from the office at 579 Ninth Ave., which WAP occupied for its first two years only (1979–1981).

[59] Women Against Pornography Slide Show Script, n.d. The Alexander's ad can be viewed in the manuscript collection of Women Against Pornography at the Schlesinger Library.

[60] Nancy Hoch, "Activists Tour Times Square to Expose Pornographic Brutality," *The Guardian* 32, no. 12, (December 26, 1979): 8.

slide show program, the WAP narrator told D'Emilio's group that pornography was about violence and it was the violence – not the sex – to which the group objected. "There is *nothing* violent about that slide," D'Emilio told the WAP representative. "I don't understand what that slide has to do with pornography or with violence against women."[61] The narrator answered that the girls were presented as sex objects, to be used and exploited by men. D'Emilio was not satisfied. "When you tell WAP that you saw very little violence, members deny your claims," he complained. "*Pornography is violent; pornography leads to violence* – inexorably … *every image, every word, leads irresistibly to the same outcome: violence against women*" (italics in original).[62] Paula Webster, a writer and a member of the pro-sex feminist movement that formed to oppose anti-pornography, also rejected WAP's analysis of the Alexander's ad. "[T]he seductive looks of the child models were offered as proof positive that the evil influence of pornography had filtered down to … even the most mundane images," she wrote. "Such photos, not unlike ones we could all find in family scrapbooks of ourselves as preteens, were indicted as encouragement to incest."[63] The WAP narrator's unbudging response frustrated some audience members who tried to challenge the organization's analysis.

A number of slide show viewers – including some who identified closely with feminism – insisted that relatively little of what they saw during the WAP slide show and on the Times Square porn tour constituted violence against women.[64] Instead, they claimed that the majority of the images featured standard sexual activity, including images of "vanilla" sex between men and women. "The picture WAP paints of the current pornographic scene as saturated by images of rape, torture and mutilation is, to put it kindly, hyperbole," a writer for *Playboy* observed.[65] Lindsy Van Gelder, a radical feminist journalist and *Ms.* editor who personally disliked pornography, agreed. After viewing the WAP slide show and taking the tour, she wrote in *Ms.* that the sex business staple was "your basic old-fashioned black garter belts and piston-rod genital close-ups" with just "a sampling" of truly violent sexual matter.[66] D'Emilio observed that the WAP narrator characterized images of anal intercourse as rape, even though there was nothing in the pictures that suggested force per se. "In the final analysis," D'Emilio concluded, "Women Against Pornography is about sex, not violence."[67] Here, the influence of cultural feminism came into play. If one accepted, as many WAP members did, that male sexuality was

[61] John D'Emilio, "Women Against Pornography," *Christopher Street* (May 1980): 21.

[62] D'Emilio, "Women Against Pornography," 24.

[63] Paula Webster, "Pornography and Pleasure," *Heresies* 12 (1981): 48.

[64] Thoughtful critical pieces include: D'Emilio, "Women Against Pornography"; Robert Shea, "Women at War," *Playboy* (February 1980): 87–92, 182–188; Jan Hoffman, "The Times Square Porn Tour," *The Village Voice*, September 17, 1979, 1–3; and Lindsy Van Gelder, "When Women Confront Street Porn," *Ms.* (February 1980): 62–67.

[65] Shea, "Women at War," 183.

[66] Van Gelder, "When Women Confront Street Porn," 62–63.

[67] D'Emilio, "Women Against Pornography," 25.

inherently violent and oppressive for women, then it was nearly impossible to look at a picture of a man and a woman having sexual intercourse and see it as anything but an exercise in brutality. This was a revolutionary type of thinking in some ways, but it closed off the possibility for positive heterosexual relationships and left many heterosexual women wondering how to reconcile their sexual desire with feminism.

Some criticisms of the slide show were valid, but the slide show program did raise the consciousness of thousands of viewers with regard to images of violence against women. WAP reached great numbers of college women in the late 1970s and early 1980s, many of whom became feminist activists, some joining the anti-pornography movement. A professor of English at Adelphi University wrote to WAP in 1982 to let the organization know that the students in her *Women in Film and Television* course had been so shaken and disturbed by the slides they saw that the dorms had "reverberated" that night with discussions about pornography. One of the students remarked that the slide show was the most important material covered that semester, and that the images had "just about engraved themselves" in her mind. "How can we not get involved after this?" the student asked the professor. "We've got to, as women, unite and say no to those images that violate and demean us!"[68] The professor noted with pride that the "first signs of activism" were emerging among the students, who were writing letters of protest regarding violent content in films and on television, and creating their own slide show presentation using movie posters. The WAP slide show did preserve and promote the core message initiated by WAVAW: Media violence legitimized and encouraged real-world violence against women.

Porn Tours

One of the most original contributions that WAP made to the campaign against media violence was the porn tour – a guided education tour of the adult establishments that lined New York City's Times Square. When WAP first formed in the spring of 1979, its leaders decided to educate themselves about the pornography industry by visiting local adult bookstores, peep shows, topless bars, and sex emporiums. Carl Weisbrod of Midtown Enforcement accompanied the WAP founders on their initial Times Square visit to see "the raw netherworld of the twenty-five-cent peeps and the glitzy, multifloored sexploitation arcades," as Brownmiller described them.[69] Once they began exploring the area, WAP members believed that they had an entirely new understanding of how the pornography industry "exploited and marketed" women.[70] "We

[68] Adelphi professor to Florence Rush, WAP, January 4, 1982, WAP Records, Box 2, Folder 76.

[69] Brownmiller, *In Our Time*, 305

[70] Grant Proposal, "1980–81 Proposal to Support the Local and National Organizing Programs of Women Against Pornography," n.d., WAP Records, Box 9, Folder 569.

began to realize that other women had to see it too," Dolores Alexander told a fellow journalist. "Women have learned to close our eyes to the stuff."[71]

Lynn Campbell suggested that WAP offer tours to the public for fundraising and consciousness raising purposes. The women's "exploratory forays" had persuaded Campbell and Alexander that people who did not frequent Times Square had no idea what was happening inside the sex shops and were too nervous to go there and see for themselves.[72] The tours would offer women the opportunity to learn firsthand amid a safe and supportive environment. For a $5 donation to WAP, members of the public could see the slide show and then move on together to tour representative Times Square establishments. It was an innovative way to empower women to confront pornography and to become sufficiently angry in the face of brazen sexism to demand change.

Beginning June 14, 1979, WAP led small groups of ten-to-twelve women (just a few tours per month were open to men) through Times Square. The tours were offered every Tuesday night at 7 P.M. and Sunday afternoon at 2 P.M. Reservations were required. The tour began at the WAP office with the slide show. Afterward, the "tourists" and two WAP guides would head out to the street, "actually invading that alien, scary, enemy territory of the sex supermarkets," Alexander recalled.[73] The tour members typically endured some jeering and harassment from Times Square natives and store managers ("Ladies, ladies! Go home! You can't come in here without escorts!"), but pressed onward.[74] The guides followed an itinerary plotted by Brownmiller that included five stops: Show World, a mixed-use sex emporium that featured live sex shows; The Dating Room, a brothel serving 400 male clients per day; Peep adult bookstore, which had a large collection of rape and incest material on display; Hollywood Twin Cinema, a XXX theater and massage parlor; and the Mardi Gras, a club featuring topless dancers. The demand for the tours was so great that in the first few months, WAP had to schedule additional sessions. In 1979, 1,200 people went on the Times Square tour. In 1980, the organization led 53 tours for more than 500 individuals. This continued throughout the early 1980s, with 700 tourgoers participating in 1982.

At the start of the tour, each person received a map showing the location of more than fifty adult bookstores, peep shows, topless bars, and sex emporiums in midtown Manhattan, plus a floor plan of one of the five massage parlors operating in the area. As they went from place to place, the tour guides encouraged everyone to leaf through the magazines in the bookstores and

[71] Letter, Dolores Alexander to *Chrysalis Magazine*, January 16, 1980, WAP Records, Box 7, Folder 376.

[72] Brownmiller, *In Our Time*, 305.

[73] Letter, Dolores Alexander to *Chrysalis Magazine*.

[74] Dullea, "In Feminists' Antipornography Drive," A12. Brownmiller advised tour groups who were denied entrance to sex establishments because they lacked male escorts to tell the proprietors that they would be happy to call for male police officers to act as their escorts. This tactic frequently won the groups entrance.

to enter the peep show booths to see film loops like *Hang Her High*, which featured a woman tortured with ropes in a dark parody of Clint Eastwood's 1968 Western film, *Hang 'Em High*. The guides pointed out materials that showed women being raped, beaten, bound, and mutilated. On one tour, Lynn Campbell and Barbara Mehrhof called attention to shelves of Nazi-themed pornography in the Peep adult bookstore, including the vile *Love and Death at Dachau*, *Rape Me Auschwitz*, and *Concentration Camp Love*.[75] At Show World, the tourgoers entered stalls and deposited four quarters to see two naked women dance on a carousel for a minute and a half. For an additional fee, viewers could touch the dancers.

Brownmiller wrote a script for tour guides to follow, using information supplied by Weisbrod and Midtown Enforcement. The script included statistics about the expansion of the sex district from 47th to 49th Street, on Seventh, Broadway, and Eighth Avenues; the city's efforts to clean up Times Square; the mob-identified men who reputedly owned most of the sex-related businesses in the area; and nuts-and-bolts information about how business was conducted at each establishment. Tourgoers learned that a basic "session" at The Dating Room cost $12. Fifteen women worked each shift. Four hundred male customers were served per day. The women turned between ten and thirty tricks in an eight-hour shift, earning $4 per trick.[76]

The WAP tour guides explained that comparatively high wages for sex work brought many women into the business. The average working woman could expect to earn about $35 a day in 1979. Topless dancers at the Mardi Gras worked eight-hour shifts, earning $56 per shift, plus as much as another $100 a day in tips. Each woman danced for half an hour, then peddled champagne to the clientele before going back on stage. For every $100 of champagne she sold, a dancer received a $25 commission.[77] Barbara Hetzel, a WAP guide who had formerly worked as a topless dancer, knew firsthand that good wages made it difficult to persuade women to leave sex work. A dancer at a top club could earn more money in eight hours than she would be paid for a forty-hour week of typing, cleaning, waitressing, or working any of the other low-wage service-sector jobs that might be available to her.[78] Certainly, for women with few good alternatives, sex work was a means of survival and a way to exercise some control over one's destiny.

[75] Jan Hoffman, "The Times Square Porn Tour," *The Village Voice*, September 17, 1979, 3.

[76] "Suggested Script for Tour Guides," June 1979, WAP Records, Box 10, Folder 595.

[77] Hoffman, "The Times Square Porn Tour," 3.

[78] On the Show World pay, see Tammy Tanaka, "The More Things Change in Times Square, Writer Learns, The More It's the Same," *Religious News Service*, July 27, 1979, clipping in WAP Papers, Box 3. A daily salary of $150 far exceeded the average working woman's daily salary in 1979. Data from the U.S. Bureau of Labor Statistics for 1979 indicate that a white woman working full time could expect to earn $184 per week, or about $37 a day. A black woman working full time would earn even less, averaging $169 per week, or about $34 a day. A good dancer at an emporium like Show World could earn $50 or $60 in two hours in tips alone. The salary data for 1979 (as well as the years 1967–1985) appears in Barbara R. Bergmann, *The Economic Emergence of Women* (New York: Basic Books, 1986): 69.

As news of the porn tours spread around the country, members of WAVPM decided to create a similar program. Lynn Campbell sent a copy of the WAP tour itinerary and script to the WAVPM office, and the group used it as a model for their own tours of San Francisco's pornography strips. Members of WAVPM prepared by reading ethnographies of the Tenderloin, the district with the greatest concentration of adult businesses, interviewing neighborhood residents and studying local crime statistics.[79] In April 1980, WAVPM began offering semimonthly tours. They began with the WAVPM slide show and followed with visits to several establishments, including an adult bookstore, a XXX movie theater, and a sex emporium that featured live shows.

The WAP and WAVPM tours were creative interventions that provided women with an opportunity to visit adult businesses to see the pornography industry in action. In the days prior to the widespread availability of cable television and in the absence of Internet porn, many women – particularly those living outside of major metropolitan areas – had no safe way to investigate the pornography industry beyond reading *Playboy*, *Hustler*, and perhaps viewing *Deep Throat*. For women who felt oppressed by the industry's growth, and for those who were trying to come to terms with the urgency of the issue, going on the tour was a way to learn and exert agency. WAP saw the tours as "an essential first step" in bringing people for perhaps the first time in their lives "face to face with pornography's misogynistic imagery and violent messages."[80] This was a significant contribution to public consciousness at a moment when feminist concern about the scope and harms of pornography was rising, and many women were feeling victimized and angry about sexual exploitation.

The tours opened up the pornography industry for many participants, but aspects of the programs created problems for the anti-pornography movement. The scripts used by both WAP and WAVPM supported the idea that all of the behavior that took place in the establishments exploited women, and that the men who frequented such places ought to feel ashamed of their sexual desires and practices. The very existence of the tours – which positioned women as outsiders who had come to discover the exotic, foreign world of the porn dens – suggested that true feminists neither used pornography nor engaged in the sexual acts that were commonly featured, especially male-identified ones like penetration and fellatio.

In both the WAVPM and WAP tours, it was clear that anti-pornography feminists felt angry that women's sexual subjectivity and self-determination were devalued in the face of men's sexual needs. WAVPM reported in *NewsPage* that a tour group had prevented men from entering a North Beach adult bookstore by forming a human logjam in the doorway. Other WAVPM tour guides and tour-goers drove men out of local establishments by staring

[79] Julie Greenberg, "Feminist Tours of a Pornography District," *WAVPM NewsPage*, 4, no. 10 (October 1980), 1.

[80] "Accomplishments of Women Against Pornography," Grant Proposal for 1983–84, n.d., WAP Records, Box 12, Folder 725, p. 32.

at them and following them around in groups of two or three. WAVPM tour leader Lily Mar, a thirty-two-year-old data entry clerk and first-generation Chinese American, was proud of her efforts to discourage male customers. "Our presence there as strong feminist women is a reality check for men who look at and buy porn," she said in a *NewsPage* interview. "Some patrons hang out and listen to our talk, then leave the store embarrassed."[81] Going a step further, the WAP tour script expressed contempt for male sexual behavior. "Show World is a masturbation palace for men," the tour guide would say to the group. "A man can masturbate in a closed booth while watching a short peep show film. [A] man can masturbate while talking dirty on the telephone to a naked woman.... In the third type of booth, the man masturbates while watching naked women dance...."[82] The aversion to what was presented as ignominious sexual conduct was clear. In these years, the movement acquired the iron-clad anti-sexual reputation that observers have linked to the rise of third-wave feminism, which rejects the sexual proscriptions that its members associate with the second wave. Porn tours that described sexual activity as "highly distasteful and embarrassing" helped create the mistaken impression that feminists in this period renounced sex as a positive and affirming part of life.[83]

The porn tours also heightened tensions between anti-pornography feminists and women working in the sex industry, some of whom had already clashed with WAP over the intended "clean up" of Times Square. The workers resented the tours because the disruptive visits and the continuing attacks on pornography put their livelihoods at stake. Others were annoyed that the guides and their groups regarded them as objects of pity. The workers did not show up at the feminists' places of business, clucking over *their* exploitation as women, and they demanded the same respect. Author Linda LeMoncheck has described the typical sex worker's response to radical feminist intervention as "self-righteous moralizing and middle-class interference."[84] WAP members recognized this problem, and they knew that the tours might act as a barrier to good relationships. "The women who work there as nude dancers or money changers ... well, their reaction [to the tours] is mixed," Dolores Alexander confessed to a fellow journalist. "Sometimes hostile, sometimes friendly. Some of them make lewd gestures. Others are interested and want to talk."[85] One Barnard College student took a WAP tour in September 1979 and recalled that the feminist guides were taken aback when a dancer at Show World told them that she enjoyed her job. "Sure, honey," came the unexpected reply. "This is great. I love it. Salary's nice. You don't get no prostitution forced at you. You can work your own hours ...," she said. "I been dancing here about two years.

[81] Madeleine Brainerd, "Why Are We Involved in WAVPM?: Interviews with Three Members," *WAVPM NewsPage*, 5, no. 2 (November 1981), 1.

[82] "Suggested Script for Tour Guides," WAP Records.

[83] "Suggested Script for Tour Guides," WAP Records.

[84] LeMoncheck, 135.

[85] Dolores Alexander to *Chrysalis Magazine*.

What else am I gonna do? Can't type. I got a good body, honey. I make good money."[86] Georgia Dullea reported in the *New York Times* that the WAP feminists described the nude dancers in the carousels at the sex emporiums as "sad," like "products coming out of vending machines."[87] This characterization was consistent with the radical feminist view that saw "unequivocal dehumanization" in sex work.[88] Radical feminists maintained that prostitution robbed women of their individual ideas, beliefs, feelings, and desires, transforming them into "empty space surrounded by flesh," blank canvasses to be used and abused as male customers saw fit.[89] This type of work degraded the individual women forced to do it, exploiting them as sex objects, and hurt women in general by reinforcing a sexist ideology that encouraged sexual objectification and sexual violence.

One additional aspect of the tours that created controversy was the inclusion of language in the tour guides' scripts that suggested that WAP intended to pursue legal solutions to the pornography problem. Although there is no way to know how closely the WAP guides followed the suggested script, Brownmiller's version praised the Midtown Enforcement Project as "a city agency that we have a good working relationship with," and added that its efforts to clean up Times Square were hindered by confusion over the definition of obscenity in the U.S. courts. According to the script, Midtown Enforcement was able to make inroads by closing massage parlors where prostitution was taking place, but they were less successful in shutting down adult bookstores and movie theaters because pornography had a claim to First Amendment protection. WAP would not be deterred in its fight. "[W]e are working for the abolition of pornography because we believe it is degrading to women," the tour leader might say, per the script.[90] The tour script did present censorship – "the abolition of pornography" – as part of the organization's overall plan, a commitment that had already proved controversial in progressive circles.

At this early juncture, most WAP members did support some form of legal action to deal with the pornography problem. Wendy Kaminer, an attorney and WAP member, wrote the group's position paper on the First Amendment in 1979. She indicated that the group did not support censorship, which was inconsistent with the tour script, and neither advocated the "summary closings" of sex-related businesses nor "general prohibitions" on the publication or production of pornographic material. Nonetheless, WAP did seek reform in the courts. Kaminer wrote that WAP wanted to change

86 Claire Martin, "Walking the Mean Streets," *Broadway: The Bi-Weekly Magazine of the Columbia Spectator*, September 13, 1979, 7.
87 Dullea, "In Feminists' Antipornography Drive," A12.
88 LeMoncheck, 135.
89 Vednita Carter and Evelina Giobbe, "Duet: Prostitution, Racism and Feminist Discourse," in *Prostitution and Pornography: Philosophical Debate about the Sex Industry*, ed. Jessica Spector (Stanford, CA: Stanford University Press, 2006), 27.
90 "Suggested Script for Tour Guides," June 1979, WAP Records.

the legal definition of obscenity to focus on violence, not sex.[91] "Most hard-core pornography consists of pictures or graphic descriptions of women being raped, bound, beaten, or mutilated," Kaminer wrote in the feminist newspaper *Plexus*.[92] Thus if the definition of obscenity were changed to focus on violence, the worst pornographic material would come within the reach of the law. Anti-pornography activist and attorney Robin Yeamans went a step further, arguing in *Take Back the Night* that pornography ought to be defined as "any use of the media that equates sex and violence" and that all such material should be suppressed.[93] In her view, pornography incited men to commit crimes of violence, making it actionable under the law.

East Coast Conference and March on Times Square

WAP made major national news with its Fall 1979 anti-pornography conference and March on Times Square. One year after WAVPM's Feminist Perspectives conference in San Francisco, WAP sponsored the East Coast Feminist Conference on Pornography, held on September 15 and 16 in New York City. The speakers and workshop leaders were among the nation's best-known feminists, including Brownmiller, Steinem, Dworkin, Congresswoman Bella Abzug, Robin Morgan, Shere Hite, Alix Kates Shulman, Lois Gould, and Barbara Seaman. The meeting attracted 750 participants, who assembled for two days at Martin Luther King Jr. High School on Manhattan's Upper West Side to talk about pornography and to hear WAP discuss what the movement against it could accomplish. Men were barred from all conference activities save a film screening.[94] WAP leaders believed that women needed their own space to discuss the pornography issue free of the divisive presence of men.

The conference opened on Saturday morning with welcoming remarks from Dolores Alexander and Lynn Campbell. Dorchen Leidholdt and Marilyn Hayes, two founding members of WAP, presented the slide show. The rest of the morning was devoted to a speak-out, which featured twelve women who offered personal testimony about their negative experiences with

[91] Wendy Kaminer, "Where We Stand on the First Amendment: Women Against Pornography," *Aegis: Magazine on Ending Violence Against Women* (September/October 1979), 52. By the mid-1980s, Kaminer had rejected MacKinnon and Dworkin's legislative solutions as a viable option for the movement. She came to view the protectionist approaches endorsed by MacKinnon/Dworkin and WAP, as well as the difference feminism exemplified by Carol Gilligan's work as wrongheaded approaches to women's rights. Kaminer's 1991 book, *A Fearful Freedom: Women's Flight from Equality*, criticized this type of thought.

[92] Wendy Kaminer, "WAP and the First Amendment," *Plexus* (December 1979): 2.

[93] Robin Yeamans, "A Political-Legal Analysis of Pornography," in *Take Back the Night*, 248.

[94] The film was the 1953 *Geisha*, by Kenji Mizoguchi, which tells a story of a relationship between two geishas and their male clients. According to WAP literature, this film "weaves in themes of feminism, sisterhood, and the male sexual exploitation of women's bodies." Registration Form for East Coast Feminist Conference Schedule, 1979, WAP Records, Box 1, Folder 8.

pornography.[95] One speaker told the audience that her father, a church-going, middle-class man, had molested her from age eight onward and routinely exposed her to pornography. "The pictures he showed me told me it was okay for men to do whatever they wanted to women," she told the audience.[96] A Cuban-born undergraduate student at Columbia University described her exposure to pornography in the dormitories. She had joined a Latin American student group that held its meetings in members' dorm rooms. There she discovered that her male classmates pinned centerfolds of naked women on their walls. Seeing these images made her feel "ashamed and humiliated" and caused her to "desexualize" herself so that men would regard her only as "one of the boys" and not as a sexual object to be used in those ways.[97]

The speak-out reflected WAP's belief that women affected by pornography were uniquely qualified to explain its harms. In a series of preconference planning meetings, the organizers debated whether to include male social scientists specializing in media effects, but ultimately decided that the most compelling evidence against pornography originated from women's personal experiences.[98] Social psychologists like Edward Donnerstein at the University of Wisconsin-Madison, Neal Malamuth at UCLA, and George Gerbner at the University of Pennsylvania were releasing data that tended to support feminist claims about the desensitizing effects of media violence and increased callousness to sexual abuse after exposure to pornography, but WAP wanted to assert women's expertise. Organization leaders did not want to turn to male experts to tell women what they already knew, namely that pornography was a dangerous force that taught men that it was socially acceptable to hurt women. Florence Denmark, president of the American Psychological Association and a self-described feminist, did mention in her WAP conference remarks that a new wave of media effects research supported feminist accounts, but the conference overall emphasized women's experiences and *their* authority to explain pornography's effects.

On Saturday afternoon and Sunday morning, conference-goers had the opportunity to attend a variety of workshops. Martha Gever and Marg Hall, two members of Rochester WAVAW who were prosecuted for protesting *Snuff*, led a session on direct action, similar to the one they had prepared for the WAVPM national conference. Brownmiller led a workshop on pornography and politics that emphasized how pornographers had won the "hearts and minds" of the liberal-left establishment. Steinem explored the topic of pornography versus erotica, a topic she had written about in *Ms.* Robin

[95] These women were selected by WAP prior to the conference and WAP members helped them prepare their testimony for the speak-out.

[96] Brady is quoted in Anne Fuller, "Women's Meeting Blasts Pornography," *The Guardian*, 31, no. 49 (September 26, 1979), 8.

[97] brooke, "Feminist Conference: Porn Again," *off our backs*, 9 (November 1979): 25.

[98] Memorandum, Women Against Pornography: Conference Planning Meeting, June 20, 1979, WAP Records, Box 1, Folder 5.

Morgan and Lynn Campbell worked with a group of women to try to create a definition of pornography.

To their credit, the WAP organizers turned over two workshops to women who had expressed reservations about the campaign against pornography. Deborah Edel and Joan Nestle, founders of the Lesbian Herstory Archives, urged tolerance for a wide range of lesbian erotic art, perhaps sensing the controversy over lesbian S/M soon to come. Ellen Willis and the feminist writer Alix Kates Shulman led a session on the appeal of the forbidden and the erotic uses of hostility.[99]

Throughout the afternoon workshops, conflicts erupted as women tried to sort out the tangle of issues surrounding pornography. Willis, who ultimately became one of WAP's most ardent critics, argued that the movement's distinction between "erotica" and "pornography" would never hold up, because no two viewers would evaluate an image in the same way. Furthermore, the use of the term "erotica" endorsed a high-minded "utopian standard" of how sex ought to be portrayed, whereas "pornography" denigrated more realistic portrayals of sex as actually practiced. "It's important in a political movement to define issues," she told workshop participants. "You can't define pornography as any eroticism you don't like."[100] Writing about this issue two weeks after the conference in the *Village Voice*, she noted that attempts to separate good erotica from bad porn would inevitably come down to: "What turns me on is erotic; what turns you on is pornographic."[101] For Willis, this veered too close to moralism, and the urge to strictly define how good feminists ought to behave in the bedroom.

The distinction between erotica and pornography was a hot-button issue at the conference, but tensions between lesbian separatists and heterosexual women were also coming to a head. Some heterosexual women felt that the anti-pornography movement unfairly condemned all "male-identified" sexual acts (e.g. fellatio, penetration), and they rejected the conflation of heterosexual sex and male violence. In one workshop, a female journalist asked whether there might be a middle ground, a way to object to male violence but not to all men. She questioned WAP's decision to exclude men from the meeting, which made it seem like they were the enemy, rather than pornography. A woman who identified herself as a lesbian separatist called out that no difference existed between pornography and heterosexuality, and that the very question showed that the journalist was male-identified. "There seemed to be an unwillingness on the part of the very vocal, very angry, radical lesbian feminists ... not to hate all men," a reporter from the *Boston Globe* who observed the incident wrote.[102] In truth, the pressure to renounce heterosexuality was still strong

99 "Conference Schedule," September 15 and 16, 1979, WAP Records, Box 1, Folder 5.

100 brooke, "Feminist Conference: Porn Again," 27.

101 Ellen Willis, "Feminism, Moralism and Pornography," *Village Voice*, October 15, 1979, 8.

102 Judy Foreman, "An Angry Conference about Pornography," *The Boston Globe*, September 17, 1979, Section 3, 24.

among radical feminists, and those politics were thriving within anti-pornography. Valerie Miner, a WAVPM board member, recalled that movement revelations about pornography were a major influence on her decision to become a lesbian. Once the violence issue had been laid bare, she found it impossible to go home to a man at night.[103] At the conference, conflicts among lesbians and heterosexual women erupted.

Issues of race and class also proved divisive, as some conference-goers criticized WAP for building a white, middle-class movement when a disproportionate number of the women working in prostitution and pornography were poor and/or women of color. *Ms.* editor Lindsy Van Gelder attended and subsequently described the conference as "virtually lily-white, with almost zero outreach."[104] The program offered little on the relationship of race to pornography, although many of the genre's worst examples exploited women of color and myths about their sexuality, including the "hot-blooded" Latina and the savage black woman. The one scheduled workshop on race, "The Black Woman and Pornography," was canceled when its moderator failed to show. The choice of an unseasoned leader, an undergraduate student at a satellite campus of the State University of New York, was proof to some that WAP did not take racial issues seriously. By contrast, the workshop on "The Heterosexual Woman and Pornography" boasted three prominent feminist leaders: authors Barbara Seaman and Barbara Grizzuti Harrison, and film critic Molly Haskell, author of the highly regarded 1974 book *From Reverence to Rape: The Treatment of Women in the Movies.*

In truth, inattention to race was a problem throughout the women's movement, although WAVAW, WAVPM, and WAP – like other predominantly white women's liberation organizations – struggled to attract feminists of color. By the early 1970s, white radical feminists had developed a universalist ideology that pointed to gender oppression as the primary force behind women's subordination. The feminist logic held that gender oppression was experienced by all women regardless of their race or class, and was thus as politically urgent as racism or the fight against capitalism. This approach consciously minimized racial and ethnic differences among women to strengthen the case for feminism and to deflect New Left criticism that women's liberation was diverting attention from broader social problems affecting the working class and people of color.[105] Given the existence of racial/ethnic and class differences that separated many feminists of color from white feminists, it was difficult for the former to embrace the idea of a universal sisterhood that downplayed non-gender-based forms of oppression. Furthermore, anti-pornography's attack on

[103] Miner discusses the choice to become a lesbian and the role of issues like pornography in Ruth Rosen, *The World Split Open: How the Modern Women's Movement Changed America* (New York: Viking Penguin, 2000), 170.

[104] Van Gelder, "When Women Confront Street Porn," 66.

[105] On the development of universal sisterhood and the strategic intent of this approach, see Benita Roth, *Separate Roads to Feminism: Black, Chicana and White Feminist Movements in America's Second Wave* (Cambridge: Cambridge University Press, 2004), esp. chapter 5.

men and male sexuality put women of color in a difficult position with regard to the men in their communities, whom they saw as allies in their struggles for racial and economic justice. Joining anti-pornography was problematic for women of color who did not embrace an uncomplicated sisterhood with white women, and who were unwilling to sever ties with men of color. Some feminists of color rejected the campaign against pornography outright, arguing that they could ill afford to focus on such a peripheral issue when their women lacked access to basic health care, education, and jobs. As a result, the anti-pornography movement remained largely white, and its analyses did not fully address the intersection of sexual and racial oppression in pornography.[106]

The question of class differences with regard to one's perspective on sex work also proved controversial. Jane Alpert, a former member of Weatherman who befriended prostitutes while serving a prison sentence for conspiracy, and Barbara Hetzel, a WAP member and former topless dancer, co-chaired a crowded Saturday afternoon workshop on "Women in the Pornography Business."[107] Some seventy-five women attended the session, and several of the most vocal speakers were prostitutes. They protested WAP's cooperation with Midtown Enforcement and insisted that organization members stand up for prostitutes' rights instead of allying themselves with city agencies. One suggested that WAP members hand out flyers to working women in the Times Square area explaining that the group had no quarrel with women in the business. A reporter for *off our backs* noted that WAP members responded that prostitution oppressed all women by promoting the belief that women were whores by nature, their bodies available to any man who wished to purchase them.

Several prostitutes rejected the WAP line and told the audience that the organization had to readjust its middle-class sensibilities to recognize that sex work provided steady jobs and decent pay for women who had few other opportunities. Even if feminists hoped to see sex work eradicated, the industry provided employment for many and those jobs had to be protected until

[106] On the relationship between feminists of color and white feminists in the second wave, see Roth, *Separate Roads to Feminism*, esp. pp. 24–46.

[107] Alpert was the infamous anti-war activist and member of the leftist group Weatherman who went underground from 1970 to 1974 to avoid capture for her involvement in several bombings of military and war-related corporate buildings in New York City in 1969. While underground in 1973, Alpert abandoned the male Left and wrote the seminal feminist essay, "Mother Right," which was published in *Ms.* magazine. Her surrender in 1975 and reported cooperation with the FBI (naming co-conspirators and flushing out underground radicals) divided the women's movement. Robin Morgan organized a "Circle of Support" for Alpert that included such future WAP members as Barbara Mehrhof and Florence Rush. Steinem, Kathy Barry, and Adrienne Rich signed a petition urging movement support for Alpert. While serving a two-year prison sentence for the bombings, Alpert wrote her autobiography, *Growing Up Underground*, and met many women working in the sex industry. Alpert's abandonment of the Left and conversion to radical feminism during this time are chronicled in Alice Echols, *Daring to Be Bad: Radical Feminism in America, 1967–1975* (Minneapolis: University of Minnesota Press, 1989).

others could be created. Prostitution, they said, was a question of economics, not morality. Another prostitute declared that she resented middle-class feminists who looked down on her line of work, especially considering that some of them relied on the marriage contract for financial support. "I mean, when you're talking about pimps, there are nice pimps," she said. "There are nice husbands."[108] Working-class women, including prostitutes, challenged middle-class feminists to think about the structural inequalities that drove women into sex work and pointed out that calls to eradicate prostitution threatened some women's survival. These kind of conflicts over class and race were endemic to the second wave, and many feminists of color/working class feminists viewed white, middle-class feminists as "insensitive to the kinds of lives that those without racial and/or class privilege had to endure," as the sociologist Benita Roth has observed.[109]

The inattention to race and class issues at the WAP conference had various sources. Some of it clearly emerged from the fact that the WAP leaders were white, middle-class women, and they were building an organization that primarily reflected their worldview regarding pornography and prostitution. Downplaying differences among women was also a hallmark of cultural feminism, which stressed that the experience of gender oppression that women had in common was the ultimate bond. Drawing from both of these strains of thought, the leaders of anti-pornography regarded pornography as *the* unifying issue, the one problem that all women would come together to fight. WAP's emergence in the years following the gay/straight split in the women's liberation movement, in the midst of numerous intramovement conflicts over race and class, influenced leaders to focus on pornography as a monolithic enemy that affected all women, eliding differences that might splinter the new effort.

Whatever the reason for the inattention, it did not sit well with some attendees. Tensions over heterosexuality, race, and class that had been brewing throughout the weekend erupted at the Sunday afternoon closing session. "Strategies for the Future" was supposed to be a panel discussion featuring leading feminist organizers, but members of the audience would not let them speak. As Brownmiller recalled, two days of painful consciousness raising about male violence combined with exposure to horrifying pornography brought "many raw emotions roiling to the surface."[110] Although she blamed the difficult conference subject matter for the Sunday afternoon uproar, it had more to do with long-standing conflicts within the women's movement. A number of women in the audience criticized WAP for privileging a narrow point of view: The conference was too white, too middle-class, and too heterosexual. Brownmiller was all of those things.

The fireworks began immediately. A woman in the audience yelled out: "What can we do to bring in more Black and Third World women?"

108 brooke, "Feminist Conference: Porn Again," 27.

109 Roth, *Separate Roads to Feminism*, 45.

110 Brownmiller, *In Our Time*, 308.

Brownmiller answered defensively: "We've been doing a lot." Before she could elaborate, cries erupted from the audience. "How? By charging $10?" A woman began shrieking that she could not afford the $10 conference registration fee.[111] Brownmiller, the reporter from *off our backs* noted, seemed to know this woman, and responded. "I'm too old, and I've been in the movement too long to believe you can't afford $10." Another woman stood up and attacked Brownmiller personally, arguing that many women of color could not pay the $10 fee, because not everyone had grown rich from a successful mass-market book (*Against Our Will*). A woman in the front row demanded to know why the WAP literature hadn't been translated into Spanish. "'You're a bunch of fucking middle-class elitists,' she yelled at Brownmiller. 'Why isn't your literature in Spanish?'"[112] Brownmiller responded that WAP was committed to making its literature available in all languages but was still struggling to get materials together in English. "First we had to build the group with one, two, ten, twenty, thirty people," she said. "Then we had to figure out what to print in the literature. After that, you can start thinking about translating into other languages, or signing, or Braille."[113] The critics would not desist. Brownmiller became frustrated and apologized to the audience for the disruption.

Within moments, the woman in the front row made her way to the stage and grabbed the microphone. Now her issue became clear. Pointing her finger at Brownmiller, she complained: "I'm sick of this elitist bullshit. Lesbians do all the work in this movement, and you go home and suck cock."[114] She was angry because she (and others) thought that the conference organizers were purposely downplaying the role of lesbians in the anti-pornography effort to protect WAP's image for the mainstream news media. WAP emphasized violent heterosexual imagery but gave far less attention to the ways that lesbian sexuality was falsely portrayed in pornography. In addition, WAP had not publicly acknowledged lesbian support for the conference nor mentioned the

[111] The conference registration fee was $10, or three and a half hours of work exchange at the WAP office during the two weeks prior to the conference. Some women in the audience yelled that this policy discriminated against working-class women, who could not afford the fee and would be forced to work a second (or third) job for WAP to pay. WAP did let many women who had neither paid the $10 nor completed work exchange attend the conference.

[112] Brownmiller, *In Our Time*, 309.

[113] Van Gelder, "When Women Confront Street Porn," 66. Brownmiller's point had merit – the conference was WAP's first major public event and the group was still relatively new. However, the WAVPM pornography conference materials had been translated into several languages, and that organization had far fewer economic resources than WAP at its disposal.

[114] Frog was denouncing Brownmiller's heterosexuality. By the mid-1970s, as discussed in Chapter 2, political lesbianism was a dominant feature of the women's movement. Heterosexual women were often treated as traitors to the feminist cause. By offering love and succor to men, heterosexual women were thought to empower the enemy. In addition, many political lesbians resented the perceived ability of heterosexual women to retain the economic and social benefits of alliances with men.

number of lesbians who worked on behalf of the anti-pornography movement. In the month prior to the conference, six New York City lesbians had handed out flyers and written to feminist newspapers to protest that WAP's "virtual silence on lesbian issues" contributed to the perception that lesbianism was shameful and deviant, and reinforced the marginalization of lesbians in the movement. "[W]hen we know large numbers of lesbians are working in WAP and are always part of every feminist street action, why have we been so noticeably excluded from the list of groups that their flyer summons to the march [on Times Square]?" they asked. The woman who stormed the stage wanted to talk about lesbian oppression.[115]

Her name was Frog. She was a lesbian separatist who attended the conference dressed in a man's suit and necktie. After pointing at Brownmiller, she complained that she was sick of the women's movement being run by "cocksucking straight women."[116] An observer paraphrased the rest of her comments in *Sinister Wisdom*, a lesbian feminist literary journal: "[H]ow could anything be accomplished to fucking abolish violence against women since the cock was fucking ultimately responsible for all violence against women, and here were all these fucking straight women right before her very eyes and they were all going to go home to their men and *suck cock!!!*" [italics in original][117] Frog denounced Brownmiller for her heterosexuality, stating that she betrayed her sisters when she organized against pornography by day but empowered men with her emotional and sexual support by night.

The crude attack infuriated Brownmiller, never one to hold her tongue, as the episode on *Donahue* had revealed. "I'd like to ask you something," she said to Frog. "If you hate men so much, why are you wearing men's clothes?"[118] Members of the audience exploded, hissing and hollering at Brownmiller: "Apologize! Apologize!"[119] In their minds, Brownmiller had used a gross anti-lesbian slur. By remarking that Frog was dressed like a man, Brownmiller insinuated that she was not really a "woman-identified woman" but was male-identified and aspired to act like and be like a man. According to the reporter from *off our backs*, when the audience pressed her for an apology, Brownmiller replied archly: "I'm sorry that I said the woman wearing a necktie was dressed in masculine attire."[120] Brownmiller added insult to injury.

Within the women's movement, Brownmiller had already earned an infamous anti-lesbian reputation. In 1970, she reportedly refused to speak at a

115 Marjory Ackerman, Quinn Bevan, Cathy Cockrell, Eileen Kane, Doris Lunden, and Marty Pottenger, "Use of Times Square," *Plexus* (February 1980): 3.

116 Susan Chute, "Backroom with the Feminist Heroes: Conference for Women Against Pornography," *Sinister Wisdom* 15 (Fall 1980), 3.

117 Chute, "Backroom with the Feminist Heroes," 3.

118 Brownmiller, *In Our Time*, 309. Susan Chute remembers Brownmiller's words somewhat differently. She wrote in *Sinister Wisdom* that Brownmiller mocked the lesbian, saying "See, she even *dresses* like a man." See Chute, "Backroom with the Feminist Heroes," 3. The reporter from *off our backs* reported Brownmiller's comment this way as well.

119 Chute, "Backroom with the Feminist Heroes," 3.

120 brooke, "Feminist Conference: Porn Again," 27.

Daughters of Bilitis convention on the grounds that lesbians were hypersexual and exhibited male behavior. According to the lesbian feminist writers Barbara Love and Sidney Abbott, Brownmiller complained that lesbians had made passes at her and were too attached to traditional sex roles (one dominant "butch" partner, one submissive "femme" partner) to be of any use to feminism. "[O]ur fight is not the same," she wrote in the early days of the women's movement. "You have bought the sex roles we are leaving behind."[121]

Along the same lines, few lesbians had forgotten the March 1970 feature story about the women's movement that Brownmiller had written for the *New York Times Magazine*. In this story, Brownmiller described Betty Friedan's fear that lesbianism would discredit feminism. Friedan had called militant lesbians like NY-NOW's Rita Mae Brown "the lavender menace" that threatened the movement's overall credibility. Employing what she thought was a clever turn of phrase, Brownmiller wrote of lesbianism: "A lavender *herring*, perhaps, but surely no clear and present danger."[122] Brownmiller writes in her memoir that she intended only to poke fun at Friedan's overblown fear of lesbianism. Nonetheless, her words ricocheted through the women's movement, devastating many lesbians. In their minds, a leading member of the women's liberation movement writing in the nation's foremost newspaper had presented lesbians as a pesky nuisance, denying the centrality of lesbianism to feminism, and whitewashing lesbians' tremendous efforts on behalf of the women's movement. Brownmiller acknowledges that she came to be thought of as "an unregenerate homophobe" in certain feminist circles.[123] Her confrontation with the lesbian separatist at the WAP conference fueled this perception.

For Brownmiller, the conference marked the beginning of the end of her association with WAP. She came under scathing attack from some quarters of the lesbian community, which denounced her "bigoted slur" as "offensive and inexcusable."[124] Within days of the conference, the lesbian-feminist poet Adrienne Rich resigned from WAP, citing Brownmiller's homophobia. Members of the lesbian community distributed a two-page account describing the "Brownmiller incident" that urged a boycott of WAP's planned March on Times Square.[125] In response, members of WAP issued an open letter to the lesbian community that stressed the organization's support for lesbians. WAP "recognizes the bitter realities of lesbian oppression, as well as the courageous efforts of our lesbian sisters to gain legal rights and respect for lesbian

121 Brownmiller is quoted in Sidney Abbott and Barbara Love, *Sappho Was a Right-On Woman* (New York: Stein and Day, 1973), 117.

122 Susan Brownmiller, "Sisterhood Is Powerful," *The New York Times Magazine*, March 15, 1979, 140. Brownmiller writes in her memoir that she meant a play on words, substituting lavender herring for red herring, which means a smokescreen or a diversion from the issue at hand. See Brownmiller, *In Our Time*, 82.

123 Brownmiller, *In Our Time*, 173.

124 A Conference Attendee to WAP, October 17, 1979, WAP Records, Box 6, Folder 296.

125 "To All Lesbians and Lesbian Supporters: About Women Against Pornography," n.d., WAP Records, Box 14, Folder 828.

women," the letter read, "and works to align its aims and efforts with the struggle for the elimination of lesbian oppression."[126] To some, this open letter to the lesbian community read like a repudiation of Brownmiller.

Brownmiller remained with WAP until the end of October to see the organization through its March on Times Square. During that time, she did receive support from a number of conference attendees, who thanked her for standing up against the constant attacks on heterosexual women that made it difficult to continue working in the movement. Nonetheless, Brownmiller would leave WAP at the end of 1979 to return full time to her writing career, publishing *Femininity* in 1984. Although she participated sporadically in special events, Brownmiller would cease to be involved on a day-to-day basis with WAP.

The March on Times Square

The March on Times Square took place on Saturday, October 20, 1979, a month after the East Coast conference. Women arrived in busloads from up and down the East Coast, many filled with college students from campuses where WAP had presented the slide show. According to newspaper estimates, the march drew 5,000 participants. They assembled at Columbus Circle at noon and then marched south on Broadway to 42nd Street, to the heart of Times Square. They were led by some of the nation's best-known feminists, including Brownmiller, Bella Abzug, Gloria Steinem, Robin Morgan, Andrea Dworkin, and WAP's Barbara Mehrhof, Dolores Alexander, Frances Patai, Amina Abdur-Rahman, and Lynn Campbell, each grasping the top of a red banner that stretched across Broadway reading: "Women Against Pornography. Stop Violence Against Women." Behind them, a sea of women waved 500 colorful placards prepared by WAP members with large, dark-lettered slogans printed on white backgrounds to create ideal visuals for the news media. The organization's savvy approach to publicity paid off. The striking image of the famous feminists carrying the banner and hundreds of women carrying posters reading "Porn Hurts Women," "Pornography is a Feminist Issue," and "Porn is Rape on Paper" were clearly visible in photos printed by the *New York Times*, *Newsweek*, and the New York *Daily News*, as well as in footage aired on CBS, ABC, and NBC. Tom Brokaw and Jane Pauley interviewed Barbara Mehrhof and Dolores Alexander for an extended segment on the *Today* show.

The march ended with a rally at Bryant Park that featured more than a dozen feminist speakers. In an effort to address some of the perspectives that had been missing from the East Coast conference, and which had caused such conflict at the closing session, WAP invited a wide range of headliners. Amina Abdur-Rahman, a black lesbian Muslim who worked as the education director for the New York Urban League, and Carolyn Reed, a member of the

[126] "Lesbian Feminist Concerns in the Feminist Anti-Pornography Movement," October 1979, WAP Records, Box 1, Folder 9.

FIGURE 7.2. The WAP March on Times Square, October 20, 1979. The march drew 5,000 participants, with women arriving in busloads from up and down the East Coast. Visible in the front row, grasping the banner from the very far left are: Gloria Steinem and Robin Morgan (both with heads turned in profile), Congresswoman Bella Abzug, Andrea Dworkin, WAP members Frances Patai, Barbara Mehrhof, Dolores Alexander, and Amina Abdur-Rahman. *Photo: Bettye Lane.*

Advisory Commission on the Status of Women in the Carter administration and an advocate for household employees, spoke about the exploitation of women of color in pornography. Urging women to unite across color lines, Abdur-Rahman told the crowd that the porn industry had "lied about all of us, libeled and defamed all of us and given us cause to fight them together."[127] Teresa Hommel, who had helped organize the New York Law School colloquium on pornography and free speech, joined Charlotte Bunch to discuss how pornography distorted lesbian sexuality and repackaged it for consumption by straight male viewers. WAP member Barbara Hetzel, a former topless dancer, told the crowd that the organization opposed the pornography industry but was mindful of the need to protect and support women who made their living through sex work. Although controversial, the possibility of controlling pornography through the legal system continued to be raised by a number of speakers. Abzug told the crowd that pornography caused violence and should be outlawed.[128]

[127] Barbara Basler, "5,000 Join Feminist Group's Rally in Times Sq. Against Pornography," *New York Times*, October 21, 1979, 41.

[128] Marcia Kramer and Brian Kates, "Get the Porn Outta Here, 4,000 Cry During March," *Daily News*, October 21, 1979, 7.

The successful march cheered WAP members who were weary after the contentious East Coast conference, and the organization's newsletter noted with pride that the march was the largest feminist demonstration to take place in New York City since the early days of the women's movement. Some members compared its "energy and enthusiasm" to that of the massive Women's Strike for Equality march led by Betty Friedan in August 1970.[129] This was a defining moment for WAP, which was enjoying national recognition for its leadership of the feminist campaign against pornography. Inside the movement, however, it was clear that serious problems were bubbling close to the surface.

Conclusion: Growing Challenges for Anti-Pornography

WAP's decision to move away from a broad movement against sexualized media violence in favor of a movement organized around pornography had lasting consequences. First, as pornography eclipsed violence as the defining movement issue, the older organizations, WAVAW and later WAVPM, were marginalized. Second, a series of controversial decisions negatively affected WAP's ability to communicate its specifically feminist objections to pornography and to build alliances with other progressive groups. These decisions included cooperating with a city agency that sought the arrest and conviction of prostitutes, taking funds from groups that promoted a Times Square clean-up, and leading porn tours that alienated women who were working in the sex industry. Third, the ideas that were emerging from WAP about the need for legal reform were creating anxiety both inside and outside of the women's movement. Just three weeks before the WAP conference, the *Village Voice* published a major attack on Brownmiller, labeling her "an enemy of the First Amendment" and ridiculing her faith in the courts. The writer urged feminists to embrace WAVAW's economic pressure and public education techniques to fight pornography.[130] Although Brownmiller was a driving force behind the idea that violent pornography should be defined as obscene and banned from public display, her exit from WAP did little to assuage fears.

Of all the problems that were emerging as WAP moved into the national spotlight, one stood out above the rest: The organization endorsed a narrow range of sexual expression and sexual behavior, arguing that sex as practiced under patriarchy was a significant source of danger to women. This position was a direct outgrowth of cultural feminism's dichotomous description of male and female nature, and it did not sit well with many feminists outside of the anti-pornography movement. Briefly stated, cultural feminists treated female and male sexuality as diametric opposites, with women valuing

129 "March a Huge Success," *Women Against Pornography NewsReport*, December 10, 1979, 1.

130 Geoffrey Stokes, "Beaver, Buggery, Brownmiller, and Black Girls: The First Amendment Bullies," *Village Voice*, August 20, 1979, 15.

"intimacy over orgasm, sensuality over genitality, psychological bonding over sexual coupling, egalitarianism and mutuality over power and domination," as the historian Jane Gerhard has characterized it.[131] As previously noted, the radical feminist critique of male sexuality as essentially brute and impersonal left little space for heterosexual women to feel good about their sexual desires and relationships.

Now, feminists outside of anti-pornography began to assert that WAP's analysis threatened to erode every woman's right to sexual variety and pleasure. Women had been denied sexual freedom for so long, some argued, that it was unfair to close off the possibility that women might find satisfaction in the activities and behaviors that WAP stigmatized as male-identified, including the use of pornography. These feminists, later known as "pro-sex" or "sex-positive," argued that pornography could serve as an important erotic outlet, affirming sexual pleasure, teaching men and women about diverse sexual behaviors, and creating visibility and community for sexual minorities. WAP's stance was evident at the East Coast conference, where a reporter from *off our backs* observed that attendees were made to follow a strict party line. "I felt a subtle pressure that the only admissible experiences with porn were real horror stories ...," she wrote, "and that women like myself who had few bad experiences directly linked to porn were out of it."[132] Ultimately, the feminist pro-sex movement would challenge what it saw as anti-pornography's monolithic approach to sexuality, arguing that it did not leave women adequate space for sexual exploration.

[131] Gerhard, *Desiring Revolution*, 179.

[132] brooke, "Feminist Conference: Porn Again," 26.

8

The New Lay of the Land

WAP Assumes Leadership of the Movement and Faces Challenges from Within and Without

At the end of 1979, WAP was the dominant organization in a national movement increasingly focused on pornography. This transition was aided by internal shifts within WAVAW and WAVPM, particularly the loss of charismatic organization leaders, which diminished the capacity of the older groups to participate on the national stage and to influence movement direction. With Julia London stepping down from WAVAW and Laura Lederer leaving WAVPM, leadership of the anti-media violence movement fell to WAP. In the years following the East Coast conference and the March on Times Square, WAP became well known as an influential feminist organization speaking out on behalf of women. "Every feminist in the New York metropolitan area has heard of Women Against Pornography," the author Paula Webster observed in 1981.[1] Indeed, WAP had attracted attention not only in New York, but also throughout the country for its commitment to fighting pornography. During this period, WAP actively sought media attention and tried to communicate a specifically feminist (as opposed to conservative-moralist) objection to pornography, namely that it was a point on the continuum of male violence and functioned as a key mechanism in the subordination of women. Pornography taught women to accept and even desire domination and objectification, and men to deny women's autonomy and subjectivity. Pornography actively reduced women to sexual objects ripe for humiliation and abuse.

At the same time that WAP assumed national leadership, the prospects for American feminist organizations dimmed as the political climate in the United States swung rightward. In the mid-1970s, the nation's Republican base was strengthened by swelling numbers of politically conservative Christians, predominantly Evangelical Protestants, who were galvanized by such social issues as abortion, women's rights, gay rights, sex education, and school prayer. Congress' approval of the Equal Rights Amendment (ERA) in 1972 and the 1973 *Roe v. Wade* decision that legalized abortion were catalysts for the formation of conservative Christian political action groups. These groups sought

[1] Paula Webster, "Pornography and Pleasure," *Heresies* 12: The Sex Issue (1981), 48.

to stem what they perceived as a dangerous liberal tide that had expanded the welfare state, eroded personal responsibility and sexual restraint, damaged the traditional family, interfered with parents who sought to teach moral values to their children, belittled faith in God, and weakened America at home and abroad.[2] Joined together in a nationwide coalition that brought older anti-communist and laissez faire free-market voters together with proponents of newer supply-side economic policies and neo-conservative intellectuals, religious conservatives made anti-feminist initiatives a major part of the New Right agenda. New Right groups launched legislative campaigns to restrict gay rights, such as the 1976 Briggs Initiative that would have barred gay and lesbian teachers from California public schools; to offer tax advantages to traditional families with stay-at-home wives; to limit abortion and to require minors seeking medical treatment for pregnancy or venereal disease to obtain parental consent.[3] Some 43 million strong in 1980, comprising almost 25 percent of the total U.S. adult population, the support of newly politicized Evangelical Christians gave New Right causes tremendous political muscle and staying power.[4]

The most influential of the conservative Christian political action committees were created by a handful of savvy leaders who were skilled at public relations, fundraising, and grassroots organizing. They used sophisticated communication strategies such as televangelism and direct-mail outreach to achieve national support for social issues on which a diverse assortment of American religious conservatives – drawn from both Catholic and Protestant ranks – generally agreed. These included opposition to feminism, pornography, and abortion. Phyllis Schlafly, a two-time congressional candidate, mother of six, and founder of the Eagle Forum (1972), organized a campaign to stop the ERA, which she condemned as an "anti-family" measure that would force women into the military and require unisex public bathrooms. Evangelical leader James Dobson founded Focus on the Family in 1977, which

[2] On the rise of conservatism and the New Right, see Sara Diamond, *Roads to Dominion: Right-Wing Movements and Political Power in the United States* (New York: Guilford Press, 1995), chapter 10; Lisa McGirr, *Suburban Warriors: The Origins of the New American Right* (Princeton, NJ: Princeton University Press, 2001); Jerome L. Himmelstein, *To the Right: The Transformation of American Conservatism* (Berkeley: University of California Press, 1990); and Sylvia Bashevkin, "Facing a Renewed Right: American Feminism and the Reagan/Bush Challenge," *Canadian Journal of Political Science*, 27, no. 4 (December 1994), 669–698.

[3] Carol Virginia Pohli defines the New Right as a coalition that includes non-Christian as well as Christian conservatives and Roman Catholic as well as Protestant Christians. However, she agrees with Jerry Falwell's assertion that the New Right is principally composed of Protestant Evangelicals. See Carol Virgina Pohli, "Church Closets and Back Doors: A Feminist View of Moral Majority Women," *Feminist Studies*, 9, no. 3 (Autumn 1983), 533. Catherine E. Rymph describes the New Right as "an attempt by a new generation of conservative leaders to merge supporters of conservative single-issue causes into a large political coalition" (p. 213). See Rymph, *Republican Women: Feminism and Conservatism from Suffrage through the Rise of the New Right* (Chapel Hill: University of North Carolina Press, 2006), chapter 8. Pornography was an example of a "single-issue" cause with staying power.

[4] Pohli, "Church Closets and Back Doors," 533.

urged parents to assert their rights to see Christian family values taught in public schools and to reject sex education, which was thought to violate parents' right to control their children's moral upbringing. Bob Billings, a church school organizer, joined Heritage Foundation cofounder Paul Weyrich to form the National Christian Action Coalition (1978) to defeat IRS efforts to limit tax exemptions for private religious schools. The fundamentalist author Beverly LaHaye organized Concerned Women for America (CWA) in 1979 to protect and promote Biblical values for women and families through prayer, education, and legislative action campaigns. Pornography was one of six core action areas that CWA targeted at the outset. Jerry Falwell, the charismatic leader of the powerful Moral Majority organization, listed pornography along with homosexuality as priority issues in the organization's 1979 founding statement. Falwell reportedly registered three million new voters and raised $100 million in 1979–1980, much of it earmarked to support Ronald Reagan's bid for the presidency.[5] Richard Viguerie, who has been dubbed the "funding father" of modern conservatism for his pioneering use of direct mail to help conservative candidates and organizations solicit contributions, urged an "all-out war against pornography" in an influential 1980 New Right manifesto.[6]

The influence of this new generation of conservative leaders rose throughout the late 1970s, as white working and lower-middle-class voters became frustrated by high inflation, unemployment, soaring interest rates, and rising taxes. Opinion polls reflected disillusionment with government spending and the expansion of what was perceived as an indulgent welfare state, and it became clear that this base of traditionally Democratic voters was unhappy with the state of national affairs. President Jimmy Carter's failed attempt to resolve the Iran hostage crisis beginning in November 1979 deepened the conviction that it was time for a change. Noting these vulnerabilities, Republican party strategists courted traditionally Democratic voters, including white southerners (the "southern strategy"), and northern working-class ethnics and Catholics, and promised a solution of social traditionalism, economic individualism, and militant anti-communism. They promoted Reagan as a pro-life, pro-family, pro-morality, and pro-America candidate who would restore the sovereignty of heterosexual marriage and motherhood and preserve the traditional institutional roles of the family, churches, and schools. As president, he would stem the tide of social and moral decay brought on by the liberation movements of the previous decade.[7] As the 1980 election drew

[5] For a detailed overview of the rise of the conservative Christian Right, and the role of these key figures, see James T. Patterson, *Restless Giant: The United States from Watergate to Bush v. Gore* (Oxford: Oxford University Press, 2005), chapter 4. See also the sources listed in note 2, above.

[6] Richard A. Viguerie, *The New Right: We're Ready to Lead* (Falls Church, VA: Viguerie, 1980), 23.

[7] This strategy is discussed in Rosalind Pollack Petchesky, "Antiabortion, Antifeminism, and the Rise of the New Right," *Feminist Studies* 7, no. 2 (Summer 1981): 206–246. She describes these four main planks of the New Right campaign on p. 215. On the deployment of the

near, it became apparent that Reagan had amassed a huge bloc of supporters, including conservative Protestants, Catholics, and disenchanted Democrats who felt a loss of status and stability in the wake of radical social change.[8]

For religious conservatives, who made up a significant segment of the New Right coalition, and some newly politicized social conservatives, pornography was a major concern. Pornography, which they defined as all sexually explicit material, including any depiction of homosexuality, was reviled as an offense to decent people that undermined the moral fabric of society. By separating sex from a larger framework of ethical conduct, pornography was said to encourage promiscuity, gay and lesbian lifestyles, and other deviant behaviors that threatened traditional values; to distort the sacred sexual relationship between husband and wife; and to interfere with the healthy moral development of children.[9] In 1977, Anita Bryant's Save Our Children crusade warned that young boys were being recruited into homosexual rings to serve adult men; this type of immoral and criminal sexual activity was linked to the spread of pornography. Pornography preyed on human weakness, promoting sexual obsession and leading men and women into sinful sexual encounters.

Given pornography's significant harms, the idea of organizing against it – and eradicating it – held tremendous appeal. As conservatives turned their attention to the preservation of the nuclear family and traditional values, pornography came under increasing scrutiny as an agent of moral decay. Furthermore, New Right activists typically endorsed the increased use of criminal law statutes (obscenity laws) against the production and dissemination of pornography as a means of protecting society from its corrupting influence.

Members of WAP always defined the pornography issue differently, repudiating the religious conservative objection to portrayals of explicit sexuality regardless of context. Instead, they criticized male-oriented, exploitative material that oppressed women and portrayed them in ways that reinforced male power. This type of material was thought to strip women of any sexual or social agency and to fan the male desire for control. Anti-pornography feminists viewed pornography as a brutal and degrading agent of predatory male sexuality that created and maintained conditions of female subordination. Pornography was a tool that men used to communicate messages about, and to enforce, traditional gender roles. Its circulation ensured women's perpetual inferior social status. In the words of the political scientist Irene Diamond, writing in *Take Back the Night*, pornography was "a medium for expressing norms about male power and domination" that functioned as a "social

Southern strategy, see Joseph Crespino, *In Search of Another Country: Mississippi and the Conservative Counterrevolution* (Princeton, NJ: Princeton University Press, 2005).

8 On these trends, see Alan Crawford, *Thunder on the Right: The "New Right" and the Politics of Resentment* (New York: Pantheon Books, 1980). See also Sidney Blumenthal and Thomas Byrne Edsall, eds. *The Reagan Legacy* (New York: Pantheon Books, 1988).

9 Charles E. Cottle et al., "Conflicting Ideologies and the Politics of Pornography," *Gender & Society* 3, no. 3 (September 1989): 303–333.

control mechanism."[10] Pornography was a form of male violence that affected all women, each falling into at least one of three categories of victimization: 1) real women were coerced to perform for the production of pornographic magazines, films, and live shows, sustaining both physical and emotional harm; 2) other women would become the "copycat" real-life victims of men who were driven to commit acts of rape, battery, incest, and other sexual violence after viewing pornography; and 3) all women were oppressed by the distorted views of women as whores, "anonymous, panting playthings, adult toys, dehumanized objects" that were disseminated in pornography.[11] To that third point, Andrea Dworkin wrote that pornography "conditions, trains, educates, and inspires men to despise women, and men despise women in part because pornography exists."[12] This was pornography's most widespread form of violence: its purposeful creation of a misogynist culture. Pornography eroticized the domination, humiliation, and objectification of women, and taught men a set of cultural attitudes that encouraged rape, incest, battering, and other acts of sexual violence that deprived women of their civil rights.

There were other important differences that separated feminist opponents of pornography from those in the right-wing conservative camp. Among them, anti-pornography feminists did make a distinction between pornography and erotica (consensual, respectful, nonviolent sexual depictions) that religious conservatives rejected. Many feminists were wary of obscenity laws because historically, upticks in enforcement had accomplished anti-feminist ends, whereas social conservatives formed groups like Morality in Media and Citizens for Decency through Law with the express purpose of increasing the number of obscenity prosecutions and supporting new obscenity laws. Regardless of the groups' philosophical differences, there were areas of overlap evident to both camps, particularly around the questions of harm and the desire to limit pornography to protect the welfare of others. The existence of right-wing support did establish a climate favorable to a public campaign against pornography at a time when other feminist goals – such as sex education and public funding for reproductive health care – were under siege.

Given the strength of the anti-porn platform and new forms of community support, the exclusive focus on pornography gathered steam. The multilayered analysis of media effects, specifically the complex relationship between mediated sexual violence and real-world attitudes and acts, and the social-psychological consequences of artificial gender roles that WAVAW had pioneered, began to fade from public conversation. As Todd Gitlin has shown in his study of the relationship between the news media and the New Left, social movement groups find it difficult to maintain complex ideas through the filters of the press, the public, movement supporters, and movement detractors.[13]

[10] Irene Diamond, "Pornography and Repression: A Reconsideration of 'Who' and 'What,' in *Take Back the Night*, 188.

[11] Brownmiller, *Against Our Will*, 394.

[12] Andrea Dworkin, "Pornography and Grief," in *Take Back the Night*, 289.

[13] Todd Gitlin, *The Whole World is Watching: Mass Media in the Making and Unmaking of the New Left*, 2nd ed. (Berkeley: University of California Press, 2003).

Sophisticated analyses, such as those produced by radical feminists to explain the social and structural factors that contributed to male violence, inevitably get boiled down into manageable soundbites. The complex analysis of the conflation of sexuality and violence in media and the related issue of the damaging role of gender stereotypes was communicated less frequently to journalists and other influential audiences than the straightforward message that: "Pornography Is Violence Against Women," a common anti-pornography poster slogan in the later phases of the movement.

Media-savvy WAP members played an important role in advancing this simplified characterization of the radical feminist theory of media effects. Dolores Alexander described the group's leaders as "women who knew how to work the press," and they assumed that a powerhouse soundbite that described pornography as an act of sexual violence and an agent of sexual exploitation would mobilize greater numbers of supporters and result in more news coverage than an academic treatise on the social construction of gender.[14] To be fair, they were right. The strategic rhetorical approach did propel WAP and the issue of pornography into the national spotlight, and organization members assessed media coverage of their various campaigns as "spectacular."[15] WAP actions were routinely covered by the nation's most influential newspapers and television news programs, including numerous in-depth stories in the *New York Times*. However, elevating pornography as the central concern also brought about an unintended effect: The group and its goals were often portrayed as being in tune with the newly conservative political climate – a characterization that only increased right-wing interest and support.

In the early 1980s, the organization staged several high-visibility public actions that focused on degrading depictions of women and the sexual exploitation of girls, departing from earlier groups' focus on overt violence. These included a series of demonstrations against *Playboy*; a 1980 news conference to call attention to the publication of Linda (Lovelace) Boreman's memoir, *Ordeal* and a related boycott of *Deep Throat*; and a 1981 protest against a Broadway adaptation of the Vladimir Nabokov novel, *Lolita*. Through these actions, WAP presented the perilous sexual environment that girls and women faced in a patriarchal society that encouraged pornography and male predation. The idea that sexual activity posed a violent threat was politically useful to right-wing activists who wanted to roll back behavioral changes associated with the sexual revolution and contain sexual relations within traditional heterosexual marriage. At the same time, feminists outside of anti-pornography began to argue that the unremitting rhetoric of sexual danger might be used as grounds to "protect" women from a wide range of expression and behavior.

[14] Dolores Alexander, oral history conducted by Kelly Anderson, Southold, New York, March 20, 2004 and October 22, 2005, Sophia Smith Voices of Feminism Oral History Project. Available online at http://www.smith.edu/library/libs/ssc/vof/vof-narrators.html

[15] "Accomplishments of Women Against Pornography," *Grant Proposal for 1983–84*, n.d., WAP Records, Box 12, Folder 725, p. 18.

In addition to the direct WAP actions, the influential 1981 Canadian documentary, *Not a Love Story*, also accomplished some of the ideological work that raised concern about anti-pornography. The film featured three of WAP's most visible theorists, Robin Morgan, Susan Griffin, and Kathy Barry, and included footage of WAP's October 1979 March on Times Square and a Times Square porn tour. *Not a Love Story* contributed to a public perception that the anti-pornography movement embraced a biblical model of redemption, wherein feminist activists were rising up to rescue pitiable girls and women from sexual slavery. The feminist film critic B. Ruby Rich characterized the film in the *Village Voice* as a "religious parable" that celebrated the moral salvation of its central character, a former stripper who had come to see the error of her ways. She described director Bonnie Klein as a missionary "unearthing the sins of the world" in order to rescue the audience's souls.[16] The same metastory was visible in WAP's *Deep Throat* event, which celebrated Linda Boreman's salvation through domesticity. Feminists outside of anti-pornography became alarmed by what they saw as similarities between anti-porn activists and nineteenth-century social purity feminists who viewed marriage as a means of saving sexually active "fallen" women, and by feminist rhetoric about victimization that right-wing activists were eager to borrow.

As WAP solidified its position at the forefront of the anti-pornography movement, serious challenges to its agenda began to emerge from feminists who questioned the organization's commitment to sexual freedom for women and criticized its reliance on gender universalism. These critics lobbed charges of sexual moralism, essentialism, and racism at WAP, and the organization's relationship with the women's movement at large began to show signs of strain. One of the most biting critiques came from pro-sex feminists such as Rich, Ellen Willis, Gayle Rubin, and Deirdre English, who accused anti-pornography of promoting conservative views that supported women's sexual oppression and argued that efforts to protect girls and women from sexuality would create a repressive climate that would interfere with every woman's right to seek sexual liberation on her own terms. Women, they insisted, needed the freedom to explore their desires using all of the tools available to them – including male-oriented pornography – if they had any hope of transcending the limits placed on women's sexuality under patriarchy. Writing in the *New York Times*, Willis also took anti-pornography feminism – and Andrea Dworkin and Susan Griffin's work in particular – to task for promoting "male sexuality as pornography as rape."[17] This equation put heterosexual women in a terrible bind, having to choose between narrowly articulated feminist

[16] B. Ruby Rich, "Antiporn: Soft Issue, Hard World," reprinted in *Chick Flicks, Theories and Memories of the Feminist Film Movement* (Durham, NC: Duke University Press, 1998), 262.

[17] Ellen Willis, "Nature's Revenge," review of *Pornography and Silence*, by Susan Griffin and *Pornography: Men Possessing Women*, by Andrea Dworkin, *New York Times Book Review*, July 12, 1981. Available online at: http://www.nytimes.com/1981/07/12/books/nature-s-revenge.html?&pagewanted=all.

principles and their own bodily lust, and ignored the reality that heterosexual couples could create nonexploitative sexual relationships.

A number of feminists of color took issue with WAP's "everywoman" argument that pornography harmed some women directly through its production and subsequently injured and debased all women through its consumption. They argued that the presentation of pornography as a universal problem whitewashed important distinctions, especially the economic and social realities that forced poor women – a disproportionate number of whom were women of color – into sex work. Some of these feminists argued that decriminalization and establishment of safe working conditions were the only valid issues.[18] Others wanted the predominantly white anti-pornography movement to recognize that women of color experienced pornography as a contemporary manifestation of an historic form of oppression, one that gave white men unlimited opportunity to sexually exploit their bodies.[19] The objections to WAP voiced by feminists located outside of anti-pornography were varied and strenuous.

Meanwhile, beyond the women's movement, another formidable challenge to the WAP agenda was brewing. The development of affordable video technology in the late 1970s began to change the American entertainment landscape in the early 1980s, and adult filmmakers were quick to recognize the utility of privately owned videocassette players. Producers of X-rated material were among the first in the entertainment industry to make their films available for purchase for home viewing. Previously, the anti-pornography movement had dealt with a geographically concentrated problem and focused attention on organizing protests against red-light districts, like the Tenderloin in San Francisco and Times Square. Now, thanks to the introduction of video technology, pornography was suddenly everywhere, all at once. The booming market for X-rated videos created a new obstacle for WAP members who, at the very least, hoped to raise public awareness of the harms of pornography so that consumers of the material would be "socially ostracized."[20] With viewing moving from public theaters to private homes, the most serious barriers to indulgence – fear of loss of social reputation and public humiliation – were fast disappearing.

[18] On the sex workers' platform, see Valerie Jenness, *Making it Work: The Prostitutes' Rights Movement in Perspective* (New York: Aldene de Gruyter, 1993); Laurie Bell, ed., *Good Girls/Bad Girls: Feminists and Sex Trade Workers Face to Face* (Toronto: The Seal Press, 1987); Priscilla Alexander, "Prostitution: A Difficult Issue for Feminists," in *Sex Work: Writings by Women in the Sex Industry*, eds. Frederique Delacoste and Priscilla Alexander (Pittsburgh, PA: Cleis Press, 1987).

[19] See for example, Lesbians of Colour, "Racism in Pornography," in *Good Girls/Bad Girls: Feminists and Sex Trade Workers Face to Face*, ed. Laurie Bell (Toronto: The Seal Press, 1987), 58–66; and Patricia Hill Collins, "Pornography and Black Women's Bodies," in *Black Feminist Thought: Knowledge, Consciousness and the Politics of Empowerment* (Boston: Unwin Hyman, 1990), 167–173.

[20] Leslie Bennetts, "Conference Examines Pornography as a Feminist Issue," *New York Times*, September 17, 1979, B10.

New Leaders, New Directions

At the end of the 1970s, each of the anti-media violence organizations faced major changes in leadership. Julia London stepped down as national coordinator of WAVAW at the conclusion of the Warner boycott in the summer of 1979. She joined the WAVAW board of directors, but relocated to the Bay Area within two years with her partner, WAVAW activist Joan Howarth, who graduated from law school at the University of Southern California in 1980 and joined the state public defender's office in San Francisco.[21] After she left WAVAW, London held a series of positions related to community organizing. She worked on behalf of energy conservation for a Santa Monica-area community association, and then conducted campus outreach for the UC-Berkeley chapter of the California Public Interest Research Group (CalPIRG), a grassroots lobbying organization that supports social justice issues, such as fair housing and voting rights. In subsequent years, she worked for Food First and the National Gay Rights Advocates.[22] In her place at WAVAW, a series of young, relatively inexperienced women stepped up to fill the role of national coordinator. None brought London's political experience and organizing skill, and the group did not carry out another major national campaign in the post-Warner years.

At WAVPM, major changes in leadership were also taking place as Laura Lederer's relationship with the organization began to decline. Lynn Campbell had departed for New York City in March 1979 to organize WAP. Lederer, now alone in the role of national coordinator, was at odds with some key members after the January 1979 structure meeting that erupted in struggles over decision-making authority and control. Several months later, on May 3, 1979, a bizarre incident set the stage for her exit from WAVPM. Lederer alleged that she had been kidnapped by a well-known American porn actress, who forcibly drugged her with the hallucinogen PCP, commonly known as angel dust.[23] Members of the WAVPM board of directors were unsure how to respond. Some thought that WAVPM members ought to picket in front of the actress's home. Attorney Jill Lippitt suggested that Lederer file a lawsuit

[21] Subsequently, Howarth worked as a staff attorney for the ACLU Foundation of Southern California, and began teaching law in 1989 at the University of California-Davis. Today, Howarth is dean of the Michigan State University College of Law, the first female dean in the history of the law school. She is nationally recognized for her scholarship on gender and the death penalty.

[22] London worked in fundraising and development for Food First, the Institute for Food and Development Policy, which is a think tank aimed at ending world hunger and returning control of farming and food production to local farmers, as opposed to transnational agribusinesses. She worked in a similar fundraising capacity for the National Gay Rights Advocates. Today, she works in the quality control assurance unit of a major American pharmaceutical corporation. She lives in the Bay Area with her partner of twenty-five years, Bridget Wynne, a co-coordinator of WAVPM in the early 1980s, and their son.

[23] WAVPM Board of Directors meeting minutes, May 9, 1979, Box 1, Folder: Board of Directors, 1979–1982, WAVPM Records, GLBT Historical Society.

seeking damages. Lederer took a leave of absence from WAVPM for the summer to go home to Detroit to recuperate and to edit the manuscript for *Take Back the Night*.

Over the next six months, conflicts over finances developed. Some stemmed from $4,000 in unreimbursed medical expenses that Lederer incurred as a result of the drugging.[24] Others were about back pay that WAVPM owed her. The majority were connected to the advance paid by publisher William Morrow for *Take Back the Night*, as disagreements ensued over Lederer's expenses in preparing the manuscript and who would receive payment of future royalties.[25] After a tense summer, member Beth Goldberg stepped up to become WAVPM's national coordinator on September 1, 1979. Four months later, Lederer submitted her resignation to the WAVPM board of directors, permanently leaving her role as national coordinator.[26]

Out of the anti-pornography spotlight, Lederer remained involved with issues surrounding violence against women. She designed grant programs as director of community and social concerns for a private philanthropic organization for ten years after leaving WAVPM. She earned a law degree from DePaul University in 1994 and subsequently founded the Protection Project, a legal research institute for the study of international trafficking of women and children that was based at Harvard University's Kennedy School of Government, and later at Johns Hopkins University's Paul H. Nitze School of Advanced International Studies. Lederer also served as a senior advisor on human trafficking to the U.S. Department of State. Once she resigned from WAVPM, Lederer ceased to play a leading public role in the anti-pornography movement per se, although her extensive work on sex trafficking emerged from the same set of radical feminist concerns.

WAP was also dealing with major changes in leadership. By April 1980, both Brownmiller and Campbell had left the organization. Brownmiller returned to her full-time writing career, alienated from many members because of the perception that she was anti-lesbian. Campbell sought a less strenuous job as her health declined from an aggressive form of skin cancer, diagnosed shortly after she arrived in New York City in 1979. She went to work with WAP member Carolyn Reed at the National Urban League, fighting to secure fair labor rights for household workers. She subsequently became program coordinator at the Funding Exchange, a national network of fourteen foundations that provided financial support for community organizing projects. Campbell moved home to Berkeley in the fall of 1983, where her family members and partner, Cheri Pies, then a graduate student in social work, were better able to

[24] WAVPM Memo from Beth Goldberg, Book Committee to Julie Greenberg, May 16, 1980, Box 1, Folder: Board of Directors, 1979–1982, WAVPM Records, GLBT Historical Society.

[25] WAVPM General Membership meeting notes, August 18, 1979, Box 1, Folder: General Meeting Minutes, 1977–1983, WAVPM Records, GLBT Historical Society.

[26] WAVPM Board of Directors meeting minutes, January 10, 1980, Box 1, Folder: General Meeting Minutes, 1977–1983, WAVPM Records, GLBT Historical Society. Lederer resigned in January 1980.

care for her as her disease progressed. She passed away in April 1984, at the age of twenty-eight.[27]

Two of WAP's four original coordinators remained at this juncture: Barbara Mehrhof and Dolores Alexander. However, the WAP steering committee would dismiss Mehrhof from her position as part-time staff coordinator in November 1981. Alexander remained with WAP until 1983, working also during this period for *Time* magazine.[28] Dorchen Leidholdt, a college textbook editor at Random House who was then an activist working with New York Women Against Rape and a founding member of New York WAVAW, stepped up to become a new leader of WAP in the 1980s.[29] Describing herself during that period as "an activist by night and an editor by day," Leidholdt moved to New York City in 1977 from the University of Virginia, where she had undertaken graduate study in English literature. Like many other anti-pornography activists, Leidholdt had experience with issues surrounding sexual violence; as a graduate student, she counseled survivors of sexual assault, including fellow students and women living in the rural areas surrounding Charlottesville.[30]

With new leaders at the helm, WAVAW and WAVPM pursued new directions. The WAVAW chapters turned their attention to motion picture advertising, protesting abusive campaigns for films like director Brian dePalma's *Dressed to Kill* (1980), Gordon Willis' *Windows* (1980), and Bob Brooks' *Tattoo* (1981), which featured themes of violence against women. WAP also protested *Dressed to Kill* and *Tattoo*, and persuaded the New York City transit authority to remove the subway posters advertising *Tattoo* on the grounds that the image of a naked female body covered with tattoos and bound at the ankles resembled a "hardcore bondage pornography display" and would increase women's fears for their personal safety in public places.[31] Toward the end of 1981, WAVAW tried unsuccessfully to persuade WAVPM to launch a joint campaign aimed at the motion picture industry. Melinda Lowrey, then WAVAW's national coordinator, contacted WAVPM's co-coordinators in hopes of support. WAVPM at this time was led by two young lesbian feminists, Julie Greenberg, a recent graduate of Swarthmore, and Bridget Wynne, a 1980 graduate of UC Berkeley who had majored in women's studies.[32] Ultimately,

[27] Jane Creighton, "Lynn Campbell, 1955–1984," *off our backs* (June 1984), 25.

[28] Personal Conversation with Dolores Alexander, November 11, 2005.

[29] Today, Leidholdt is an attorney and Director of the Center for Battered Women's Legal Services at Sanctuary for Families in New York City. This is the largest legal services program for domestic violence victims in the country, providing legal representation to battered women in family law, criminal, civil rights, and immigration cases. The Center is an advocate for policy and legislative reform on behalf of battered women.

[30] Taylor Smith, "NYU Alumna of the Month, February 2009: Dorchen Leidholdt" Available online at http://www.law.nyu.edu/alumni/almo/pastalmos/2008–09almos/dorchenleidholdt/index.htm/ (accessed January 27, 2010).

[31] "Accomplishments of Women Against Pornography," *Grant Proposal for 1983–84*, n.d., WAP Records, Box 12, Folder 725, p. 22.

[32] Leadership of WAVPM changed rapidly during this period. In January 1980, Julie Greenberg was a a full time coordinator; Luisah Teish, a black feminist poet who had helped WAVPM

WAVPM decided that ads for the movie industry were too ephemeral, coming and going so quickly that it would be difficult to organize and sustain a campaign. In a letter to Lowrey explaining their rationale, Greenberg wrote that WAVPM sought targets that were likely to have greater "national impact."[33]

WAVPM returned to its roots in advertising, launching a *Write Back! Fight Back!* letter writing campaign against the Maidenform lingerie company in February 1982. The organization objected to the "Maidenform Woman" campaign that depicted women as doctors, lawyers, stockbrokers, and athletes at work in public settings, but showed them with their clothing pushed aside, revealing Maidenform bras and panties. Each advertisement in the series included the slogan: "The Maidenform woman. You never know where she'll turn up." WAVPM members believed that these words, coupled with the passive and vacuous images of women in lingerie, encouraged men to regard all women as willing targets, just waiting for men to discover the raw animal sexuality brimming beneath their prim exteriors. The result might be unwanted sexual advances, or worse, rape.

One execution of this campaign showed a female physician standing in front of a patient, her white lab coat hanging open, providing a full frontal view of her lacy red lingerie. Two male physicians stood behind her, fully clothed. Dr. Anne L. Barlow, president of the American Medical Women's Association, condemned the ad in *Time* magazine as "extremely distasteful."[34] Another woman wrote to Maidenform and criticized the lingerie company for depicting the female doctor as an "unprofessional, intellectually lacking, exhibitionistic woman on the periphery of the male world."[35] The chauvinist quality of the campaign and its subtle invitation to sexual violence also raised WAP's ire, and earned Maidenform the organization's first annual, and soon to be infamous, ZAP award for sexist advertising (a plastic statuette in the shape of a pig) in 1982.[36] That year, ZAPs were also presented to Jordache and to Calvin Klein

with the slideshow and its presentation of women of color, was a half-time coordinator, and member Lani Silver was also a half-time coordinator. Within the year, Julie Greenberg and Bridget Wynne became national co-coordinators. Greenberg and Wynne were young lesbian activists, both in their twenties during this period, without significant prior feminist experience. Both would graduate rabbinical school and become ordained as rabbis post-WAVPM. Wynne and WAVAW's Julia London would eventually become partners, and they now reside in the Berkeley, California area with their son.

33 Letter, Julie Greenberg to Melinda Lowrey, November 12, 1981, Box 9, LA WAVAW Papers.

34 "Maidenform Blushes," *Time*, April 25, 1983, available online at http://www.time.com/time/magazine/article/0,9171,923573,00.html (accessed December 15, 2008).

35 Letter, an angry customer to Mrs. Beatrice Coleman, President, Maidenform, Inc., May 11, 1983, WAP Records, Box 3, Folder 101.

36 The WAP Annual Advertising Awards, which began in 1982, showed the organization's ties to the work of WAVAW and WAVPM, and the collective interest in the portrayal of women in advertising. WAP presented both Ms. Liberty Awards (the "Libby") for nonsexist advertisements that promoted women's dignity, and ZAP Awards for sexist advertisements that degraded women or used sexual violence to sell a product. WAP honored shoe designer Joe Famolare in 1982 for switching from sexist shoe ads to his well-known "Footloose and Famolare" campaign. In subsequent years, WAP dispensed ZAP awards to companies like

Jeans, the latter for its sexually provocative ads featuring teen actress-model Brooke Shields, who coyly whispered: "Nothing comes between me and my Calvins." Maidenform did withdraw the "Maidenform Woman" in 1983, but there was no evidence that feminist protest motivated this change.

WAP in the Early 1980s

In the early 1980s, WAP was very active on the local and national scenes, envisioning and carrying out an ambitious anti-pornography agenda. Membership reached 3,500 by 1982, and the organization created a new structure led by a steering committee of active members who volunteered at least twenty hours per month. Group actions during this period ranged from protesting the sale of *Playboy*, *Penthouse*, and *Oui* magazines at Sloans supermarkets in Manhattan, to developing the WAP Annual Advertising Awards program that bestowed ZAPs for sexist ads and Ms. Liberty ("Libbie") awards for woman-positive campaigns, to expanding the tour program to the city's Upper East Side, where sex businesses catering to affluent male customers flourished. To accomplish the latter, WAP members Frances Patai, Renee Mittler, and Dorchen Leidholdt visited East Side sex establishments such as the Peep n' Palace on 53rd Street off Lexington Avenue, and the Harem and Tahitia massage parlors on Third Avenue between 50th and 51st Streets, in March 1980 to establish a new tour route. During this period, the organization also revised the slide show to include more images of softcore, *Playboy*-style pornography to better illustrate the concept of sexual objectification and the "covert and psychological" violence against women present in porn.[37] In January 1980, WAP protested the premiere of *Windows*, a United Artists film that featured a violent lesbian killer who hired a man to rape the woman she secretly loved, hoping that the woman would turn to her in the aftermath for help and support.[38] WAP criticized the film for presenting rape as a woman's crime and for encouraging viewers to enjoy the depiction of sexual violence. The early 1980s were prolific and energetic organizing years for WAP, as the group established itself as the leading national feminist voice on questions of pornography and sexuality.

Anti-*Playboy* Demonstrations

During these years, WAP was also involved in a series of anti-*Playboy* demonstrations, and the attack on pornography expanded to include nonviolent

Huggies diapers, Gillette razors, and Hanes hosiery for its "Gentlemen Prefer Hanes" campaign. Ms. Liberty awards went to Ford, Bell Telephone, and Crest toothpaste, among others. WAP member Frances Patai, an actress with academic training in cultural criticism, was a major organizer of this awards ceremony. In 1985, the group received more than 500 nominations for the awards, and the event was covered by both the general and trade press. For more on the WAP Zaps, see Sandra Dhois, "WAP ZAPs Ads," *Women Against Pornography NewsReport* (Spring/Summer 1984): 1, 6.

[37] Dana Lobell, "Slide Show Revision," *WAP NewsReport*, March 24, 1980, 3.

[38] Sheila Roher, "Smashing 'Windows,'" *WAP NewsReport*, March 24, 1980, 1.

expressions (no overt violence) of male-identified desire. The first *Playboy* protest occurred in February 1980. WAP objected to a promotional Valentine's Day event that asked couples to submit applications to take part in a mass wedding ceremony. A full-page *Playboy* ad in the *New York Times* describing the upcoming event depicted a bride and groom with a caption: "She wanted hearts and flowers; he just wanted a good time." WAP insisted that the ad revealed the essence of the Playboy philosophy, namely that women were "entertaining pets" for men and that "male sexual exploitation of women is both humorous and inevitable." About fifty people joined the February 14 picket in front of the New York City Playboy Club, chanting "*Playboy* Calls It Liberation/Women Call It Exploitation" and brandishing signs with slogans such as "*Playboy* Degrades Women," "A *Playboy* Wedding is a Life Sentence," and "Porn is Visual Assault."[39]

The first two slogans reiterated well-known WAP beliefs about the sexual objectification and dehumanization of women in pornography, and the punishing nature of the institution of heterosexuality for women, but the "visual assault" sign revealed a significant movement shift. Whereas members of Denver WAVAW defined pornography in 1977 as "the *visual portrayal* of the humiliation and physical, mental and economic violence against women" [emphasis added], pornography was now regarded as the act of violence *in and of itself*: a form of assault.[40] WAP now treated pornographic *images* and real world *acts* of violence (e.g., rape, battery), as if there were no difference between the two.[41] The idea that pornography was more than the representation of assault, but assault itself, gathered steam among movement supporters in the early 1980s, building on the influential argument advanced by Catharine MacKinnon and Andrea Dworkin that the viewing of pornographic images constituted an *act* of male supremacy and domination. Writing in 1983, MacKinnon defined pornography as "a form of forced sex."[42] That same year, MacKinnon and Dworkin introduced their model anti-pornography civil rights ordinance in Minneapolis, which defined pornography as an act: "the graphic sexually explicit subordination of women," not as an image that depicted or caused the subordination of women.[43] Cindy Jenefsky has described this turn in Dworkin's thinking as a move from interpreting pornography as an influential cultural artifact to interpreting it as an institutional practice of subordination. As Jenefsky wrote of Dworkin's

[39] Dorchen Leidholdt, "Valentine's Day Demonstration Against *Playboy*," *WAP NewsReport*, March 24, 1980, 1.

[40] Denver WAVAW, "We Are Women Against Violence Against Women," *Big Mama Rag* 5, no. 8 (October 1977): 1.

[41] This critique appears in Gayle Rubin, Dierdre English, and Amber Hollibaugh, "Talking Sex: A Conversation on Sexuality and Feminism," *Socialist Review* 58, no. 4 (July-August 1981): 43–62.

[42] Catharine A. MacKinnon, "Not a Moral Issue," in *Feminism Unmodified: Discourses on Life and Law* (Cambridge, MA: Harvard University Press, 1987), 148.

[43] Andrea Dworkin and Catharine A. MacKinnon, *Pornography and Civil Rights: A New Day for Women's Equality* (Minneapolis, MN: Organizing Against Pornography, 1988), 138.

FIGURE 8.1. WAP members and supporters protest outside of the New York City Playboy Club on February 14, 1980. The poster describing pornography as "visual assault" expressed an idea that was gathering steam among movement supporters in the early 1980s, namely that pornography was more than the graphic depiction or representation of assault, but a form of assault itself. *The Schlesinger Library, Radcliffe Institute, Harvard University. Photo by Stephanie Cohen.*

later approach, "What pornography *is*, therefore, is always also what it *does* to women."[44]

The *Playboy* mass wedding protest illustrated the gradual shift within the movement from WAVAW and WAVPM's focus on overt acts of physical violence to WAP's concern with a more diffuse standard of harm. Looking back to WAVPM's 1978 action against *Hustler*, when women opposed the depiction of a woman's body being ground up into bloody hamburger meat, a change was discernible. Within the *Playboy* demonstration, one could see a new objection to the violation of the positive aspects of female nature, women's innate nurturing and loving values ("she wanted hearts and flowers"), for the sake of men's base desires ("he wanted a good time"). This transition was tied to theoretical changes within feminism itself, namely the rise of cultural feminism and its assertion of women's distinct and superior virtues. The selection of *Playboy* as a target for WAP action communicated the organization's broader operating definition of violence against women.

[44] Cindy Jenefsky, "Andrea Dworkin's Reconstruction of Pornography as a Discriminatory Social Practice," in *Violence and its Alternatives*, eds. Manfred B. Steger and Nancy S. Lind (New York: St. Martin's, 1999), 140.

FIGURE 8.2. WAVPM national coordinator and WAP founder Lynn Campbell at the February 14, 1980 *Playboy* demonstration. The young radical feminist would step down from her leadership position with WAP just weeks after this protest, due to declining health. She subsequently worked with WAP member Carolyn Reed at the National Urban League, fighting to secure fair labor rights for household workers. Campbell passsed away in April 1984, at the age of twenty-eight. *Photo: Bettye Lane.*

During the spring of 1980, WAP participated in two other anti-*Playboy* actions. *Playboy*'s softcore pictorial approach, although certainly not a favorite among feminists, had previously attracted less movement criticism than its overtly violent and misogynistic competitor, *Hustler*. Now, WAP took on *Playboy* for advancing an ideology that presented women as unequal to men, objects to be used at will for sexual gratification. In April 1980, the New York City Playboy Club created a promotional event inviting executives to bring their secretaries in for lunch in honor of National Secretaries Week. Members of WAP were outraged. The magazine regularly presented cartoons and other editorial material depicting secretaries as sexual playthings for their male supervisors, often being chased around their bosses' desks. *Playboy* routinely made light of sexual advances in the workplace and presented office sex as a welcome fringe benefit. The "insulting invitation" to lunch at the Playboy Club, where they would be served by women dressed in skimpy bunny costumes (an experience reported by an undercover Gloria Steinem in 1963), robbed women office workers of their dignity, reinforced their subordination to men in general, and left them ever more vulnerable to sexual harassment.[45]

On Friday, April 25, fifty members and supporters of WAP formed a picket line in front of the Playboy Club on 59th Street. They carried signs reading: "Secretaries Want Respect, Not More *Playboy* Jokes," and "Raises not Roses," as well as numerous "Women Against Pornography" and "Fight Back!" posters. Andrea Dworkin picketed with WAP, carrying a poster featuring the slogan: "*Playboy* Degrades Secretaries." The women handed out leaflets with examples of *Playboy*'s sexist workplace cartoons. In truth, the issues at stake, such as sexual harassment and marginalizing women in low-paid, dead-end clerical positions, were ones that enjoyed broad-based feminist support. However, within the context of a demonstration against *Playboy*, it was difficult to train public attention on the question of fair and equal treatment of working women. In selecting *Playboy* as a target – a rational choice given the women's movement history of antipathy for the publication – WAP likely strengthened the public perception that the organization was opposed to any sexually explicit portrayals of women. In fact, it was the persistent, sexist portrayal of women as subordinate to men, as "bunnies" with no higher function than serving men's sexual needs, that infuriated WAP. The protest was meant to criticize *Playboy* for demeaning women and helping create and maintain their lesser social standing relative to men, "fit only for sexual use, unfit for human life," as MacKinnon later characterized such harm.[46]

In June 1980, WAP joined with WAVAW and WAVPM in a Los Angeles protest against *Playboy*, aimed this time at the Hugh M. Hefner First Amendment Awards. The Playboy Foundation under the direction of Christie Hefner established the awards to honor individuals who were thought to have made significant contributions to the protection and enhancement of First Amendment rights. From its founding in 1965, the Foundation promoted itself as a defender of free speech and provided financial support to progressive and liberal organizations including the ACLU and the National Coalition Against

[45] Maggie Smith, "Demonstration at Playboy Club," *WAP NewsReport* (July/August 1980): 3. Steinem worked "undercover" at the Manhattan Playboy club in 1963 and published an account of her experiences in the arts and culture magazine, *Show*. Her article is described in Watts, *Mr. Playboy*, 237–238.

[46] Catharine A. MacKinnon, "The Roar on the Other Side of Silence," in *In Harm's Way: The Pornography Civil Rights Hearings* (Cambridge, MA: Harvard University Press, 1997), 5.

Censorship, and feminist organizations such as the Women's Equity Action League, Planned Parenthood, and groups supporting ratification of the Equal Rights Amendment (ERA). The Foundation purposely gave as much as 65 percent of its funding dollars to women's organizations, which was widely interpreted within the movement as a way of quieting criticism and "classing up" *Playboy* to divert attention from its trade in pornography.[47] Dorchen Leidholdt, quoted in a WAVAW newsletter, argued that *Playboy* had carefully constructed a "façade of liberalism" by celebrating progressive people and causes to ensure that people would not question or challenge its core business of "trafficking in the flesh of women."[48]

On June 26, Hefner and a representative from the Southern California ACLU were slated to present the First Amendment awards at the Playboy Mansion in Los Angeles to select writers and public figures. In the days prior to the event, members of WAVAW reached out to awardee Sonia Johnson, a feminist activist who had been excommunicated from the Mormon church in the late 1970s for exposing illegal lobbying efforts to block the ratification of the ERA. Citing the magazine's distortion of female sexuality, and its light-hearted treatment of rape, child molestation, battering, and sexual harassment, WAVAW urged Johnson to refuse the *Playboy* award and the accompanying $3,000 check. She agreed. During the ceremony, Johnson told Hefner and the 200 guests and media representatives assembled for the event that she was a "feminist first" and that she disapproved of the way that *Playboy* depicted women.[49] In an Associated Press story that ran in newspapers around the country, Johnson condemned the "non-loving and non-committed relationships" that the magazine promoted.[50]

During the awards ceremony, members of WAVAW and WAVPM's Beth Goldberg held a counterceremony outside of the Los Angeles Playboy Club. They handed out a series of "Hefner Awards" to individuals whom they recognized for encouraging sexual harassment, trivializing the sexual abuse of girls, ridiculing older woman, encouraging racism, and promoting violence against women. Recipients included Louis Malle, director of the the 1978 film *Pretty Baby*, which starred twelve-year-old Brooke Shields as a young girl born into a life of prostitution; and Larry Flynt, publisher of *Hustler* and the Chester the Molester cartoons. Both men were recognized for promoting the sexual abuse of children. They gave awards for "S & M Chic" to fashion photographers Richard Avedon and Helmut Newton. Hefner received an award for contributing to the sexual harassment of working women.

[47] On *Playboy* and funding of women's organizations, see Kathleen S. Kelly, *Fund Raising and Public Relations: A Critical Analysis* (Mahwah, NJ: Lawrence Erlbaum, 1991), 372–373.

[48] Quoted in "WAVAW/WAP Take on Hefner," *WAVAW Speaks* (April 1982), 4.

[49] Quoted in Elizabeth Fraterrigo, *Playboy and the Making of the Good Life in Modern America* (New York and Oxford: Oxford University Press, 2009), 199.

[50] Quoted in "WAVAW/WAP Take on Hefner," *WAVAW Speaks* (April 1982), 4. See also Dorchen Leidholdt, "WAVAW Shames Playboy," *WAP NewsReport* (July/August 1980): 3; and Letter, Jeanette Silvieria, WAVAW to Playboy awardees, June 20, 1980, WAP Records, Box 6, Folder 272.

In 1982, WAP and WAVAW would tangle with Hefner again, persuading three high-profile judges set to participate in the First Amendment Award contest to resign.[51] At that time, Andrea Dworkin wrote to former California congresswoman Yvonne Brathwaite-Burke, and urged her to refrain from judging. Dworkin condemned *Playboy* for championing free speech absolutism as a means of protecting its right to sell women's bodies and for robbing women of the chance to participate as citizens on equal footing with men. "What *Playboy* promotes – the sexual objectification of women, the sexual exploitation of women – keeps women from being able to exercise the rights of speech *Playboy* pretends to honor," Dworkin wrote. She urged Brathwaite-Burke not to lend her name to the "purveyors of pornographic speech" and to recognize that Playboy used its power "to promote the exclusion of women from humanity."[52] Dworkin was unsuccessful. Citing *Playboy*'s fundraising for the ERA in California and support for her own electoral campaigns, Braithwaite-Burke concluded that it would be "hypocritical" for her to turn down the invitation.[53]

Anti-*Playboy* actions sent a series of messages to the general public that members of the anti-pornography movement may not have intended. As noted above, *Playboy* had not previously been a major target for action, as the first generation of leaders of WAVAW and WAVPM had focused their attention on depictions of overt violence against women, which *Playboy* typically avoided. Now, anti-pornography feminists also expressed their commitment to eradicating sexually themed material that objectified girls and women. *Playboy* centerfolds, for example, portrayed women as sexual objects for the express purpose of evoking a male sexual response. As such, the women within the magazine's pages were stripped of their humanity, reduced to "things" meant for male use.

The belief that explicit sexuality of this sort was harmful seemed to link anti-pornography feminists and religious conservatives, although their reasons for opposing *Playboy* were very different. When Sonia Johnson, now publicly aligned with WAP, condemned *Playboy* on the grounds that it showed men and women in "non-loving and non-committed relationships," her statement

[51] See both Leidholdt, "WAVAW Shames Playboy," and "Playboy Actions," in *Grant Proposal for 1983–84*, n.d., WAP Records, Box 12, Folder 725, 19. In 1982, the feminist groups were able to persuade the following individuals to resign as judges for the First Amendment Awards: Charles Nesson, professor, Harvard Law School; Gene Reynolds, television producer; and Donna Shalala, then-president of Hunter College and future Secretary of Health and Human Services under the Clinton Administration. Judges who refused to decline included: Yvonne Brathwaite Burke, California's first African American congresswoman; Hamilton Fish III, publisher, the *Nation*; Florence McMullin, chair of the Washington Library Association Intellectual Freedom Committee; and Aryeh Neier, professor of law at New York University and vice chairman of the U.S. Helsinki Watch Committee and the Fund for Free Expression.

[52] Letter, Andrea Dworkin to Yvonne Brathwaite-Burke, March 16, 1982, WAP Records, Box 8, Folder 426.

[53] Letter, Yvonne Brathwaite-Burke to Andrea Dworkin, March 26, 1982, WAP Records, Box 8, Folder 426.

reflected conservative Christian beliefs that engaging in casual sex for physical gratification was wrong. From a radical feminist standpoint, one of the achievements of the sexual revolution had been the separation of sex from reproduction and marriage, and the embrace of sex as an affirming part of life that could be freely chosen on the basis of desire. Johnson's statement, now publicly linked *with* feminism, was certainly open to a conservative interpretation that sex belonged only within the framework of marriage – an argument that many feminists would have rejected outright.

To be clear, WAP was always careful to try to distinguish its official issue positions from those held by the religious Right. Some WAP supporters, notably Andrea Dworkin, were less scrupulous about this line in the sand, citing the value of right-wingers who saw themselves on the same side as feminists with regard to pornography.[54] Over time, however, some of the marked differences between the two groups did seem to collapse. Social conservatives learned to appropriate feminist rhetoric about degradation and harm to women and children, and the anti-pornography movement devised actions that were likely to garner conservative support. For example, WAP's protest against the *Playboy* mass wedding and the newspaper advertisement that poked fun at men and women's different motives for marriage seemed to echo the new conservative rhetoric of restoring respect for the family. Religious conservatives defended marriage as a sacred bond established by God and rooted in procreational purposes. It was an unselfish partnership in which the husband exercised authority and the wife reached her fullest potential as a helper who willingly submitted to her husband and followed him with "a servant's heart."[55] Members of WAP would never have endorsed such a view, but through the *Playboy* action they did engage in a critique that supported attention to the emotional and spiritual harm done to women by male sexual license in a libidinal culture. With their emphasis firmly rooted in the dangers that sex posed for women, and offering very little in the way of an alternative, liberatory vision of sexual freedom, members of WAP did promote an unintended public view of anti-pornography as a place of some agreement between radical feminists and New Right activists.

Protesting *Deep Throat*: Linda Lovelace's *Ordeal*

The publication of Linda "Lovelace" Boreman's memoir, *Ordeal* (1980), provided an opportunity for WAP to draw attention to sexual exploitation and to advance the "everywoman" argument that pornography's first victims were

[54] See Judy Klemesrud, "Joining Hands in the Fight Against pronorgraphy (sic)," *New York Times*, August 26, 1985, available online at http://www.nytimes.com/1985/08/26/style/joining-hands-in-the-fight-against-pronorgraphy.html?scp=1&sq=joining+hands+in+the+fight+against&st=nyt (accessed June 29, 2009).

[55] Daniel W. Zink, "The Practice of Marriage and Family Counseling and Conservative Christianity," in *The Role of Religion in Marriage and Family Counseling*, ed. Jill Onedera (New York: Taylor and Francis, 2007), 63.

the women featured in it, but all women suffered harm. In the best-selling book, Boreman debunked the myth that she had willingly and enthusiastically starred in *Deep Throat*. Instead, she described herself as the prisoner of Chuck Traynor, a violent and abusive husband who drugged and beat her, and forced her to work as a prostitute and perform on camera in X-rated films. Boreman had tried to escape three times, only to be tracked down and forcibly returned to her life of sexual servitude. Years later, Boreman initiated her fourth – and final – escape attempt. She spent weeks hiding out alone, fearing that Traynor would find her. When she eventually emerged, she found that Traynor was promoting Marilyn Chambers, the former Ivory soap model who would star in the 1970s porn classic, *Behind the Green Door*. In *Ordeal*, Boreman characterized *Deep Throat* as filmed rape.

WAP planned a demonstration and a news conference to promote the book and to call for a nationwide boycott of *Deep Throat*. Although the film had been released seven years prior, it remained a steady attraction at adult theaters. At the time of *Ordeal*'s release, patrons of the Frisco theater at 48th Street and Seventh Avenue could see daily showings of *Deep Throat* on a double bill with another classic film of the porno chic era, *The Devil in Miss Jones* (1973). On May 31, 1980, about 100 WAP members and supporters picketed the Frisco and asked passers-by to boycott *Deep Throat* to protest the exploitation and abuse of women in pornography. Picketers carried posters with slogans including: "No More Profits Off Our Bodies" and "The First Victims of Pornography are the Women in It!" The latter slogan captured WAP's "everywoman" argument.

Following the demonstration, WAP held a news conference at the Times Square storefront. The event featured Boreman as well as Andrea Dworkin, Susan Brownmiller, actress Valerie Harper (of *Rhoda* fame), Dorchen Leidholdt, and WAP member Marilyn Hayes.[56] Dworkin invited the feminist attorney Catharine MacKinnon to attend, and according to Brownmiller's account, the two began discussing whether Boreman might sue Traynor and the producers of *Deep Throat*, a conversation that ultimately led to the creation of their model anti-pornography ordinances.[57]

Each panelist gave a statement. Dworkin described *Deep Throat* as a documentary of rape. "The millions upon millions of men – especially those freedom-loving liberals – who found 'Deep Throat' so much fun must now be told what they should have known all along: that they have been enjoying

[56] Brownmiller returned to full-time writing in 1979 following the East Coast conference and March on Times Square, and ceased to play an active role in the daily affairs of WAP. She occasionally participated in special events. By May 1980, her presence at the WAP office was so infrequent that Dana Lobell, a steering committee member, sent Brownmiller a note thanking her for her help on the *Deep Throat* action and reminding her: "Remember, you're always welcome to stop in." Letter, Dana Lobell to Susan Brownmiller, June 9, 1980, WAP Records, Box 6, Folder 270A.

[57] Brownmiller, *In Our Time*, 316–317.

FIGURE 8.3. A May 31, 1980 WAP protest at the Frisco adult movie theater at 48th Street and Seventh Avenue, where the XXX classic *Deep Throat* played daily. The picketers urged passers-by to boycott *Deep Throat* to protest the exploitation and abuse of women in pornography. The event was designed to coincide with the publication of Linda "Lovelace" Boreman's autobiography, in which she revealed that her performance in the famous film had been coerced. *Photo: Bettye Lane.*

and defending and laughing at the sexual abuse of a woman," Dworkin said.[58] Brownmiller hammered home the idea that the myth of the sexually liberated

[58] Statement by Andrea Dworkin, Press Release, "Protest *Deep Throat*," May 31, 1980, WAP Records, Box 9, Folder 540. Liberals typically value First Amendment freedoms over concerns about pornography, but agree that pornography could justifiably be restricted if such action were necessary to avoid injuring others. Once Lovelace revealed the harm she had sustained in the making of *Deep Throat*, it seemed like liberals might have to agree that there was sufficient evidence to set new limits.

FIGURE 8.4. WAP holds a news conference on May 31, 1980 to announce the publication of Linda "Lovelace" Boreman's autobiography and to call attention to the victimization of women in pornography. Top row, left to right: WAP founder Dolores Alexander, actress Valerie Harper, attorney Catharine MacKinnon. Bottom row, left to right: Linda "Lovelace" Boreman, WAP member Marilyn Hayes, author Andrea Dworkin. Susan Brownmiller also participated. *Photo: Bettye Lane.*

American woman concealed the reality of violence and force. "*Ordeal* says more about sex in America than Gay Talese's *Thy Neighbor's Wife*," she claimed.[59] Talese had lionized Lovelace in the pages of his book, which celebrated the free-wheeling sexual culture of the late 1960s and 1970s, as an X-rated film heroine who "used men for [her] pleasure, even beckoning a second or third actor after the first had exhausted himself."[60] Boreman spoke last. Her words completed the debunking of Linda Lovelace. She said that she hoped that anyone who chose to view *Deep Throat* would "sense my pain and degradation." She connected her exploitation with that of children, strengthening a new pattern within anti-pornography that portrayed women and girls as equally vulnerable in the sexual sphere. "Not for a minute do I feel I'm the only victim of this so-called 'victimless' crime," Boreman said. "What about the filmed sexual abuse of children five years old or seven years old or nine years old? ... And does a person become any less of a victim at age eleven or thirteen or nineteen? Or ever?"[61] By the end of the news conference, WAP had clearly communicated its position that pornography was violence against

[59] Joseph Pratt, "Deep Six *Deep Throat*," *The New York Daily News*, June 1, 1980, clipping in the WAP Records, Box 9, Folder 540.

[60] Gay Talese, *Thy Neighbor's Wife* (Garden City, NY: Doubleday, 1980), 534.

[61] "Linda Lovelace's Personal Statement," *WAP NewsReport* (July/August 1980): 2.

women: The first victims were those who were filmed in its production, and all women subsequently suffered degradation and harm from its consumption.

The star power of WAP's spokespersons ensured public attention. The *Ordeal* news conference was covered by every major New York television news program, and the publication of Boreman's book was reported by dozens of influential newspapers and magazines, including a sympathetic five-page feature story in *Ms.* penned by Gloria Steinem.[62] The article celebrated Boreman's new life as a wife and mother, and gave a favorable accounting of her daily routines of prayer and housecleaning. Steinem marveled at Boreman's strength escaping a life of sexual slavery: "In the microcosm of this one woman is the familiar miracle; the way in which women survive – and fight back," she wrote.[63]

Boreman was a powerful spokesperson for WAP. Her story proved the existence of the coercion and brutal treatment (male power backed by force) that members of WAP believed were endemic to prostitution and pornography. She presented a compelling, possibly irrefutable counterargument to those who maintained that sex work could be a source of erotic and economic power for women, and that the women shown in pornography were just acting. When the most famous porn star of all time revealed that she had filmed *Deep Throat* under barbaric conditions – imprisoned, beaten, raped, tortured, and threatened with a loaded gun – she confirmed for members of WAP and many others that images of sexual violence on film and real-world sexual violence were one and the same. "*Deep Throat* is more than the account of the abuse of one woman," WAP wrote in response to *Ordeal*. "It bears witness to the slavery of thousands of women and girls trapped by poverty, violence, and fear in an industry that reaps four billion dollars a year from their degradation."[64]

Speaking about Boreman in 1982, MacKinnon held her up as an example of women's experience with heterosexual relations more generally. In having to smile and show "apparent enjoyment" during what was actually a terrible, abusive sexual encounter, MacKinnon saw a situation that she believed many women endured. Boreman's story was on one hand "individually extreme, specifically horrible and unusually brutal," yet on the other hand was, "a very common, everywoman kind of experience."[65] Sex was a dangerous proposition for women under patriarchy, laced with the threat of punishment to be exacted should women not comply with male demands. "From pornography one learns that forcible violation of women is the essence of sex," MacKinnon later wrote.[66] If Lovelace's experience was typical, and widespread physical

62 Gloria Steinem, "Linda Lovelace's 'Ordeal,'" *Ms.* (May 1980): 72–76.

63 Steinem, "Linda Lovelace's 'Ordeal,'" 76.

64 Press Release, "Protest *Deep Throat*," May 31, 1980, WAP Records, Box 9, Folder 540.

65 Catharine A. MacKinnon, "Linda's Life and Andrea's Work," in *Feminism Unmodified: Discourses on Life and Law* (Cambridge, MA: Harvard University Press, 1987), 128.

66 Catharine A. MacKinnon, "Sexuality, Pornography and Method: 'Pleasure Under Patriarchy,'" in Cass Sunstein, ed., *Feminism and Political Theory* (Chicago: University of Chicago Press, 1990), 219.

abuse of women occurred in and resulted from pornography, creating a constant and inescapable state of sexual inequality, then the regulation of pornography would be necessary to ensure women's basic rights under the law.

Even male liberals who had publicly clashed with WAP had to acknowledge that Boreman's testimony offered strong support for restrictions on pornography. It became easier to believe that physical abuse was pervasive in the pornography industry when Lovelace said so than if the same complaint had been lodged "by a performer in some obscure film," observed Aryeh Neier, who had just stepped down as the national director of the ACLU.[67] Writing in the *Nation*, Neier concluded that Boreman's revelations provided the "elusive link" between pornography and actual harm to women, which supported the feminist argument that pornography was a form of forced sex and provided a basis for its prohibition through censorship. Traditionally, liberals maintained that if pornography could be proven to have harmful consequences, restrictions on its production and distribution would be justifiable. Boreman's story offered such proof, and it shattered the myth of the "happy hooker" and replaced it with a view of women who plied their trade under extreme duress. This too was important, as it relieved anti-pornography feminists of the burden of condemning women who claimed to freely choose sex work, and allowed them to frame these women as vulnerable victims of gender oppression.[68]

The *Ordeal* news conference did help WAP mount a serious challenge to those who argued that pornography was harmless and even liberating sexual entertainment. Boreman was not a sexual radical, but an exploited woman coerced into prostitution and pornography. "How many Linda Lovelaces

[67] Aryeh Neier, "Memoirs of a Woman's Displeasure," *The Nation*, August 16, 1980, 156.

[68] The story of Linda Lovelace's forced descent into prostitution and pornography, and ultimately her return to respectability through marriage reminded feminist historians critical of anti-pornography of 19th century middle-class feminist accounts of female sexual victimization. Ellen DuBois and Linda Gordon pointed out in response to the anti-pornography movement that 19th-century feminists viewed prostitution (a category that included all women engaged in extramarital sex) as so degrading that no woman could choose it of her own free will. The prostitute was "a direct victim, not only of male dominance in general, but of kidnapping, sexual imprisonment, starvation, and/or seduction in particular." The feminist reformers aimed to rescue these "fallen" women through marriage, which would put an end to sexually impure ways and allow natural purity and piety to emerge. The prostitutes, however, had to acknowledge their status as victims if they wished to avail themselves of feminist aid. As DuBois and Gordon observed: "The 'white slavery' interpretation of prostitution – that prostitutes had been forced into the business – allowed feminists to see themselves as rescuers of slaves." See Ellen Carol DuBois and Linda Gordon, "Seeking Ecstasy on the Battlefield: Danger and Pleasure in Nineteenth-Century Feminist Thought," in Carole Vance, ed., *Pleasure and Danger: Exploring Female Sexuality* (Boston: Routledge and Kegan Paul, 1984), 33, 38. See also Peggy Pascoe, "Gender Systems in Conflict: The Marriages of Mission-Educated Chinese American Women, 1874–1939," *Journal of Social History* 33, no. 3 (1989): 631–652. For a discussion of contemporary feminist historians' view of similarities between the two campaigns, see Lisa Duggan, "Feminist Historians and Antipornography Campaigns: An Overview," in *Sex Wars: Sexual Dissent and Political Culture*, eds. Lisa Duggan and Nan D. Hunter (New York: Routledge, 1995), 65–70.

will never be able to tell of their ordeals?" WAP mused in the press release for the *Ordeal* news conference.[69] Critical observers worried, however, that the depiction of women working in the sex trade as utterly bereft of agency created a debilitating stereotype. A fuller perspective on women working in prostitution or as pornography models had to allow for a multifaceted portrait to emerge, one that acknowledged elements of power as well as victimization. As the feminist philosopher Linda LeMoncheck has written of this tension, "[W]omen's sexuality under patriarchy constitutes a dialectical relation between defining sexual subject and abused sexual object."[70] The organization's unremitting focus on the dangers women faced in the sexual sphere would become a focus of feminist criticism, but one of the organization's most significant accomplishments in the early 1980s was giving voice to women who did find themselves imprisoned in a life of prostitution and pornography. WAP made important inroads in public consciousness as it called attention to the potential for coercion in the production of pornography.

Fighting "The Lolita Syndrome" and the Sexual Exploitation of Girls

As previously noted, one of the themes that characterized WAP activity in the early 1980s was concern over the increased sexualization of girls in mainstream and adult-themed media. WAP leader Dorchen Leidholdt had expressed this worry at the organization's 1979 East Coast conference, and was quoted in the *New York Times* to the effect that an increase in kiddie porn and child sexual abuse could be interpreted as a male reaction to the gains of the women's movement. "Part of the backlash," she told the *Times*, "is men who are unable to relate to women as equal human beings turning to little girls."[71] WAP members worried that men who could not accommodate to the new reality of liberated women demanding equal treatment would take their frustration out on immature girls with few defenses. Media presentations of young girls as sexually experienced and desirable seemed likely to escalate the potential for real-life exploitation.

These concerns found strong advocates within WAP, as the organization was home to a number of prominent writers and therapists centrally concerned with the problem of child molestation. Most notably, WAP steering committee member Florence Rush was the author of *The Best Kept Secret: The Sexual Abuse of Children*. In this 1980 book, Rush claimed that almost 20 percent of children engaged in a sexual encounter with an adult before the age of fourteen. Rush had also contributed an essay on child pornography to WAVPM's *Take Back the Night* collection. She was a leading voice within WAP regarding the sexual exploitation of children, and was instrumental in pointing out

[69] Press Release, "Protest *Deep Throat*," May 31, 1980, WAP Records, Box 9, Folder 540.

[70] LeMoncheck, "Loose Women, Lecherous Men," 209.

[71] Leslie Bennetts, "Conference Examines Pornography as a Feminist Issue," *New York Times*, September 17, 1979, B10.

that the erotic images of girls typically present in magazines like *Hustler* had come to pervade mainstream advertising and entertainment, putting young girls at great risk.

In the spring of 1981, members of WAP became concerned about a new Broadway production of the 1958 Vladimir Nabokov novel, *Lolita.* The novel had been adapted for the stage by playwright Edward Albee, creator of *Who's Afraid of Virginia Woolf,* the 1962 play regarded as sexually bold in its time. Following the Nabokov novel, *Lolita* told the story of a sexual relationship between a middle-aged man and his twelve-year-old stepdaughter, but the Albee version took liberties with the characters' roles.[72] The *Village Voice* reported that Albee departed from the original story and cast Lolita, rather than Humbert, as the active agent in the love affair.[73] Members of WAP criticized the play for portraying pubescent Lolita "as a deliberate seductress" and Humbert as her powerless victim in an attempt to "justify pedophilia" and ignore the damage associated with child molestation.[74] WAP's Leidholdt characterized this Lolita as a "demon nymphette" who "prances seductively around the stage, seduces her middle-aged stepfather ... delightedly rides him in intercourse, and is unharmed by their 'relationship.'"[75] Scheduled to open on March 19 following dismal previews in Boston, members of WAP saw an opportunity to protest media depictions of little girls as sexual temptresses and to point out that sexual abuse of girls, including incest and rape, were the real-life consequences.[76]

On March 2, 1981, WAP held a news conference and announced a picket to protest the Broadway premiere of *Lolita.* At the news conference, WAP insisted that the sexual objectification of girls present in mainstream media as well as pornography was creating a climate where such depictions were considered "normal."[77] The participants included Florence Rush, Dorchen

[72] The actress who played Lolita in the Broadway stage version was twenty-four years old.

[73] Richard Goldstein, "Kids Do the Darndest Things," *The Village Voice*, September 24, 1981, quoted in Leidholdt, "Women Against Pornography Protests 'The *Lolita* Syndrome,' *WAP NewsReport* (Spring-Summer 1981): 2. In the Nabokov novel, the emphasis is on Humbert's sexual preoccupation.

[74] "Press Conference on the Lolita Syndrome," in *Grant Proposal for 1983–84*, n.d., WAP Records, Box 12, Folder 725, 20.

[75] Leidholdt, "Women Against Pornography Protests 'The *Lolita* Syndrome,'" *WAP NewsReport* (Spring-Summer 1981): 3. The degree to which the novel's Lolita was a sexual agent in her own right is open to interpretation. Certainly, Lolita's escape from a cross-country motel-hopping trek with Humbert into the arms of another lover, the playwright Clare Quilty, shed some doubt on the characterization of her as a helpless victim. In a classic review of the novel that appeared in *the Atlantic Monthly* in 1958, Lolita is described as fatally seductive. During their first sexual encounter, Humbert is shocked to discover that she turns out to be utterly depraved. See Charles Rolo, review of *Lolita*, by Vladimir Nabokov, *Atlantic Monthly*, September 1958, 78.

[76] The majority of the theater critics in Boston panned the play. See, for example, Kevin Kelly, "Albee Trashes Nabokov's Classic," *The Boston Globe*, February 2, 1981, 24, clipping in the WAP Records, Box 9, Folder 541.

[77] Judy Klemesrud, "'*Lolita* Syndrome' is Denounced," *The New York Times*, March 3, 1981, B24.

Leidholdt, Katherine Brady, author of *Father's Days*, a memoir describing her ten-year sexual relationship with her father; writer Louise Armstrong, whose 1978 book, *Kiss Daddy Goodnight*, presented the personal narratives of women who had survived incest; and pediatricians and social workers familiar with child sexual abuse.

During the news conference, the participants condemned the production of *Lolita* and the social problem of the sexual exploitation of girls. Dr. Helen Rodriguez-Trias, a Puerto Rican-born pediatrician who was active in the anti-sterilization abuse movement and who served as the director of a child sexual abuse unit at a New York City hospital, was quoted in the *New York Times* describing the play as "a vehicle for an ideology that says it's all right to exploit youngsters."[78] Dee Livingston, a social worker, said that *Lolita* gave men "encouragement and permission" to have sex with children.[79] Members of WAP introduced the idea of "the *Lolita* syndrome," a wide-ranging cultural phenomenon that they defined as "eroticized images of little girls which now flourish in every form of the media," including adult magazines like *Playboy*, *Penthouse*, and *Hustler*, advertisements, movies such as *Pretty Baby*, and Broadway plays.[80] They argued that seductive appeals such as the Calvin Klein jeans campaign featuring a partially-clad, fifteen-year-old Brooke Shields portrayed girls as sexually willing and mature, and implicitly sanctioned their sexual abuse.[81]

Two weeks later, WAP staged a demonstration on the play's opening night. About fifty people showed up to picket outside the Brooks Atkinson theater, waving posters with slogans reading: "The Lolita Syndrome Exploits Girls" and "Twenty-Five Percent of All Rape Victims are Under Twelve." The demonstrators shouted: "Lolita is a lie, pass it by!" to discourage theatergoers.[82] Media coverage of the news conference and picket was widespread, appearing in the *New York Times*, *Time*, *People*, the *New York Post*, and *The New York Daily News*, as well as on broadcasts of *Good Morning America* and *The Today Show*. The play closed after one week in the face of lukewarm reviews, WAP protest, and poor ticket sales.[83] The organization reported in its

78 Klemesrud, "'*Lolita* Syndrome' is Denounced.".

79 Klemesrud, "'*Lolita* Syndrome' is Denounced."

80 Press Release, "The *Lolita* Syndrome," n.d., WAP Records, Folder 411, Box 8.

81 Calvin Klein received the organization's 1982 ZAP award for sexist advertising for this campaign, which WAP denounced as "child pornography" and as "sexualizing a very young model as a mature, experienced seductress." "ZAP!" *WAVPM NewsPage* 6, no. 3 (March 1982): 2.

82 The placards are described in Dorchen Leidholdt, "Women Against Pornography Protests 'The *Lolita* Syndrome': Anatomy of an Action," *WAP NewsReport* (Spring-Summer 1981): 1. The picketers' shouts are described in T. E. Kalem, "Lo and Hum as Ho and Hum," *Time*, March 30, 1981, 65.

83 Many reviewers thought that Albee took excessive artistic license with Nabokov's work, rewriting a classic exploration of human sexual desire. Most panned the play on the grounds that the stage adaptation was boring, that it lacked the nuanced psychological elements of the novel and featured witless dialogue. See for example, Jack Kroll, "Albee's Humbert Humbug," *Newsweek*, 30 March 1981, 85; Kalem, "Lo and Hum as Ho and Hum.".

newsletter that the telephone at the WAP storefront was "ringing with calls" from people who wanted to know how they could fight "the Lolita syndrome," and members agreed that it had been one of WAP's most successful actions. By 1982, the organization was listing the sexual exploitation of children as one of its core organizing issues, and members intended to stage one major action per year to raise awareness about this problem.[84]

Although the production was a critical flop, worried observers noted that the selection of *Lolita* as an object of protest flew in the face of previous WAP assurances that the organization was anti-censorship. Dolores Alexander had assured party-goers at the 1979 East Hampton fundraiser that WAP had "no quarrel" with art or literature "or reasonable facsimiles thereof."[85] Whether or not one appreciated Albee's stage version of the novel, it did seem to qualify as a "reasonable facsimile" of literature, and the WAP protest played a role in its demise. Writing in the *Nation* nine months prior, Neier had described anti-pornography feminists as part of a tide of "new censors" whose program for combatting oppression was focused on silencing speech that they found offensive or harmful. "These days," he commented, "it sometimes seems that the oppressed aggressively exercise their own First Amendment rights only when trying to interfere with the expression of those whom they see as exploiting their suffering."[86] WAP had never officially supported censorship, but in the wake of the publication of *Ordeal*, new talk of legal action against pornographers filled the air.

As in the *Deep Throat* and *Playboy* actions, there seemed to be within the *Lolita* protest an easy point of entry for members of the religious Right to join their voices with anti-pornography feminists. The sexual abuse of children had become a national hot-button issue in the mid-1970s; law enforcement figures from 1976–1977 revealed that child pornography was more readily available than ever before in adult bookstores, much of it featuring graphic images of sexual acts between children and adults. Anita Bryant's Save Our Children crusade claimed that tens of thousands of teenage boys were being recruited into homosexual rings to service adult male customers. In response, Congress passed the Sexual Exploitation of Children Act of 1977, which outlawed the commercial production and dissemination of visual or print depictions of minors engaged in sexually explicit conduct.[87] According to the historian

[84] "Accomplishments of Women Against Pornography," *Grant Proposal for 1983–84*, n.d., WAP Records, Box 12, Folder 725, 34.

[85] Letter, Dolores Alexander to East Hampton party host, August 3, 1979, WAP Records, Box 6, Folder 270.

[86] Aryeh Neier, "Expurgating the First Amendment," *The Nation* 230, no. 24, (June 21, 1980): 737.

[87] Because it failed to address the noncommercial trading of pornography and nonobscene pornography, the first iteration of the law proved largely ineffectual. In 1982, the Supreme Court began interpreting child pornography legislation in *New York v. Ferber*, when the Court upheld a state statute outlawing the promotion of a sexual performance of a child by selling nonobscene material depicting minors engaged in sexual conduct. In response to *Ferber* and problems with the noncommercial enforcement under the 1977 Act, Congress passed the

FIGURE 8.5. WAP members picket outside of New York City's Brooks Atkinson theater in March 1981 to protest a Broadway adaptation of Vladimir Nabokov's *Lolita* that portrayed the adolescent title character as a deliberate seductress. The play closed after one week. Middle: WAP member Marilyn Hayes; right: WAP founder Dolores Alexander. *Photo: Bettye Lane.*

Philip Jenkins, the late 1970s witnessed the rise of a powerful right-wing child protection lobby that presented American society as damaged by the cultural excesses of the 1960s liberation movements, and blamed such social problems as pedophilia, child pornography, child sex rings, preschool sex scandals, and satanic rock music on the "libertinism" of previous years.[88] By 1982, largely

Child Protection Act of 1984. This version eliminated the need for the material to be obscene, raised the age of protection to under 18, and included material traded noncommercially as well as commercial sales.

[88] Philip Jenkins, *Decade of Nightmares: The End of the Sixties and the Making of Eighties America* (New York: Oxford University Press, 2006), 257.

due to pressure from religious conservative interest groups, the U.S. courts were interpreting the 1977 Act in ways that made it almost impossible to explore issues of youth sexuality – even fantasy representations – without fear of prosecution. Prosecutors were empowered to convict individuals for simple possession of indecent images of children, rather than limiting criminal charges to the producers or distributors of such material.

The movement to protect children from a perceived epidemic of sexual abuse and kiddie porn was part of a larger desire on the part of the religious Right to reinstitute gender norms and impose strict limits on sexuality after a period of social and political upheaval. According to historian Lisa McGirr, who has chronicled the origins of the New Right, conservative middle-class men and women in these years were desperate to restore "a properly ordered world," the one that had been turned upside down by sexual liberation, Civil Rights, the growth of the Left, the rise of the women's movement, and the emergence of a youth counterculture.[89] By championing family values and patriarchal authority, they saw a means of challenging new social and sexual freedoms. Anti-pornography's presentation of girls like Lolita as helpless victims of male sexual predators was useful for activists who demanded parental notification for teens seeking reproductive health care and those fighting to raise the age of sexual consent.[90] During the WAP conference protesting *Lolita*, Rodriguez-Trias was quoted as saying that "conscious men and women are uniting to expose these evils," which sounded like a clarion call for broad participation across the political spectrum.[91] Once again, feminists and right-wing interest groups seemed to be supporting the same goals.

Feminists outside of anti-pornography feared the rhetoric of female victimization and the need for state-supervised protection, warning that feminist-supported state regulation of girls' sexual activity in the late 19th century had spiraled into oppressive paternalism. Between 1886 and 1895, social purity campaigners succeeded in raising the age of sexual consent to between fourteen and eighteen years of age in twenty-nine states, and enshrining the idea that sexually active girls were always victims of male coercion.[92] This focus on girls' sexual activity resulted in the creation of "teenage sex delinquents," a new category of female offenders, and juvenile detention homes established at the beginning of the 20th century were used to incarcerate teenage girls almost exclusively for sexual activity.[93] The age-of-consent legislation denied

89 Lisa McGirr, *Suburban Warrior: The Origins of the New American Right* (Princeton, NJ: Princeton University Press, 2001), 242.

90 Cottle et al., "Politics of Pornography," 313. See also Jenkins, *Decade of Nightmares*, 269, 120–121.

91 Klemesrud, "'*Lolita* Syndrome' Is Denounced," B24.

92 On the links between social purity politics and anti-pornography feminism, see Ellen Carol DuBois and Linda Gordon, "Seeking Ecstasy on the Battlefield: Danger and Pleasure in Nineteenth-Century Feminist Sexual Thought," in *Pleasure and Danger: Exploring Female Sexuality*, ed. Carole S. Vance (Boston: Routledge and Kegan Paul, 1984), 31–49.

93 Jeffrey Weeks, *Sexuality and Its Discontents: Meanings, Myths and Modern Sexualities* (London: Routledge, 1985), 230.

older girls the right to engage in sex unless they married, and could not accommodate the social changes that accompanied industrialization, including the development of a subculture of urban girls who traded sexual favors for treats, such as gifts and entertainment.[94] When religious conservatives joined WAP in objecting to sexualized portrayals of children, they did so in hopes of resurrecting a set of controls over sexuality, enforced through the family, the law, and social morality. At its root, this agenda contradicted the radical feminist drive to free women from a culture of male dominance maintained through force.

Challenges From Within: Early Women's Movement Critiques of Anti-Pornography Feminism

WAP was energetic and ambitious, and fast became the nation's most prominent feminist group speaking out on issues of female sexuality. The star power of the membership and WAP's creative, media-driven actions ensured publicity, and the group's reputation and authoritative voice developed quickly. Nonetheless, strong criticism of the anti-pornography movement emerged in the early 1980s. Women who identified as feminists but took issue with elements of anti-pornography were taken aback by the movement's hostility to alternative viewpoints and warnings about right-wing encroachment. These feminists began to write and speak about what they saw as the limitations of anti-pornography, going beyond the free speech and right-wing "bedfellows" critiques to examine the heart of cultural feminism's view of women. Much criticism was directed at the movement's conceptualization of a universal sisterhood uncomplicated by race and class, and the ensuing rejection of men and male values.

The embrace of a universal sisterhood and the lack of attention to race and class was not unique to anti-pornography feminism. American feminism from

94 These girls were wage earners by day but devoted their nights to commercial amusements, such as bars and dance halls, that offered an intriguing world of pleasure and sexual companionship. Historian Kathy Peiss has demonstrated that the girls found in both their places of employment and leisure a milieu that openly accepted physical contact between men and women, and encouraged the exchange of sexual favors for social and economic rewards. Among working girls, there was a subculture that participated in a system of treating – trading sexual favors of varying degrees for gifts and entertainment. These women, Peiss explains, were known as "charity girls," a term that differentiated them from prostitutes because they did not accept money for their sexual encounters with men. historian Beth Bailey confirms that many working class girls in urban-industrial turn-of-the-century America "fled the squalor, drabness and crowdedness of their homes to seek amusement and intimacy elsewhere." Working girls did not have sufficient wages to go out for the evening and relied on men's "treats," which were offered in exchange for sexual contact. See Beth L. Bailey, *From Front Porch to Back Seat: Courtship in Twentieth-Century America* (Baltimore: The Johns Hopkins University Press, 1989) and Kathy Peiss, "'Charity Girls' and City Pleasures: Historical Notes on Working-Class Sexuality, 1880–1920," in *Powers of Desire: The Politics of Sexuality*, eds. Ann Snitow, Christine Stansell and Sharon Thompson (New York: Monthly Review Press, 1983): 74–87.

the early 1970s forward was splintered by these questions. Feminists of color who desired a multicultural approach that placed race, ethnicity, class, and other structural inequalities on a level playing field with gender criticized white feminists for ignoring meaningful differences among women. They argued that gender-focused feminism defined oppression in ways that spoke primarily to the experiences of white, middle class, well-educated, heterosexual women.[95] By the late 1970s, the cultural feminist emphasis on valorizing women's sameness to one another and difference from men positioned divisions among women such as race and class as less significant than their sex-based commonalities. For women of color, this was a critical shortcoming. The issues of pornography and sexual violence excited many white radical feminists precisely because they seemed to affect all women, possibly uniting women across race and class in the fight. But as the sociologist Benita Roth has documented, women of color were disenchanted with this approach, feeling that white feminists lacked consciousness about class and race privilege, and emphasized cultural change (e.g., ridding society of pornography) over economic change that would have radically improved the lot of working-class people.

Each of the feminist anti-pornography groups was sincere in its desire to see women of color join, but the theoretical construct of universal sisterhood made the organizations "uncomfortable places" for feminists of color.[96] A cohesive group identity based on the idea of a sisterhood united against sexual violence seemed like a powerful basis for action, but women of color could not, even temporarily, shelve their racial and class identities, nor ignore vital connections to men of color and working-class communities, in order to build a single-issue movement with middle-class, white women. WAVPM's Judith Reisman argued in an interview in the organization's newsletter in 1978 that women needed to do just that, setting aside differences to focus on the war against pornography. "A coalition of all women needs to be established, regardless of race, color, creed or political persuasion," she wrote. "Disagreements on other issues can be dealt with when fewer of us are being murdered, beaten, tortured and raped."[97] For many women of color, this kind of untenable directive confirmed that anti-pornography was a movement whose leaders lacked

[95] See Rosemarie Tong, *Feminist Thought: A More Comprehensive Introduction*, 3rd ed. (Boulder, CO: Westview Press, 2009). These tensions are thoroughly explored in Benita Roth's book, *Separate Roads to Feminism: Black, Chicana, and White Feminist Movements in America's Second Wave* (Cambridge, UK: Cambridge University Press, 2004). See also Gloria I. Joseph and Jill Lewis, *Common Differences: Conflicts in Black and White Feminist Perspectives* (New York: Doubleday/Anchor Books, 1981). The feminist theorist Hester Eisenstein has described this aspect of cultural feminism as a "false universalism" that suggested to women that the similarity of their situation as females was more fundamental than economic, racial, or cultural differences. Cultural feminism led to analysis that "in spite of its narrow base of white, middle-class experience purported to speak about and on behalf of all women, black or white, poor or rich." See Hester Eisenstein, *Contemporary Feminist Thought* (Boston: G.K. Hall & Co., 1983), 132.

[96] Roth, *Separate Roads to Feminism*, 198.

[97] "An Interview with Judith Reisman," *WAVPM NewsPage* 2, no. 3 (April 1978): 5.

awareness of race and class issues and were insensitive to the gendered form of racism prevalent in pornography. Brownmiller had been on the receiving end of some of this anger and frustration when she tried to share WAP's strategies for the future at the 1979 East Coast conference. Audience members denounced her as a middle-class elitist and criticized WAP for not doing enough to bring in women of color, for charging a higher conference fee than working-class women could afford, and for failing to provide literature in Spanish.

Both WAVPM and WAP found it difficult to recruit women of color to their organizations and to the anti-pornography cause. In 1979, Dolores Alexander personally invited a group of Latina and black activists to attend a WAP open house, and was dismayed by the turnout. "Unhappily, not one showed up," she confided in a letter to the friend who had provided the list of names.[98] WAVPM hired Noreen McDermott, a thirty-year-old white woman, to canvass door-to-door for new organization members in 1981. McDermott found that women of color did not typically respond with enthusiasm when she described WAVPM and its beliefs and goals. Many expressed feelings of alienation from the mainstream women's movement because its groups seemed to focus on problems that were framed in terms of white women's needs, such as abortion on demand, rather than ending sterilization abuse. Black women frequently saw the movement as reluctant to deal with their sexualized oppression, and with the reality of rape as a crime of sexual violence that was intertwined with myths about race. Within pornography, the depiction of black women as savage and lustful animals who desired brutal treatment was part of the legacy of slavery, recalling that it was not illegal in the United States during the time of slavery to rape an African-American woman slave.[99] African women were legally sanctioned targets for male sexual abuse and were cast as immoral and undeserving of respect to facilitate their sexual exploitation by white men. McDermott wrote in *NewsPage* that she tried to overcome this chasm by sharing WAVPM's analysis of racist images in pornography. "I talk about ... how black women are pictured being raped by white men, and how this portrayal of the master/slave relationship evolved as a tactic of political terrorism," she reported. "I talk about how Asian women are pictured in pornography as childish and exotic sex toys."[100] Although McDermott did her best to communicate the group's commitment to analyzing the intersections of class, race, and sexual oppression, few women of color elected to join.[101]

[98] Letter, Dolores Alexander to a feminist friend, September 28, 1979, WAP Records, Box 6, Folder 270.

[99] See Thomas D. Morris, *Southern Slavery and the Law, 1619–1860* (Chapel Hill: University of North Carolina Press, 1996), 305. See also Amii Larken Barnard, "The Application of Critical Race Feminism to the Anti-Lynching Movement: Black Women's Fight Against Race and Gender Ideology, 1892–1920," *UCLA Women's Law Journal* 1, no. 2–3 (1993).

[100] "Why Are We Involved in WAVPM? Interviews with Three Members," *WAVPM NewsPage*, 5, no. 2 (November 1981): 2.

[101] Women of color were actively engaged in sex-related issues that affected the everyday health of women in their communities, including sterilization abuse, and access to reproductive

The slide show presentations offered another opportunity for anti-pornography feminists to reach out to women of color, but some viewers pointed out that the accompanying scripts offered limited analyses of racism in pornography. This included both the sexual abuse of women of color by white men and the related problem that images of white women engaged in sexual intercourse with men of color were seen as especially brutal and corrupting. This seemed like further evidence to many women of color that anti-pornography's agenda was anti-sexist but not actively anti-racist. A member of a NOW chapter in Lubbock, Texas, wrote to WAP in 1980 to share audience feedback. "There were some criticisms of the show, and a couple that I thought were especially valid," she wrote. "One had to do with the assumption that the black magazines were necessarily aimed toward the black male. I realize that *Black Bondage* states that it is, but we wondered if there isn't another thing going on with the white male-black woman that is unexplored in the show."[102] The NOW viewers thought that the images of black women in bondage were linked to slavery and perpetuated the racist historic right of white male sexual access to black women's bodies. The scripted WAP commentary to be read along with that slide said only that the magazine was trying to create a new market among black men for bondage pornography by featuring black women tied up in ropes. The NOW audience members argued that this material was produced for white men and complained that the WAP analysis downplayed the discussion of racism to protect the idea that all women were equally oppressed by, and all men were equally implicated in, the production and consumption of pornography.

In 1982, WAP received a lengthy letter from a member of Cleveland WAVAW, who expressed her dissatisfaction with the analysis of racism in the WAP slide show. Like other women of color who tried to participate in the anti-pornography movement, she felt tremendous isolation. "I have been from the inception, and remain, the only Black member," she wrote of her WAVAW chapter. For more than a year, members of Cleveland WAVAW had been presenting the WAP slide show all over northeastern Ohio. From her perspective, the show's discussion of black women in pornography was incomplete because it did not provide sufficient social and historical context regarding their sexual exploitation. "There are five slides of Black women in the slide show," she wrote. "Yet during each presentation, during each discussion, they/I/we remain invisible."[103]

care as well as abortion, but not anti-pornography. Many saw the white, middle-class leadership of anti-pornography as disconnected from the realities in their communities, having no firsthand experience with sex-related issues that were directly tied to class and race, such as what it was like to be a Latina who consented to a tubal ligation because the medical explanation and consent forms were available only in English. These kind of distinctions separated anti-pornography and other white radical feminists from working-class and Third World feminists throughout the women's movement.

102 Letter, NOW member in Lubbock, Texas to WAP, 29 April 1980, WAP Records, Box 6, Folder 268.

103 The slide show consisted of approximately forty slides. Letter, Black female member of Cleveland WAVAW to WAP, February 23, 1982, WAP Records, Box 3, Folder 100.

The Cleveland WAVAW member offered a series of observations about common portrayals of black women in pornography that WAP did not articulate. These included that black women were rarely depicted in softcore pornography, but almost exclusively in hardcore, where they were shown as "base, brutal, sadistic, savage, and willing to submit to any sexual practice." She believed that WAP needed to explain that these images were ritual reenactments of the sexual subjugation of African women produced for white men to enjoy. This contemporary depiction of black women as promiscuous, or as the sociologist Barbara Omolade has described this distortion, "whorish and loose," had to be connected to slavery and the continuing sexual exploitation of black women's bodies.[104] The WAVAW member pointed out that the slide show ignored these issues. "Why does the slide show script avoid the implication of active white racism in the production as well as consumption of such materials?" she asked [emphasis in original]. This "benign negligence" was harmful and left audiences with the impression that the material was produced solely for black men. It allowed white, middle-class women to comfort themselves with the thought that their husbands and sons were not the ones using the crude and savage porn featuring black women. "The point is that pornography tells lies about women; our bodies, our feelings, our lives," she concluded. "But it tells more lies, and more revealing lies, about some of us than others."[105]

Five years after its founding, WAVPM's membership was not diverse, a situation also encountered in WAVAW and WAP. "White women need to put energy into learning from women of color and their struggles," two WAVPM members urged in *NewsPage* in 1981. "A group whose active members are 95 percent white will always need to beware of ignoring the connections between sexism and racism."[106] These writers pressed WAVPM to build coalitions with women of color, but anti-pornography (like most radical feminist groups of the second wave) remained predominantly white. Furthermore, movement actions tended to focus on the exploitation of white women and children like Linda Boreman and *Lolita*, and advanced a sexually conservative ethic that harked back to Victorian notions of "passionlessness," or the belief that women had less innate sexual desire than men and thus were morally superior. Indeed, when interviewed by Steinem for *Ms.*, Boreman rejected any sexual feeling associated with her performance in *Deep Throat*: "It wasn't

[104] Barbara Omolade, "Hearts of Darkness," in Ann Snitow, Christine Stansell and Sharon Thompson, eds. *Powers of Desire: The Politics of Sexuality* (New York: Monthly Review Press, 1983), 362. Patricia Hill Collins has argued that the treatment of black women's bodies in 19th-century Europe and the United States is the very foundation upon which contemporary pornography is based. See Patricia Hill Collins, *Black Feminist Thought: Knowledge, Consciousness and the Politics of Empowerment* (New York: Routledge, 1990). See also bell hooks, "Continued Devaluation of Black Womanhood," in *Ain't I a Woman: Black Women and Feminism* (Boston: South End Press, 1981).

[105] Letter, Black female member of Cleveland WAVAW to WAP, February 23, 1982, WAP Records, Box 3, Folder 100.

[106] Linda Shields and Julianne Chatelain, "WAVPM's First Five Years," *WAVPM NewsPage* 6, no. 5 (May 1982): 3.

sexual. I never experienced any sexual pleasure, not one orgasm, nothing."[107] The ideal of true womanhood, of which passionlessness was an integral part, excluded women of color. Their collective histories as victims of racist sexual violence whose bodies were sanctioned targets for male lust made it impossible to claim the asexual high ground upon which passionlessness depended.[108]

At this juncture, anti-pornography was also coming under attack for its dichotomous characterization of men (as victimizers) and women (as victims), which followed cultural feminist theories of women's difference. Feminist authors including Dorothy Dinnerstein, Carol Gilligan, and Nancy Chodorow argued that women's experience of sexism set them fundamentally apart from men and created within them an alternative set of values, character traits, and interpersonal styles. Cultural feminists viewed these gender differences favorably and valorized female nature as moral, spiritual, and attuned to the needs of others. Women learned to "value relationships over separation, mothering over work, love over sex, mutuality over individuation," as the historian Jane Gerhard has described these supposed gender traits.[109] On the flip side, cultural feminism regarded men and "male values" as aggressive, violent, and power-hungry, and as the source of women's oppression. According to the historian Linda Gordon, cultural feminism assumed that "most social and individual evils derived from some aspect of maleness," whether rooted in male biology (testosterone) or social learning that encouraged men to dominate.[110]

Anti-pornography feminists grafted views of fixed male and female values onto sexuality, finding theories of women's innate desire for intimacy,

[107] Steinem, "Feminist Notes," 76.

[108] According to historian Nancy Cott, Victorians believed that women did not possess a sexual drive equivalent to that of men, and were inherently more pure. The stronger moral character they derived from this "passionlessness" enabled women to keep male sexuality in check and to view unrestrained sexuality as a dangerous and base force that could corrupt innocent women. The denial of a female sexual drive became an integral component of the ideal of "true womanhood." Both 19th-century and anti-pornography feminists sought to improve women's status through desexualization, emphasizing women's greater moral and spiritual character. Anti-pornography feminists celebrated "female values" like integrity, sensuality and reciprocity, and rejected the pursuit of sex as male. In *Ordeal*, Boreman cast herself as a victim of seduction and white slavery, who participated in immoral sexual activity against her will. She rejected any association between her filmed acts and physical pleasure, and when reporters asked her how her new husband could stand to have a wife with such an infamous sexual past, Boreman would deny that she had experienced any part of *Deep Throat* as sexual. In this way, Boreman embraced "passionlessness" in her drive to assert her purity. On "passionlessness," see Nancy Cott, "Passionlessness: An Interpretation of Victorian Sexual Ideology, 1790–1850," in *A Heritage of Her Own: Toward a New Social History of American Women*, eds. Nancy F. Cott and E. H. Pleck (New York: Touchstone, 1979). For Boreman comments, see Steinem, "Linda Lovelace's 'Ordeal,'" 76.

[109] Gerhard, *Desiring Revolution*, 172.

[110] Linda Gordon, "Killing in Self-Defense," *The Nation*, March 24, 1997, 27.

mutuality, and care "enormously useful" in their fight.[111] These theories supported a sexual dichotomy and allowed feminists to describe male sexuality (and its cultural expression: pornography) as violent, brutal, and alienated whereas female sexuality was gentle, interpersonally oriented, and reciprocal.[112] This dualism was first evident in WAVPM; the August 1977 issue of *NewsPage* described pornography as depicting brutal sexual behaviors that no woman would enjoy, including spanking and bondage. Pornography celebrated raw male sexuality and presented scenarios that were:

> ... for the most part totally contrary to what we know about female sexuality, i.e. it is almost totally penis-oriented, often devoid of 'foreplay,' tenderness, or caring, to say nothing of love and romance....[113]

Two years later, WAVPM conducted a series of workshops to try to figure out the distinction between erotica and pornography, terms that came to stand in for female and male sexuality. Members concluded that erotica was "personal," "natural," "fulfilling," "circular," and tapped into the "emotional, creative part of self." Pornography, by contrast, was for the "titillation of men – not with women's interests in mind," "defined by penis, men," and produced "violence," a "power imbalance," "no reciprocity," and "gratification at someone else's expense."[114]

Over time, WAVPM definitions of female sexuality moved farther away from the physical realm to embrace the spiritual. In a 1981 *NewsPage* article, a WAVPM member defined the erotic for women as a celebration of "a woman's wholeness and integrity."[115] Most anti-pornography feminists could agree that erotica was nonsexist and nondegrading, but as the movement progressed, it became almost impossible to look at any heterosexual image (especially images featuring "male-defined" acts like fellatio or penetrative sex) without seeing subordination. Critics of the movement began to argue that anti-pornography had circumscribed the range of sexual behavior deemed nonexploitative, restricting the definition of acceptable female sexual behavior to monogamous lesbianism and defining male and female sexuality in ways that recalled the Victorian ideology of "separate spheres."[116] They warned that associating a strong sexual drive with men and a concern for emotional bonding and deep spiritual connection with women, would threaten women's right to pursue an active sexual life.

[111] Gerhard, *Desiring Revolution*, 173.

[112] Alice Echols has written the major critique of anti-pornography's views of sexuality as reflecting cultural feminism. See Echols, "The Taming of the Id," 50–72.

[113] *WAVPM NewsPage*, 1, no. 3 (August 1977).

[114] Sue Scope, "Erotica Versus Pornography: An Exploration," *WAVPM NewsPage*, 3, no. 6 (July 1979), 1.

[115] Lisa Falls, "Leslie Simon on: The Erotic," *WAVPM NewsPage*, 5, no. 3 (March 1981), 1.

[116] Judith Walkowitz, *Prostitution and Victorian Society: Women, Class and the State* (Cambridge, UK: Cambridge University Press, 1980), 256. On monogamous lesbianism as the only feminist choice, see Tong, *Feminist Thought*, 68–73.

Conclusion: A Difficult Dance for WAP

The early 1980s were complex years for WAP, full of accomplishment and national recognition, but also marked by mounting criticism emerging from within the women's movement and the Left. The organization was attacked for advancing a politics that was open to right-wing cooptation; for racism and essentialism; for undermining free speech; and for devaluing the liberatory potential of female sexuality. At the same time that WAP struggled to defend itself against these charges, the pornography problem only deepened. WAP members looked with anger and dismay at the cable television boom, the spread of home video technology, and the introduction of 1–900 recorded and live adult chat telephone sex lines, all of which made it easier to purchase access to women's bodies. WAP members were committed to improving the material conditions of womens' lives, but were increasingly caught up in internecine feuds that sapped time and energy.

In 1980, Dolores Alexander and other WAP steering committee members found themselves in conflict with members of a recently formed feminist anti-pornography group based in Pittsburgh. The Pittsburgh women had been influenced by WAP's 1979 East Coast conference and March on Times Square, and had organized a satellite chapter the following month using the name Pittsburgh Women Against Pornography.[117] They were showing a modified version of the WAP slideshow and selling WAP buttons, giving credit to the New York group. After several months, the Pittsburgh group decided to abandon the original name, and call themselves Women Against Sexist Violence in Pornography and Media (WASVP/M) instead. They also jettisoned a WAP policy that held that women, not men, were to speak on behalf of the movement as experts on pornography and its effects on women's lives. The Pittsburgh women planned an anti-pornography conference and invited the psychologists Edward Donnerstein and Neal Malamuth to share their nationally recognized experimental laboratory research demonstrating that exposure to sexually violent material increased the likelihood of sexual aggression. In New York, WAP steering committee members were infuriated, feeling that discarding the organization's name was tantamount to ignoring WAP's influence and national leadership, and turning to male experts devalued women's hard-won authority on the question of pornography's harms.

Members of the Pittsburgh group tried to mend fences with WAP by explaining the rationale behind the changes. In a lengthy letter to Alexander, Pittsburgh founding member Heidi Swarts defended the invitation to Donnerstein and Malamuth on the grounds that the scientists offered useful "hard data" regarding pornography's effects on male attitudes and behavior that only strengthened the feminist case. Regarding the name change, she explained that right-wing anti-pornography groups in the Pennsylvania area

[117] Letter, Heidi Swarts, Pittsburgh Women Against Pornography to Dorchen Leidholdt, November 11, 1979, WAP Records, Box 14, Folder 862.

were trying to incorporate the WAP name and message into their efforts, scaring away potential feminist supporters. "Some are right now trying to use us and our slideshow to push their repressive anti-porn bill," Swarts wrote. "Many leftists, progressives, and feminists here have been leery of us and our goals (NOW chapters have even avoided us!) and a lot of it has been the name."[118] In a statement about the name change distributed at their May 1980 conference, WASVP/M noted that the Right was concerned with many of the same issues as the women's movement, especially sexuality, pornography, and abortion, and wanted to claim common ground with feminists to disguise their sexist goals. Religious conservatives planned "to use our materials, our energy, our devotion to this issue in ways that might take the feminist struggle several steps backward," the group warned.[119] Ultimately, the Pittsburgh women wanted a name that would discourage right-wing affiliation and would differentiate the feminist struggle against sexist violence from the conservative-moralist battle against sexual freedom and women's rights.

As this episode reveals, the early 1980s brought trying times to WAP. Conservative political action committees formed in the late 1970s had transformed huge numbers of religious conservatives to activists, with tens of thousands flooding into the secular arena of anti-pornography activity. Although WAP was always careful to affirm its feminist principles, it was difficult to ignore such a large, well-funded, politically organized movement that courted anti-pornography feminists and shared outrage about pornography at the same time that supposed allies on the male Left and even fellow feminists challenged the organization and its goals. Mutual feelings about pornography's harms encouraged some WAP members to see women of the New Right as part of feminism's unreached constituency, and opened up the possibility for coalition building. Others, however, feared such alliances. A WAP member wrote to friends in the Boston WAVAW chapter in the early 1980s and expressed her concern that the feminist anti-pornography groups would soon find themselves among "stronger bedfellows." She thought that it was urgent for feminists to "be real clear about why we are opposed to porn so we don't get lost in <u>their</u> argument,"[emphasis in original] differentiating between feminist and right-wing opposition to pornography in recognition of the potential for slippage. "Goddess forbid," she shuddered, "that we should be aligned with Reagan."[120]

By the early 1980s, WAP had to execute a difficult dance: The organization wanted to draw more mainstream support to increase its numbers,

118 Letter, Heidi Swarts of Women Against Sexist Violence in Pornography and Media to Dolores Alexander, May 1980, WAP Records, Box 6, Folder 270.

119 WASVP/M conference handout, "Two Frequently Asked Questions Regarding This Conference and Our Group's Name," WAP Records, Box 14, Folder 862.

120 Letter, Woman in Olympia, WA to Boston WAVAW, November 13, no year. Boston WAVAW Papers, Box 1, Folder: Correspondence Undated. The letter describes possible action from the new federal administration on anti-pornography legislation, so the date is most likely 1980–1981, as Reagan assumed office.

membership, and influence, but was also keenly aware of the need to keep the message feminist and not allow the organization's work to be co-opted. The Pittsburgh women stepped away from the WAP name and WAP's national leadership to prevent any right-wing encroachment, a move that was possible only because this satellite group assumed no responsibility for bringing the anti-pornography message to the national stage. The pressure to lead sat firmly on WAP's shoulders, and by the early 1980s it weighed heavily.

As the ties linking anti-pornography feminists and religious conservatives seemed to tighten, feminists outside of anti-pornography began moving against the tide. Feminists who identified themselves as "pro-sex" took up the question of the revolutionary potential of women's sexual pleasure and advocated for more open and frank exploration of women's sexual desires. These individuals worried that WAP's emphasis on the potential for violence and coercion in sexual matters threatened to overtake appreciation for sex as a pleasurable, fulfilling, and life-affirming activity. They expressed concern that greater restrictions on sexually explicit material might limit a woman's ability to pursue an active sexual life. They also looked with dismay at a feminist organization that spoke little about enlarging women's rights to seek sexual pleasure, but primarily about women's sexual victimization under patriarchy. In the following chapter, I examine the rise of organized pro-sex feminist dissent. The establishment of a formal countermovement was an "agonizing" development for WAP, the radical feminist activist Sheila Jeffreys has observed, as anti-pornography feminists found themselves under full frontal attack from former allies in the women's movement.[121]

[121] Jeffreys, *Anticlimax*, 261.

9

Anti-Pornography Comes Undone

The Rise of the Feminist Pro-Sex Countermovement

The election of Ronald Reagan in 1980 and the ascendance of the New Right offered an important new political context for thinking about anti-pornography efforts. Feminists across the nation looked with grave concern at the growth of right-wing reactionism and the emergence of a power structure and a grassroots political culture openly hostile to liberal and feminist ideas. Reagan made it clear that his administration would launch an assault on the liberal state, challenging the New Deal principle that government has an obligation to help its citizens meet basic economic and social needs. Within months of taking office, the president had recommended more than $9 billion in budget cuts, taking aim at programs that provided money for day care, welfare, Medicaid and foster care, among other social services. Grant money from federal agencies that had previously funded local rape crisis centers, battered women's shelters and other anti-violence initiatives dried up. Feminist activists used to a more supportive climate under Carter's administration looked on with dismay, fear, and anger as the budgets for government-sponsored initiatives to support poor people and women were slashed.

Connected to this attack on liberalism and social welfare was an equally virulent popular backlash aimed at abortion rights, sexual freedom, gay rights, sex education, and all visible aspects of sexuality in U.S. culture that fell outside of traditional heterosexual marriage. This two-pronged approach was part of an overall program to challenge progressive ideas and to roll back some of the rights hard won by women in the arena of sexuality. As the political scientist Rosalind Petchesky has argued, the fight to deny women the right to abortion was critical to overturning women's progress toward sexual and social autonomy, and was a direct attack on women's bid for equality. "[T]he meanings resonating from abortion politics have more to do with compulsory heterosexuality, family structure, the relationship between men and women and parents and children, and women's employment," Petchesky wrote in

1981, "than they do with the fetus."[1] Feminism's threat to male power was linked to women's ability to control reproduction, and restricting abortion was a means of reasserting the supremacy of the patriarchal family and women's subordinate role within it. In response, the religious Right launched a major attack on the nation's more tolerant sexual climate and the enlarged sets of rights that the revolution had wrought, pledging to strengthen America and cure the spiritual ills created by women who had jettisoned their traditional roles as wives and mothers; homosexuals; pornography; and immoral sexual content in the arts and popular media like movies and television. Indeed, by the early 1980s, many politicized Evangelical Christians regarded the sexual revolution and the changes that accompanied it as a phenomenon that was "causing the downfall of Western civilization," as the historian David Allyn has described it.[2]

Given this frightening new revelation, many feminists cautioned that the anti-pornography movement promoted gender stereotypes and repressive sexual ideas that served right-wing interests, namely that men possessed uncontrollable sexual drives, that women were more oriented to emotional nurturing than physical release, and that sex itself was a dangerous, violent force from which vulnerable women required protection. Feminists could already see that the description of pornography as violence against women was useful to religious conservatives who wanted to eradicate nonmarital, nonreproductive sexuality and return women to the "safe" space of the home, where sex was said to be properly constrained within the bounds of marriage. These conservatives extended their use of feminist rhetoric, casting pornography, along with abortion, sex education, and divorce, as "violence against the family" that interfered with husbands' traditional control over their wives and parents' traditional control over their children.

This situation motivated pro-sex feminists to argue that a feminist campaign against pornography was a risky proposition, being undertaken at a politically inopportune moment. The state had turned sharply away from promoting women's rights and women's equality, and it was a dangerous time for women to cede sexual territory. They opposed any effort that might give the state additional power to regulate sexual expression, fearing that such power would likely be used to censor feminist, gay, and lesbian materials. Instead, they argued, feminists needed to mount a rigorous defense of female sexual pleasure, sexual variation, and the rights of sexual minorities, all of which were under attack by the Right. In sum, feminist concern coalesced around three major sets of issues: first, the potential threat to freedom of expression; second, the likelihood that anti-pornography activity would

[1] A definitive discussion of this two-headed New Right attack on feminism and social welfare policy is found in Rosalind Pollack Petchesky, "Antiabortion, Antifeminism, and the Rise of the New Right," *Feminist Studies* 7, no. 2 (Summer 1981): 206–246. The quote is found on p. 210.

[2] Allyn, *Make Love, Not War*, 274.

lead to alliances with religious conservatives whose views on sexuality were decidedly anti-feminist; and third, the failure to claim the positive aspects of sexuality for women and to defend women's right to authentic sexual liberation.

At this juncture, there was significant disquiet in the larger feminist community about the potential social ramifications of anti-pornography politics. Although pro-sex challengers opposed the movement for the reasons previously described, many were sympathetic to the fundamental claim that mass-market pornography was bad for women and agreed that its dominant messages were hateful and objectifying. They also shared anti-pornography feminists' anguish over the appalling problem of violence against women. Reflecting in 1998 on her disparaging review of the anti-pornography documentary, *Not a Love Story*, the film critic B. Ruby Rich acknowledged that she herself was "not immune to the feelings of outrage and dismay" that led women to want to stop the production and dissemination of pornography.[3] Ellen Willis also found the average piece of pornography detestable. She criticized *Deep Throat* soundly at the time of its debut, and she protested the relentless commodification of women's bodies and the obnoxious displays that had become commonplace in public spaces. In a published conversation with fellow pro-sex activists Gayle Rubin and Amber Hollibaugh, Deirdre English stated that most pornography was "deeply sexist and contains a hideous and misogynistic view of women."[4]

Thus, pro-sex feminists were not indifferent to the ills of mass-market pornography, nor did they summarily dismiss every argument advanced by the anti-pornography movement. Instead, they tended to reject the conflation of pornography and violence, to point out that the relationship between representation and action was more complex than anti-pornography allowed, and to demand that feminism must not approach sex unilaterally as an act that men craved and women feared. Most saw the potential for government censorship of sexual material as a greater danger to women than pornography itself. They worried that an attack on pornography at a time when politically powerful religious conservatives had declared their intent to restore morality to the nation (e.g., quash sexual freedom and the rights of sexual minorities) was likely to result in counterfeminist ends. The rise of organized pro-sex feminism was also intended to diversify the conversation about sexuality, which had been almost exclusively focused on male violence, women's fears, sexism, and objectification; to carve out some space for women to talk about sexual pleasure, lust, fantasy, and desire; and to challenge anti-pornography's growing control over the feminist discourse about sexuality.

[3] B. Ruby Rich, "Prologue: Sex, Gender and Consumer Culture," in *Chick Flicks: Theories and Memories of the Feminist Film Movement* (Durham, NC: Duke University Press, 2004), 260.

[4] Deirdre English, Amber Hollibaugh, and Gayle Rubin, "Talking Sex: A Conversation on Sexuality and Feminism," in *My Dangerous Desires: A Queer Girl Dreaming Her Way Home*, ed. Amber L. Hollibaugh (Durham, NC: Duke University Press, 2000), 135.

In this chapter, I explore the origins of the organized pro-sex countermovement. I begin with the clash between S/M-identified lesbians and WAVPM activists on the West Coast in the late 1970s, which intensified when NOW passed a 1980 resolution condemning pornography and sadomasochism, rejecting both as elements of healthy female sexuality. The lesbian sexual radicals maintained that anti-pornography feminists were unfairly attacking their consensual sexual practice, and they complained that persecuting a group of lesbians for their sexual behavior was antithetical to feminism's commitment to authentic sexual liberation. The radicals also argued that anti-pornography's promotion of restrictive codes for appropriate feminist sexual behavior – what they labeled vanilla sex – threatened women's need for sexual exploration and their right to pursue an active and varied sexual life without shame. Next, I look at the publication of the 1981 "Sex Issue" of the feminist journal *Heresies*, and its brazen investigation of questions of sexual desire. Finally, I turn to the Scholar and the Feminist IX conference, "Towards a Politics of Sexuality," held at Barnard College in 1982. The organizers of the Barnard Conference, as it is known, sought to shift the discourse away from themes of danger, coercion, and victimization and to create some space within feminism to return to a consideration of women's sexual pleasure. The Barnard Conference was bitterly divisive, but it brought the conflict between anti-pornography and pro-sex feminists squarely into public view and created the conditions necessary for open debate within American feminism.

The Battle Over Lesbian S/M

As discussed in Chapter 2, lesbian feminism was a product of the political climate of the early 1970s, when homophobia threatened to deny lesbians their rightful place in the women's movement. Some national leaders of NOW, most prominently Betty Friedan, perceived lesbianism early on as a "lavender menace" that threatened movement credibility, and lesbians were pushed to the margins of many women's organizations. As a result, theorists like Rita Mae Brown, Jill Johnston, and Charlotte Bunch began to theorize lesbianism's relationship to feminism, and proposed that lesbianism was a revolutionary alternative to heterosexuality. Lesbianism was recast as a challenge to the patriarchal order and male power.[5]

In keeping with radical feminism, lesbian feminists argued that heterosexuality was characterized by an ideology of sexual objectification that cast women into subordinate roles as objects and slaves. The lesbian feminist community, with which most radical feminists identified by the mid-1970s,

[5] Emma Healey writes: "Lesbian feminism and political lesbianism had initially been created as a way to bring all women, gay or straight, into a political movement that could challenge the power of patriarchy through the collective power of women's energy." Healey, *Lesbian Sex Wars* (London: Virago Press, 1996), 79.

thus rejected all forms of sexuality that perpetuated an unequal distribution of power between partners and sexual practices that relied on sexual objectification. These included S/M, which cast partners into dominant (master) and submissive (slave) roles and involved the inflicting and receiving of pain and the ritual exchange of power; and butch/femme, a form of lesbian eroticism that mimicked the gender divisions of heterosexual life, with a sexually aggressive partner whose physical appearance and clothing were masculine (butch), and a sexually passive partner who was traditionally feminine in her clothing style and self-presentation (femme).[6] Lesbian feminists urged community members to assert a proud female sexuality by rejecting these behaviors and other aspects of sex that were thought to reflect the male sexual style, particularly a focus on genital contact and orgasm, and the use of pornography. Instead, ideal lesbian sexuality elevated women's sexual priorities, which were thought to center around emotional intimacy and gentle touching. Over time, a narrow view of politically correct sexual behavior developed; critics complained that it left room for nothing more than affectionate petting.

By the late 1970s, a subculture of West Coast lesbian sexual radicals who were committed to personal sexual exploration, especially S/M, was chafing under these restrictions. They rejected lesbian feminism's parameters for acceptable sexual behavior and argued that feminists ought to reject any theoretical analyses, laws, or moral judgments that stigmatized sexual minorities. This was particularly important at a time when sexual repression was on the rise, as evidenced by Anita Bryant's successful drive in June 1977 to repeal a local ordinance in Dade County, Miami, that prohibited discrimination on the basis of sexual orientation. Others pointed to the case of the Canadian gay and lesbian magazine, *The Body Politic*, which saw three members of its editorial collective arrested in 1977 on obscenity charges for publishing an essay in defense of sexual relationships between adult men and adolescent boys. The sexual radicals warned that gay and lesbian sexuality – in both its more marginalized and conventional forms – was under forceful attack by the Right. Lesbians in this climate belonged at the forefront of the fight

[6] Lesbians were said to reinforce the ideology of objectification that characterized heterosexual relationships by adopting butch-femme roles. In their history of working-class lesbian life in Buffalo, New York, in the 1930s, 1940s, and 1950s, Elizabeth Lapovsky Kennedy and Madeline D. Davis write that the butch-femme erotic system shared some patterns with heterosexuality. "The obvious similarity between butch-fem and male-female eroticism was that they were both based on gender polarity: In lesbian culture, masculine and feminine imagery identified the objects of desire; aggressiveness and passivity were crucial to the erotic dynamic." Elizabeth Lapovsky Kennedy and Madeline D. Davis, *Boots of Leather, Slippers of Gold: The History of a Lesbian Community* (New York: Penguin Books, 1994), 192. Joan Nestle has argued that butch/femme has been described too simplistically as relying on active and passive partners, and she defines these relationships as complex erotic and social statements that were filled with a "deeply lesbian language of stance, dress, gesture, love, courage and autonomy." See Joan Nestle, "The Fem Question," in *Pleasure and Danger*, 232.

for sexual freedom, defending the right of consenting partners to engage in sexual behavior that brought them pleasure and satisfaction, without fear of condemnation or recrimination.

The historian Lillian Faderman has explored the motivations that led sexual radicals to launch a critique of lesbian feminist sexual politics. She argues that these women wanted to free lesbians from the sexual limitations that had been imposed on them as females and increase the variety and intensity of lesbian sexual pleasure. In other words, the sexual radicals recognized that lesbians were doubly oppressed, first *as women* in a culture that denied them the freedom to explore an active, desire-driven sexual life; and second *as lesbians*, constrained by a heterosexual society that defined their sexuality as criminal and perverse, and now by lesbian feminist standards that restricted permissible sexual behavior. They wanted to transcend these boundaries to create a sexual revolution by and for women. The sexual radicals intended to persuade lesbians that it was important to enjoy "the most imaginative and exciting sex their minds and bodies could construct," Faderman wrote.[7]

Given their emphasis on pleasure and power for women, it was difficult for some members of the lesbian S/M subculture to fathom that other lesbian feminists interpreted their sexuality as oppressive and male-identified. They did not agree with a feminist critique that saw S/M as a dehumanizing practice that perpetuated roles associated with male dominance, where the "top" exercised violent and sadistic control over a powerless, submissive "bottom." Practitioners defended their sexuality, arguing that lesbian S/M took place between fully consenting, equal partners who maximized each other's sexual pleasure, provided therapeutic and cathartic sexual release, and allowed women to explore positions of power denied them in male-dominated society.[8] "Why must we all love the same way?" asked Barbara Ruth, who announced in a provocative December 1975 essay that she was a feminist and a lesbian sadomasochist. "Aren't we, in fact, by having stringent 'rules' for sexual behavior miming the coercive situation of enforced heterosexuality, the sexual hell in which we all grew up?"[9] Gayle Rubin, who emerged as a leading theorist of sexuality, urged feminists to look more carefully and nonjudgmentally at alternative sexual practices, and not to characterize S/M as "the epitome of sexual hierarchy" without developing an

[7] Lillian Faderman, *Odd Girls and Twilight Lovers: A History of Lesbian Life in Twentieth-Century America* (New York: Penguin, 1991), 253.

[8] For a detailed discussion of the positive social uses of lesbian S/M, see Shane Phelan, *Identity Politics: Lesbian Feminism and the Limits of Community* (Philadelphia: Temple University Press, 1989), chapter 6. See also Weeks, *Sexuality and its Discontents*, chapter 9.

[9] Barbara Ruth, "Cathexis: A Preliminary Investigation into the Nature of S/M," in *What Color is Your Handkerchief? A Lesbian S/M Sexuality Reader*, ed. Samois (Berkeley, CA: Samois, 1979), 11. Reprinted from *Hera*, 1, no. 5 (December 1975).

understanding for the challenge it posed to sexual norms and sexual repression.[10] Foreshadowing the argument that she would advance in the influential 1984 essay, "Thinking Sex," Rubin warned that valorizing certain types of sexual behavior over others – particularly at a moment of right-wing conservative political power – would license the persecution of those who fell outside the charmed circle of state-sanctioned, legitimate sex, which privileged heterosexual, married, procreative relations. She urged feminists to develop a sexual politics that could support and defend individuals' rights to engage in a wider range of expression and behavior.

Within the later phase of the anti-pornography movement, lesbian feminists were typically not swayed by these arguments. They viewed S/M dominance and submission rituals, and the purposeful infliction of physical pain and humiliation, as well as psychological intimidation, as glorifying the unequal relations of power fundamental to a patriarchal society.[11] The assumption of master/slave sexual roles in S/M and masculine and feminine roles in butch/femme, which was also caught up in this debate, validated and reinforced social inequalities. Eroticizing these imbalances would create in women a subconscious emotional and physical attachment to an oppressive, hierarchical gender system. "We feel that S&M essentially involves one person voluntarily surrendering control ... to another," Deb Friedman and Lois Yankowski wrote in *Aegis*, a feminist anti-violence journal. "We could not accept as 'healthy' sexuality, the practice of willingly submitting to a condition similar to rape."[12] Poet and anti-pornography activist Audre Lorde also rejected S/M as a feminist option. "Even in play," she insisted, "to affirm

[10] Gayle Rubin, "Sexual Politics, The New Right, and the Sexual Fringe," in *What Color is Your Handkerchief?*, 34. Reprinted from *The Leaping Lesbian* (February 1978).

[11] See, for example, Sheila Jeffreys, "Eroticizing Women's Subordination," in *The Sexual Liberals and the Attack on Feminism*, eds. Dorchen Leidholdt and Janice G. Raymond (Elmsford, NY: Pergamon Press, 1990), 132–135. For the most complete radical feminist analysis of S/M, see Robin Linden et al., eds., *Against Sadomasochism: A Radical Feminist Analysis* (East Palo Alto, CA: Frog in the Well, 1982).

[12] Deb Friedman and Lois Yankowski, "Ban Porno?" *Aegis: Magazine on Ending Violence Against Women* (Winter/Spring 1981), 48. Lesbian feminists urged women to resist sadomasochistic thoughts and desires, even as they acknowledged that domination, control, and violence were so much a part of our cultural environment that they shaped women's sexual fantasies and desires. Lesbians could not simply indulge these desires in the name of pleasure and sexual exploration, but had to recognize the origins of those feelings and the ways in which a celebration of submission and dominance perpetuated the inequalities and oppressions of a patriarchal society. On this point, see Ann Snitow's exploration of how Harlequin romance novels use commonly experienced psychological and social elements in the daily lives of women to create their erotic pull. As Snitow describes it, Harlequins illustrate "the particular nature of the satisfactions we are all led to seek by the conditions of our culture" (247). Ann Barr Snitow, "Mass Market Romance: Pornography for Women is Different," in Ann Snitow, Christine Stansell and Sharon Thompson, eds., *Powers of Desire: The Politics of Sexuality* (New York: Monthly Review Press, 1983), 245–263.

that the exertion of power over powerlessness is erotic, is empowering, is to set the emotional and social stage for the continuation of that relationship, politically, socially, and economically."[13] Anti-pornography feminists insisted that these polarized behaviors normalized the social dichotomy of male power and female powerlessness, and that women who participated were encouraging sexual objectification, and through it male sexual violence, and were supporting the patriarchal patterns of racist and sexist domination that feminists sought to eradicate.[14]

Samois Battles WAVPM

The battles between anti-pornography feminists and lesbian sexual radicals began on the West Coast in the late 1970s, as groups on the sexual fringe empowered by gay liberation began to emerge and demand recognition. Samois, which identified itself as a lesbian feminist S/M support group, marched in the 1978 Gay Freedom Day Parade in San Francisco.[15] During the march, members of Samois and the Society of Janus, an S/M educational organization, handed out copies of "Don't Close the Closet Door Just Because There's Leather Inside," an essay that demanded acknowledgment from the gay and lesbian communities. "While others were marching militantly out of their closets, we were urged to keep a low profile, leave our leather at home, and keep quiet about the whole business," the essay read.[16] The political scientist Shane Phelan has argued that gay liberation made sadomasochists think

[13] Audre Lorde and Susan Leigh Star, "Interview with Audre Lorde," in *Against Sadomasochism*, 4.

[14] The most complete analysis of the anti-pornography movement's beliefs about lesbian sadomasochism appears in *Against Sadomasochism*, which grew out of a 1980 WAVPM forum, and to which several WAVPM members contributed. The truth about S/M probably lies somewhere in-between the anti-pornography (lesbian feminist) and sexual radical perspectives. Lynn Chancer has argued that S/M is best described as "*both* sometimes a legitimate form of consensual activity *and* a practice that is often rendered especially attractive, maybe even predictably seductive, precisely because of its resonance with common experiences of our everyday lives." These common experiences include teacher/student, doctor/patient, employer/employee relationships and other common relationships of power that structure our lives. See Lynn Chancer, *Reconcilable Differences: Confronting Beauty, Pornography, and the Future of Feminism* (Berkeley: University of California Press, 1998), 201–202.

[15] Samois was an offshoot of Cardea, an S/M group that was open to heterosexual women and lesbians. Members split off to form Samois in response to the special problems of isolation and stereotyping experienced by lesbian sadomasochists, including their vilification in the lesbian feminist movement. The formation of Samois is discussed in K. Kaufmann, "Playing with Samois," *Plexus* 8 (August 1980): 13. The group's stated purposes included: 1) circulating information on safe S/M techniques and practices; 2) developing lesbian feminist perspectives on S/M; 3) promoting discussion of S/M in the women's community; and 4) creating a network of personal support for S/M lesbians to build community, lessen isolation, and sharpen consciousness.

[16] Skip A., "Don't Close the Closet Door Just Because There's Leather Inside," in *What Color is Your Handkerchief?*, 26.

that a proud "coming out" was their right and responsibility. These individuals were ready to proclaim their sexual identities and receive community support and respect.

As West Coast organizations, both WAVAW and WAVPM encountered Samois, but only WAVPM saw the issue of lesbian sadomasochism as having some bearing on their cause. Members of WAVAW were aware of the controversy over lesbian S/M by the mid-1970s, but members determined at that time that no connection existed between sadomasochism and the fight against media violence. In 1976, WAVAW leaders instructed regional chapter spokespersons to ignore questions about S/M and to stay focused on the organization's priority: the Warner music boycott. "There's still nothing wrong, per se, with what people do alone, in privacy," WAVAW leaders advised. "If they're into S&M and that's what they want to do, it's none of your business."[17]

WAVPM, on the other hand, repeatedly clashed with Samois and the San Francisco-based lesbian sadomasochist community in the late 1970s. Members of WAVPM interpreted lesbian S/M as eroticizing male supremacy and they did not agree with practitioners who labeled this behavior as feminist. "[W]e need to examine the issue of *fantasy violence*," two members observed in *NewsPage*. "Can we support S&M erotica that portrays consensual power and pleasure, while opposing portrayals of victimization that reinforce widespread oppression? [italics in original]."[18] The answer for many was: No. WAVPM members reasoned that if lesbians were freely engaging in S/M, they were doing so because women were socialized in the dominant culture to be submissive and to expect and desire domination. This patriarchal training made women think that dominance and submission were natural and desirable erotic states. As such, many WAVPM members rejected the defense of S/M as consensual, arguing that just because some women said that they enjoyed being whipped and chained did not mean that conditions for meaningful consent were actually present, but only that women internalized their oppression in order to accommodate to victimization. "Wanting or consenting to domination and humiliation does not make it non-oppressive," WAVPM founder Diana Russell said during the course of a 1980 forum on S/M, "... it merely demonstrates how deep and profound the oppression is."[19] For many activists within the anti-pornography movement, there was no way to reconcile lesbian S/M with feminism.

[17] WEA Boycott, "Questions That People Will Ask," December 1976, WAVAW Papers, Los Angeles Correspondence file. In 1983, members of WAVAW did take a stand against sadomasochism as violence against women, but the women who led the group at that time were not part of the original WAVAW, nor did they share the same interpretation of violence against women. The group had drifted so far from its roots by 1983 that founding member Joan Howarth signed a letter with a group calling itself Women on the Sexual Fringe that demanded a meeting to discuss WAVAW's negative position on S/M.

[18] Linda Shields and Julianne Chatelain, "WAVPM's First Five Years," *WAVPM NewsPage* 6, no. 5 (May 1982): 3.

[19] Diana Russell, "Sadomasochism as a Contra-Feminist Activity," *Plexus* (November 1980): 13.

In August 1978, WAVPM announced plans for its first national conference, Feminist Perspectives on Pornography, which would take place in San Francisco that fall. Pat Califia, a Bay Area lesbian sexual radical and a founding member of Samois, recalled that her group wrote to WAVPM requesting permission to lead a conference workshop on lesbian S/M. The letter was never answered, and members of Samois heard through the community grapevine that WAVPM leaders wanted no Samois presence at the conference. This shocked many Samois members, including some who were also members of WAVPM. According to Califia, these women knew that WAVPM opposed heterosexual S/M pornography, but they believed that WAVPM could and should have a "different, supportive position" on lesbian S/M.[20] In November 1978, Califia and Rubin tried to attend the WAVPM conference but were turned away at the door. According to Rubin, WAVPM's Laura Lederer and Lynn Campbell told them that sadomasochists were not welcome at a feminist meeting. "Not only the program, but the *audience* was restricted to true believers," Rubin observed several years later [italics in original].[21] According to the WAVPM women, however, neither Califia nor Rubin had registered for the conference. They tried to enter as journalists representing the Bay Area feminist newspaper *Plexus*, but had not requested press privileges ahead of time.

Following the conference, Samois began contacting WAVPM in hopes of discussing the organization's position on S/M. First, Samois asked for a presentation of the WAVPM slide show, "Abusive Images of Women in Mass Media and Pornography." According to Califia, WAVPM responded with a letter that asked Samois to explain why its members wanted to see it. After a flurry of letters and telephone calls, Califia recalled, WAVPM refused the Samois request "because our group 'glamourized violence against women,'" and because members of Samois might find the slide show "erotic."[22]

Califia and other Samois members were determined to see the slide show. They attended presentations that WAVPM put on for other community groups and were devastated to hear anti-pornography feminists describe S/M as violence against women. Rubin was troubled by an image that showed a woman tied up in S/M bondage play juxtaposed with an image of a battered woman from an actual police file. She found this "guilt-by-association

[20] Pat Califia, "A Personal View of the History of the Lesbian S/M Community and Movement in San Francisco," in *Coming to Power: Writings and Graphics on Lesbian S/M*, eds. Samois (Boston: Alyson Publications, 1981), 253. Pat Califia is now Patrick Califia. He is a female-to-male (FTM) transgendered person. Because Califia's identity as a lesbian was central to the events described in this chapter, and because he was known as Pat Califia at that time, I am using his former name and gender identity in keeping with the historical record.

[21] Gayle Rubin, "Letter to the Editors," *Feminist Studies* 9, no. 3 (Fall 1983): 599. Rubin recounted this incident in response to anti-pornography protests at the 1982 Barnard Conference, a sexuality conference planned by pro-sex feminists who consciously excluded anti-pornography feminists.

[22] Califia, "A Personal View," 254.

theory of pornography" to be "manipulative" because the WAVPM presenter implied that the batterer had been exposed to S/M images in pornography and then tried to recreate at home what he had seen.[23] Rubin complained that anti-pornography feminists were looking at material produced for a particular subculture with a particular set of conventions and beliefs, and were both interpreting it through their own framework to mean something very different and asserting that their interpretation was authoritative.[24] It worried her, and other members of Samois, that members of WAVPM contradicted experienced members of the lesbian S/M community, describing as violent and sexist the same set of images that S/M-identified lesbians interpreted as consensual.

Meanwhile, WAVPM was expanding its public critique of S/M. On January 29, 1979, the organization picketed the privately owned UC Theatre in Berkeley, which was showing the French film, *The Story of O*, based on Pauline Réage's S/M literary classic. Forty WAVPM members and supporters carried signs with slogans including "Who Says Pain is Erotic?" while chanting "The Story of O has got to go!"[25] WAVPM's *NewsPage* lambasted the film for portraying a woman who enjoyed S/M encounters, willingly wore a leather collar around her neck, and endured whippings. WAVPM founder Susan Griffin noted that *The Story of O* was largely about overpowering and silencing women, and pointed out that the heroine in the story was silenced, instructed by her master not to speak at all. Members of Samois were especially incensed at the attack on this film; the group took the name "Samois" after a lesbian dominatrix in Réage's book.[26]

Intense anger and distrust developed between Samois and WAVPM during this period. The lesbian sexual radicals believed that the anti-pornography feminists had no right to assert that their sexual practices perpetuated violence, nor to persist in harassment that might jeopardize women living on the sexual fringe. Califia recalled that others were angry because they used and enjoyed some pornography and didn't want to see all of it banned or driven underground. There was also fear among community members who wanted to produce erotic S/M lesbian literature that WAVPM opposition would make it more difficult to publish and circulate their work.[27] Samois requested a meeting shortly after the Berkeley protest to discuss WAVPM's portrayal of S/M, but were denied. Samois remained determined to confront the anti-pornography feminists.

23 Deirdre English, Amber Hollibaugh, and Gayle Rubin, "Talking Sex: A Conversation on Sexuality and Feminism," in *My Dangerous Desires: A Queer Girl Dreaming Her Way Home*, ed. Amber L. Hollibaugh (Durham: Duke University Press, 2000), 133.

24 English, Hollibaugh and Rubin, "Talking Sex," 134.

25 Angela Gennino, "WAVPM Protests 'The Story of O,'" *WAVPM NewsPage*, 3, no. 2 (March 1979), 1.

26 K. Kaufmann, "Playing with Samois," 13.

27 Califia, "A Personal View of the History of the Lesbian S/M Community and Movement in San Francisco," 255.

In July 1979, Samois sent a letter to *Plexus* and aired its complaint against WAVPM. In the letter, Samois addressed WAVPM's characterization of S/M as a sexual practice that supported male sexual violence against women. Samois asserted its right to call itself a feminist organization and criticized WAVPM for portraying S/M as "the opposite of feminism," which unfairly positioned lesbian sexual radicals as outsiders to the women's movement. Next, the group objected to WAVPM's conflation of sadomasochism and violence in its slide show presentations, pointing out that images of S/M in pornography produced for male consumers no more accurately reflected S/M practice than images of lesbians in pornography reflected real lesbianism. "Consensual s/m is no more violent than consensual lovemaking is rape," the letter claimed. Finally, Samois asked WAVPM to stop picketing films like *The Story of O* and clubs that welcomed S/M patrons, and to recognize the S/M community's right to exist.[28] The Samois letter brought the escalating feud between the groups in plain view of the larger women's movement.

Plexus asked WAVPM to answer the Samois letter. WAVPM's co-coordinators, Beth Goldberg and Bridget Wynne, did send a response, but it was brief and did not directly address Samois' major points. Goldberg and Wynne chose to reiterate WAVPM's basic goals in hopes of ending "Samois' apparent misunderstanding of our group." They wrote that WAVPM had not adopted a specific organizational policy on S/M, which seemed disingenuous after the *Story of O* protest. They also maintained that their decision to refuse Samois a meeting reflected only WAVPM's "limited amount of time and energy."[29] Goldberg and Wynne implied that Samois' quarrel with the anti-pornography movement was a marginal issue for WAVPM. Their members wanted to concentrate on the fight against pornography, not see their agenda derailed by time-consuming interactions with fringe groups whose issues had nothing to do with solving the problem of violence against women. "We believe that our priority – as WAVPM members – is putting an end to the woman-hating propaganda that threatens us all," they explained in *Plexus*, trying to reorient the conversation to the fight against pornography.[30] Furthermore, Samois' insistence that their sexual practices were "feminist" simply by virtue of the fact that they were carried out by lesbians who claimed to consciously desire them held no water with WAVPM. In an April 1980 WAVPM forum, Diana Russell confirmed the organization's dim view of S/M and groups like Samois who promoted its virtues. "Defending such behavior as healthy and compatible with feminism, even proselytizing in favor of it is about the most contra-feminist ... stance that I can imagine," Russell told the audience.[31]

28 Samois to *Plexus*, "Samois Tries to Meet WAVPM," *Plexus* (October 1979): 4.

29 Beth Goldberg and Bridget Wynne to *Plexus*, "Two Respond to Samois," *Plexus* (October 1979): 4.

30 Goldberg and Wynne to *Plexus*, "Two Respond to Samois," *Plexus*, 4.

31 Diana Russell, "Sadomasochism as a Contra-Feminist Activity," *Plexus* (November 1980): 13. WAVPM sponsored a forum on S/M held at the University of California at Berkeley on April

Two months after WAVPM's response to Samois appeared in *Plexus*, Califia published an angry account that challenged dominant anti-pornography ideas. Writing in *The Advocate*, a leading gay periodical, she warned that restrictive new codes for ideal feminist sexual behavior would limit female sexual agency and deny women the right to seek sexual pleasure on their own terms. Califia mocked "the women's groups, the political clones, the Dworkinites" as anti-sexual. She described their ideal sexual encounter as one of "holding hands, taking their shirts off and dancing in a circle." Then, she added, these "high priestesses of feminism" would be sure to fall asleep prior to orgasm, a physical response that was looked upon with disfavor as "male identified, objectifying, pornographic, noisy and undignified."[32] She and other pro-sex feminists in this period feared that enshrining the idea of female sexuality as primarily spiritual, more concerned with love and connection than physical desire, would fuel the idea that sexual variations were shameful and dangerous and would further stigmatize sexual minorities. "I don't know how long we will continue to let women's groups who believe that S/M and pornography are the same thing and cause violence against women go unchallenged because they are ostensibly feminist," she wrote, her words tangibly bitter.[33] As the anti-pornography movement expanded over the next few years, the battles between Samois and WAVPM would heat up considerably. The intense personal conflict between members of these organizations alerted many feminists to the growth of intramovement opposition to the sexual ideology that fueled anti-pornography.

Feminists of color were also exposed to the high-profile debates over S/M, which added fuel to the fire for those who believed that anti-pornography was a white women's movement that was insensitive to political realities affecting others. Many women of color felt alienated from anti-pornography efforts because they did not believe that the movement's major groups were seriously engaged in a dual struggle against racism and sexism. As discussed in the previous chapter, educational materials like the slide shows were criticized for failing to explain how racism contributed to stereotypical portrayals of women of color in pornography, such as black women shown in chains. For feminists of color, particularly black feminists, the emergence of serious debates over the use of master and slave roles in sex fantasy was offensive and insulting. The idea that feminists were fighting over whether or not it was liberating to adopt these roles, after African people had been for decades forcibly and violently thrust into slavery, was sickening.

18, 1980. This forum was a fundraiser for WAVPM and featured prominent anti-pornography feminists and WAVPM founders, including Susan Griffin and Diana Russell. Another panelist, Susan Leigh Starr, would begin work with Russell and others on the edited collection *Against Sadomasochism*, which would be published in 1982.

32 Pat Califia, "A Secret Side of Lesbian Sexuality," *The Advocate*, December 27, 1979, 20.

33 Califia, "A Secret Side of Lesbian Sexuality," 23.

Many women of color became infuriated when the S/M feminist community portrayed itself as an oppressed minority; the fact that S/M women could *voluntarily* assume positions of powerlessness and subjugation underscored how different their oppression was. Karen Sims, a black lesbian feminist, described her response to descriptions of S/M as a feminist activity as "devastating for me as a Black woman, having grown up in Black culture and being subjected to someone else's power, and having to live with that all my life," she said.[34] Others responded with similar acrimony. "How dare you take the privilege at my expense," said Rose Mason, also a black lesbian feminist. "I've never had a choice as to whether I want to deal with power issues around my life.... [I]t is a privilege that goes along with your skin color, being able to make that choice and then to make it in a decadent way is disgusting."[35] Although these women were in agreement with members of anti-pornography that S/M was an anti-feminist activity that reinforced the oppressive relations of power that structured a racist, patriarchal, capitalist society, some were less sanguine about the sheer amount of time and energy that was devoted to this debate. Ultimately, anti-pornography feminists and lesbian sexual radicals, most of whom were white, were clashing over an issue that contributed to the alienation of women of color from anti-pornography.

NOW Condemns Pornography

The backlash against anti-pornography feminism took many forms in the early 1980s. The movement and its leaders were attacked by male intellectuals on the Left who decried any effort to limit pornography as a dangerous threat to freedom of speech. And within the women's movement at large, feminists outside of anti-pornography were speaking up in defense of sexual variation and criticizing anti-porn politics as repressive and moralistic. Critics from both camps asserted that newly emerging connections among anti-pornography feminists and Evangelical Christian activists were troubling and misguided. These antagonisms were disheartening to anti-pornography activists, many of whom had difficulty understanding how a movement dedicated to eradicating hateful propaganda against women could be so vilified. Movement activists were buoyed by a significant victory in 1980, however, when NOW formally condemned pornography for the first time in a resolution adopted at the organization's national convention.

The NOW resolution affirmed the organization's support for lesbian rights but endorsed a narrow definition of appropriate lesbian sexual behavior that hewed closely to cultural feminist views. Specifically, the resolution condemned pornography, sadomasochism, public sex, and pederasty (a

[34] Karen Sims and Rose Mason, with Darlene R. Pagano, "Racism and Sadomasochism: A Conversation with Two Black Lesbians," in *Against Sadomasochism*, 100.

[35] Sims and Mason, 103.

sexual relationship between an adult man and an adolescent boy) as issues that had been "mistakenly correlated with Lesbian/Gay rights" by "some gay organizations." The influence of anti-pornography was unmistakable. Using the familiar language of the movement, the NOW resolution defined pornography as "an issue of exploitation and violence" and sadomasochism as "an issue of violence," whereas lesbianism was a matter of one's "affectional/sexual preference" that bore no relationship to those other issues. To confuse pornography and sadomasochism with lesbian rights, the NOW resolution stated, "would violate the feminist principles upon which this organization was founded."[36] The resolution caused an "immediate uproar," dividing sexual radicals like the Samois women and other sexual libertarians from cultural feminists, including lesbian feminists and anti-pornography feminists, who sanctioned some types of sexual behavior as more feminist than others.[37] The NOW resolution drew a line in the sand.

Critics of the resolution urged caution and argued that people should not be denigrated for exploring their sexuality, including sampling pornography, S/M, and other stigmatized sexual behaviors en route to a fuller understanding of their needs and desires. American society offered women precious little freedom and opportunity to be sexual in the first place, and now *feminists* of all groups were heaping shame on women who practiced unorthodox sex and were calling for restrictions. "[W]e are dealing with the complex and shadowy area of sexuality, an area where little is known or understood," read one response signed by close to 200 individuals. "People making tentative forays into new realms of experience are being treated as if they were monsters and criminals."[38] Opponents saw the NOW resolution promoting a feminism that demanded ideological conformity, and found this inconsistent with the goals of the movement. Why were feminists now trying to enforce a "correct" way to think and feel and behave sexually, they asked, when the movement had previously put so much effort into challenging society's right to impose a heterosexual, marital, procreative norm for women?

Opponents of the resolution also rejected NOW's authority to speak for all feminists on these vital questions related to sexuality, most of which had not yet received a full airing in the women's movement at large. Pro-sex feminists objected that the organization had adopted the cultural feminist perspective with little debate and insufficient examination of its potential effects, and that women who questioned this analysis were subject to trashing and attacked as

[36] The NOW Resolution on Lesbian and Gay Rights is reprinted in Mark Blasius and Shane Phelan, eds., *We Are Everywhere: A Historical Sourcebook of Gay and Lesbian Politics* (New York: Routledge, 1997), 468.

[37] The "immediate uproar" is described by Blasius and Phelan, *We Are Everywhere*, 468. The valorization of types of sex as more feminist than others is described in Gerhard, *Desiring Revolution*, 186.

[38] This response appeared in *Plexus* in May 1981, and was signed by 196 people. See "Response #1," *Plexus* (May 1981): 3.

anti-feminist. "In its appeal to 'feminist principles,' the resolution enshrines the political views of one faction of the women's movement as *the* feminist position," one group of pro-sex feminists pointed out. "It implies the existence of a non-existent consensus and suggests that those of us whose feminist principles have led us to different conclusions need not be taken seriously."[39] Those words, signed by a group of ten prominent feminists, including Ellen Willis, Rosalyn Baxandall, Alix Kates Shulman, and Ann Snitow, foreshadowed the emergence of a countermovement in light of the pressing need for more thorough feminist analysis of sexuality.

The NOW resolution left feminists who disagreed with cultural feminist theories about sexuality more concerned than ever about the rising ideological influence of anti-pornography feminism. Although most pro-sex feminists could accept some of anti-pornography's claims, especially the idea that pornography perpetuated an ideology of male dominance, and that most of the mass-market material was sexist, they flatly rejected others. When the NOW resolution passed in 1980, and when New York-NOW gave WAP a Susan B. Anthony Award the following year for educating the public about pornography, raising national consciousness, and improving the status of women, it was clear that battles over sexuality were making their way to the forefront of the women's movement.

Heresies #12: The Sex Issue

The publication of the *Heresies* "Sex Issue" in 1981 moved the split between anti-pornography feminists and pro-sex feminists, including lesbian sex radicals, into plain view of the women's movement. *Heresies* was a quarterly periodical founded by feminist artists. Each issue was devoted to a single theme and edited by a different collective. The "Sex Issue" collective was made up of twelve women who collaborated for nearly two years to produce a literary and graphic response to anti-pornography. In an attempt to produce something politically incorrect about sex, the collective explored female sexual desire and the question of sexual pleasure with little or no mention of sexual danger. Sheila Jeffreys, a British radical feminist and anti-pornography activist, noted that the publication of the *Heresies* special issue was the first hint that many English radical feminists had of the development of the pro-sex current of thought.

The contributors explored erotic experience in a way that was lighthearted, adventuresome, and risqué, using "hot porn-playing graphics" to catch attention and stimulate new thinking.[40] The issue featured sexually explicit

[39] This response appeared in *Plexus* in May 1981, and was signed by ten prominent New York feminists, including Ellen Willis, Ann Snitow, Rosalyn Baxandall, Karen Durbin, Brett Harvey, and Alix Kates Shulman. Most of these women were members of the abortion rights group, No More Nice Girls. Willis and Snitow emerged as leading members of the pro-sex feminist movement. See "Response #2," *Plexus* (May 1981): 3.

[40] For a discussion of the issue, see B. Ruby Rich, "Review Essay: Feminism and Sexuality in the 1980s," *Feminist Studies*, 12 (Fall 1986): 526–561.

cartoons, photographs, and drawings, as well as stories, poems, satire, and essays. One image depicted a woman's hand in a zippered glove, which suggested S/M. Another showed nearly naked women wrestlers. Other entries described sexual fantasies, such as an explicit cartoon about a woman's desire to wear a strap-on dildo and have anal intercourse with a man. In a review of the "Sex Issue," B. Ruby Rich wrote that what stood out was "its spirit of *daring* in both senses of the word, the taking of a risk and the accepting of a 'dare,' here requiring a jump across the old boundary of respectability."[41] The *Heresies* collective threw down a gauntlet with the publication of this issue, challenging cultural feminist views about appropriate sexual behavior, specifically the gentle, nongenital lesbian sex that Gayle Rubin derided in 1981 as "the missionary position of the women's movement."[42]

The *Heresies* collective tried to speak to fantasy and pleasure, and to create a magazine that reflected positive, alternative views of what women *craved* from sex, as opposed to what they *feared*. "If there can be said to have been a majority interest in the collective," the editors wrote, "it was in examining that aspect of sexuality which might be called 'desire.'"[43] The contributors were trying to stimulate discussions that would help empower women to know and claim what they wanted and needed from sex. In a published conversation about "sexual silences," Cherríe Moraga, a butch-identified Chicana poet, and Amber Hollibaugh, a femme-identified white activist, spoke about feminists' failure to talk openly about their sexual practices and to be accepting of sexual diversity. They agreed that the construction of lesbianism as the "'perfect' vision of egalitarian sexuality" was generating shame and confusion for women who did not conform. They also worried that the movement looked with disfavor on lesbians who displayed an aggressive sexuality or who admitted to strong physical, rather than emotional, desires. Hollibaugh was angry that a sexually androgynous form of lesbianism was being promoted within the movement as politically correct, while butch/femme and S/M-identified lesbians were marginalized and disenfranchised. The conversation ended with a call for women to return to consciousness raising groups to talk openly and honestly about sexual desire, and to create spaces where women could "feel free to say what we do sexually or what we want to do or have done to us," because little freedom of this kind existed at that juncture within the mainstream of the women's movement.[44]

Paula Webster, a member of the "Sex Issue" collective, contributed an article that criticized the anti-pornography movement for closing off dialogue. In "Pornography and Pleasure," she argued that anti-pornography feminism was too focused on controlling male vice, leaving little room for women to

41 Rich, "Review Essay: Feminism and Sexuality," 528.

42 English, Hollibaugh and Rubin, "Talking Sex," 125.

43 The Sexuality Issue Collective, "Editorial," *Heresies* 12: The Sex Issue (1981), 1.

44 Amber L. Hollibaugh and Cherrí Moraga, "What We're Rollin' around in Bed With," in *My Dangerous Desires: A Queer Girl Dreaming Her Way Home* (Durham, NC: Duke University Press, 2000), 82–83.

consider the positive and pleasurable aspects of sex. Like many of the *Heresies* contributors, Webster maintained that greater freedom for women lay in more candid discussions of pleasure, and that pornography should be regarded with a degree of openness as a means of enlarging one's range of sexual experiences and encouraging sexual experimentation. When it came to sexual desire, the *Heresies* editors argued, women were not peas in a pod, with identical needs and wants. In a direct challenge to cultural feminism's emphasis on the existence of unique, shared female qualities, the editors wrote that it was not true that women shared "a uniform relationship to sexuality, sexual identity, fantasy, and sexual practice."[45]

Webster also pointed to a difficult problem that had never been satisfactorily answered with regard to pornography: How to define it. The burgeoning debate over lesbian s/m and butch/femme sexuality showed that the distinction between pornography and erotica depended on the social and cultural experiences that one brought to the viewing experience. "There are no universal, unchanging criteria for drawing the line between acceptable and unacceptable sexual images," Webster wrote. "As feminists, we might question the very impulse to make such a rigid separation, to let a small group of women dictate the boundaries of our morality and our pleasure."[46] She echoed Ellen Willis' conclusion that efforts to differentiate erotica from pornography would always depend on personal interpretive frameworks, or as Willis had put it: "What turns me on is erotic; what turns you on is pornographic."[47] Webster's essay challenged anti-pornography feminists – the "small group of women" to whom she referred – and made it clear that critics viewed anti-pornography as a repressive movement. It was time, she wrote, to inaugurate a conversation about female sexual pleasure and desire, turning attention to a topic that many feminists agreed had been "underexplored and underemphasized."[48]

As expected, the appearance of the *Heresies* "Sex Issue" generated controversy. Anti-pornography feminists were angry and dismayed at this attack, shocked at the suggestion that there had been enough talk about sexual violence and distraught by the growth of a vocal feminist opposition that seemed intent on stopping the movement in its tracks. Anti-pornography activist Sheila Jeffreys described the emotional blow. "To feminists who had been working for years, immersed in the realities of women's pain at the hands of men in childhood, in marriage and in relationships," she wrote, "this cheerful concentration on an unproblematic 'desire' seemed like a brutal callousness and indifference to the real material situation of women's

[45] The *Heresies* collective, "Editorial," *Heresies* 12: The Sex Issue (1981), 94.

[46] Webster, "Pornography and Pleasure," 50.

[47] Ellen Willis, "Feminism, Moralism and Pornography," in *Beginning to See the Light: Sex, Hope and Rock-and-Roll* (Hanover, MA: Wesleyan University Press, 1992), 223.

[48] Chancer, *Reconcilable Differences*, 63.

lives."[49] It was unthinkable that after everything that the anti-violence movements had uncovered about female sexual oppression under patriarchy, feminists would turn away from the analysis of women's victimization to advocate for sexual variation and pleasure. The lack of any discussion of sexual violence in the *Heresies* issue appalled anti-pornography feminists.

Members of the *Heresies* collective were aware that an exploration of female sexual desire would be viewed in some feminist quarters as frivolous, if not reprehensible. Many anti-pornography feminists were deeply suspicious of claims that sex could be a liberatory force for women, and were more likely to endorse WAVPM member Kathy Barry's view that sexual slavery "lurks in the corners of every woman's life."[50] WAVPM included in its anti-pornography literature packet an essay by the radical feminist and political lesbian Ti-Grace Atkinson that characterized sex as expendable. "I do not know any feminist worthy of that name who, if forced to choose between freedom and sex, would choose sex," she wrote. "She'd choose freedom every time."[51] This was the type of thought that pro-sex feminists sought to challenge. They wanted to eradicate the idea that sex itself could be a barrier to freedom and that there was glory attached to a willingness to jettison it from women's lives. They saw a need to fight sexism and sexual repression while simultaneously claiming sex for women. The *Heresies* collective did not argue that women should ignore the dangerous aspects of sex, nor give up the fight against female oppression, but that women should also fight for their right to be sexual on their own terms.

The Barnard Conference

The growing sentiment of pro-sex feminists up until this time had primarily been expressed in private conversations among concerned women, through letters to the editor published in alternative periodicals, such as the anti-NOW resolution responses published in *Plexus* and other feminist newspapers, and through sporadic essays published by writers espousing a radical sexual ethic, such as Ellen Willis, Deirdre English, and Gayle Rubin. The *Heresies* "Sex Issue" represented a major step forward, but the pro-sex camp still existed primarily as a loose, informal network of women who opposed

[49] Sheila Jeffreys, *Anticlimax: A Feminist Perspective on the Sexual Revolution* (New York: New York University Press, 1990), 263–264.

[50] Barry, *Female Sexual Slavery*, 103.

[51] Ti-Grace Atkinson, "Why I'm Against S/M Liberation," in *Against Sadomasochism*, 91. Atkinson first published this piece in *Majority Report* in 1977, and WAVPM included it in an anti-pornography literature packet available to the public. The historian Jane Gerhard discusses how far cultural feminists had come by this time from the theories of radical feminists like Anne Koedt, Kate Millett, and Germaine Greer who had argued in 1970 that sexual pleasure was an important aspect of women's empowerment. See Gerhard, *Desiring Revolution*, 184–185.

cultural feminism's sexual ideas and anti-pornography politics. These pro-sex women represented a wide range of political positions within feminism, including such groups as lesbian sexual radicals, early radical feminists such as Ellen Willis and Kate Millett, and women – many of them academics – influenced by Marxism, structuralism, and psychoanalysis.[52] Although the "Sex Issue" brought some of the pro-sex voices together, the countermovement needed a major event to build theory, solidify its arguments, and claim a presence on the national stage. The 1982 Barnard Conference provided that opportunity.

Since 1974, the Barnard College Women's Center had worked with activists and academics to plan the Scholar and the Feminist conference, an annual meeting to explore the relationship between feminist scholarship and practice. Carole S. Vance, a Columbia University professor with expertise in human sexuality and gender, was selected as the academic coordinator for the ninth annual conference, and she helped choose the conference theme: sexuality. Vance invited about 100 women to join the planning committee. They would work together to select speakers, develop workshops, and produce a conference diary. Her efforts produced a working group of twenty-five academics and activists who met from September 1981 to April 1982 to organize the conference.[53] Alarmed by the ways that a broad feminist agenda on sexuality and sexual rights seemed to have given way to a single-minded campaign against pornography, the planning committee sought to restore some balance to the feminist conversation. They hoped to reintroduce questions of sexual pleasure, drawing on women's positive sexual experiences to imagine "the textures and contours [of sexual life] that would unfurl and proliferate in a safer space," Vance wrote of their intent.[54] The conference planners did not ignore danger, but saw the meeting's emphasis on pleasure as an intellectual and political intervention needed to challenge the conservative feminist sexual discourse that held sway in the women's movement. This was considered

[52] Anti-pornography feminists, on the other hand, were primarily cultural feminists who were influenced by lesbian feminist theory and the idea that men and male values were the greatest threat to women's freedom.

[53] The estimate of 100 original invitations appears in Tacie Dejanikus, "Charges of Exclusion and McCarthyism at Barnard Conference," *off our backs* (June 1982): 19. Active members of the planning committee included: Julie Abraham, Hannah Alderfer, Meryl Altman, Jan Boney, France Doughty, Ellen DuBois, Kate Ellis, Judith Friedlander, Julie German, Faye Ginsburg, Diane Harriford, Beth Jaker, Mary Clare Lennon, Sherry Manasse, Nancy K. Miller, Marybeth Nelson, Esther Newton, Claire Riley, Susan R. Sacks, Ann Snitow, Quandra P. Stadler, Judith R. Walkowitz, Ellen Willis, and Patsy Yaeger. Although Vance has described these women as "virtual strangers" at the outset, a number of them had already declared their opposition to anti-pornography politics. Carole S. Vance, "More Danger, More Pleasure: A Decade After the Barnard Sexuality Conference," *New York Law School Law Review*, 38, no. 1–4 (1993): 294.

[54] Carole S. Vance, "Pleasure and Danger: Towards a Politics of Sexuality," in *Pleasure and Danger: Exploring Female Sexuality*, ed. Carole S. Vance (Boston: Routledge and Kegan Paul, 1984), 3.

particularly pressing given the rising power of the religious Right and their "family values" campaign, which lent credibility and support to the feminist anti-pornography position.

By the time that the planning group assembled in 1981, the existence of a strong backlash against the women's movement and women's rights was evident. The intense battles around the ERA, a congressional bill in support of the anti-feminist, anti-gay federal Family Protection Act; attacks on abortion rights, including the 1980 Supreme Court decision in *Harris v. McRae* that affirmed the constitutionality of the 1976 Hyde Amendment, which left 44 million poor women without access to funding for abortion; and massive reductions in social services that affected women who were poor, underemployed, and/or on welfare, and their children, were achieved in a culture that had grown openly hostile to feminism. In 1980, for the first time, under pressure from groups like Phyllis Schlafly's Eagle Forum and Jerry Falwell's Moral Majority, the Republican platform adopted anti-ERA and anti-abortion positions. Under Reagan's leadership, Congress authorized drastic cuts to federal government programs and transferred responsibility for funding social services like homeless shelters, rape crisis centers, and food pantries from federal authorities to state and local government and the private sector, causing a national crisis for these organizations and their clients. Women's organizations that had relied on federal funding saw their resources dry up as the budgets of the Equal Employment Opportunity Commission, the U.S. Civil Rights Commission, the Department of Labor, and the State Department, along with many others, were slashed.[55] The federal government stalled funding for battered women's programs, voted down bills to fund shelters, and closed down the Office of Domestic Violence, which had been created just two years earlier in 1979 under Carter's administration.

Feminist gains of the 1970s were being eroded under constant pressure from the Right, and by some accounts, feminist activists were marginalized and demoralized in the 1980s. The increasing reluctance of many women to identify as feminist amid media pronouncements of a "postfeminist" decade peopled by young women who rejected the women's movement left some veteran activists feeling threatened and defeated.[56] In the face of dried-up resources, loss of feminist organizations and paying staff jobs, a federal government that espoused traditional family values, cultural backlash, and a deep recession through 1983 that forced individuals to prioritize earning a living as the national unemployment rate surged past 10 percent, anti-pornography seemed to many like the wrong path for the times. Critics warned that anti-pornography was too much in concert with a right-wing government that

[55] Nancy Whittier, *Feminist Generations: The Persistence of the Radical Women's Movement* (Philadelphia: Temple University Press, 1995), 85–91.

[56] Susan Faludi, *Backlash: The Undeclared War Against American Women* (New York: Crown Publishers, 1991).

quickly proved itself no friend of feminism, and too focused on one set of issues at a time of broad economic and social crisis for many American women.

Amid the context of the rise of right-wing power and an organized attack on sexual freedom, sexuality was a timely and important subject for a conference. But within New York City's tightly-knit feminist community, it soon became known that no one affiliated with WAP or the anti-pornography movement had been asked to join the planning committee. Anti-pornography feminists were furious that they had been excluded from a conference that was supposed to represent all quarters, and complained that the event was biased. The organizers later conceded these points. They acknowledged that anti-pornography activists had been kept out, but defended that decision on the grounds that the feminist debate on sexuality was already dominated by the anti-pornography position. Ellen Willis and others fought back that it was hard to argue that the views of radical feminist theorists like Andrea Dworkin and Adrienne Rich had been excluded, when their views were widely known and were referenced in every feminist conversation about sex. Vance pointed out that the conference planners wanted to have a forum where a wide range of views on sexuality could be explored, and that anti-pornography feminists were not tolerant of others who challenged their opinions.[57] Joan Nestle, a cofounder of the Lesbian Herstory Archives and a leader of the conference workshop on politically incorrect sexuality, supported the decision to keep WAP members out. "This conference was about pleasure and sexuality and WAP has nothing to say on this and they are not interested in discussion," she told a reporter from *off our backs*. "I don't think this conference was closed to any point of view but focused on points of view not heard with any regularity.... WAP is used to having the territory all to themselves."[58] The organizers believed that the anti-pornography activists were so unrelenting in their opposition to pro-sex thought that their presence on the planning committee would have eroded the possibility for open conversation.

[57] The organizers' decision is discussed in Elizabeth Wilson, "The Context of 'Between Pleaure and Danger': The Barnard Conference on Sexuality," *Feminist Review* 13 (February 1983): 35–41.

[58] Joan Nestle, quoted in Dejanikus, "Charges of Exclusion & McCarthyism," 20. The conference organizers maintained that anti-pornography was not wholly excluded because the movement's views were so well-known in the feminist community that it was not possible to discuss sexuality without discussing WAP and its primary theorists. Ellen Willis explained it as follows to a reporter from *off our backs*: "'The anti-pornography movement and its particular kind of ideology of sex have been a dominant and visible feminist position. Not a single person on the planning committee is unfamiliar with WAP's position. Although there was a lot of different points of view, we agreed that the discussion about sexual violence was too limited. WAP was excluded in the sense that their position was a given. We wanted to open up the debate. For example, you can't talk about excluding Adrienne Rich when her views are extremely well known." Ellen Willis, quoted in Dejanikus, "Charges of Exclusion & McCarthyism," 20. The WAP activists rejected this explanation, and pointed out that the Scholar and the Feminist conference was supposed to include all viewpoints.

Vance's letter of invitation to prospective planning committee members framed the conference theme as a challenge to anti-pornography. She asked women to think about the paradox of the sexual domain as an arena for both pleasure *and* danger, introducing for the first time a provocative phrase still used today to describe the risks and rewards that women must balance when dealing with sexual matters.[59] She offered a list of questions that the planners might discuss at their first group meeting, beginning with: "How do women get sexual pleasure in patriarchy?" in hopes of stimulating conversation about the liberating aspects of sexuality for women.[60]

Anti-pornography, by contrast, focused on women's sexual oppression under patriarchy, and the relentless cycle of sexual violence that ensured the continuation of male power and female victimization. Returning to Ti-Grace Atkinson's words to the effect that a feminist worthy of her name would choose freedom over sex, anti-pornography feminists typically found questions regarding sexual pleasure less pressing and even frivolous when compared to those dealing with danger. Writer Dorothy Allison, who led a conference workshop that explored the concepts of politically correct and politically incorrect sex, reflected on the conference in an oral history conducted in 1995. At that time, she offered a description of the climate surrounding the event and anti-pornography feminists' reluctance to explore pleasure until the issue of danger was resolved. "Everybody's gonna have to refrain from enjoying sexuality or women's pursuit of sexual pleasure, or heterosexual women teaching heterosexual men how to actually make them have an orgasm," Allison cracked. "We can't talk about any of that until we stop pornography and stop violence against women. These are the only two subjects we can discuss about sexuality."[61] This was her characterization of anti-pornography feminists' mindset as the Barnard Conference loomed.

Vance's letter to the conference planners also brought up the question of feminist alliances with right-wing conservatives and made this discussion an integral part of the conference agenda. She asked the planners to think about points of similarity between feminist analyses of pornography, incest, and male and female sexual nature and the Right's position on sexuality. In so doing, she was urging them to consider these movements' parallel affirmations of gender difference and the limitations of this ideology for women. Pro-sex feminists feared that the celebration of traditionally feminine qualities evident in cultural feminist thought played into the Right's comprehensive plan to protect women from the ills of free-wheeling sexuality, and they were eager to expose points of overlap.

59 Vance, "More Danger, More Pleasure," 289.

60 Carole S. Vance, "Invitational Letter," in *Diary of a Conference on Sexuality*, eds. Hannah Alderfer, Beth Jaker, and Marybeth Nelson (New York: Faculty Press, 1982), 1.

61 Dorothy Allison, oral history conducted by Susanne Dietzel, New Orleans, Louisiana, November 1995, Zale Writer in Residence Program at the Newcomb College Center for Research on Women. Available online at http://www.tulane.edu/~wc/zale/allison/allison.html

Overall, it was clear that many of the members of the planning committee had antipathy for anti-pornography politics. The committee members' thoughts about the anti-pornography movement were sprinkled throughout their meeting notes, which were to be published and distributed to conference attendees as the *Diary of a Conference on Sexuality*. The *Diary* contained minutes and reading lists from the planning sessions, personal statements from committee members, a conference concept paper, and abstracts describing the planned workshops. Three members of the *Heresies* "Sex Issue" collective contributed feisty graphics and photographs. In her *Diary* comment, the historian Judith Walkowitz celebrated the conference's pro-sex orientation and saw it as a needed corrective to anti-pornography: "It should be a very exciting event: a coming out party for feminists who have been appalled by the intellectual dishonesty and dreariness of the anti-pornography movement."[62] Ellen Willis attacked anti-pornography for restricting women's sexual choices. "The tendency of some feminists to regard women purely as sexual victims rather than sexual subjects … reinforces women's oppression and plays into the hands of the new right," she wrote. "It is a dead end, a politics of despair."[63] Activist Frances Doughty took aim at the movement's dim view of heterosexuality in a satirical announcement of a "pioneering conference" on "heterophilia."[64] Like other members of the planning committee, Doughty expressed her anger at the poor treatment that many heterosexual women had received. The idea that a woman who willingly had sex with men capitulated not just in her own oppression, but in the oppression of all women left many heterosexual women feeling self-conscious and ashamed. Whether they objected to anti-pornography's anti-sexual aspects or its endorsement of a limited range of sexual behavior, its ideas about gender difference or its portrayal of women as sexual victims, the conference planners were hostile to the anti-pornography movement.

In the weeks leading up to the April 24 conference, the conflict between the planners and the excluded anti-pornography activists intensified. A group of anti-pornography feminists, most of whom were associated with WAP, launched a protest that resulted in the confiscation of the *Diary*. WAP members telephoned Barnard College officials and trustees and complained that the conference was endorsing anti-feminist ideas and sexual perversions, including sadomasochism. They reportedly denounced particular members of the planning committee by name on the basis of their sexual preferences.[65] Vance

[62] Judith Walkowitz, comment in *Diary of a Conference on Sexuality*, 72.

[63] Ellen Willis, comment in *Diary of a Conference on Sexuality*, 72.

[64] Frances Doughty, comment in *Diary of a Conference on Sexuality*, 72.

[65] There are many pro-sex accounts of WAP's activity in the days leading up to the Barnard Conference. WAP did not deny that its leaders contacted Barnard officials. See Lisa Orlando, "Bad Girls and 'Good' Politics," *The Village Voice Literary Supplement* (December 1982): 1, 16–17; Marcia Pally, "The Fireworks at the Sexuality Conference: Whom Should Feminists Fuck?" *New York Native*, May 24–June 6, 1982: 14–16; and Carole S. Vance,

has described the episode that followed as "a full-scale sexual panic" in which representatives of the college interrogated the staff of the Barnard Women's Center and demanded to review the conference program and materials. Their attention became focused on the *Diary*. Two days before the conference, Ellen V. Futter, the president of Barnard, decided to suppress all 1,500 copies. She insisted that the use of Barnard's name implied endorsement of controversial points of view, and might jeopardize future conference funding. The administration agreed to pay for the *Diary* to be reprinted – although not in time for the conference – if all references to Barnard and to the Scholar and the Feminist's major funding organization, the Helena Rubinstein Foundation, were removed.[66] Participants received the sanitized version of the *Diary* months after the actual meeting.

On the day of the conference, WAP members and supporters formed a picket line outside the gates of Barnard College. Wearing t-shirts which read "For a Feminist Sexuality" on the front and "Against S/M" on the back, the protesters greeted more than 800 registrants with a two-page leaflet. This leaflet charged that the conference promoted a minority perspective on sexuality and silenced the views of the majority of radical feminists and lesbian feminists. It condemned the conference for recognizing organizations that supported and produced pornography, that promoted sex roles and S/M, and that lobbied alongside straight and gay pedophile organizations (e.g., North American Man/Boy Love Association) to end laws that protected children from adult sexual abuse.[67] In addition, the leaflet argued that the organizers consciously excluded the women who had pioneered the feminist analysis of sexual violence, including those who had built the anti-pornography movement, those who fought media images that legitimized sexual violence, and

"Epilogue," in *Pleasure and Danger*, 431–446. Accounts that privilege the WAP point of view include: Deborah Sherman and Harriet Hirshorn, "Feminists and Sexuality: Background to a Debate," *WIN*, October 15, 1982, 9–11; Claudette Charbonneau, "Sexual Confusion at Barnard," *off our backs* (June 1982): 25, 29.

66 The Helena Rubinstein Foundation withdrew funding from future Scholar and the Feminist conferences, but the *Diary* was not the cause so much as the furor and negative publicity surrounding the event in the wake of the WAP protests.

67 The organizations themselves – No More Nice Girls, Samois, and The Lesbian Sex Mafia – were not officially part of the conference. Rather, members of these organizations were invited to the conference because of their activist and academic work around the question of sexuality. Ellen Willis, for example, was a founder of No More Nice Girls, an abortion rights group, but was invited to be a conference planner on the basis of her writings on sexuality. Gayle Rubin was not invited as a representative of Samois, but as an academic well known for her writing on gender and sex, especially her seminal 1975 essay, "The Traffic in Women: Notes on the 'Political Economy' of Sex." The organization that supposedly lobbied for pedophilia was Samois. Samois had signed a petition protesting FBI harassment of NAMBLA. NAMBLA opposes age-of-consent laws that place legal restrictions on minors who wish to engage in sexual activity and argues that sex per se is not abusive, and that young people should have the right to engage in sexual contact if they so choose. NAMBLA is not supported by the mainstream gay rights movement. For more on this group, see Weeks, *Sexuality and Its Discontents*, 225–231.

those who believed that S/M was a reactionary and patriarchal form of sexuality. Critics of the leaflet, like Carole Vance and Ellen Willis, pointed out that it characterized a conference that addressed a wide range of topics in sexuality as a vehicle for just three issues: pornography, S/M, and butch-femme.[68] Gayle Rubin saw the leaflet as consistent with the anti-pornography movement's "pattern of intimidation" to silence critics and preserve its control of the feminist discourse on sexuality. "What was really at stake with the Sex Conference is that it marked the end of this anti-porn monopoly," Rubin wrote. "The leaflet was a squeal of distress from those who could no longer have their way with impunity."[69]

In addition to criticizing the conference, the leaflet singled out a handful of associated feminists by name and "outed" them as practitioners of stigmatized sexual behaviors like S/M.[70] These attacks on individual feminists – some of whom were conference organizers or workshop leaders, and one of whom merely attended – were described by the conference organizers as "McCarthyite tactics" meant to silence dissenting voices.[71] Willis pointed out that the anti-pornography movement did not tolerate criticism well, and that

[68] Carole Vance made this point in a letter to the editors of *Feminist Studies*. See Carole Vance, "Letter to the Editors," *Feminist Studies* 9, no. 3 (Fall 1983): 590. The conference featured workshops, papers, and poetry dealing with childhood sexuality, anti-abortion activism, the quest for bodily perfection, sexual taboo, butch-femme roles, class/race/cultural influences on sexuality, sex and money, language and desire, the relationship between representation and desire, teenage romance, politically correct and incorrect sexuality, popular sex literature, and various other topics. There was no scheduled workshop on S/M, although Dorothy Allison, a workshop leader, invited conference attendees to attend a separate event on April 25, 1982: the Lesbian Sex Mafia speak-out on politically incorrect sexuality. Allison was a founder of the Lesbian Sex Mafia, a support group for women engaged in "politically incorrect sex." The speakers were asked to address two questions: "How are you a sexual outlaw?" and "What is it about sex that makes you feel whole and strong." The proceeds from the speakout were donated to Kitchen Table: Women of Color Press, and the literature packet handed out to attendees included guidelines for political organizing. About twenty women spoke out, according to the reporter from *off our backs*, in celebration of their varied "politically incorrect" sexual practices. Many wore garments associated with S/M or butch/femme. See Fran Moira, "Lesbian Sex Mafia Speakout," *off our backs* (June 1982): 23–24.

[69] Rubin, "Letter to the Editors," 598.

[70] The editors of the academic journal *Feminist Studies* reprinted the WAP leaflet in full, which further publicized its descriptions of individual women. The journal's editors subsequently apologized, stating that the publication of those names endangered women who may have been "out" to the lesbian and feminist communities about their sexuality, but not "out" to the general public. Conference organizers pointed out that women identified as sadomasochists or other sexual minorities could face serious consequences, from job loss to personal violence. Carole Vance wrote to the editors: "You don't seem to understand that the sexual margin is a very dangerous place, peopled by employers who fire you, landlords who evict you, and police who arrest you. If you are not on, or accused of being on, a sexual margin, you need to educate yourself about the situation of women who are, be aware of the very real threats they face, and act responsibly in protecting them." For the text of the leaflet, see *Feminist Studies*, 9, no. 1 (Spring 1983): 180–182. For the editors' apology and letters of response from women named in the leaflet, see *Feminist Studies* 9, no. 3 (Fall 1983): 589–602.

[71] Letter of protest against the WAP leaflet, *Feminist Studies* 9, no. 1 (Spring 1983): 180.

any woman who dared to contradict movement opinion was vilified as anti-feminist.[72] "This is nothing less than a demand for a blacklist, which no radical movement worthy of the name can countenance," she wrote.[73] Indeed, the pamphlet became so controversial that several of its supposed authors quickly distanced themselves.

The official author of the leaflet was The Coalition for a Feminist Sexuality and Against Sadomasochism, an ad hoc group made up of WAP, WAVAW and New York Radical Feminists. It became obvious, however, that members of WAP were the authors. Lisa Orlando described the Coalition as "a WAP Front" in an article in *Gay Community News*.[74] New York Radical Feminists was essentially defunct; the group had not met regularly for years and its sole organizational vestige consisted of a post office box.[75] Los Angeles WAVAW reportedly agreed to lend its name to the leaflet without having seen it, but only after being assured that it contained a statement about S/M and no attack on individuals.[76] At the time of the Barnard Conference, LA WAVAW was in a state of disarray and so short of funds that the chapter had not published its national newsletter since 1980. The issue that came out in April 1982 was the first one in two years, and it acknowledged "lack of on-going communication with our members."[77] Thus, any support for the leaflet could not be said to truly represent the views of a national membership. Members of Cleveland WAVAW were sufficiently upset by the contents of the leaflet that the chapter wrote to *off our backs* to dissociate themselves from it. "Because several of us were upset about the leafleting and the part the so-called anti-pornography movement groups played in it, we wanted to make it known that the action taken was not indicative of the opinions of all women associated with the anti-pornography movement," they wrote.[78] Even within the loose structure of the anti-pornography movement, consensus was beginning to break down.

[72] In later years, when Catharine MacKinnon became one of the leading anti-pornography theorists and the proponent of anti-pornography legislation, she perpetuated the movement's refusal to deal with feminist critics. MacKinnon refused to debate women who disagreed with her about pornography. She said: "I do not allow myself to be used to orchestrate and legitimate a so-called 'debate within feminism' over whether pornography harms women. It is my analysis that that is the pimps' current strategy for legitimizing a slave trade in women. I do not need to be sucked into the pornographers' strategy, period." MacKinnon, quoted in Nadine Strossen, *Defending Pornography: Free Speech, Sex and the Fight for Women's Rights* (New York: Scribner, 1995), 85.

[73] Ellen Willis, Letter to the Editors, *Feminist Studies* 9, no. 3 (Fall 1983): 594.

[74] Lisa Orlando, "Lust at Last, Or Spandex Invades the Academy," *Gay Community News* 15 (May 1982): 16.

[75] This information about NYRF came from Ellen Willis, an original member of the group from its founding in 1968. See Willis, "Letter to the Editors," 593–594. Lisa Orlando, a former member of NYRF, also confirmed that the group was defunct. See Orlando, "Lust at Last," 16.

[76] Reported in Pat Califia, "In Response to Dorchen Leidholdt's 'Lesbian S/M: Radicalism or Reaction,'" *New Women's Times* (October 1982): 13.

[77] Melinda Lowrey, "WAVAW In Motion," *WAVAW Newsletter*, 9 (April 1982): 1.

[78] Cleveland WAVAW, "Cleveland WAVAW Clarifies," *off our backs* (November 1982): 26.

Members of WAP did extensive public relations work in the wake of the conference, arguing that forceful tactics had been necessary to defend their organization and the reputation of the anti-pornography movement from pro-sex assault. Dorchen Leidholdt told a reporter from *off our backs* that the Barnard Conference had been rigged. She said that the organizers were trying to wrest feminism away from its conflict with existing sexual institutions in order to reorient it in the direction of sexual liberation.[79] WAP members argued that the conference did not fairly represent feminist sexual thought, promoting just one perspective on sexuality and silencing the views of a major sector of the women's movement and many of its preeminent theorists. In a separate effort defending the anti-pornography movement, Andrea Dworkin reportedly sent out photocopies of the *Diary* with a letter expressing concern over its editorial content and explicit images.[80]

No matter which side one chose with regard to questions about sexuality, the Barnard Conference contributed to a widening rift among American feminists and created a bitter climate that would take years to subside. One account of the events surrounding the conference described "scarring divisions" and "consternation, anger and uproar" among feminists on both sides.[81] Even today, the mention of the event stirs up unpleasant feelings and memories. Speaking about Barnard more than a decade after it took place, Dorothy Allison recounted the pain and high personal cost that she and others endured for their participation. "It turned into a nightmare," she said. "I know people who lost their lives because of that conference. A lot of people lost their jobs. Plenty of people had nervous breakdowns, left town, disappeared.... And a lot of us lost our religion.... The Women's Movement was not the safe place we imagined it to be. Open discussion was not the rule as we had imagined."[82]

Notwithstanding the personal fallout associated with the meeting, the Barnard Conference made an impact on American feminism by creating new avenues for talking about sexuality. The organizers challenged the dominance of the anti-pornography analysis and insisted that the conversation about sex had to be opened up to free women to approach sex in more affirmative ways. Writing about the event in the *Village Voice*, one feminist pointed out positive uses of pornography in a society where women were raised to regard sex as a source of oppression. "Porn may represent women as passive victims," she remarked, "but it also shows us taking and demanding pleasure, aggressive and powerful in a way rarely seen in our culture."[83] Like many pro-sex feminists, she acknowledged that pornography could be misogynistic, but she insisted that it could serve a social good in helping

[79] See Dejanikus, "Charges of Exclusion & McCarthyism,"19–20.

[80] This is reported in Elizabeth Wilson, "The Context of 'Between Pleaure and Danger': The Barnard Conference on Sexuality," *Feminist Review* 13 (February 1983): 40.

[81] This is reported in Wilson, "The Context of 'Between Pleaure and Danger,'" 35.

[82] Dorothy Allison, oral history.

[83] Orlando, "Bad Girls and 'Good' Politics," 16.

women discover and express their sexual desires and show them that women could be sexual actors. This perspective on pornography – and on a larger scale, sexuality – as a venue for both pleasure and danger was the central theoretic proposition that animated the Barnard Conference. The debut of organized pro-sex feminism at Barnard signaled an end to uncontested anti-pornography politics; anti-pornography feminists who tried to speak about sexuality with carte blanche for the women's movement from that moment forward found themselves challenged at every turn.[84] Indeed, the Barnard Conference jump-started the "sex wars" of the 1980s, the rancorous, all-consuming debates over sexuality that continued well past the defeat of Dworkin and MacKinnon's anti-pornography ordinances in 1986. Although these wars were terribly divisive and were instrumental in the collapse of second-wave feminism, they did provide an important opportunity for feminists representing very different schools of thought to begin a conversation about sexuality that moved beyond the parameters of violence.

Conclusion: Searching for the Light

In the post-Barnard period, WAP kept on with its anti-pornography work. One could argue that the organization exerted its greatest influence over the next few years, lending support and providing testimony on behalf of both Dworkin and MacKinnon's civil rights ordinances and Attorney General Edwin Meese's 1985 Commission on Pornography. But the organization was forever changed in the wake of Barnard. WAP was at permanent odds with some sectors of the women's movement after the conference, and its agenda was often characterized as repressive and anti-sexual. Much of the organization's attention and energy had to be diverted from the anti-pornography cause and redirected to dealing with conflicts with groups who advocated on behalf of pornography and free sexuality.

On the weekend of October 8, 1982, six months post-Barnard, this change was evident as WAP held a two-day protest of Sexpo '82, the first northeast convention and trade show for magazine, video, and film pornographers. Open to the general public, the convention organizers billed Sexpo as an erotica festival furthering sexual liberation. WAP members protested pornography as liberation and picketed the event with posters that featured sexually violent photographs and cartoons from the magazines *Hustler*, *Screw*, and *Velvet*, each of which participated in Sexpo.[85] What made this event notable, however,

[84] It should be noted that Catharine MacKinnon and Andrea Dworkin, who began drafting their model anti-pornography ordinance just six months after Barnard, refused to acknowledge the existence of legitimate perspectives in defense of pornography within the women's movement. They have maintained that there is no legitimate "pro-pornography" feminism. After Barnard, however, it was clear that the WAP analysis and campaigns, and the MacKinnon-Dworkin ordinance, were actively contested by organized pro-sex forces. FACT, the Feminist Anti-Censorship Taskforce, was started by pro-sex feminists to educate other feminists and the public about the dangers of the ordinance, and played a major role in defeating it in several cities.

[85] Dorchen Leidholdt, "WAP Exposes Sexpo," *WAP NewsReport* (Fall 1982): 1–2, 7.

FIGURE 9.1. Sex workers at Sexpo '82, a trade show for the adult magazine, video, and film industries, staged a counterprotest against WAP picketers. They derided anti-pornography feminists as "witch hunters" who sought to deny women their erotic rights. *Photo: Bettye Lane.*

was the eruption of a counterprotest led by Sexpo registrants. Carrying bare-bones signs that consisted of black lettering on white posterboard, and slogans defending women's erotic rights, they jeered WAP members and denounced them as neo-Puritans and prudes conducting a sexual witch hunt. The conflict between the groups attracted significant media attention. WAP members were interviewed on New York's WPIX and WNBC radio stations. The New York *Daily News* covered the story for three days. Members of WAP appeared on a midday television news program to debate Sexpo organizer and pornography distributor Vivian Forlander and the adult film actor Harry Reems (*Deep Throat*). In the wake of Barnard, WAP faced a new wave of challengers beyond the circle of pro-sex, primarily academic, feminists. Increasingly, the men and women who saw the sex business as big business offered vocal opposition to the anti-pornography movement. With the video revolution taking hold in American culture at precisely that moment, infinitely expanding the pornography industry's reach, the voices of pornography's proponents would continue to rise.

Conclusion

Porn Is Here to Stay

The Feminist Anti-Pornography Movement in the 1980s and Beyond

Gloria Leonard had a big idea. It was 1982, and the federal government had ordered AT&T to sell off its regional "Baby Bell" telephone companies and to give up its monopoly on 900 numbers in the wake of a landmark antitrust court case. People typically called the 900 numbers to find out the time or the weather. Some local phone companies even offered "Dial-a-Joke." But now the 900 lines were up for grabs, and outside information providers would get a chance to determine their content and keep a share of the profits. Leonard, a former nightclub manager and X-rated movie star who became the publisher of the adult magazine *High Society*, hoped to secure one. She didn't know if many people called in for the time or the weather. But she had a hunch that lots of people would call in for sex.

New York Telephone used a lottery system to award the leases for its 900 lines, and *High Society* was one of 21 lucky winners. Leonard set about creating the first erotic telephone service featuring sexually suggestive messages that were supposedly recorded by the magazine's glamorous models. The women described titillating scenarios and sexual encounters, complete with moaning and groaning. The messages changed three times a day. Leonard promoted the new service in the magazine, and waited to see if anyone would call.

By the spring of 1983, half a million callers were dialing *High Society*'s 900 number every day. Each call cost seven cents per minute. New York Telephone kept five cents and paid *High Society* the other two, netting $25,000 a day for the telephone company and $10,000 a day for the magazine.[1] The business was so lucrative that the magazine took over the 900-number leases held by two other lottery winners. By July 1983, a number of other adult magazines, including *Penthouse*, *Oui*, *Swank*, and *Playgirl*, had followed in *High Society*'s footsteps, offering sexually explicit recorded messages on 900 numbers leased from lottery winners.[2]

[1] "Aural Sex," *Time*, May 9, 1983, p. 39.

[2] Larry Sutton, "Phone Pornucopia," *The New York Daily News*, July 19, 1983, 9.

Less than a year after the Barnard Conference, WAP identified *High Society*'s "degrading dispatches" as a matter of serious concern. "[A]nyone, child or adult, who dials 976–2727 in New York will hear a female voice inviting males to have sex with her ...," WAP leader Florence Rush complained. This form of entertainment was dangerous to women's physical and emotional well-being because it reduced them to nothing more than sexual objects. "Such a message," she wrote in *NewsReport* in 1983, "suggests to men that women are willing, available, and anxious to submit to any form of sexual use."[3] In a subsequent issue, WAP objected to the telephone lines because they portrayed women as wanting and desiring anonymous, unemotional sexual contact – an erotic style that cultural feminists assigned to men. "We believe that it promotes a distorted perception of women as sexually ravenous creatures who enjoy brutal and impersonal sex," the organization stated.[4] A member of WAP sent a letter to NBC News that characterized the messages available through "'dial-a-porn'" as "shockingly descriptive."[5] WAP hoped the Federal Communications Commission might ban these "pornographic phone calls" and urged members to demand FCC action by sending letters and telegrams to the agency, providing contact information in *NewsReport*.[6] By bringing its case to the FCC, WAP sought direct government action to protect women from sexually explicit material – a major shift in the movement that was also taking place via the MacKinnon-Dworkin anti-pornography ordinance introduced in Minneapolis that year.

By the time that WAP began to protest the *High Society* 900-numbers, there were external factors working against the anti-pornography movement that reduced the likelihood as well as the advisability of achieving legal suppression of pornography. First, the possibility of eradicating or even controlling pornography seemed increasingly implausible as up-and-coming video and cable technology encouraged viewers to enjoy a steady stream of programming right in their own homes. Second, the emergence of a virulent anti-feminist and anti-gay New Right legislative agenda that threatened prior gains gave new urgency to efforts to protect liberal values of freedom of choice, individual self-determination, and equality before the law. Although MacKinnon and Dworkin presented the ordinances as a means of correcting a shortcoming of classic liberalism, namely its reliance on gender-blind standards and principles that prevented meaningful equality, other feminists and progressives argued that it was simply too dangerous in a right-wing political climate to call on the state to regulate sexual expression in the name of women's rights.

[3] Florence Rush, "The Latest Trend – Telephone Pornography," *WAP NewsReport* 5, no. 1 (Spring/Summer 1983): 10.

[4] "Protest Dial-a-Porn," *WAP NewsReport*, vol. 5, no. 2, (Fall/Winter 1983): 2.

[5] Member of WAP to NBC News, n.d., WAP Records, Box 2, Folder 83.

[6] See both Rush, "The Latest Trend – Telephone Pornography," and "Protest Dial-a-Porn" *WAP NewsReport*.

In this concluding chapter, I review these cultural and political changes, the status of the anti-pornography movement groups, and the effort to achieve legal reform. From 1983 onward, WAP lent its support to the passage of civil rights legislation against pornography pioneered by MacKinnon and Dworkin, and to the arch-conservative 1985 Commission on Pornography, led by Attorney General Edwin Meese. These actions, widely viewed as bringing feminists into imprudent alliances with right-wing activists and legislators, inaugurated the final chapter in feminist anti-pornography organizing.

Porn Is Here to Stay

Changes in technology throughout the 1970s and early 1980s made access to pornography relatively inexpensive and private – factors that worked in favor of its dissemination and against the possibility of suppression. The development of video technology, including videocassette players and portable video cameras that encouraged amateur production, meant that pornography could move out of public theaters and adult bookstores that were targets for police raids and were often located in run-down areas of town. "[N]o cinema patrons would want to watch a porn film while sitting next to a cop from the local vice squad," two industry observers noted, "when they could be viewing more or less the same thing in the comfort and privacy of their own homes."[7] The adult film industry was quick to embrace video, recognizing its tremendous potential to bring pornography to all Americans. Observing these technological and cultural changes, the sociologist Amitai Etzioni declared on the *New York Times* op-ed page in 1977: "Porn is here to stay."[8]

Video technology became available to the American market in the early 1970s, growing more popular and affordable toward the end of the decade. Sony manufactured the first home videocassette player in 1972. The 0.75-inch U-Matic device sold for $1,600. In 1975, Sony introduced the popular Betamax videocassette recorder (VCR). The following year, JVC, a subsidiary of Matsushita, marketed a less-expensive VHS system VCR. By Christmas 1977, the competition between the two systems drove the price of VCRs below $1,000, making them more affordable. Zenith, Sylvania, Magnavox, and RCA soon flooded the market with cheaper models.[9] In 1981, three million American homes had a VCR, comprising about 5 percent of the total number of homes equipped with television sets.[10] By the end of the decade, 87 percent of American homes featured at least one VCR.

7 Hebditch and Anning, 227.

8 Amitai Etzioni, "Porn is Here to Stay," *New York Times*, May 17, 1977, 33.

9 Bruce C. Klopfenstein, "The Diffusion of the VCR in the United States," in *The VCR Age: Home Video and Mass Communication*, ed. M.R. Levy (Newbury Park, CA: Sage, 1989), 23.

10 Tony Schwartz, "The TV Pornography Boom," *New York Times*, September 13, 1981, available online at: http://www.nytimes.com/1981/09/13/magazine/the-tv-pornography-boom.html. Accessed June 25, 2009.

Adult film industry entrepreneurs recognized that the videocassette was the perfect medium for pornography. Whereas the mainstream motion picture industry fought to keep the new technology at bay and refused to transfer studio pictures, the producers of X-rated films rushed to get features like *Deep Throat* and *Behind the Green Door*, and even the "loops" that predated full-length features, onto videotape.[11] By the mid-1970s, fans could purchase adult video titles through the mail or in adult bookstores. The men's magazines *Oui* and *Penthouse* advertised mail-order cassettes of Russ Meyer's *Vixen* for $299.95 each. *Deep Throat* sold for $100. In the mid-1980s, the price had dropped to about $70 per title. The purchase of adult tapes could be accomplished discreetly; mail-order goods arrived in plain brown wrappers that concealed their contents. In 1978 and 1979, an estimated 75 percent of all prerecorded tapes sold were X-rated.[12]

Once Americans became accustomed to video pornography, industry experts predicted that public demand would increase. David Friedman, chairman of the 260-member Adult Film Association of America, described the appeal of building up a personal collection of hardcore films to a reporter for *Forbes* in 1978. "It's an absolute natural for homes, for parties, when the boys come over for a beer," he declared. "The man who buys a copy of *Patton* may look at it one or two times, but one who buys *Seven Into Snowy* [an X-rated version of *Snow White*] is going to look at it 10 or 15 times."[13] The reporter added that manufacturers marketed the devices by claiming that they would allow people to enjoy more cultural and sports events, knowing that this was not the primary intended use. It is an "open secret," he noted, that the biggest market for VCRs and camcorders was "among those for whom visual sex is a turn-on or entertainment or both."[14]

In the early 1980s, the introduction of sexually oriented cable television services accelerated the spread of erotic entertainment. In 1981, some 21 million American homes were wired for cable, with fewer than a million served by cable systems that offered one of six available premium networks showing adult fare. Even so, an entertainment reporter for the *New York Times* observed in 1981 that an "extraordinarily high" percentage of viewers were willing to pay additional monthly fees for adult content. When a separate network devoted to sexual fare, like the 1982 *Playboy* channel, was made available through a cable television system or as a late-night addition to a premium channel, such as Cinemax's *Max After Dark*, more than 50 percent of cable subscribers – and as many as 95 percent – typically signed up. The *Times* described cable television as a "pipeline" that brought sexually explicit entertainment "into the bedrooms of couples across America."[15] By 1988, about 53

[11] James Lardner, *Fast Forward: Jollywood, the Japanese and the Onslaught of the VCR* (New York: W. W. Norton & Co., 1987), 170–175.

[12] Klopfenstein, 30.

[13] James Cook, "The X-Rated Economy," *Forbes*, September 18, 1978, 85.

[14] Cook, "The X-Rated Economy," 82.

[15] Schwartz, "The TV Pornography Boom."

percent of all American homes with televisions received their service through cable providers.[16]

The technology-driven pornography boom created an insurmountable obstacle for anti-pornography feminists and other opposition groups, akin to removing television sets from U.S. homes. The right-wing decency organization Morality in Media led an unsuccessful campaign in Buffalo, New York, in 1981 to force the local city council to revoke the license for the *Escapade* adult entertainment cable channel, only to discover that their efforts publicized the availability of the service and increased subscriptions.[17] One could hazard a guess that WAP protests against the *High Society* 900-numbers produced a similar result. Once advances in technology brought pornography directly and privately into Americans' homes, while netting untold millions for the producers, distributors, and media companies who were eager for the higher profit margins associated with adult entertainment, there was no turning back.

Anti-Feminism and the New Right

In the early 1980s, the feminist anti-pornography movement also had to navigate the challenges of a repressive social and political climate created by the New Right. A defining feature of this neoconservative and religious coalition was its organized anti-feminism, expressed as a "pro-family" platform that opposed abortion, homosexuality, child care, sex education, sexual freedom, and pornography. New Right leaders desired a return to traditional religious and moral values, and a recommitment to the supremacy of the heterosexual, patriarchal family. Ronald Reagan centered his 1980 presidential campaign around these themes, speaking about the need to make America strong again by reconstituting the authority of the family and the state, at home and abroad. In addition to securing the loyal support of an anti-feminist segment of the population who could be counted on for high voter turnout, he gave powerful new legitimacy to the ideology of the nuclear family and to a gender hierarchy that feminists opposed.

Right-wing concern with pornography, long a feature of conservative civic reform efforts led by groups like Citizens for Decent Literature in the 1960s, gathered new strength. According to conservative Christian beliefs, God intended for men and women to practice sexual intercourse exclusively within marriage for the purposes of procreation and intimacy. Pornography encouraged sexual activity outside those bounds, stimulating immoral thoughts that could lead decent people to engage in destructive behaviors like promiscuity, adultery, and homosexuality, each of which exerted a devastating effect on families. The use of pornography within marriage was equally contaminating, encouraging lust rather than love and reducing a sacred sexual union to the

[16] Jonathan Coopersmith, "Pornography, Technology and Progress," *ICON* 4 (1988): 10.
[17] Coopersmith, 10.

level of an "animal" act.[18] As the legal scholar Eric Hoffman has explained, the conservative emphasis on sexual containment was one aspect of a larger worldview that saw "virtue, self-control, and dignity" as critical elements of a moral society.[19] As such, the government had an important role to play in restricting the availability of pornography.

In the late 1970s, New Right leaders attempted to pass new laws to achieve their vision of moral order. Senators Paul Laxalt, Orrin Hatch, and Jack Garn introduced the Family Protection Act to Congress in September 1979. This sweeping "pro-family" bill proposed to strengthen the two-parent, heterosexual family through a range of education, tax, and federal funding initiatives. Among its many provisions, the bill stipulated that no organization that endorsed homosexuality, challenged the significance of traditional sex roles, or provided contraception, abortion services, or counseling to a minor without parental consent could receive federal funding. Discrimination against gay people would not comprise an "unlawful employment practice." Legal Assistance offices, which offered government-supported legal aid to the lowest-income Americans, would be stripped of federal funds if they offered any advice regarding divorce, abortion services, gay rights, or practical advice to accomplish school desegregation. Although defeated, this bill and a wave of other anti-feminist and anti-gay ballot initiatives shaped an ideological context favorable to discrimination and intolerance. The burgeoning AIDS crisis in the 1980s intensified the backlash against alternative sexualitics and practices. AIDS was interpreted as proof that gay sex violated the laws of nature, and pornography was tied to this discourse as harmful material that encouraged homosexual conduct. As the anti-pornography ordinance campaigns went forward, feminists, gays, and lesbians saw their civil rights hanging in jeopardy, facing the threat of discriminatory laws and state-sanctioned harassment.

Internal Challenges for Anti-Pornography

Amid the pitfalls of the challenging external landscape, the feminist anti-pornography movement found itself dealing with internal problems that also affected its trajectory. By 1983, the feminist community that had supported the emergence and development of the anti-pornography movement was badly splintered. The women who had joined to object to depictions of sexual violence now found themselves part of a movement that objected to depictions of sex. Those who had demanded corporate responsibility through economic boycotts, pickets, and national letter-writing campaigns now found themselves

[18] See for example, the statement on pornography put forward by the General Council of the Assemblies of God Church, available online at: http://www.ag.org/top/beliefs/contempissues_06_pornography.cfm. Accessed March 20, 2010.

[19] Eric Hoffman, "Feminism, Pornography, and Law," *University of Pennsylvania Law Review* 497, no. 133 (1985); 505.

part of a movement publicly associated with censorship. Intramovement disagreements over the use of legal strategies had never been resolved, meaning that there was no consensus for how the movement should proceed. Leading members of WAP had professed interest in exploring legal solutions, but the organization as a whole had not endorsed this approach. To make matters worse, the national WAVAW and WAVPM chapters were in shambles. When MacKinnon and Dworkin introduced their ordinances defining pornography as a practice of sex discrimination, WAP was the only one of the three founding organizations in a position to decide how the movement ought to respond.

The first major shift that fractured the movement prior to 1983 was the growth of opposition to images that depicted sex rather than violence. When members of WAVAW opposed *Snuff* and *Black and Blue*, they did so because these images falsely constructed female and male sexuality and encouraged violence. Men were presented as motivated by an aggressive sexual drive, and women were aroused in turn by their own passivity and victimization. This type of portrayal justified and encouraged men's use of sexual force. The model in *Black and Blue* was battered and tied with ropes, and she enjoyed this brutal treatment: "I Love It!" she proclaimed. This image perpetuated a sexual ideology that damaged men as badly as women. The women who founded the anti-media violence branch of the movement were committed to eradicating these socially constructed gender differences as part of the struggle for true sexual liberation for both sexes, and they believed that this goal was within reach.

As the movement progressed, members of later groups like WAP were far less sanguine that sex, or at least heterosexual sex as constructed under patriarchy, could be a positive and empowering force for women. Instead of rejecting socially constructed gender differences, members of WAP built their analyses around them. Once they embraced cultural feminist ideas that described male values and female values as separate and fixed, where men were said to be inherently violent, lustful, and oppressive and women were emotional, caring, and nurturing, it became just as logical to oppose depictions of nonviolent heterosexual sex as those of overt sexual violence. Following influential theorists like Susan Griffin, Andrea Dworkin, and Catharine MacKinnon, members of WAP came to view pornography itself as an act of male violence. Real women were coerced in the making of pornography, sustaining both physical and emotional harm. Other women were victimized by men who were driven to rape after exposure to pornography. By sexualizing domination and subordination, pornography also objectified all women as subhuman "things" to be used, effectively consigning all women as a sex class to an inferior social position.

Under the terms of the WAP analysis, the *High Society* telephone messages constituted pornography because they encouraged men to regard women as panting, willing sexual objects. One of the *High Society* models recorded a message that described how she wanted the caller to meet her in Central Park at noon the following day and strip off her panties. For WAP, this message was not sexual fantasy, but a clarion call to men to fan out over New York City and rape. WAP also opposed the message because it suggested that some women might actually seek out and enjoy casual, no-strings sexual contact, which created a distorted view of women overall as "sexually ravenous creatures who enjoy brutal and impersonal sex." The concept of a "sexually ravenous" woman who desired "brutal and impersonal sex" was a male invention, and women who claimed to choose this sexuality suffered from false consciousness. No woman set free from the corrupt and male-defined world of eroticism under patriarchy would consent to such an objectifying encounter. To many WAP members, a sexually avid, lustful woman was a lie created by a pornographic culture.

Within the community of anti-pornography feminism, the transition from the focus on violence to the focus on sex was deeply troubling. Sexually repressive ideas had not been a part of the anti-media violence campaign. Members of WAVAW had defended women's right to be sexual, and to be sexual without fear of violence. When WAVAW said, "We are not *Black and Blue* and we do not love it when we are," it was debunking the myth that women enjoy sexual abuse, not saying that women did not enjoy sex.[20] Early members of WAVAW and WAVPM came into the movement with a commitment to the positive aspects of sexuality, and women's need to claim space to discover their sexuality free from the artificial gender differences foisted upon them by heterosexist media. As the movement changed over time, and as cultural feminist beliefs about gender polarity took hold, many of the early members felt a disconnect between their initial organizing efforts, and new movement directions.

WAVAW's decision to limit its campaign to images of overt sexual violence should not be interpreted as a whole-hearted endorsement of the kind of nonviolent sexually explicit materials, such as *Playboy* centerfolds, that proliferated in American society from the 1970s onward. If the community of anti-pornography feminists agreed on anything, it was that the majority of commercially available sexual fare was heterosexist, created with the male consumer in mind. The *High Society* phone lines were a perfect example. Gloria Leonard designed the system to make "aural" sex easily available to men, to give them access to women and sexual satisfaction anywhere five minutes of privacy and a telephone were available. That said, the founders of WAVAW also believed that women who challenged the myth of female sexuality as passive had to be free to use the cultural materials available to begin the process of imagining something better. In this way, they resembled pro-sex feminists, who argued that the kind of raw eroticism expressed through the *High Society* lines had been off-limits for too long. "It is precisely sex as an aggressive, unladylike activity, an expression of violent and unpretty emotion,

[20] Press Release, "No More Black and Blue," June 22, 1976, Branch Literature file, WAVAW Papers.

an exercise of erotic power, and a specifically genital experience that has been taboo for women," Ellen Willis wrote in defense of pornography.[21] WAVAW also hoped to free women to demand sexual pleasure on their own terms.

The second major shift that fractured anti-pornography feminism prior to 1983 concerned changes in preferred strategies, specifically the shift from public education techniques to demands for legal action. WAVAW wanted to empower every individual to create change. The organization asked everyone who viewed their slide show during the Warner boycott to write a protest letter on the spot. "The letters don't have to be polished," the slide show narrator would tell the audience, encouraging average citizens to let their voices be heard. "People should state if they are mothers, work with or know abused or raped women or have been themselves abused, or if they are men who don't like being portrayed as brutes."[22] The slide show script encouraged the narrator to help people understand the power of collective action. "While people are writing ask them to imagine being Mo Ostin or Ahmet Ertegun and receiving 1,000 letters. The presence of 1,000 letters ... all hand written! They cannot be ignored."[23] Every person could demand better media representation by writing to offending corporations, by joining WAVAW, by refusing to buy Warner-label records, and by spreading the word about the boycott. WAVAW's Joan Howarth, then a newly minted law school graduate, was an ardent supporter of these tactics. She encouraged the movement to stick with consumer action and public education, to demand fair and responsible representation of women, and to expose offending corporations to "the glare of publicity and the heat of women's rage."[24] WAVPM also pursued this course when it initiated the *Write Back, Fight Back!* letter-writing network.

The initial movement discussion of legal strategies took place at WAVPM's 1978 conference, when Brownmiller and others argued that restriction of pornography was consistent with First Amendment principles because obscenity was not protected speech. WAVPM leader Diana Russell said at that time that feminists should not allow free speech concerns to "short-circuit" their thinking about pornography. The debate heated up in 1979 when Brownmiller published an essay in a New York-area newspaper that argued that images that degraded, humiliated, and dehumanized women ought to be declared legally obscene and banned from public display.

By 1980–1981, many anti-pornography feminists were wary of the pursuit of legal strategies, finding them too dangerous in a conservative climate. They feared the well-mobilized New Right and its nationwide efforts to purge public libraries and schools of books and curricular materials containing sexual themes and presentations of nontraditional gender roles. History also offered

[21] Ellen Willis, "Feminism, Moralism and Pornography," in *Beginning to See the Light: Pieces of a Decade* (New York: Alfred Knopf, 1981), 224.

[22] WAVAW Slide Show, 1977, Boston WAVAW Papers.

[23] WAVAW Slide Show, 1977, Boston WAVAW Papers. Ostin was president of Warner Records, Ertegun was president of Atlantic Records.

[24] Joan Howarth, "Response by Joan Howarth," *WAVAW Newsletter* 8 (1980), 6

important lessons: The first federal anti-obscenity statute, known as the "Comstock" law of 1873, criminalized the interstate mailing of sexually oriented literature and devices, and was used to prosecute birth control advocates like Margaret Sanger.[25] Wendy Kaminer, a feminist attorney who resigned her membership in WAP in 1980 over First Amendment concerns, published a statement in WAVPM's *NewsPage* that year arguing that anti-pornography should remain a movement committed to education and consciousness raising. Feminists should not entrust a right-wing government with the legal right to ban pornography, she argued, because "[t]he power it will assume to do so will be far more dangerous to us all than the 'power' of pornography."[26] Attorney and WAVPM member Jill Lippitt, who had advocated legal action at the 1978 national conference, also rejected this approach in 1980.[27] "I simply do not trust what the patriarchal, racist and elitist state would do with the expanded powers of suppression which we feminists might give to them," she wrote in *NewsPage*.[28] WAVPM formally rejected the pursuit of new legislation or government action against pornography in 1981.[29] WAP, by contrast, did not reject the possibility of seeking legal reform and was associated with high-profile movement leaders who advocated the idea that pornography should be suppressed or banned.

The internal struggles over ideology, goals, and strategy, combined with the difficulty of maintaining sufficient resources for social action, took a heavy toll on the feminist anti-pornography movement in the early 1980s. At the time of the Barnard Conference in April 1982, the Los Angeles office of WAVAW was in a state of disarray and so short of funds that the chapter had not published its national newsletter for two years. Seven months later, the situation was no better. Melinda Lowrey, then the organization's national coordinator, sent a letter to the regional chapters recommending that WAVAW disband to

[25] For the history of women's efforts to communicate about sexual matters, especially birth control, see Linda Gordon, *Woman's Body, Woman's Right: A Social History of Birth Control in America*, 2nd ed. (New York: Penguin Books, 1990).

[26] Wendy Kaminer, "Pornography and the First Amendment: Prior Restraint and Private Action," *WAVPM NewsPage* 5, no. 4 (May 1980), 6.

[27] Lippitt's comments at the 1978 Feminist Perspectives on Pornography Conference are preserved in an NPR report on the conference. See Rosenbluth, *Fair Sex, Fair Game*, 1979. See also the discussion of the conference in Chapter 5.

[28] Jill Lippitt, "Choosing a Strategy to Fight Pornography," *WAVPM NewsPage* 5, no. 4 (May 1980), 5.

[29] "[T]hrough study and discussion of this issue, our position has now developed towards an emphasis on community education and direct action with no recourse to legal remedies," WAVPM's national coordinators advised in *NewsPage*. See Julie Greenberg and Bridget Wynne, "Learning to Organize Against Pornography," *WAVPM NewsPage* 5 no. 1 (January 1981), 4. For an extended discussion of WAVPM's change of heart, see Julie Greenberg, "An Activist's Analysis of the First Amendment," *WAVPM NewsPage* 5, no. 4 (May 1980), 5. Some WAVPM members privately supported legislation to ban pornography, even though the organization as a whole rejected this option. Diana Russell, a WAVPM founder, went on record in *The New York Times* in 1984 as favoring legal prohibitions. See Walter Goodman, "Battle on Pornography Spurred by New Tactics," *The New York Times*, July 3, 1984, A8.

allow local chapters to pursue projects with total autonomy. Lowrey pointed out that all of the chapters, including Los Angeles, were pursuing local projects in the absence of a unifying national campaign; that the national office lacked the womanpower, money, and time needed to coordinate activities and communication; and that some chapters were taking up pornography as their main focus, which violated the organization's founding principles.[30]

Over at WAVPM, the situation was also gloomy. According to the organization's meeting notes from January 1982, the group was experiencing severe financial difficulties and lack of participation by members, including the board of directors. Staff members had not been paid since the middle of October. Julie Greenberg, one of the two national coordinators, had left her position in May 1981. Bridget Wynne, the other national coordinator, resigned in April 1982. The committees that were responsible for WAVPM's core functions, such as presenting the slide show and coordinating special actions, had "dwindled in membership" and could not sustain the group's work.[31]

WAVPM tried to rally its members after an August 1982 retreat where the problems of lack of consensus on a long-term strategy were raised. The organization announced that it was inaugurating a new campaign focused on abusive television programming and advertising. Less than a year later, however, members expressed "low morale" about the television campaign, which had never gotten off the ground, and the fact that the organization was not accomplishing any goals. At a March 1983 general membership meeting, potential new targets were considered, including video pornography, sexual oppression in the office, or another *Take Back the Night* march, but there was little momentum for action.[32] At the end of 1983, the national chapter could no longer afford to publish the *NewsPage* newsletter.

WAP emerged as the dominant feminist anti-pornography group in the early 1980s, at the same time that consensus about the goals of anti-pornography overall broke down among movement groups. In the preceding period, especially from 1978–1980, WAVAW, WAVPM, and WAP regarded each other as "sister organizations" and tried to support one another's campaigns. By 1981, however, WAVAW and WAVPM had rejected legal methods for controlling pornography, and the transition from a focus on sexual violence to a focus on sex caused further consternation. These internal inconsistencies, as I have shown throughout the book, contributed to the demise of the earlier groups, as confusion and disagreements ensued over the changing nature of anti-pornography rhetoric and analysis. By the early 1980s, a loosely connected national network of feminist anti-pornography groups remained, but did not share a coherent vision for future organizing.

[30] Melinda Lowrey, National Coordinator, Los Angeles WAVAW, to all chapters, 3 November 1982, LA WAVAW Papers, Box 14A.

[31] Board of Directors Meeting Minutes, January 16, 1982, WAVPM Papers, Box 1 Administrative Files, Folder 3.

[32] WAVPM General Membership Meeting Notes, March 20, 1983 and April 17, 1983, WAVPM Papers, Box 1, Administrative Files, Folder: "General Meeting, 1977–1983."

Right-Wing Membership Growth for WAP

With WAVAW and WAVPM in serious decline by 1982, WAP was the most visible national feminist anti-pornography group. Newly politicized religious conservatives were eager to take action on issues of concern, and they saw in WAP a well-mobilized, well-publicized organization that was fighting the scourge of pornography.

Over the course of the early 1980s, WAP received hundreds of letters from religious conservatives and their groups expressing admiration for their work and seeking information on anti-pornography efforts. In September 1982, a member of Odessans for Decency (Odessa, Texas) wrote and asked for materials to hand out at the county fair. In March 1983, a staff member of Citizens for Decency Through Law (Fort Wayne, Indiana) wrote to let WAP know that his chapter had been putting forth "quite an effort to fight against pornography" and requested that WAP send pamphlets and a copy of their newsletter. The cofounder of the National Christian Outcry (Sierra Madre, California) wrote a few months later and asked to be added to the WAP mailing list and to receive literature about pornography. "My associates and I have recently become aware of your organization because of our own efforts in the morality legislation and education field," he advised. WAP did its share of outreach to this community as well. WAP steering committee member Alexandra Matusinka wrote in November 1983 to a Cincinatti woman who was working with the Presbyterian Church to introduce an anti-pornography bill in Ohio, and asked to receive a copy. That same month, WAP's Frances Patai, another member of the steering committee, sent petitions protesting the "Dial-a-Porn" telephone lines to a Catholic priest in New Jersey. She asked him to gather signatures from churchgoers that the organization could add to its portfolio for the FCC.[33] In most cases, when an individual or organization reached out to WAP or otherwise crossed WAP's path, organization members responded by mailing out literature and a membership form.

In May 1983, WAP received a letter signed by fourteen women living in Columbia, South Carolina. The women identified themselves as members of the Ola B. Taylor Circle of the Shandon United Methodist Church, a Christian denomination with evangelical roots that bars gays and lesbians from the ministry and prohibits same-sex unions. "It is apparent that explicit sex often coupled with sadistic or masochistic behavior have had a very detrimental effect on our society as a whole," they wrote. "We feel this is particularly true among the younger people and is attested by the rising crime rate [among] this group." The women also stated that it did not seem likely that the media

[33] These letters are: Odessans for Decency to WAP, August 25, 1982, WAP Records, Box 3, Folder 100; CDL Staffer to WAP, March 18, 1983, WAP Records, Box 2, Folder 86; cofounder National Christian Outcry to WAP, WAP Records, October 25, 1983, Box 2, Folder 86; Alexandra Matusinka to Cincinatti woman, WAP Records, November 14, 1983, Box 2, Folder 86; Frances Patai to Catholic priest, November 17, 1983, WAP Records, Box 2, Folder 86.

could practice sufficient restraint with regard to the portrayal of sex, making censorship inevitable. "While we are a small group, we do believe we are representative of a large majority of Middle America," they added.[34]

The Ola B. Taylor women clearly found pornography objectionable. Yet their antipathy for this material arose from a moralist perspective, not a feminist one. Their words echoed those of the three clergymen who founded the decency group Morality in Media in 1962 to address the effects of pornography "on children, youth and the family."[35] Exposure to pornography was frequently described by conservatives in the 1980s as a special threat to youth, leading them away from healthy relationships to a lifestyle characterized by deviant sexual practices and sexual addiction.

By way of response, WAP did not send a letter that explained the differences between the feminist and conservative Christian perspectives. It did not clarify the organization's support for gay and lesbian rights, abortion, sex education, and a host of other feminist commitments that might have caused the Taylor women to take a step back. Instead, steering committee member Florence Rush sent off a delighted note. "Dear All You Wonderful People," she wrote, "Thank you so much for your interest and support. A letter like yours makes all our hard work worthwhile." Rush enclosed literature and a membership form. "Please join us with your membership," she urged. "You will receive our newsletters and we could use your additional support."[36] Regardless of whether or not the Taylor women sent back their form, what is clear is that some portion of the 10,000 members that WAP claimed by 1985 opposed pornography on religious and moral grounds but were added to the WAP rolls, inflating the appearance of feminist support. This demographic shift had important political ramifications in the 1980s, as the organization publicly endorsed the MacKinnon-Dworkin anti-pornography ordinances and provided witnesses for Attorney General Edwin Meese's 1985 Commission on Pornography.

In sharing the story of the Taylor women, I am not trying to argue that WAP and anti-pornography feminism lacked feminist supporters. Rather I am suggesting that the total community of members that WAP claimed as it advocated for both a version of anti-pornography that was increasingly focused on sex, not violence, and for government restriction, was not strictly feminist in orientation. It was comprised of heterogeneous groups and individuals who opposed pornography on different sets of ideological grounds, including religious conservatives who believed that explicit sexuality encouraged immoral behavior. When WAP condemned pornography and urged the passage of ordinances that would have made it vulnerable to censorship, the organization did so in the

[34] Fourteen members of the Ola B. Taylor Circle of Shandon United Methodist Church to Women Against Pornography, May 3, 1983, WAP Records, Box 2, Folder 86.

[35] Quoted in Franklin Mark Osanka and Sara Lee Johann, *Sourcebook on Pornography* (Lexington, MA: Lexington Books, 1989), 255.

[36] Florence Rush, WAP Steering Committee, to Fourteen members of the Ola B. Taylor Circle of Shandon United Methodist Church, May 17, 1983, WAP Records, Box 2, Folder 86.

name of its feminist base. Yet its membership – the numbers that gave the organization such clout – was clearly drawn from a much broader set of constituents.[37] Their numbers – 7,000 members in 1983, rising to 10,000 members in 1985 – concealed a significant population whose attraction to anti-pornography was based on a desire to curb the free flow of pictures and information that dealt with sexually explicit themes, homosexuality, lesbianism, abortion, and birth control, none of which squared with feminist frameworks.

Social movement literature confirms that these patterns of cooperation among different kinds of movement actors are common. Social action groups often create alliances with outsiders when they seem, in principle, to share affinities on issues of concern. Religious conservatives brought strengths to the anti-pornography movement, including access to political elites, funding, and the potential to exercise substantial influence on public opinion. In return, the religious conservatives benefited from collaboration with a feminist movement that provided fresh rhetoric and innovative legal approaches. The right was quick to adopt feminist terminology, particularly the language of degradation and violence against women, both of which were central features of feminist and fundamentalist approaches but carried different meanings for the respective groups.[38]

At the time that these events unfolded, and in the years since, a range of observers have argued that the feminist anti-pornography movement made a dire mistake when it forged alliances with members of the religious and political right. Although I do not disagree with that assertion, the movement trajectory established in this book offers some context for understanding such decisions. By the early 1980s, WAP had few social supports. WAVAW and WAVPM were in tatters, for the most part, with no appreciable national leadership and organizational structure. Criticism rained down from the Left, with free speech advocates arguing that everyone – including pornographers – had an equal right to communicate their ideas, offensive and reprehensible as they might be, and pro-sex feminists rising up to demand women's right to claim sex and sexuality, even if that meant using male-oriented pornography for their own purposes. In addition, U.S feminism in general, as Susan Faludi has argued, was experiencing an intense public backlash supercharged by popular media portrayals of liberated women as angry, unhappy, lonely creatures who pined for the family life they had dismissed years prior. This smear campaign

[37] "Feminists Pioneer New Legislation Against Pornography," *WAP NewsReport* 6, no. 1 (Spring/Summer 1984), 1.

[38] On this dynamic in social movement theory, see Dieter Rucht, "Movement Allies, Adversaries, and Third Parties," in David A. Snow, Sarah A. Soule, and Hanspeter Kriesi, eds., *The Blackwell Companion to Social Movements* (Malden, MA: Blackwell Publishing, 2007), 197–216. On the use of the rhetoric of "degradation" see Vance, "More Danger, More Pleasure," 308. Feminists argued that pornography degraded women when it put men's pleasure and sexual needs first, and when it suggested that women were sexual objects whose primary purpose was to serve men. Fundamentalists argued that pornography degraded women by exposing them to depictions of sexually explicit acts that violated the sexual and moral integrity of human beings.

created a new wave of "fear and loathing" of feminism that turned potential new recruits away in droves.[39] This was the cultural climate surrounding WAP as the organization tried to address the pornography problem – a problem that its leadership sincerely believed was central to women's social, political, and economic subordination. As a result, they looked to others who opposed pornography and built bridges, seeking linkages to individuals and groups who were also committed to doing something concrete about pornography.

The MacKinnon-Dworkin Anti-Pornography Ordinance

When MacKinnon and Dworkin introduced their anti-pornography ordinance in 1983, they seemed to breathe new life into a stalled movement, offering a groundbreaking legal approach that warranted serious attention.[40] Dworkin, a radical feminist anti-pornography theorist with long-standing ties to WAP, and MacKinnon, a feminist legal scholar, cotaught a course on pornography at the University of Minnesota Law School in the fall of 1983, where they presented their analysis of the role of pornography in the oppression of women. This analysis included the idea that pornography is the graphic, sexually explicit subordination of women, and that it harms women by conditioning men to view women as inferior, as sex objects to be used. Pornography sexualizes and institutionalizes women's inequality by actively creating women's inferiority on the basis of their sex. In this way, pornography transcends defamation or hate speech and becomes an act of sex discrimination.[41] The political scientist Donald A. Downs has explained that MacKinnon and Dworkin interpreted pornography as the "literal expression" of male dominance, making pornography "more than simply a form of expression distinct from action: it is intricately and inextricably bound up with the subordination of women."[42] Pornography sexualizes the conditions of women's subordination, namely hierarchy, objectification, submission, and violence, and creates a society organized around male domination.[43] The free-flowing trade in pornography and pornographers themselves – the "secret police of male

[39] Faludi, *Backlash*, xix.

[40] For a complete analysis of the development of the ordinance and the related campaigns, see Donald Alexander Downs, *The New Politics of Pornography* (Chicago: The University of Chicago Press, 1989); Paul Brest and Ann Vandenberg, "Politics, Feminism and the Constitution: The Anti-Pornography Movement in Minneapolis," *Stanford Law Review* 39 (February 1987): 607–661; Lisa Duggan and Nan D. Hunter, *Sex Wars: Sexual Dissent and Political Culture* (New York: Routledge, 1995). For a comprehensive analysis by the leaders of this final phase, see Andrea Dworkin and Catharine A. MacKinnon, *Pornography and Civil Rights: A New Day for Women's Equality* (Minneapolis, Minn.: Organizing Against Pornography, 1988).

[41] For MacKinnon's description, see Catharine A. MacKinnon, *Only Words* (Cambridge, Mass: Harvard University Press, 1993), 3–41.

[42] Downs, *The New Politics of Pornography*, 38, and more generally, chapter 2.

[43] See Dworkin, "Against the Male Flood: Censorship, Pornography and Equality," in Drucilla Cornell, ed., *Feminism and Pornography* (Oxford, UK: Oxford University Press, 2000), 19–38.

supremacy" – made it impossible for women to exercise their civil rights and claim equality with men.[44]

At the same time that MacKinnon and Dworkin were teaching their seminar, Minneapolis residents were struggling to find a legal means to control the spread of adult bookstores, massage parlors, and other sexually oriented businesses. Members of a neighborhood task force invited MacKinnon and Dworkin to testify at a public hearing intended to persuade city officials to restructure the local adult-business zoning ordinance, which had been struck down by a federal district court in 1982. They appeared at the October 18, 1983 hearing and argued that zoning approaches failed to take account of the effect of pornography on women. Pornography, MacKinnon argued, was a form of sex discrimination that ought to be eliminated, not regulated with real estate rules.[45] Several weeks later, city officials hired MacKinnon and Dworkin to draft an amendment to the Minneapolis Civil Rights Ordinance.

MacKinnon and Dworkin drafted a model ordinance that introduced a definition of pornography rooted in the concept of civil rights. Pornography was a practice of sex discrimination against women, the "sexually explicit subordination of women, graphically depicted, through pictures and/or words." To warrant action under the law, a specific piece of pornography had to meet one of a series of ten additional conditions, such as the presentation of women "as whores by nature" or "as sexual objects, things or commodities" or "in postures of sexual submission" or "being penetrated by objects." If the material conformed to the definition, the ordinance provided four actionable claims of discrimination: trafficking in pornography, coercing someone to perform in pornography, forcing pornography on someone, or assaulting someone as a direct result of pornography. In the majority of instances, individuals could bring lawsuits for damages against producers, sellers, exhibitors, and distributors, and for an injunction against the further exhibition, distribution, or sale of the offending material.[46]

The ordinance was controversial from the start. Supporters hailed it as a feminist approach to the restriction of sexually explicit material that would finally give women the power to claim equality with men. Opponents warned that the language used to define pornography was vague and open-ended, and could be applied not only to violent material, but also to sexual images that did not feature overt violence. Individuals interested in the eradication of sex education materials, information about abortion, and other materials that feminists did not regard as pornographic could make a persuasive case using the language of the ordinance that such materials subordinated women and ought to be suppressed.

[44] Dworkin, "Against the Male Flood," 29.

[45] For the text of MacKinnon's comments, see Downs, *The New Politics of Pornography*, 58.

[46] The model ordinance is reprinted in Osanka and Johann, *Sourcebook on Pornography*, 519–521. It is also reprinted along with the Indianapolis and Cambridge ordinances in Catharine A. MacKinnon and Andrea Dworkin, eds., *In Harm's Way: The Pornography Civil Rights Hearings* (Cambridge, Mass.: Harvard University Press, 1997).

Throughout the mid-1980s, WAP was a strong advocate for the MacKinnon-Dworkin anti-pornography ordinances. When the Minneapolis city council held hearings on the proposed measure in December 1983, the WAP steering committee sent a passionate telegram to Mayor Donald Fraser urging him to approve it. "Unless you sign this amendment into law, the women of Minneapolis will continue to be second-class citizens and will continue to be subjected to a reign of sexual terror," they warned, noting the support of 7,000 members nationwide.[47] Members of a newly formed WAVPM chapter at Mankato State University wrote to WAP to let them know that the telegram had been read aloud at the public hearing on December 12, and had been very effective. High-profile feminists associated with WAP, including Robin Morgan, Gloria Steinem, and Phyllis Chesler, and WAVPM's Kathy Barry also sent letters of support to the city council that became part of the formal record.[48] Fraser claimed that the ordinance jeopardized free speech and vetoed it on January 5, 1984. WAP's Dorchen Leidholdt flew to Minneapolis to help organize a petition drive for a veto override. Upon her return to New York City, according to Brownmiller's account, she persuaded WAP to donate several thousand dollars to help support the effort.[49] Fraser established a task force to modify the ordinance in accordance with First Amendment protections, but he ultimately vetoed the measure when it came before him for a second time in July 1984.

Meanwhile, MacKinnon was drafting a version of the ordinance to be introduced in Indianapolis. Mayor William Hudnut III, a religious conservative who opposed pornography on obscenity grounds, had been watching the situation unfold in Minneapolis. He alerted Beulah Coughenour, a member of the Indianapolis city council who had spearheaded the successful fight against the ERA in Indiana, and who opposed abortion and laws against rape in marriage, to the new civil rights approach. Coughenour established contact with MacKinnon and hired her – but not Dworkin, whose passionate radical feminist rhetoric and unruly appearance would not have been well received in the conservative town – as a consultant to the city to develop the new legislation. MacKinnon and Coughenour worked together on a modified version of the ordinance, without much input from community members. As the historian Lisa Duggan has pointed out, MacKinnon did no outreach to local feminists, and took Coughenour's word that right-wing fundamentalists were not the ones backing the ordinance at the city council level.[50]

47 WAP Steering Committee to Minneapolis City Council, December 7, 1983, WAP Records, Box 12, Folder 718. The organization experienced steady membership growth in this period, and claimed 10,000 members in 1985.

48 These letters are reprinted in MacKinnon and Dworkin, *In Harm's Way*, in the section titled: Minneapolis: Exhibits.

49 Brownmiller, *In Our Time*, 319.

50 See Lisa Duggan, "Censorship in the Name of Feminism," in Duggan and Hunter, eds., *Sex Wars*, 29–39.

The Indianapolis city council passed the ordinance in April 1984, although it was opposed locally by feminists, members of the gay community, Democrats on the city council, and African-American politicians. Local feminists were incensed that an outsider had been brought in to represent the feminist position, and that this had been done by anti-feminist right-wingers like Coughenour. In an essay on the Indianapolis campaign, Duggan noted that local feminists were offended by the use of feminist rhetoric to "cloak" fundamentalist efforts to stifle sexual expression, and by the pretense that conservative city council members cared about women's rights.[51] In Indianapolis, unlike Minneapolis, the majority of grassroots support came from social conservatives and Evangelical Christians, including the Rev. Greg Dixon, a Baptist pastor and a cofounder with Jerry Falwell of the national Moral Majority, who used his influence to persuade city council members that the ordinance would be a powerful weapon in the war against smut. Hudnut signed the ordinance into law on May 1, 1984. A coalition of media groups led by the American Booksellers Association filed an immediate lawsuit. Ultimately, the Indianapolis ordinance was struck down as unconstitutional by the Indiana district court and the federal appeals court for the Seventh Circuit, a decision affirmed without oral argument by the Supreme Court in 1986.[52]

As the ordinance made its way around the country, WAP stepped up its efforts to promote and support the passage of civil rights legislation against pornography. The organization printed appeals in *NewsReport* for contributions to the Women Against Pornography Civil Rights Fund, which would be used in support of ordinance campaigns, especially to fund travel for "feminist legal scholars and organizers" to visit cities interested in pursuing feminist legislation against pornography. These scholars and organizers – who surely included MacKinnon and Dworkin – would provide local governments with expert advice to ensure that any laws drafted would accomplish feminist goals. WAP would also use some portion of the Civil Rights Fund to help gather testimony about pornography's harms that could subsequently be used in city council hearings and other government proceedings. The organization's steering committee – the eight women who ran WAP and charted its course of action – believed that legislation had become a necessary component of the anti-pornography campaign.[53] Women hurt by pornography had insufficient recourse without it. "[O]ur analysis of the condition of women ... has convinced us that education alone is not enough to help women who have been subordinated and abused through pornography," they wrote. Sending money to the fund would directly aid the passage of civil rights legislation against

[51] Duggan, "Censorship in the Name of Feminism," in Duggan and Hunter, eds., *Sex Wars*, 33.

[52] On Indianapolis, see Downs, *The New Politics of Pornography*, 95–143.

[53] The steering committee members in 1984 included: Evelina Kane, Dorchen Leidholdt, Alexandra Matusinka, Judy Ogden, Frances Patai, Kristen Reilly, Lesley Rimmel, and Florence Rush. None of the original full-time coordinators, namely Lynn Campbell, Susan Brownmiller, Dolores Alexander or Barbara Mehrhof sat on the committee.

pornography in cities around the country, an outcome that would constitute "a victory for women everywhere."[54]

The appeal for donations to the legislative fund was indicative of a larger transformation taking place within the feminist anti-pornography movement in the mid-1980s. As WAP and the movement as a whole directed attention to the effort to pass new legislation, the opportunities for individual activists to participate in feminist anti-pornography efforts declined. Organized anti-pornography groups like WAP shifted into new modes of action, largely playing supporting roles in the mid-1980s on behalf of ordinance campaigns and other government actions, like the 1985 Attorney General's Commission on Pornography. To aid the Commission, WAP provided a list of twenty-eight potential witnesses who were willing to testify at federal hearings about the personal harm they had sustained. These included a woman whose former husband was "an obsessive consumer of pornography" who forced her to act out scenarios from bondage magazines, and a University of Iowa cheerleader who had been seduced by a photographer into posing for nude pictures, which he subsequently sold to *Playboy*.[55] For their efforts, WAP received a certificate of appreciation from the U.S. Department of Justice for outstanding assistance to the Commission. Membership in the feminist anti-pornography movement in this period more often meant donating money, following coverage of the ordinances and other legislative efforts in the national media, writing support letters on behalf of other organizations' actions, and reading about First Amendment debates taking place on the national stage, rather than active participation in grassroots campaigns like the Warner boycott.

This was a major change for WAP, which had initially adopted tactics that gave women ownership of the anti-pornography issue and numerous opportunities to participate in grassroots actions. In its first year, WAP sponsored a march on Times Square that attracted thousands of participants, a feminist conference with 750 registrants, and an active education program of slide shows and porn tours that enabled members to play a hands-on role in building the movement and exerting influence over its direction. After 1983, however, the anti-pornography movement was primarily conducted through formal events like university forums and news conferences that featured select, high-profile feminists, often MacKinnon and Dworkin. The feminist position on pornography was articulated by a handful of leaders who were removed from the diverse community of grassroots organizers. Without the benefit of regular channels of communication, there were no "coherent procedures" for establishing representative group opinion and acting on it, a situation that the sociologist Todd Gitlin has described as also affecting the New Left.[56] The situation intensified throughout the 1980s, as the news media inflated

[54] "An Appeal to Members and Friends," *WAP NewsReport* 6, no. 1 (Spring/Summer 1984), 4.

[55] "Potential Witness List, prepared for Alan Sears," n.d. WAP Records, Box 5, Folder 246, "Attorney General's Commission."

[56] Gitlin, *The Whole World Is Watching*, 165.

the perception of feminist consensus around legislative action as the preferred solution to the pornography problem.

The Feminist Anti-Censorship Taskforce

Following the introduction of the ordinance in Indianapolis, the idea of using a civil rights approach to regulating the spread of sexually oriented materials caught conservatives' attention. Phyllis Schlafly endorsed the ordinance in 1984 in her national newsletter as an inspired means of controlling pornography in American communities. A right-wing legislator in Suffolk County, New York, introduced a version of the ordinance in 1984 that asserted that pornography caused "sodomy" and the "destruction of the family unit."[57] The language of the proposed ordinance was so anti-feminist that WAP opposed it.[58] The measure was defeated by just one vote. According to Carole Vance, the large turnout of Bible-toting fundamentalists who favored the ordinance galvanized concerned feminists to act, spurring the formation of the Feminist Anti-Censorship Taskforce (FACT). FACT was organized by New York and Madison, Wisconsin-area activists who were committed to opposing the ordinance on feminist grounds.

As the ordinance spread to other cities around the country, FACT helped organize local opposition. In 1985, the Los Angeles County Board of Supervisors considered and rejected a Minneapolis-style version, again failing to pass the measure by just one vote. FACT-LA formed to oppose the ordinance, joined by leaders of the Feminist Women's Health Centers who helped establish WAVAW in 1976. Voters in Cambridge, Massachusetts, turned the ordinance down in 1985 when it appeared as a referendum question on their ballots. In Cambridge, a coalition of feminist groups worked to defeat the ordinance, including FACT, the Greater Boston Area NOW chapter, sex industry workers, and the founders of the Boston chapter of WAVAW.[59] In 1985, FACT submitted an amicus curiae brief to the U.S. Appeals Court that was reviewing the constitutionality of the Indianapolis ordinance. The brief contained the argument that sexually explicit speech was not in and of itself harmful to

57 This is described in Lisa Duggan, "Censorship in the Name of Feminism," 39.

58 The Suffolk County version recast the ordinance as a way to restore respect for women, and inserted language about immorality, sodomy, and family values. As such, the revised version lacked feminist intent and few feminists supported it. The majority of the Suffolk County support came from fundamentalists.

59 The complexity of the Minneapolis and Indianapolis ordinance campaigns has been chronicled extensively by other scholars, and the account offered here is purposely brief. For MacKinnon and Dworkin's own view of the hearings, see MacKinnon and Dworkin, eds., *In Harm's Way: The Pornography Civil Rights Hearings*; for a First Amendment perspective, see Downs, *The New Politics of Pornography*; and Nadine Strossen, *Defending Pornography: Free Speech, Sex and the Fight for Women's Rights* (New York: Scribner, 1995); for a pro-sex account, as well as information about the formation of FACT, see Vance, "More Danger, More Pleasure," and Lisa Duggan and Nan D. Hunter, eds. *Sex Wars: Sexual Dissent and Political Culture* (New York: Routledge, 1995).

women, and that the vague terminology used to define pornography under the ordinance would result in state suppression of a wide range of sexual expression, including feminist presentations.[60] It criticized the ordinance for reinforcing sexist stereotypes that presented women as too fragile, and men too lustful and uncontrollable, to be trusted to negotiate sexuality without state intervention. FACT condemned the perpetuation of gender-based roles as a true barrier to achieving women's equality and ending sexual violence.

The FACT brief carried the signatures of more than 200 prominent feminists. Many of the founders of the pro-sex movement lent their names, including Carole Vance, Gayle Rubin, Amber Hollibaugh, Linda Gordon, and Ellen Willis. To anti-pornography feminists' chagrin, the list also contained the names of feminists who had turned away from the cause. The radical feminists Adrienne Rich and Kate Millett, the gender and violence experts Del Martin and Susan Schecter, the lesbian feminist Rita Mae Brown, NOW founder Betty Friedan, and LA-WAVAW founder Joan Howarth signed the brief. Although the anti-pornography feminists summoned support from Gloria Steinem, Phyllis Chesler, and Robin Morgan, the FACT brief exposed the extent of organized feminist opposition to anti-pornography legislation. MacKinnon and Dworkin tried to discredit those who supported FACT, but as Vance has observed, this tactic backfired. As more and more women who had devoted their lives to feminist causes began to appear on the "enemies list," the anti-pornography movement could no longer persuasively claim to speak on behalf of American feminism.[61]

In the years following the Supreme Court's 1986 finding that the Indianapolis anti-pornography ordinance was unconstitutional, the feminist anti-pornography movement ground to a halt. When efforts to continue pushing for legal reform proved futile, there was little to nothing left of the grassroots feminist anti-media violence movement to resuscitate. WAP survived on paper until 1989, but the group gradually collapsed along with much of organized second-wave feminism, which came apart over the battles around sexuality that engulfed the women's movement in the 1980s. Players on both sides of the pornography question were worn out by the bitter sex wars and despondent over mounting evidence of a full-scale crusade against plural forms of sexuality and sexual practices. The late 1980s witnessed a moral panic around AIDS, abstinence-only programs in schools, and struggles around the National Endowment for the Arts and its funding for "obscene" sexually themed work. In the face of this multipronged, large-scale backlash that included attacks on daycare centers, reproductive freedom, gay rights, affirmative action, privacy, and a host of other civil rights, it was clear that the state's interest in restricting sexual expression had nothing to do with a commitment to enlarging women's rights.

[60] The FACT brief was authored by two feminist law professors, Nan D. Hunter and Sylvia A. Law. It is reprinted in Duggan and Hunter, eds. *Sex Wars*, Appendix A.

[61] Vance, "More Danger, More Pleasure," 304.

Several years after the demise of WAP, anti-pornography feminism rallied again when the Canadian Supreme Court embraced MacKinnon and Dworkin's theory that pornography was a practice of sex discrimination. In the 1992 case, *Butler v. The Queen*, the Court interpreted Canadian obscenity laws as compatible with newer feminist concepts and upheld a statute that outlawed materials that "degraded" or "dehumanized" women. Anti-pornography feminists throughout North America hailed the decision as a victory for women. Feminists who had opposed the MacKinnon-Dworkin ordinances in the U.S. argued that it illustrated just how far the Right had come in appropriating feminist rhetoric and feminist approaches for their own purposes, giving the traditional anti-obscenity agenda a modern gloss that helped it achieve widespread social acceptance.

Years earlier, pro-sex feminists had warned that anti-pornography laws would be used to persecute women and sexual minority communities. Events in Canada confirmed their suspicions. Authorities moved to suppress a number of gay and lesbian materials; *Bad Attitude*, a lesbian sex magazine published by a Boston women's collective, was the first prosecution for obscenity under *Butler*.[62] More than half of all Canadian feminist bookstores had shipments confiscated by customs agents within two and a half years of the *Butler* decision, and the majority of seized materials dealt with gay, lesbian, and feminist themes. The Canadian feminists who initially celebrated the law as a powerful weapon in the war against female subordination lamented that it had become an engine for oppression. In an ironic twist, two books written by Andrea Dworkin, *Pornography: Men Possessing Women* and *Woman Hating*, were impounded at the U.S.-Canada border on the grounds that they contained obscene pornographic material.[63] According to Nadine Strossen, a legal scholar and the former president of the American Civil Liberties Union, neither the *Butler* decision nor any version of the MacKinnon-Dworkin anti-pornography ordinances contained a loophole for sexually explicit depictions that were part of a feminist presentation.[64]

Much like 19th-century feminists who mobilized an offensive against male vice, the anti-pornography feminists were overpowered in the end by conservative interests who redirected the feminist intent of the MacKinnon-Dworkin ordinance.[65] Feminists lost control of the movement as its support base moved to the right, and they were unable to compel the courts and the government to adopt the feminist worldview of the pornography problem. Anti-pornography

[62] On the effect of *Butler*, see Brenda Cossman, *Bad Attitudes on Trial: Pornography, Feminism, and the Butler Decision* (Toronto: University of Toronto Press, 1997); see also Dany Lacombe, *Blue Politics: Pornography and the Law in the Age of Feminism* (Toronto: University of Toronto Press, 1994).

[63] See Strossen, 237.

[64] On *Butler* and censored materials, see Strossen, 230–246; Carl Wilson, "Northern Closure: Anti-Pornography Campaign in Canada," *The Nation*, December 27, 1993, 788.

[65] On the nineteenth-century case, see Judith Walkowitz, *Prostitution and Victorian Society: Women, Class and the State* (Cambridge, UK: Cambridge University Press, 1980).

feminists saw their rhetoric and strategies co-opted and redirected to serve the interests of conservative moralists who hoped to suppress sexually explicit materials. This about-face quashed any movement hope that a new law might forcibly eradicate material that some activists saw as blocking the path to women's equality.

Epilogue: Evaluating Anti-Pornography Feminism in Historical Context

In the spring of 2007, a controversial print advertisement for the Italian fashion house of Dolce & Gabbana appeared in the United States in the men's magazine, *Esquire*. The ad depicted a stylized gang rape that featured a woman lying on the ground in the prone position with her dress hiked up above her hips. A partially-clothed man knelt beside her, physically restraining her by pinning her wrists to the ground. Four other men towered above them, watching the action unfold with coolly detached expressions, clearly waiting to take a turn. When public furor erupted in the United States and Europe, the designers Domenico Dolce and Stefano Gabbana defended the ad as a representation of an erotic dream or a sexual game. This explanation failed to quell protest. In response, the fashion house canceled the campaign and pulled the ad from its scheduled global print run.

As I have pondered the lasting impact of the feminist anti-pornography movement, the Dolce & Gabbana episode has often returned to my thoughts. Although it is discouraging to realize that such sexually violent representations continue to surface, and not just in advertising, but in mainstream films and television, music videos, video games, and of course in pornography, as well as other popular media, an important social change has occurred that deserves note. Whereas feminists in the 1970s had to launch a national protest and a three-year consumer boycott of a major media corporation to make the point that advertisements like *Black and Blue* glorified violence against women, it was immediately apparent to contemporary audiences that a glamorous depiction of rape was a dangerous proposition. The Dolce & Gabbana advertisement promoted the stereotypical gender roles that the early anti-pornography movement groups criticized as unhealthy for women and men, and it normalized sexual violence as something that men enjoy and women accept as their due. One important legacy of the feminist anti-pornography movement is this improved public understanding that the symbolic environment that we create has concrete effects on the quality of men's and women's lives. Our culture has become sensitized to the problem of mediated representation of sexual violence against women and its connection to real-world attitudes and acts, and this heightened awareness is a result, at least in part, of the public education and consciousness-raising efforts of the feminist anti-pornography movement.

Connecting the Dolce & Gabbana ad to the work of the anti-pornography movement also offers an important reminder that the movement evolved out of a feminist commitment to oppose images that portrayed sexual violence, not sex. This distinction is often absent from contemporary discussions of the anti-pornography movement, especially those influenced by a body of mid-1990s postfeminist work by such well-known authors as Katie Roiphe, Naomi Wolf, and Rene Denfeld. Focusing on the last few years of the movement as if they represented the whole, these authors have portrayed anti-pornography activists as "victim feminists" who saw only the potential for oppression and coercion in the sexual realm, and who equated sexual relations with men to a violent physical and emotional invasion.

Each of these authors has promulgated a vision of second-wave feminism, particularly anti-pornography feminism, as anti-sexual, a representation that does not accurately capture the diversity of thought among movement activists. In *Fire with Fire*, Wolf argued that the anti-pornography generation constructed a view of women as powerless, so cowed by the sheer magnitude of male tyranny that they could not begin to fight back. The pathway forward for feminism, she argued, was for women to overcome the limitations of the victim mindset by recognizing – and seizing – their power, including sexual power. For Wolf, seizing sexual power meant letting go of a version of feminism that was "sexually judgmental, even anti-sexual" and one that held that "sensuality cannot coincide with seriousness."[66] Roiphe and Denfeld's accounts fanned the anti-sexual flames. Roiphe, in *The Morning After*, argued that the feminism she encountered as a college student existed primarily to scare women away from sex by conjuring up an epidemic of date rape and other forms of sexual coercion on campus. Roiphe took particular aim at MacKinnon, whom she dubbed the "antiporn star," characterizing the legal theorist and her followers as anti-sexual puritans who sought to impose a conservative sexual morality on society as a whole.[67] Denfeld, in turn, described the entire "feminist agenda" as a "holy crusade" bent on eradicating sexually explicit material at any cost, "even at the expense of women's rights."[68] According to Denfeld, the anti-pornography movement devised a novel solution to the ongoing problem of rape, namely the systematic "destruction and censorship of sexual words and ideas."[69]

Influenced in part by these popular texts, the third wave of feminism today positions itself as a response to a sexually repressive second wave. The mainstream news media have celebrated this shift, congratulating the third wave for inaugurating a lighter and brighter version of feminism that encourages women to reject the second wave's dour fixation on gender oppression.[70] In

[66] Naomi Wolf, *Fire with Fire: The New Female Power and How It Will Change the 21st Century* (New York: Random House, 1993), 137.

[67] On this tendency in third-wave writing, see Astrid Henry, *Not My Mother's Sister: Generational Conflict and Third-Wave Feminism* (Bloomington: Indiana University Press, 2004), chapter 3.

[68] Rene Denfeld, *The New Victorians: A Young Woman's Challenge to the Old Feminist Order* (New York: Warner Books, 1995), 58, 99.

[69] Denfeld, 89.

[70] I have discussed current media constructions of second and third wave feminists in a previous work. See Carolyn Bronstein, "Representing the Third Wave: Mainstream Print Media

a recent *Guardian* interview with the writer Ariel Levy, who has described the rise of a commercialized porn-star culture that young women embrace, the third wave was praised for rescuing sexual pleasure and diversity. "[T]he wider third-wave project of reclaiming and embracing female sexuality, after generations in which women weren't allowed to admit to any sexual feelings or interest at all," the interviewer noted, "has been a genuinely positive progression."[71] In response to a multitude of similar pronouncements, each of which obliterates advocacy of "sexual feelings or interest" among second-wavers, the feminist philosopher Cathryn Bailey has pointed out that such statements do not hold up against the historical record. Too often, third-wave authors – and journalists writing about third-wavers – portray the second wave as a monolith, as if there were some "agreed-upon party line" that every second-wave feminist endorsed. This is certainly false with regard to sexual thought, as many historians including Linda Gordon, John D'Emilio, Estelle Freedman, Ellen Carol DuBois, Alice Echols, and Jane Gerhard have shown that there were always voices within the second wave "crying out for diversity and individual variance" in defense of women's erotic rights.[72] Gerhard states this succinctly, characterizing the notion that feminists are anti-sex as "breathtakingly wrong."[73]

In this book, I have constructed a history of the evolution of the anti-pornography movement that emphasizes its roots in a broad-based, grassroots effort to protest commercial images of sexual violence against women. By doing so, I intended to show that the majority of movement participants were interested in eradicating depictions of violence, not depictions of sex. Beginning with protests against *Snuff* in 1975, WAVAW members built on the radical feminist critique of heterosexuality to argue that false gender stereotypes that portrayed men as lustful, brutish beasts and women as vulnerable, willing victims distorted relationships between the sexes and encouraged sexual violence and sexual inequality. The proliferation of violent, sadistic images of women in the 1970s, such as the *Hustler* meat-grinder cover and countless other dehumanized images of the female body that reduced women to objects – or "specimens" as Ellen Willis observed in 1979 – showed a total disregard for women's bodily integrity and their quest for political and social rights. Violent pornography emerged as the consummate male cultural product of the sexual revolution, marketed unapologetically by an industry that commodified women's bodies without concern for social consequences. For the early anti-pornography activists, sexually violent images of women represented a fierce backlash against women's attempts to claim equality with men and a powerful reminder of their vulnerability to physical abuse.

Framing of a New Feminist Movement," *Journalism and Mass Communication Quarterly* 82, no. 4 (Winter 2005): 783–803.

[71] Kira Cochrane, "Interview with Ariel Levy," *The Guardian*, available online at: http://www.ariellevy.net/about.php?press=y&article=12 (accessed August 12, 2009).

[72] Bailey, "Unpacking the Mother/Daughter Baggage," 139, 150.

[73] Gerhard, *Desiring Revolution*, 11.

The anti-sexual attitudes that have won anti-pornography negative popular and academic appraisals were a feature of late movement discourse, to be sure, but they were not endorsed in all corners. Most WAVAW, WAVPM, and WAP feminists were trying to undo the climate of acceptability around sexual violence – the epidemic of rape, incest, battering, and coercion discovered in consciousness raising groups – so that they, and generations of women to come, might actually enjoy the sexual freedom that the sexual revolution promised but had not fully delivered. WAVAW, in protesting *Black and Blue*, opposed the myth that knocking a woman around would awaken her slumbering desire precisely because it threatened women's ability to pursue sexual experiences without being exposed to violence. The activists who founded anti-pornography recognized that the artificial gender divisions created by the institution of heterosexuality – including the stereotypes of male aggression and female passivity – blocked everyone's path to authentic sexual liberation. In restoring the intent and activities of the earlier phase of the movement, I sought to challenge the unwarranted condemnation of all anti-pornography activists as anti-sexual. Within each anti-pornography movement group, there were always voices challenging the slide toward opposition to images that depicted sex, rather than overt violence, and contesting the censorship route. These voices warned that such a path would endanger sexual freedom.

In restoring the historical context of the evolution of anti-pornography, this book also offers a needed corrective to accounts that treat the MacKinnon-Dworkin period from 1983 to 1986 as the sum total of the movement. Denfeld, for example, dates the beginning of the anti-pornography movement to the introduction of the Minneapolis ordinance in 1983. The women's studies scholar Astrid Henry has pointed out an important limitation of this truncated chronology, noting that it has fostered a common perception that MacKinnon and Dworkin were the movement's "supreme leaders," who stood in for second-wave feminism as a whole.[74] In my own formulation, I would change that to read that MacKinnon and Dworkin have come to stand in for *the anti-pornography movement as a whole*, a representation that I seek to challenge. As this book shows, the effort in Minneapolis inaugurated the movement's final phase, and the ordinance campaigns signaled a major departure from the tactics and strategies endorsed by the majority of earlier movement activists. Accounts that start with the tail end of the anti-pornography movement, failing to take what I have called a "long view" of the movement that incorporates its formative years, erase the better part of a decade of organizing against sexualized media violence and obscure the complex set of political and cultural factors that led *some* feminists to support legal strategies.

By the time that MacKinnon and Dworkin introduced the ordinances, movement energy and resources were ebbing. The prospect of a new approach appealed to many activists who were discouraged that alternative feminist strategies had failed to curb sexually violent and heterosexist expression. It

[74] Henry, *Not My Mother's Sister*, 101.

is not clear, however, whether the majority of grassroots support for anti-pornography in 1983 and beyond was feminist support. What is clear is that feminist anti-pornography organizations like WAP enjoyed significant, but mixed, membership including religious conservatives who saw an opportunity to join hands with others opposed to pornography. WAP, in turn, lent support to the ordinances with the weight of its membership behind it. The anti-pornography movement as a whole, however, did not support legal measures to control pornography.

I will close by returning briefly to the question of power and powerlessness in the anti-pornography movement. As discussed earlier, postfeminist accounts take anti-pornography feminism to task for robbing women of their power. Such an indictment is only possible if one considers the final phase of the anti-pornography movement in a vacuum, divorcing it from its roots. The MacKinnon-Dworkin ordinance did position women as powerless, and it sought special government protection on the basis of the inferior social status that pornography supposedly created for all women as a sex class. Yet, as this book shows, the MacKinnon-Dworkin ordinance was not the sum total of anti-pornography organizing. It comprised the final phase of a movement that originated in inspiring anti-media violence protest led by groups who did not endorse visions of powerlessness, but believed in women's power to achieve social change.

When early movement activists organized against mediated images of sexual violence, they asserted their power to challenge the glorification of violence against women and the promotion of gender stereotypes that blocked their path to equality. They initiated a boycott of the record industry. They held news conferences. They created a slide show to teach members of the public about the antisocial effects of sexually violent images. They bought corporate stock and spoke up at shareholders' meetings. They established a national letter-writing network to persuade media corporations to cancel abusive advertising campaigns. They created street theater performances, marched en masse, organized conferences, and published newsletters and books. The women who built the movement were empowered agents who were committed to doing something concrete to end sexual violence against women, and to improve the material conditions of women's lives. They strove to reduce gender oppression, creating social change that would allow women to claim real sexual freedom, long overdue.

Bibliography

Aagerstoun, Mary Jo and Elissa Auther. "Considering Feminist Activist Art." *NWSA Journal* 19, no. 1 (Spring 2007): vii–xiv.

Abbott, Sidney, and Barbara Love. *Sappho Was a Right-On Woman: A Liberated View of Lesbianism*. New York: Stein and Day, 1972.

Alderfer, Hannah, Beth Jaker, and Marybeth Nelson, eds. *Diary of a Conference on Sexuality*. New York: Faculty Press, 1982.

Alexander, Dolores. Oral History conducted by Kelly Anderson, Southold, New York, March 20, 2004 and October 22, 2005, Sophia Smith Voices of Feminism Oral History Project. Available online at http://www.smith.edu/library/libs/ssc/vof/vof-narrators.html

Alexander, Priscilla. "Prostitution: A Difficult Issue for Feminists." In *Sex Work: Writings by Women in the Sex Industry*, edited by Frederique Delacoste and Priscilla Alexander, 248–263. Pittsburgh: Cleis Press, 1987.

Allen, Pamela. "Free Space." In *Radical Feminism*, edited by A. Koedt, E. Levine, and A. Rapone, 271–279. New York: Quadrangle Books, 1973.

Allison, Dorothy. Oral History conducted by Susanne Dietzel, Tulane University, New Orleans, Louisiana, November 1995, Zale Writer in Residence Program at the Newcomb College Center for Research on Women. Available online at http://www.tulane.edu/~wc/zale/allison/allison.html

Allyn, David. *Make Love, Not War: The Sexual Revolution: An Unfettered History*. New York: Routledge, 2001.

Altman, Clara. "All of These Rights: Equality, Free Speech, and the Feminist Anti-Pornography Movement, 1976–1986." Paper presented at the annual meeting of the Law and Society Association, Grand Hyatt, Denver, Colorado, May 25, 2009.

Appleford, Steve. *The Rolling Stones: It's Only Rock and Roll, Song by Song*. New York: Schirmer Books, 1997.

Atkinson, Ti-Grace. *Amazon Odyssey*. New York: Links Books, 1974.

"Why I'm Against S/M Liberation." In *Against Sadomasochism: Radical Feminist Analysis*, edited by R. Linden, D. Pagano, D. Russell, and S. Star, 90–92. East Palo Alto, CA: Frog In the Well, 1982.

Attorney General's Commission on Pornography. *Final Report*. Washington, DC: U.S. Department of Justice, 1986.

Bailey, Beth. *From Front Porch to Back Seat: Courtship in Twentieth-Century America*. Baltimore: The Johns Hopkins University Press, 1989.

Sex in the Heartland. Cambridge, MA: Harvard University Press, 1999.

Bailey, Cathryn. "Making Waves and Drawing Lines: The Politics of Defining the Vicissitudes of Feminism." *Hypatia: A Journal of Feminist Philosophy* 12, no. 3 (1997): 17–28.

"Unpacking the Mother/Daughter Baggage: Reassessing Second-and Third-Wave Tensions." *Women's Studies Quarterly* 30, no. 3–4 (Fall 2002): 138–154.

Barnard, Amii Larken. "The Application of Critical Race Feminism to the Anti-Lynching Movement: Black Women's Fight Against Race and Gender Ideology, 1892–1920." *UCLA Women's Law Journal* 1, no. 2–3 (1996): 1–38.

Barry, Kathleen. *Female Sexual Slavery*. Englewood Cliffs, NJ: Prentice Hall, 1979.

Bashevkin, Sylvia. "Facing a Renewed Right: American Feminism and the Reagan/Bush Challenge." *Canadian Journal of Political Science* 27, no. 4 (December 1994): 669–698.

Baughman, James L. *The Republic of Mass Culture: Journalism, Filmmaking and Broadcasting in America Since 1941*, 2nd ed. Baltimore: The Johns Hopkins University Press, 1997.

Henry R. Luce and the Rise of the American News Media. Baltimore: The Johns Hopkins University Press, 2001.

Baumer, Eric P., Richard B. Felson, and Steven F. Messner, "Changes in Police Notification for Rape, 1973–2000." *Criminology* 41, no. 3 (August 2003): 841–872.

Baxandall, Rosalyn and Linda Gordon. *Dear Sisters: Dispatches from the Women's Liberation Movement*. New York: Basic Books, 2000.

Baxandall, Rosalyn, Linda Gordon, and Susan Reverby, eds. *America's Working Women*. New York: Random House, 1976.

Belkaoui, Ahmed and Janice M. Belkaoui. "A Comparative Analysis of the Roles Portrayed by Women in Print Advertisements: 1958, 1970, 1972." *Journal of Marketing Research* 13 (May 1976): 168–172.

Bell, Laurie, ed. *Good Girls, Bad Girls: Feminists and Sex Trade Workers Face to Face*. Toronto: Seal Press, 1987.

Benedict, Helen. *Virgin or Vamp: How the Press Covers Sex Crimes*. New York: Oxford University Press, 1992.

Bergmann, Barbara. *The Economic Emergence of Women*. New York: Basic Books, 1986.

Berson, Ginny. "The Furies." In *Lesbianism and the Women's Movement*, edited by Nancy Myron and Charlotte Bunch, 15–19. Baltimore: Diana Press, 1975.

Blasius, Mark and Shane Phelan, eds. *We Are Everywhere: A Historical Sourcebook on Gay and Lesbian Politics*. New York: Routledge, 1997.

Blumenthal, Ralph. "Porno Chic." *New York Times Magazine*, January 21, 1973, 28–34.

Blumenthal, Sidney and Thomas Byrne Edsall, eds. *The Reagan Legacy*. New York: Pantheon, 1988.

Blumler, Jay, Michael Gurevitch, and Elihu Katz. "Reaching Out: A Future for Gratifications Research." In *Media Gratifications Research: Current Perspectives*, edited by Karl E. Rosengren, L. Wenner, and P. Palmgreen, 255–273. Beverly Hills, CA: Sage Publications, 1985.

Bradley, Patricia. *Mass Media and the Shaping of American Feminism, 1963–1975*. Jackson: University of Mississippi Press, 2005.

Brest, Paul and Ann Vandenberg. "Essay: Politics, Feminism, and the Constitution: The Anti-Pornography Movement in Minneapolis." *Stanford Law Review* 39 (February 1987): 607–661.

Bronstein, Carolyn. "Representing the Third Wave: Mainstream Print Media Framing of a New Feminist Movement." *Journalism and Mass Communication Quarterly* 82, no. 4 (Winter 2005): 783–803.

"No More Black and Blue: Women Against Violence Against Women and the Warner Communications Boycott, 1976–1979." *Violence Against Women* 14, no. 4 (April 2008): 418–436.

brooke. "Feminist Conference: Porn Again." *off our backs* (November 1979): 24–27.

"Life, Liberty, & the Pursuit of Porn." *off our backs* (January 1979): 5–6.

Brown, Helen Gurley. *Sex and the Single Girl.* New York: Pocket Books, 1962.

Brown, Rita Mae. "The Shape of Things to Come." In *Lesbianism and the Women's Movement*, edited by Nancy Myron and Charlotte Bunch, 69–78. Baltimore: Diana Press, 1975.

A Plain Brown Rapper. Oakland, CA: Diana Press, 1976.

Brownmiller, Susan. *Against Our Will: Men, Women and Rape.* New York: Simon & Schuster, 1975.

"Pornography and the First Amendment." *New York University Review of Law and Social Change* 8 (1978–1979): 255–257.

"Let's Put Pornography Back in the Closet." *Newsday*, July 17, 1979, 16.

In Our Time: Memoir of a Revolution. New York: The Dial Press, 1999.

Bryan, Shirley K. "Venereal Disease and the Teenager." *Journal of Clinical Child Psychology* 3 (1974): 24–36.

Bunch, Charlotte. *Passionate Politics: Feminist Theory in Action.* New York: St. Martin's Press, 1987.

Burstyn, Varda, ed. *Women Against Censorship.* Vancouver and Toronto: Douglas & McIntyre, 1985.

Califia, Pat. "A Secret Side of Lesbian Sexuality." *The Advocate* (December 27, 1979): 19–23.

Chancer, Lynn S. *Reconcilable Differences: Confronting Beauty, Pornography, and the Future of Feminism.* Berkeley: University of California Press, 1998.

Clark, Wendy. "The Dyke, the Feminist and the Devil." *Feminist Review* 11 (June 1982): 30–39.

Clayton, Richard and Harwin Voss. "Shacking Up: Cohabitation in the 1970's." *Journal of Marriage and the Family* 39 (1977): 273–283.

Cmiel, Kenneth. "The Politics of Civility." In *The Sixties: From Memory to History*, edited by David Farber, 263–290. Chapel Hill and London: University of North Carolina Press, 1994.

Collins, Patricia Hill. *Black Feminist Thought: Knowledge, Consciousness and the Politics of Empowerment.* New York: Routledge, 1990.

Comfort, Alex. *The Joy of Sex.* New York: Simon & Schuster, 1972.

Commission on Obscenity and Pornography. *Final Report.* Washington, DC: U. S. Government Printing Office, 1970.

Cook, James. "The X-Rated Economy." *Forbes*, September 18, 1978: 81–92.

Coopersmith, Jonathan. "Pornography, Technology and Progress." *ICON* 4 (1988): 94–125.

Corliss, Richard. "That Old Feeling: When Porno Was Chic." *Time.com.* Available online at http://www.time.com/time/columnist/prinout/0881610432670o.html (accessed March 29, 2005).

Cornell, Drucilla. *At the Heart of Freedom: Feminism, Sex, and Equality*. Princeton, NJ: Princeton University Press, 1998.

ed. *Feminism & Pornography*. New York: Oxford University Press, 2000.

Cossman, Brenda. *Bad Attitudes on Trial: Pornography, Feminism, and the Butler Decision*. Toronto: University of Toronto Press, 1997.

Cott, Nancy F. "Passionlessness: An Interpretation of Victorian Sexual Ideology, 1790–1850." In *A Heritage of Her Own: Toward a New Social History of American Women*, edited by Nancy F. Cott and E. H. Pleck, 162–181 New York: Touchstone, 1979.

Cottle, Charles E., et al. "Conflicting Ideologies and the Politics of Pornography." *Gender & Society* 3, no. 3 (September 1989): 303–333.

Courtney, Alice E. and Sarah Wernick Lockeretz. "A Woman's Place: An Analysis of the Roles Portrayed by Women in Magazine Advertisements." *Journal of Marketing Research* 8 (February 1971): 92–95.

Craft, Nikki. "Kitty Genovese Women's Project: Statement of Purpose." In *Fight Back! Feminist Resistance to Male Violence*, edited by F. Delacoste and F. Newman, 242–246. Minneapolis, MN: Cleis Press, 1981.

Craig, Stephen. "Madison Avenue versus *The Feminine Mystique*: How the Advertising Industry Responded to the Onset of the Modern Women's Movement." Paper presented to the Popular Culture Association, annual meeting, San Antonio, Texas, March 27, 1997. Available online at http://www.rtvf.unt.edu/people/craig/madave.htm (accessed January 20, 2010).

Crawford, Alan. *Thunder on the Right: The "New Right" and the Politics of Resentment*. New York: Pantheon Books, 1980.

Creighton, Jane. "Lynn Campbell, 1955–1984." *off our backs* (June 1984): 25.

Crespino, Joseph. *In Search of Another Country: Mississippi and the Conservative Counterrevolution*. Princeton, NJ: Princeton University Press, 2007.

Cronan, Sheila. "Marriage." In *Radical Feminism*, edited by Anne Koedt, Ellen Levine, and Anita Rapone, 213–221. New York: Quadrangle Books, 1973.

Cuklanz, Lisa M. *Rape on Prime Time: Television, Masculinity and Sexual Violence*. Philadelphia: University of Pennsylvania Press, 2000.

Daly, Mary. "Deep Throat." *Variety*, June 28, 1972, 26.

Gyn/Ecology: The Meta-Ethics of Radical Feminism. Boston: Beacon, 1978.

de Grazia, Edward. *Censorship Landmarks*. New York: Bowker, 1969.

Girls Lean Back Everywhere: The Law of Obscenity and the Assault on Genius. New York: Random House, 1992.

Delacoste, Frederique and Felice Newman, eds. *Fight Back! Feminist Resistance to Male Violence*. Minneapolis, MN: Cleis Press, 1981.

Delaplaine, Jo. "Stabbing the Beast in the Belly: Women Against Violence Against Women." *off our backs* 7 (November 1977): 9.

D'Emilio, John. "Women Against Pornography." *Christopher Street* (May 1980): 19–26.

D'Emilio, John and Estelle B. Freedman. *Intimate Matters: A History of Sexuality in America*. New York: Harper & Row, 1988.

Denfeld, Rene. *The New Victorians: A Young Woman's Challenge to the Old Feminist Order*. New York: Warner Books, 1995.

Densmore, Dana. "Independence from the Sexual Revolution." In *Radical Feminism*, edited by Anne Koedt, Ellen Levine, and Anita Rapone, 107–118. New York: Quadrangle Books, 1973.

Diamond, Irene. "Pornography and Repression: A Reconsideration of 'Who' and 'What'," In *Take Back the Night: Women on Pornography*, edited by Laura Lederer, 187–203. New York: William Morrow, 1980.

Diamond, Sara. *Roads to Dominion: Right-Wing Movements and Political Power in the United States*. New York: Guilford Press, 1995.

Dow, Bonnie J. *Prime Time Feminism: Television, Media Culture and the Women's Movement since 1970*. Philadelphia: University of Pennsylvania Press, 1996.

Downs, Donald Alexander. *The New Politics of Pornography*. Chicago: University of Chicago Press, 1989.

DuBois, Ellen and Linda Gordon. "Seeking Ecstasy on the Battlefield: Danger and Pleasure in Nineteenth-Century Feminist Sexual Thought." In *Pleasure and Danger: Exploring Female Sexuality*, edited by Carole S. Vance, 31–49. Boston: Routledge & Kegan Paul, 1984.

Duggan, Lisa and Nan D. Hunter. *Sex Wars: Sexual Dissent and Political Culture, 10th Anniversary Edition*. New York: Routledge, 1995.

Dullea, Georgia. "In Feminists' Antipornography Drive, 42nd Street Is the Target," *The New York Times*, July 6, 1979, A12.

Dworkin, Andrea. *Woman Hating*. New York: E. P. Dutton, 1974.

"For Men, Freedom of Speech; For Women, Silence Please." In *Take Back the Night: Women on Pornography*, edited by Laura Lederer, 256–258. New York: William Morrow, 1980.

"Pornography and Grief." In *Take Back the Night: Women on Pornography*, edited by Laura Lederer, 286–292. New York: William Morrow, 1980.

"Why So-Called Radical Men Love and Need Pornography." In *Take Back the Night: Women on Pornography*, edited by Laura Lederer, 148–154. New York: William Morrow, 1980.

Right-Wing Women. New York: Perigee Books, 1983.

Intercourse. New York: The Free Press, 1987.

Pornography: Men Possessing Women. 1979. Reprint, with a foreword by Andrea Dworkin, New York: Penguin Books, 1989.

"Biological Superiority: The World's Most Dangerous and Deadly Idea." In *Letters from a War Zone*, 110–116. New York: Lawrence Hill Books, 1993.

"Violence Against Women: It Breaks the Heart, Also the Bones." In *Letters from a War Zone*, 172–184. New York: Lawrence Hill Books, 1993.

"Against the Male Flood: Censorship, Pornography, and Equality." In *Feminism and Pornography*, edited by Drucilla Cornell, 19–38. Oxford: Oxford University Press, 2000.

Dworkin, Andrea and Catharine A. MacKinnon. *Pornography and Civil Rights: A New Day for Women's Equality*. Minneapolis, MN: Organizing Against Pornography, 1988.

Echols, Alice. "The New Feminism of Yin and Yang." In *Powers of Desire: The Politics of Sexuality*, edited by Ann Snitow, Christine Stansell, and Sharon Thompson, 439–459. New York: Monthly Review Press, 1983.

Daring to Be Bad: Radical Feminism in America, 1967–1975. Minneapolis: University of Minnesota Press, 1989.

"The Taming of the Id: Feminist Sexual Politics, 1963–83." In *Pleasure and Danger: Exploring Female Sexuality*, edited by Carole S. Vance, 50–72. Boston: Routledge & Kegan Paul, 1989.

Ehrenreich, Barbara. "What Is Socialist Feminism?" *WIN* 3 (June 1976): 4

Ehrenreich, Barbara, Elizabeth Hess, and Gloria Jacobs. *Re-Making Love: The Feminization of Sex*. Garden City, NY: Anchor Press, 1986.

Eisenstein, Hester. *Contemporary Feminist Thought*. Boston: G. K. Hall, 1983.

Eisenstein, Zillah R. "Antifeminism in the Politics and Election of 1980." *Feminist Studies* 7, no. 2 (Summer 1981): 187–205.

The Female Body and the Law. Berkeley: University of California Press, 1988.

Elshtain, Jean Bethke. "Ethics in the Women's Movement." *Annals of the American Academy of Political and Social Science* 515 (May 1991): 126–139.

English, Deirdre. "The Politics of Porn: Can Feminists Walk the Line?" *Mother Jones* (April 1980): 20–23, 43–44, 48–50.

English, Deirdre, Amber Hollibaugh, and Gayle Rubin. "Talking Sex: A Conversation on Sexuality and Feminism." In *My Dangerous Desires: A Queer Girl Dreaming Her Way Home*, edited by Amber L. Hollibaugh, 118–137. Durham, NC: Duke University Press, 2000. First published in *Socialist Review* 58, 11, no. 4 (July-August 1981): 43–62.

Ephron, Nora. "Women." *Esquire* (February 1973): 14–22.

Evans, Sara. "Socialist Feminism and NAM: A Political Debate Whose Time Has Come." *NAM Discussion Bulletin* 8 (1974): 36–37.

Personal Politics: The Roots of Women's Liberation in the Civil Rights Movement and the New Left. New York: Vintage, 1979.

Born for Liberty: A History of Women in America. New York: Free Press, 1989.

Faderman, Lillian. *Odd Girls and Twilight Lovers: A History of Lesbian Life in Twentieth-Century America*. New York: Penguin, 1991.

Faludi, Susan. *Backlash: The Undeclared War Against American Women*. New York: Crown, 1991.

Farland, Maria. "Total System, Total Solution, Total Apocalypse: Sex Oppression, Systems of Property, and 1970s Women's Liberation Fiction." *Yale Journal of Criticism* 18, no. 2 (Fall 2005): 381–407.

Farley, Lin. *Sexual Shakedown: The Sexual Harassment of Women on the Job*. New York: McGraw Hill, 1978.

Ferguson, Ann. "Sex War: The Debate between Radical and Libertarian Feminists." *Signs: Journal of Women in Culture and Society* 10, no. 1 (Autumn 1984): 106–135.

Blood at the Root: Motherhood, Sexuality and Male Dominance. London: Pandora, 1989.

Ferree, Myra M. and Beth B. Hess. *Controversy and Coalition: The New Feminist Movement* Boston: Twayne Publishers, 1985.

Firestone, Shulamith. *The Dialectic of Sex: The Case for Feminist Revolution*. New York: Bantam, 1970.

Foucault, Michel. *The History of Sexuality, Volume 1: An Introduction*. Robert Hurley, trans. New York: Pantheon, 1977.

Frank, Thomas. *The Conquest of Cool: Business Culture, Counterculture, and the Rise of Hip Consumerism*. Chicago: The University of Chicago Press, 1997.

Fraterrigo, Nancy. *Playboy and the Making of the Good Life in Modern America*. New York and Oxford: Oxford University Press, 2009.

Freeman, Jo. *The Politics of Women's Liberation: A Case Study of an Emerging Social Movement and Its Relation to the Policy Process*. New York: David McKay Co., 1975.

Friday, Nancy. *My Secret Garden: Women's Sexual Fantasies*. New York: Pocket Books, 1974.
Friedman, Deb. "Rape, Racism and Reality." *FAAR and NCN News* (July/August 1978): 14–19.
Friedman, Deb and Lois Yankowski. "Snuffing Sexual Violence." *Quest* 3, no. 2 (Fall 1976): 25–30.
Fryd, Vivien Green. "Suzanne Lacy's *Three Weeks in May*: Feminist Activist Performance Art as 'Expanded Public Pedagogy.'" *NWSA Journal* 19, no. 1 (Spring 2007): 23–36.
Gagnon, John H. and William Simon. *The Sexual Scene*. Chicago: Aldine, 1970.
Gale, Mary Ellen. Review of *Against Our Will: Men, Women and Rape*, by Susan Brownmiller. *The New York Times Book Review*, October 12, 1975, sec. 7, pp. 1–3.
Gerhard, Jane. *Desiring Revolution: Second-Wave Feminism and the Rewriting of American Sexual Thought, 1920–1982*. New York: Columbia University Press, 2001.
Giddens, Anthony. *The Transformation of Intimacy: Sexuality, Love and Eroticism in Modern Societies*. Stanford, CA: Stanford University Press, 1992.
Gitlin, Todd. "The Politics of Communication and the Communication of Politics." In *Mass Media and Society*, edited by James Curran and Michael Gurevitch, 329–341. New York: Edward Arnold, 1991.
The Whole World Is Watching: Mass Media in the Making and Unmaking of the New Left, 2nd ed. Berkeley: University of California Press, 2003.
Goffman, Erving. *Gender Advertisements*. Cambridge, MA: Harvard University Press, 1976.
Gordon, Linda. *Woman's Body, Woman's Right: Birth Control in America*. 2nd ed. New York: Penguin Books, 1990.
"Killing in Self-Defense." *The Nation*, March 24, 1997, 25–28.
Griffin, Susan. "Sadism and Catharthis: The Treatment Is the Disease." In *Take Back the Night*, edited by L. Lederer, 141–147. New York: William Morrow, 1980.
Pornography and Silence: Culture's Revenge Against Nature. New York: Harper and Row, 1981.
"Rape: The All-American Crime." *Ramparts* 10 (1971), republished as "The Politics of Rape," in *Made From This Earth: An Anthology of Writings* (New York: Harper & Row, 1982), 39–58.
Hall, Jacqueline D. "The Mind That Burns in Each Body: Women, Rape, and Racial Violence." In *Powers of Desire: The Politics of Sexuality*, edited by Ann Snitow, Christine Stansell, and Sharon Thompson, 328–349. New York: Monthly Review Press, 1983.
Handy, Bruce. "Ye Olde Smut Shoppe." *Time*. November 17, 1997, 54.
Healey, Emma. *Lesbian Sex Wars*. London: Virago Press, 1996.
Hebditch, David and Nick Anning. *Porn Gold: Inside the Pornography Business*. London: Faber & Faber, 1988.
Henry, Astrid. *Not My Mother's Sister: Generational Conflict and Third-Wave Feminism*. Bloomington: Indiana University Press, 2004.
Heresies: A Feminist Publication on Art & Politics, 3, no. 4: Issue 12 "The Sex Issue" (1981).
Hite, Shere. *The Hite Report: A Nationwide Study on Female Sexuality*. New York: Macmillan, 1976.

Hoffman, Eric. "Feminism, Pornography, and Law." *University of Pennsylvania Law Review* 497, no. 133 (1985): 497–534.

Hoffman, Jan. "The Times Square Porn Tour," *The Village Voice*, September 17, 1979, 1–3.

Hole, Judith and Ellen Levine. *Rebirth of Feminism*. New York: Quadrangle Books, 1971.

Hollibaugh, Amber L. and Cherríe Moraga, "What We're Rollin Around in Bed With." In *Dangerous Desires: A Queer Girl Dreaming Her Way Home*, 62–84. First published in *Heresies 12: The Sex Issue* (1981): 58–62.

Hommel, Teresa. "Images of Women in Pornography and Media." *New York University Review of Law and Social Change* 8 (1978–1979): 207–214.

hooks, bell. *Ain't I A Woman: Black Women and Feminism*. Boston: South End Press, 1981.

Howard, Janet. "Battered and Raped: The Physical/Sexual Abuse of Women." In *Fight Back! Feminist Resistance to Male Violence*, edited by F. Delacoste and F. Newman. Minneapolis, MN: Cleis Press, 1981.

Hunt, Morton. *Sexual Behavior in the 1970's*. New York: Dell Books, 1974.

Ivins, Molly. "Feminist Leaders Join Anti-Smut Campaign Despite Reservations," *The New York Times*, July 2, 1977, 18.

Jackson, Stevi and Sue Scott, eds. *Feminism and Sexuality: A Reader*. New York: Columbia University Press, 1996.

Jacoby, Susan. "Hers." *The New York Times*, January 26, 1978, C2.

Jeffreys, Sheila. *Anticlimax: A Feminist Perspective on the Sexual Revolution*. New York: New York University Press, 1990.

Jenefsky, Cindy. "Andrea Dworkin's Reconstruction of Pornography as a Discriminatory Social Practice." In *Violence and Its Alternatives*, edited by Manfred B. Steger and Nancy S. Lind, 133–144. New York: St. Martin's, 1999.

Jenkins, Philip. *Decade of Nightmares: The End of the Sixties and the Making of Eighties America*. Oxford: Oxford University Press, 2006.

Jenness, Valerie. *Making It Work: The Prostitutes' Rights Movement in Perspective*. New York: Aldene de Gruyter, 1993.

Johnson, Allan Griswold. "On the Prevalence of Rape in the United States." *Signs* 6, no. 1, Women: Sex and Sexuality, Part 2 (Autumn, 1980): 136–146.

Joseph, Gloria I. and Jill Lewis. *Common Differences: Conflicts in Black and White Feminist Perspectives*. New York: Doubleday/Anchor Books, 1981.

Kalven, Harry Jr. *A Worthy Tradition: Freedom of Speech in America*. Edited by Jamie Kalven. New York: Harper and Row, 1987.

Kaminer, Wendy. "Where We Stand on the First Amendment: Women Against Pornography," *Aegis: Magazine on Ending Violence Against Women* (September/October 1979), 52–53.

"WAP and the First Amendment." *Plexus* (December 1979): 2.

Keetley, Dawn and John Pettegrew, eds. *Public Women, Public Words: A Documentary History of American Feminism*. New York: Rowman & Littlefield, 2002.

Kelly, Kathleen S. *Fund Raising and Public Relations: A Critical Analysis*. Mahwah, NJ: Lawrence Erlbaum, 1991.

Kempton, Murray. "A Feelthy Commission." *New York Review of Books*, November 19, 1970.

Kendrick, Walter. *The Secret Museum: Pornography in Modern Culture*. New York: Penguin Books, 1987.

Kennedy, Elizabeth Lapovsky and Madeline D. Davis. *Boots of Leather, Slippers of Gold: The History of a Lesbian Community*. New York: Penguin Books, 1994.

King, Karl, Jack O. Balswick, and Ira Robinson. "The Continuing Sexual Revolution Among College Females." *Journal of Marriage and the Family* 39 (1977): 455–459.

Kipnis, Laura. *Bound and Gagged: Pornography and the Politics of Fantasy in America*. New York: Grove Press, 1996.

Klein, Frances. "Violence Against Women." In *The Women's Annual 1981: The Year in Review*, edited by Barbara Haber, 270–293. Boston: G. K. Hall, 1982.

Klein, Jeffrey. "Born Again Porn." *Mother Jones* (February/March 1978): 12–29.

Klopfenstein, Bruce C. "The Diffusion of the VCR in the United States." In *The VCR Age: Home Video and Mass Communication*, edited by Mark R. Levy, 21–39. Newbury Park, CA: Sage, 1989.

Koedt, Anne. "Lesbianism and Feminism." In *Radical Feminism*, edited by Anne Koedt, Ellen Levine, and Anita Rapone, 246–258. New York: Quadrangle Books, 1973.

"The Myth of the Vaginal Orgasm." In *Radical Feminism*, edited by Anne Koedt, Ellen Levine, and Anita Rapone, 198–207. New York: Quadrangle Books, 1973.

"Politics of the Ego: A Manifesto for N. Y. Radical Feminists." In *Radical Feminism*, edited by Anne Koedt, Ellen Levine, and Anita Rapone, 379–383. New York: Quadrangle Books, 1973.

Komisar, Lucy. "The Image of Woman in Advertising." In *Woman in Sexist Society: Studies in Power and Powerlessness*, edited by Vivian Gornick and Barbara K. Moran, 207–217. New York: Basic Books, 1971.

Kreps, Bonnie. "Radical Feminism 1." In *Radical Feminism*, edited by Anne Koedt, Ellen Levine, and Anita Rapone, 234–239. New York: Quadrangle Books, 1973.

LaBelle, Beverly. "*Snuff* – The Ultimate in Woman-Hating." In *Take Back the Night*, edited by Laura Lederer, 272–278. New York: William Morrow, 1980.

Labowitz, Leslie and Suzanne Lacy. "Evolution of a Feminist Art." *Heresies* 6 (1978): 78–84.

Lacombe, Dany. *Blue Politics: Pornography and the Law in the Age of Feminism*. Toronto: University of Toronto Press, 1994.

Lacy, Suzanne. *Oral history interview with Suzanne Lacy*, conducted by Moira Roth, Berkeley, California, 1990 Mar. 16 & 24 and Sept. 27, Archives of American Art, Smithsonian Institution. Available online at http://www.aaa.si.edu/collections/oralhistories/transcripts/lacy90.htm

"The Name of the Game." *Art Journal* 50, no. 2 (1991): 64–68.

Leaving Art: Writings on Performance, Politics, and Publics, 1974–2007. Durham, NC: Duke University Press, 2010.

Lacy, Suzanne and Leslie Labowitz. "Feminist Media Strategies for Political Performance." In *The Feminism and Visual Culture Reader*, edited by Amelia Jones, 302–313. London: Routledge, 2003.

Lane III, Frederick S. *Obscene Profits: The Entrepreneurs of Pornography in the Cyber Age*. New York: Routledge, 2000.

Laner, Mary R. and Steve L. Housker. "Sexual Permissiveness in Younger and Older Adults." *Journal of Family Issues* 1 (1980): 103–124.

Lardner, James. *Fast Forward: Hollywood, the Japanese and the Onslaught of the VCR*. New York: W.W. Norton & Co., 1987.

Largen, Mary Anne. "Grassroots Centers and National Task Forces: A Herstory of the Anti-Rape Movement." *Aegis: Magazine on Ending Violence Against Women* 32 (Autumn 1981): 46–52.

Lederer, Laura. "Introduction." In *Take Back the Night: Women on Pornography*, edited by Laura Lederer, 15–20. New York: William Morrow, 1980.

"*Playboy* Isn't Playing: An Interview with Judith Bat-Ada." In *Take Back the Night: Women on Pornography*, edited by Laura Lederer, 121–133. New York: William Morrow, 1980.

Leidholdt, Dorchen. "The Sexual Exploitation of Women and Girls: A Violation of Human Rights." In *Feminism and Pornography*, edited by Drucilla Cornell, 418–422. London: Oxford University Press, 2000.

Leidholdt, Dorchen and Janice G. Raymond, eds. *The Sexual Liberals and the Attack on Feminism*. Elmsford, NY: Pergamon Press, 1990.

LeMoncheck, Linda. *Loose Women, Lecherous Men: A Feminist Philosophy of Sex*. Oxford: Oxford University Press, 1997.

Lesbians of Colour. "Racism in Pornography." In *Good Girls/Bad Girls: Feminists and Sex Trade Workers Face to Face*, edited by Laurie Bell, 58–66. Toronto: The Seal Press, 1987.

Levine, Elana. *Wallowing in Sex: The New Sexual Culture of 1970s American Television*. Durham, NC: Duke University Press, 2007.

Levy, Ariel. *Female Chauvinist Pigs: Women and the Rise of Raunch Culture*. New York: Free Press, 2006.

Lewin, Tamar. "Feminist Scholars Spurring a Rethinking of Law." *New York Times*, September 30, 1988, p. B9.

Linden, Robin, Darlene R. Pagano, Diana E. H. Russell, and Susan Leigh Star, eds. *Against Sadomasochism: A Radical Feminist Analysis*. East Palo Alto, CA: Frog in the Well, 1982.

Lindner, Katharina. "Images of Women in General Interest and Fashion Magazine Advertisements from 1955 to 2002." *Sex Roles* 51, no. 7/8 (October 2004): 409–421.

London, Julia. "Images of Violence Against Women." *Victimology: An International Journal* 3–4 (1977–1978): 510–524.

London, Julia and Lynn Heidelberg. "'*Snuff*' Shut Down by Protests, Stink Bombs, Bricks." *The Lesbian Tide* (May/June 1976): 4–7.

Longino, Helen. "Pornography, Oppression and Freedom: A Closer Look." In *Take Back the Night: Women on Pornography*, edited by Laura Lederer, 40–54. New York: William Morrow, 1980.

Lovelace, Linda with Mike McGrady. *Ordeal*. Secaucus, NJ: Citadel Press, 1980.

MacKinnon, Catharine A. *Sexual Harassment of Working Women: A Case of Sex Discrimination*. New Haven, CT: Yale University Press, 1979.

"Linda's Life and Andrea's Work." In *Feminism Unmodified: Discourses on Life and Law*, 127–133. Cambridge, MA: Harvard University Press, 1987.

"Not a Moral Issue." In *Feminism Unmodified: Discourses on Life and Law*, 146–162. Cambridge, MA: Harvard University Press, 1987.

"Liberalism and the Death of Feminism." In *The Sexual Liberals and the Attack on Feminism*, edited by Dorchen Leidholdt and Janice G. Raymond, 3–13. Elmsford, NY: Pergamon Press, 1990.

"Sexuality, Pornography, and Method: 'Pleasure Under Patriarchy." In *Feminism and Political Theory*, edited by Cass Sunstein, 207–239. Chicago: University of Chicago Press, 1990.

Only Words. Cambridge, MA: Harvard University Press, 1993.
"Prostitution and Civil Rights." *Michigan Journal of Gender and Law* 1 (1993): 13–31.
"Sexuality." In *Theorizing Feminism: Parallel Trends in the Humanities and Social Sciences*, edited by Eileen Hermann and Abigail J. Stewart, 257–287. Boulder, CO: Westview Press, 1994.

MacKinnon, Catharine A. and Andrea Dworkin, eds. *In Harm's Way: The Pornography Civil Rights Hearings*. Cambridge, MA: Harvard University Press, 1997.

Makagon, Daniel. *Where the Ball Drops: Days and Nights in Times Square*. Minneapolis: University of Minnesota Press, 2004.

Marchand, Roland. *Advertising the American Dream: Making Way for Modernity, 1920–1940*. Berkeley: University of California Press, 1985.

Marcuse, Herbert. *Eros and Civilization: A Philosophical Inquiry into Freud*. Boston: Beacon Press, 1955.

Marks, J. "Women in Rock: Don't Sing Me No Bad Songs 'Bout Bad Women!" *Vogue* (March 1971), 112.

Marshall, Susan E. "Who Speaks for American Women? The Future of Antifeminism." *Annals of the American Academy of Political and Social Science*, 515 (May 1991): 50–62.

Martin, Del and Phyllis Lyon. *Lesbian/Woman*. 2nd ed. Volcano, CA: Volcano Press, 1991.

Masters, William H. and Virginia E. Johnson. *Human Sexual Response*. Boston: Little, Brown, 1966.

Matthews, Nancy A. *Confronting Rape: The Feminist Anti-Rape Movement and the State*. New York: Routledge, 1994.

Matrix, Cherie, ed. *Tales from the Clit: A Female Experience of Pornography*. San Francisco: AK Press, 1996.

McDonnell, Evelyn and Ann Powers, eds. *Rock She Wrote*. New York: Delta Books, 1995.

McGirr, Lisa. *Suburban Warriors: The Origins of the New American Right*. Princeton, NJ: Princeton University Press, 2001.

Meade, Marion. "Does Rock Degrade Women?" *The New York Times*, March 14, 1971, sect. 2: 13, 22.

Medea, Andra and Kathleen Thompson. *Against Rape*. New York: Farrar, Straus and Giroux, 1974.

Mehrhof, Barbara and Pam Kearon. "Rape: An Act of Terror." In *Radical Feminism*, edited by Anne Koedt, Ellen Levine, and Anita Rapone, 228–233. New York: Quadrangle Books, 1973 (Reprinted).

Melucci, A. *Nomads of the Present: Social Movements and Individual Needs in Contemporary Society*. London: Hutchinson Radius, 1988.

Merit Systems Protection Board. *Sexual Harassment in the Federal Workplace: Is It A Problem?* Washington, DC: U.S. Government Printing Office, 1981.

Morgan, Marabel. *The Total Woman*. Old Tappan, NJ: Fleming H. Revell, 1973.
Total Joy. Old Tappan, NJ: Fleming H. Revell, 1976.

Morgan, Robin. *Going Too Far: The Personal Chronicle of a Feminist*. New York: Vintage Books, 1978.
"Lesbianism and Feminism: Synonyms or Contradictions?" In *Going Too Far: The Personal Chronicle of a Feminist*, 170–188. New York: Vintage Books, 1978 (Reprinted).

"Theory and Practice: Pornography and Rape." In *Take Back the Night: Women on Pornography*, edited by Laura Lederer, 134–140. New York: William Morrow, 1980 (Reprinted).

Morris, Thomas D. *Southern Slavery and the Law, 1619–1860*. Chapel Hill: University of North Carolina Press, 1996.

Myron, Nancy and Charlotte Bunch, eds. *Lesbianism and the Women's Movement*. Baltimore: Diana Press, 1975.

Neier, Aryeh. "Expurgating the First Amendment." *The Nation* (June 21, 1980): 1, 751–754.

"Memoirs of a Woman's Displeasure." *The Nation* (August 16–23, 1980): 154–157.

Nestle, Joan. "The Fem Question." In *Pleasure and Danger: Exploring Female Sexuality*, edited by Carole S. Vance, 232–241. Boston: Routledge & Kegan Paul, 1984.

Nussbaum, Martha C. *Sex and Social Justice*. New York: Oxford University Press, 1999.

Omolade, Barbara. "Hearts of Darkness." In *Powers of Desire: The Politics of Sexuality*, edited by Ann Snitow, Christine Stansell, and Sharon Thompson, 350–367. New York: Monthly Review Press, 1983.

Orlando, Lisa. "Bad Girls and 'Good' Politics." *The Village Voice Literary Supplement* (December 1982): 1, 16–17.

Osanka, Franklin Mark and Sara Lee Johann. *Sourcebook on Pornography*. Lexington, MA: Lexington Books, 1989.

Overall, Christine. "What's Wrong with Prostitution? Evaluating Sex Work." *Signs* 17, no. 4 (Summer, 1992): 705–724.

Pascoe, Peggy. "Gender Systems in Conflict: The Marriages of Mission-Educated Chinese American Women, 1874–1939." *Journal of Social History* 33, no. 3 (1989): 631–652.

Pateman, Carole. *The Sexual Contract*. Stanford, CA: Stanford University Press, 1988.

Patterson, James T. *Restless Giant: The United States from Watergate to Bush v. Gore*. Oxford: Oxford University Press, 2005.

Peiss, Kathy. "'Charity Girls' and City Pleasures: Historical Notes on Working-Class Sexuality, 1880–1920," in *Powers of Desire: The Politics of Sexuality*, edited by Ann Snitow, Christine Stansell, and Sharon Thompson, 74–87. New York: Monthly Review Press, 1983.

Petchesky, Rosalind P. "Antiabortion, Antifeminism, and the Rise of the New Right," *Feminist Studies* 7, no. 2 (Summer 1981): 206–246.

Phelan, Shane. *Identity Politics: Lesbian Feminism and the Limits of Community*. Philadelphia: Temple University Press, 1989.

Phelps, Linda. "Patriarchy and Capitalism." *Quest: A Feminist Quarterly* 2 (1975): 35–48.

Pingree, Suzanne, Robert Hawkins, Matilda Butler, and William Paisley. "Equality in Advertising: A Scale for Sexism." *Journal of Communication* 26, no. 4 (1976): 193–200.

Pleck, Elizabeth. *Domestic Tyranny: The Making of Social Policy Against Family Violence from Colonial Times to the Present*. New York and Oxford: Oxford University Press, 1987.

Pohli, Carol Virginia. "Church Closets and Back Doors: A Feminist View of Moral Majority Women." *Feminist Studies* 9, no. 3 (Autumn 1983): 529–558.

Radicalesbians. "The Woman-Identified-Woman." In *Radical Feminism*, edited by Anne Koedt, Ellen Levine, and Anita Rapone, 240–245. New York: Quadrangle Books, 1971.

Redstockings. *Feminist Revolution*. New Paltz, NY: Redstockings, 1975.

Reich, Wilhelm. *The Sexual Revolution: Toward a Self-Governing Character Structure*. Translated by T. P. Wolfe. 2nd edition. New York: Octagon Books, 1971.

Reiss, Ira L., Albert Banwart, and Harry Foreman. "Premarital Contraceptive Usage: A Study and Some Theoretical Explorations." *Journal of Marriage and the Family* (August 1975): 619–629.

Report of the 1970 Commission on Obscenity and Pornography. New York: Bantam Books, 1970.

Rich, Adrienne. "Afterword." In *Take Back the Night: Women on Pornography*, edited by Laura Lederer, 313–320. New York: William Morrow, 1980.

"Compulsory Heterosexuality and Lesbian Existence." *Signs: Journal of Women in Culture and Society* 5 (1980): 631–660.

Rich, B. Ruby. "Review Essay: Feminism and Sexuality in the 1980s." *Feminist Studies* 12 (Fall 1986): 525–561.

"Anti-Porn: Soft Issue, Hard World." In *Chick Flicks: Theories and Memories of the Feminist Film Movement*. Durham, NC: Duke University Press, 1998.

Robinson, Paul. *The Freudian Left: Wilhelm Reich, Geza Roheim, Herbert Marcuse*. 2nd ed. Ithaca, NY and London: Cornell University Press, 1990.

Roiphe, Katie. *The Morning After: Sex, Fear and Feminism on Campus*. New York: Little, Brown, 1993.

Rolo, Charles. Review of *Lolita*, by Vladimir Nabokov. *The Atlantic Monthly* (September 1958): 78.

Rosen, Ruth. *The World Split Open: How the Modern Women's Movement Changed America*. New York: Viking Penguin, 2000.

Rosenbluth, Helene, narrator. *Fair Sex, Fair Game: Women Say No to the Sexual Safari*. 1979. Los Angeles: Pacifica Tape Library. Sound Recording.

Ross, Ellen. "'The Love Crisis': Couples Advice Books of the Late 1970s." *Signs: Journal of Women in Culture and Society* 6, no. 1 (1980): 109–122.

Roth, Benita. *Separate Roads to Feminism: Black, Chicana and White Feminist Movements in America's Second Wave*. Cambridge, UK: Cambridge University Press, 2004.

Royalle, Candida. "Porn in the USA." In *Feminism & Pornography*, edited by Drucilla Cornel, 540–550. Oxford and New York: Oxford University Press, 2000.

Ruth, Barbara. "Cathexis: A Preliminary Investigation into the Nature of S/M." In *What Color Is Your Handkerchief? A Lesbian S/M Sexuality Reader*, edited by Samois, 8–11. Berkeley, CA: Samois, 1979.

Rubin, Gayle. "Sexual Politics, The New Right, and the Sexual Fringe." In *What Color Is Your Handkerchief? A Lesbian S/M Sexuality Reader*, edited by Samois, 28–35. Berkeley, CA: Samois, 1979.

"The Leather Menace: Comments on Politics and S/M." In *Coming to Power: Writings and Graphics on Lesbian S/M*, edited by Samois, 192–227. Palo Alto, CA: Alyson, 1982.

"Thinking Sex: Notes for a Radical Theory of the Politics of Sexuality." In *Pleasure and Danger: Exploring Female Sexuality*, edited by Carole S. Vance, 267–319. Boston: Routledge and Kegan Paul, 1985.

Rubin, Gayle; Deirdre English, and Amber Hollibaugh. "Talking Sex: A Conversation on Sexuality and Feminism." *Feminist Review* 11 (June 1982): 40–52.

Rubin, Lillian B. *Worlds of Pain: Life in the Working Class Family*. New York: Basic Books, 1976.

Rush, Florence. "Child Pornography." In *Take Back the Night: Women on Pornography*, edited by Laura Lederer, 71–81. New York: William Morrow, 1980.

Russell, Diana E. H. *The Politics of Rape: The Victim's Perspective*. New York: Stein & Day, 1975.

"Pornography and the Women's Liberation Movement." In *Take Back the Night: Women on Pornography*, edited by Laura Lederer, 301–312. New York: William Morrow, 1980.

Sexual Exploitation. Beverly Hills, CA: Sage, 1984.

Ryan, Barbara. "Ideological Purity and Feminism: The U.S. Women's Movement from 1966 to 1975." *Gender & Society* 3 (1989): 239–257.

Rymph, Catherine E. *Republican Women: Feminism and Conservatism from Suffrage through the Rise of the New Right*. Chapel Hill: University of North Carolina Press, 2006.

Safran, Carolyn. "What Men Do to Women on the Job." *Redbook* (October 1976): 217–223.

Samois, eds. *Coming to Power: Writings and Graphics on Lesbian S/M*. Boston: Alyson Publications, 1981.

What Color Is Your Handkerchief? A Lesbian S/M Sexuality Reader. Berkeley, CA: Samois, 1979.

Schauer, Frederick F. *The Law of Obscenity*. Washington DC: The Bureau of National Affairs, Inc., 1976.

Schechter, Susan. *Women and Male Violence: The Visions and Struggles of the Battered Women's Movement*. London: Pluto Press, 1982.

Schipper, Henry. "Filthy Lucre: A Tour of America's Most Profitable Frontier." *Mother Jones* (April 1980): 31–33, 60–62.

Schrage, Laurie. "Prostitution and the Case for Decriminalization." In *Prostitution and Pornography: Philosophical Debate about the Sex Industry*, edited by Jessica Spector, 240–246. Stanford, CA: Stanford University Press, 2006.

Schulman, Bruce J. *The Seventies: The Great Shift in American Culture, Society, and Politics*. New York: The Free Press, 2001.

Schulman, Mark A. *A Survey of Spousal Violence Against Women in Kentucky*. U. S. Department of Justice, Law Enforcement Assistance Administration: Study No. 792701 (July 1979).

Schwartz, Tony. "The TV Pornography Boom," *New York Times*, September 13, 1981, available online at http://select.nytimes.com/search/restricted/article?res=FA081EFE3C5D0C708DDDA00894D9484D81 (accessed June 25, 2009).

Segal, Lynne. *Straight Sex: Rethinking the Politics of Pleasure*. Berkeley: University of California Press, 1994.

Seidman, Steven. *Romantic Longings: Love in America, 1830–1980*. New York and London: Routledge, 1991.

Embattled Eros: Sexual Politics and Ethics in Contemporary America. New York and London: Routledge, 1992.

Self, Robert O. "Sex in the City: The Politics of Sexual Liberalism in Los Angeles, 1963–79," *Gender & History* 20, no. 2 (August 2008): 288–311.

Shulman, Alix Kates. "Sex and Power: Sexual Bases of Radical Feminism." *Signs* 5, no. 4, Women: Sex and Sexuality (Summer 1980): 590–604.

Sides, Josh. "Excavating the Postwar Sex District in San Francisco." *Journal of Urban History* 32 (March 2006): 355–379.

Simson, Rennie. "The Afro-American Female: The Historical Context of the Construction of Sexual Identity." In *Powers of Desire: The Politics of Sexuality*, edited by Ann Snitow, Christine Stansell, and Sharon Thompson, 229–235. New York: Monthly Review Press, 1983.

Slade, Joseph. "Pornographic Theaters Off Times Square." In *The Sexual Scene*, rev. ed., edited by John H. Gagnon and William Simon, 263–289. New Brunswick, NJ: Transaction Books, 1973.

Smith, Marjorie M. "'Violent Pornography' and the Women's Movement." *The Civil Liberties Review* (January/February 1978): 46–59.

"Private Action Against Pornography: An Exercise of First Amendment Rights," *New York University Review of Law and Social Change* 8 (1978–1979): 247–250.

Snitow, Ann. "Mass Market Romance: Pornography for Women Is Different." In *Powers of Desire: The Politics of Sexuality*, edited by Ann Snitow, Christine Stansell, and Sharon Thompson, 245–263. New York: Monthly Review Press, 1983.

"Retrenchment Versus Transformation: The Politics of the Antipornography Movement." In *Women Against Censorship*, edited by Varda Burstyn, 107–120. Vancouver and Toronto: Douglas & McIntyre, 1985.

Snitow, Ann, Christine Stansell, and Sharon Thompson. "Introduction." In *Powers of Desire: The Politics of Sexuality*, edited by Ann Snitow, Christine Stansell, and Sharon Thompson, 9–47. New York: Monthly Review Press, 1983.

Spector, Jessica, ed. *Prostitution and Pornography: Philosophical Debate about the Sex Industry*. Stanford, CA: Stanford University Press, 2006.

Stacey, Judith. "The New Conservative Feminism." *Feminist Studies* 9, no. 3 (Autumn 1983): 559–583.

Stafford, Rebecca, Elaine Backman, and Pamela Dibona. "The Division of Labor among Cohabiting and Married Couples." *Journal of Marriage and the Family* (February 1977): 43–57.

Stansell, Christine. "Films" (review of Deep Throat), *off our backs* 3 (April 1973): 11.

Stearns, Peter. *Battleground of Desire: The Struggle for Self-Control in Modern America*. New York: New York University Press, 1999.

Steinem, Gloria. "Erotica and Pornography: A Clear and Present Difference," *Ms.* (November 1978): 53–54, 75.

"Feminist Notes: Linda Lovelace's '*Ordeal*,'" *Ms.* (May 1980): 72–76.

Steiner, Linda. "Oppositional Decoding as an Act of Resistance." *Critical Studies in Mass Communication* 5, no. 1 (March 1988): 1–15.

Stokes, Geoffrey. "Beaver, Buggery, Brownmiller, and Black Girls: The First Amendment Bullies." *The Village Voice*, August 20, 1979: 14–15.

Strossen, Nadine. *Defending Pornography: Free Speech, Sex, and the Fight for Women's Rights*. New York: Scribner, 1995

Strub, Whitney. "Perversion for Profit: Citizens for Decent Literature and the Arousal of an Antiporn Public in the 1960s," *Journal of the History of Sexuality*, 15, no. 2 (May 2006): 258–291.

Perversion for Profit: The Politics of Pornography and the Rise of the New Right. New York: Columbia University Press, 2011.

Swedberg, Deborah. "What Do We See When We See Woman/Woman Sex in Pornographic Movies." *NWSA Journal* 1 (1989): 602–616.

Symposium: The Sex Panic: Women, Censorship and "Pornography." *New York Law School Law Review* 38, no. 1–4 (1993).

Talese, Gay. *Thy Neighbor's Wife*. New York: Doubleday, 1980.

Taylor, Verta and Sheila J. Rupp. "Women's Culture and Lesbian Feminist Activism: A Reconsideration of Cultural Feminism." In *Community Activism and Feminist Politics: Organizing Against Race, Class, and Gender*, edited by Nancy A. Naples, 57–79. New York: Routledge, 1998.

Taylor, Verta and Nancy Whittier. "Collective Identity in Social Movement Communities: Lesbian Feminist Mobilization." In *Frontiers in Social Movement Theory*, edited by Aldon Morris and Carol McClurg Mueller, 104–129. New Haven, CT: Yale University Press, 1992.

The Feminists. "The Feminists: A Political Organization to Annihilate Sex Roles." In *Notes from the Second Year: Women's Liberation*, edited by Shulamith Firestone and Anne Koedt, 114–118. New York: Radical Feminism, 1970.

Tong, Rosemarie. *Women, Sex, and the Law*. Baltimore: Rowman & Littlefield, 1984.

Feminist Thought: A More Comprehensive Introduction, 3rd ed. Boulder, CO: Westview Press, 2009.

Tsoulas, Diane L. "Women Against Violence Against Women." *Sister Courage* 3, no. 4 (June 1978): 1, 7.

Tuchman, Gaye, Arlene Kaplan Daniels, and James Benet, eds. *Hearth and Home: Images of Women in the Mass Media*. New York: Oxford University Press, 1978.

Turan, Kenneth and Stephen F. Zito. *Sinema: American Pornographic Films and the People Who Make Them*. New York: Praeger Publishers, 1974.

Vance, Carole S. "Pleasure and Danger: Towards a Politics of Sexuality." In *Pleasure and Danger: Exploring Female Sexuality*, edited by Carole S. Vance, 1–27. Boston: Routledge and Kegan Paul, 1984.

"More Danger, More Pleasure: A Decade After the Barnard Sexuality Conference," *New York Law School Law Review* 38, no. 1–4 (1993): 289–317.

"Negotiating Sex and Gender in the Attorney General's Commission on Pornography." In *The Gender and Sexuality Reader: Culture, History, Political Economy*, edited by Roger N. Lancaster and Micaela di Leonardo, 440–452. New York: Routledge, 1997.

Wagner, Lewis C. and Janis B. Banos. "A Woman's Place: A Follow-Up Analysis of the Roles Portrayed by Women in Magazine Advertisements." *Journal of Marketing Research* 10 (1973): 213–214.

Walker, Lenore E. *The Battered Woman*. New York: Harper & Row, 1979.

Walkowitz, Judith. *Prostitution and Victorian Society: Women, Class and the State*. Cambridge, UK: Cambridge University Press, 1980.

Walter, Barbara Boyer, narrator. *Women Against Violent Pornography*. 1978. Washington, DC: National Public Radio. Sound Recording.

Wandersee, Winifred D. *On the Move: American Women in the 1970s*. Boston: Twayne Publishers, 1988.

Watts, Steven. *Mr. Playboy: Hugh Hefner and the American Dream*. New York: Wiley, 2009.

Webster, Paula. "Pornography and Pleasure." *Heresies 12: The Sex Issue* (1981): 48–50.

Weedon, Chris. *Feminism, Theory and the Politics of Difference.* New York: John Wiley, 1999.

Weeks, Jeffrey. *Sexuality and Its Discontents: Meanings, Myths and Modern Sexualities.* London: Routledge, 1985.

Whittier, Nancy. *Feminist Generations: The Persistence of the Radical Women's Movement.* Philadelphia: Temple University Press, 1995.

Williams, Linda. *Hard Core: Power, Pleasure and the "Frenzy of the Visible."* Berkeley: University of California Press, 1989.

Willis, Ellen. "Sexual Counterrevolution I." *Rolling Stone*, March 24, 1977, 29.

Beginning to See the Light: Pieces of a Decade. New York: Alfred Knopf, 1981.

"Nature's Revenge." Review of *Pornography and Silence*, by Susan Griffin, and *Pornography: Men Possessing Women*, by Andrea Dworkin. *New York Times Book Review*, July 12, 1981. Available online at http://www.nytimes.com/1981/07/12/books/nature-s-revenge.html?&pagewanted=all

"Lust Horizons: Is the Women's Movement Pro-Sex?" *The Village Voice* 26, no. 25 (June 17, 1981): 1, 36–41. Reprinted in Ellen Willis, *No More Nice Girls: Countercultural Essays.* Hanover, NH: Wesleyan University Press, 1992, 3–14.

Wilson, Bill. *The Adult Business Mail Marketing Guide.* Washington, DC: RPE Associates, 1979. The Kinsey Institute for Research in Sex, Gender and Reproduction. Bloomington, Indiana.

Wilson, Elizabeth. "The Context of 'Between Pleasure and Danger': The Barnard Conference on Sexuality." *Feminist Review* 13 (February 1983): 35–41.

Winick, Charles. "The Desexualized Society." In *The New Eroticism: Theories, Vogues and Canons*, edited by Philip Nobile, 201–207. New York: Random House, 1970.

Wolf, Naomi. *The Beauty Myth: How Images of Beauty are Used Against Women.* New York: Doubleday, 1991.

Fire with Fire: The New Female Power and How It Will Change the 21st Century. New York: Random House, 1993.

Women Against Pornography. Records, 1979–1989, #90-M153. Schlesinger Library, Radcliffe Institute, Harvard University, Cambridge, MA.

Women Against Pornography. *NewsReport.* New York, NY: WAP (1979–1987). Historical Society Library Pamphlet Collection, State Historical Society of Wisconsin, Madison, Wis., and Women Against Pornography Records, 1979–1989, #90-M153. Schlesinger Library, Radcliffe College, Cambridge, Mass.

Women Against Violence Against Women (Boston chapter). Papers, 1977–1984. Northeastern University Libraries, Archives and Special Collections, Boston, MA.

Women Against Violence Against Women, Papers (Los Angeles national office), 1976–1986. June L. Mazer Lesbian Archives, West Hollywood, CA.

Women Against Violence Against Women. *Newsletter.* Los Angeles, CA: The Women, no. 1-no. 8 (1977–1982). Historical Society Library Pamphlet Collection, State Historical Society of Wisconsin, Madison, WI.

Women Against Violence in Pornography and Media. *NewsPage.* Berkeley, CA: WAVPM, vol. 1, no. 2- vol. 7, no. 9 (July 1977-October 1983). Historical Society Library Microforms Collection, State Historical Society of Wisconsin, Madison, WI.

Women Against Violence in Pornography and Media. Records, 1977–1983. #96–21. The Gay, Lesbian, Bisexual, Transgender Historical Society, San Francisco, CA.

Yeamans, Robin. "A Political-Legal Analysis of Pornography." In *Take Back the Night: Women on Pornography*, edited by Laura Lederer, 248–251. New York: William Morrow, 1980.

Zelnik, Melvin and John F. Kantner. "Sexual and Contraceptive Experience of Young Unmarried Women in the United States, 1976 and 1971." *Family Planning Perspectives* 9 (March/April 1977): 55–71.

"First Pregnancies to Women Aged 15–19: 1976 and 1971." *Family Planning Perspectives* 10 (January/February 1978): 11–20.

Zelnik, Melvin, Young J. Kim, and John F. Kantner. "Probabilities of Intercourse and Conception Among U. S. Teenage Women, 1971 and 1976." *Family Planning Perspectives* 11 (May/June 1979): 177–183.

Zink, Daniel W. "The Practice of Marriage and Family Counseling and Conservative Christianity." In *The Role of Religion in Marriage and Family Counseling*, edited by Jill Onedera, 55–72. New York: Taylor & Francis, 2007.

Index